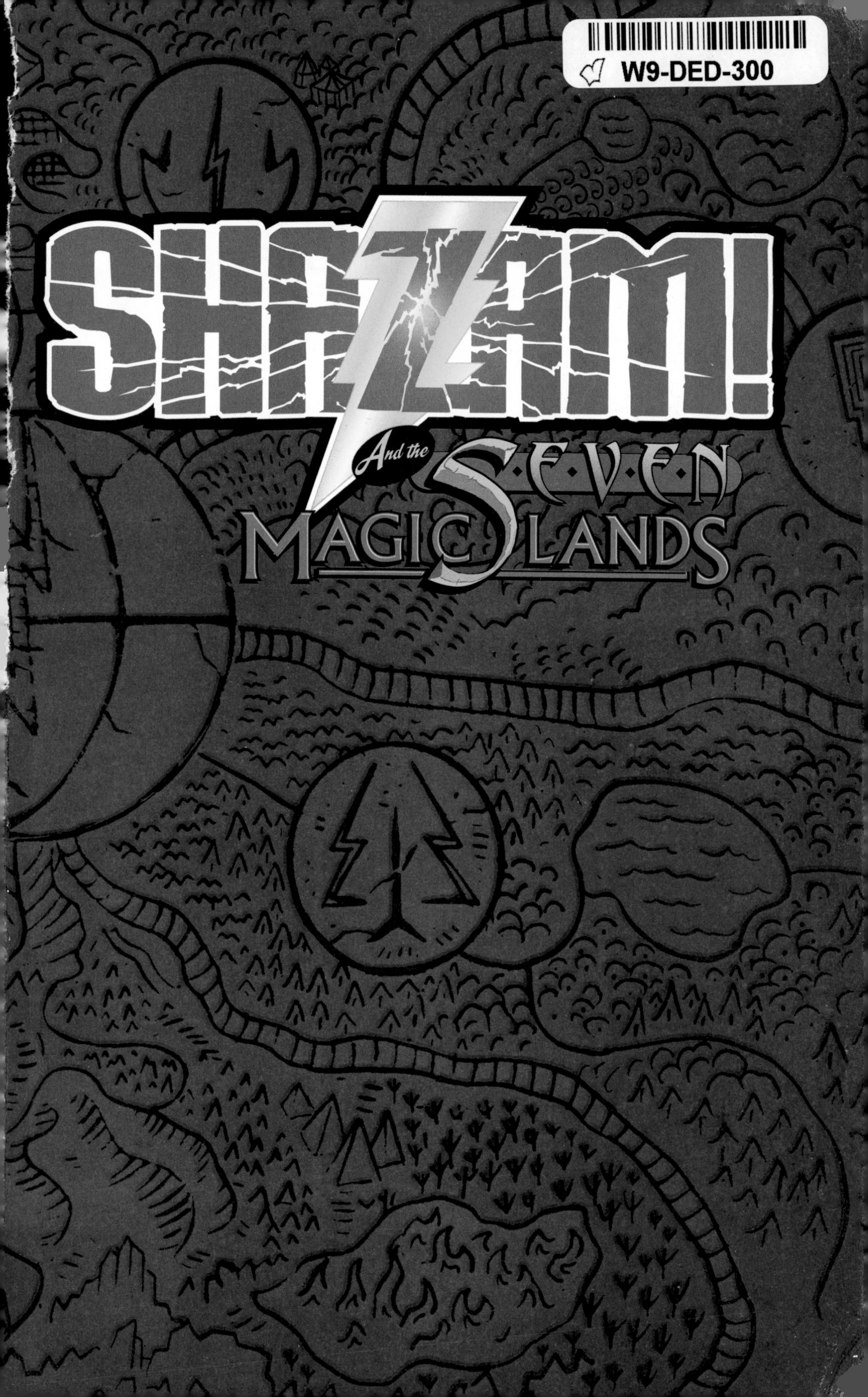
SHAZAM!
And the SEVEN MAGIC LANDS

# SHAZAM

## and the SEVEN MAGIC LANDS

**GEOFF JOHNS**
WRITER

**MICHAEL ATIYEH**
**MAYO "SEN" NAITO**
COLORISTS

**DALE EAGLESHAM**
**SCOTT KOLINS**
**MARCO SANTUCCI**
**MAYO "SEN" NAITO**
**MAX RAYNOR**
ARTISTS

**ROB LEIGH**
LETTERER

**DALE EAGLESHAM**
**AND ALEX SINCLAIR**
COLLECTION COVER ARTISTS

SHAZAM! CREATED BY
C. C. BECK AND BILL PARKER

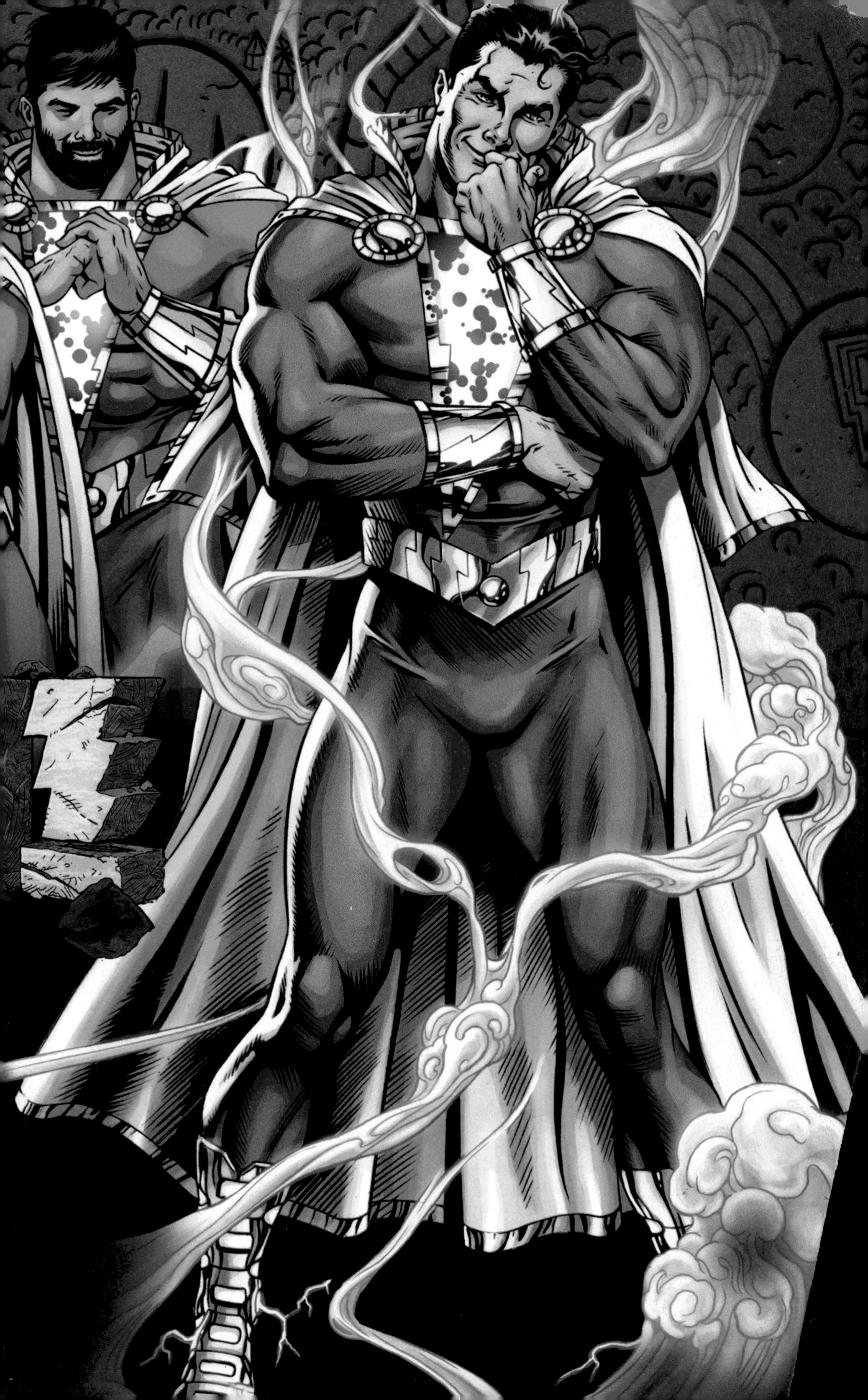

BRIAN CUNNINGHAM, MOLLY MAHAN, MIKE COTTON Editors - Original Series
ANDREA SHEA, HARVEY RICHARDS Associate Editors - Original Series
MARQUIS DRAPER Assistant Editor - Original Series
JEB WOODARD Group Editor - Collected Editions
ROBIN WILDMAN Editor - Collected Edition
STEVE COOK Design Director - Books
AMIE BROCKWAY-METCALF Publication Design
CHRISTY SAWYER Publication Production

BOB HARRAS Senior VP - Editor-in-Chief, DC Comics

JIM LEE Publisher & Chief Creative Officer
BOBBIE CHASE VP - Global Publishing Initiatives & Digital Strategy
DON FALLETTI VP - Manufacturing Operations & Workflow Management
LAWRENCE GANEM VP - Talent Services
ALISON GILL Senior VP - Manufacturing & Operations
HANK KANALZ Senior VP - Publishing Strategy & Support Services
DAN MIRON VP - Publishing Operations
NICK J. NAPOLITANO VP - Manufacturing Administration & Design
NANCY SPEARS VP - Sales
JONAH WEILAND VP - Marketing & Creative Services
MICHELE R. WELLS VP & Executive Editor, Young Reader

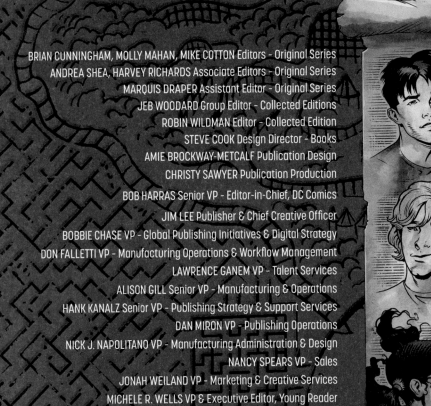

SHAZAM! AND THE SEVEN MAGIC LANDS

DC Comics, 2900 West Alameda Ave., Burbank, CA 91505

Printed by LSC Communications, Owensville, MO, USA. 10/30/20. First Printing.

ISBN: 978-1-77950-459-3

Library of Congress Cataloging-in-Publication Data is available.

PEFC Certified

This product is from
sustainably managed
forests and controlled
sources

PEFC/29-31-337    www.pefc.org

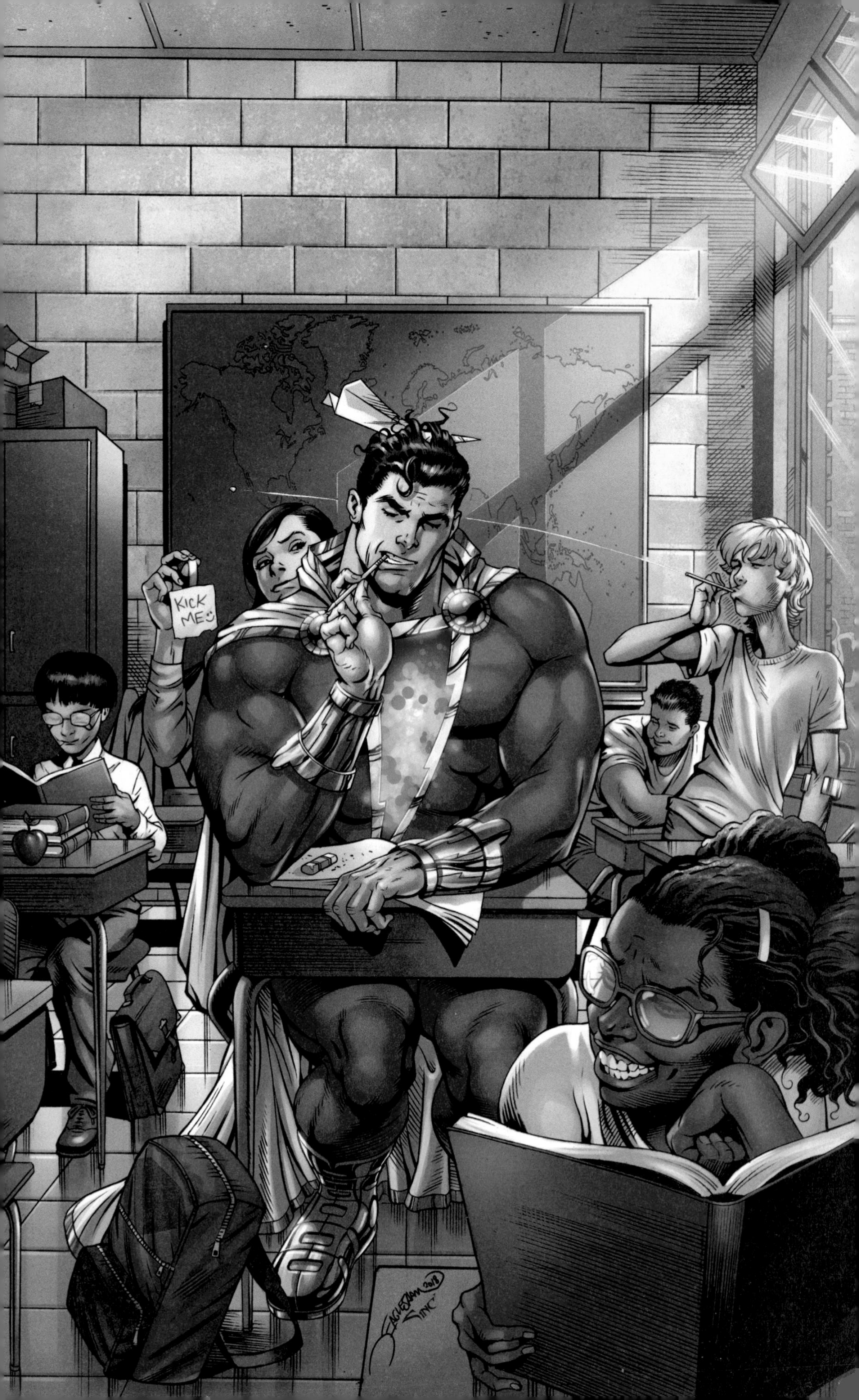
KICK ME

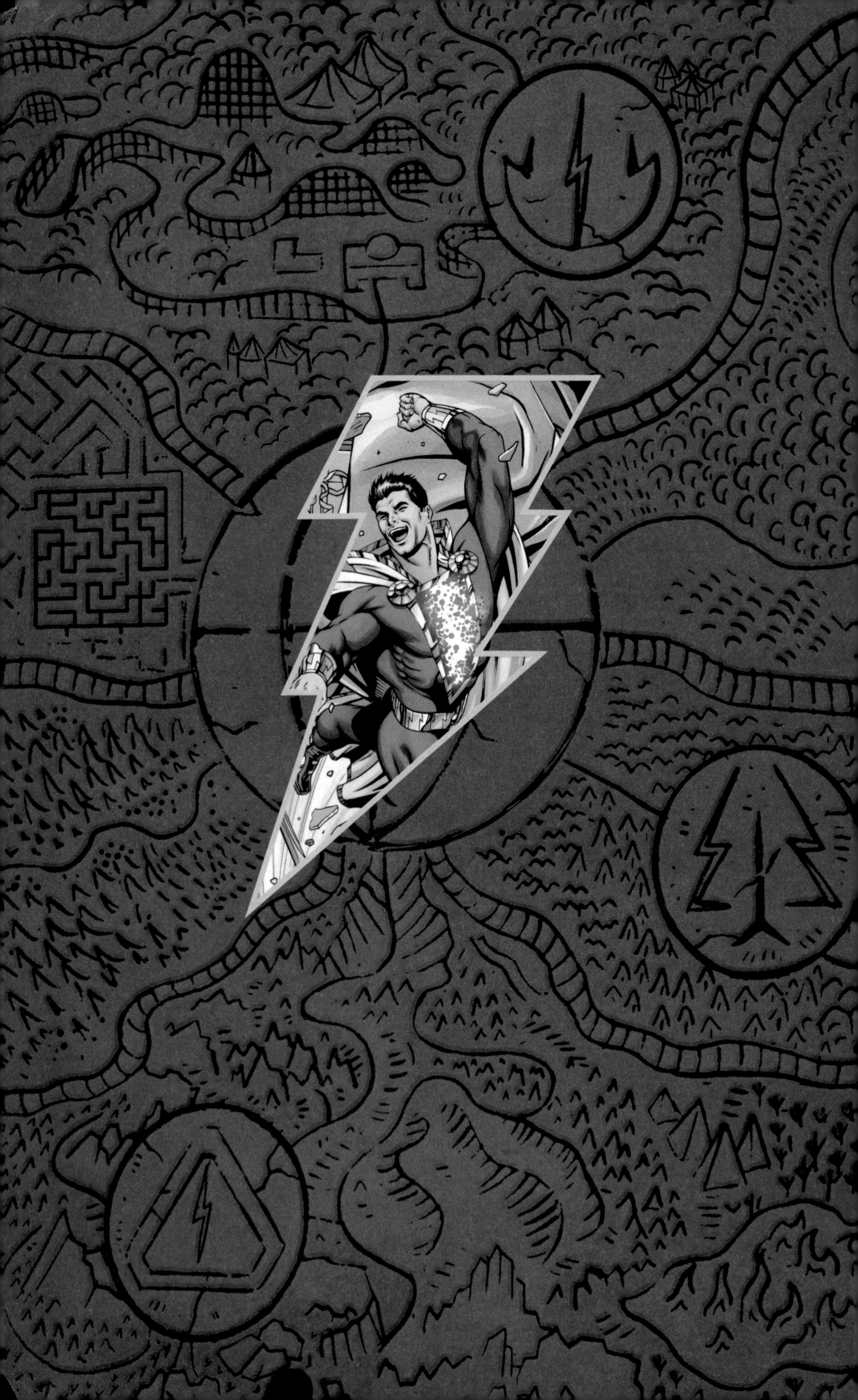

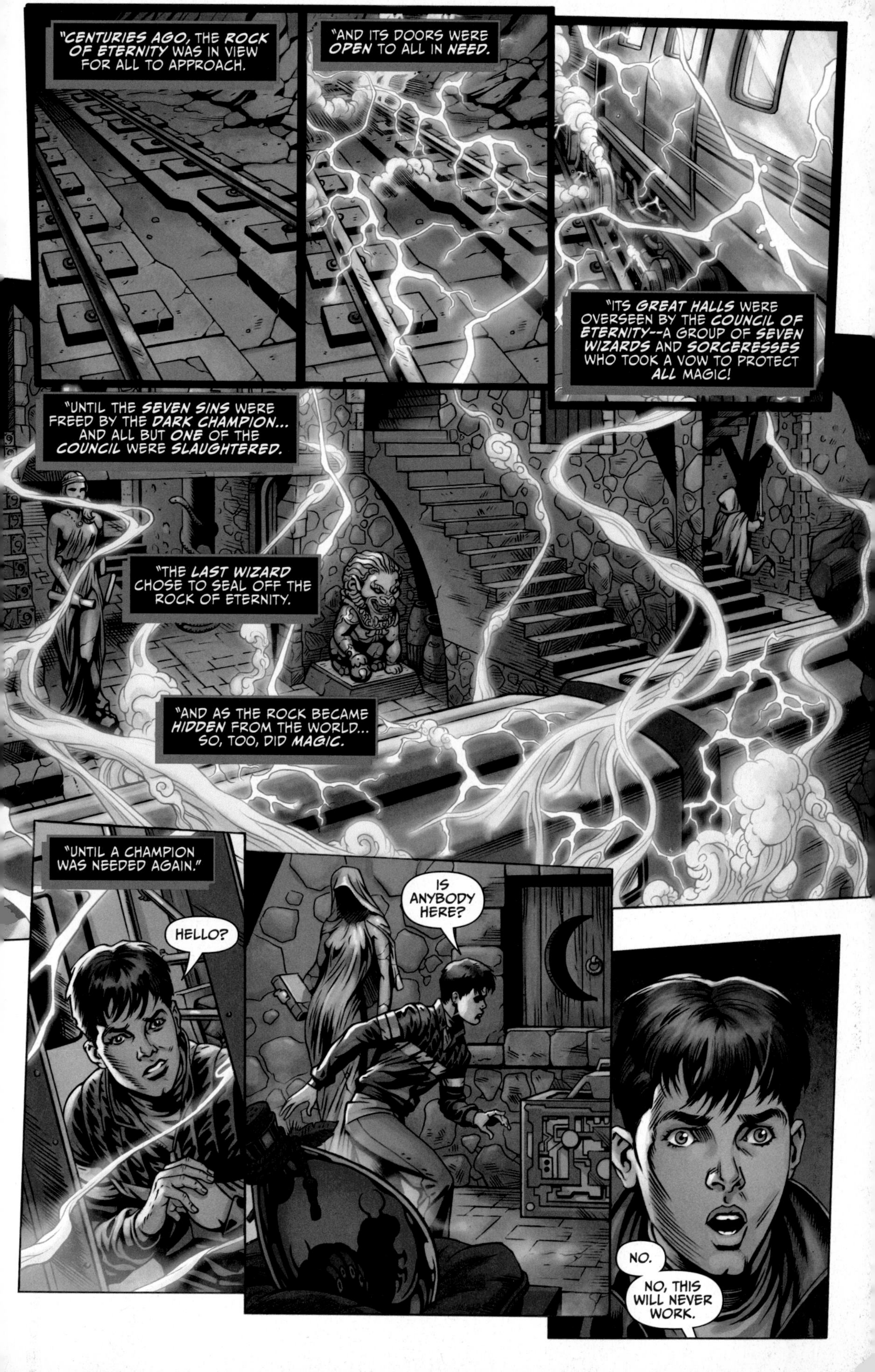
"CENTURIES AGO, THE ROCK OF ETERNITY WAS IN VIEW FOR ALL TO APPROACH.
"AND ITS DOORS WERE OPEN TO ALL IN NEED.
"ITS GREAT HALLS WERE OVERSEEN BY THE COUNCIL OF ETERNITY--A GROUP OF SEVEN WIZARDS AND SORCERESSES WHO TOOK A VOW TO PROTECT ALL MAGIC!
"UNTIL THE SEVEN SINS WERE FREED BY THE DARK CHAMPION... AND ALL BUT ONE OF THE COUNCIL WERE SLAUGHTERED.
"THE LAST WIZARD CHOSE TO SEAL OFF THE ROCK OF ETERNITY.
"AND AS THE ROCK BECAME HIDDEN FROM THE WORLD... SO, TOO, DID MAGIC.
"UNTIL A CHAMPION WAS NEEDED AGAIN."
HELLO?
IS ANYBODY HERE?
NO.
NO, THIS WILL NEVER WORK.

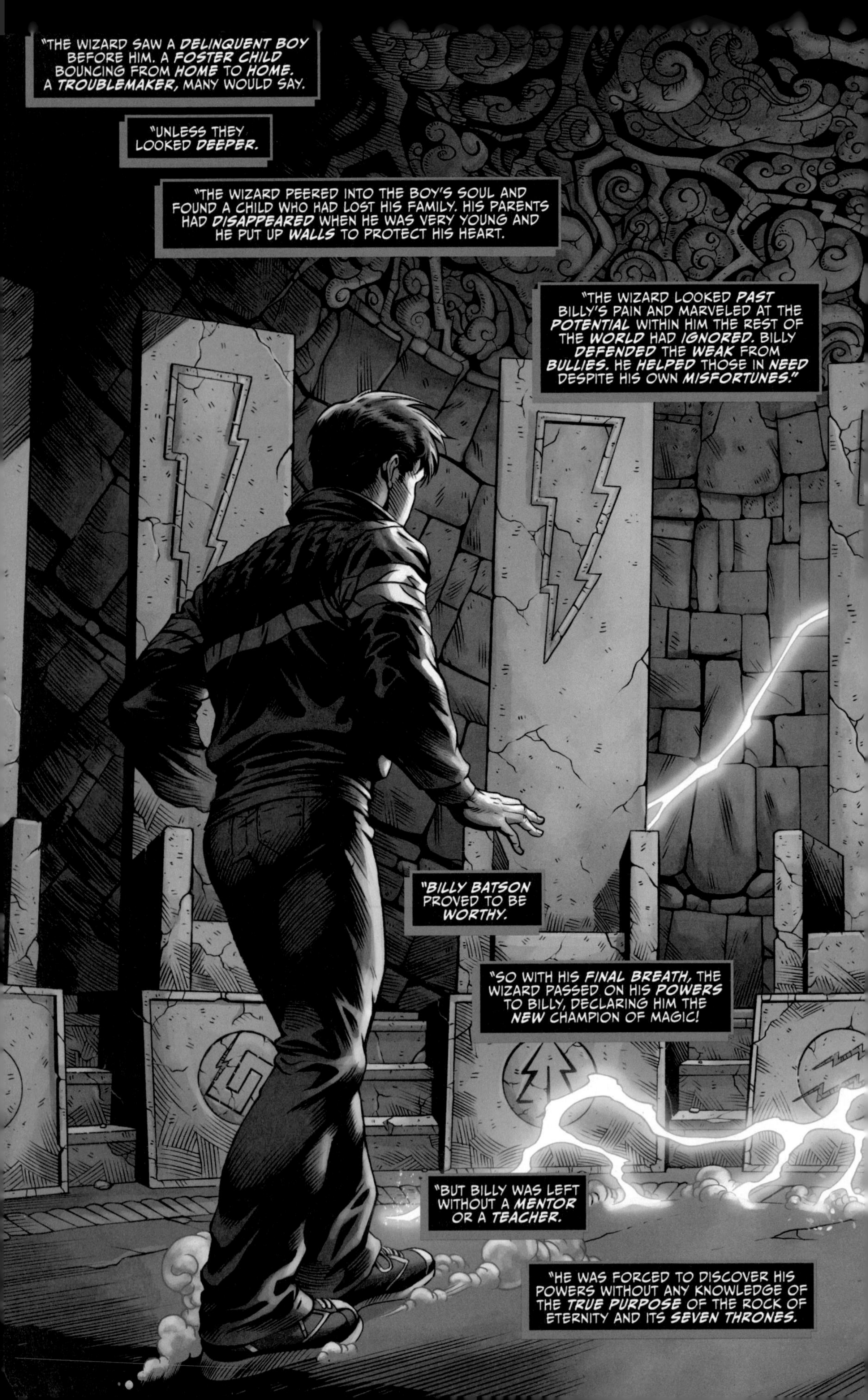
"THE WIZARD SAW A DELINQUENT BOY BEFORE HIM. A FOSTER CHILD BOUNCING FROM HOME TO HOME. A TROUBLEMAKER, MANY WOULD SAY.
"UNLESS THEY LOOKED DEEPER.
"THE WIZARD PEERED INTO THE BOY'S SOUL AND FOUND A CHILD WHO HAD LOST HIS FAMILY. HIS PARENTS HAD DISAPPEARED WHEN HE WAS VERY YOUNG AND HE PUT UP WALLS TO PROTECT HIS HEART.
"THE WIZARD LOOKED PAST BILLY'S PAIN AND MARVELED AT THE POTENTIAL WITHIN HIM THE REST OF THE WORLD HAD IGNORED. BILLY DEFENDED THE WEAK FROM BULLIES. HE HELPED THOSE IN NEED DESPITE HIS OWN MISFORTUNES."
"BILLY BATSON PROVED TO BE WORTHY.
"SO WITH HIS FINAL BREATH, THE WIZARD PASSED ON HIS POWERS TO BILLY, DECLARING HIM THE NEW CHAMPION OF MAGIC!
"BUT BILLY WAS LEFT WITHOUT A MENTOR OR A TEACHER.
"HE WAS FORCED TO DISCOVER HIS POWERS WITHOUT ANY KNOWLEDGE OF THE TRUE PURPOSE OF THE ROCK OF ETERNITY AND ITS SEVEN THRONES.

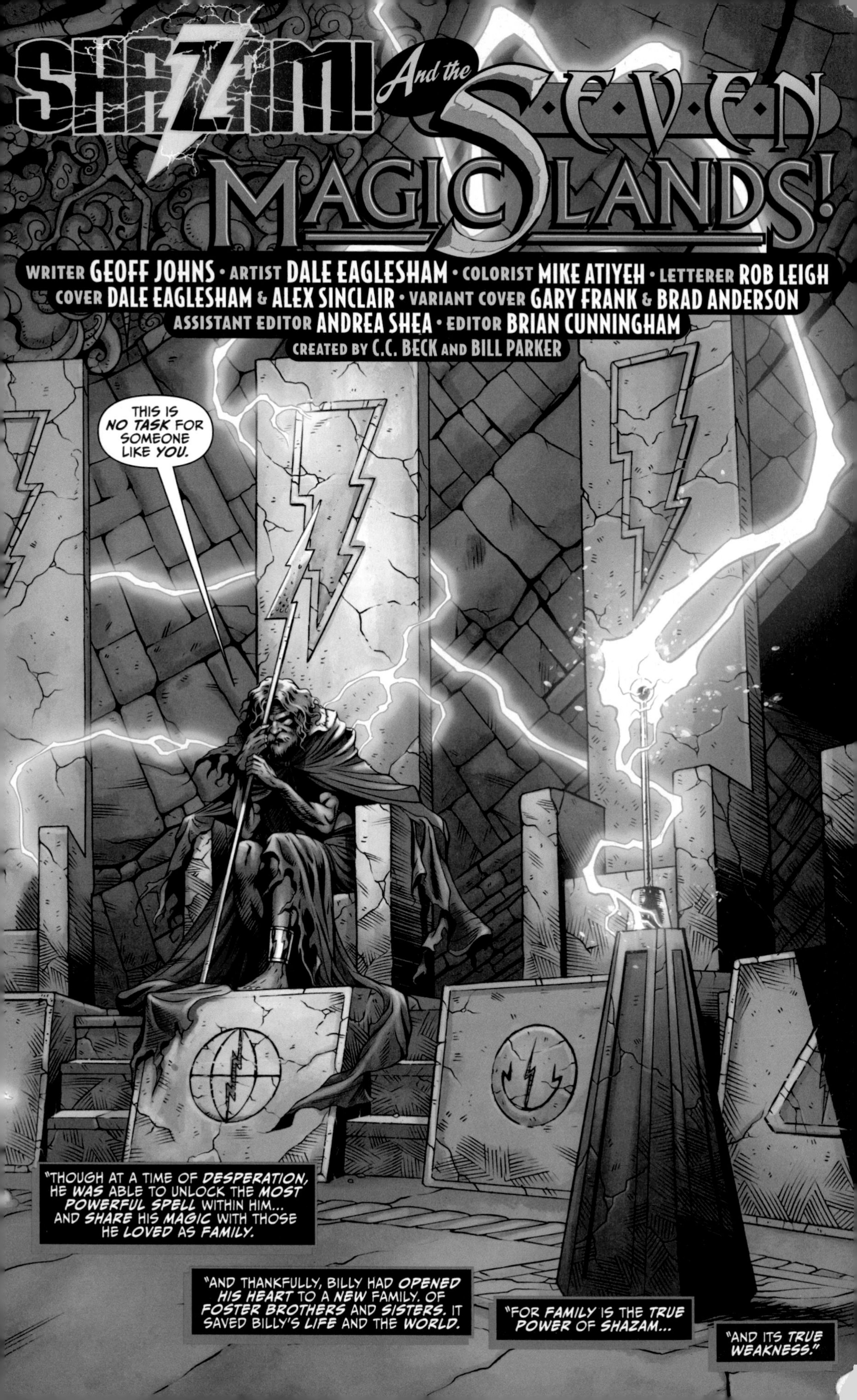
SHAZAM! And the SEVEN MAGIC LANDS!
WRITER GEOFF JOHNS • ARTIST DALE EAGLESHAM • COLORIST MIKE ATIYEH • LETTERER ROB LEIGH
COVER DALE EAGLESHAM & ALEX SINCLAIR • VARIANT COVER GARY FRANK & BRAD ANDERSON
ASSISTANT EDITOR ANDREA SHEA • EDITOR BRIAN CUNNINGHAM
CREATED BY C.C. BECK AND BILL PARKER
THIS IS NO TASK FOR SOMEONE LIKE YOU.
"THOUGH AT A TIME OF DESPERATION, HE WAS ABLE TO UNLOCK THE MOST POWERFUL SPELL WITHIN HIM... AND SHARE HIS MAGIC WITH THOSE HE LOVED AS FAMILY.
"AND THANKFULLY, BILLY HAD OPENED HIS HEART TO A NEW FAMILY. OF FOSTER BROTHERS AND SISTERS. IT SAVED BILLY'S LIFE AND THE WORLD.
"FOR FAMILY IS THE TRUE POWER OF SHAZAM...
"AND ITS TRUE WEAKNESS."

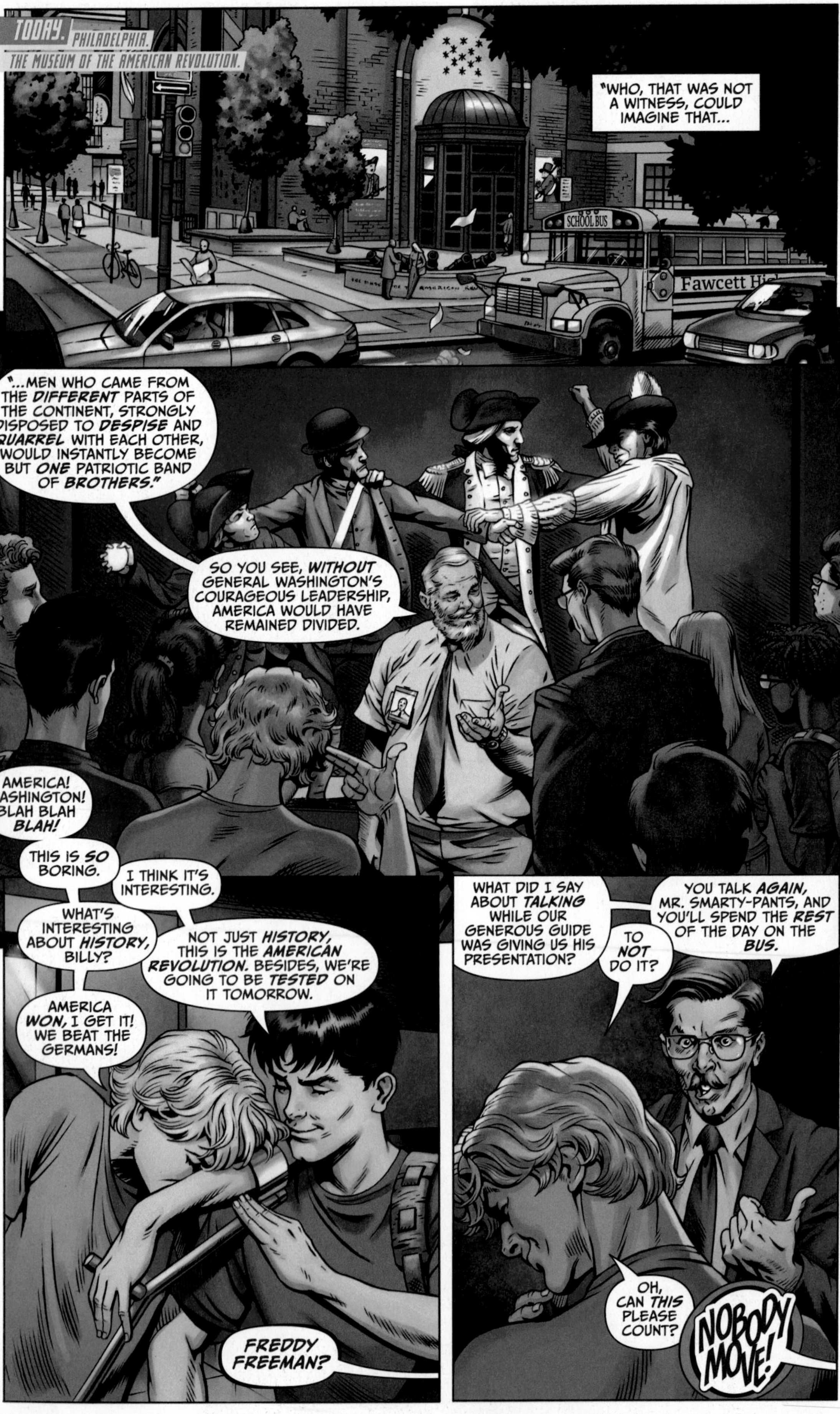
TODAY. PHILADELPHIA.
THE MUSEUM OF THE AMERICAN REVOLUTION.
"WHO, THAT WAS NOT A WITNESS, COULD IMAGINE THAT...
SCHOOL BUS
Fawcett Hi
"...MEN WHO CAME FROM THE DIFFERENT PARTS OF THE CONTINENT, STRONGLY DISPOSED TO DESPISE AND QUARREL WITH EACH OTHER, WOULD INSTANTLY BECOME BUT ONE PATRIOTIC BAND OF BROTHERS."
SO YOU SEE, WITHOUT GENERAL WASHINGTON'S COURAGEOUS LEADERSHIP, AMERICA WOULD HAVE REMAINED DIVIDED.
AMERICA! WASHINGTON! BLAH BLAH BLAH!
THIS IS SO BORING.
I THINK IT'S INTERESTING.
WHAT'S INTERESTING ABOUT HISTORY, BILLY?
NOT JUST HISTORY, THIS IS THE AMERICAN REVOLUTION. BESIDES, WE'RE GOING TO BE TESTED ON IT TOMORROW.
AMERICA WON, I GET IT! WE BEAT THE GERMANS!
FREDDY FREEMAN?
WHAT DID I SAY ABOUT TALKING WHILE OUR GENEROUS GUIDE WAS GIVING US HIS PRESENTATION?
TO NOT DO IT?
YOU TALK AGAIN, MR. SMARTY-PANTS, AND YOU'LL SPEND THE REST OF THE DAY ON THE BUS.
OH, CAN THIS PLEASE COUNT?
NOBODY MOVE!

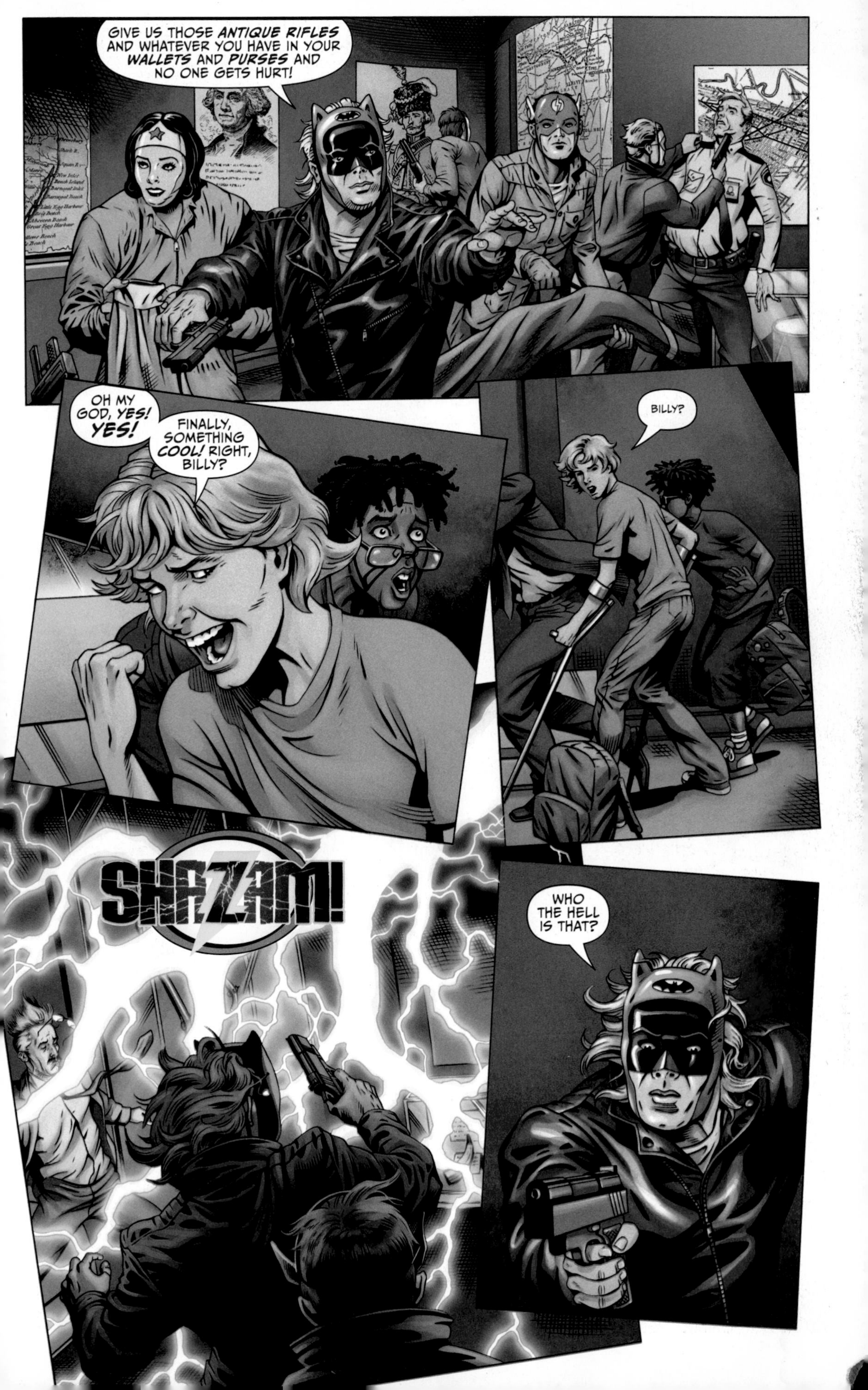
GIVE US THOSE ANTIQUE RIFLES AND WHATEVER YOU HAVE IN YOUR WALLETS AND PURSES AND NO ONE GETS HURT!
OH MY GOD, YES! YES!
FINALLY, SOMETHING COOL! RIGHT, BILLY?
BILLY?
SHAZAM!
WHO THE HELL IS THAT?

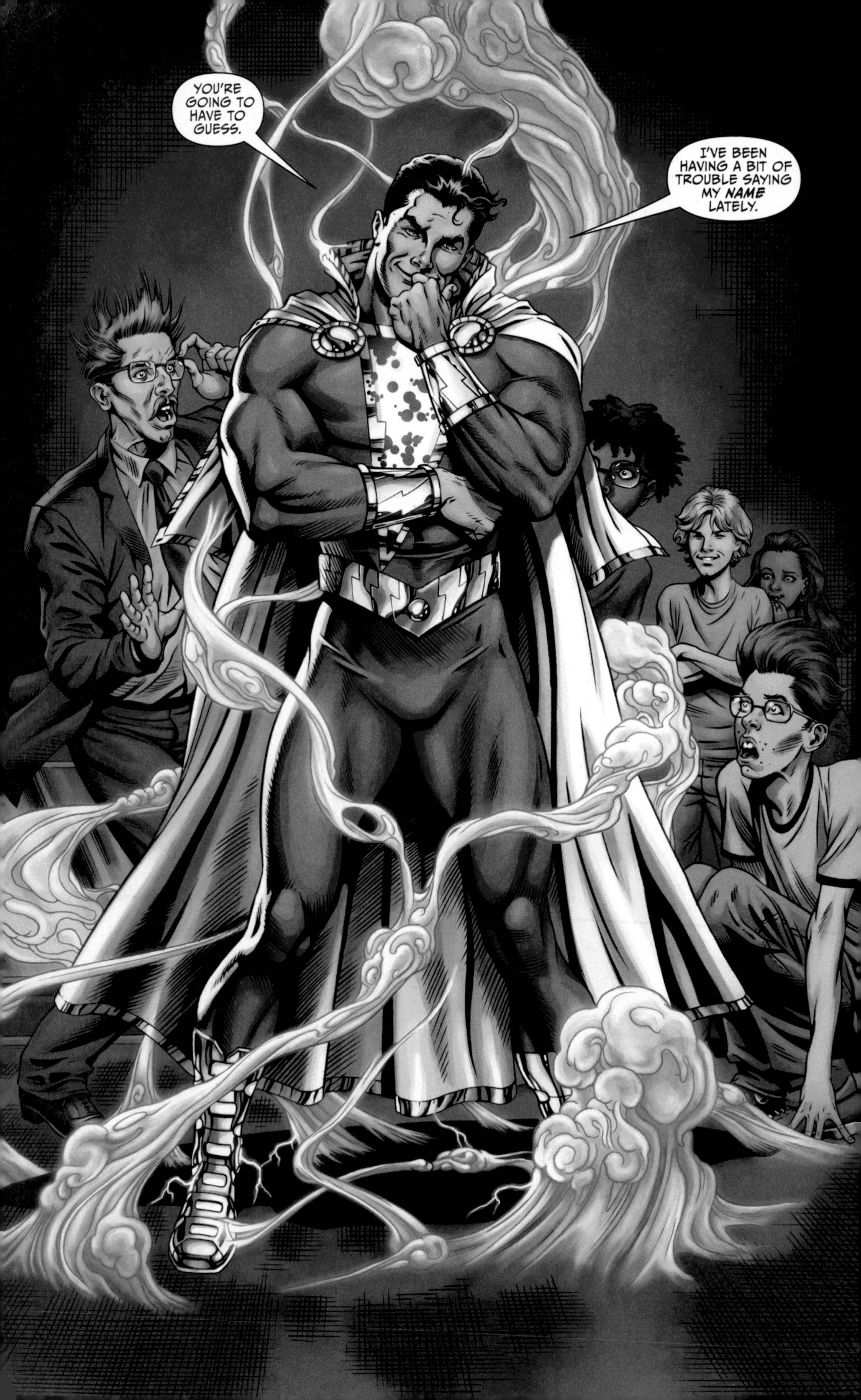
YOU'RE GOING TO HAVE TO GUESS.
I'VE BEEN HAVING A BIT OF TROUBLE SAYING MY **NAME** LATELY.

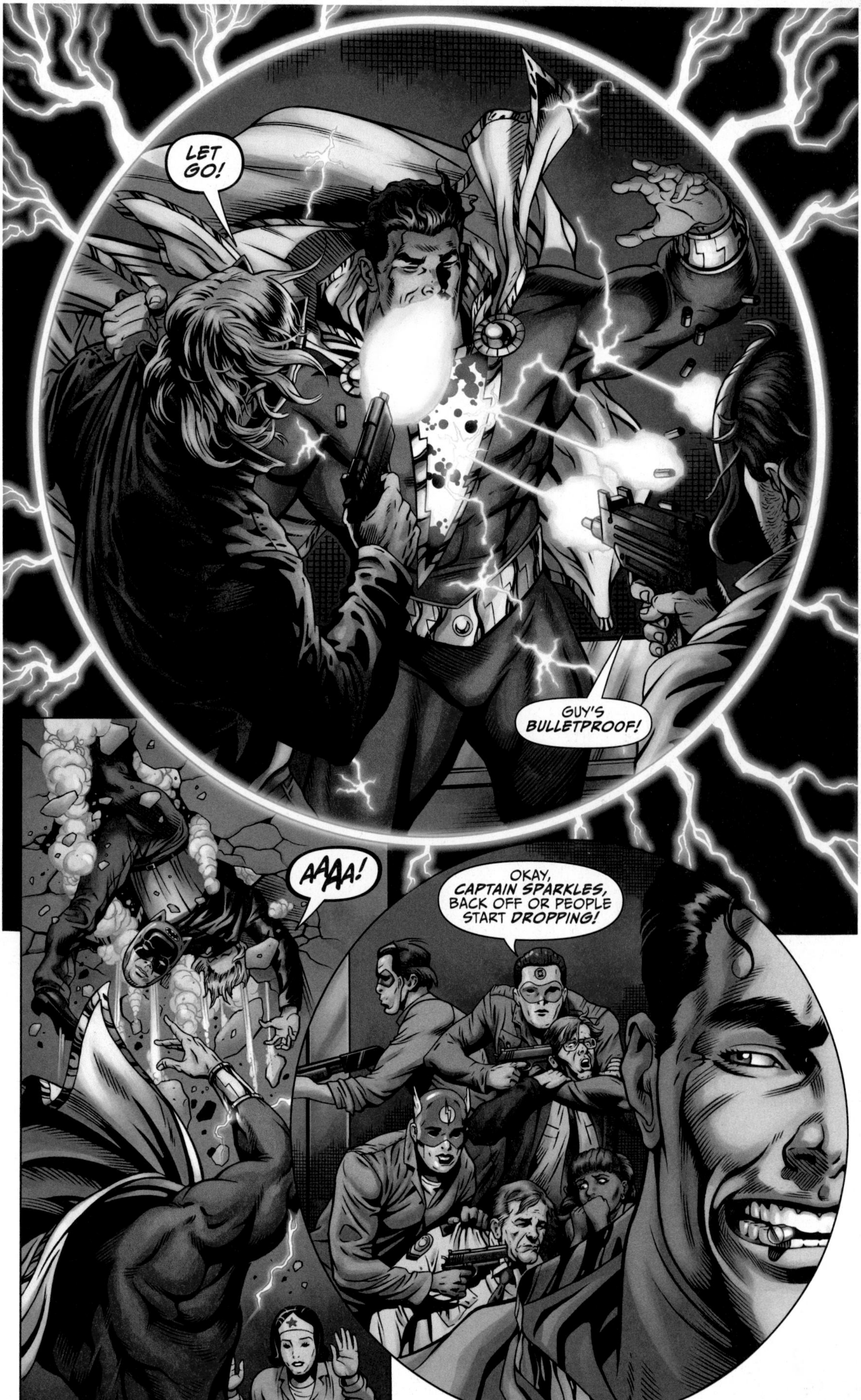
LET GO!
GUY'S BULLETPROOF!
AAAA!
OKAY, CAPTAIN SPARKLES, BACK OFF OR PEOPLE START DROPPING!

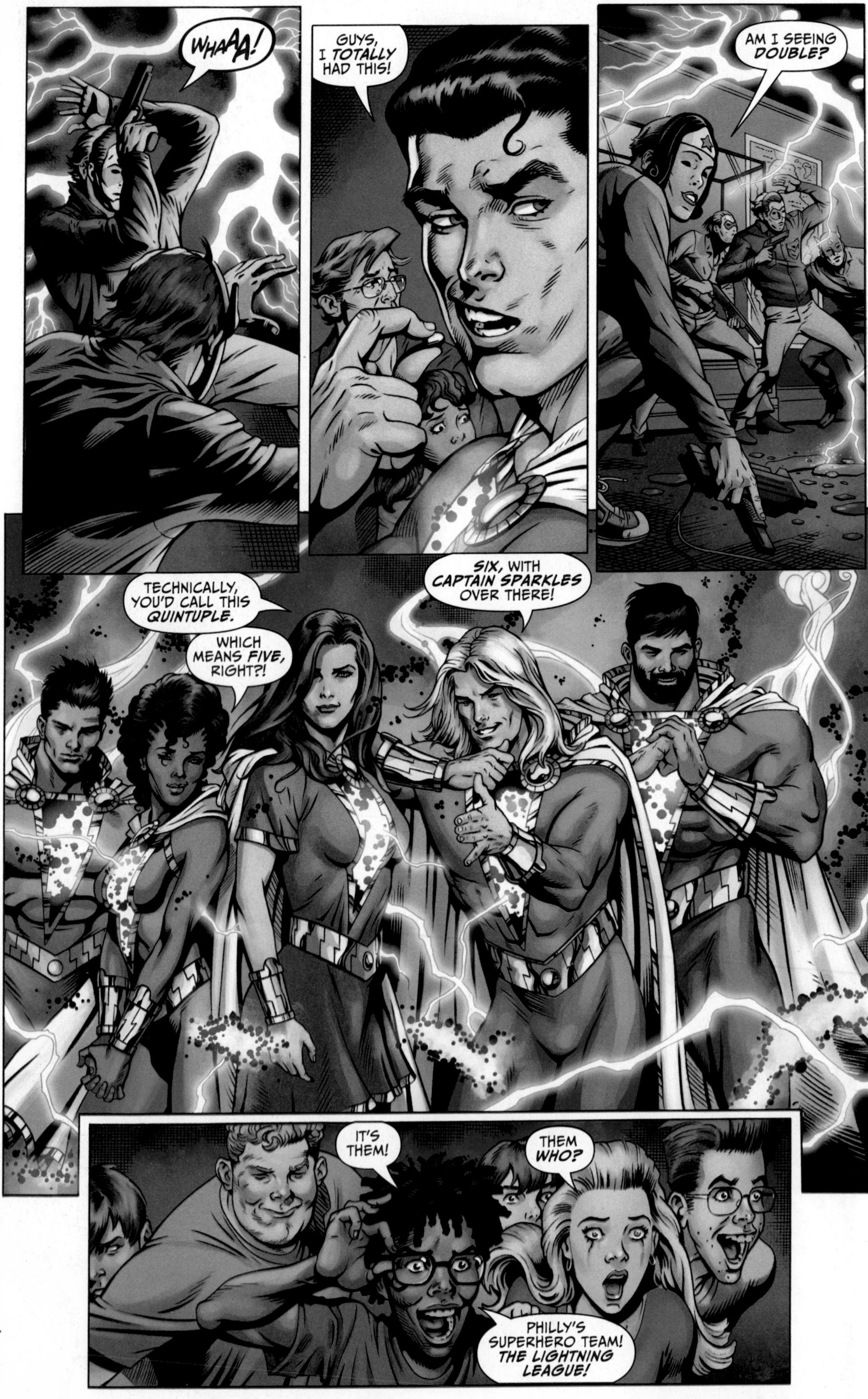
WHAAA!
GUYS, I TOTALLY HAD THIS!
AM I SEEING DOUBLE?
TECHNICALLY, YOU'D CALL THIS QUINTUPLE.
WHICH MEANS FIVE, RIGHT?!
SIX, WITH CAPTAIN SPARKLES OVER THERE!
IT'S THEM!
THEM WHO?
PHILLY'S SUPERHERO TEAM! THE LIGHTNING LEAGUE!

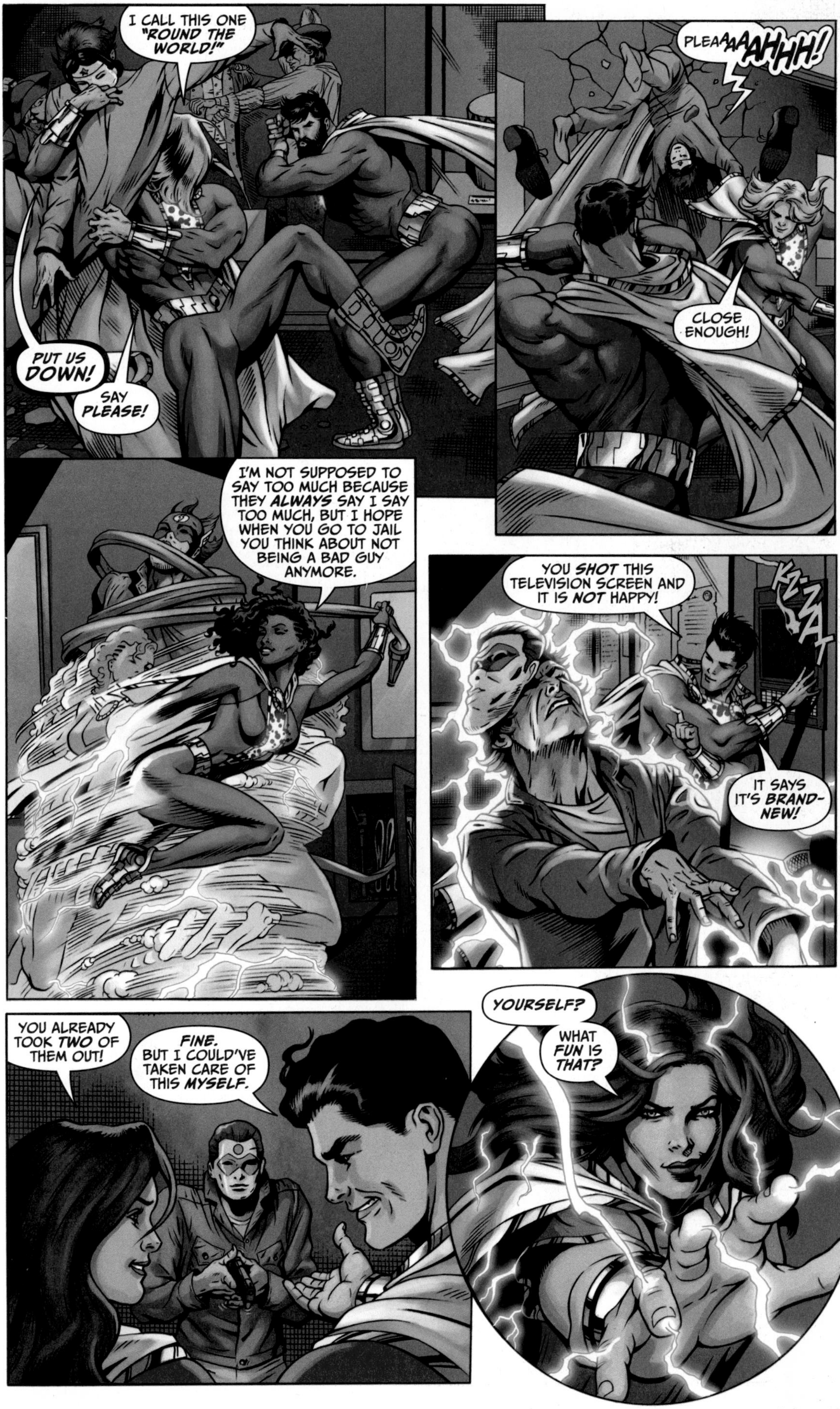
I CALL THIS ONE "ROUND THE WORLD!"
PUT US DOWN!
SAY PLEASE!
PLEAAAAAHHH!
CLOSE ENOUGH!
I'M NOT SUPPOSED TO SAY TOO MUCH BECAUSE THEY ALWAYS SAY I SAY TOO MUCH, BUT I HOPE WHEN YOU GO TO JAIL YOU THINK ABOUT NOT BEING A BAD GUY ANYMORE.
YOU SHOT THIS TELEVISION SCREEN AND IT IS NOT HAPPY!
IT SAYS IT'S BRAND-NEW!
YOU ALREADY TOOK TWO OF THEM OUT!
FINE. BUT I COULD'VE TAKEN CARE OF THIS MYSELF.
YOURSELF?
WHAT FUN IS THAT?

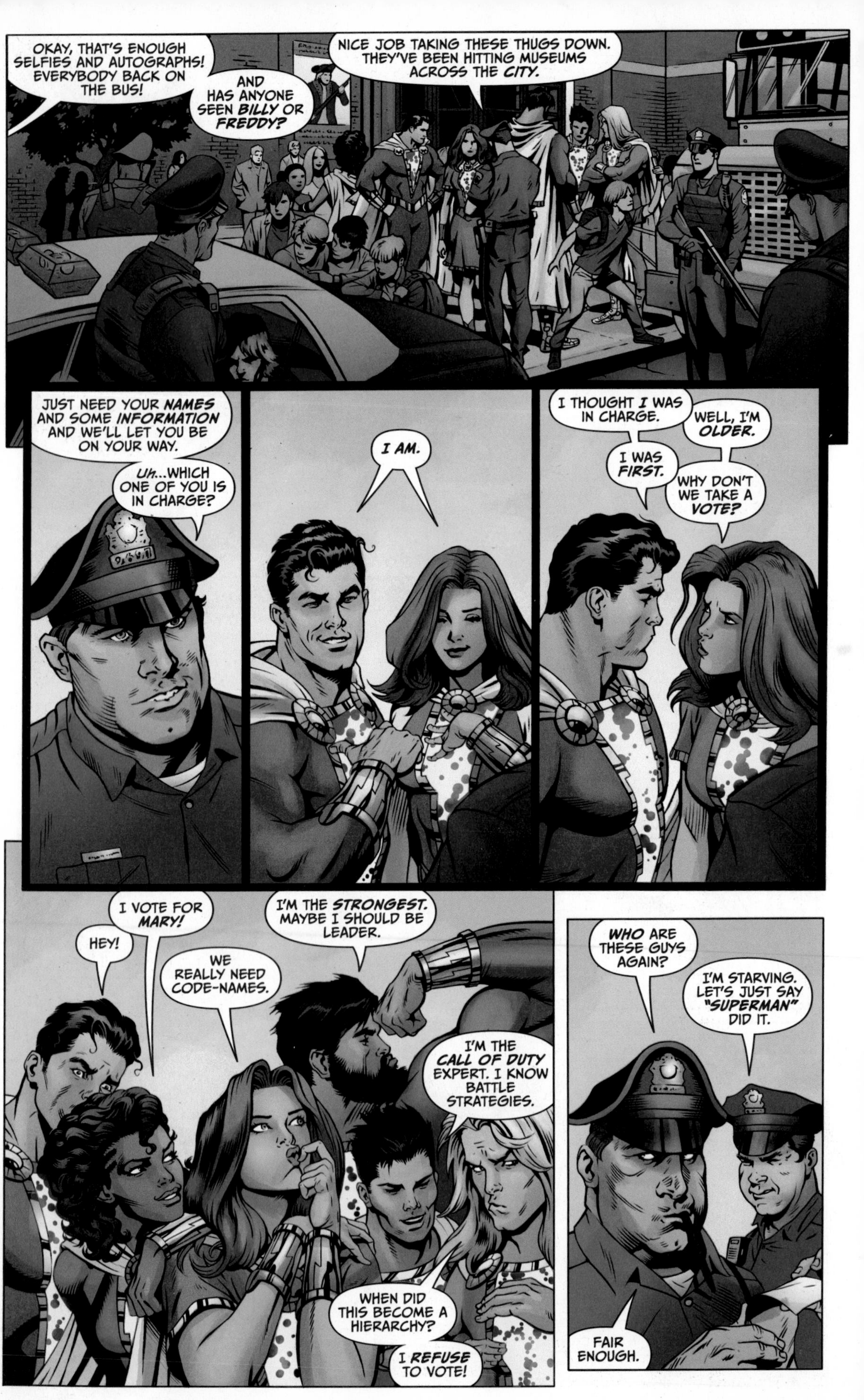
OKAY, THAT'S ENOUGH SELFIES AND AUTOGRAPHS! EVERYBODY BACK ON THE BUS!
AND HAS ANYONE SEEN BILLY OR FREDDY?
NICE JOB TAKING THESE THUGS DOWN. THEY'VE BEEN HITTING MUSEUMS ACROSS THE CITY.
JUST NEED YOUR NAMES AND SOME INFORMATION AND WE'LL LET YOU BE ON YOUR WAY.
Uh...WHICH ONE OF YOU IS IN CHARGE?
I AM.
I THOUGHT I WAS IN CHARGE.
I WAS FIRST.
WELL, I'M OLDER.
WHY DON'T WE TAKE A VOTE?
HEY!
I VOTE FOR MARY!
WE REALLY NEED CODE-NAMES.
I'M THE STRONGEST. MAYBE I SHOULD BE LEADER.
I'M THE CALL OF DUTY EXPERT. I KNOW BATTLE STRATEGIES.
WHEN DID THIS BECOME A HIERARCHY?
I REFUSE TO VOTE!
WHO ARE THESE GUYS AGAIN?
I'M STARVING. LET'S JUST SAY "SUPERMAN" DID IT.
FAIR ENOUGH.

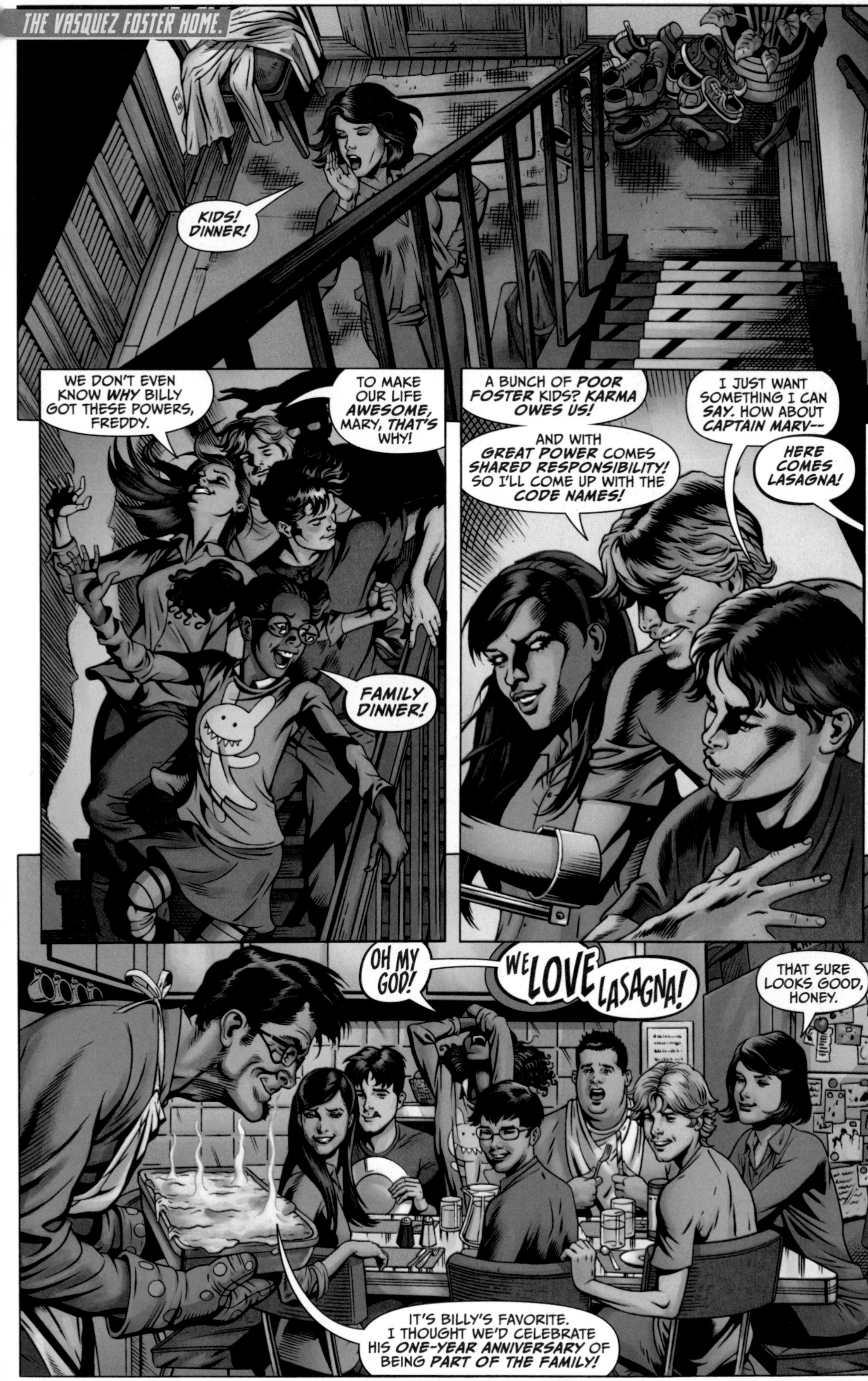
THE VASQUEZ FOSTER HOME.
KIDS! DINNER!
WE DON'T EVEN KNOW WHY BILLY GOT THESE POWERS, FREDDY.
TO MAKE OUR LIFE AWESOME, MARY, THAT'S WHY!
FAMILY DINNER!
A BUNCH OF POOR FOSTER KIDS? KARMA OWES US!
AND WITH GREAT POWER COMES SHARED RESPONSIBILITY! SO I'LL COME UP WITH THE CODE NAMES!
I JUST WANT SOMETHING I CAN SAY. HOW ABOUT CAPTAIN MARV--
HERE COMES LASAGNA!
OH MY GOD!
WE LOVE LASAGNA!
THAT SURE LOOKS GOOD, HONEY.
IT'S BILLY'S FAVORITE. I THOUGHT WE'D CELEBRATE HIS ONE-YEAR ANNIVERSARY OF BEING PART OF THE FAMILY!

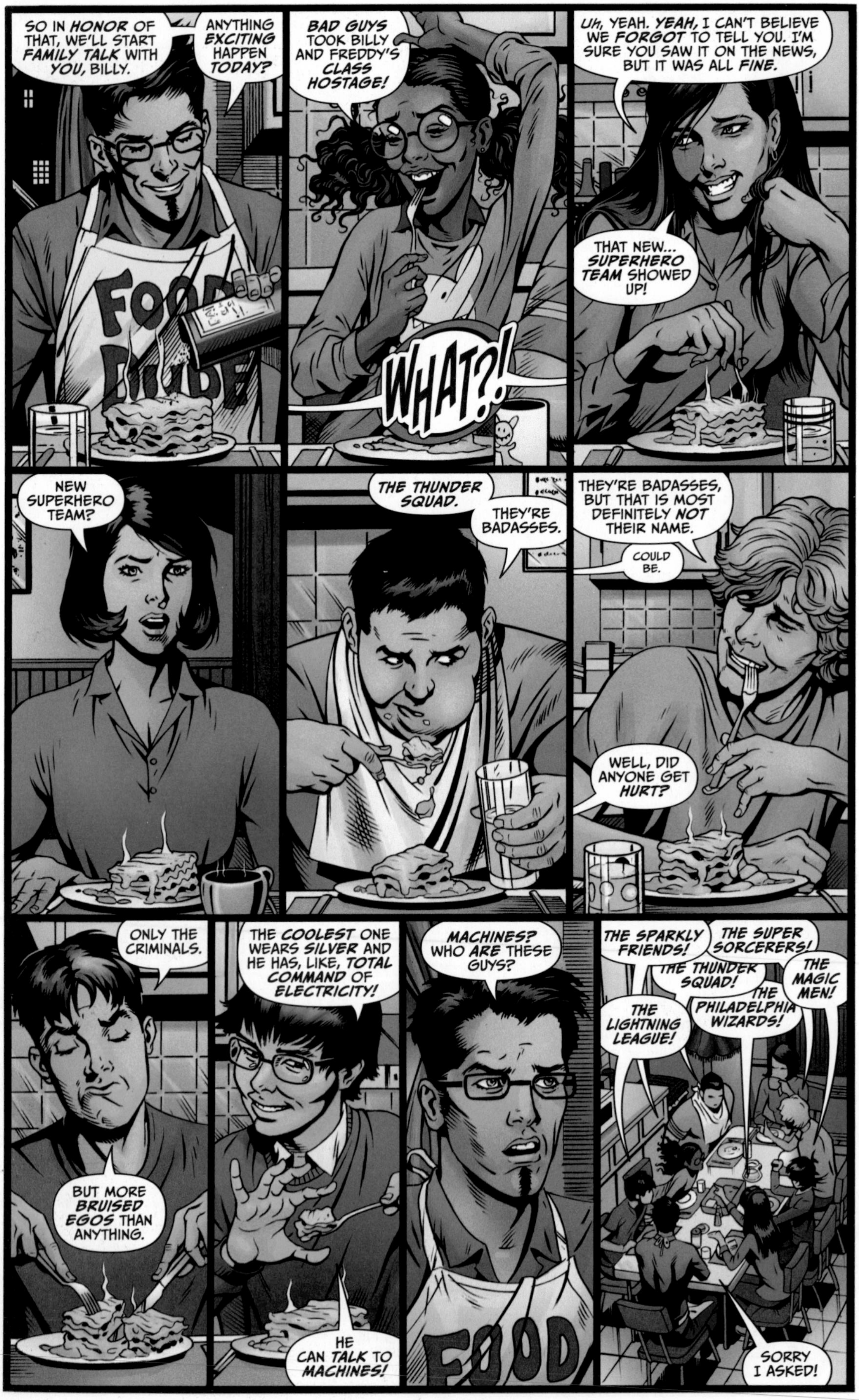
SO IN HONOR OF THAT, WE'LL START FAMILY TALK WITH YOU, BILLY.
ANYTHING EXCITING HAPPEN TODAY?
BAD GUYS TOOK BILLY AND FREDDY'S CLASS HOSTAGE!
WHAT?!
Uh, YEAH. YEAH, I CAN'T BELIEVE WE FORGOT TO TELL YOU. I'M SURE YOU SAW IT ON THE NEWS, BUT IT WAS ALL FINE.
THAT NEW... SUPERHERO TEAM SHOWED UP!
NEW SUPERHERO TEAM?
THE THUNDER SQUAD.
THEY'RE BADASSES.
THEY'RE BADASSES, BUT THAT IS MOST DEFINITELY NOT THEIR NAME.
COULD BE.
WELL, DID ANYONE GET HURT?
ONLY THE CRIMINALS.
BUT MORE BRUISED EGOS THAN ANYTHING.
THE COOLEST ONE WEARS SILVER AND HE HAS, LIKE, TOTAL COMMAND OF ELECTRICITY!
HE CAN TALK TO MACHINES!
MACHINES? WHO ARE THESE GUYS?
THE SPARKLY FRIENDS!
THE SUPER SORCERERS!
THE THUNDER SQUAD!
THE MAGIC MEN!
THE PHILADELPHIA WIZARDS!
THE LIGHTNING LEAGUE!
SORRY I ASKED!

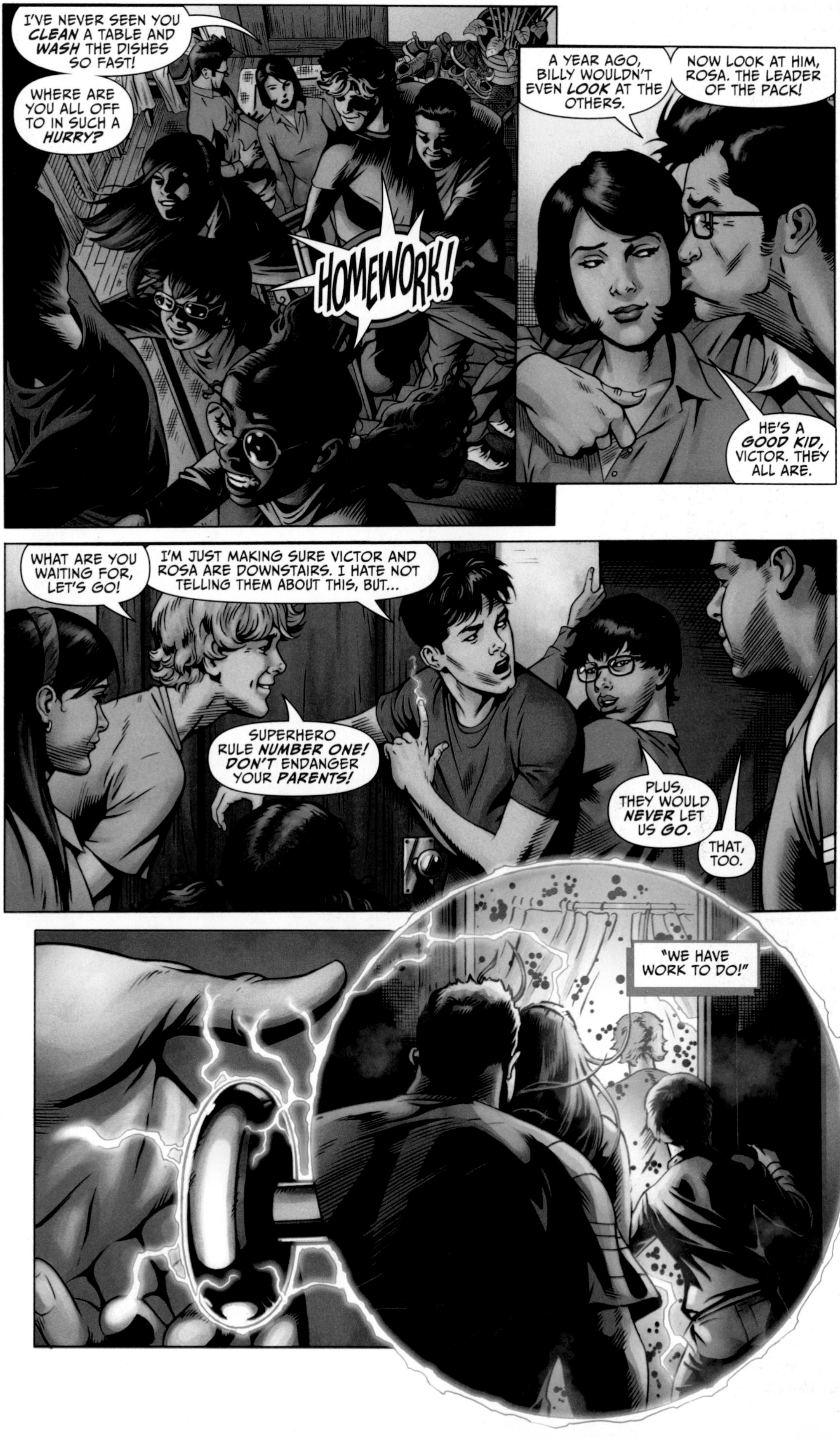
I'VE NEVER SEEN YOU CLEAN A TABLE AND WASH THE DISHES SO FAST!
WHERE ARE YOU ALL OFF TO IN SUCH A HURRY?
HOMEWORK!
A YEAR AGO, BILLY WOULDN'T EVEN LOOK AT THE OTHERS.
NOW LOOK AT HIM, ROSA. THE LEADER OF THE PACK!
HE'S A GOOD KID, VICTOR. THEY ALL ARE.
WHAT ARE YOU WAITING FOR, LET'S GO!
I'M JUST MAKING SURE VICTOR AND ROSA ARE DOWNSTAIRS. I HATE NOT TELLING THEM ABOUT THIS, BUT...
SUPERHERO RULE NUMBER ONE! DON'T ENDANGER YOUR PARENTS!
PLUS, THEY WOULD NEVER LET US GO.
THAT, TOO.
"WE HAVE WORK TO DO!"

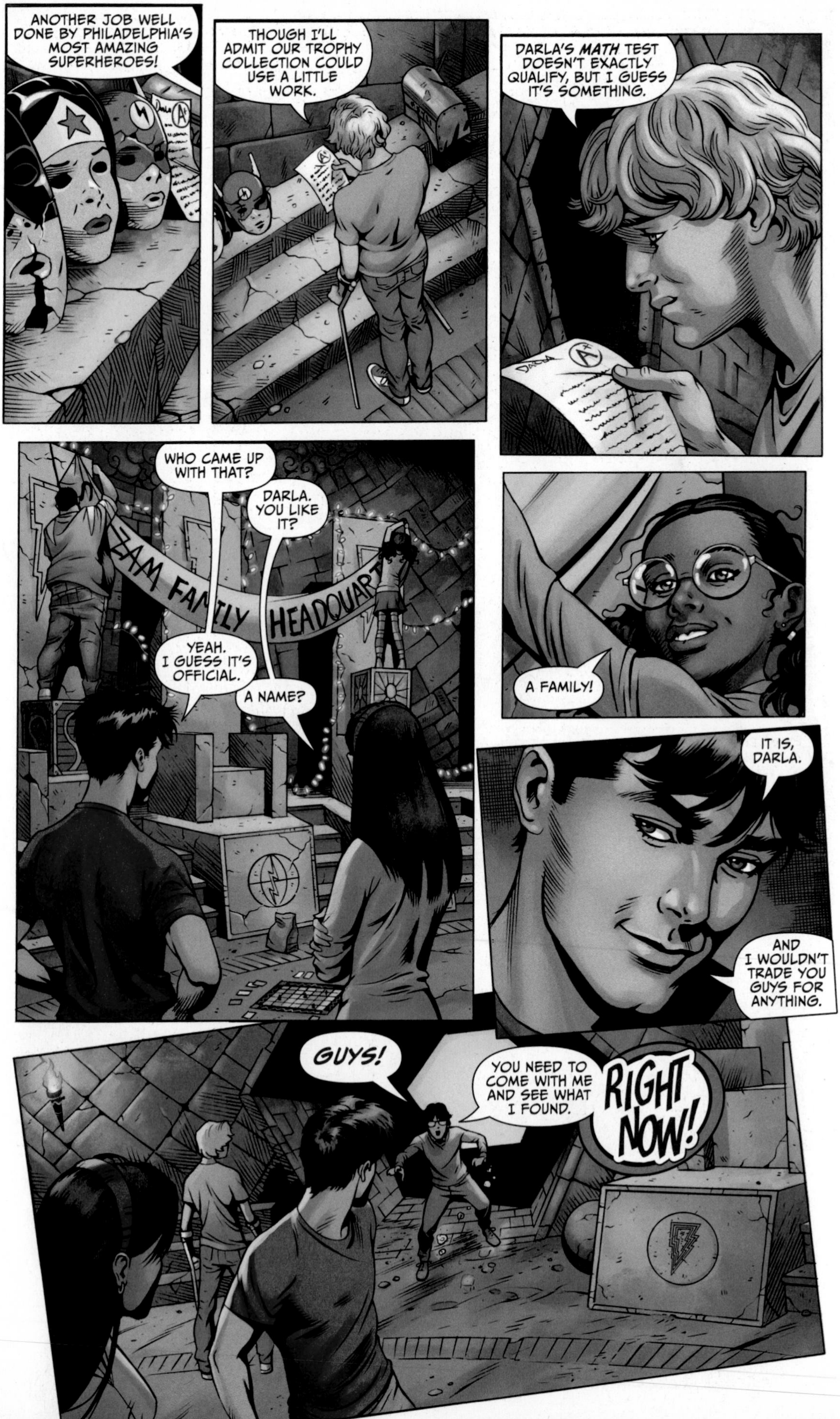
ANOTHER JOB WELL DONE BY PHILADELPHIA'S MOST AMAZING SUPERHEROES!
THOUGH I'LL ADMIT OUR TROPHY COLLECTION COULD USE A LITTLE WORK.
DARLA'S MATH TEST DOESN'T EXACTLY QUALIFY, BUT I GUESS IT'S SOMETHING.
WHO CAME UP WITH THAT?
DARLA. YOU LIKE IT?
YEAH. I GUESS IT'S OFFICIAL.
A NAME?
A FAMILY!
IT IS, DARLA.
AND I WOULDN'T TRADE YOU GUYS FOR ANYTHING.
GUYS!
YOU NEED TO COME WITH ME AND SEE WHAT I FOUND.
RIGHT NOW!

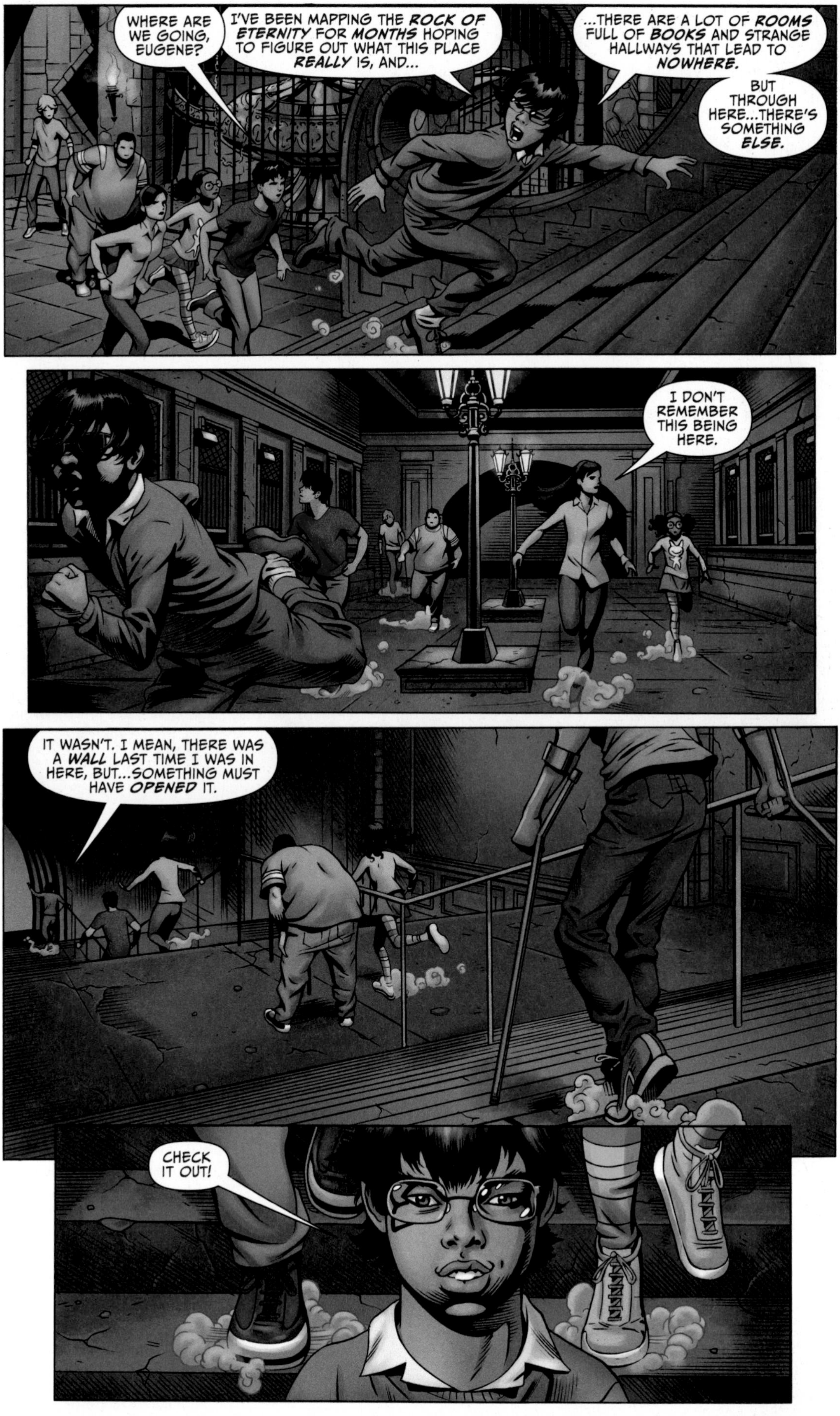
WHERE ARE WE GOING, EUGENE?
I'VE BEEN MAPPING THE ROCK OF ETERNITY FOR MONTHS HOPING TO FIGURE OUT WHAT THIS PLACE REALLY IS, AND...
...THERE ARE A LOT OF ROOMS FULL OF BOOKS AND STRANGE HALLWAYS THAT LEAD TO NOWHERE.
BUT THROUGH HERE...THERE'S SOMETHING ELSE.
I DON'T REMEMBER THIS BEING HERE.
IT WASN'T. I MEAN, THERE WAS A WALL LAST TIME I WAS IN HERE, BUT...SOMETHING MUST HAVE OPENED IT.
CHECK IT OUT!

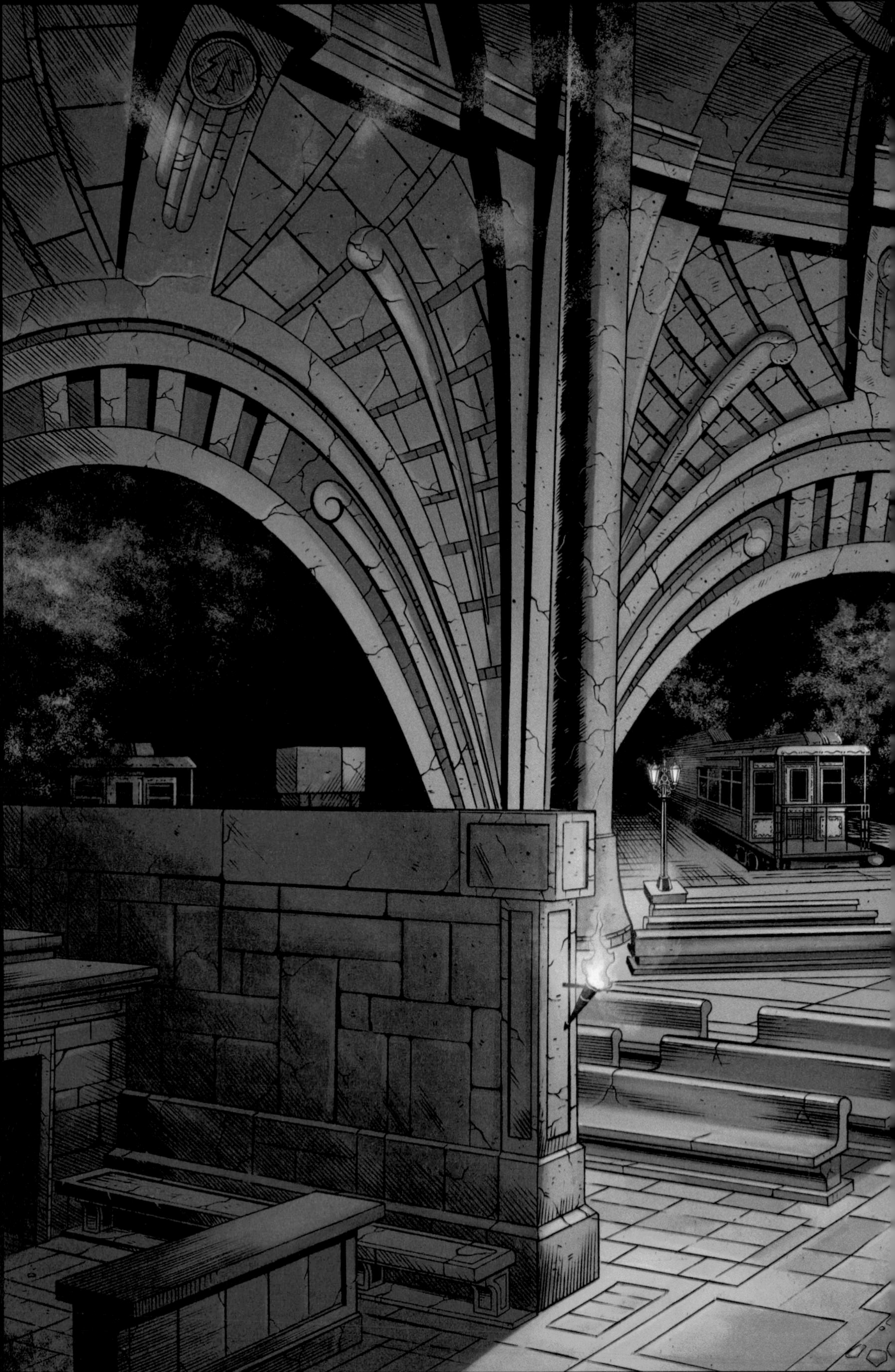

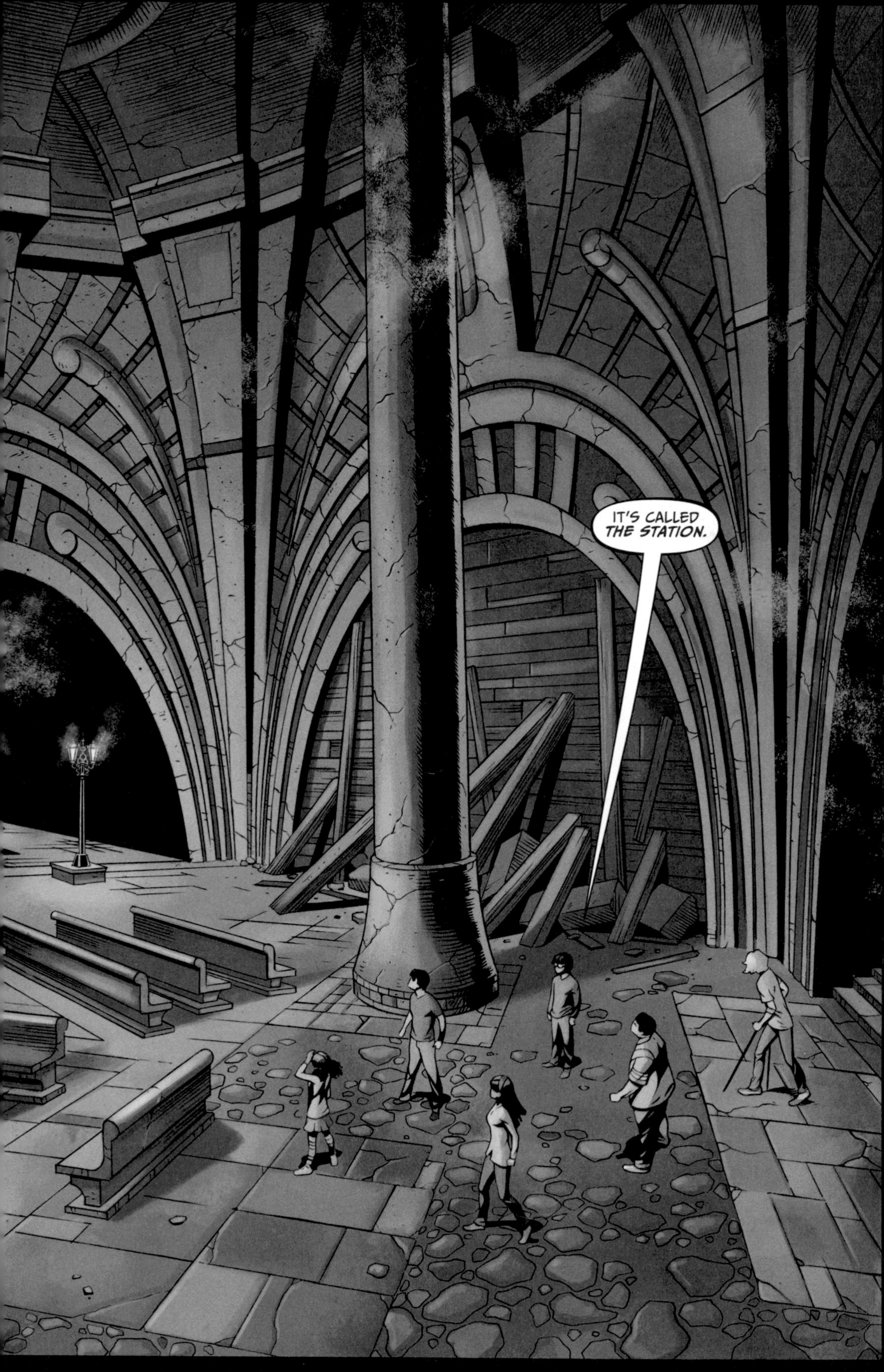
IT'S CALLED *THE STATION.*

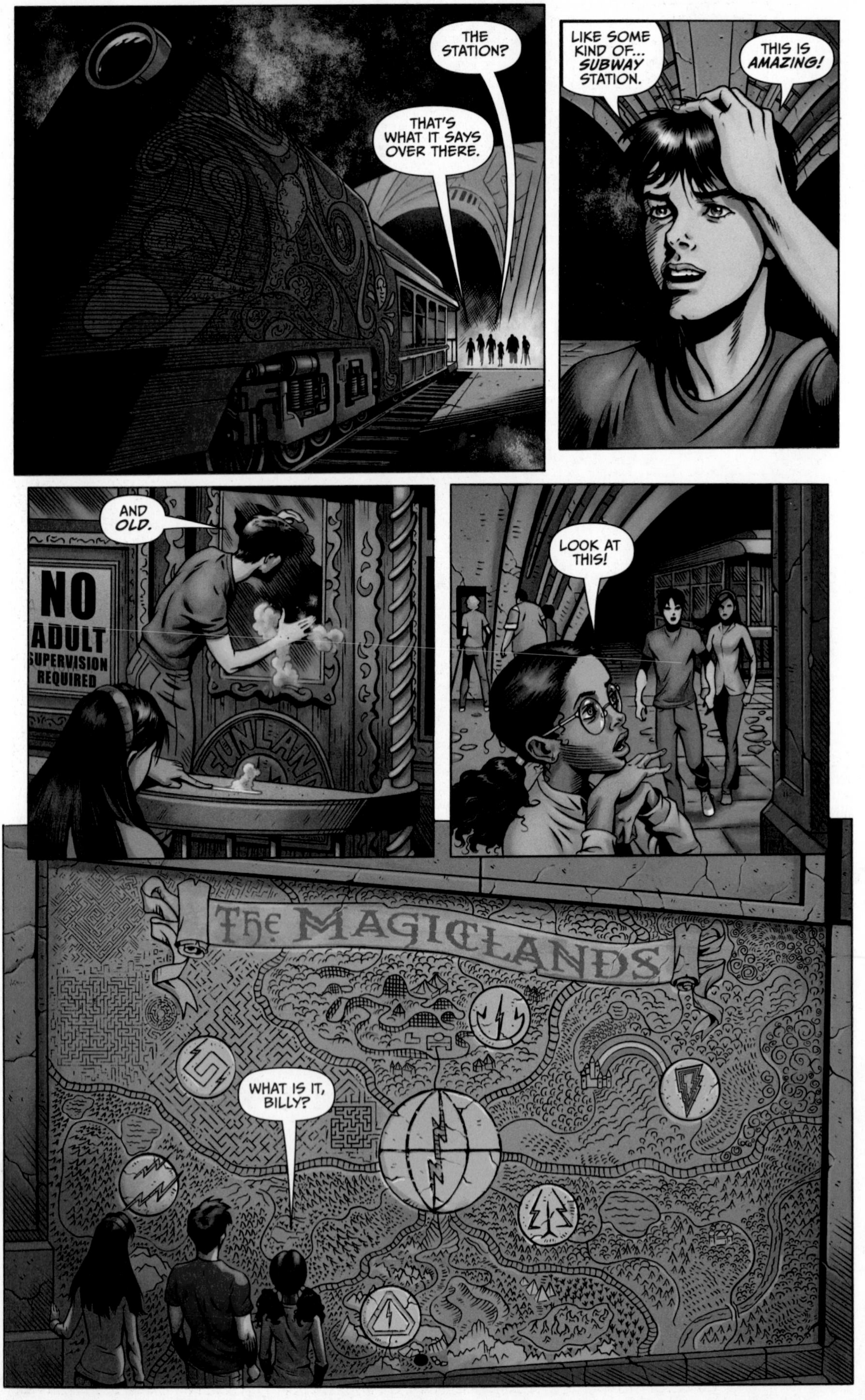
THE STATION?
THAT'S WHAT IT SAYS OVER THERE.
LIKE SOME KIND OF... *SUBWAY* STATION.
THIS IS *AMAZING!*
AND *OLD.*
NO ADULT SUPERVISION REQUIRED
LOOK AT THIS!
THE MAGICLANDS
WHAT IS IT, BILLY?

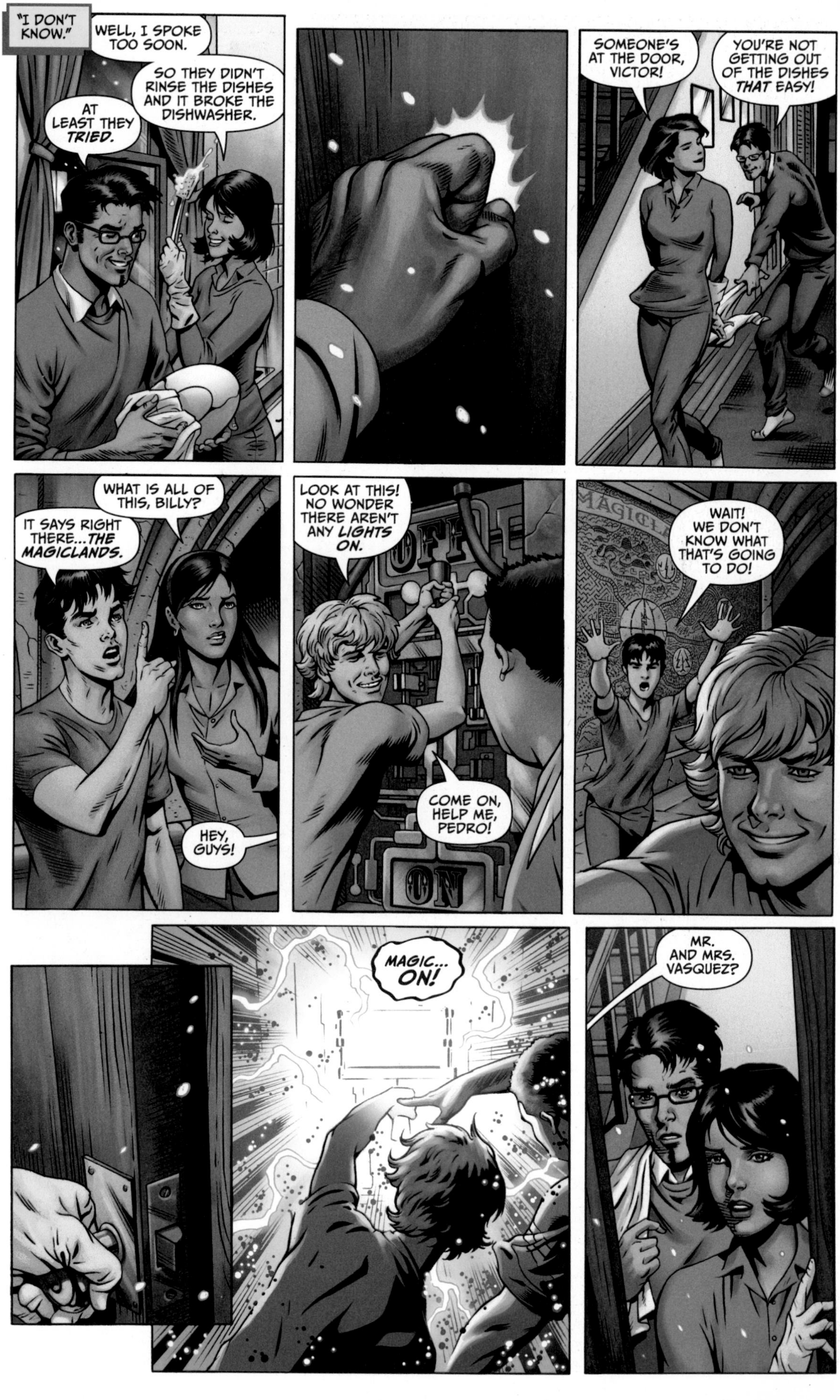
"I DON'T KNOW."
WELL, I SPOKE TOO SOON.
SO THEY DIDN'T RINSE THE DISHES AND IT BROKE THE DISHWASHER.
AT LEAST THEY *TRIED.*
SOMEONE'S AT THE DOOR, VICTOR!
YOU'RE NOT GETTING OUT OF THE DISHES *THAT* EASY!
WHAT IS ALL OF THIS, BILLY?
IT SAYS RIGHT THERE...*THE MAGICLANDS.*
HEY, GUYS!
LOOK AT THIS! NO WONDER THERE AREN'T ANY *LIGHTS ON.*
COME ON, HELP ME, PEDRO!
OFF
ON
WAIT! WE DON'T KNOW WHAT THAT'S GOING TO DO!
MAGIC... *ON!*
MR. AND MRS. VASQUEZ?

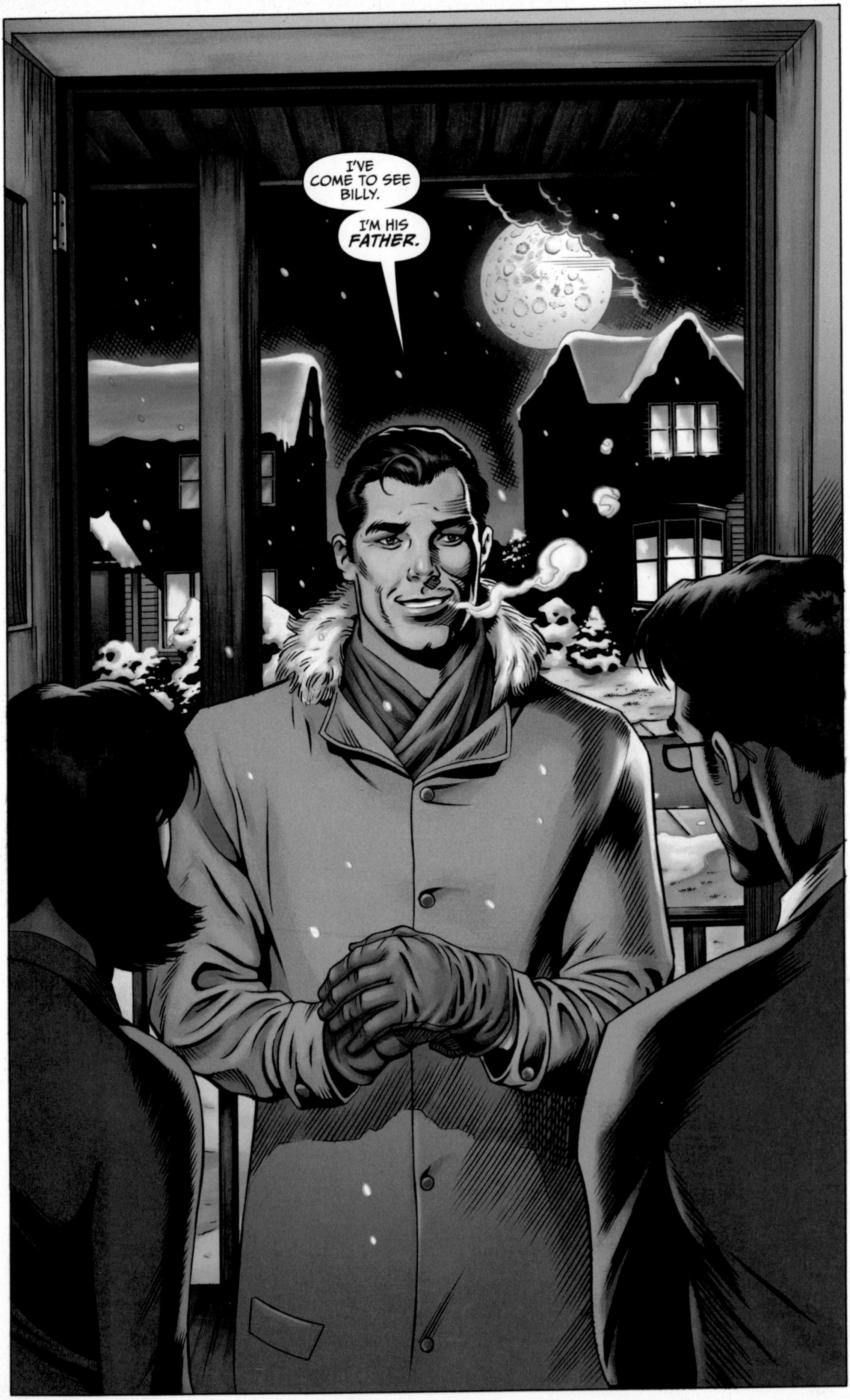
I'VE COME TO SEE BILLY.
I'M HIS FATHER.

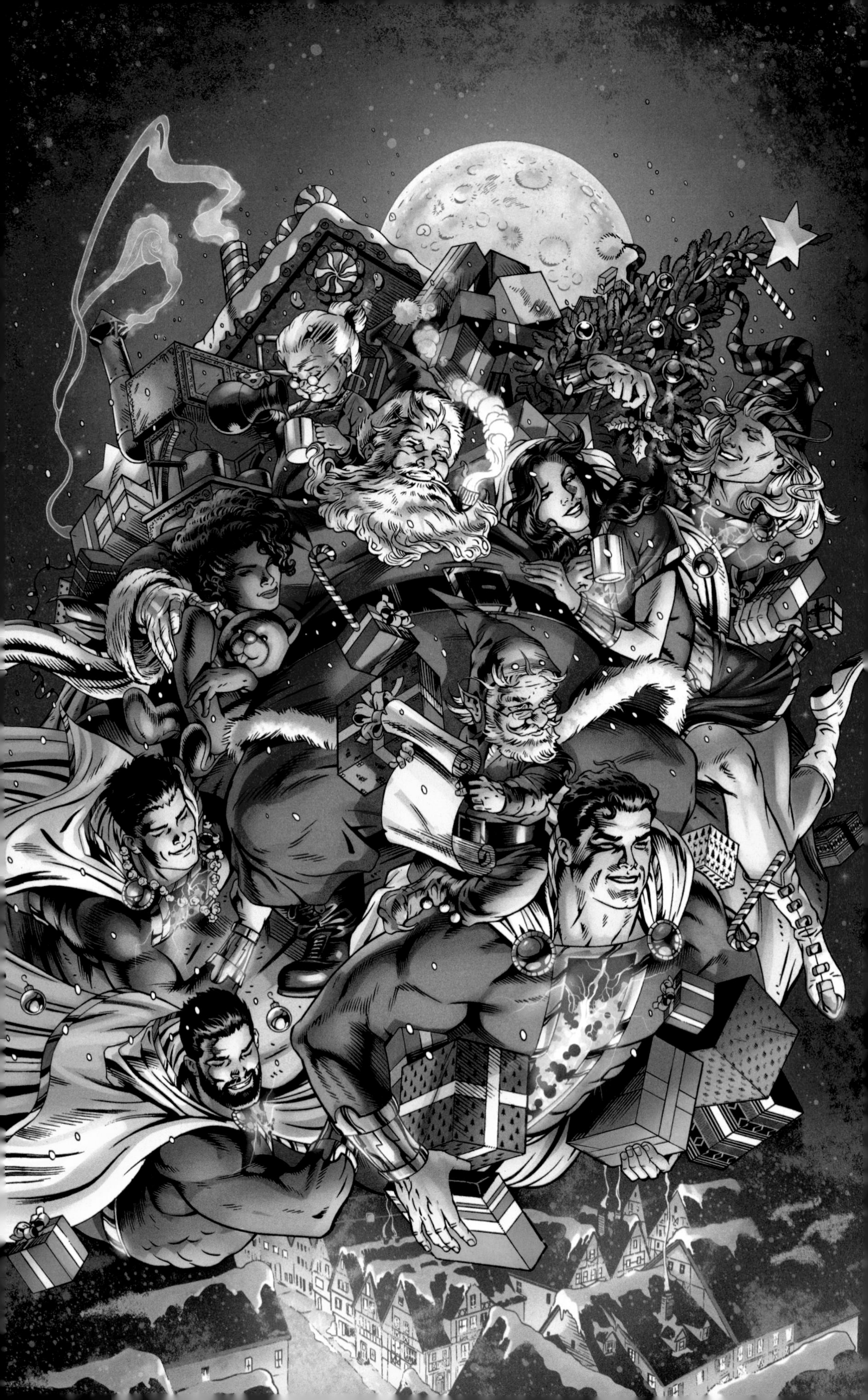

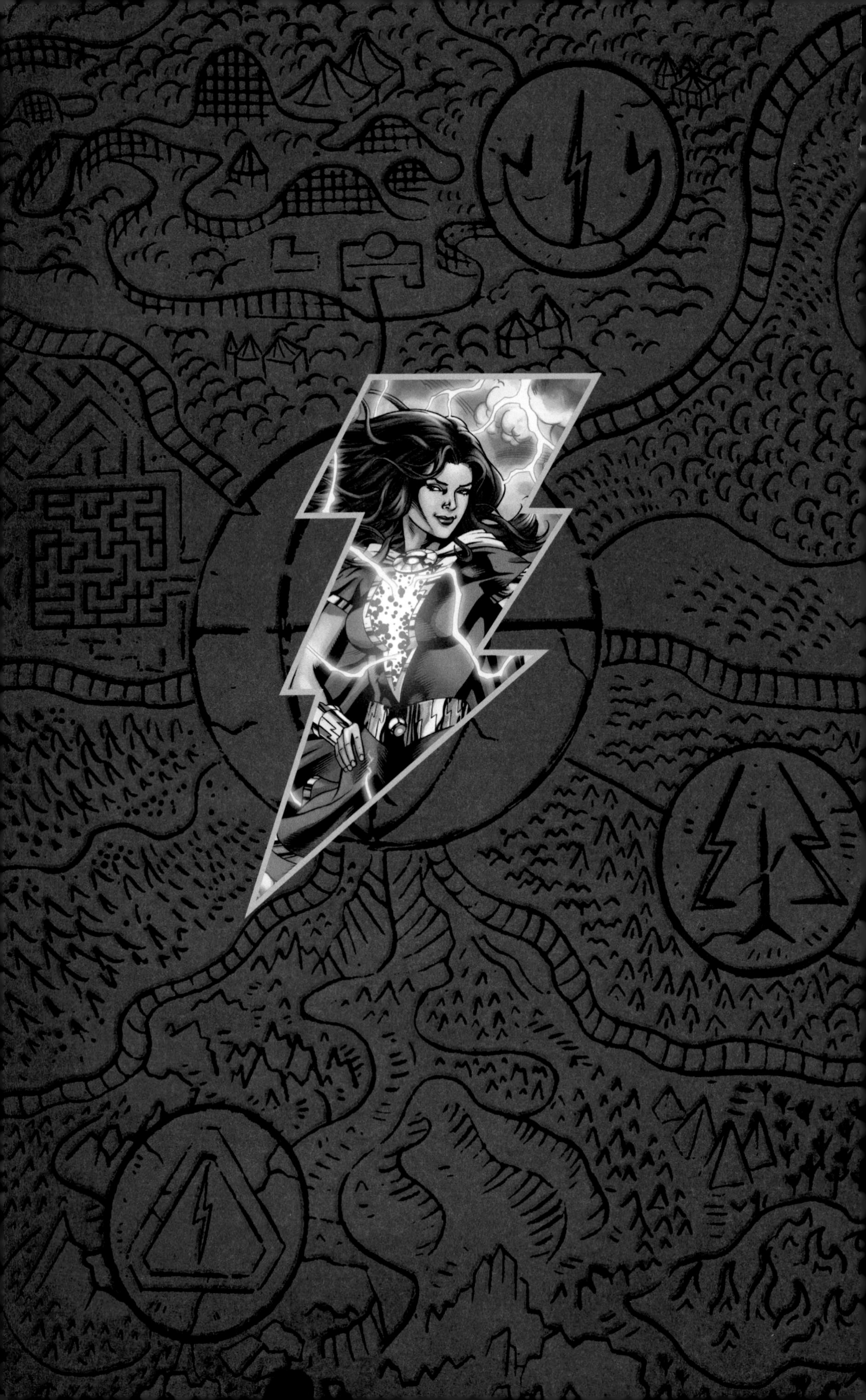

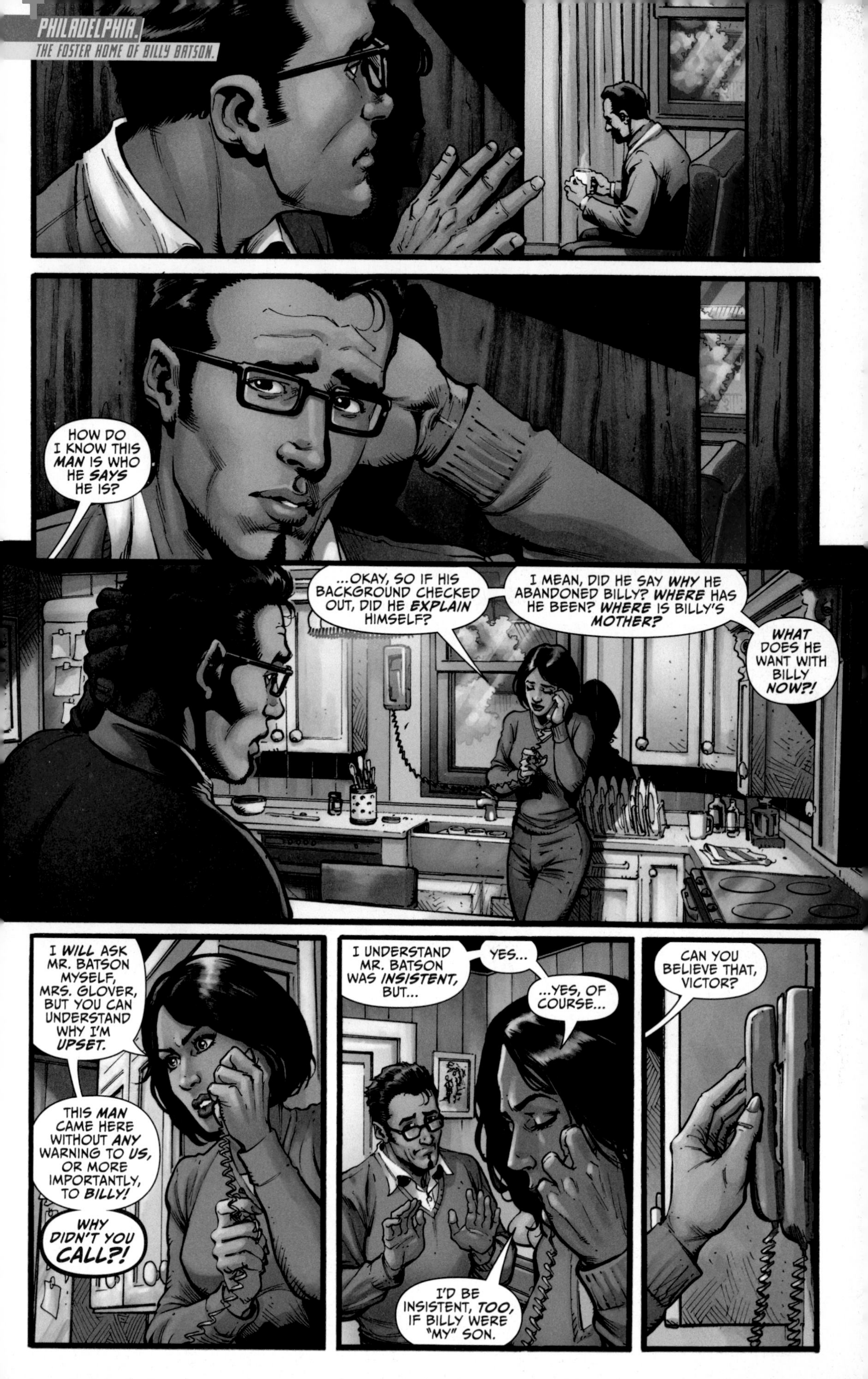
PHILADELPHIA.
THE FOSTER HOME OF BILLY BATSON.
HOW DO I KNOW THIS MAN IS WHO HE SAYS HE IS?
...OKAY, SO IF HIS BACKGROUND CHECKED OUT, DID HE EXPLAIN HIMSELF?
I MEAN, DID HE SAY WHY HE ABANDONED BILLY? WHERE HAS HE BEEN? WHERE IS BILLY'S MOTHER?
WHAT DOES HE WANT WITH BILLY NOW?!
I WILL ASK MR. BATSON MYSELF, MRS. GLOVER, BUT YOU CAN UNDERSTAND WHY I'M UPSET.
THIS MAN CAME HERE WITHOUT ANY WARNING TO US, OR MORE IMPORTANTLY, TO BILLY!
WHY DIDN'T YOU CALL?!
I UNDERSTAND MR. BATSON WAS INSISTENT, BUT...
YES...
...YES, OF COURSE...
I'D BE INSISTENT, TOO, IF BILLY WERE "MY" SON.
CAN YOU BELIEVE THAT, VICTOR?

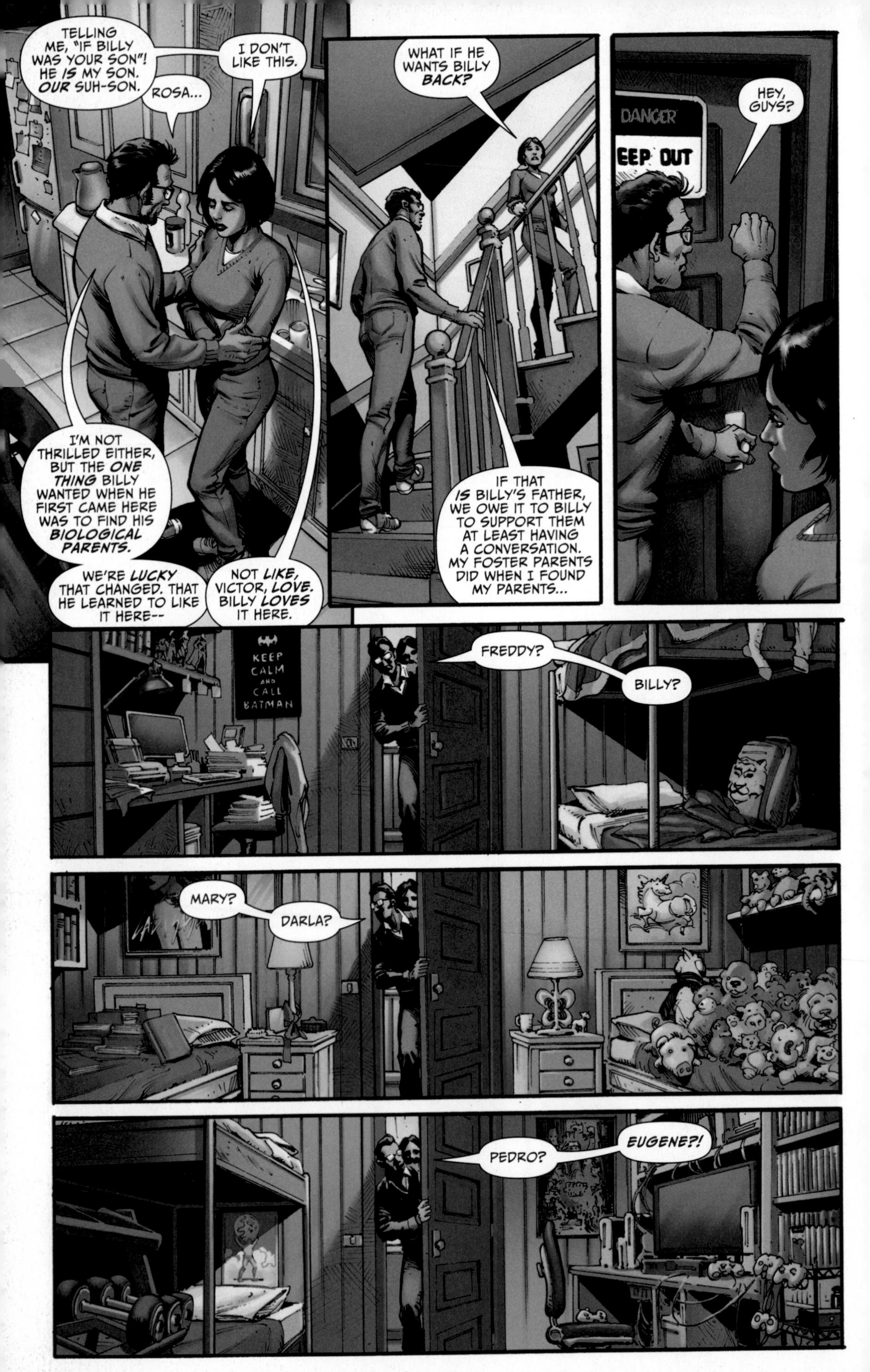
TELLING ME, "IF BILLY WAS YOUR SON"! HE IS MY SON. OUR SUH-SON.
I DON'T LIKE THIS.
ROSA...
I'M NOT THRILLED EITHER, BUT THE ONE THING BILLY WANTED WHEN HE FIRST CAME HERE WAS TO FIND HIS BIOLOGICAL PARENTS.
WE'RE LUCKY THAT CHANGED. THAT HE LEARNED TO LIKE IT HERE--
NOT LIKE, VICTOR, LOVE. BILLY LOVES IT HERE.
WHAT IF HE WANTS BILLY BACK?
IF THAT IS BILLY'S FATHER, WE OWE IT TO BILLY TO SUPPORT THEM AT LEAST HAVING A CONVERSATION. MY FOSTER PARENTS DID WHEN I FOUND MY PARENTS...
DANGER
EEP OUT
HEY, GUYS?
KEEP CALM AND CALL BATMAN
FREDDY?
BILLY?
MARY?
DARLA?
PEDRO?
EUGENE?!

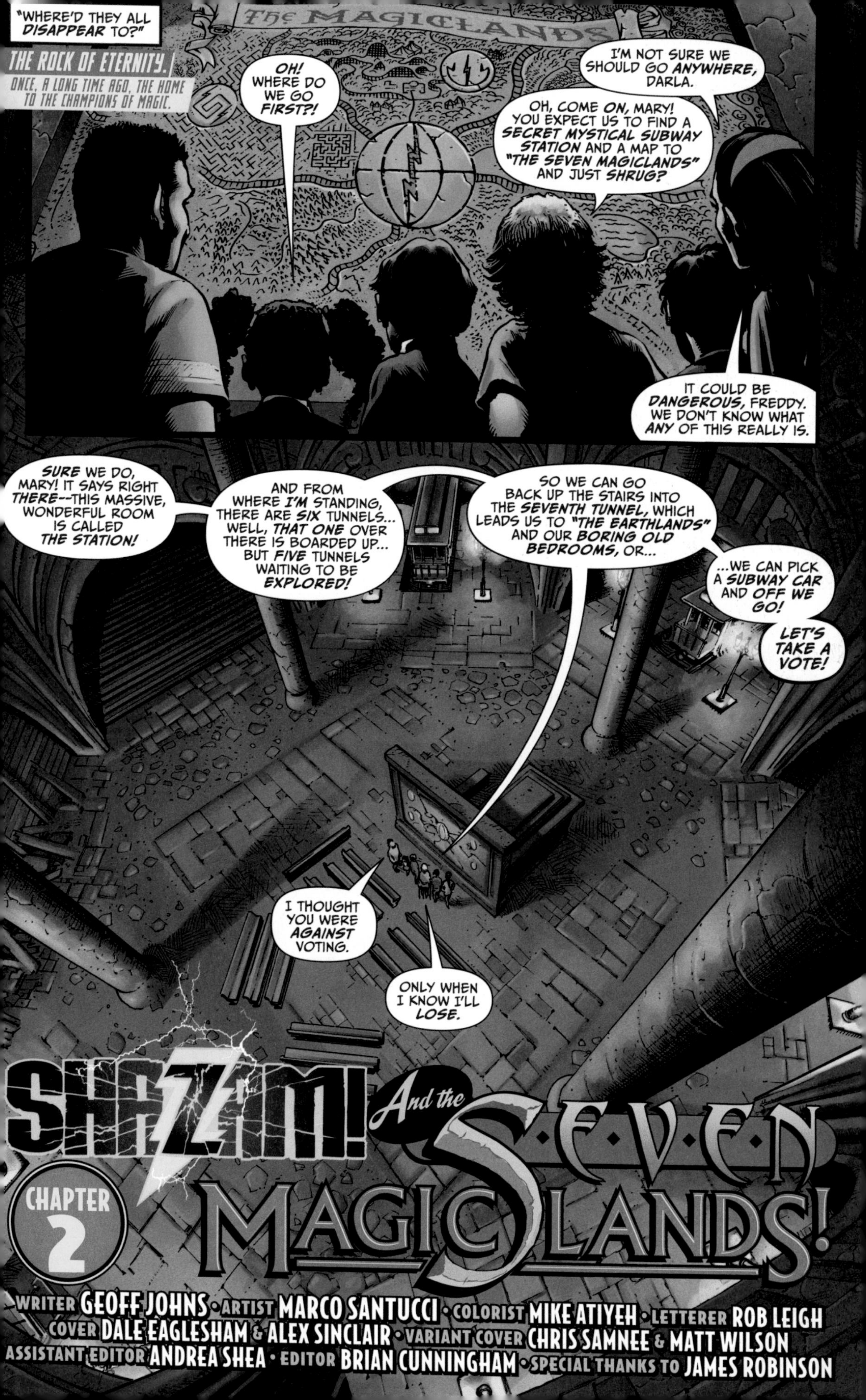
"WHERE'D THEY ALL DISAPPEAR TO?"
THE ROCK OF ETERNITY.
ONCE, A LONG TIME AGO, THE HOME TO THE CHAMPIONS OF MAGIC.
THE MAGICLANDS
OH! WHERE DO WE GO FIRST?!
I'M NOT SURE WE SHOULD GO ANYWHERE, DARLA.
OH, COME ON, MARY! YOU EXPECT US TO FIND A SECRET MYSTICAL SUBWAY STATION AND A MAP TO "THE SEVEN MAGICLANDS" AND JUST SHRUG?
IT COULD BE DANGEROUS, FREDDY. WE DON'T KNOW WHAT ANY OF THIS REALLY IS.
SURE WE DO, MARY! IT SAYS RIGHT THERE--THIS MASSIVE, WONDERFUL ROOM IS CALLED THE STATION!
AND FROM WHERE I'M STANDING, THERE ARE SIX TUNNELS... WELL, THAT ONE OVER THERE IS BOARDED UP... BUT FIVE TUNNELS WAITING TO BE EXPLORED!
SO WE CAN GO BACK UP THE STAIRS INTO THE SEVENTH TUNNEL, WHICH LEADS US TO "THE EARTHLANDS" AND OUR BORING OLD BEDROOMS, OR...
...WE CAN PICK A SUBWAY CAR AND OFF WE GO!
LET'S TAKE A VOTE!
I THOUGHT YOU WERE AGAINST VOTING.
ONLY WHEN I KNOW I'LL LOSE.
SHAZAM! And the SEVEN MAGICLANDS!
CHAPTER 2
WRITER GEOFF JOHNS • ARTIST MARCO SANTUCCI • COLORIST MIKE ATIYEH • LETTERER ROB LEIGH
COVER DALE EAGLESHAM & ALEX SINCLAIR • VARIANT COVER CHRIS SAMNEE & MATT WILSON
ASSISTANT EDITOR ANDREA SHEA • EDITOR BRIAN CUNNINGHAM • SPECIAL THANKS TO JAMES ROBINSON

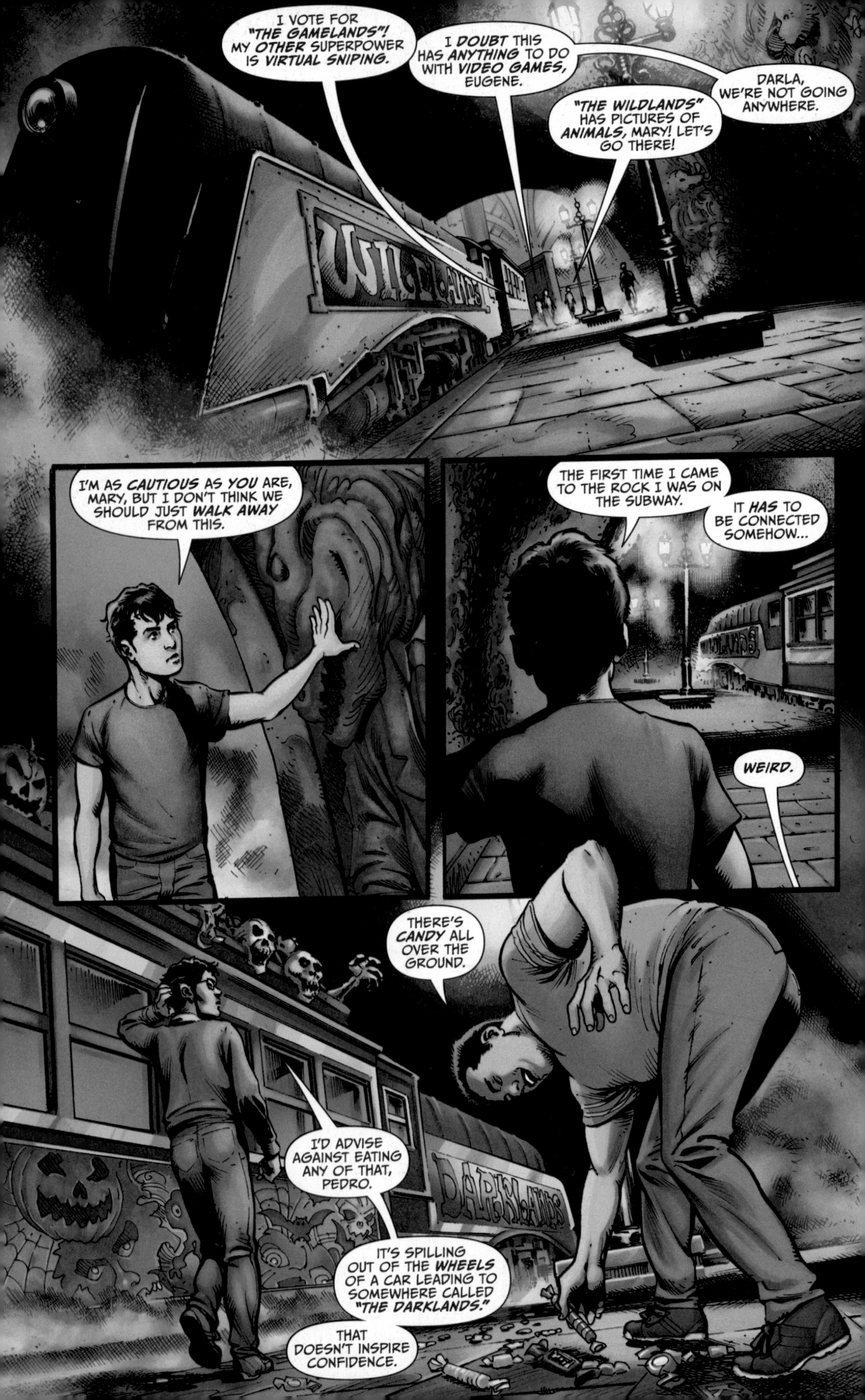
I VOTE FOR "THE GAMELANDS"! MY OTHER SUPERPOWER IS VIRTUAL SNIPING.
I DOUBT THIS HAS ANYTHING TO DO WITH VIDEO GAMES, EUGENE.
DARLA, WE'RE NOT GOING ANYWHERE.
"THE WILDLANDS" HAS PICTURES OF ANIMALS, MARY! LET'S GO THERE!
WILDLANDS
I'M AS CAUTIOUS AS YOU ARE, MARY, BUT I DON'T THINK WE SHOULD JUST WALK AWAY FROM THIS.
THE FIRST TIME I CAME TO THE ROCK I WAS ON THE SUBWAY.
IT HAS TO BE CONNECTED SOMEHOW...
WEIRD.
THERE'S CANDY ALL OVER THE GROUND.
I'D ADVISE AGAINST EATING ANY OF THAT, PEDRO.
IT'S SPILLING OUT OF THE WHEELS OF A CAR LEADING TO SOMEWHERE CALLED "THE DARKLANDS."
THAT DOESN'T INSPIRE CONFIDENCE.
DARKLANDS

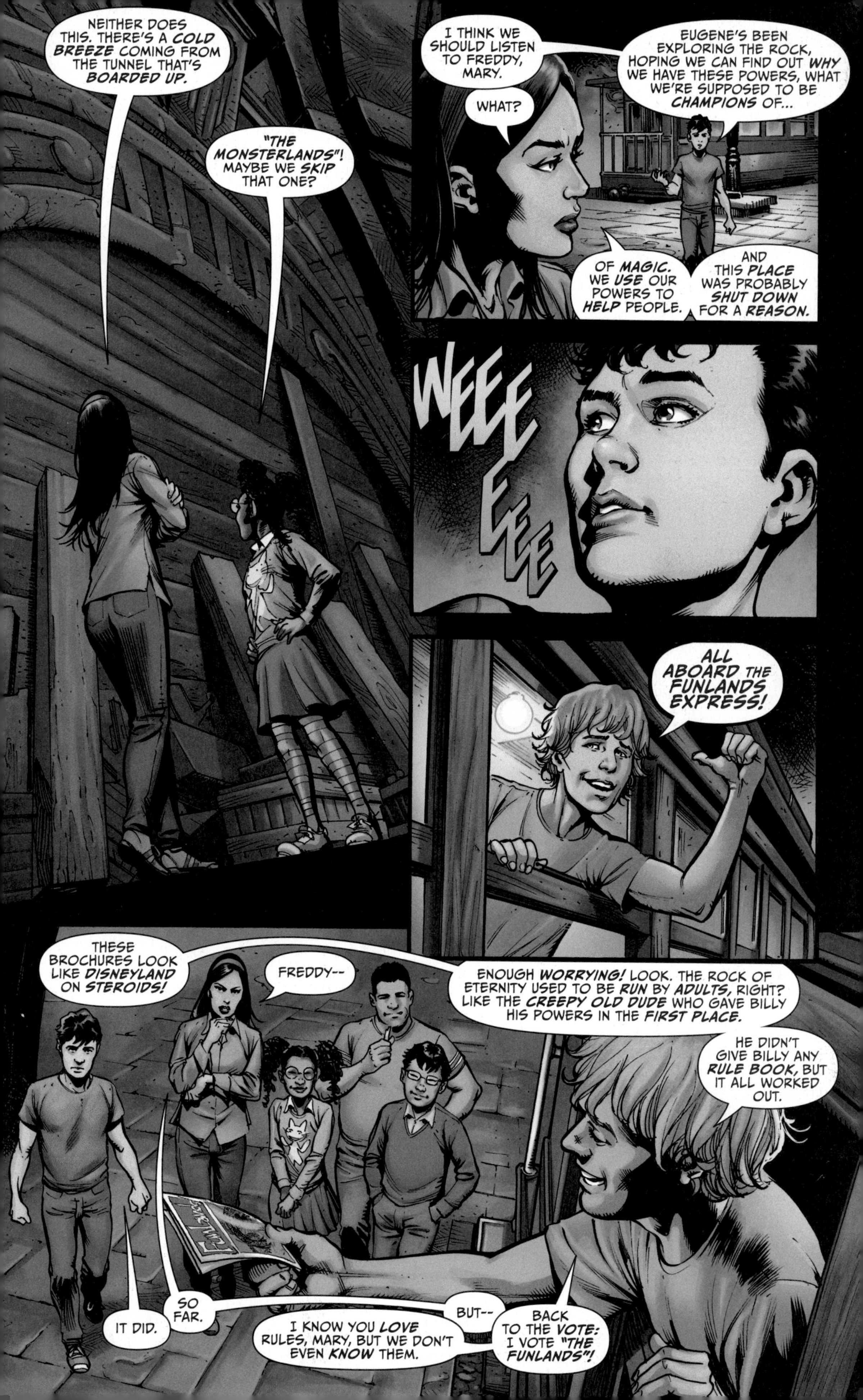
NEITHER DOES THIS. THERE'S A COLD BREEZE COMING FROM THE TUNNEL THAT'S BOARDED UP.
"THE MONSTERLANDS"! MAYBE WE SKIP THAT ONE?
I THINK WE SHOULD LISTEN TO FREDDY, MARY.
EUGENE'S BEEN EXPLORING THE ROCK, HOPING WE CAN FIND OUT WHY WE HAVE THESE POWERS, WHAT WE'RE SUPPOSED TO BE CHAMPIONS OF...
WHAT?
OF MAGIC. WE USE OUR POWERS TO HELP PEOPLE.
AND THIS PLACE WAS PROBABLY SHUT DOWN FOR A REASON.
WEEEEEEE
ALL ABOARD THE FUNLANDS EXPRESS!
THESE BROCHURES LOOK LIKE DISNEYLAND ON STEROIDS!
FREDDY--
ENOUGH WORRYING! LOOK. THE ROCK OF ETERNITY USED TO BE RUN BY ADULTS, RIGHT? LIKE THE CREEPY OLD DUDE WHO GAVE BILLY HIS POWERS IN THE FIRST PLACE.
HE DIDN'T GIVE BILLY ANY RULE BOOK, BUT IT ALL WORKED OUT.
IT DID.
SO FAR.
BUT--
I KNOW YOU LOVE RULES, MARY, BUT WE DON'T EVEN KNOW THEM.
BACK TO THE VOTE: I VOTE "THE FUNLANDS"!

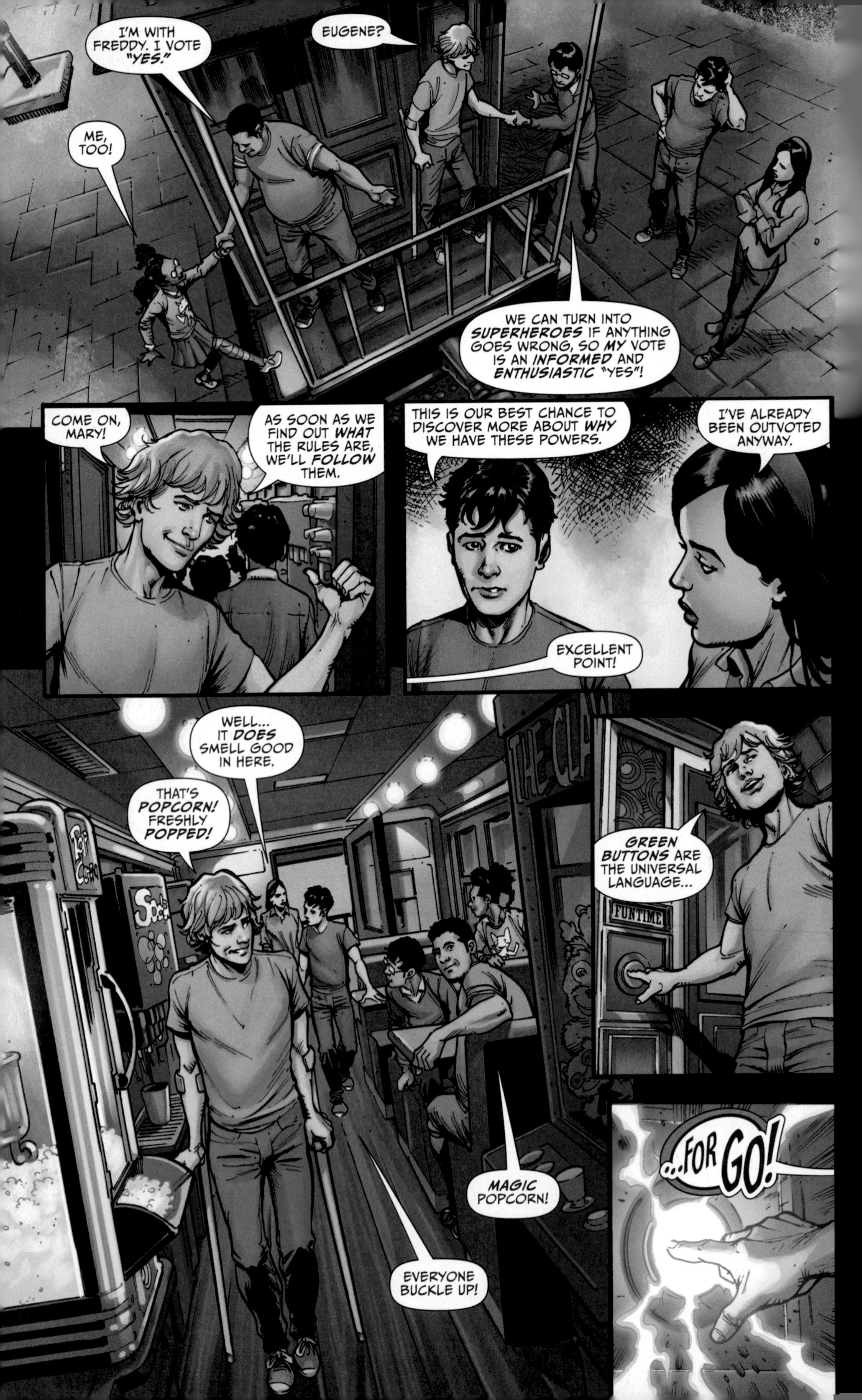

I'M WITH FREDDY. I VOTE "YES."
EUGENE?
ME, TOO!
WE CAN TURN INTO SUPERHEROES IF ANYTHING GOES WRONG, SO MY VOTE IS AN INFORMED AND ENTHUSIASTIC "YES"!
COME ON, MARY!
AS SOON AS WE FIND OUT WHAT THE RULES ARE, WE'LL FOLLOW THEM.
THIS IS OUR BEST CHANCE TO DISCOVER MORE ABOUT WHY WE HAVE THESE POWERS.
I'VE ALREADY BEEN OUTVOTED ANYWAY.
EXCELLENT POINT!
WELL... IT DOES SMELL GOOD IN HERE.
THAT'S POPCORN! FRESHLY POPPED!
MAGIC POPCORN!
EVERYONE BUCKLE UP!
GREEN BUTTONS ARE THE UNIVERSAL LANGUAGE...
FUNTIME
...FOR GO!

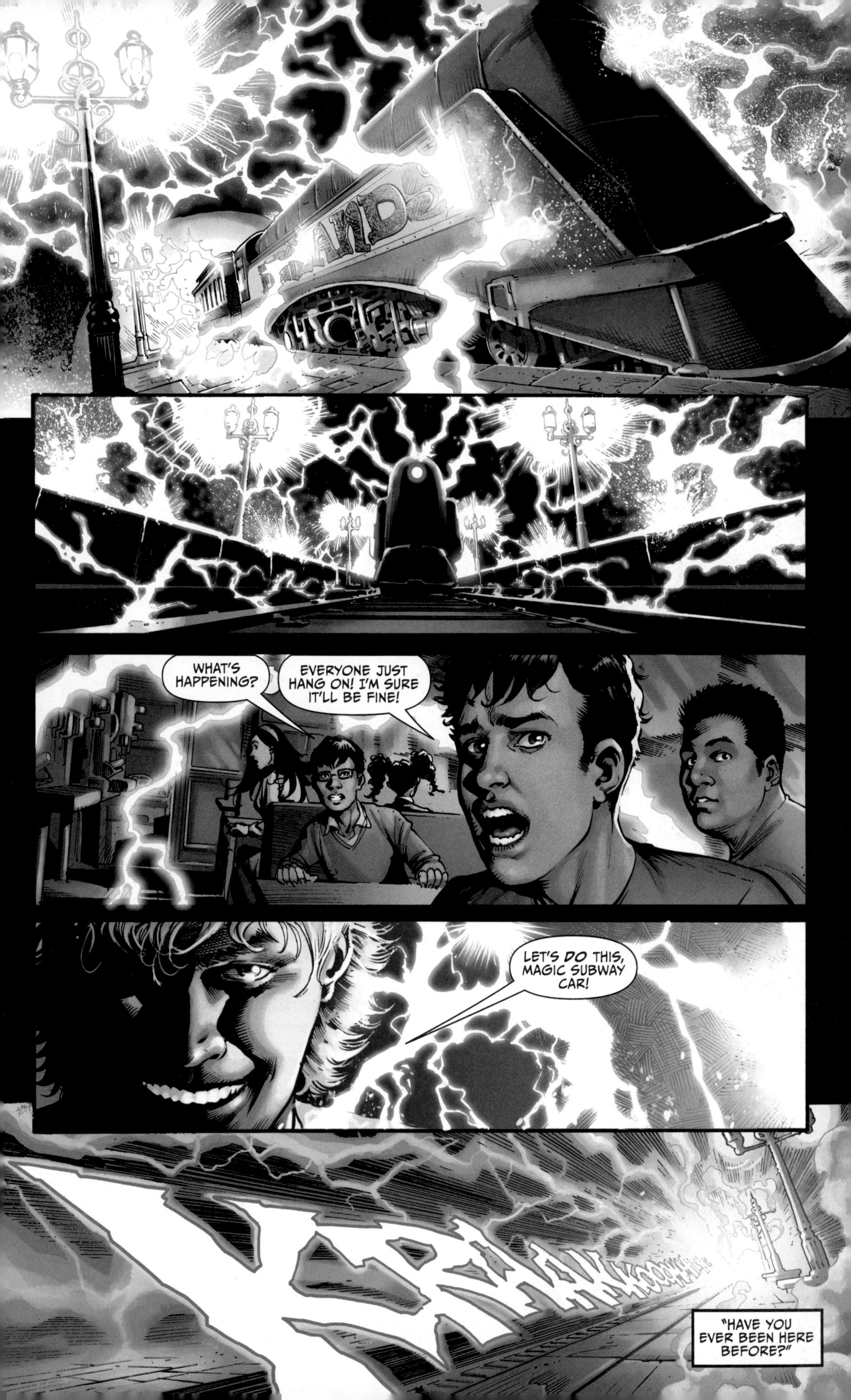
WHAT'S HAPPENING?
EVERYONE JUST HANG ON! I'M SURE IT'LL BE FINE!
LET'S *DO* THIS, MAGIC SUBWAY CAR!
"HAVE YOU EVER BEEN HERE BEFORE?"

THIS IS MY FIRST TIME.

JUST FILL THESE FORMS OUT, THEN, MR. SIVANA.

*Dr. Thaddeus Sivana*

IT'S DOCTOR.

MY APOLOGIES.

WOULD YOU LIKE A *MAGAZINE* WHILE YOU WAIT?

NO THANK YOU.

I BROUGHT MY OWN READING MATERIAL.

THE ENCYCLOPEDIA OF MAGICAL MONSTERS!

A TREASURE IF THERE EVER WAS ONE! RECOVERED FROM THE LOST LIBRARY OF LUOYANG!

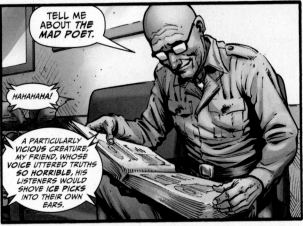

TELL ME ABOUT *THE MAD POET.*

HAHAHAHA!

A PARTICULARLY VICIOUS CREATURE, MY FRIEND, WHOSE VOICE UTTERED TRUTHS SO HORRIBLE, HIS LISTENERS WOULD SHOVE ICE PICKS INTO THEIR OWN EARS.

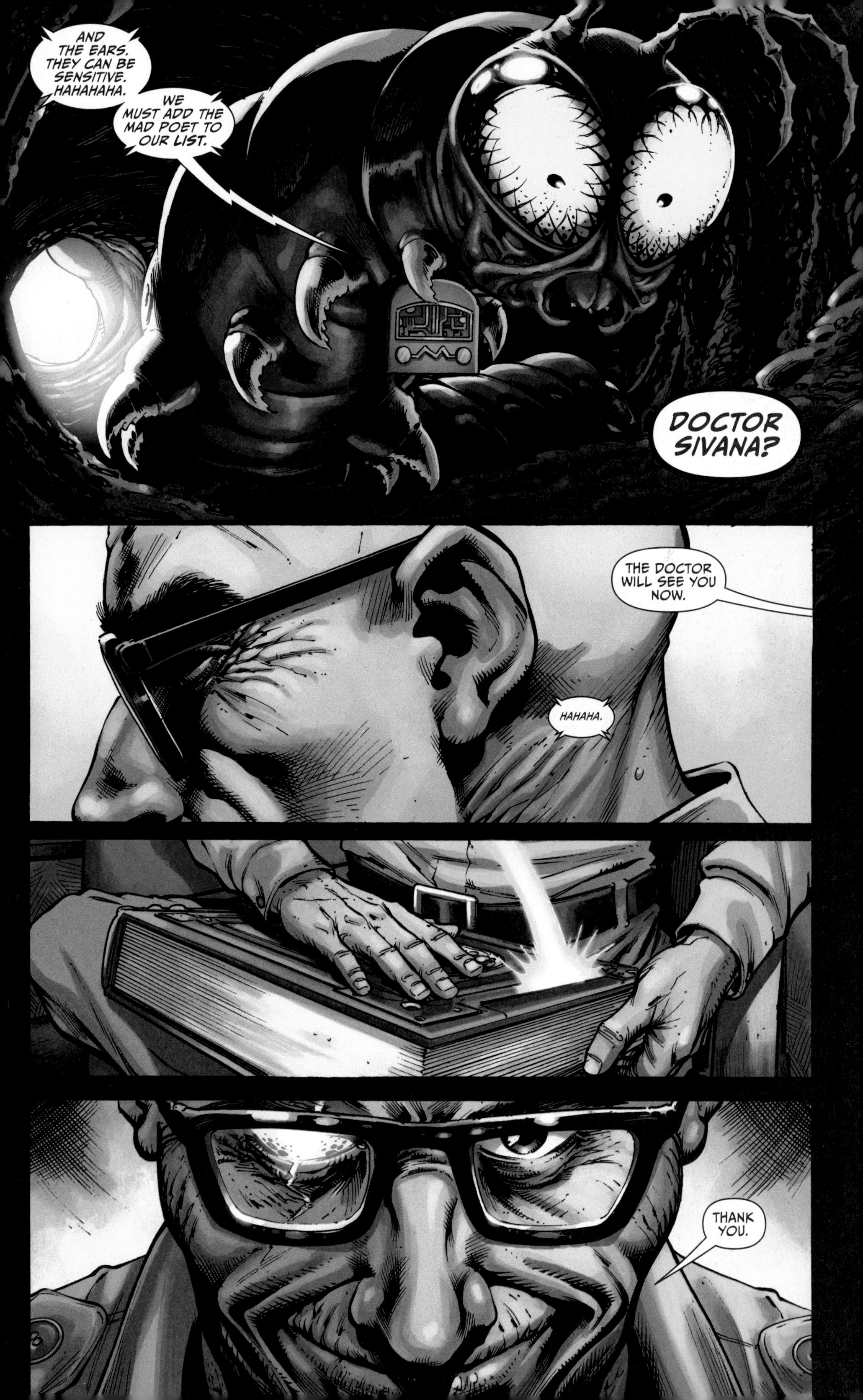
AND THE EARS. THEY CAN BE SENSITIVE. HAHAHAHA.
WE MUST ADD THE MAD POET TO OUR LIST.
DOCTOR SIVANA?
THE DOCTOR WILL SEE YOU NOW.
HAHAHA.
THANK YOU.

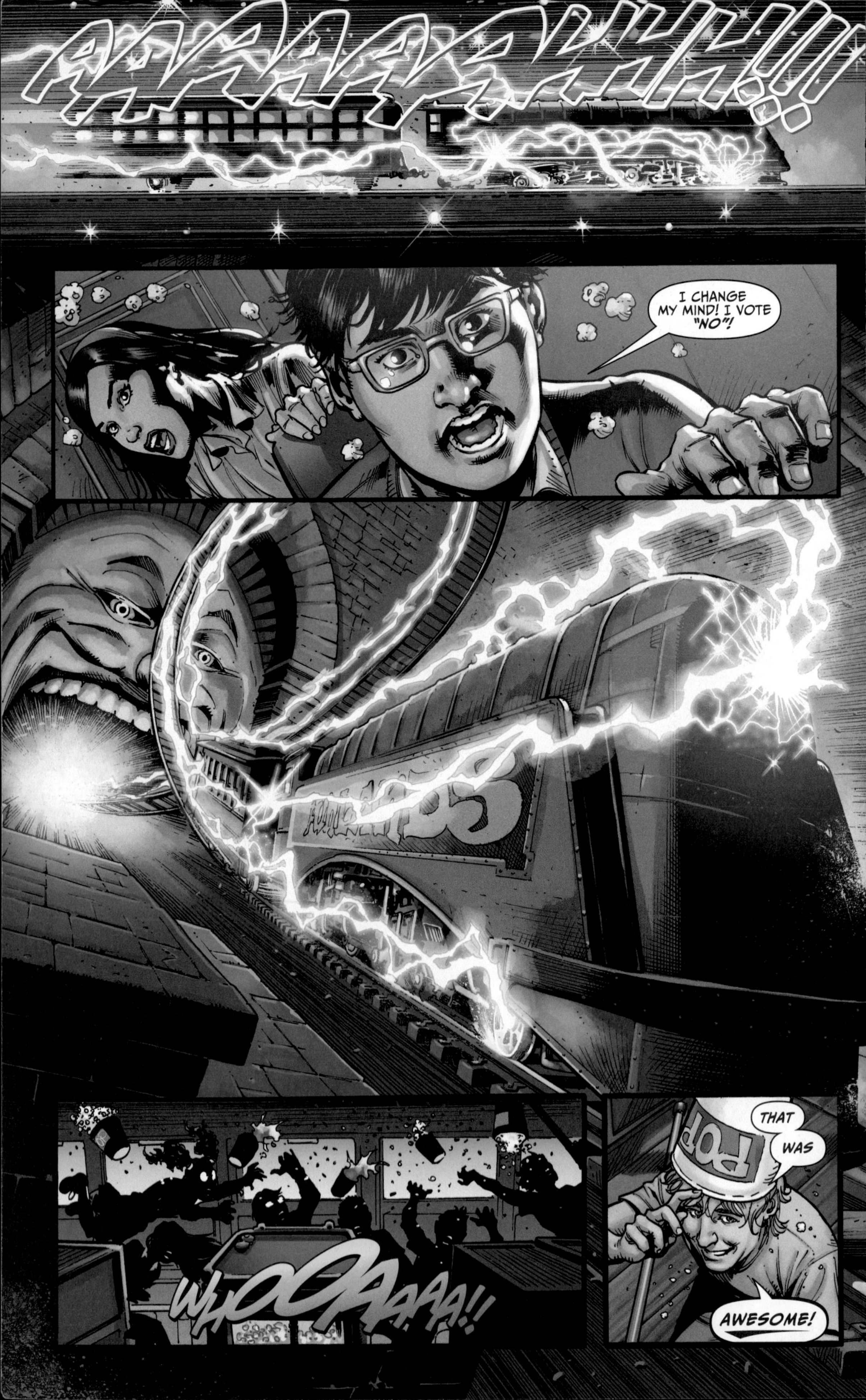
AAAAAAAHHH!!!
I CHANGE MY MIND! I VOTE "NO"!
WHOOAAAAA!!
POP
THAT
WAS
AWESOME!

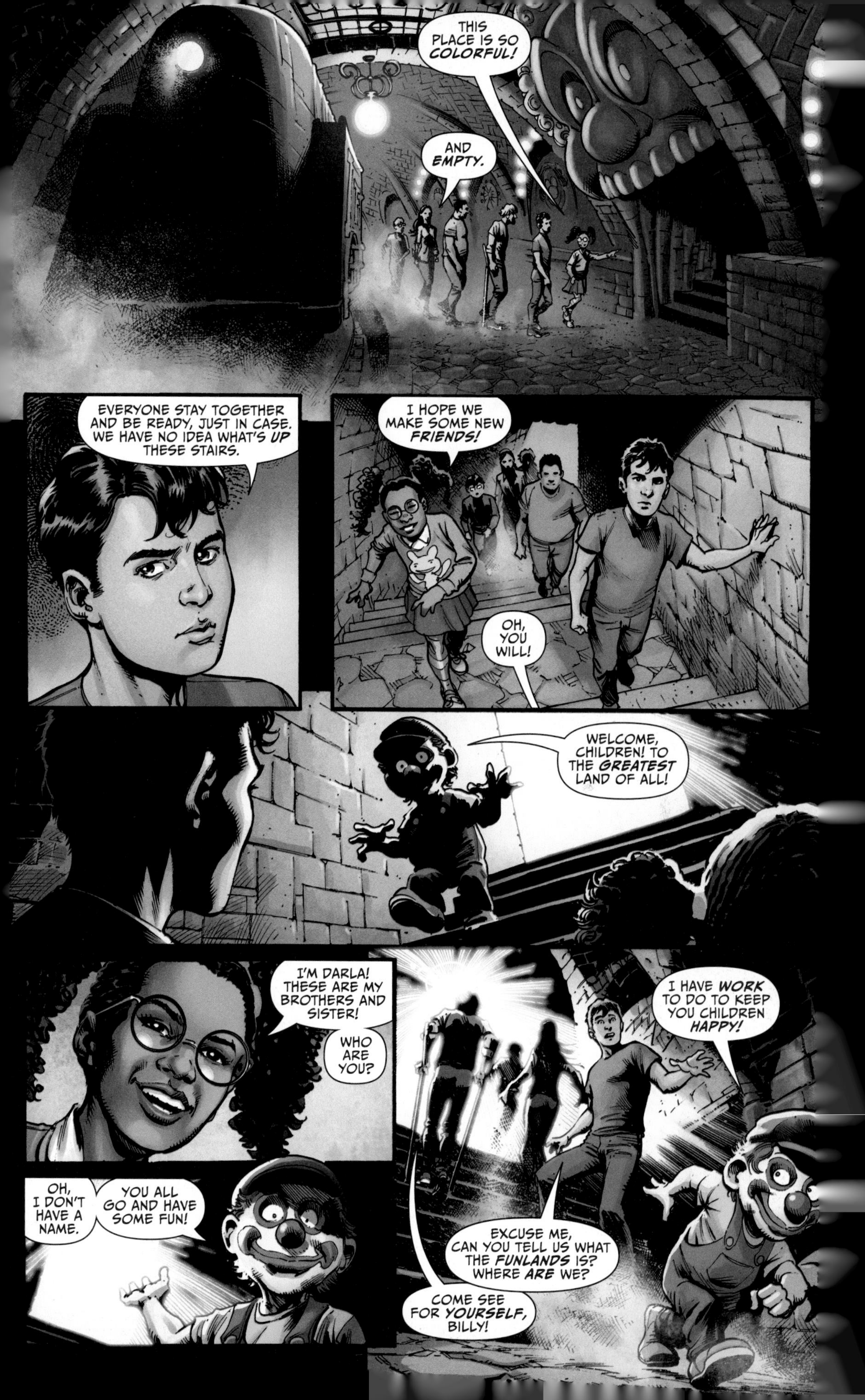
THIS PLACE IS SO *COLORFUL!*
AND *EMPTY.*
EVERYONE STAY TOGETHER AND BE READY, JUST IN CASE. WE HAVE NO IDEA WHAT'S *UP* THESE STAIRS.
I HOPE WE MAKE SOME NEW *FRIENDS!*
OH, YOU WILL!
WELCOME, CHILDREN! TO THE *GREATEST* LAND OF ALL!
I'M DARLA! THESE ARE MY BROTHERS AND SISTER!
WHO ARE YOU?
OH, I DON'T HAVE A NAME.
YOU ALL GO AND HAVE SOME FUN!
I HAVE *WORK* TO DO TO KEEP YOU CHILDREN *HAPPY!*
EXCUSE ME, CAN YOU TELL US WHAT THE *FUNLANDS* IS? WHERE *ARE* WE?
COME SEE FOR *YOURSELF,* BILLY!

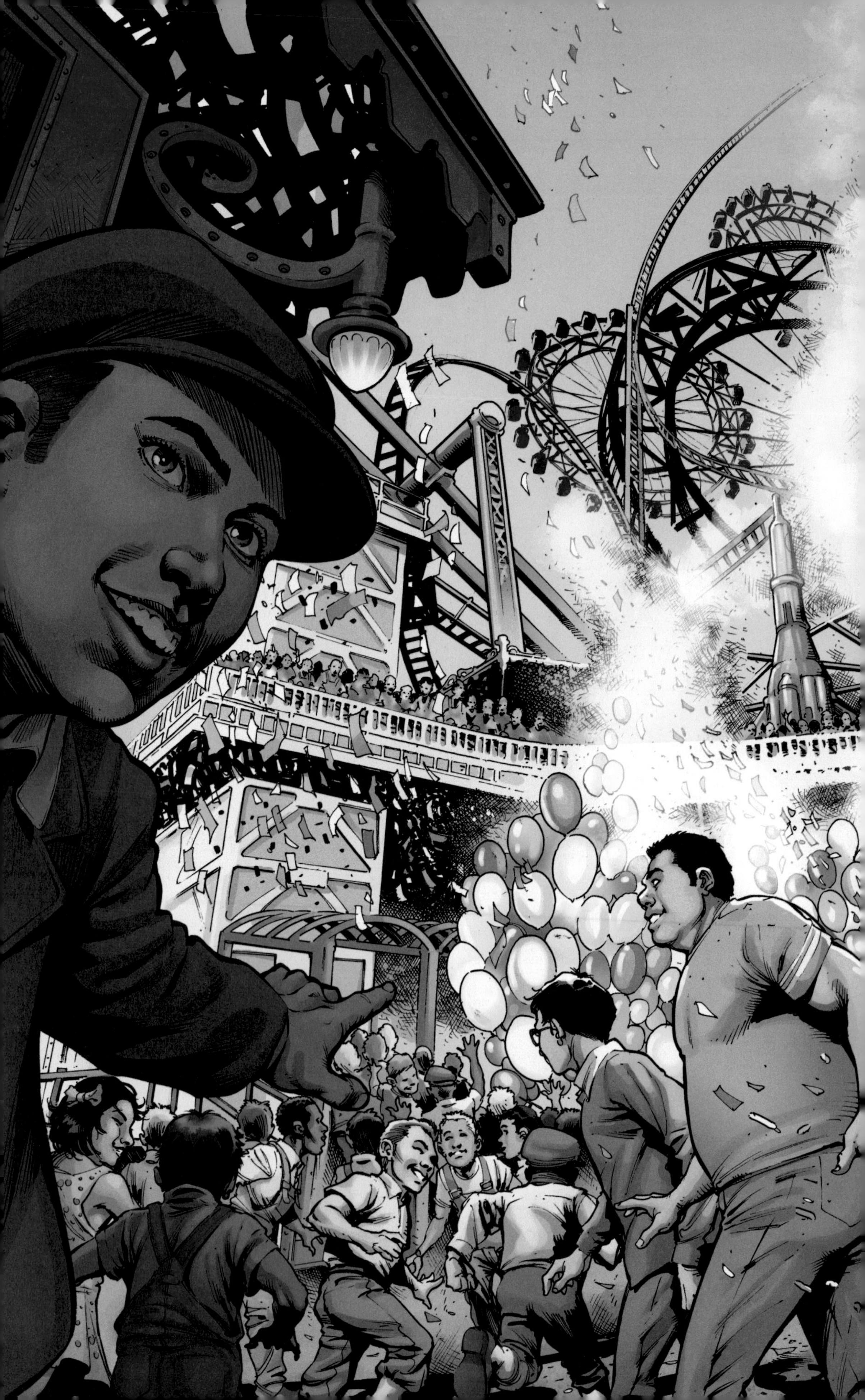

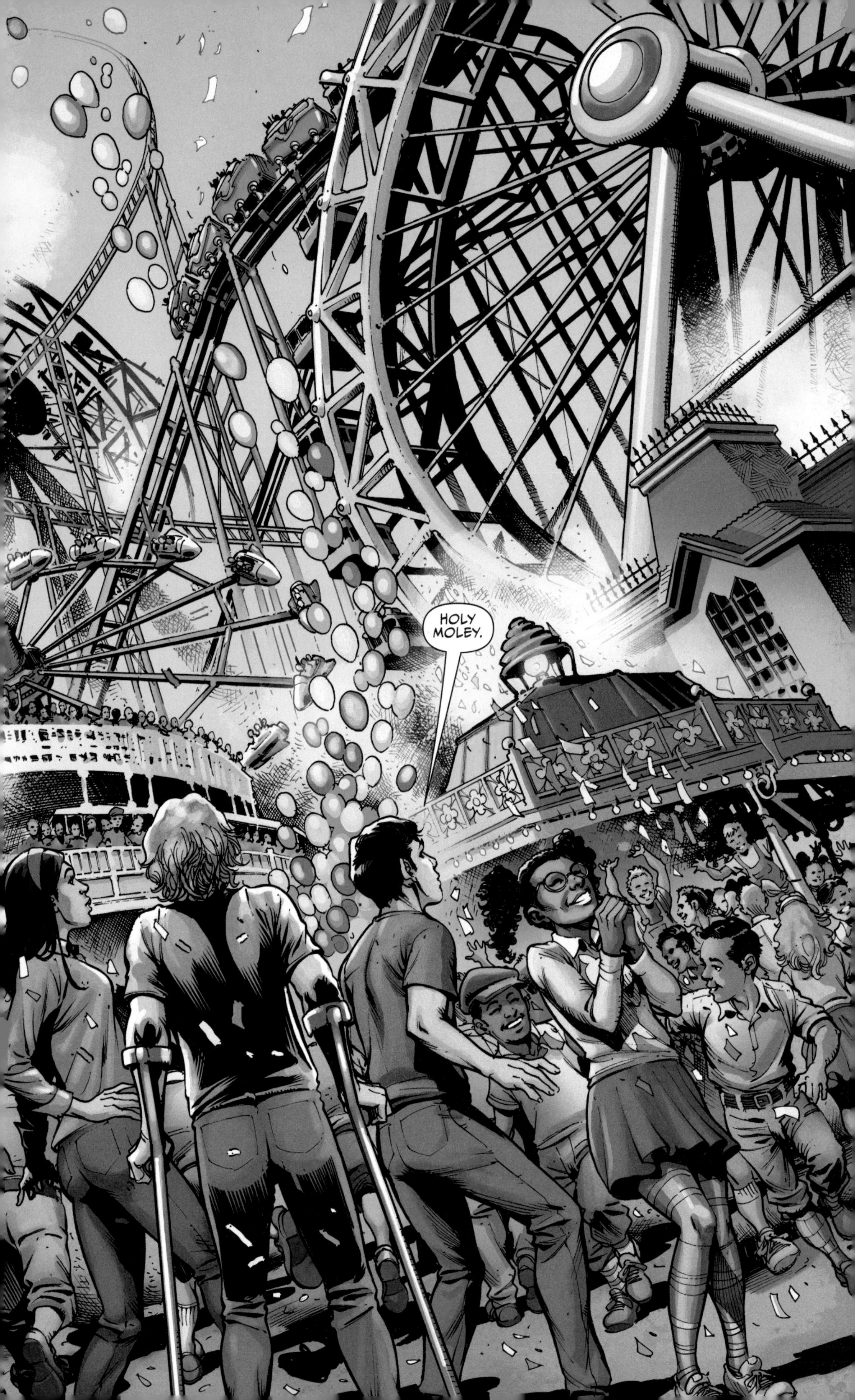
HOLY MOLEY.

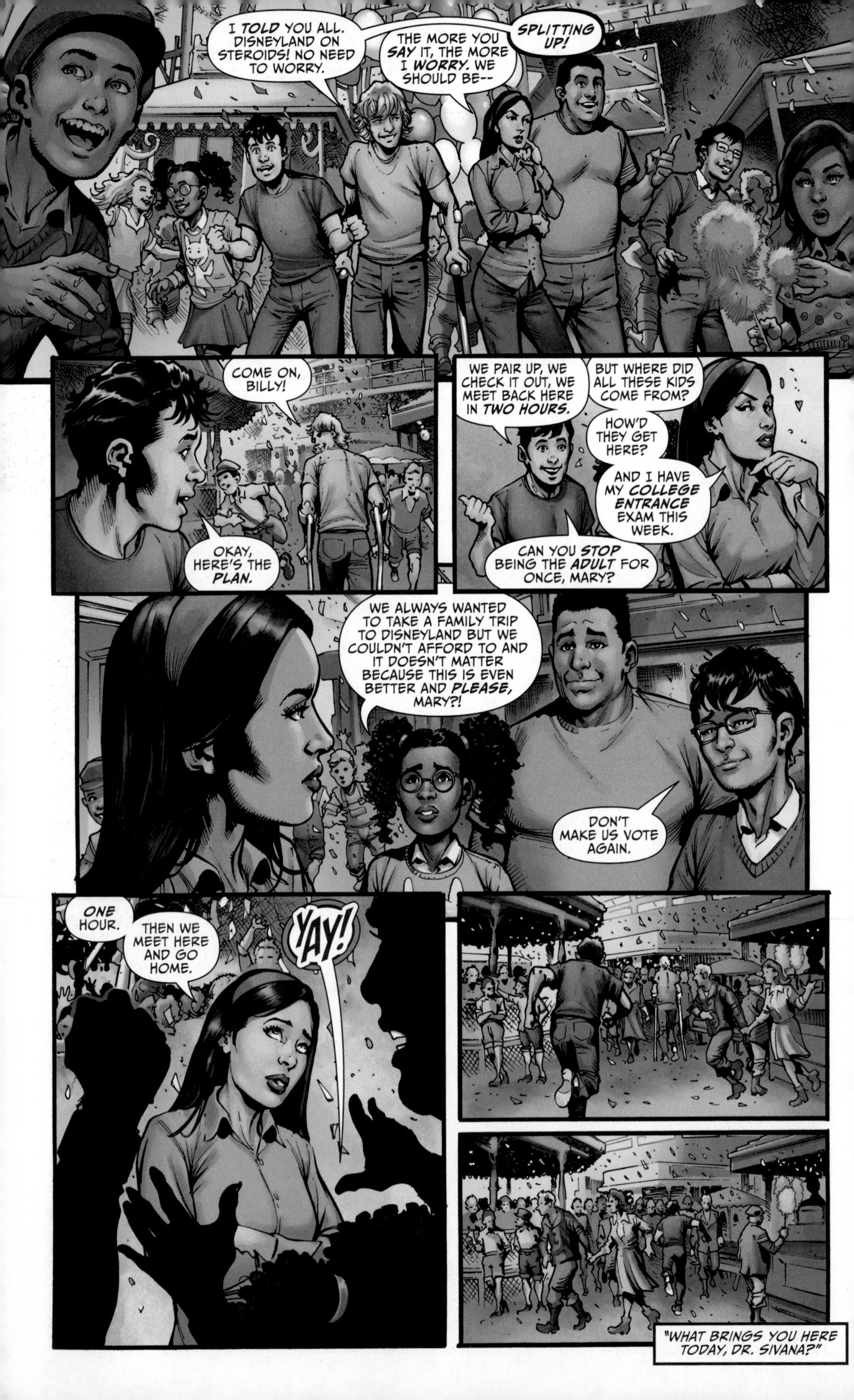
I TOLD YOU ALL. DISNEYLAND ON STEROIDS! NO NEED TO WORRY.
THE MORE YOU SAY IT, THE MORE I WORRY. WE SHOULD BE--
SPLITTING UP!
COME ON, BILLY!
OKAY, HERE'S THE PLAN.
WE PAIR UP, WE CHECK IT OUT, WE MEET BACK HERE IN TWO HOURS.
BUT WHERE DID ALL THESE KIDS COME FROM?
HOW'D THEY GET HERE?
AND I HAVE MY COLLEGE ENTRANCE EXAM THIS WEEK.
CAN YOU STOP BEING THE ADULT FOR ONCE, MARY?
WE ALWAYS WANTED TO TAKE A FAMILY TRIP TO DISNEYLAND BUT WE COULDN'T AFFORD TO AND IT DOESN'T MATTER BECAUSE THIS IS EVEN BETTER AND PLEASE, MARY?!
DON'T MAKE US VOTE AGAIN.
ONE HOUR.
THEN WE MEET HERE AND GO HOME.
YAY!
"WHAT BRINGS YOU HERE TODAY, DR. SIVANA?"

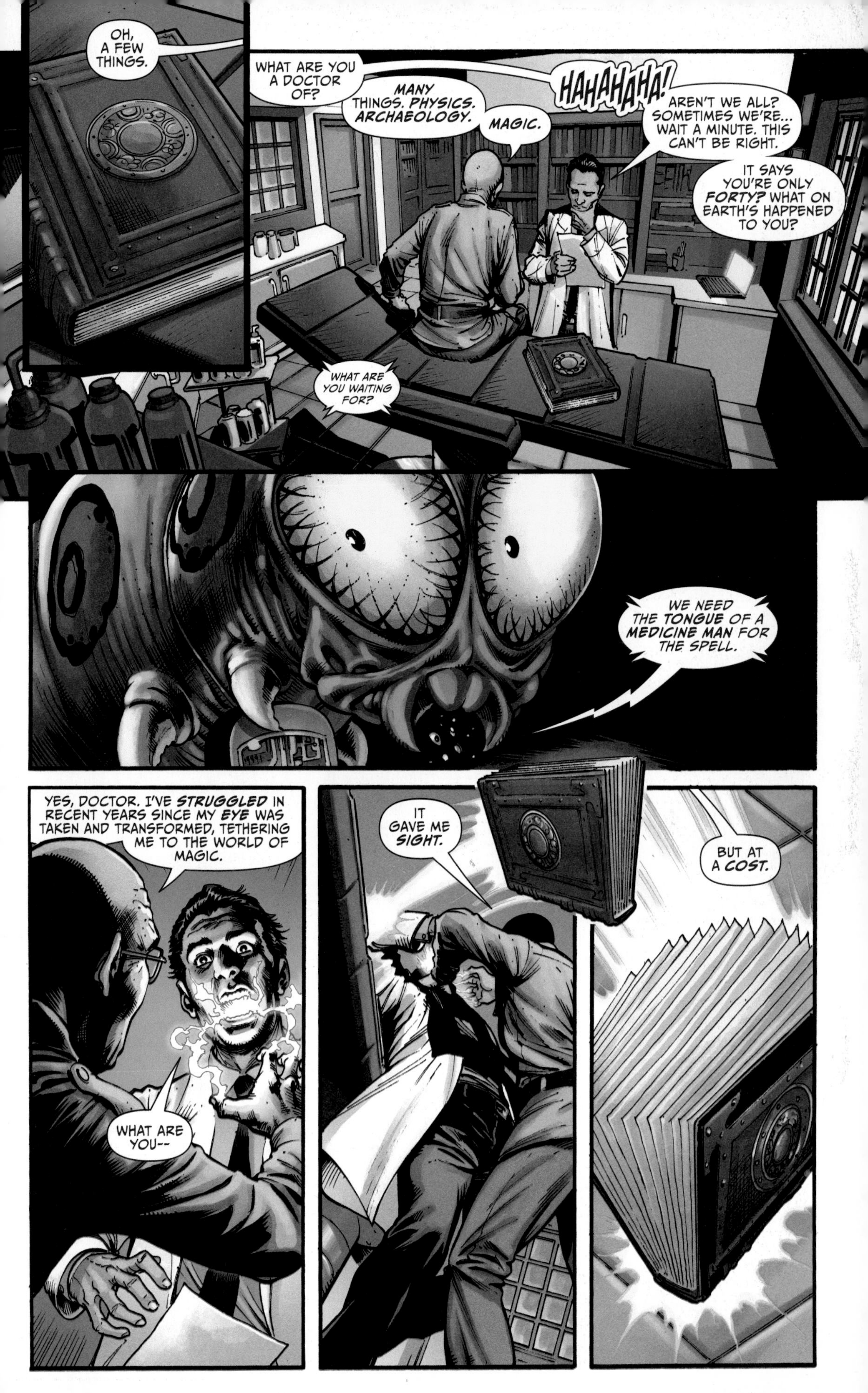
OH, A FEW THINGS.
WHAT ARE YOU A DOCTOR OF?
MANY THINGS. PHYSICS. ARCHAEOLOGY.
MAGIC.
HAHAHAHA!
AREN'T WE ALL? SOMETIMES WE'RE... WAIT A MINUTE. THIS CAN'T BE RIGHT.
IT SAYS YOU'RE ONLY FORTY? WHAT ON EARTH'S HAPPENED TO YOU?
WHAT ARE YOU WAITING FOR?
WE NEED THE TONGUE OF A MEDICINE MAN FOR THE SPELL.
YES, DOCTOR. I'VE STRUGGLED IN RECENT YEARS SINCE MY EYE WAS TAKEN AND TRANSFORMED, TETHERING ME TO THE WORLD OF MAGIC.
WHAT ARE YOU--
IT GAVE ME SIGHT.
BUT AT A COST.

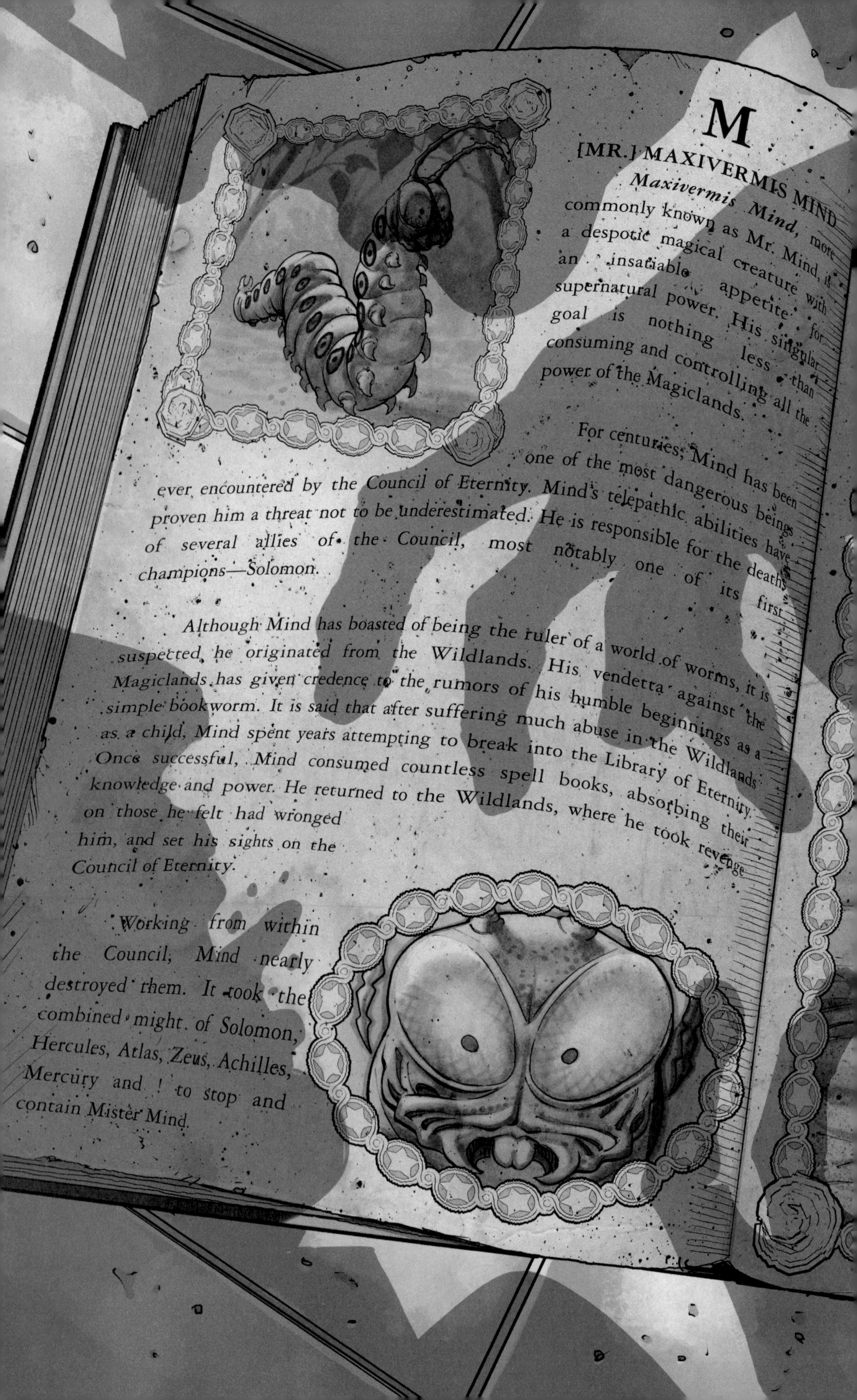
M
[MR.] MAXIVERMIS MIND
Maxivermis Mind, more commonly known as Mr. Mind, is a despotic magical creature with an insatiable appetite for supernatural power. His singular goal is nothing less than consuming and controlling all the power of the Magiclands.
For centuries, Mind has been one of the most dangerous beings ever encountered by the Council of Eternity. Mind's telepathic abilities have proven him a threat not to be underestimated. He is responsible for the deaths of several allies of the Council, most notably one of its first champions—Solomon.
Although Mind has boasted of being the ruler of a world of worms, it is suspected he originated from the Wildlands. His vendetta against the Magiclands has given credence to the rumors of his humble beginnings as a simple bookworm. It is said that after suffering much abuse in the Wildlands as a child, Mind spent years attempting to break into the Library of Eternity. Once successful, Mind consumed countless spell books, absorbing their knowledge and power. He returned to the Wildlands, where he took revenge on those he felt had wronged him, and set his sights on the Council of Eternity.
Working from within the Council, Mind nearly destroyed them. It took the combined might of Solomon, Hercules, Atlas, Zeus, Achilles, Mercury and ! to stop and contain Mister Mind.

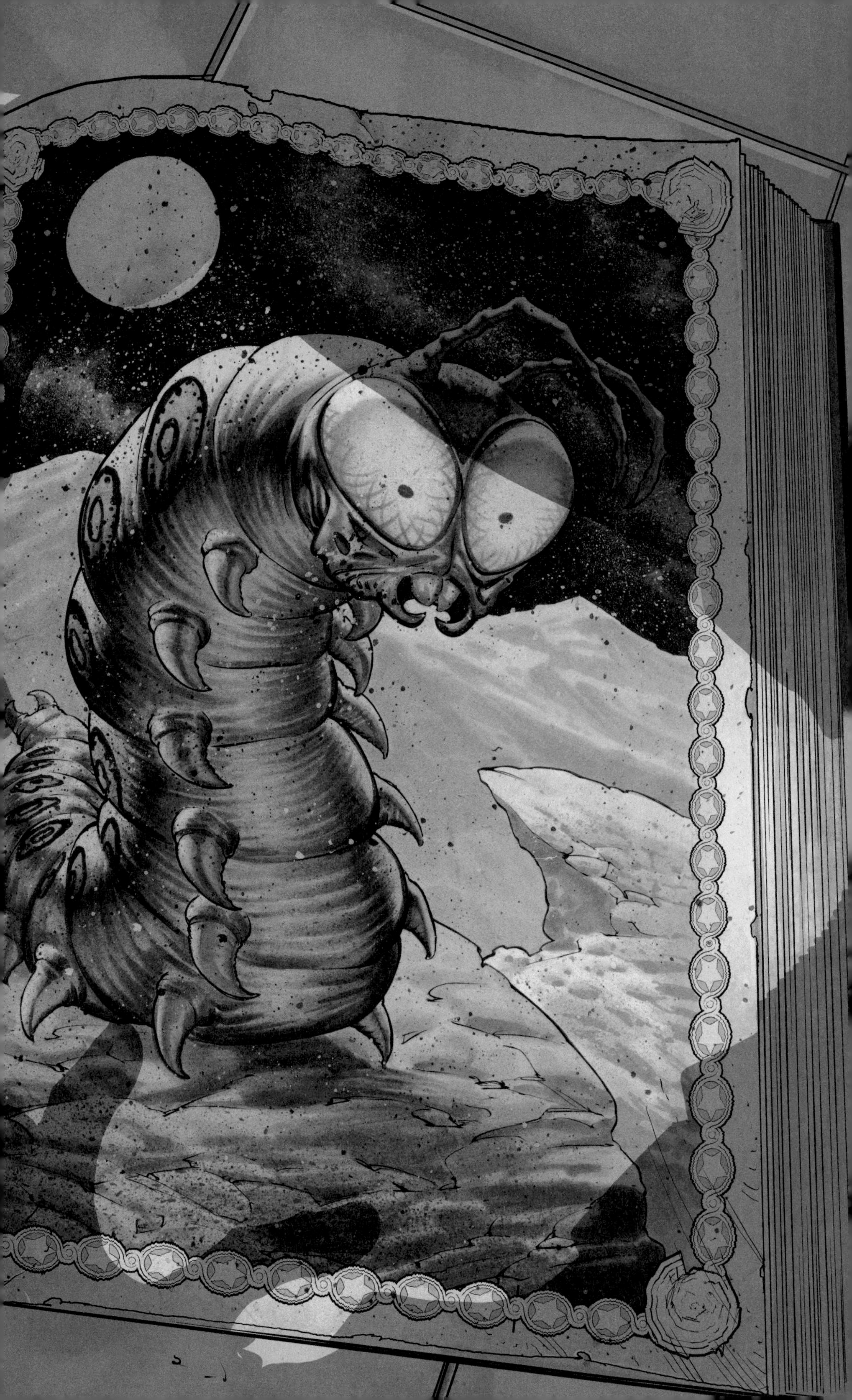

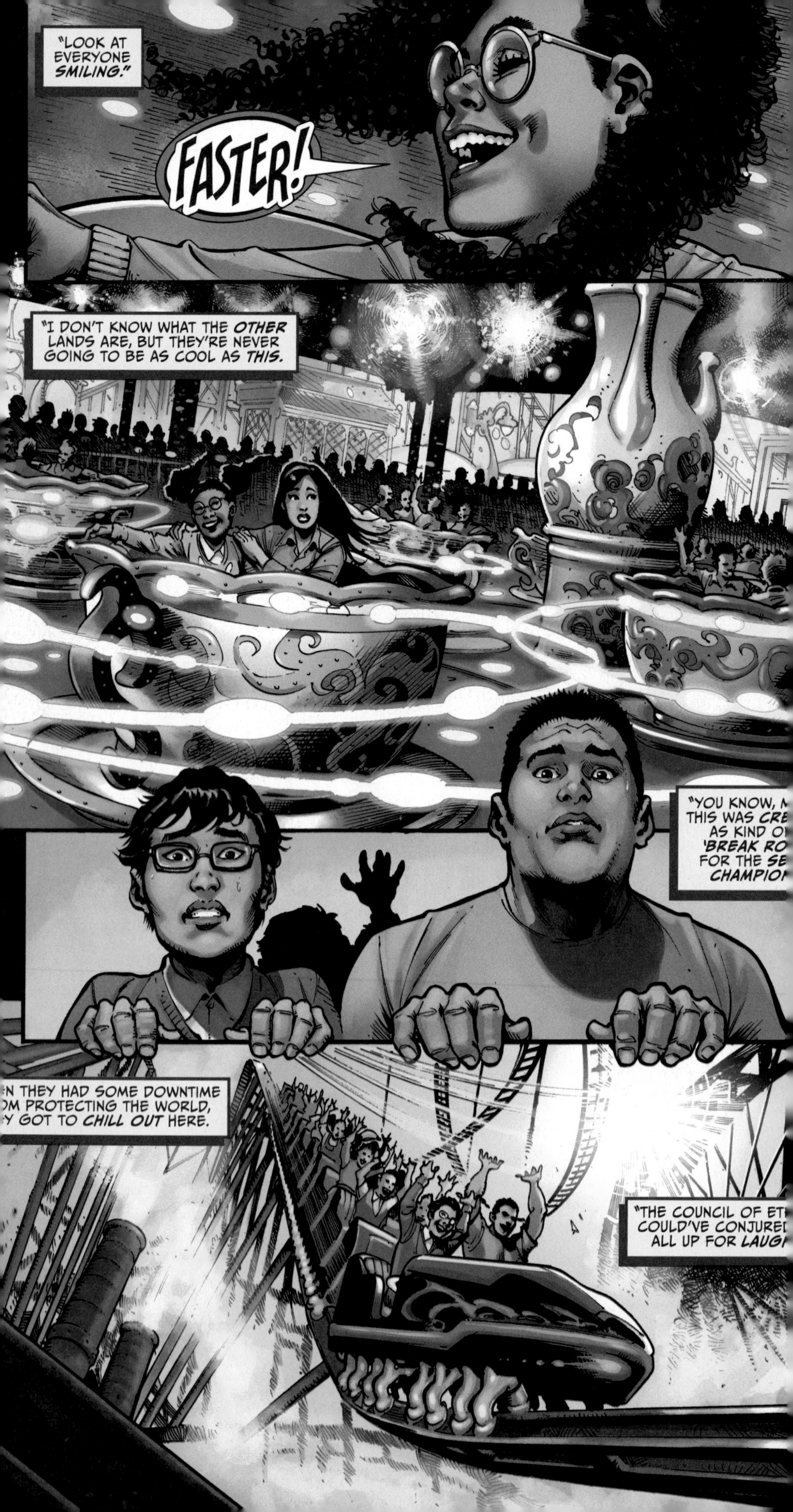
"LOOK AT EVERYONE SMILING."
FASTER!
"I DON'T KNOW WHAT THE OTHER LANDS ARE, BUT THEY'RE NEVER GOING TO BE AS COOL AS THIS.
"YOU KNOW, M THIS WAS CRE AS KIND OF 'BREAK RO FOR THE SE CHAMPIO
EN THEY HAD SOME DOWNTIME OM PROTECTING THE WORLD, Y GOT TO CHILL OUT HERE.
"THE COUNCIL OF ET COULD'VE CONJURED ALL UP FOR LAUG

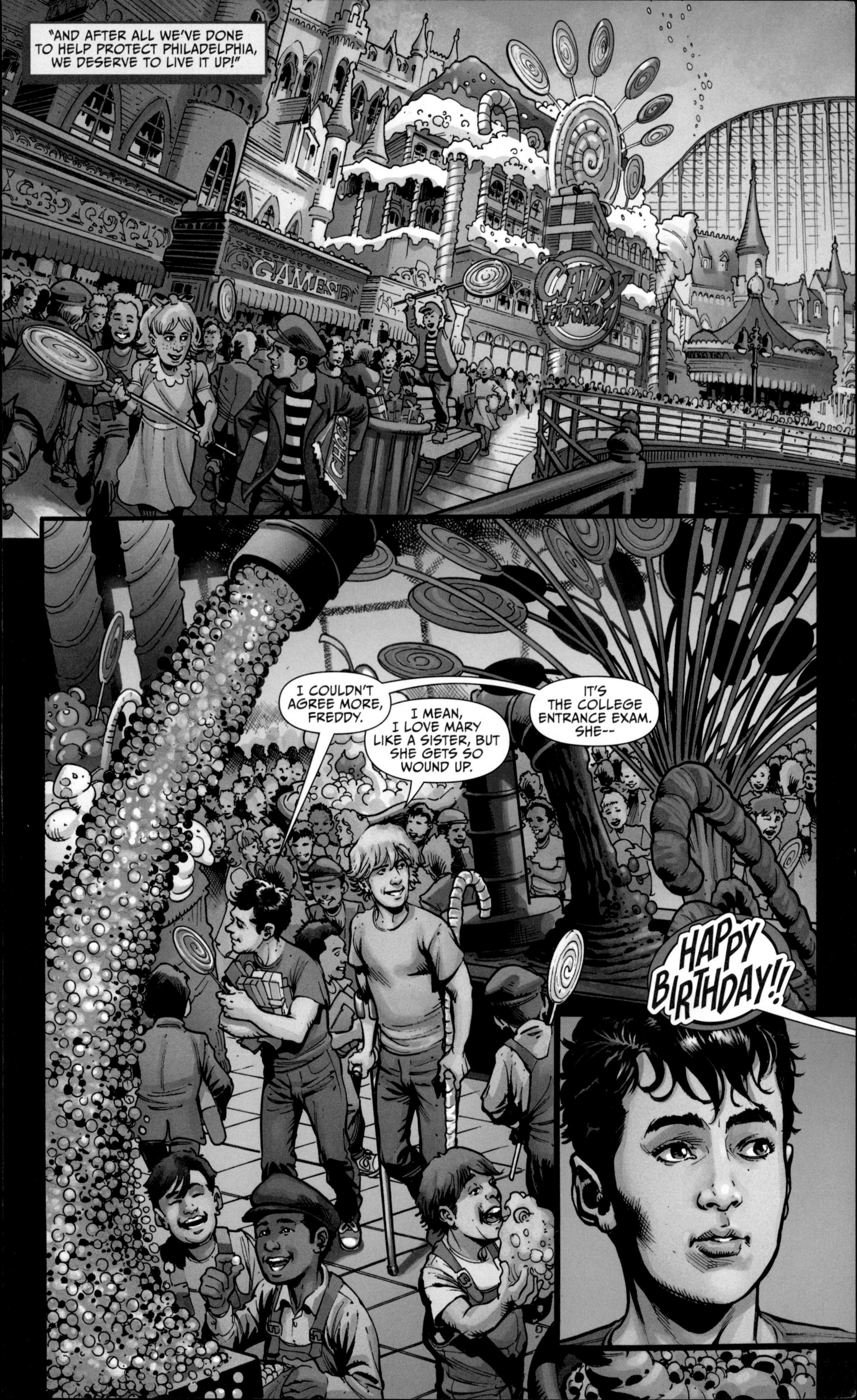
"AND AFTER ALL WE'VE DONE TO HELP PROTECT PHILADELPHIA, WE DESERVE TO LIVE IT UP!"
GAMES
CANDY EMPORIUM
I COULDN'T AGREE MORE, FREDDY.
I MEAN, I LOVE MARY LIKE A SISTER, BUT SHE GETS SO WOUND UP.
IT'S THE COLLEGE ENTRANCE EXAM. SHE--
HAPPY BIRTHDAY!!

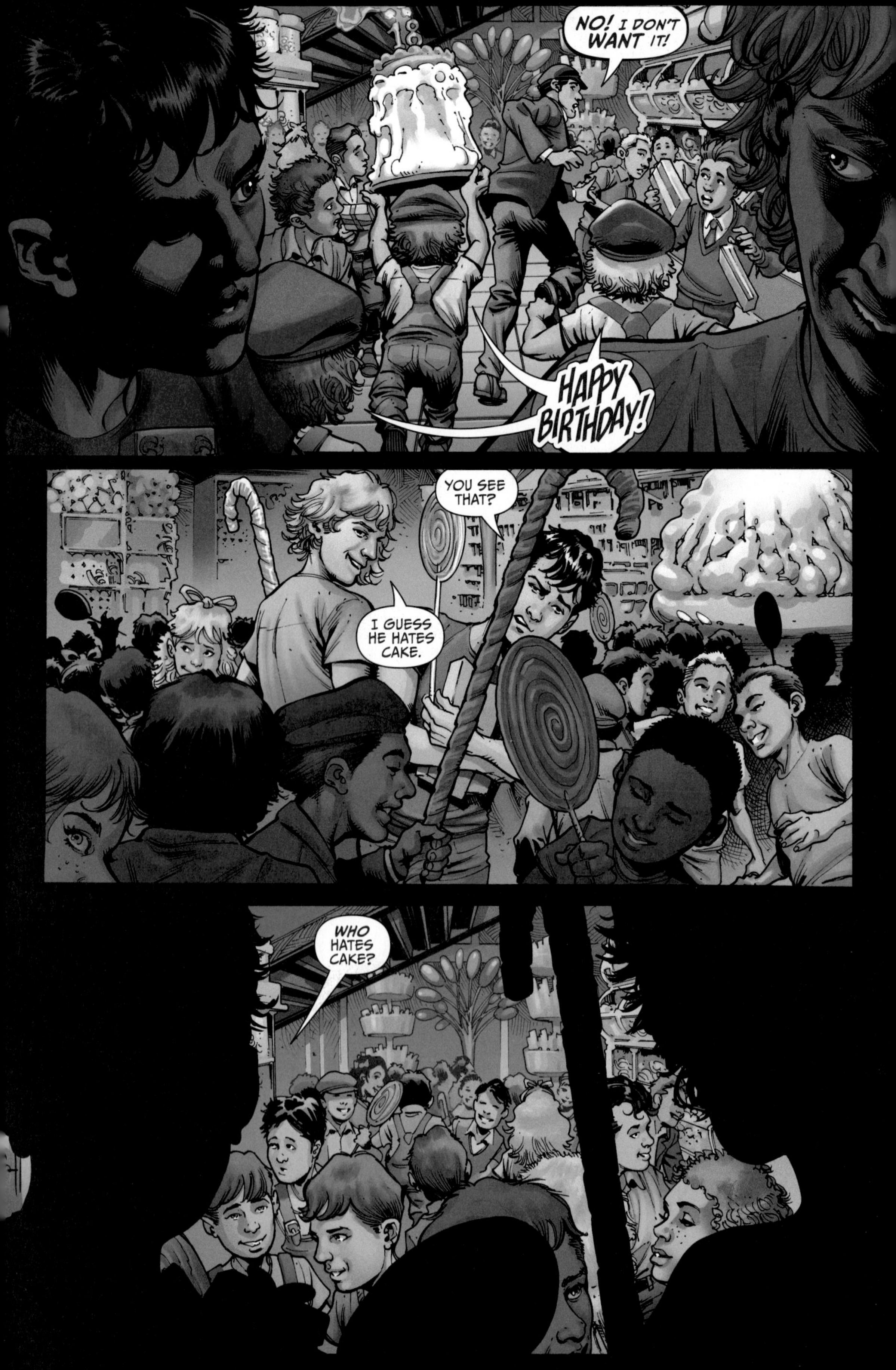
NO! I DON'T WANT IT!
HAPPY BIRTHDAY!
YOU SEE THAT?
I GUESS HE HATES CAKE.
WHO HATES CAKE?

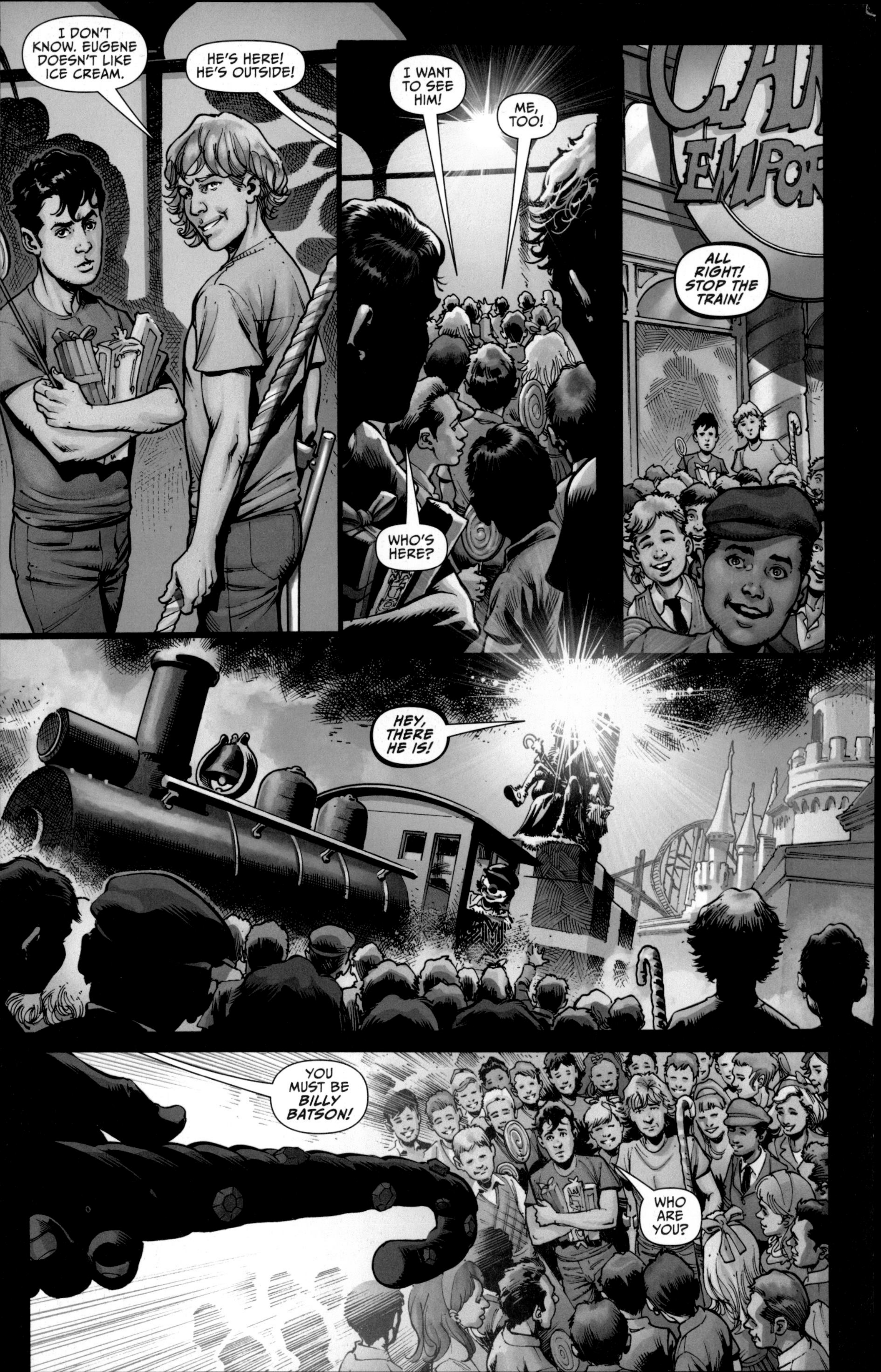
I DON'T KNOW. EUGENE DOESN'T LIKE ICE CREAM.
HE'S HERE! HE'S OUTSIDE!
I WANT TO SEE HIM!
ME, TOO!
WHO'S HERE?
EMPOR
ALL RIGHT! STOP THE TRAIN!
HEY, THERE HE IS!
YOU MUST BE BILLY BATSON!
WHO ARE YOU?

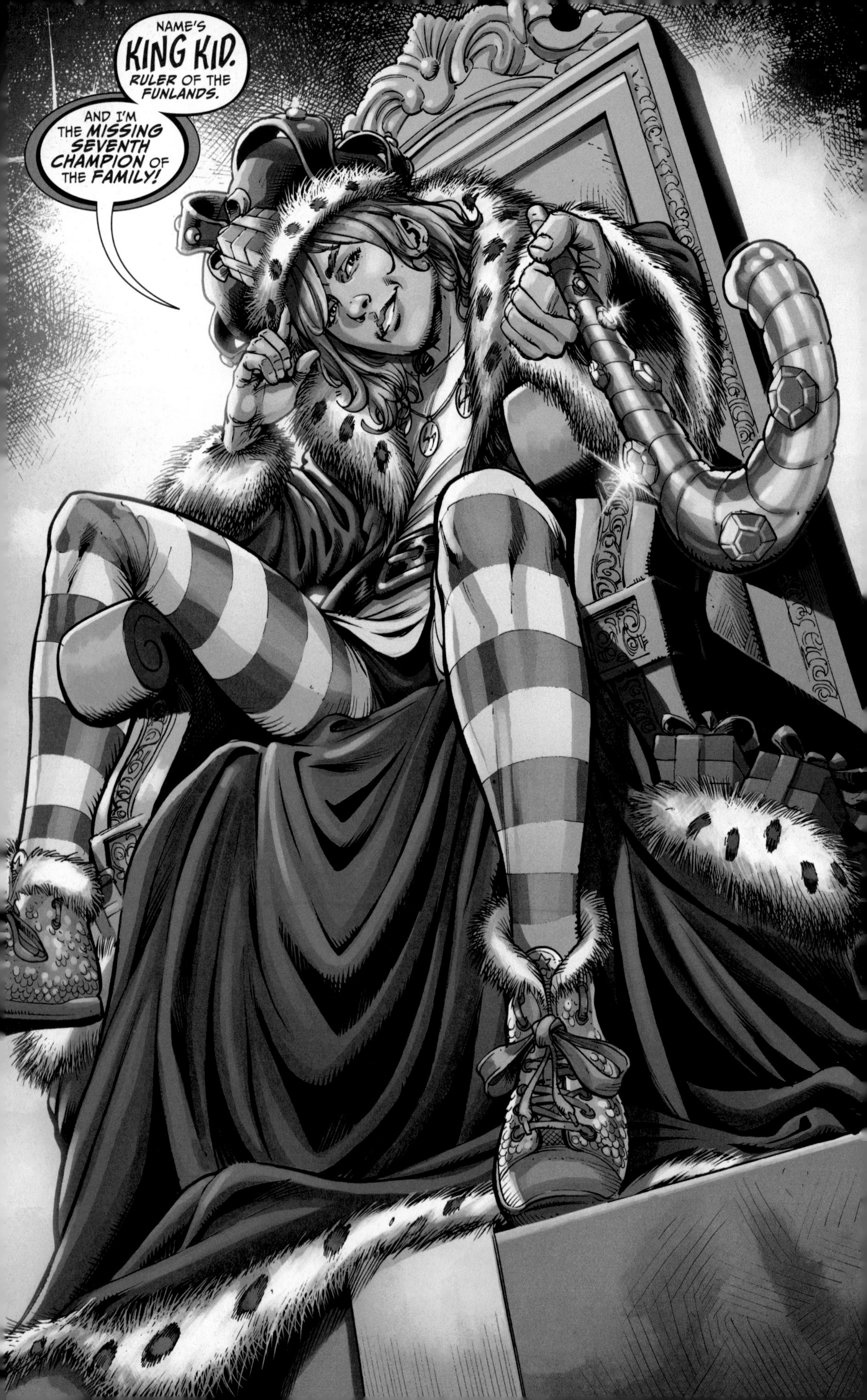
NAME'S KING KID. RULER OF THE FUNLANDS.
AND I'M THE MISSING SEVENTH CHAMPION OF THE FAMILY!

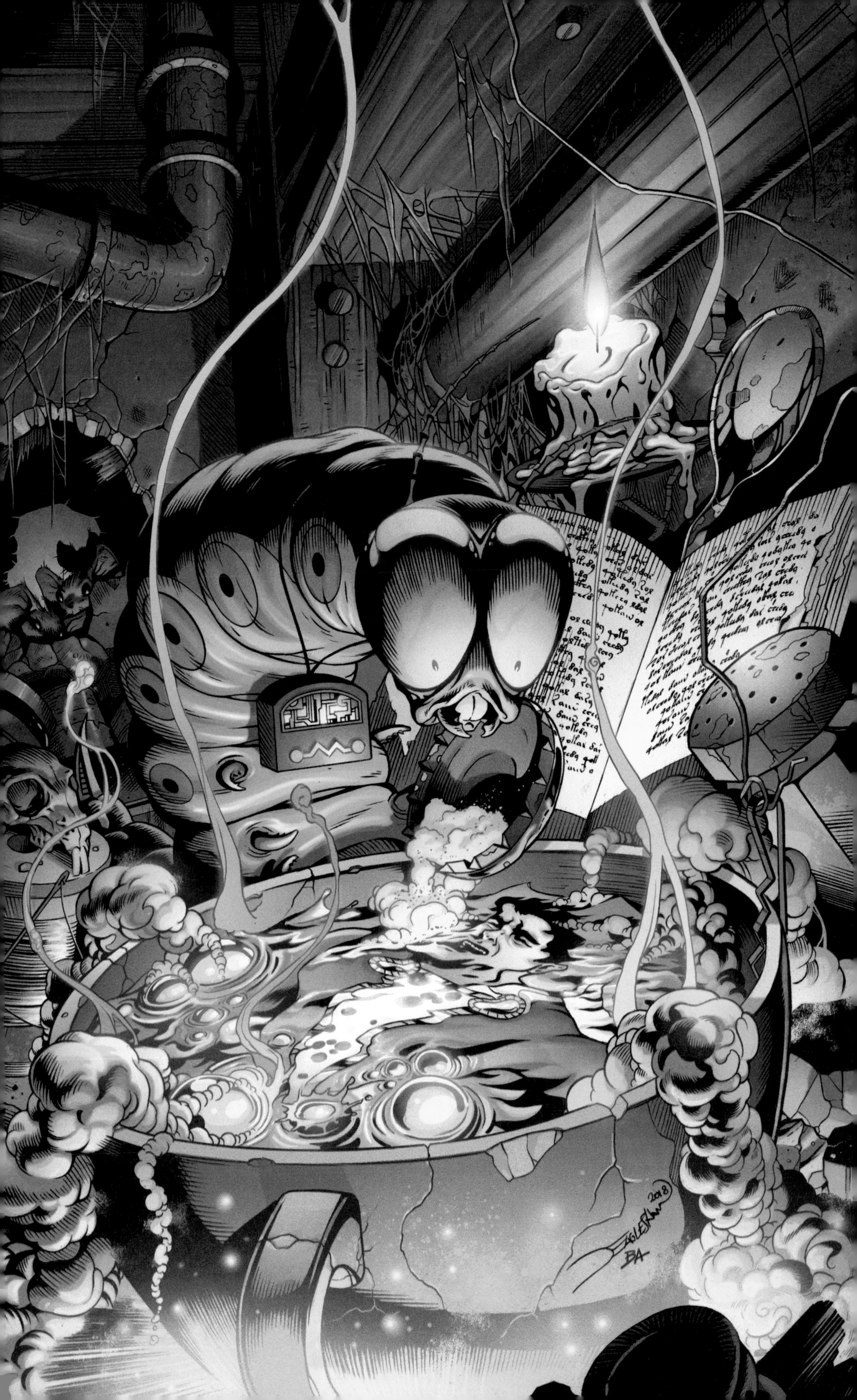

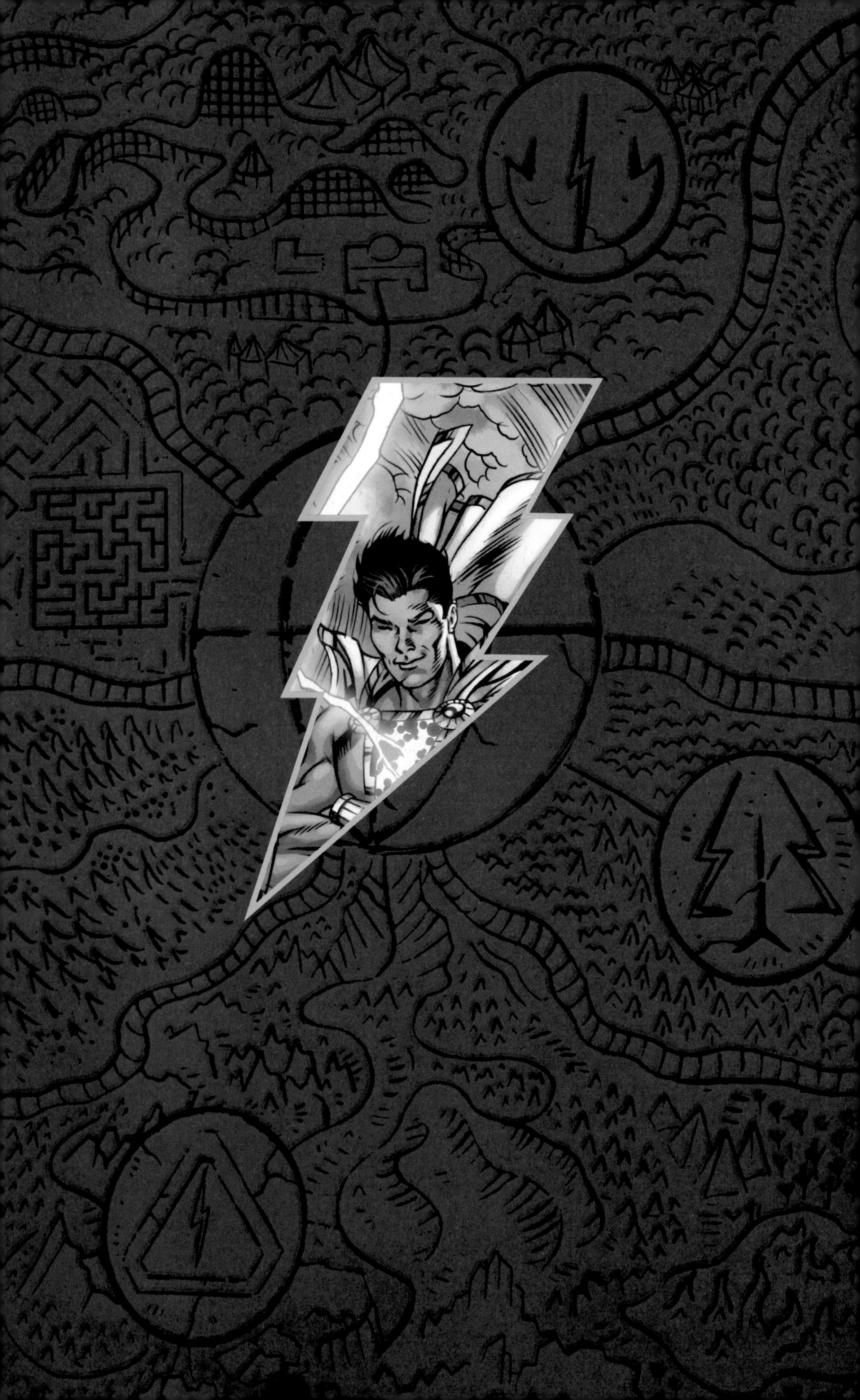

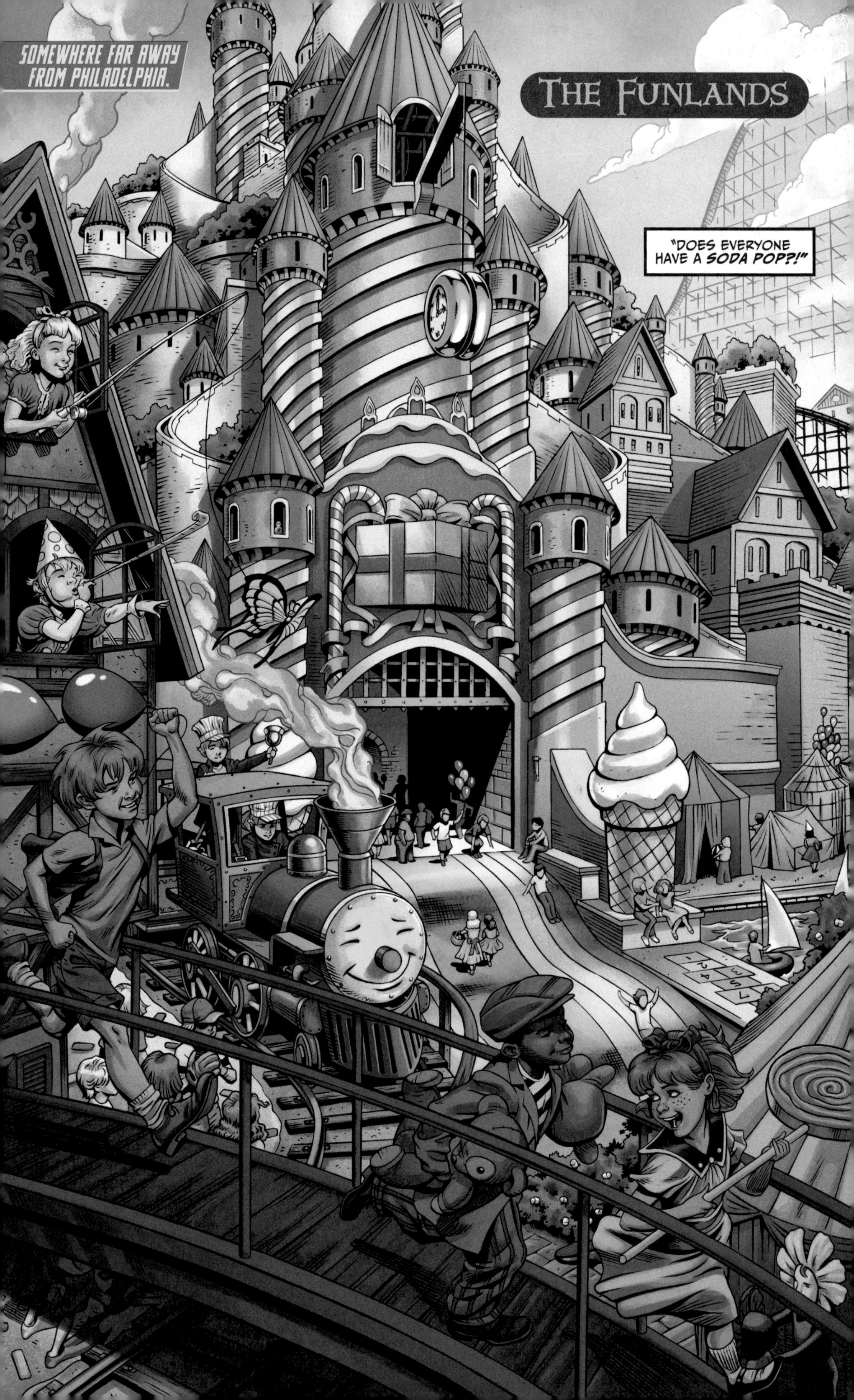

SOMEWHERE FAR AWAY FROM PHILADELPHIA.
THE FUNLANDS
"DOES EVERYONE HAVE A SODA POP?!"

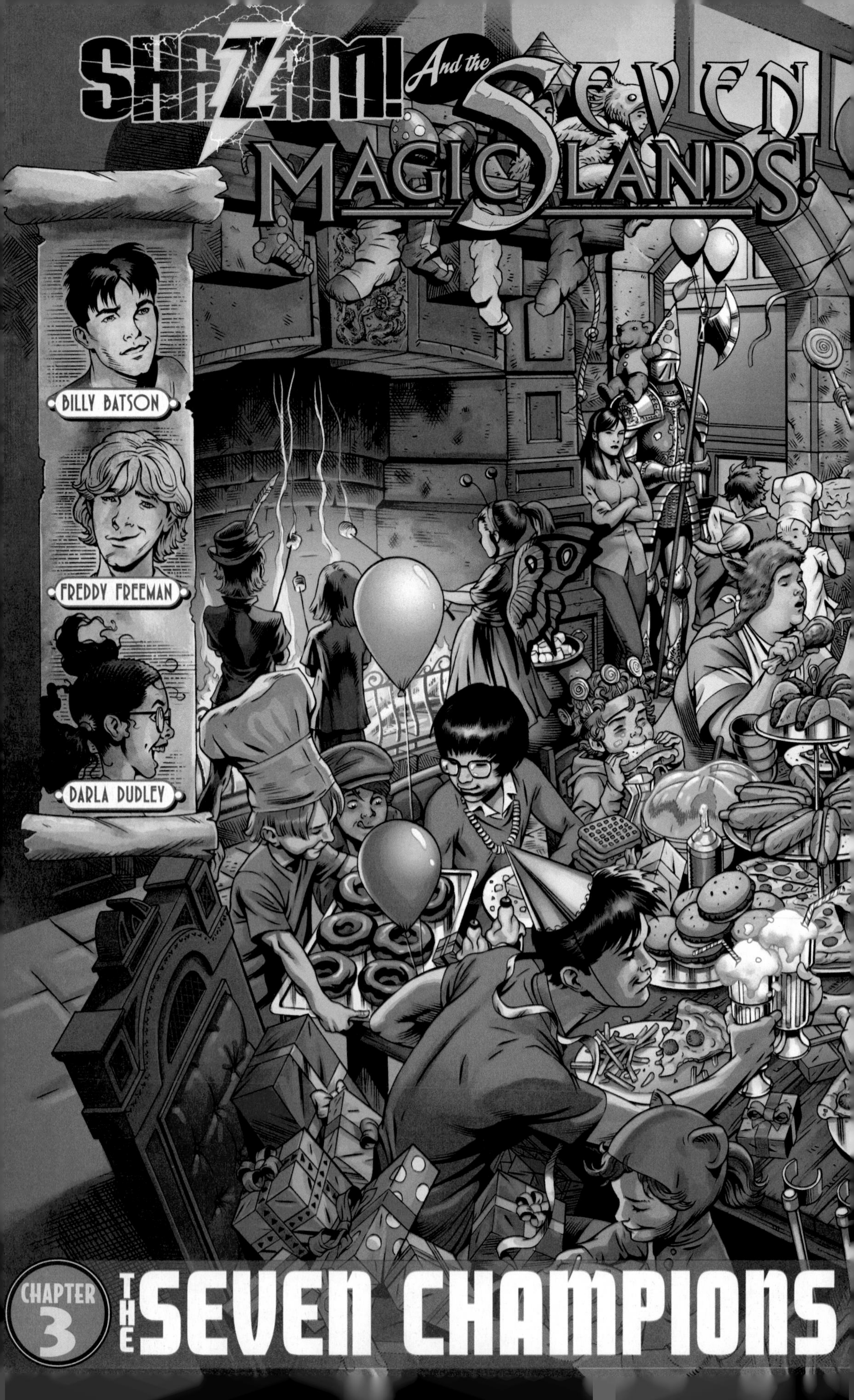

SHAZAM! And the SEVEN MAGIC LANDS!
BILLY BATSON
FREDDY FREEMAN
DARLA DUDLEY
CHAPTER 3
THE SEVEN CHAMPIONS

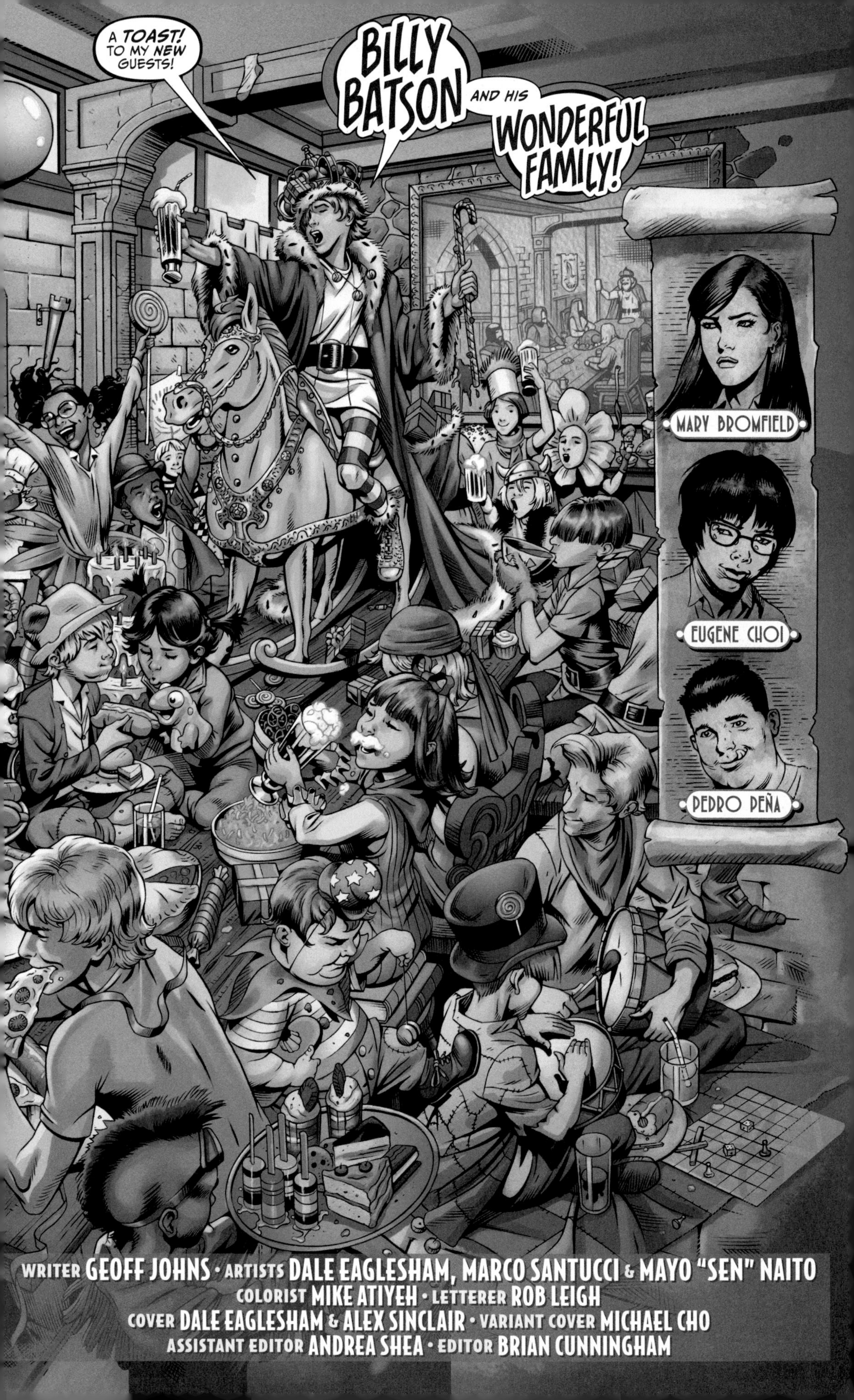
A TOAST! TO MY NEW GUESTS!
BILLY BATSON AND HIS WONDERFUL FAMILY!
MARY BROMFIELD
EUGENE CHOI
PEDRO PEÑA
WRITER GEOFF JOHNS · ARTISTS DALE EAGLESHAM, MARCO SANTUCCI & MAYO "SEN" NAITO
COLORIST MIKE ATIYEH · LETTERER ROB LEIGH
COVER DALE EAGLESHAM & ALEX SINCLAIR · VARIANT COVER MICHAEL CHO
ASSISTANT EDITOR ANDREA SHEA · EDITOR BRIAN CUNNINGHAM

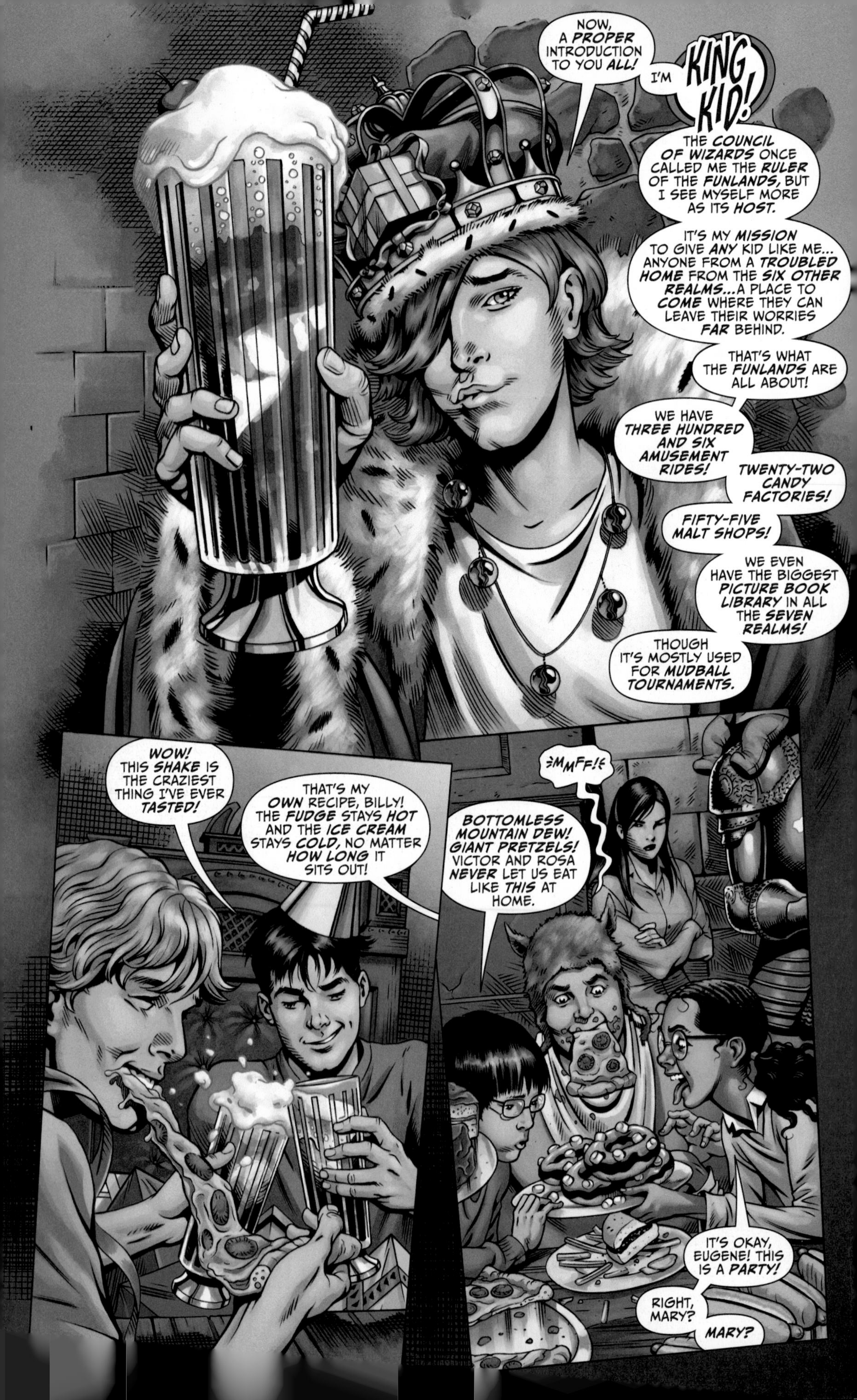
NOW, A PROPER INTRODUCTION TO YOU ALL!
I'M KING KID!
THE COUNCIL OF WIZARDS ONCE CALLED ME THE RULER OF THE FUNLANDS, BUT I SEE MYSELF MORE AS ITS HOST.
IT'S MY MISSION TO GIVE ANY KID LIKE ME... ANYONE FROM A TROUBLED HOME FROM THE SIX OTHER REALMS...A PLACE TO COME WHERE THEY CAN LEAVE THEIR WORRIES FAR BEHIND.
THAT'S WHAT THE FUNLANDS ARE ALL ABOUT!
WE HAVE THREE HUNDRED AND SIX AMUSEMENT RIDES!
TWENTY-TWO CANDY FACTORIES!
FIFTY-FIVE MALT SHOPS!
WE EVEN HAVE THE BIGGEST PICTURE BOOK LIBRARY IN ALL THE SEVEN REALMS!
THOUGH IT'S MOSTLY USED FOR MUDBALL TOURNAMENTS.
WOW! THIS SHAKE IS THE CRAZIEST THING I'VE EVER TASTED!
THAT'S MY OWN RECIPE, BILLY! THE FUDGE STAYS HOT AND THE ICE CREAM STAYS COLD, NO MATTER HOW LONG IT SITS OUT!
MMFF!
BOTTOMLESS MOUNTAIN DEW! GIANT PRETZELS! VICTOR AND ROSA NEVER LET US EAT LIKE THIS AT HOME.
IT'S OKAY, EUGENE! THIS IS A PARTY!
RIGHT, MARY?
MARY?

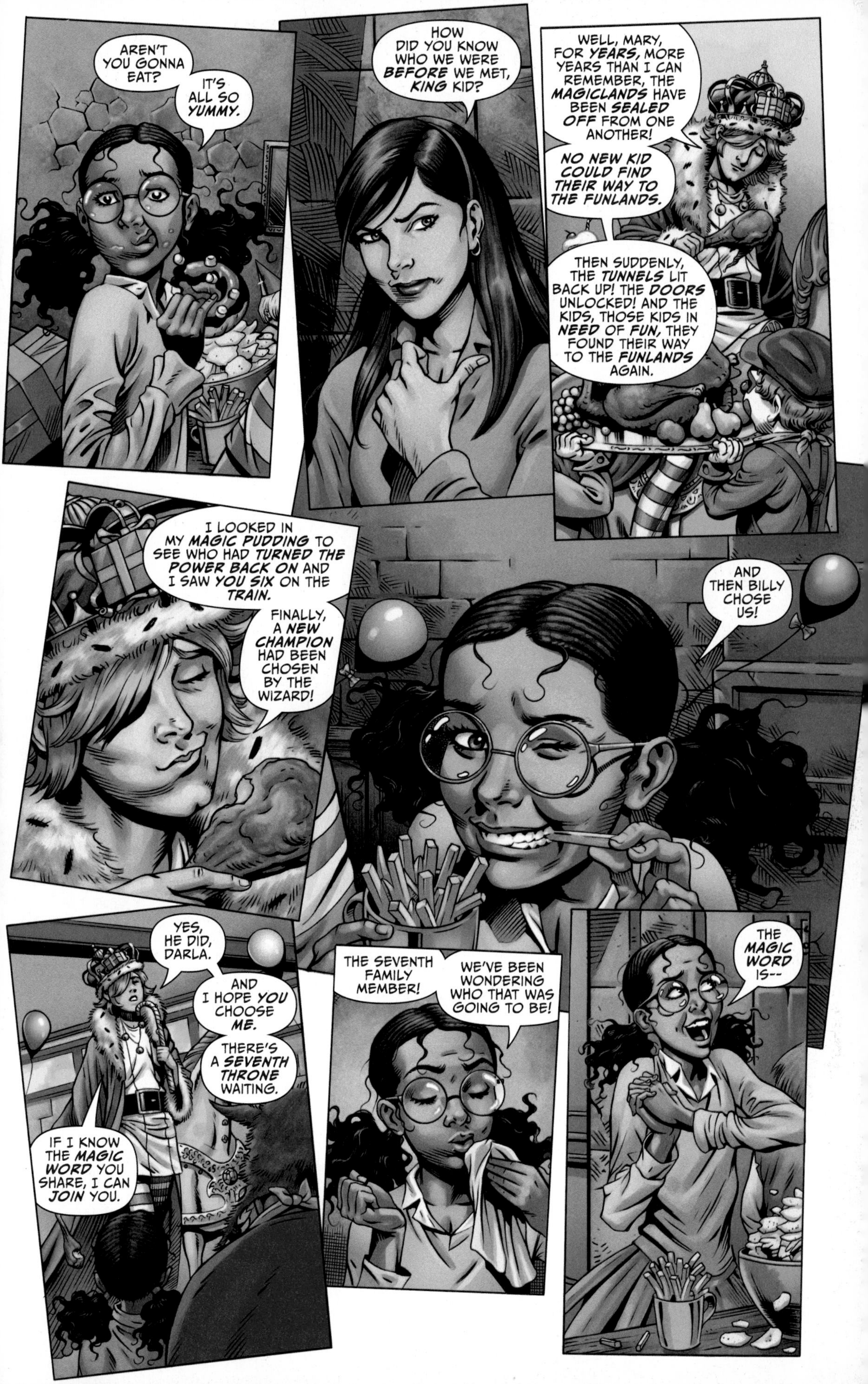
AREN'T YOU GONNA EAT?
IT'S ALL SO YUMMY.
HOW DID YOU KNOW WHO WE WERE BEFORE WE MET, KING KID?
WELL, MARY, FOR YEARS, MORE YEARS THAN I CAN REMEMBER, THE MAGICLANDS HAVE BEEN SEALED OFF FROM ONE ANOTHER!
NO NEW KID COULD FIND THEIR WAY TO THE FUNLANDS.
THEN SUDDENLY, THE TUNNELS LIT BACK UP! THE DOORS UNLOCKED! AND THE KIDS, THOSE KIDS IN NEED OF FUN, THEY FOUND THEIR WAY TO THE FUNLANDS AGAIN.
I LOOKED IN MY MAGIC PUDDING TO SEE WHO HAD TURNED THE POWER BACK ON AND I SAW YOU SIX ON THE TRAIN.
FINALLY, A NEW CHAMPION HAD BEEN CHOSEN BY THE WIZARD!
AND THEN BILLY CHOSE US!
YES, HE DID, DARLA.
AND I HOPE YOU CHOOSE ME.
THERE'S A SEVENTH THRONE WAITING.
IF I KNOW THE MAGIC WORD YOU SHARE, I CAN JOIN YOU.
THE SEVENTH FAMILY MEMBER!
WE'VE BEEN WONDERING WHO THAT WAS GOING TO BE!
THE MAGIC WORD IS--

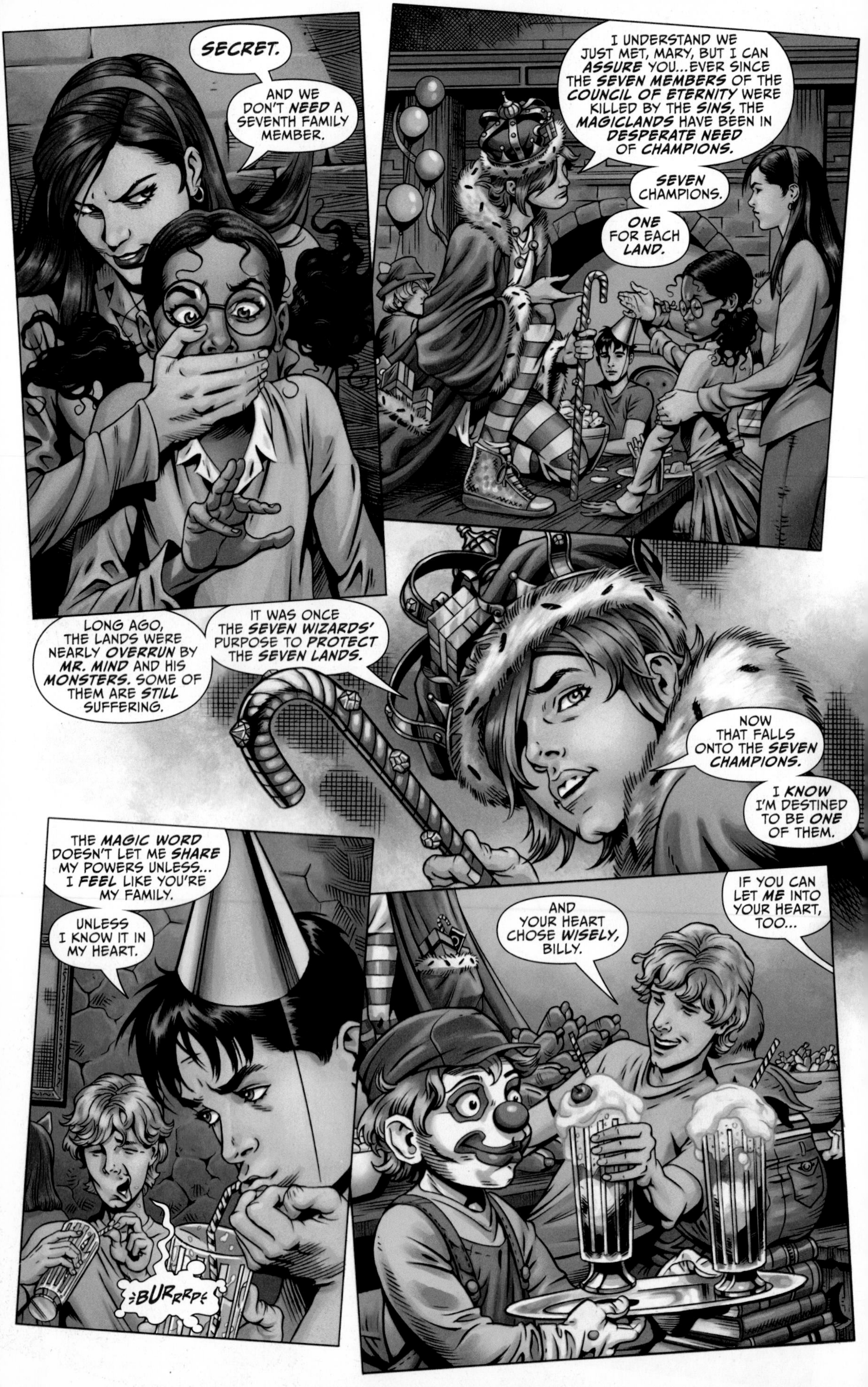
SECRET.
AND WE DON'T NEED A SEVENTH FAMILY MEMBER.
I UNDERSTAND WE JUST MET, MARY, BUT I CAN ASSURE YOU...EVER SINCE THE SEVEN MEMBERS OF THE COUNCIL OF ETERNITY WERE KILLED BY THE SINS, THE MAGICLANDS HAVE BEEN IN DESPERATE NEED OF CHAMPIONS.
SEVEN CHAMPIONS.
ONE FOR EACH LAND.
LONG AGO, THE LANDS WERE NEARLY OVERRUN BY MR. MIND AND HIS MONSTERS. SOME OF THEM ARE STILL SUFFERING.
IT WAS ONCE THE SEVEN WIZARDS' PURPOSE TO PROTECT THE SEVEN LANDS.
NOW THAT FALLS ONTO THE SEVEN CHAMPIONS.
I KNOW I'M DESTINED TO BE ONE OF THEM.
THE MAGIC WORD DOESN'T LET ME SHARE MY POWERS UNLESS... I FEEL LIKE YOU'RE MY FAMILY.
UNLESS I KNOW IT IN MY HEART.
BURRRP
AND YOUR HEART CHOSE WISELY, BILLY.
IF YOU CAN LET ME INTO YOUR HEART, TOO...

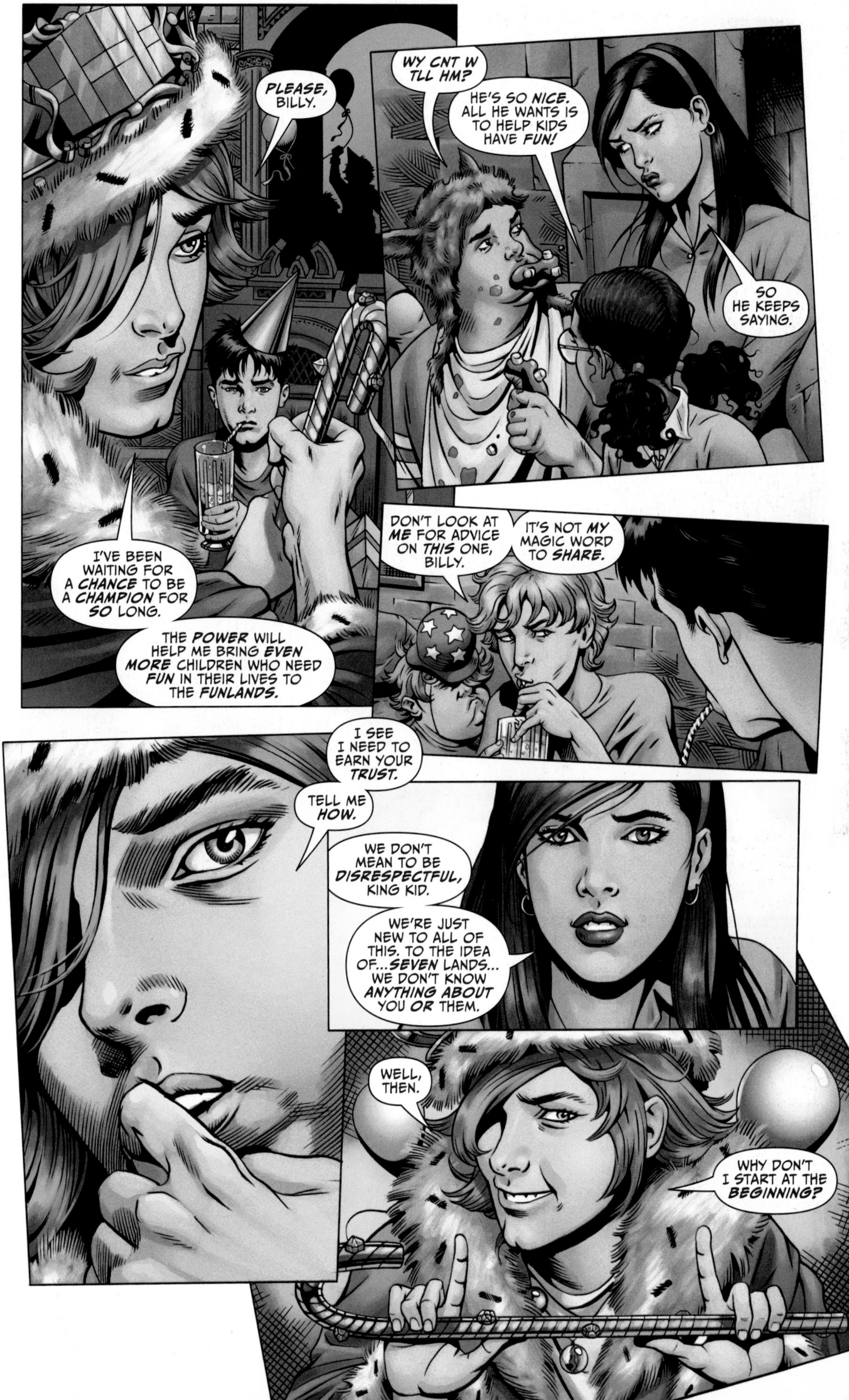
PLEASE, BILLY.
I'VE BEEN WAITING FOR A CHANCE TO BE A CHAMPION FOR SO LONG.
THE POWER WILL HELP ME BRING EVEN MORE CHILDREN WHO NEED FUN IN THEIR LIVES TO THE FUNLANDS.
WY CNT W TLL HM?
HE'S SO NICE. ALL HE WANTS IS TO HELP KIDS HAVE FUN!
SO HE KEEPS SAYING.
DON'T LOOK AT ME FOR ADVICE ON THIS ONE, BILLY.
IT'S NOT MY MAGIC WORD TO SHARE.
I SEE I NEED TO EARN YOUR TRUST.
TELL ME HOW.
WE DON'T MEAN TO BE DISRESPECTFUL, KING KID.
WE'RE JUST NEW TO ALL OF THIS. TO THE IDEA OF...SEVEN LANDS... WE DON'T KNOW ANYTHING ABOUT YOU OR THEM.
WELL, THEN.
WHY DON'T I START AT THE BEGINNING?

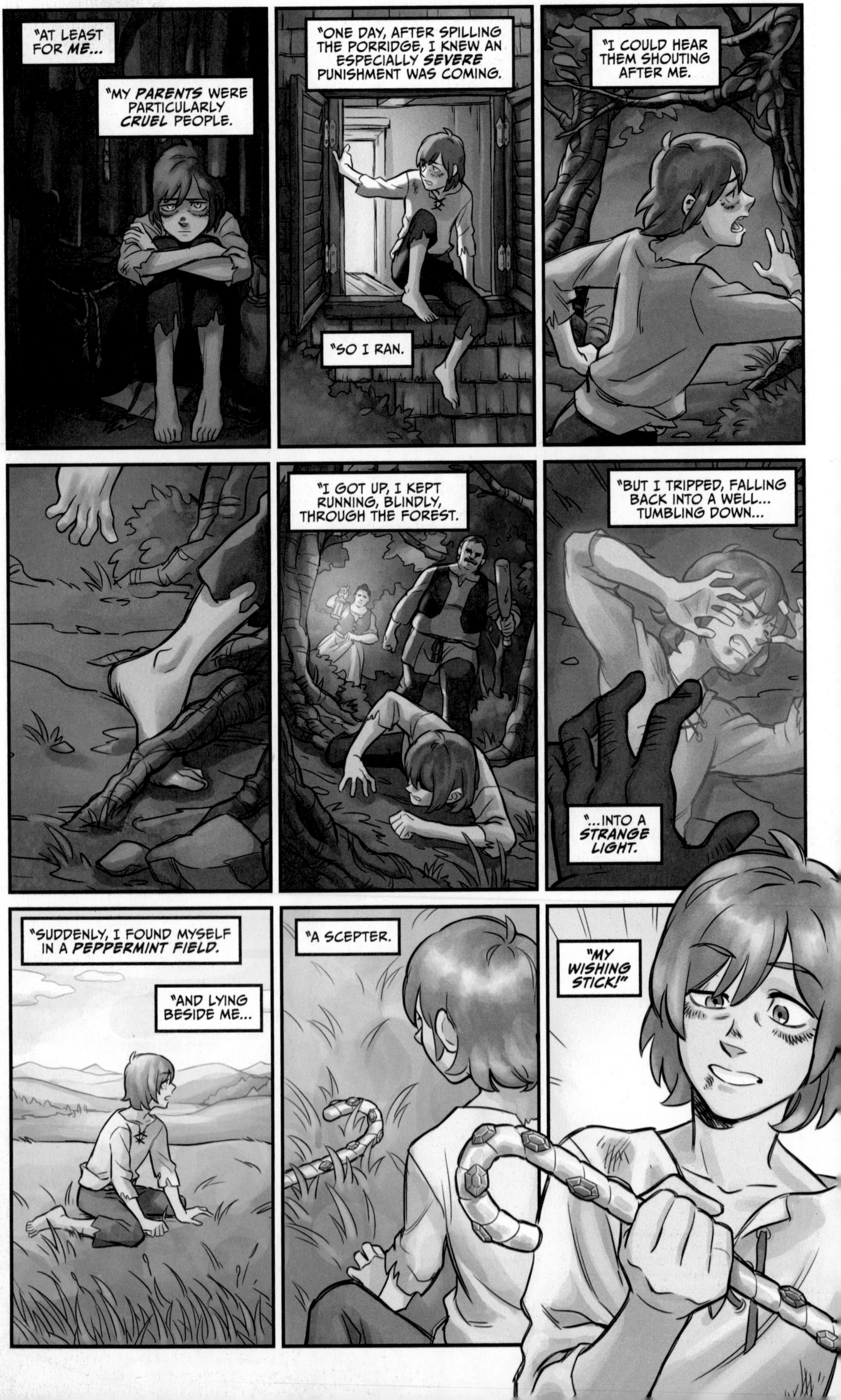
"AT LEAST FOR ME...
"MY PARENTS WERE PARTICULARLY CRUEL PEOPLE.
"ONE DAY, AFTER SPILLING THE PORRIDGE, I KNEW AN ESPECIALLY SEVERE PUNISHMENT WAS COMING.
"SO I RAN.
"I COULD HEAR THEM SHOUTING AFTER ME.
"I GOT UP, I KEPT RUNNING, BLINDLY, THROUGH THE FOREST.
"BUT I TRIPPED, FALLING BACK INTO A WELL... TUMBLING DOWN...
"...INTO A STRANGE LIGHT.
"SUDDENLY, I FOUND MYSELF IN A PEPPERMINT FIELD.
"AND LYING BESIDE ME...
"A SCEPTER.
"MY WISHING STICK!"

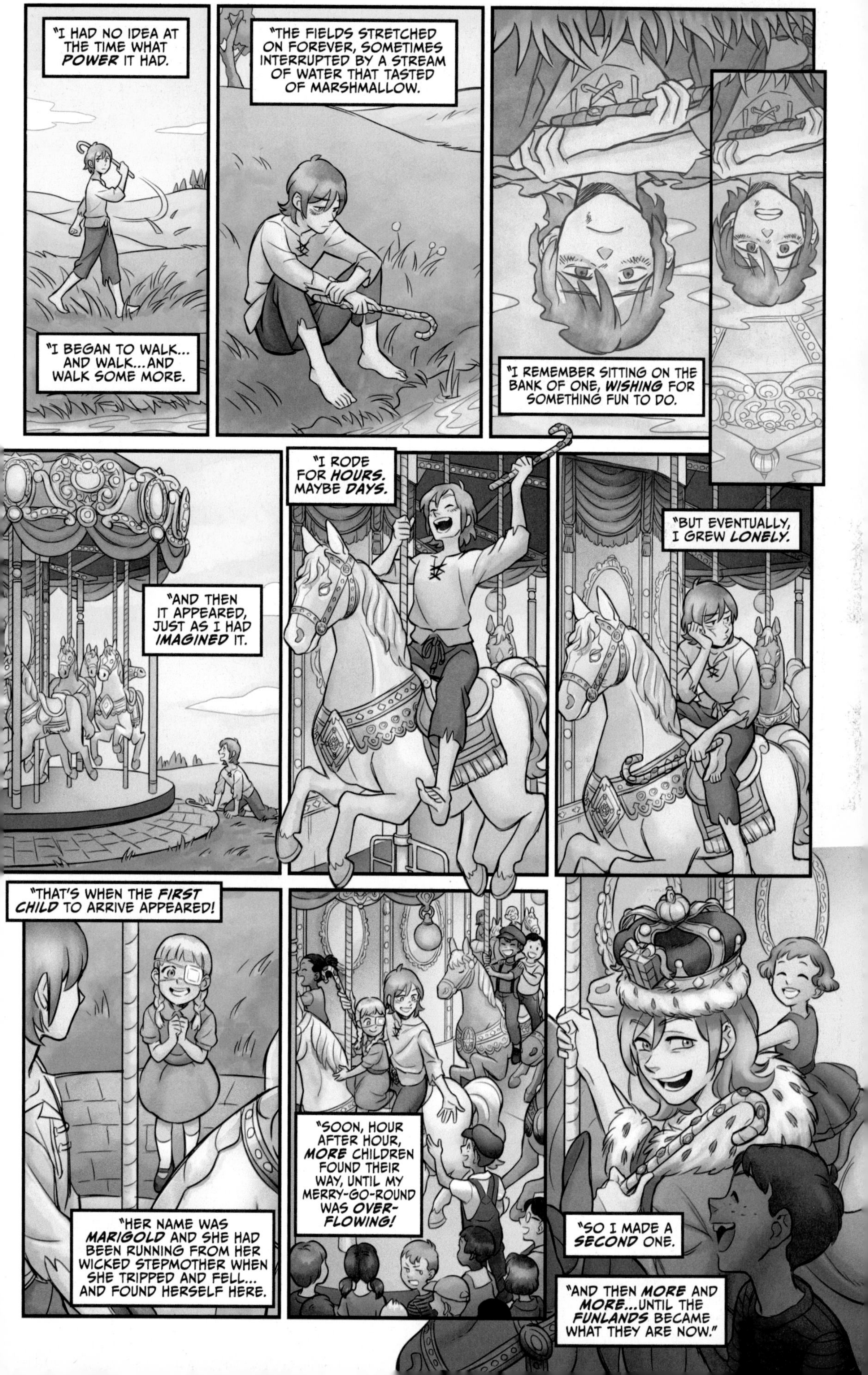
"I HAD NO IDEA AT THE TIME WHAT POWER IT HAD.
"I BEGAN TO WALK... AND WALK... AND WALK SOME MORE.
"THE FIELDS STRETCHED ON FOREVER, SOMETIMES INTERRUPTED BY A STREAM OF WATER THAT TASTED OF MARSHMALLOW.
"I REMEMBER SITTING ON THE BANK OF ONE, WISHING FOR SOMETHING FUN TO DO.
"AND THEN IT APPEARED, JUST AS I HAD IMAGINED IT.
"I RODE FOR HOURS. MAYBE DAYS.
"BUT EVENTUALLY, I GREW LONELY.
"THAT'S WHEN THE FIRST CHILD TO ARRIVE APPEARED!
"HER NAME WAS MARIGOLD AND SHE HAD BEEN RUNNING FROM HER WICKED STEPMOTHER WHEN SHE TRIPPED AND FELL... AND FOUND HERSELF HERE.
"SOON, HOUR AFTER HOUR, MORE CHILDREN FOUND THEIR WAY, UNTIL MY MERRY-GO-ROUND WAS OVER-FLOWING!
"SO I MADE A SECOND ONE.
"AND THEN MORE AND MORE... UNTIL THE FUNLANDS BECAME WHAT THEY ARE NOW."

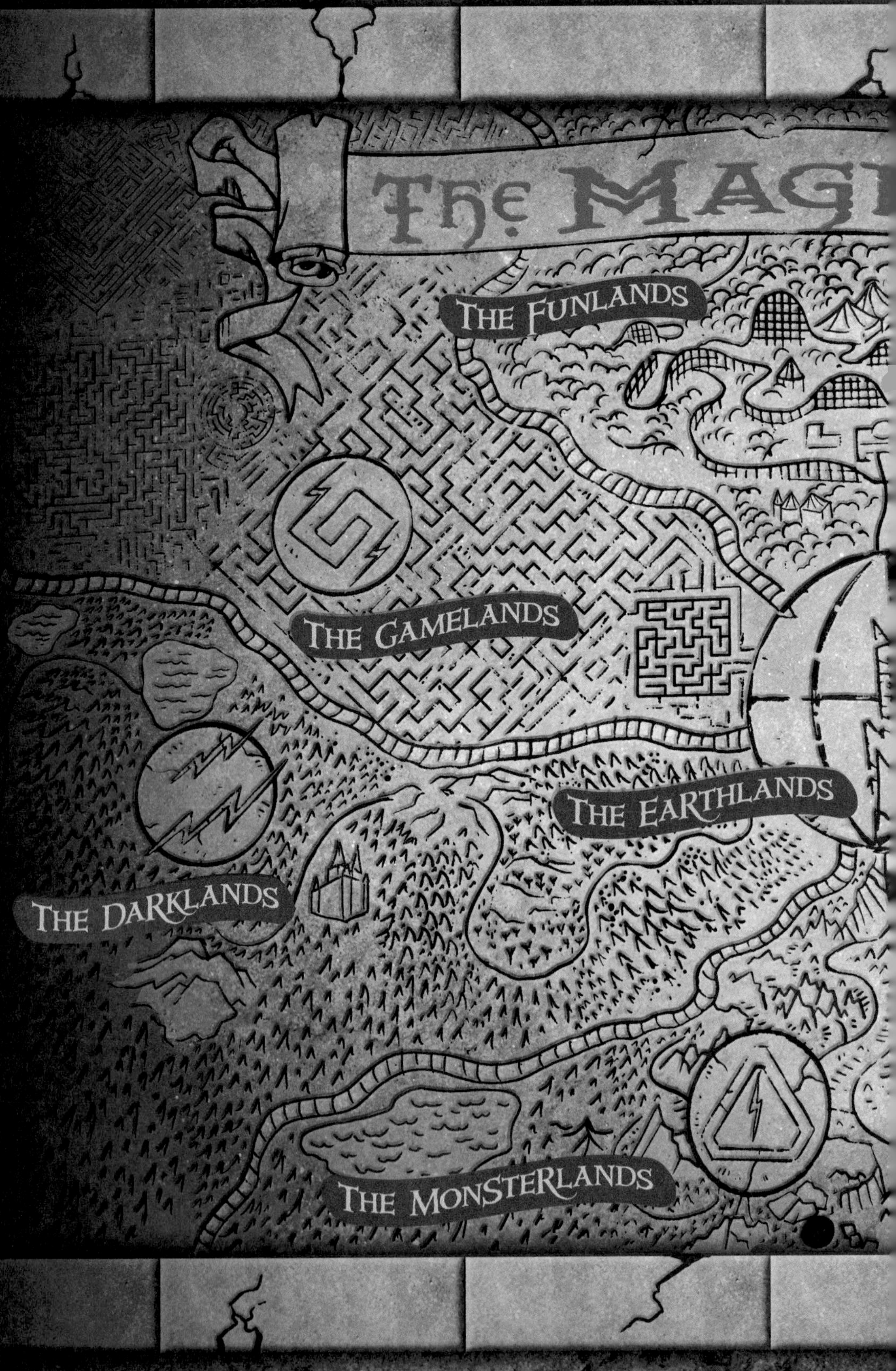
The Mag
The Funlands
The Gamelands
The Earthlands
The Darklands
The Monsterlands

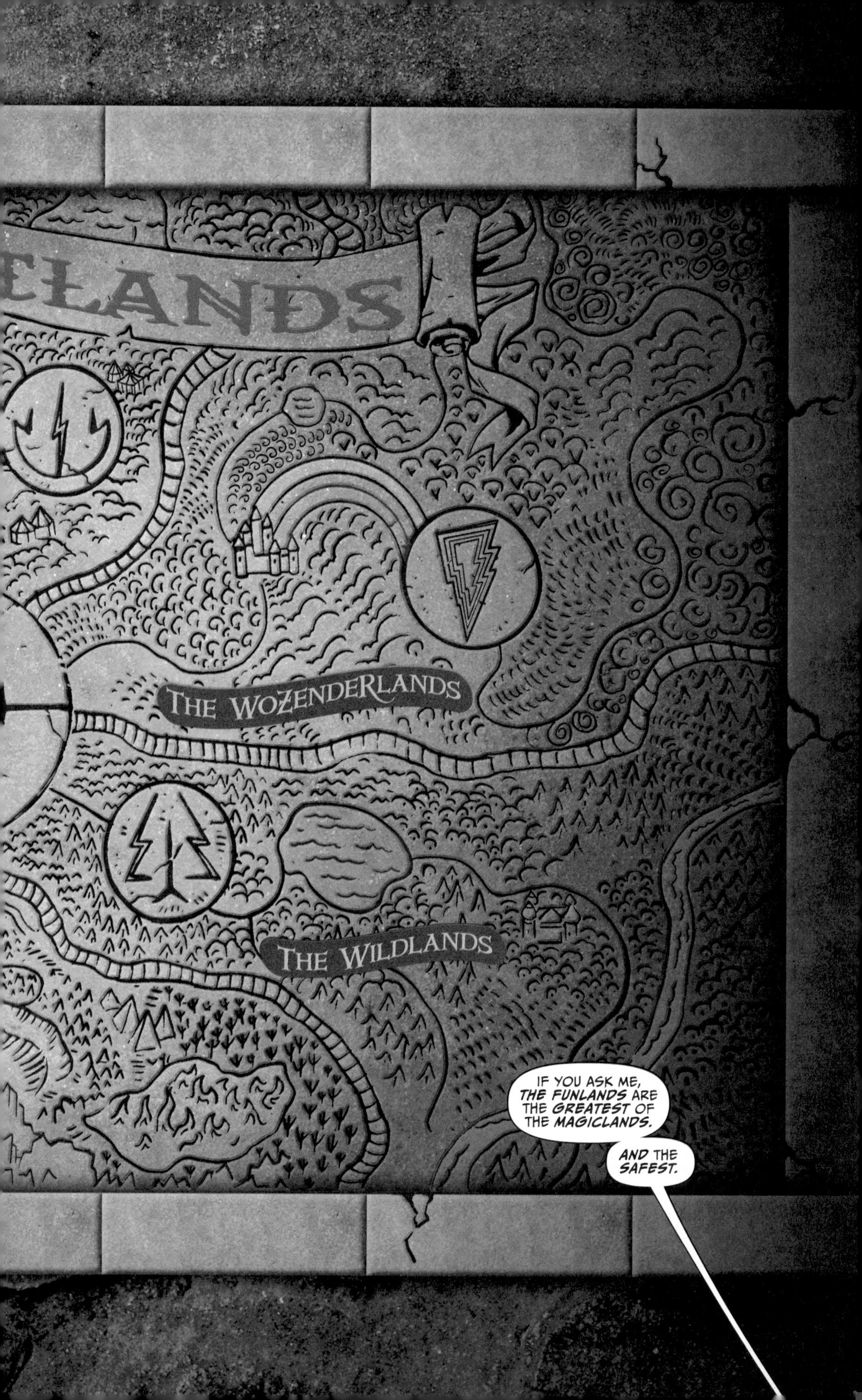
ELANDS
THE WOZENDERLANDS
THE WILDLANDS
IF YOU ASK ME, THE FUNLANDS ARE THE GREATEST OF THE MAGICLANDS.
AND THE SAFEST.

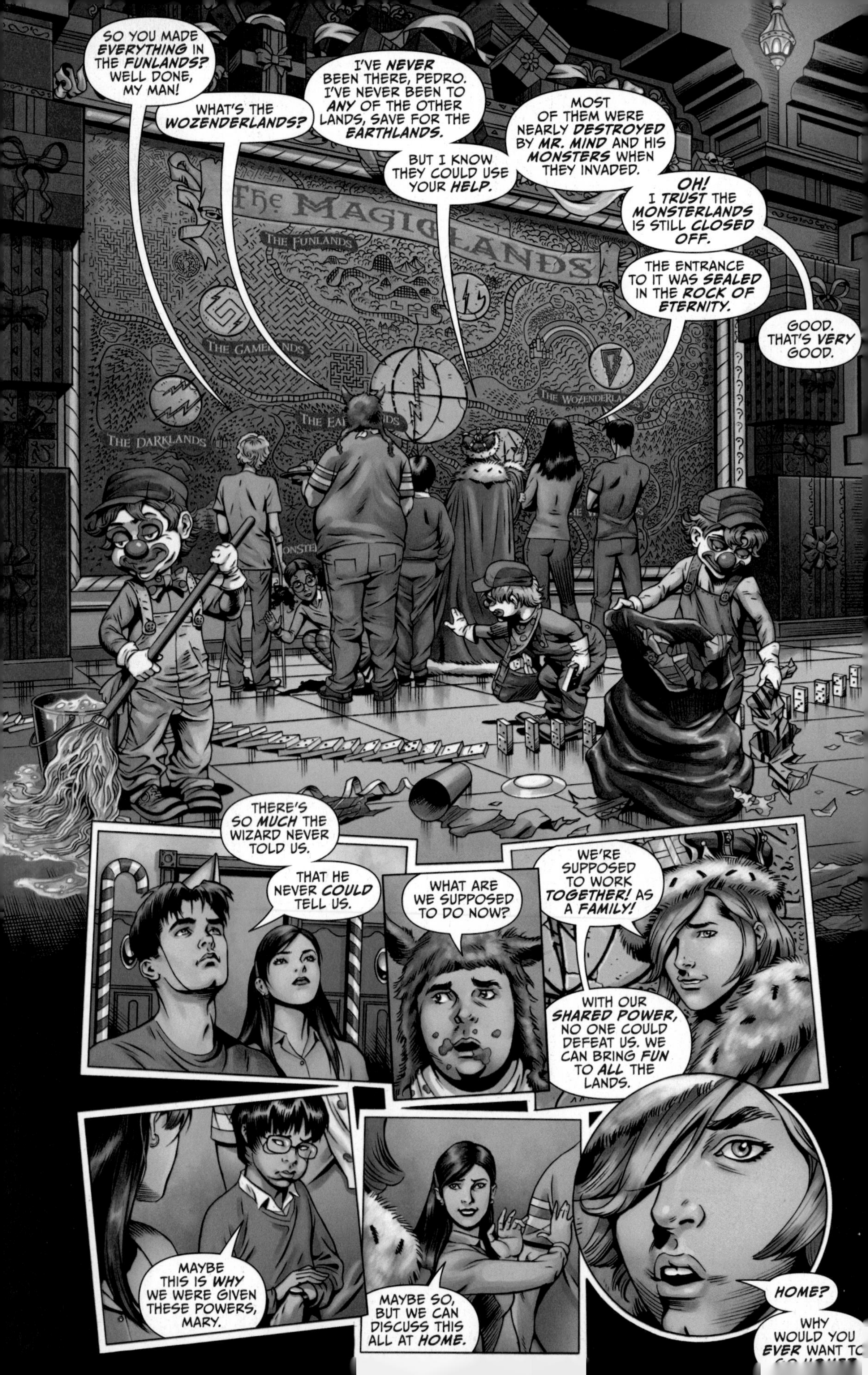
SO YOU MADE *EVERYTHING* IN THE *FUNLANDS?* WELL DONE, MY MAN!
WHAT'S THE *WOZENDERLANDS?*
I'VE *NEVER* BEEN THERE, PEDRO. I'VE NEVER BEEN TO *ANY* OF THE OTHER LANDS, SAVE FOR THE *EARTHLANDS.*
BUT I KNOW THEY COULD USE YOUR *HELP.*
MOST OF THEM WERE NEARLY *DESTROYED* BY *MR. MIND* AND HIS *MONSTERS* WHEN THEY INVADED.
*OH!* I *TRUST* THE *MONSTERLANDS* IS STILL *CLOSED OFF.*
THE ENTRANCE TO IT WAS *SEALED* IN THE *ROCK OF ETERNITY.*
GOOD. THAT'S *VERY* GOOD.
THE FUNLANDS
THE DARKLANDS
THERE'S SO *MUCH* THE WIZARD NEVER TOLD US.
THAT HE NEVER *COULD* TELL US.
WHAT ARE WE SUPPOSED TO DO NOW?
WE'RE SUPPOSED TO WORK *TOGETHER!* AS A *FAMILY!*
WITH OUR *SHARED POWER,* NO ONE COULD DEFEAT US. WE CAN BRING *FUN* TO *ALL* THE LANDS.
MAYBE THIS IS *WHY* WE WERE GIVEN THESE POWERS, MARY.
MAYBE SO, BUT WE CAN DISCUSS THIS ALL AT *HOME.*
*HOME?*
WHY WOULD YOU *EVER* WANT TO

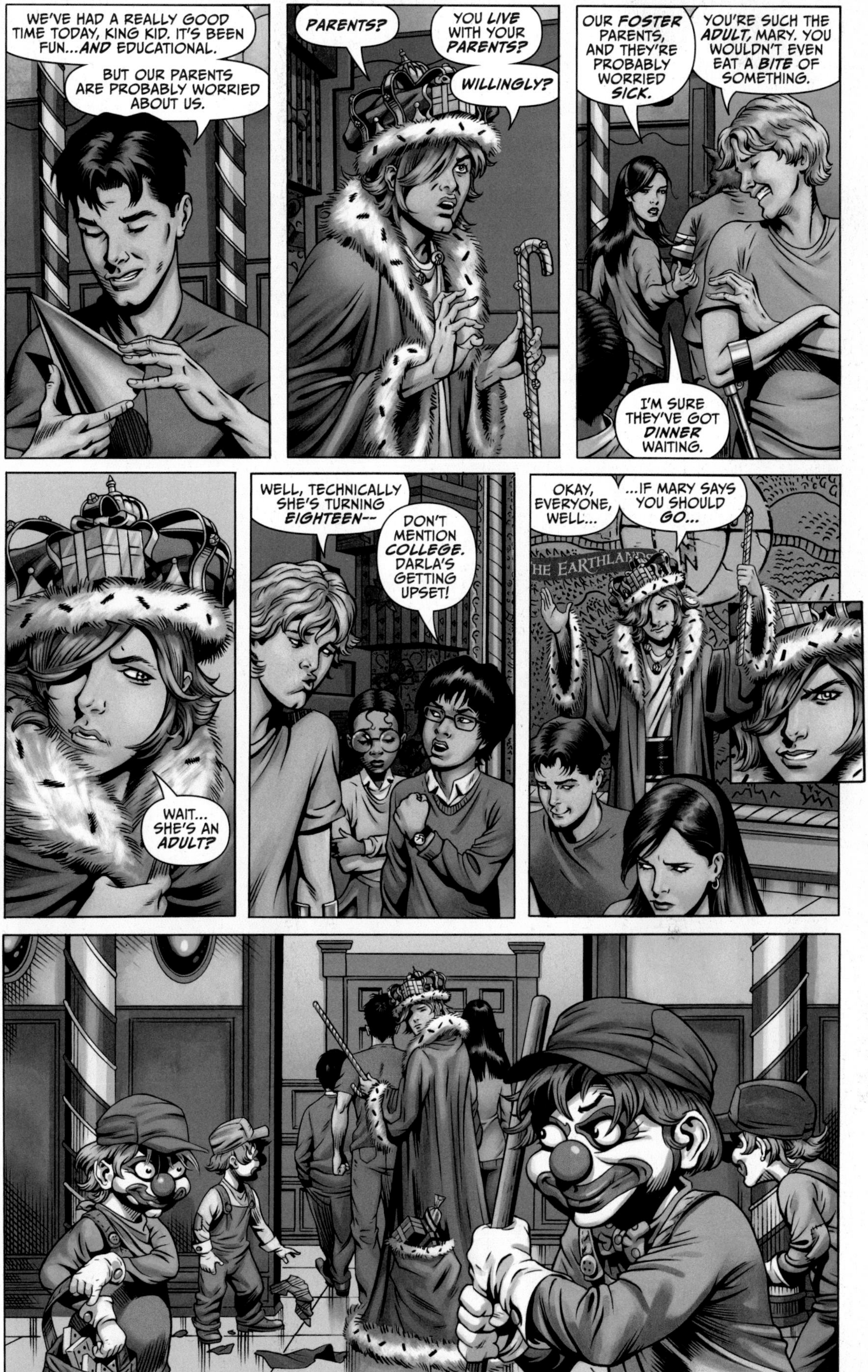
WE'VE HAD A REALLY GOOD TIME TODAY, KING KID. IT'S BEEN FUN...AND EDUCATIONAL.
BUT OUR PARENTS ARE PROBABLY WORRIED ABOUT US.
PARENTS?
YOU LIVE WITH YOUR PARENTS?
WILLINGLY?
OUR FOSTER PARENTS, AND THEY'RE PROBABLY WORRIED SICK.
YOU'RE SUCH THE ADULT, MARY. YOU WOULDN'T EVEN EAT A BITE OF SOMETHING.
I'M SURE THEY'VE GOT DINNER WAITING.
WAIT... SHE'S AN ADULT?
WELL, TECHNICALLY SHE'S TURNING EIGHTEEN--
DON'T MENTION COLLEGE. DARLA'S GETTING UPSET!
OKAY, EVERYONE, WELL...
...IF MARY SAYS YOU SHOULD GO...
THE EARTHLANDS

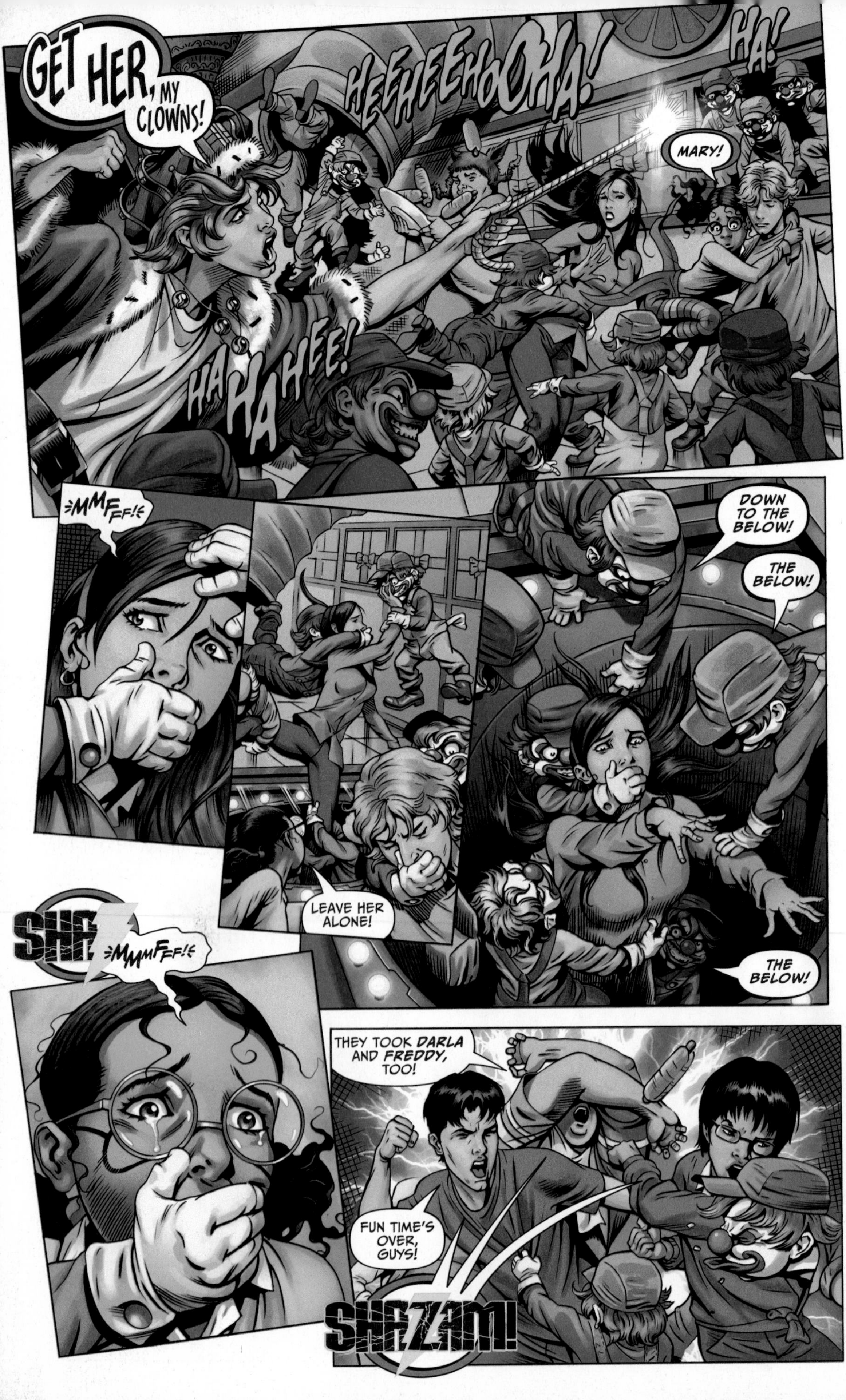
GET HER, MY CLOWNS!
HEEHEEHEEHOOHA!
HA!
MARY!
HA HA HAHEE!
MMFFF!
DOWN TO THE BELOW!
THE BELOW!
LEAVE HER ALONE!
THE BELOW!
SHA
MMMFFF!
THEY TOOK DARLA AND FREDDY, TOO!
FUN TIME'S OVER, GUYS!
SHAZAM!

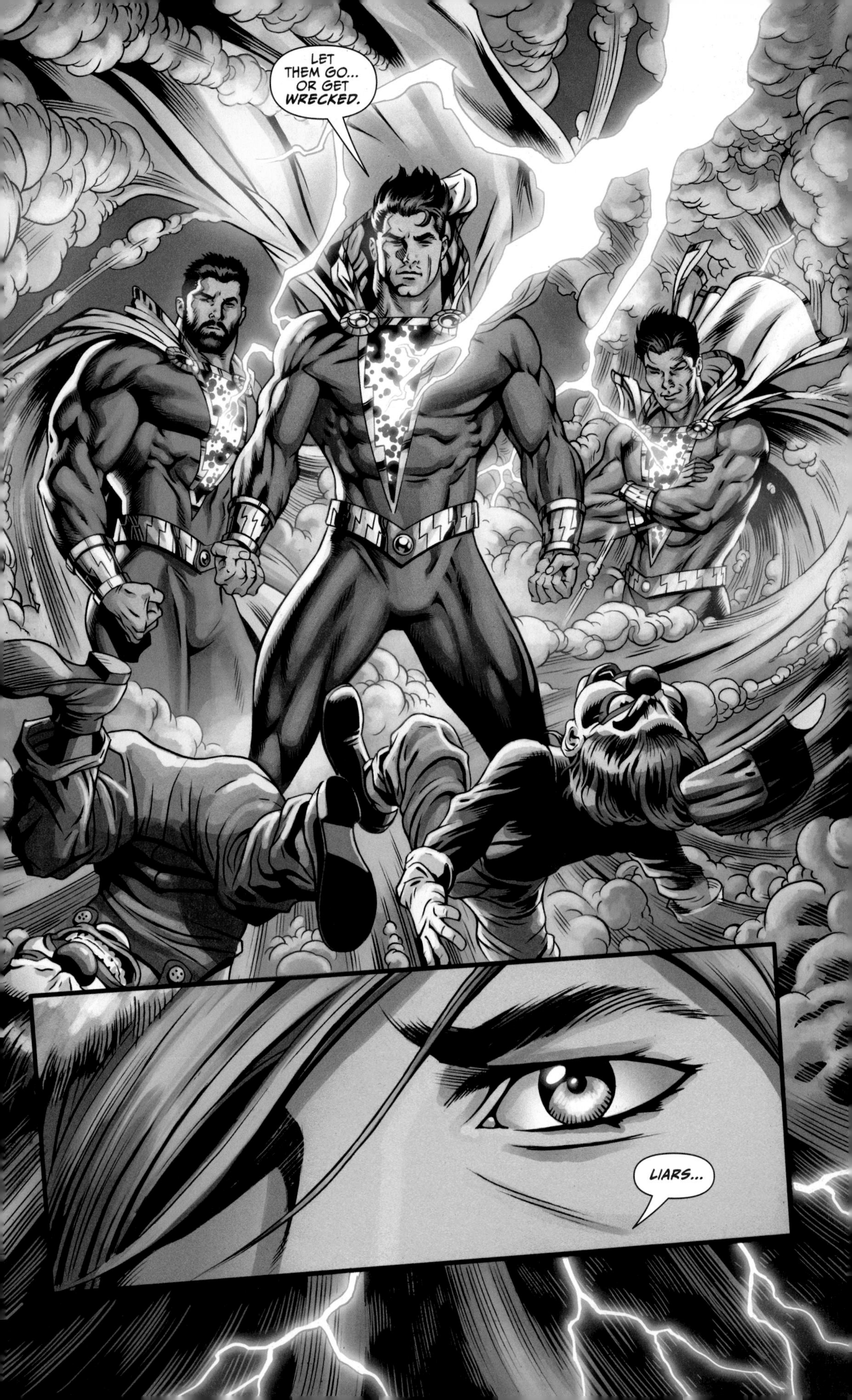

LET THEM GO... OR GET WRECKED.
LIARS...

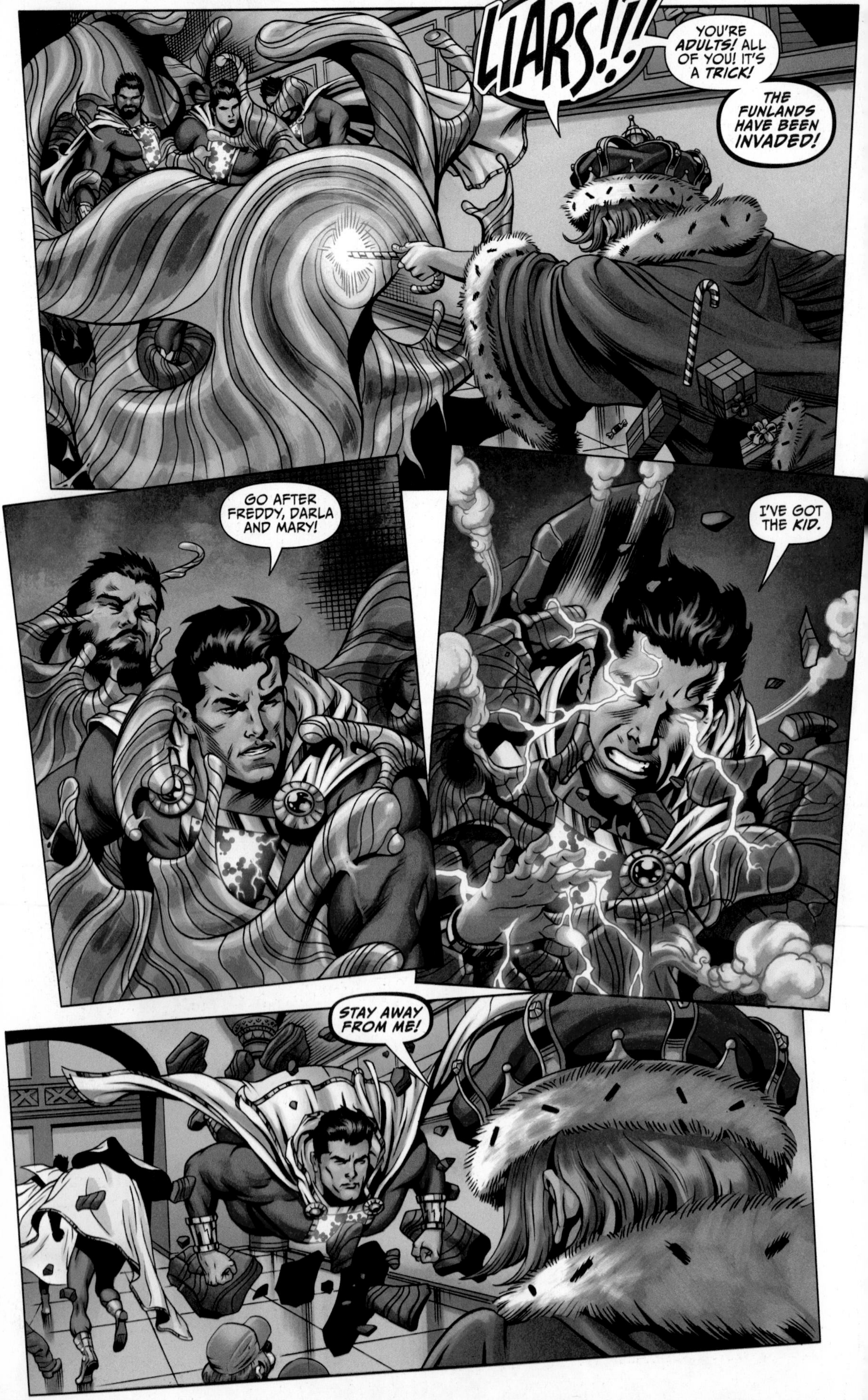
LIARS!!!
YOU'RE ADULTS! ALL OF YOU! IT'S A TRICK!
THE FUNLANDS HAVE BEEN INVADED!
GO AFTER FREDDY, DARLA AND MARY!
I'VE GOT THE KID.
STAY AWAY FROM ME!

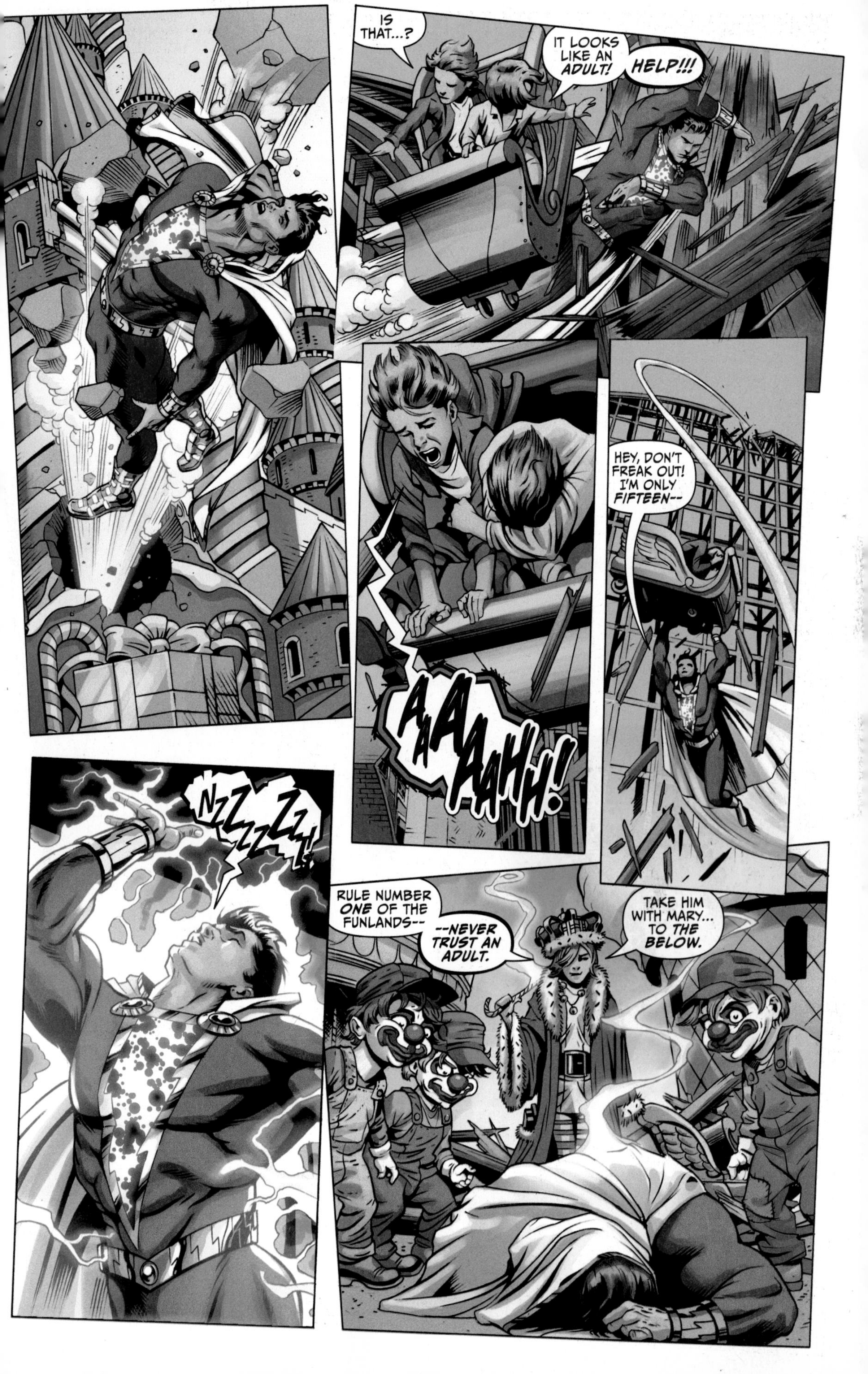
IS THAT...?
IT LOOKS LIKE AN ADULT!
HELP!!!
AAAAAAHHH!
HEY, DON'T FREAK OUT! I'M ONLY FIFTEEN--
NZZZZZZT!
RULE NUMBER ONE OF THE FUNLANDS--
--NEVER TRUST AN ADULT.
TAKE HIM WITH MARY... TO THE BELOW.

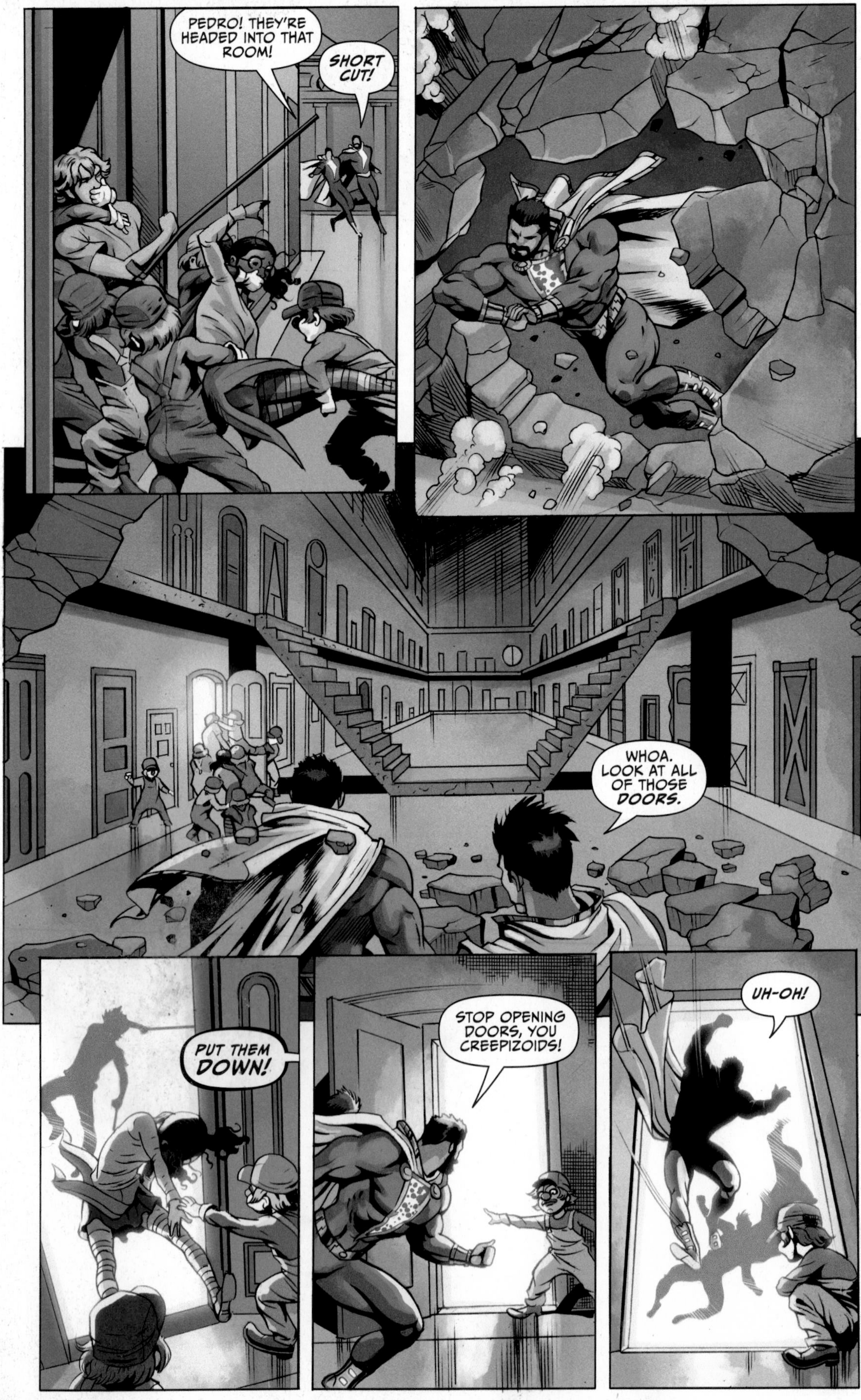
PEDRO! THEY'RE HEADED INTO THAT ROOM!
SHORT CUT!
WHOA. LOOK AT ALL OF THOSE DOORS.
PUT THEM DOWN!
STOP OPENING DOORS, YOU CREEPIZOIDS!
UH-OH!

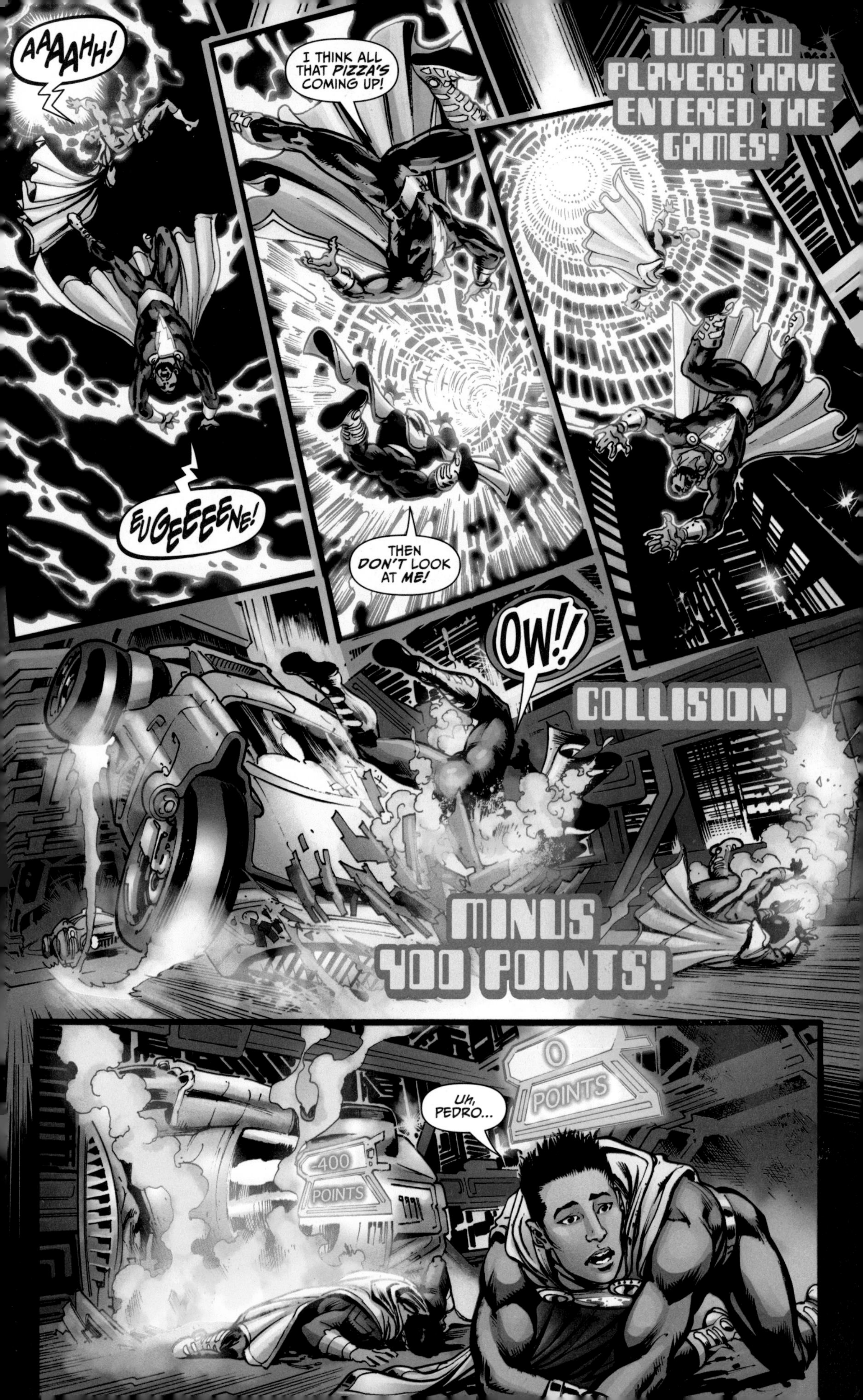
AAAAHH!
I THINK ALL THAT PIZZA'S COMING UP!
TWO NEW PLAYERS HAVE ENTERED THE GAMES!
EUGEEEENE!
THEN DON'T LOOK AT ME!
OW!!
COLLISION!
MINUS 400 POINTS!
0 POINTS
UH, PEDRO...
-400 POINTS

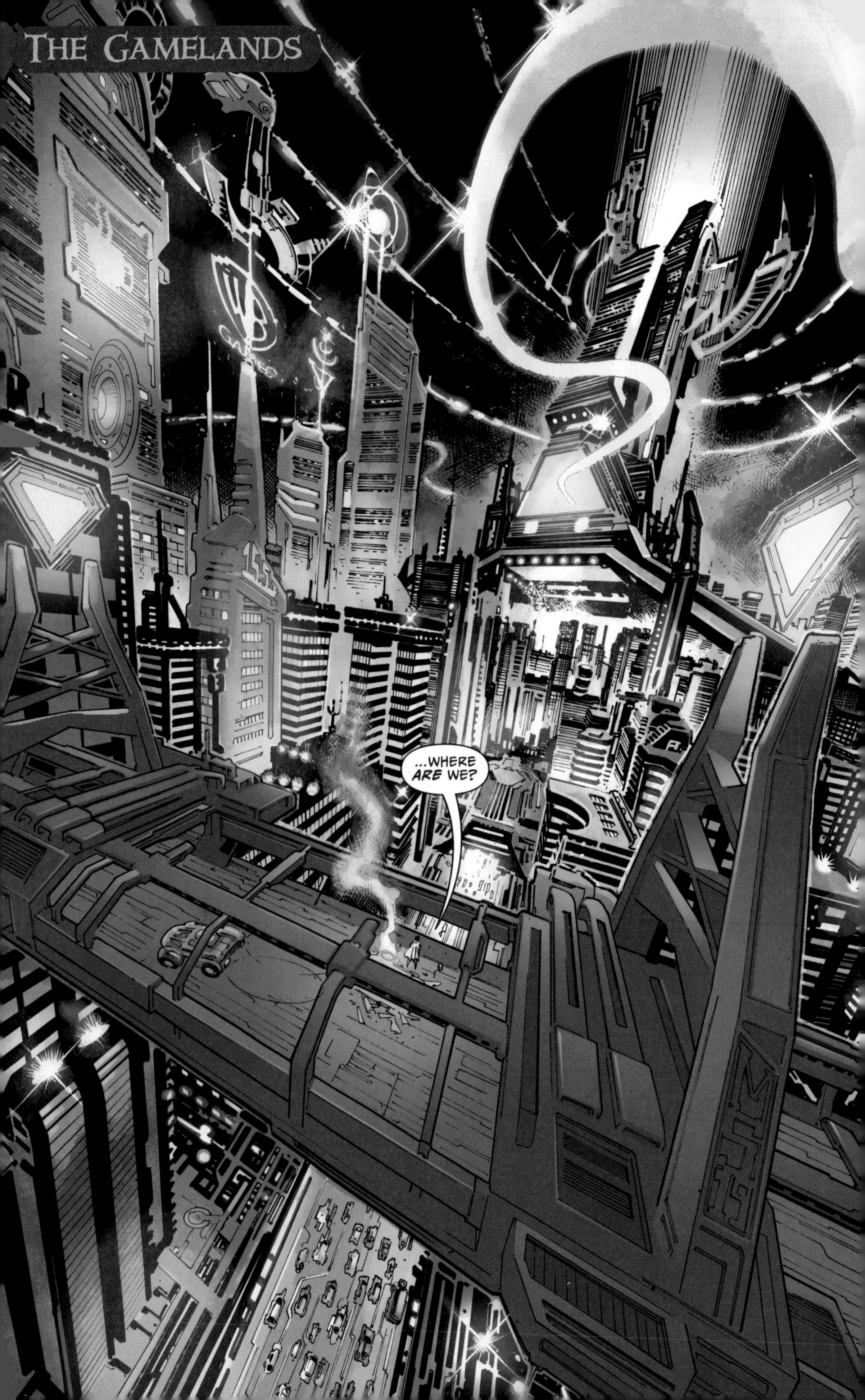
THE GAMELANDS
...WHERE ARE WE?

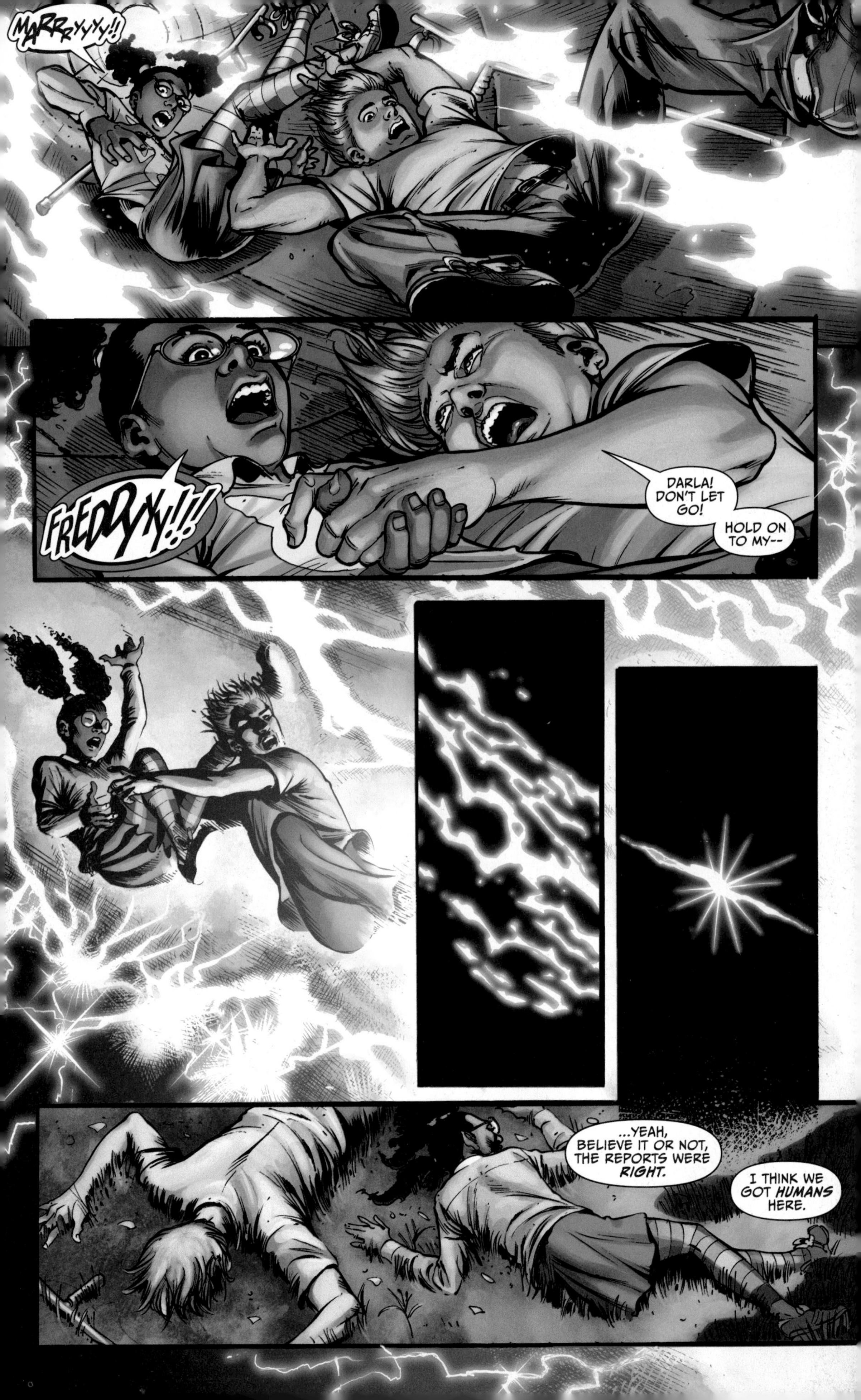
MARRRYYYY!!
FREDDYYY!!!
DARLA! DON'T LET GO!
HOLD ON TO MY--
...YEAH, BELIEVE IT OR NOT, THE REPORTS WERE *RIGHT.*
I THINK WE GOT *HUMANS* HERE.

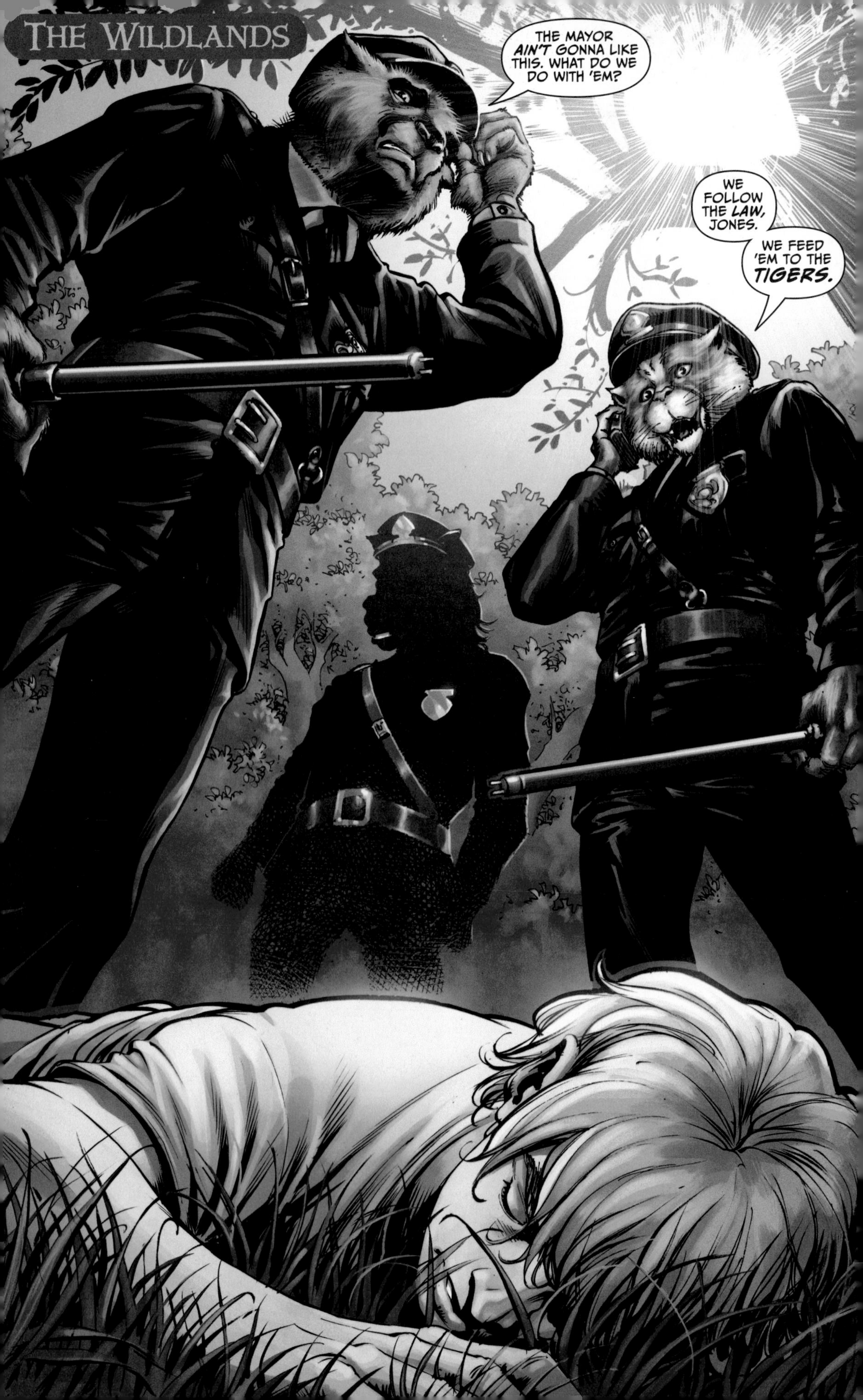
THE WILDLANDS
THE MAYOR AIN'T GONNA LIKE THIS. WHAT DO WE DO WITH 'EM?
WE FOLLOW THE LAW, JONES.
WE FEED 'EM TO THE TIGERS.

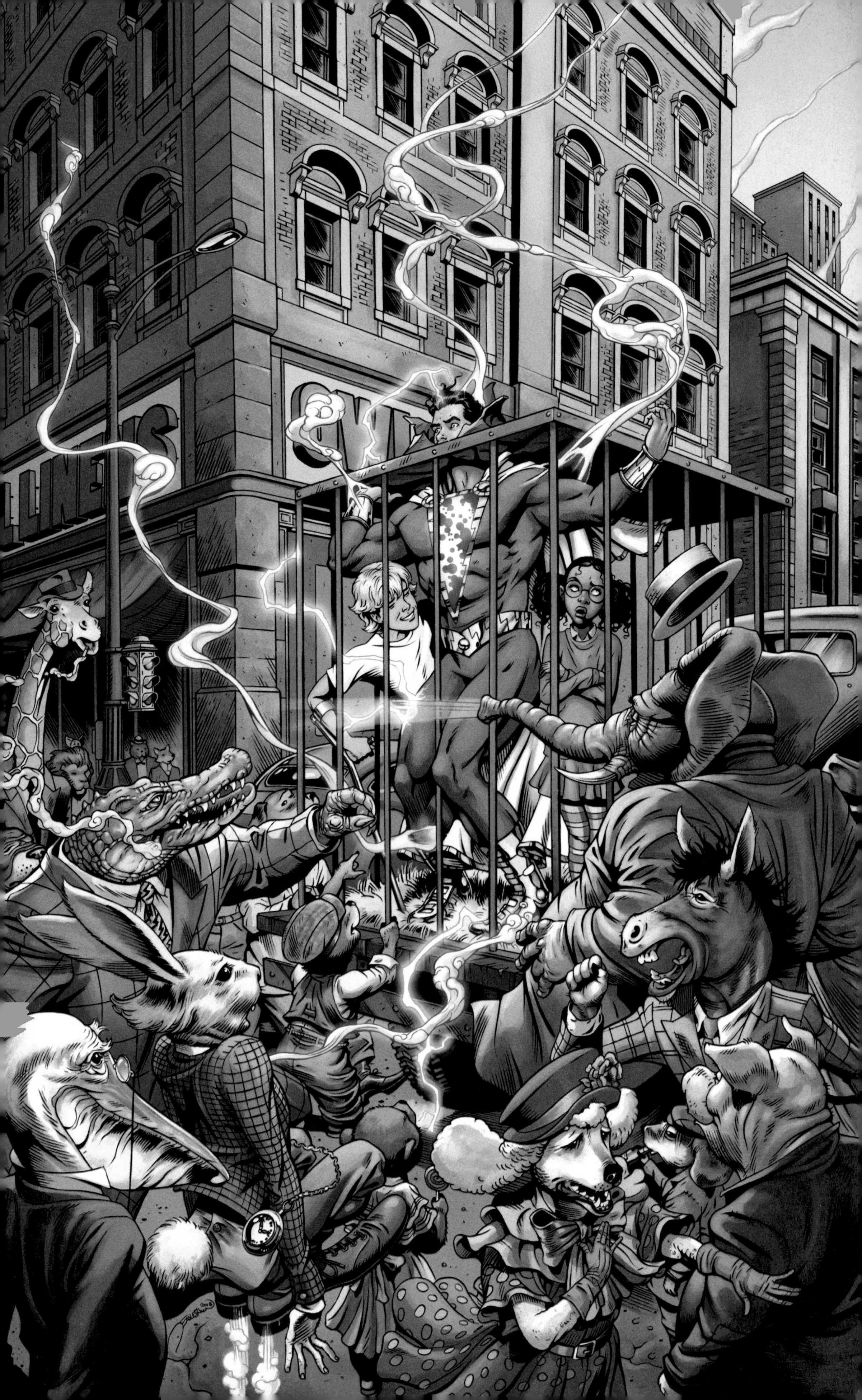

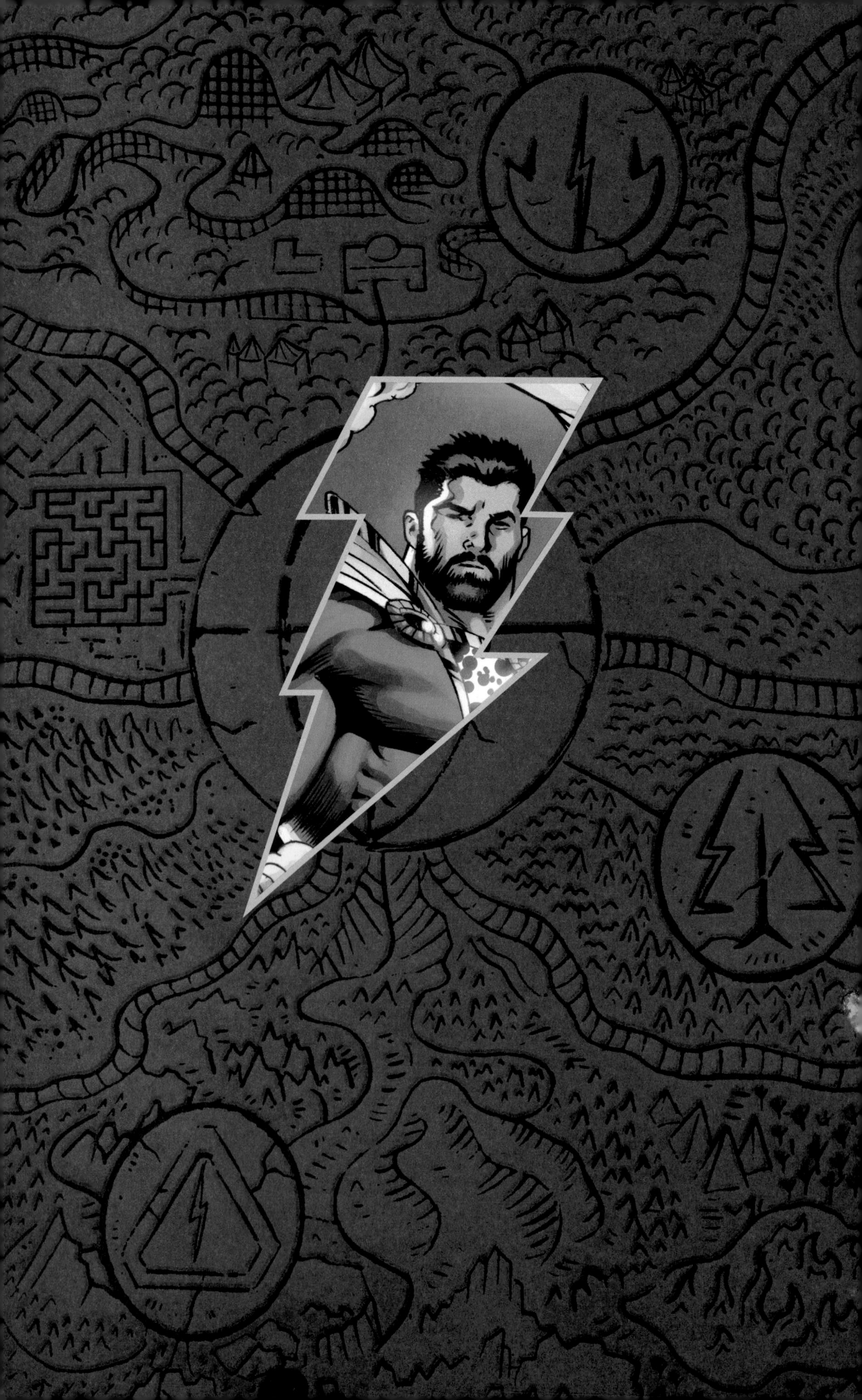

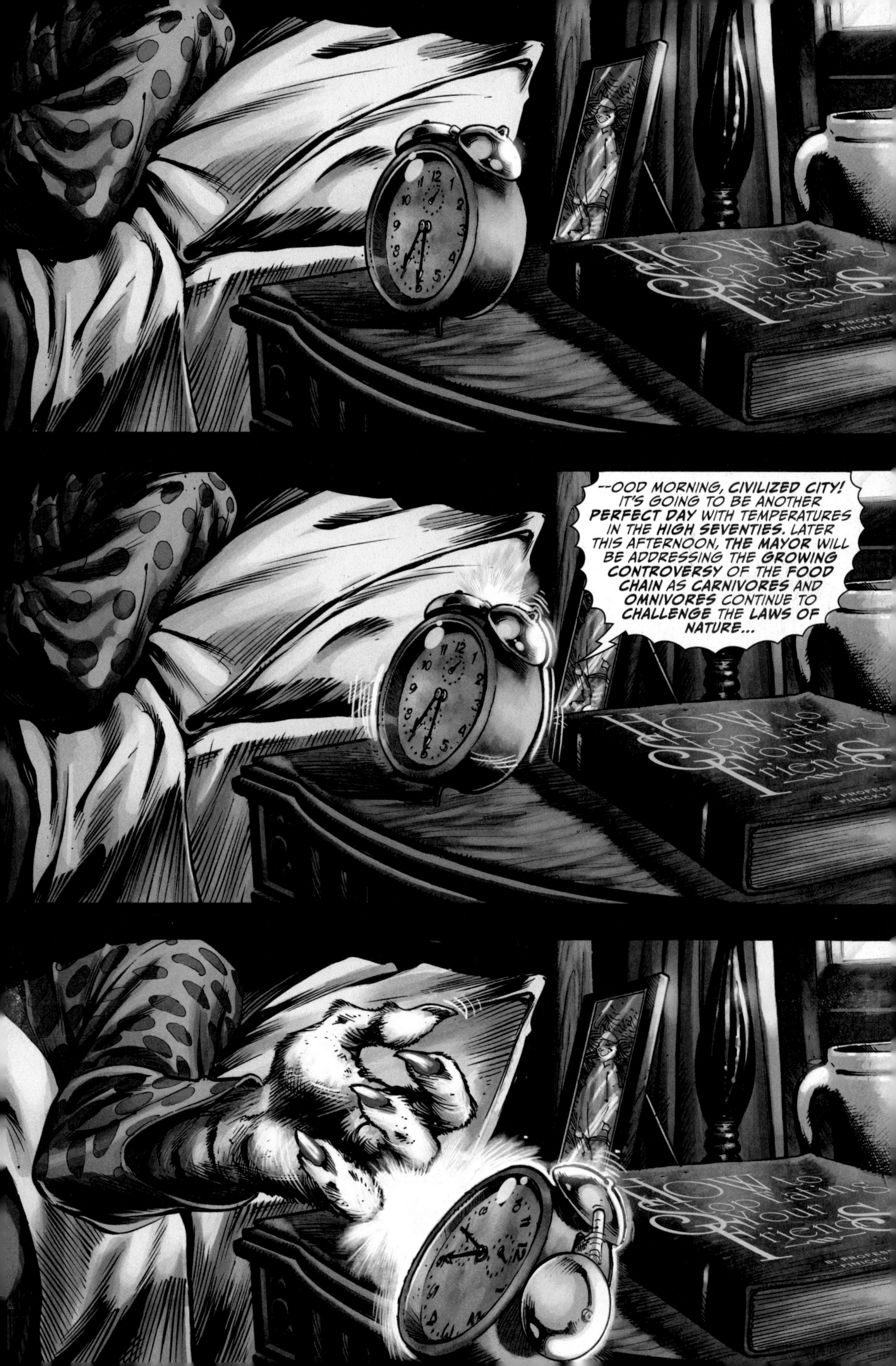
--OOD MORNING, CIVILIZED CITY! IT'S GOING TO BE ANOTHER PERFECT DAY WITH TEMPERATURES IN THE HIGH SEVENTIES. LATER THIS AFTERNOON, THE MAYOR WILL BE ADDRESSING THE GROWING CONTROVERSY OF THE FOOD CHAIN AS CARNIVORES AND OMNIVORES CONTINUE TO CHALLENGE THE LAWS OF NATURE...

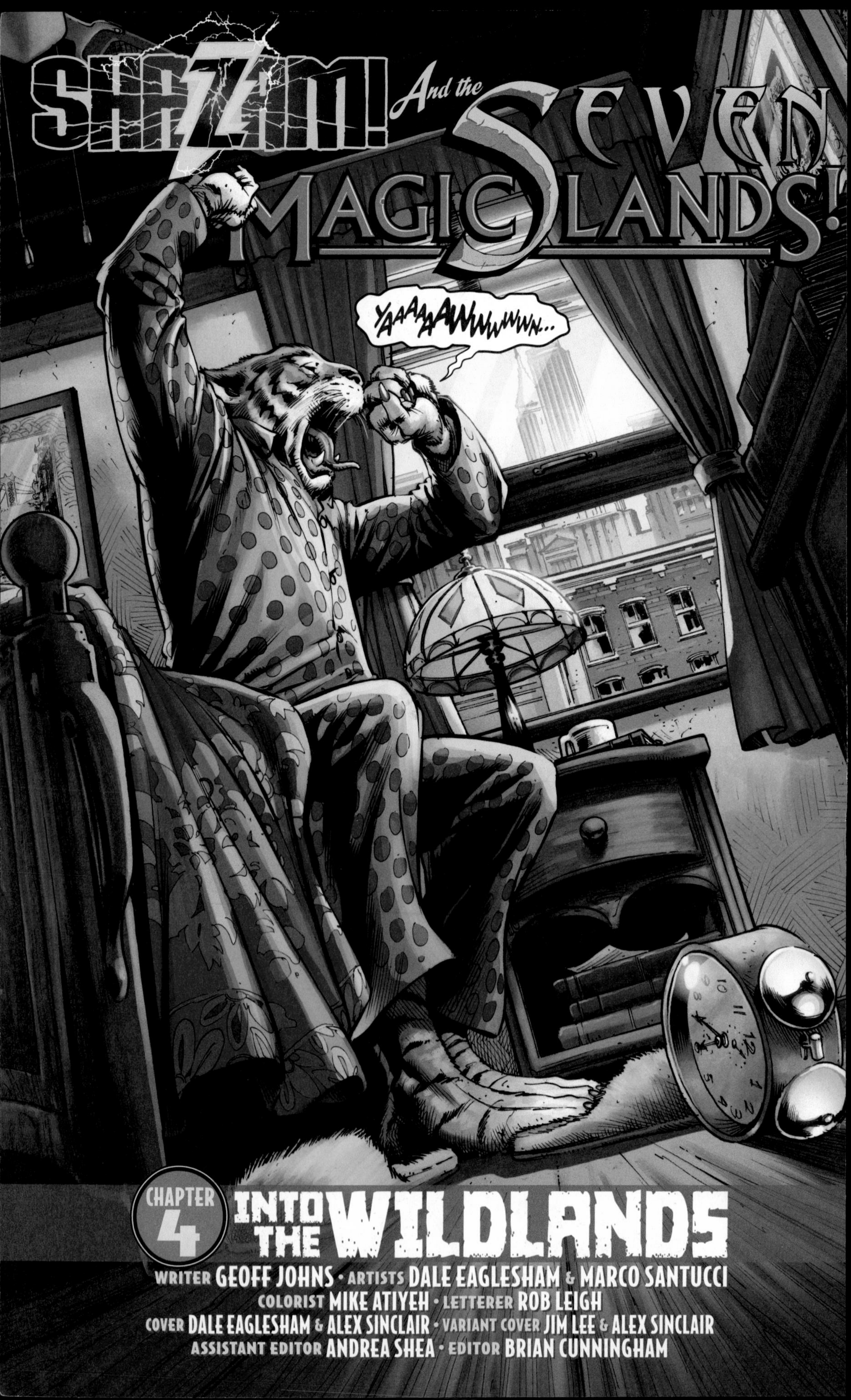
SHAZAM! And the SEVEN MAGIC LANDS!
YAAAAAWWWWWN...
CHAPTER 4
INTO THE WILDLANDS
WRITER GEOFF JOHNS · ARTISTS DALE EAGLESHAM & MARCO SANTUCCI
COLORIST MIKE ATIYEH · LETTERER ROB LEIGH
COVER DALE EAGLESHAM & ALEX SINCLAIR · VARIANT COVER JIM LEE & ALEX SINCLAIR
ASSISTANT EDITOR ANDREA SHEA · EDITOR BRIAN CUNNINGHAM

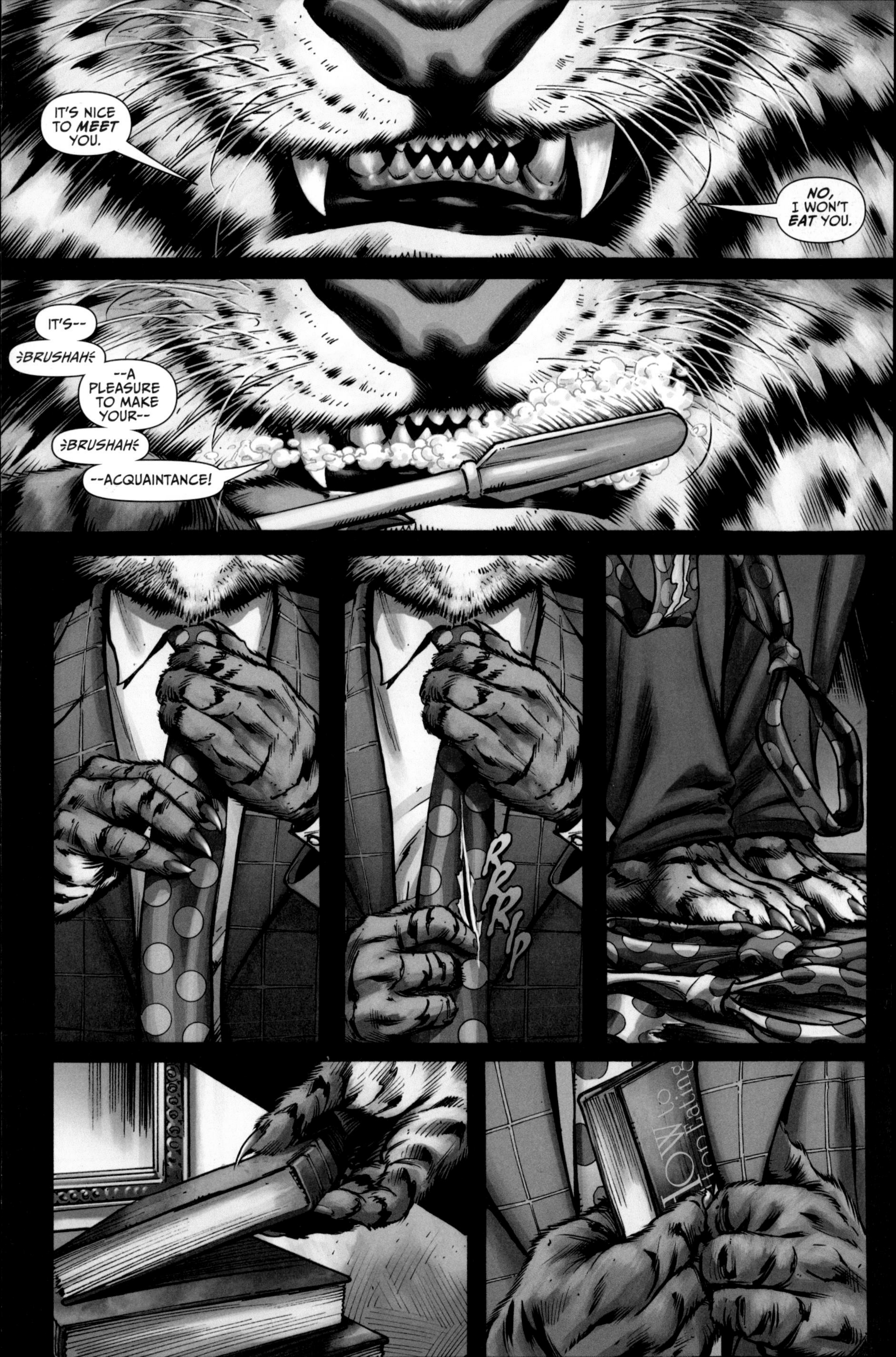
IT'S NICE TO MEET YOU.
NO, I WON'T EAT YOU.
IT'S--
BRUSHAH
--A PLEASURE TO MAKE YOUR--
BRUSHAH
--ACQUAINTANCE!
RRRIP

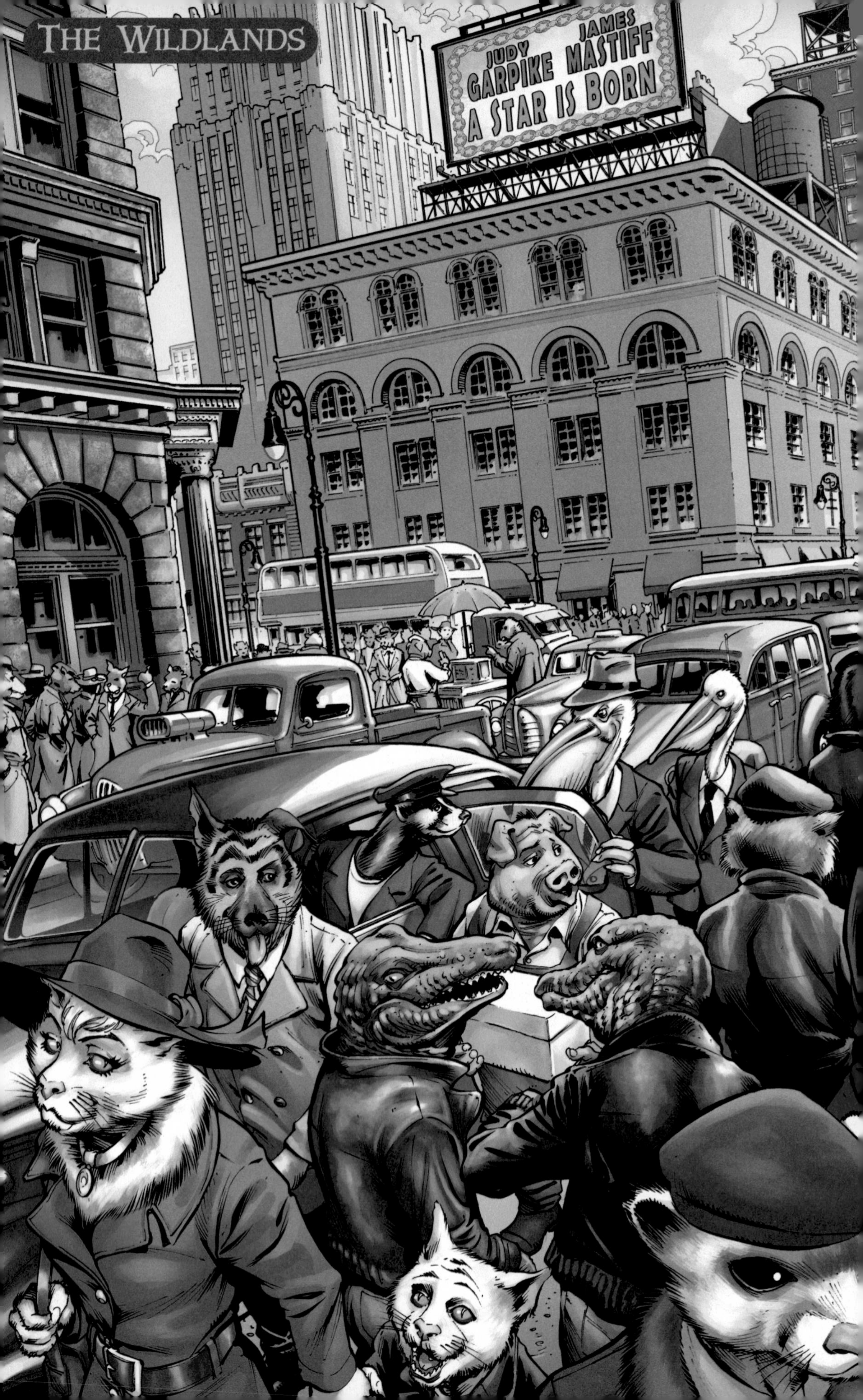
THE WILDLANDS
JUDY GARPIKE
JAMES MASTIFF
A STAR IS BORN

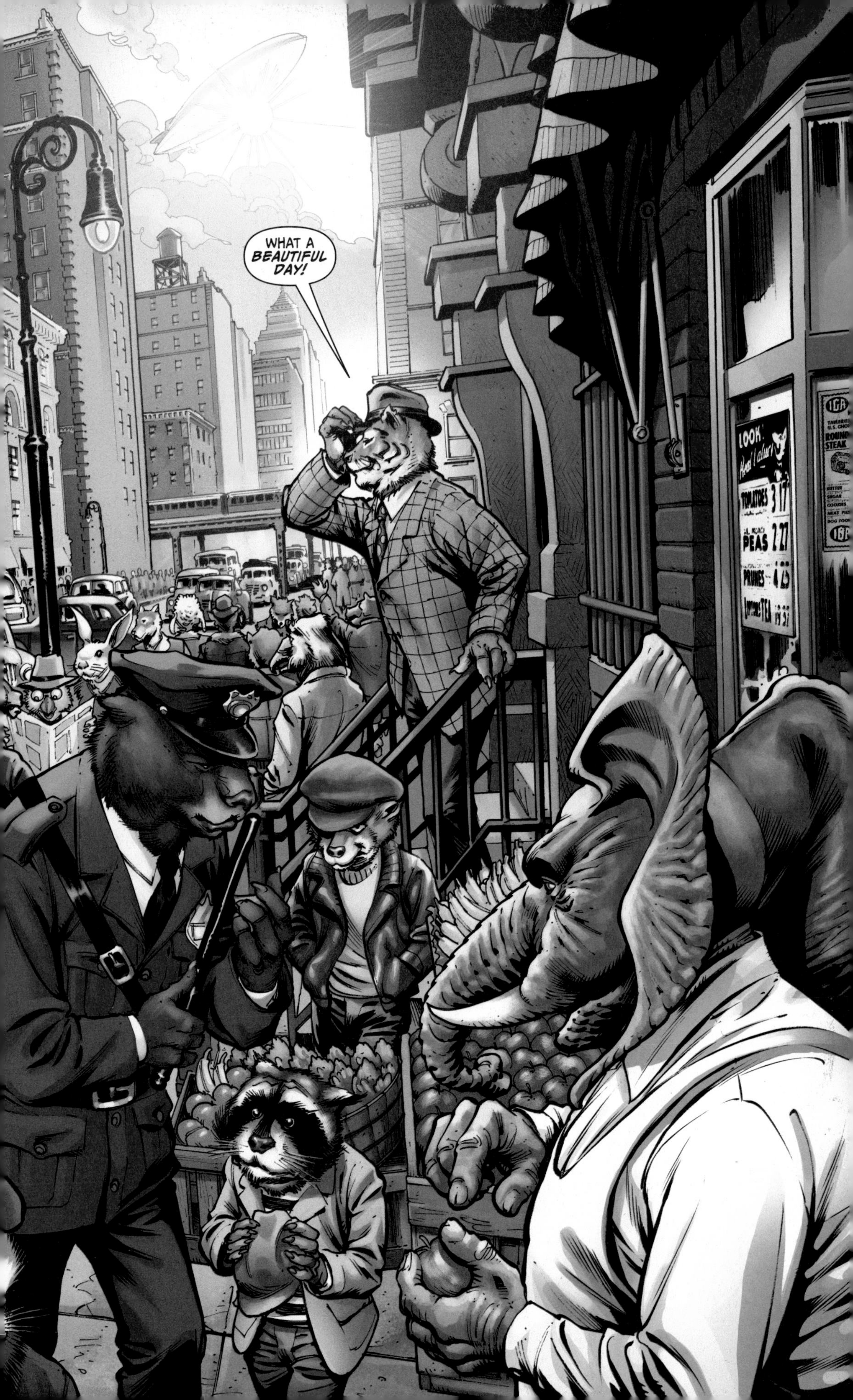
WHAT A BEAUTIFUL DAY!
LOOK!
TOMATOES
PEAS
PRUNES

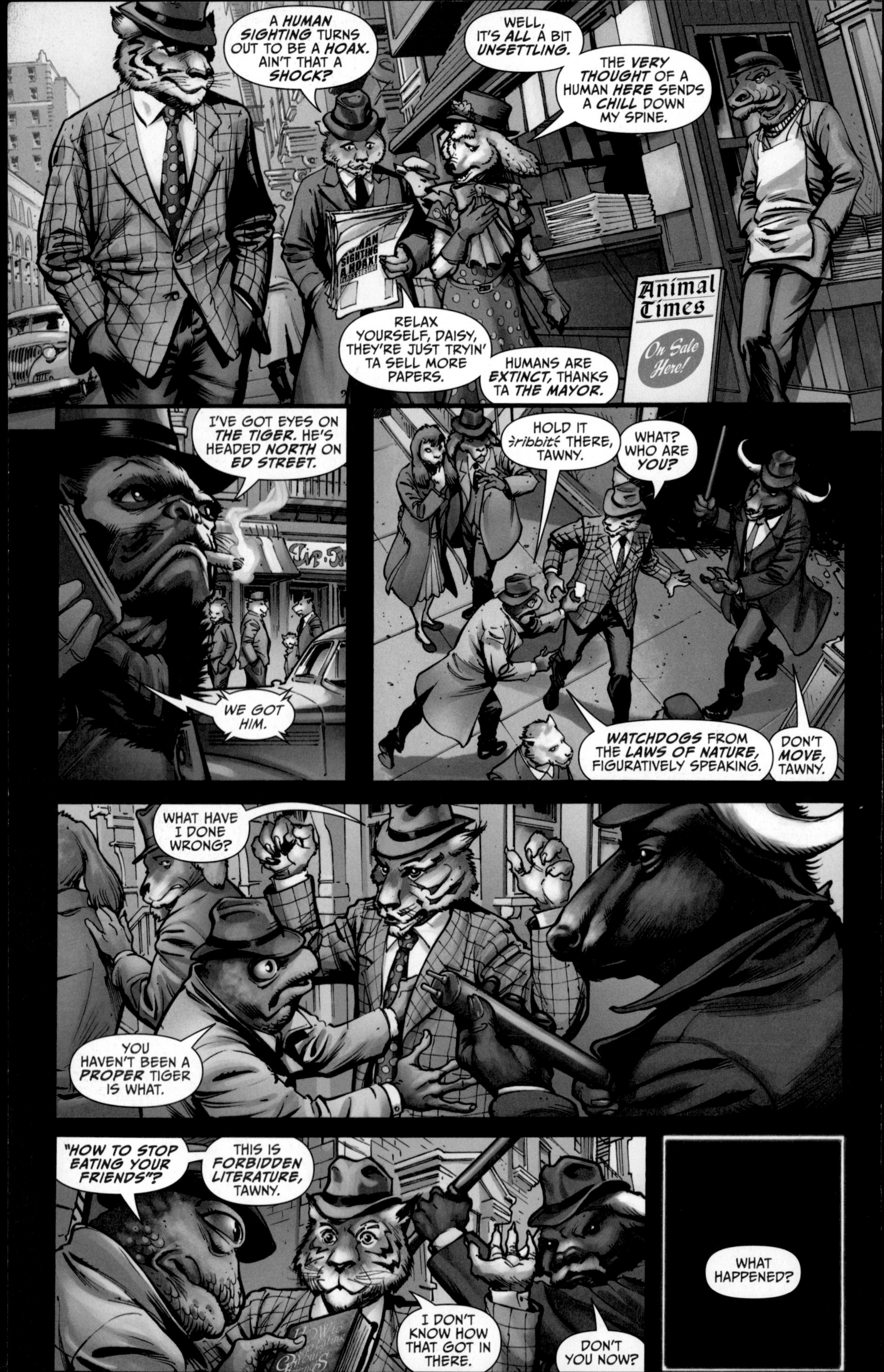

A HUMAN SIGHTING TURNS OUT TO BE A HOAX. AIN'T THAT A SHOCK?
WELL, IT'S ALL A BIT UNSETTLING.
THE VERY THOUGHT OF A HUMAN HERE SENDS A CHILL DOWN MY SPINE.
HUMAN SIGHTING A HOAX!
Animal Times
On Sale Here!
RELAX YOURSELF, DAISY, THEY'RE JUST TRYIN' TA SELL MORE PAPERS.
HUMANS ARE EXTINCT, THANKS TA THE MAYOR.
I'VE GOT EYES ON THE TIGER. HE'S HEADED NORTH ON ED STREET.
WE GOT HIM.
HOLD IT ⫶ribbit⫶ THERE, TAWNY.
WHAT? WHO ARE YOU?
WATCHDOGS FROM THE LAWS OF NATURE, FIGURATIVELY SPEAKING.
DON'T MOVE, TAWNY.
WHAT HAVE I DONE WRONG?
YOU HAVEN'T BEEN A PROPER TIGER IS WHAT.
"HOW TO STOP EATING YOUR FRIENDS"?
THIS IS FORBIDDEN LITERATURE, TAWNY.
I DON'T KNOW HOW THAT GOT IN THERE.
DON'T YOU NOW?
WHAT HAPPENED?

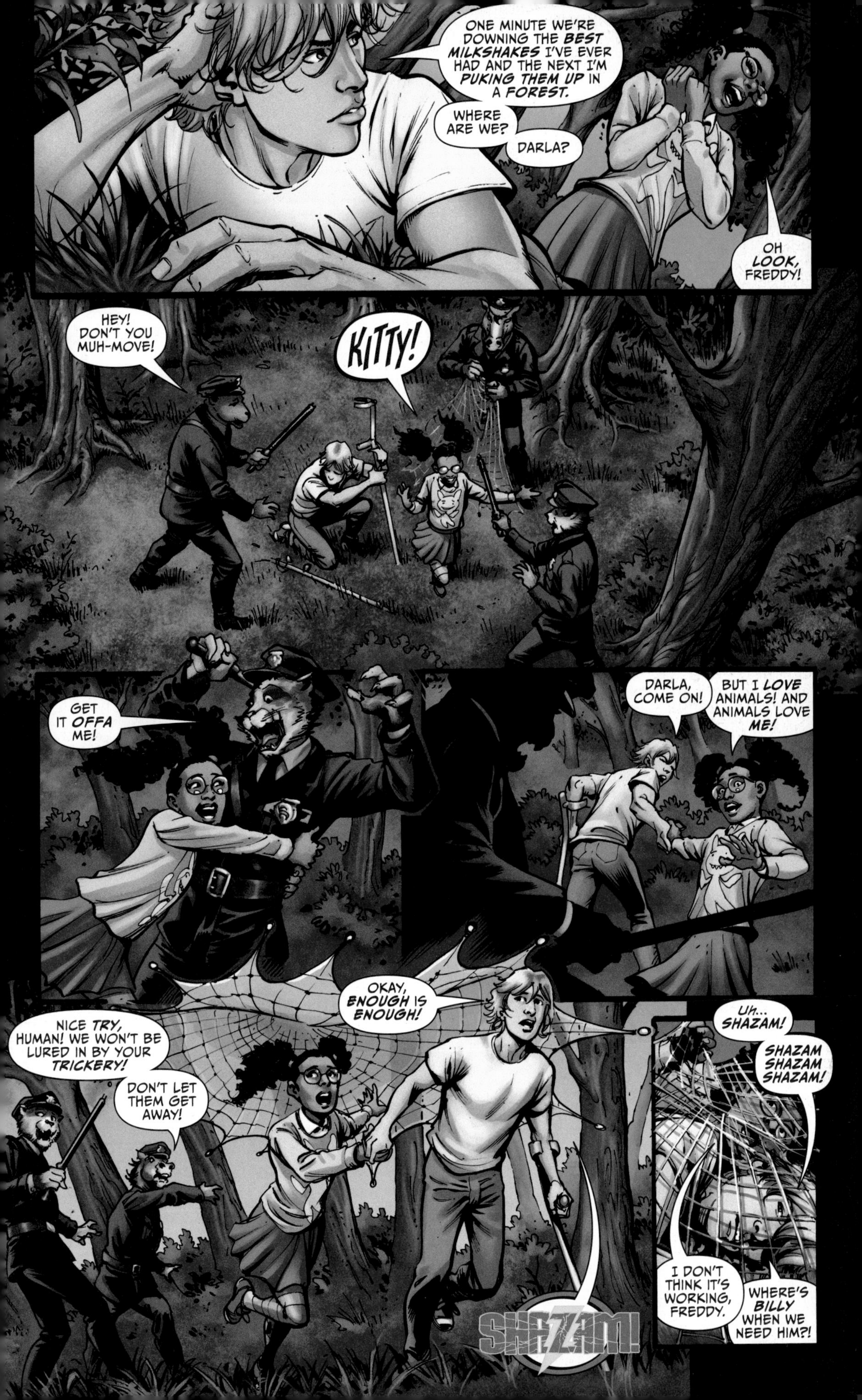
ONE MINUTE WE'RE DOWNING THE BEST MILKSHAKES I'VE EVER HAD AND THE NEXT I'M PUKING THEM UP IN A FOREST.
WHERE ARE WE?
DARLA?
OH LOOK, FREDDY!
HEY! DON'T YOU MUH-MOVE!
KITTY!
GET IT OFFA ME!
DARLA, COME ON!
BUT I LOVE ANIMALS! AND ANIMALS LOVE ME!
OKAY, ENOUGH IS ENOUGH!
NICE TRY, HUMAN! WE WON'T BE LURED IN BY YOUR TRICKERY!
DON'T LET THEM GET AWAY!
Uh... SHAZAM!
SHAZAM SHAZAM SHAZAM!
I DON'T THINK IT'S WORKING, FREDDY.
WHERE'S BILLY WHEN WE NEED HIM?!
SHAZAM!

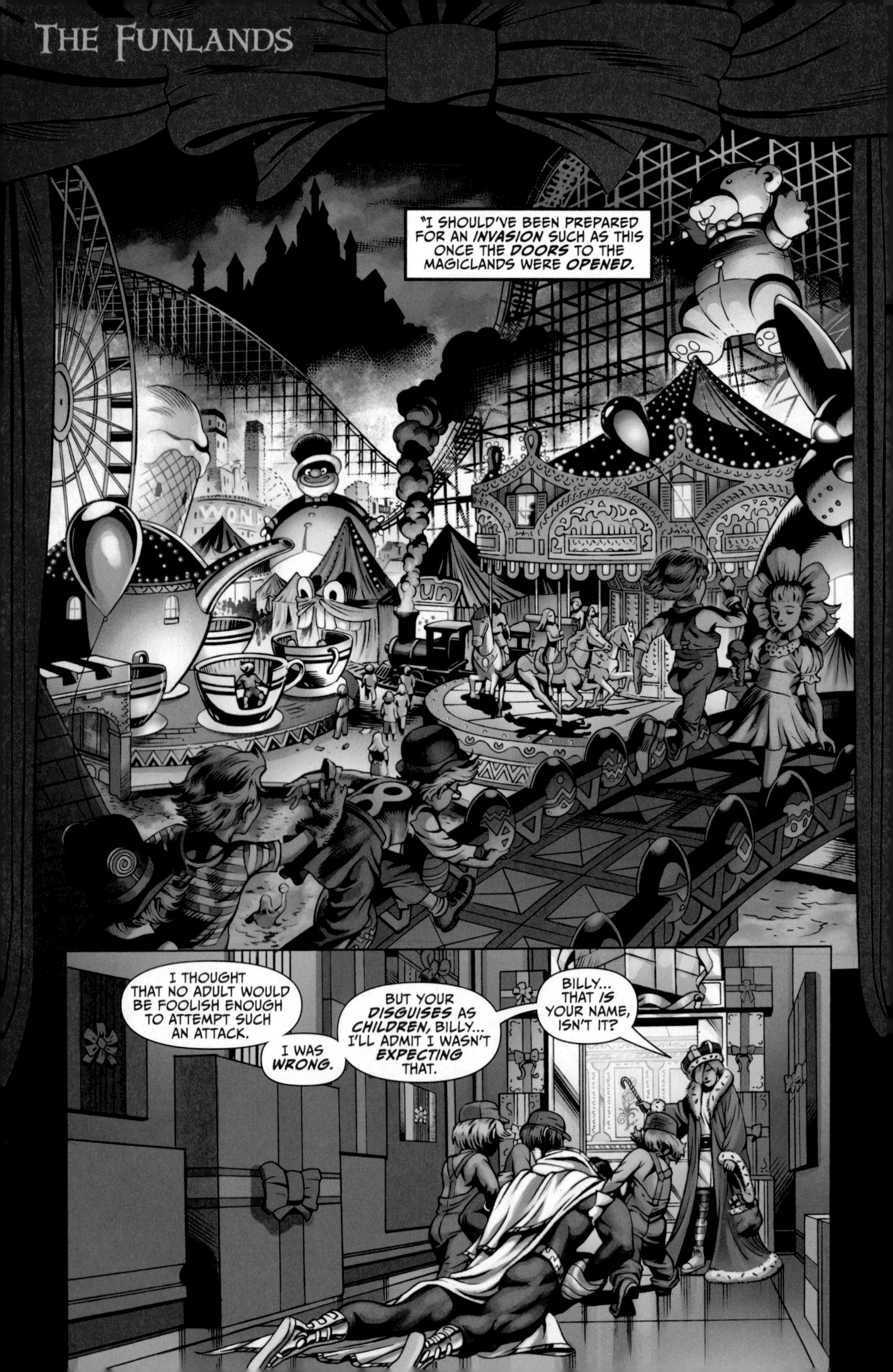
THE FUNLANDS
"I SHOULD'VE BEEN PREPARED FOR AN INVASION SUCH AS THIS ONCE THE DOORS TO THE MAGICLANDS WERE OPENED.
WON
I THOUGHT THAT NO ADULT WOULD BE FOOLISH ENOUGH TO ATTEMPT SUCH AN ATTACK.
I WAS WRONG.
BUT YOUR DISGUISES AS CHILDREN, BILLY... I'LL ADMIT I WASN'T EXPECTING THAT.
BILLY... THAT IS YOUR NAME, ISN'T IT?

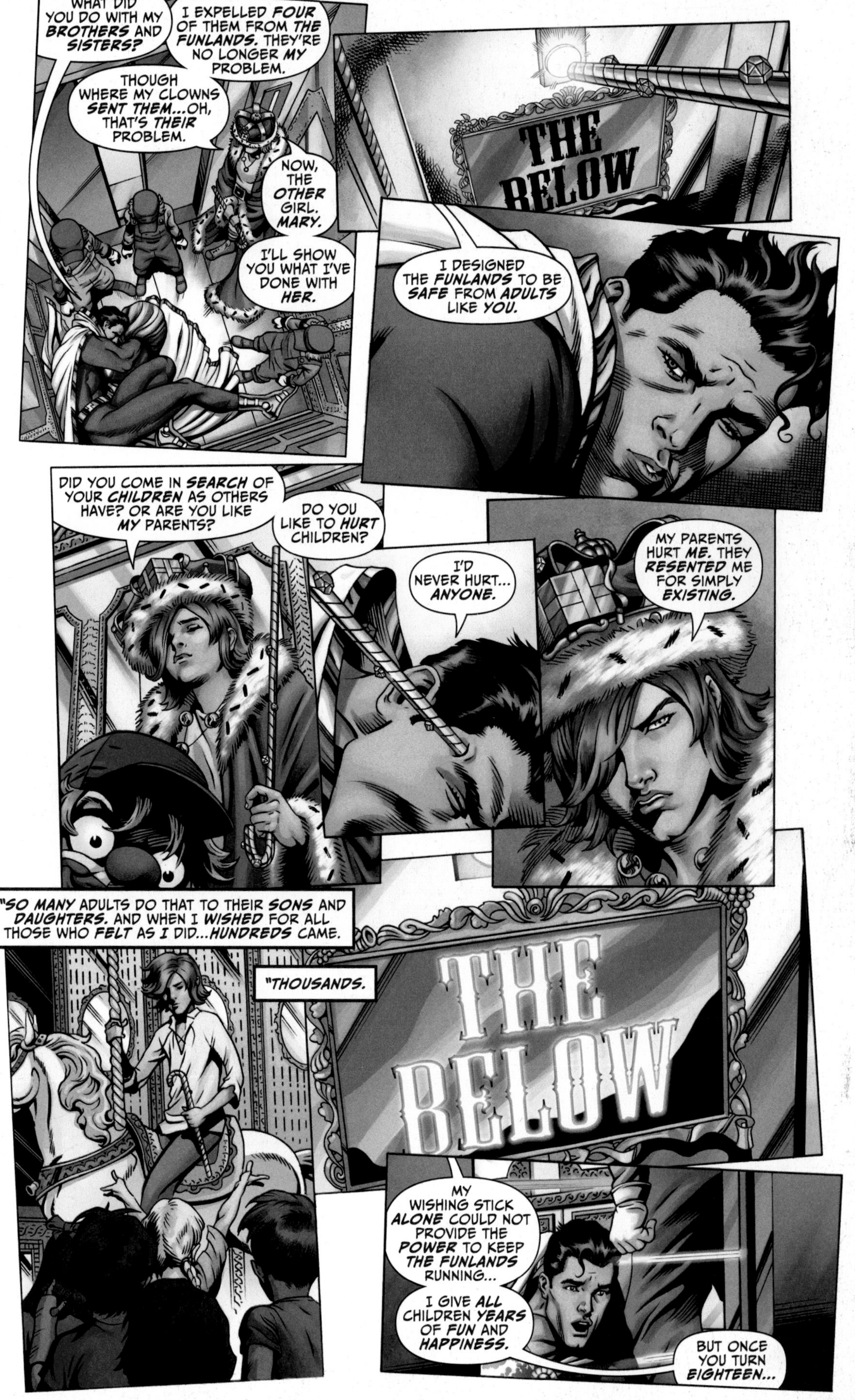
WHAT DID YOU DO WITH MY BROTHERS AND SISTERS?
I EXPELLED FOUR OF THEM FROM THE FUNLANDS. THEY'RE NO LONGER MY PROBLEM.
THOUGH WHERE MY CLOWNS SENT THEM...OH, THAT'S THEIR PROBLEM.
NOW, THE OTHER GIRL. MARY.
I'LL SHOW YOU WHAT I'VE DONE WITH HER.
THE BELOW
I DESIGNED THE FUNLANDS TO BE SAFE FROM ADULTS LIKE YOU.
DID YOU COME IN SEARCH OF YOUR CHILDREN AS OTHERS HAVE? OR ARE YOU LIKE MY PARENTS?
DO YOU LIKE TO HURT CHILDREN?
I'D NEVER HURT... ANYONE.
MY PARENTS HURT ME. THEY RESENTED ME FOR SIMPLY EXISTING.
"SO MANY ADULTS DO THAT TO THEIR SONS AND DAUGHTERS. AND WHEN I WISHED FOR ALL THOSE WHO FELT AS I DID...HUNDREDS CAME.
"THOUSANDS.
THE BELOW
MY WISHING STICK ALONE COULD NOT PROVIDE THE POWER TO KEEP THE FUNLANDS RUNNING...
I GIVE ALL CHILDREN YEARS OF FUN AND HAPPINESS.
BUT ONCE YOU TURN EIGHTEEN...

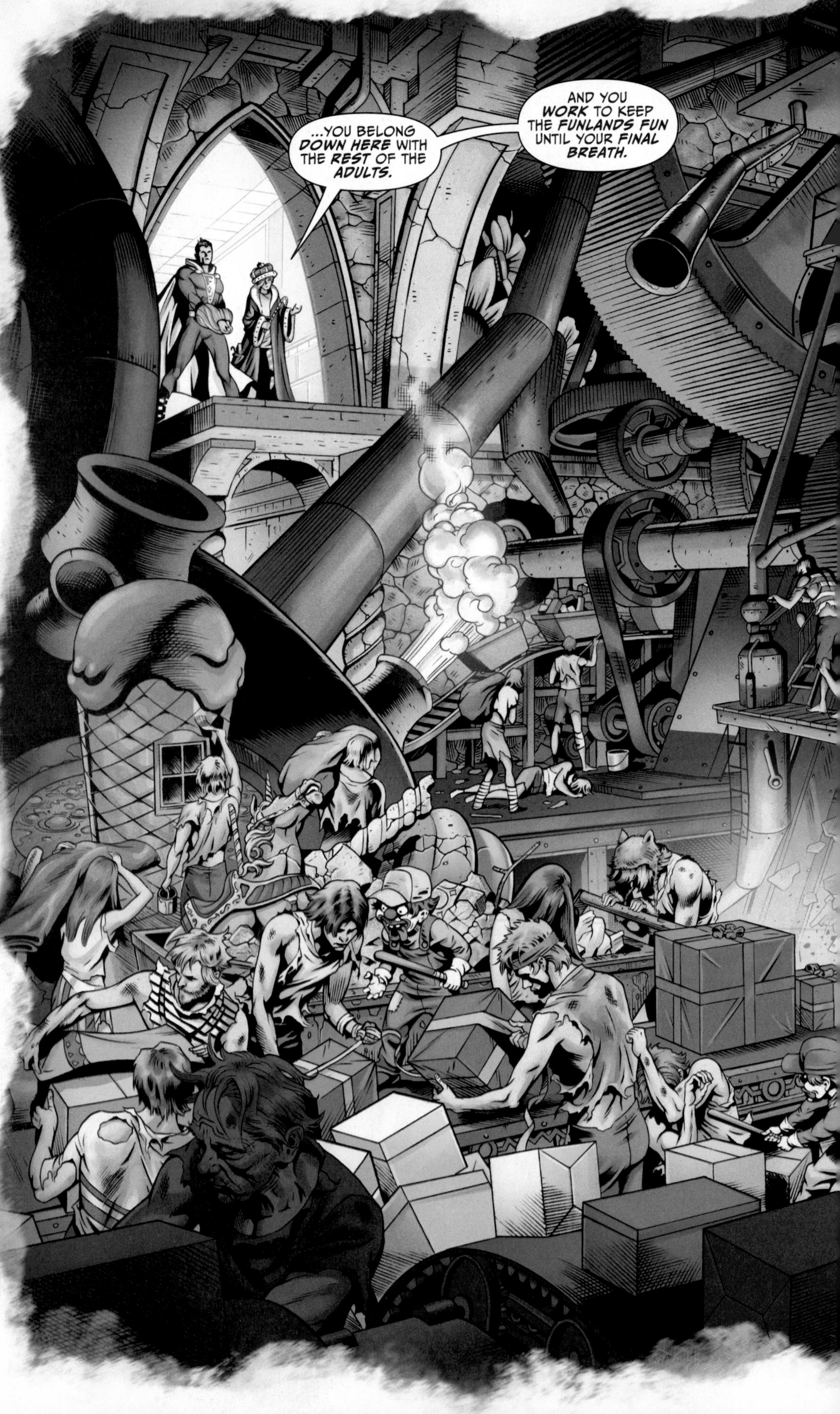
...YOU BELONG DOWN HERE WITH THE REST OF THE ADULTS.
AND YOU WORK TO KEEP THE FUNLANDS FUN UNTIL YOUR FINAL BREATH.

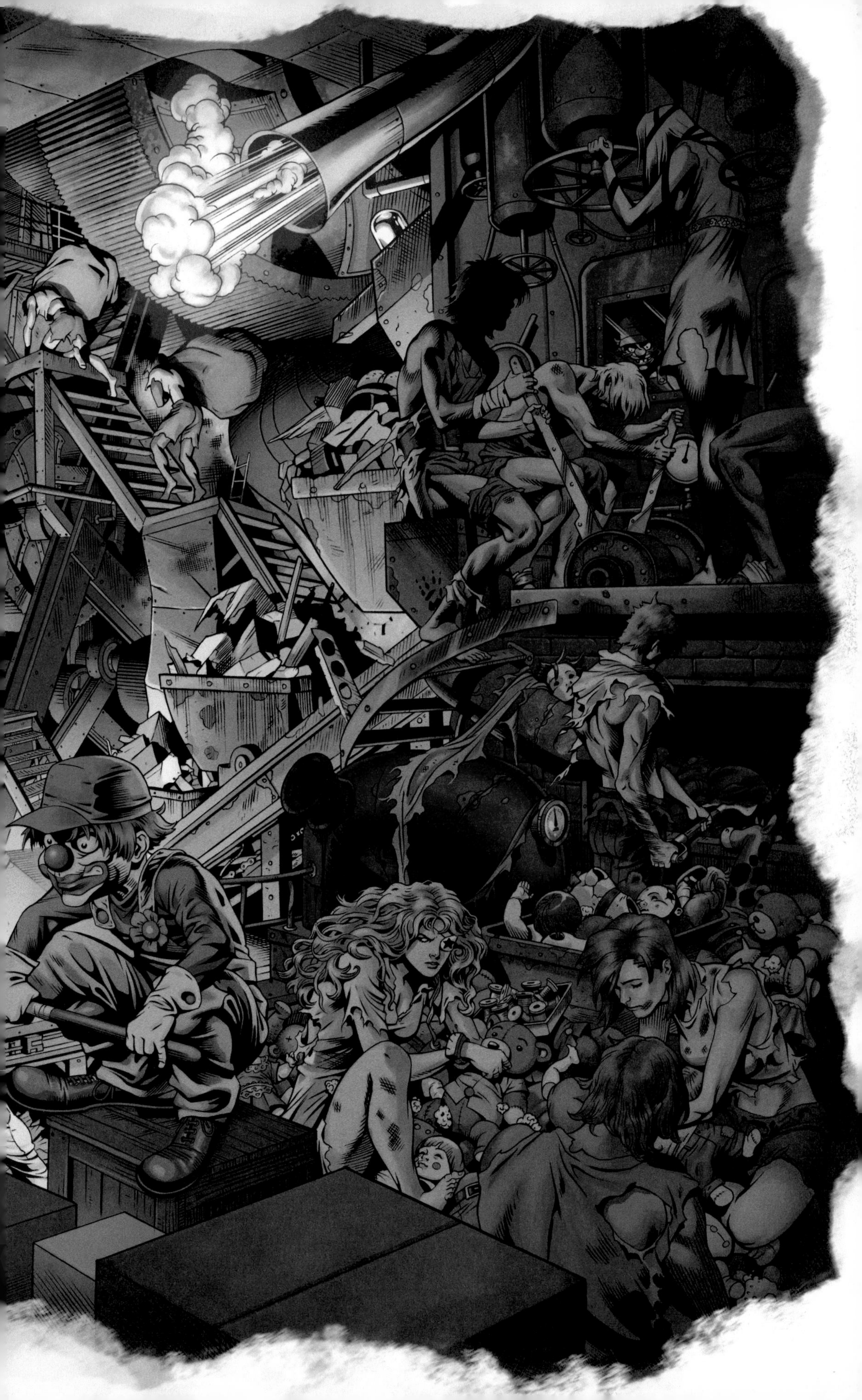

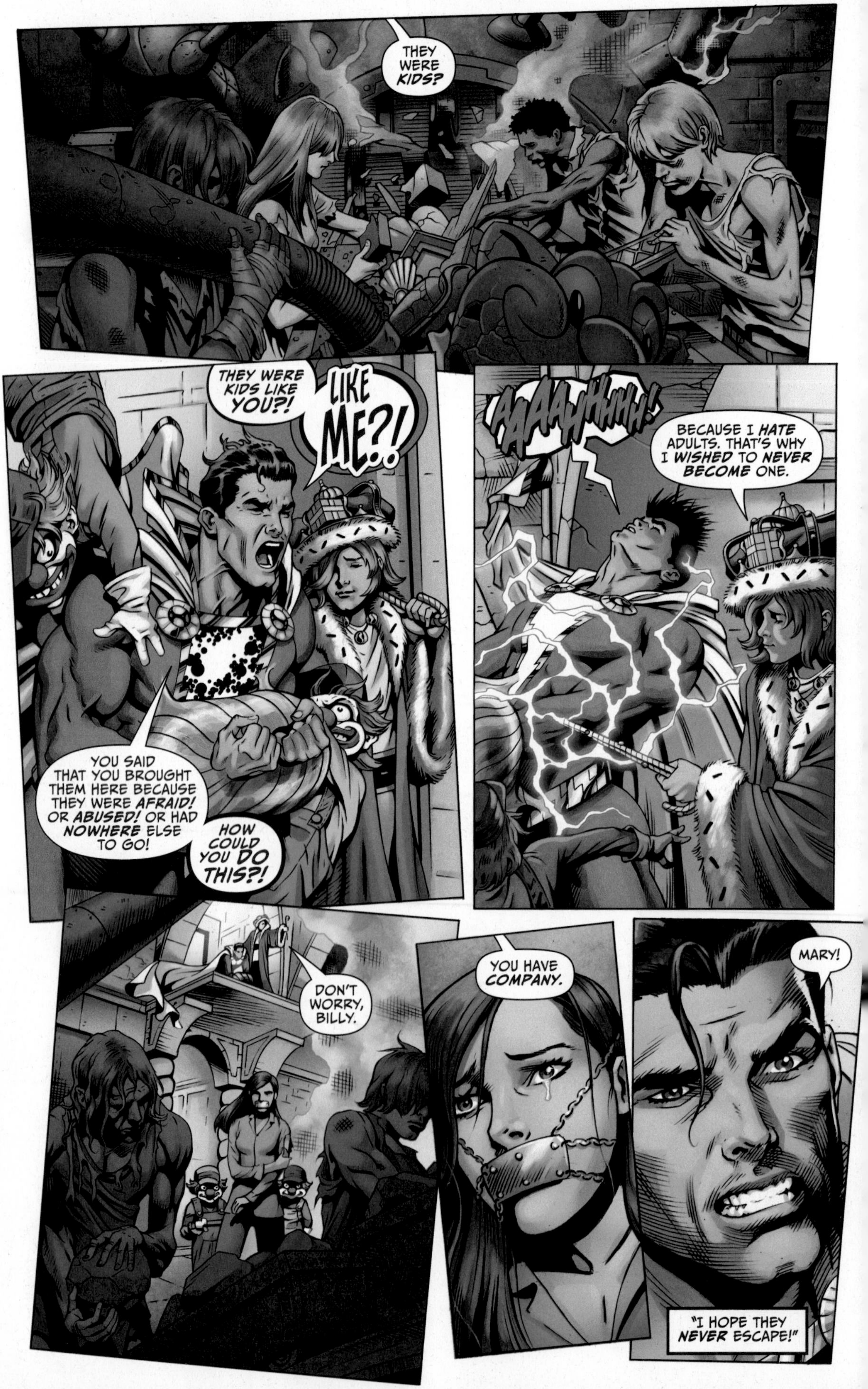
THEY WERE KIDS?
THEY WERE KIDS LIKE YOU?!
LIKE ME?!
YOU SAID THAT YOU BROUGHT THEM HERE BECAUSE THEY WERE AFRAID! OR ABUSED! OR HAD NOWHERE ELSE TO GO!
HOW COULD YOU DO THIS?!
AAAAUHHHH!
BECAUSE I HATE ADULTS. THAT'S WHY I WISHED TO NEVER BECOME ONE.
DON'T WORRY, BILLY.
YOU HAVE COMPANY.
MARY!
"I HOPE THEY NEVER ESCAPE!"

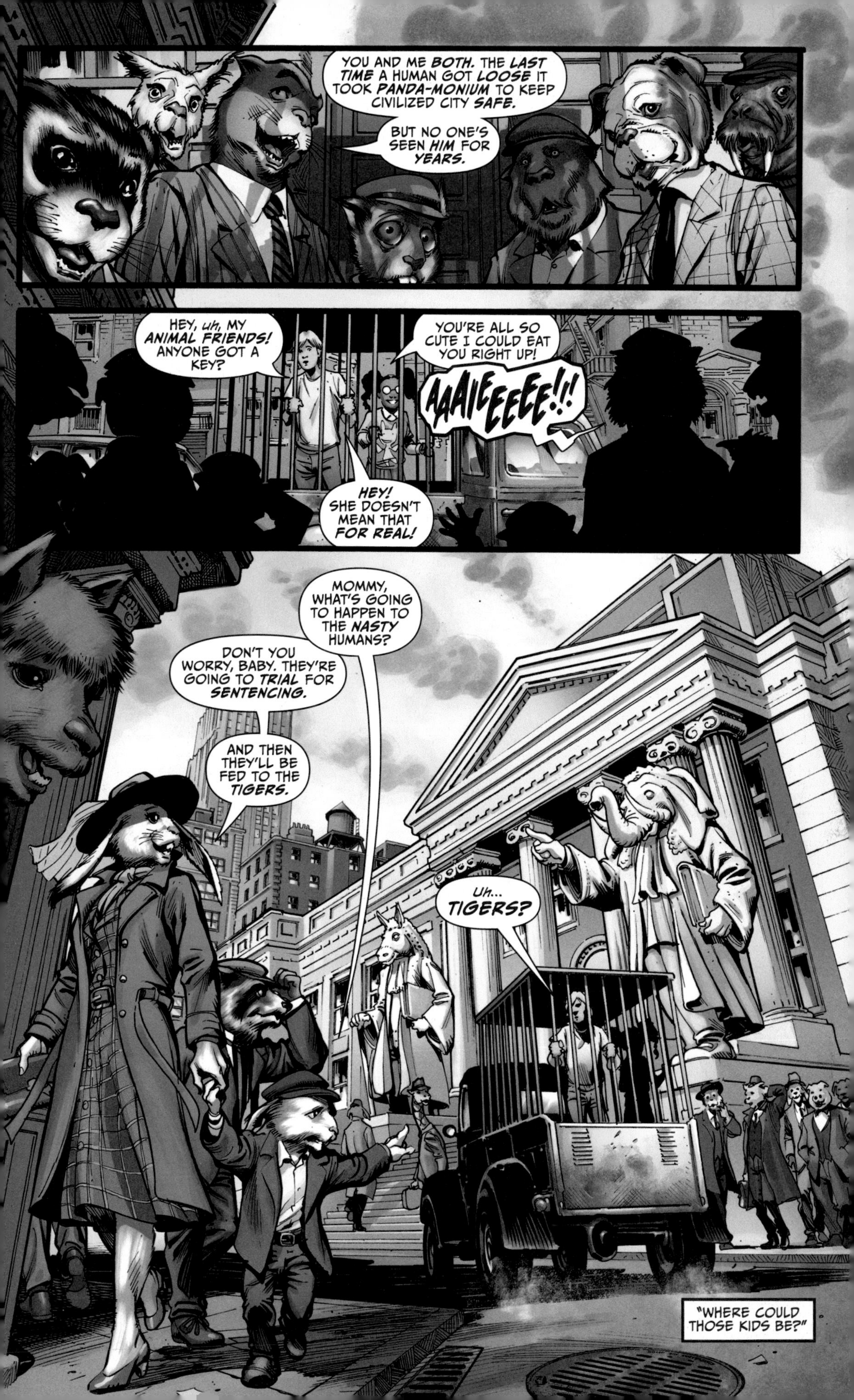
YOU AND ME BOTH. THE LAST TIME A HUMAN GOT LOOSE IT TOOK PANDA-MONIUM TO KEEP CIVILIZED CITY SAFE.
BUT NO ONE'S SEEN HIM FOR YEARS.
HEY, uh, MY ANIMAL FRIENDS! ANYONE GOT A KEY?
YOU'RE ALL SO CUTE I COULD EAT YOU RIGHT UP!
AAAIEEEEE!!!
HEY! SHE DOESN'T MEAN THAT FOR REAL!
MOMMY, WHAT'S GOING TO HAPPEN TO THE NASTY HUMANS?
DON'T YOU WORRY, BABY. THEY'RE GOING TO TRIAL FOR SENTENCING.
AND THEN THEY'LL BE FED TO THE TIGERS.
Uh... TIGERS?
"WHERE COULD THOSE KIDS BE?"

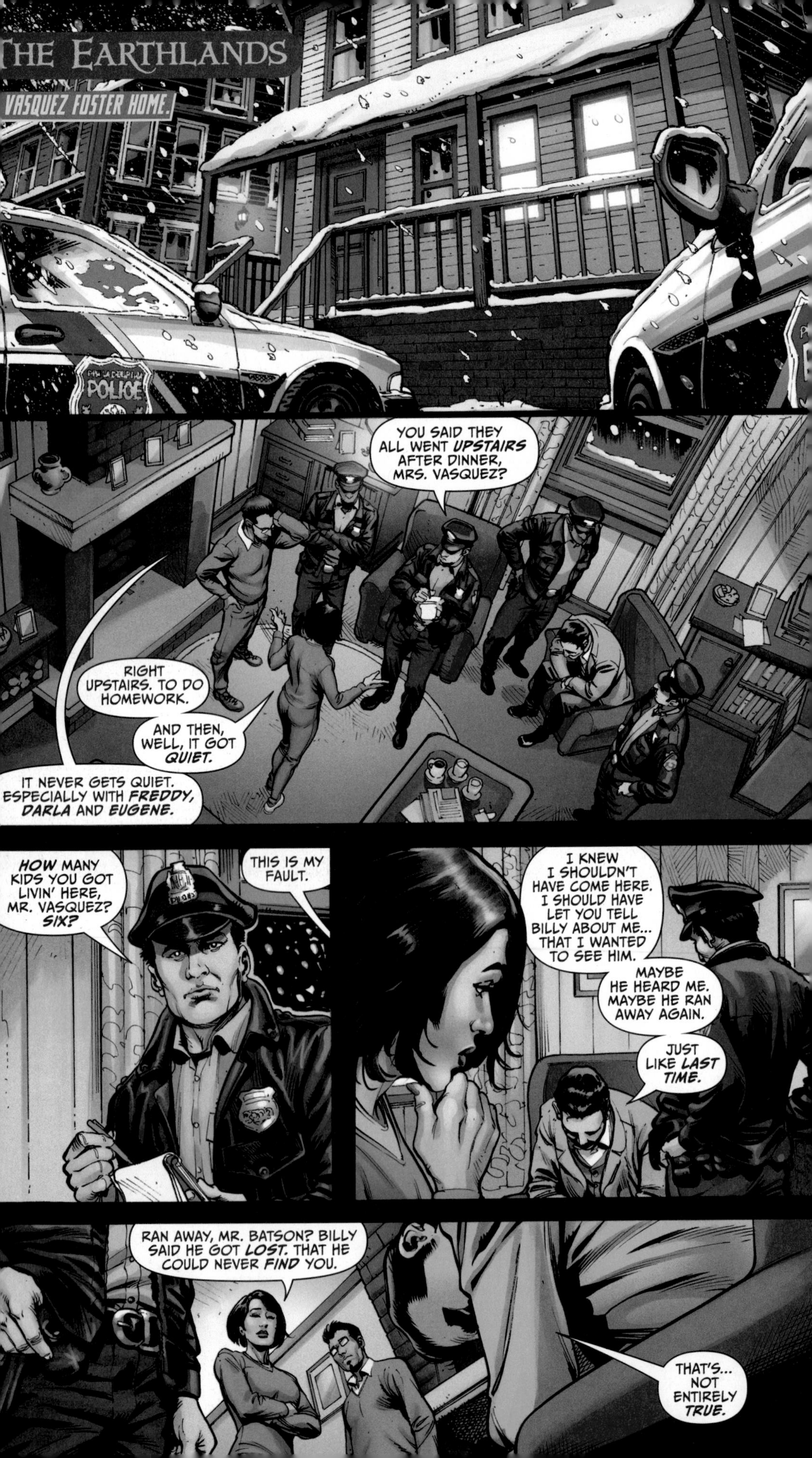

THE EARTHLANDS
VASQUEZ FOSTER HOME.
POLICE
YOU SAID THEY ALL WENT UPSTAIRS AFTER DINNER, MRS. VASQUEZ?
RIGHT UPSTAIRS. TO DO HOMEWORK.
AND THEN, WELL, IT GOT QUIET.
IT NEVER GETS QUIET. ESPECIALLY WITH FREDDY, DARLA AND EUGENE.
HOW MANY KIDS YOU GOT LIVIN' HERE, MR. VASQUEZ? SIX?
THIS IS MY FAULT.
I KNEW I SHOULDN'T HAVE COME HERE. I SHOULD HAVE LET YOU TELL BILLY ABOUT ME... THAT I WANTED TO SEE HIM.
MAYBE HE HEARD ME. MAYBE HE RAN AWAY AGAIN.
JUST LIKE LAST TIME.
RAN AWAY, MR. BATSON? BILLY SAID HE GOT LOST. THAT HE COULD NEVER FIND YOU.
THAT'S... NOT ENTIRELY TRUE.

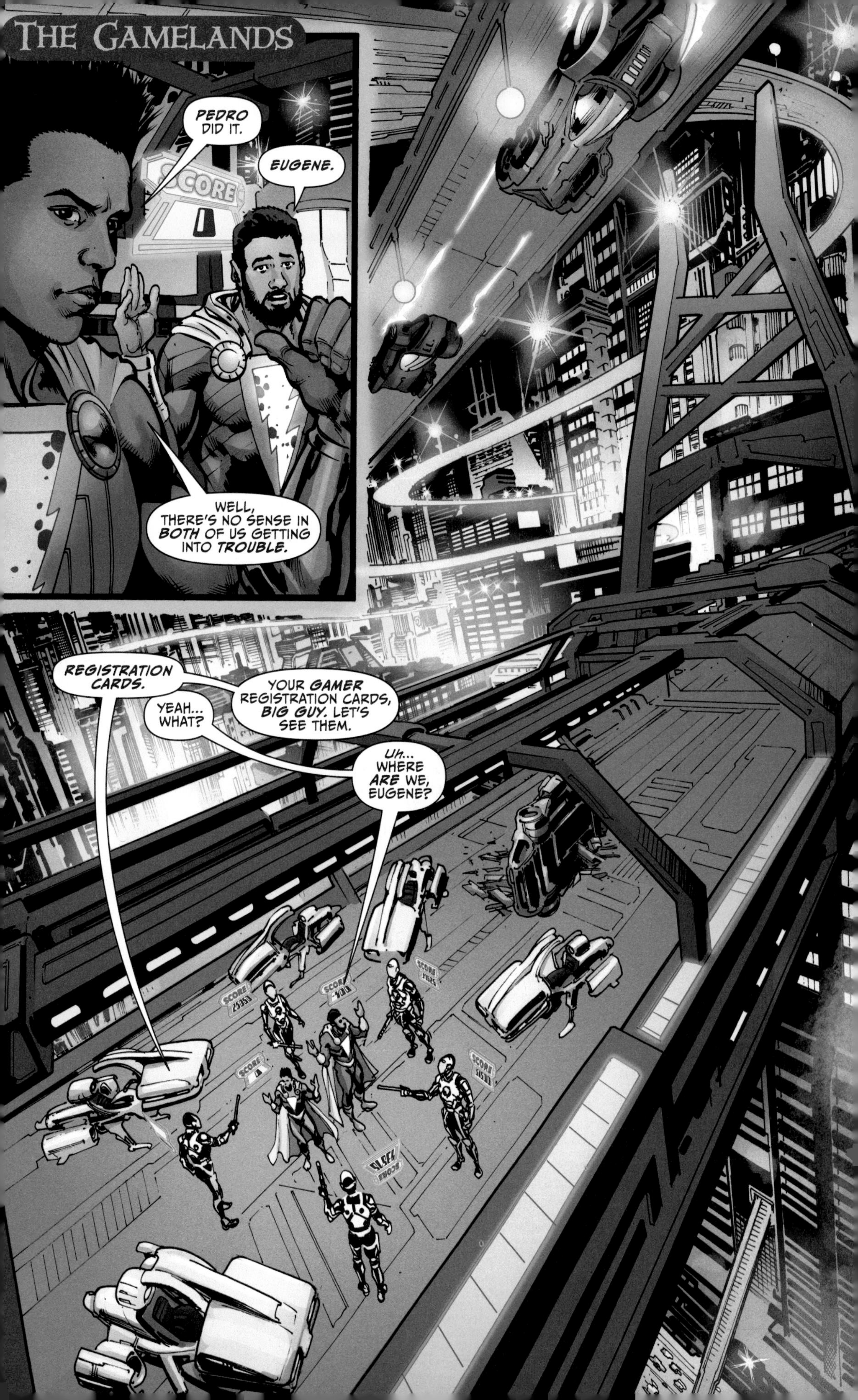
THE GAMELANDS
PEDRO DID IT.
EUGENE.
WELL, THERE'S NO SENSE IN BOTH OF US GETTING INTO TROUBLE.
REGISTRATION CARDS.
YEAH... WHAT?
YOUR GAMER REGISTRATION CARDS, BIG GUY. LET'S SEE THEM.
Uh... WHERE ARE WE, EUGENE?

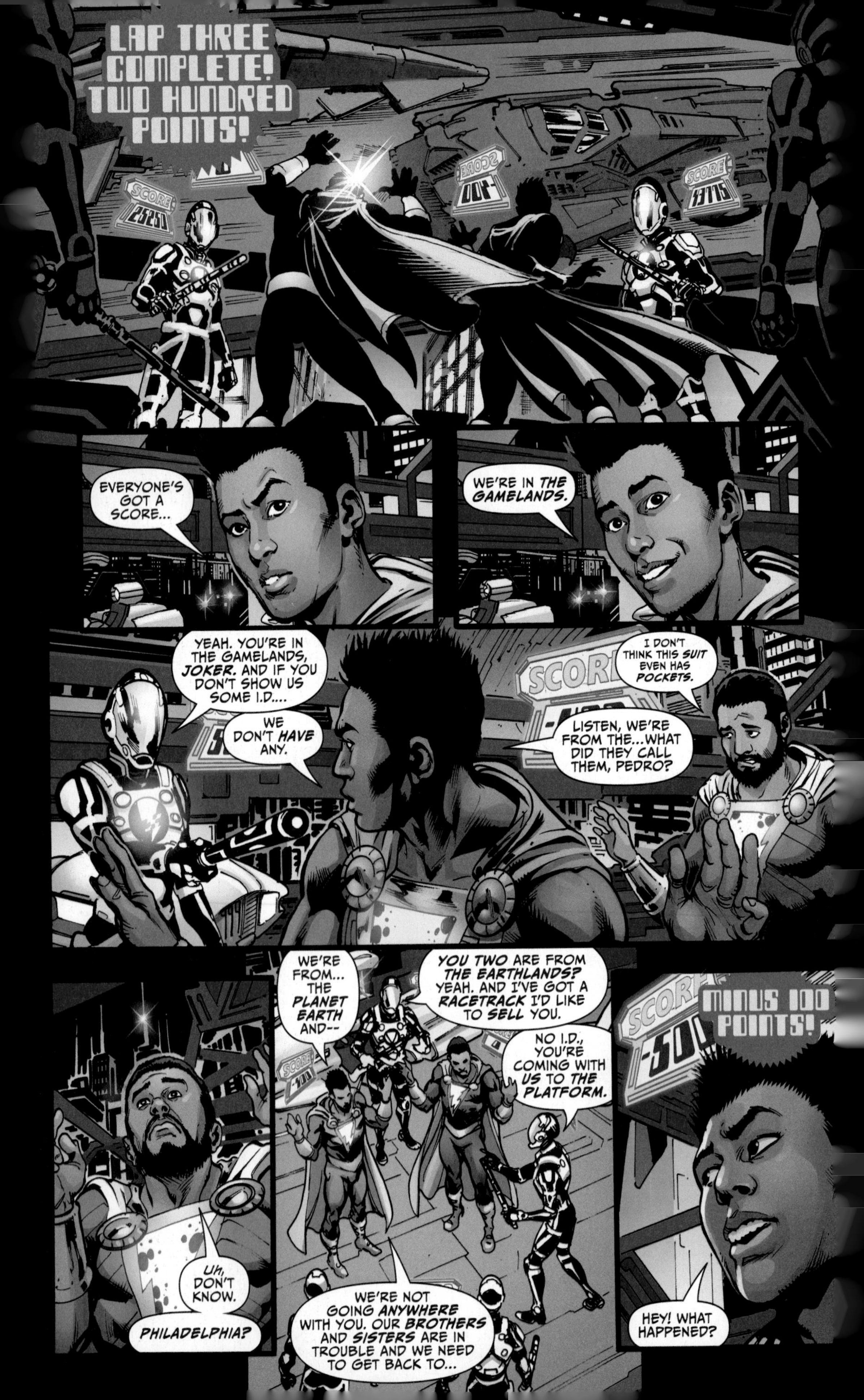

LAP THREE COMPLETE! TWO HUNDRED POINTS!
SCORE 25250
SCORE -400
SCORE 13775
EVERYONE'S GOT A SCORE...
WE'RE IN THE GAMELANDS.
YEAH. YOU'RE IN THE GAMELANDS, JOKER. AND IF YOU DON'T SHOW US SOME I.D....
WE DON'T HAVE ANY.
I DON'T THINK THIS SUIT EVEN HAS POCKETS.
LISTEN, WE'RE FROM THE...WHAT DID THEY CALL THEM, PEDRO?
UH, DON'T KNOW.
PHILADELPHIA?
WE'RE FROM... THE PLANET EARTH AND--
YOU TWO ARE FROM THE EARTHLANDS? YEAH. AND I'VE GOT A RACETRACK I'D LIKE TO SELL YOU.
NO I.D., YOU'RE COMING WITH US TO THE PLATFORM.
WE'RE NOT GOING ANYWHERE WITH YOU. OUR BROTHERS AND SISTERS ARE IN TROUBLE AND WE NEED TO GET BACK TO...
MINUS 100 POINTS!
HEY! WHAT HAPPENED?

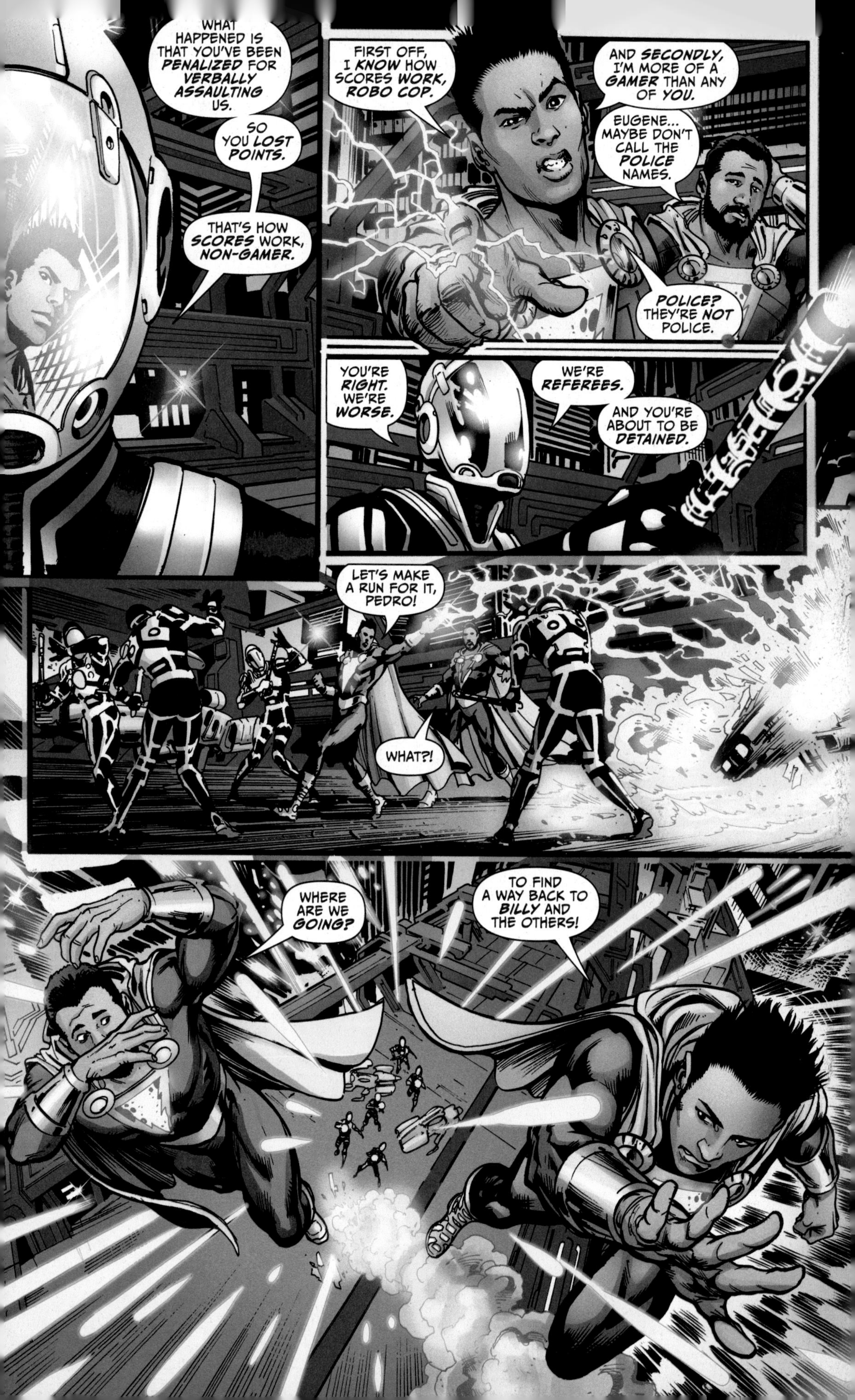
WHAT HAPPENED IS THAT YOU'VE BEEN PENALIZED FOR VERBALLY ASSAULTING US.
SO YOU LOST POINTS.
THAT'S HOW SCORES WORK, NON-GAMER.
FIRST OFF, I KNOW HOW SCORES WORK, ROBO COP.
AND SECONDLY, I'M MORE OF A GAMER THAN ANY OF YOU.
EUGENE... MAYBE DON'T CALL THE POLICE NAMES.
POLICE? THEY'RE NOT POLICE.
YOU'RE RIGHT. WE'RE WORSE.
WE'RE REFEREES.
AND YOU'RE ABOUT TO BE DETAINED.
LET'S MAKE A RUN FOR IT, PEDRO!
WHAT?!
WHERE ARE WE GOING?
TO FIND A WAY BACK TO BILLY AND THE OTHERS!

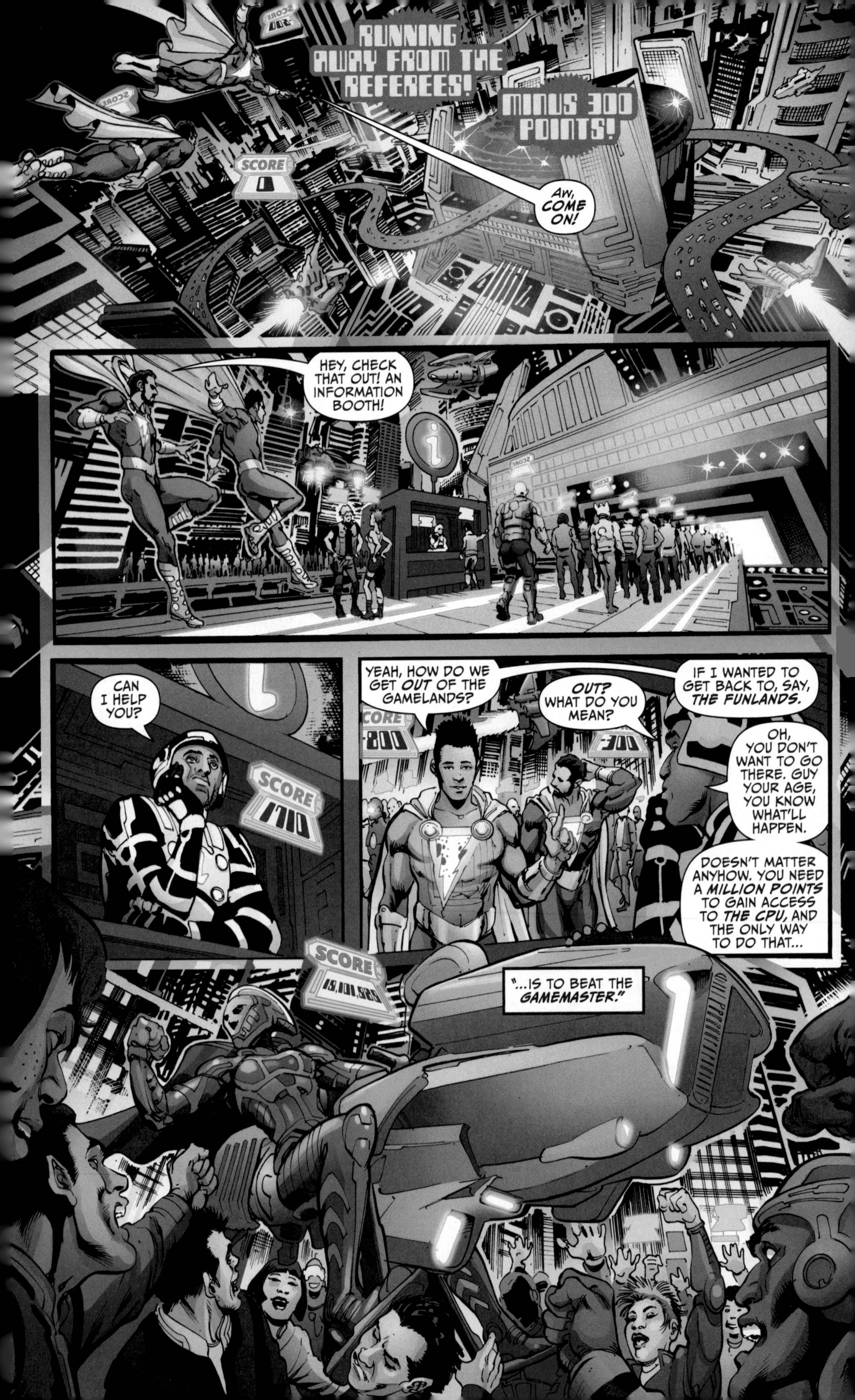
SCORE
-300
SCORE
0
RUNNING AWAY FROM THE REFEREES!
MINUS 300 POINTS!
AW, COME ON!
HEY, CHECK THAT OUT! AN INFORMATION BOOTH!
CAN I HELP YOU?
SCORE
1710
YEAH, HOW DO WE GET OUT OF THE GAMELANDS?
OUT? WHAT DO YOU MEAN?
IF I WANTED TO GET BACK TO, SAY, THE FUNLANDS.
OH, YOU DON'T WANT TO GO THERE. GUY YOUR AGE, YOU KNOW WHAT'LL HAPPEN.
DOESN'T MATTER ANYHOW. YOU NEED A MILLION POINTS TO GAIN ACCESS TO THE CPU, AND THE ONLY WAY TO DO THAT...
SCORE
19,101,585
"...IS TO BEAT THE GAMEMASTER."

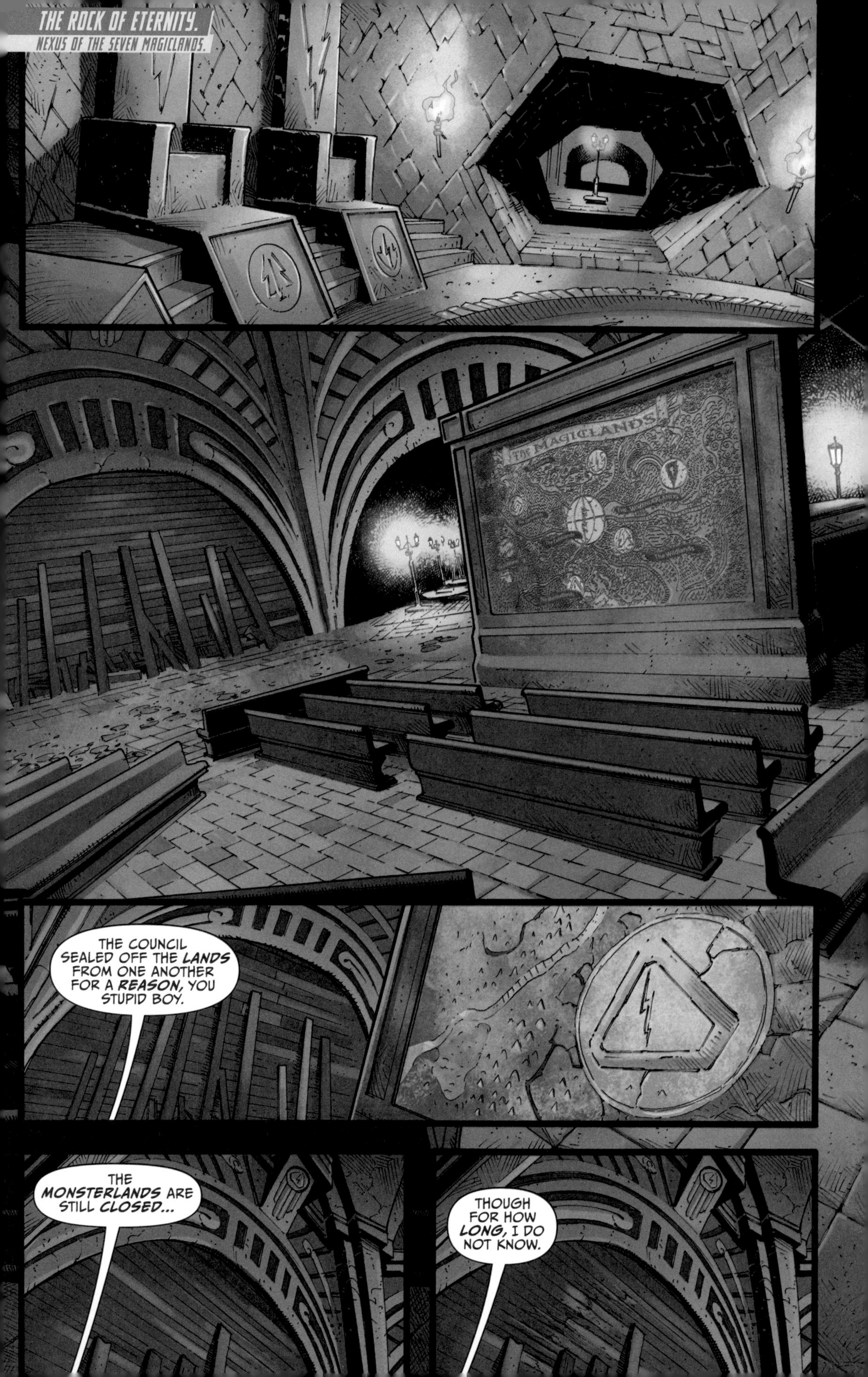
THE ROCK OF ETERNITY.
NEXUS OF THE SEVEN MAGICLANDS.
THE MAGICLANDS
THE COUNCIL SEALED OFF THE LANDS FROM ONE ANOTHER FOR A REASON, YOU STUPID BOY.
THE MONSTERLANDS ARE STILL CLOSED...
THOUGH FOR HOW LONG, I DO NOT KNOW.

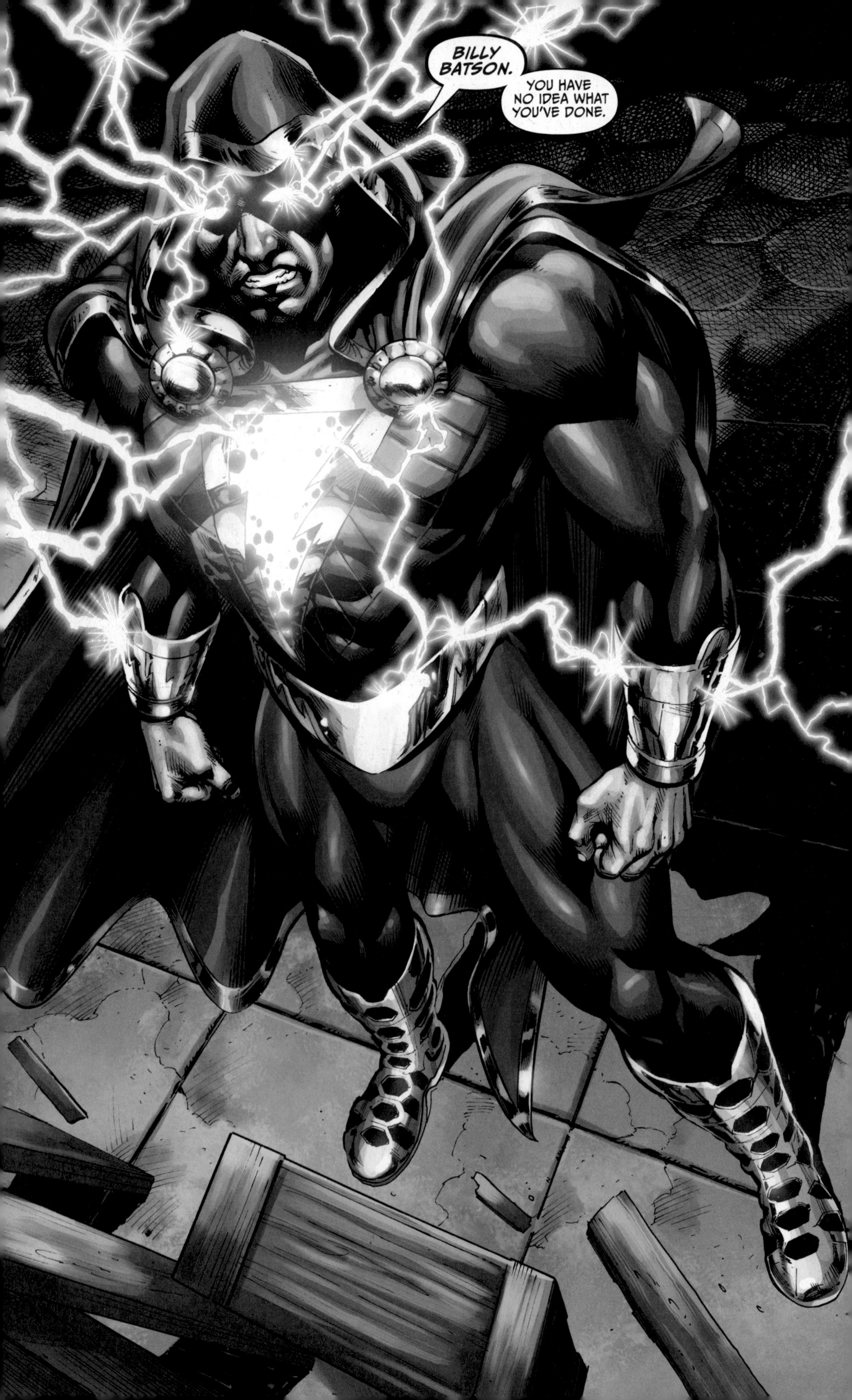
BILLY BATSON.
YOU HAVE NO IDEA WHAT YOU'VE DONE.

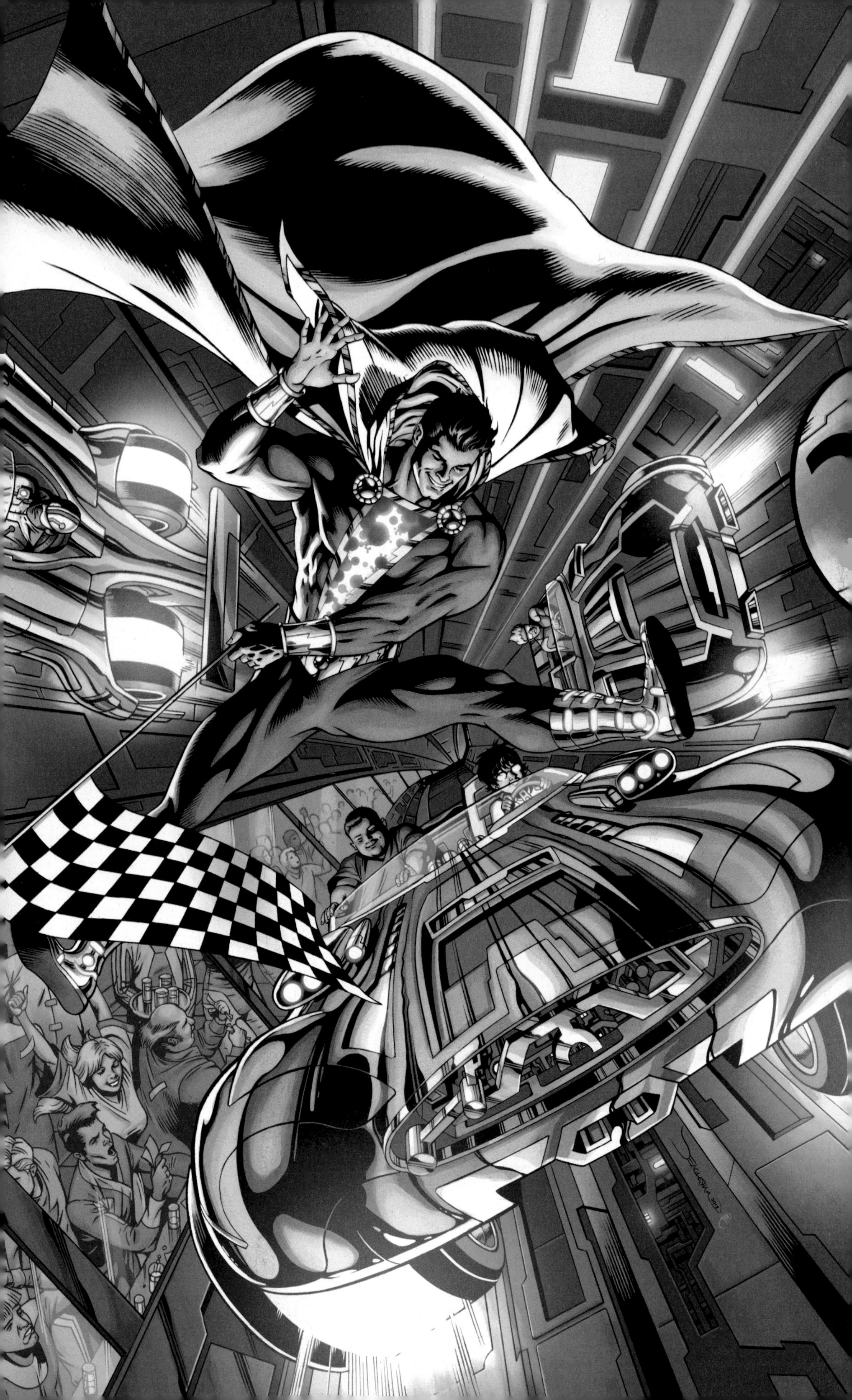

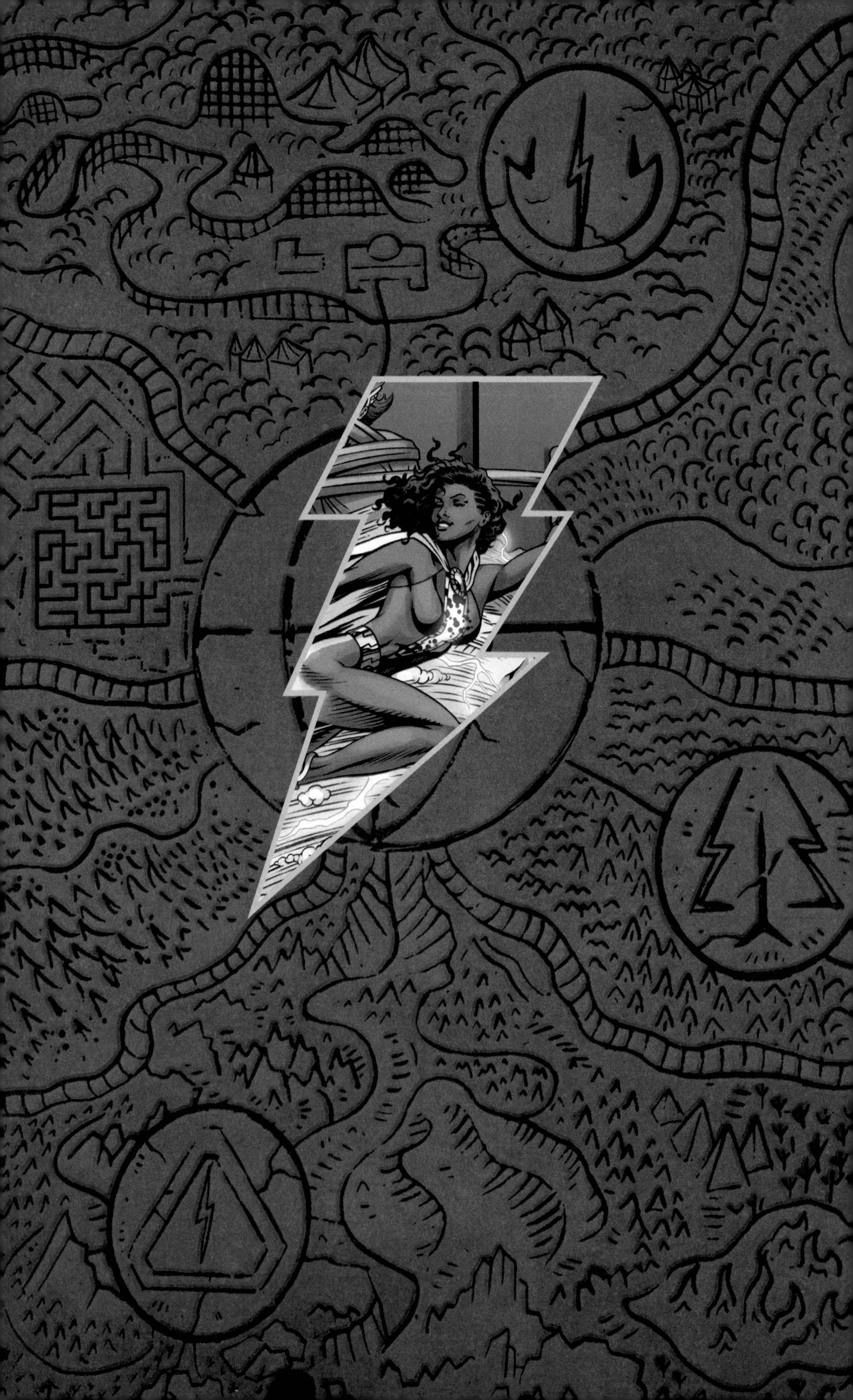

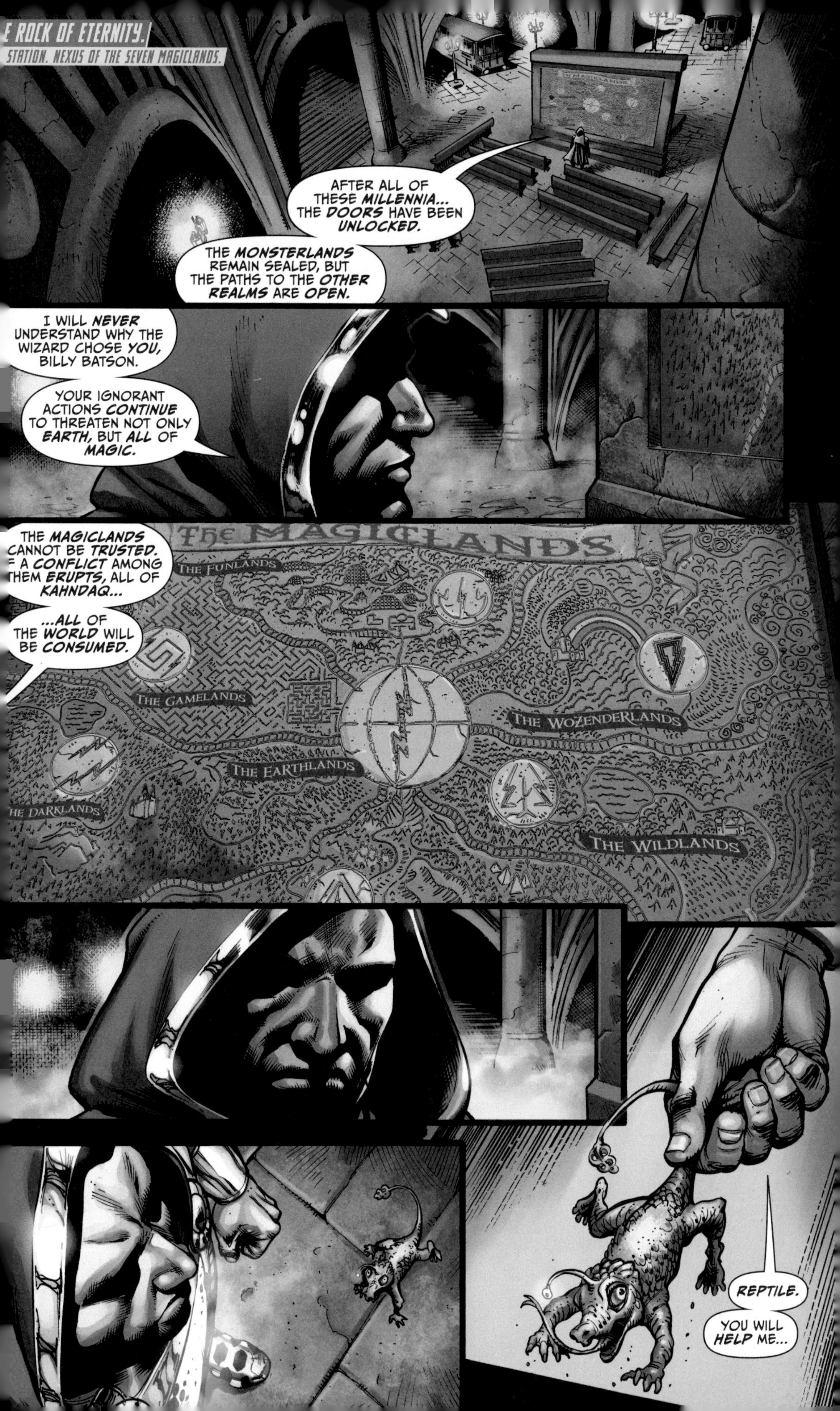
E ROCK OF ETERNITY.
STATION. NEXUS OF THE SEVEN MAGICLANDS.
AFTER ALL OF THESE MILLENNIA... THE DOORS HAVE BEEN UNLOCKED.
THE MONSTERLANDS REMAIN SEALED, BUT THE PATHS TO THE OTHER REALMS ARE OPEN.
I WILL NEVER UNDERSTAND WHY THE WIZARD CHOSE YOU, BILLY BATSON.
YOUR IGNORANT ACTIONS CONTINUE TO THREATEN NOT ONLY EARTH, BUT ALL OF MAGIC.
THE MAGICLANDS CANNOT BE TRUSTED. F A CONFLICT AMONG THEM ERUPTS, ALL OF KAHNDAQ...
...ALL OF THE WORLD WILL BE CONSUMED.
THE MAGICLANDS
THE FUNLANDS
THE GAMELANDS
THE WOZENDERLANDS
THE EARTHLANDS
HE DARKLANDS
THE WILDLANDS
REPTILE.
YOU WILL HELP ME...

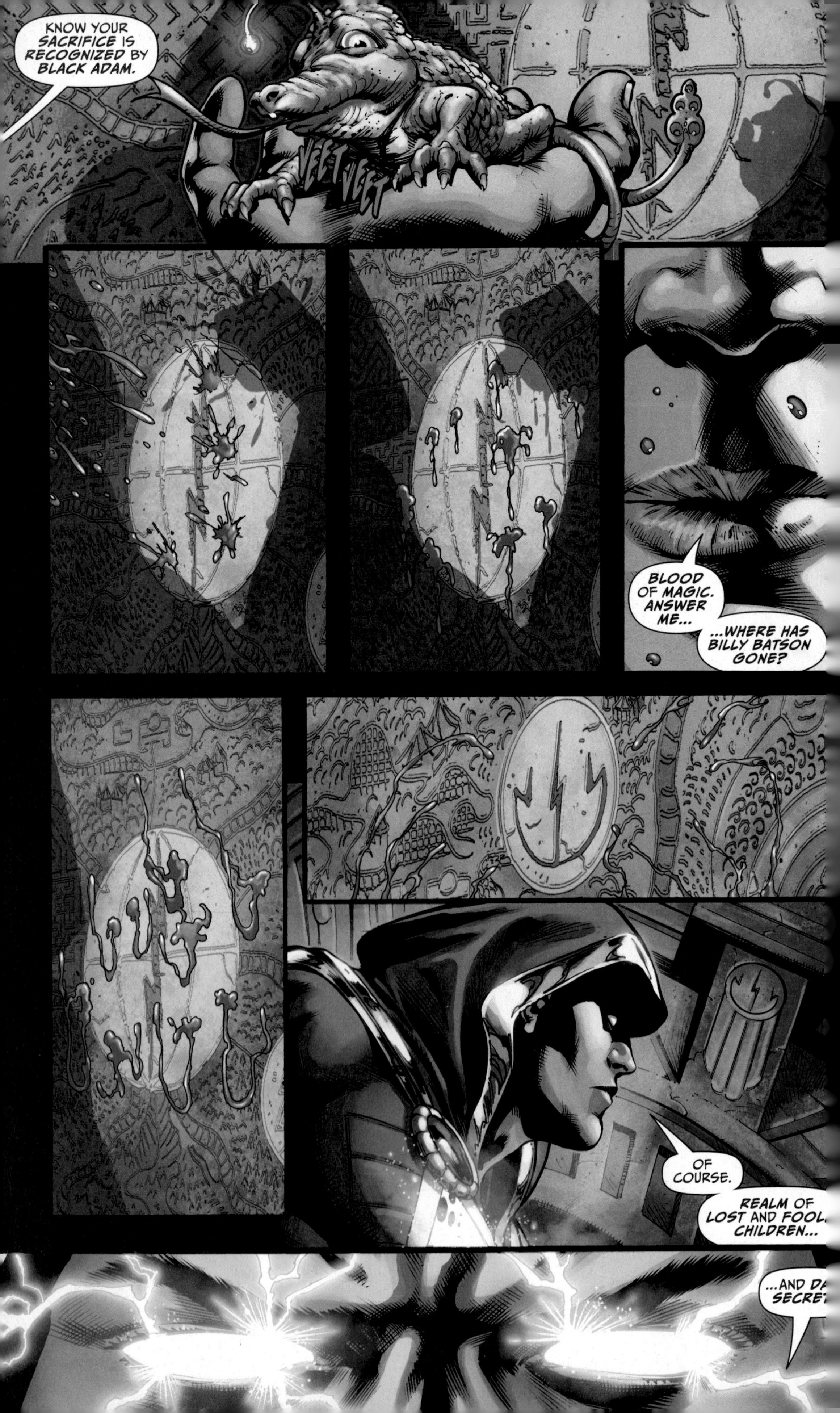

KNOW YOUR SACRIFICE IS RECOGNIZED BY BLACK ADAM.
VEET VEET
BLOOD OF MAGIC. ANSWER ME...
...WHERE HAS BILLY BATSON GONE?
OF COURSE.
REALM OF LOST AND FOOL CHILDREN...
...AND DA SECRE

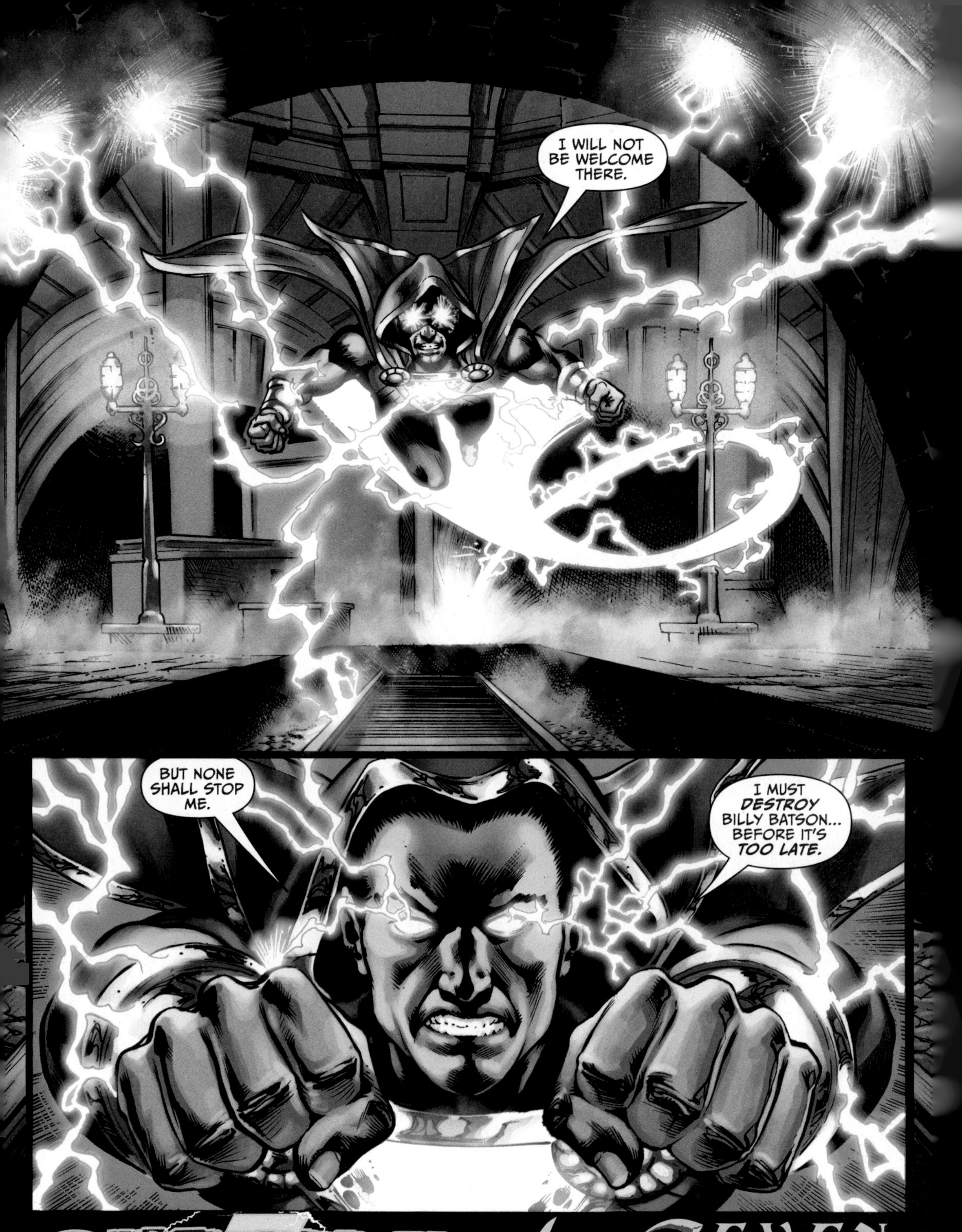
I WILL NOT BE WELCOME THERE.
BUT NONE SHALL STOP ME.
I MUST DESTROY BILLY BATSON... BEFORE IT'S TOO LATE.

# SHAZAM! And the SEVEN MAGIC LANDS!

CHAPTER 5

WRITER
GEOFF JOHNS

ARTISTS
MARCO SANTUCCI PP. 1–3, 21, 22 · DALE EAGLESHAM PP. 4–10, 20.3 · SCOTT KOLINS PP. 11–13, 16, 20.2 · MAX RAYNOR PP. 14–15, 17–20.1

COLORIST MIKE ATIYEH · LETTERER ROB LEIGH · COVER EAGLESHAM WITH ATIYEH · VARIANT COVER RAFAEL ALBUQUERQUE

ASSOCIATE EDITOR HARVEY RICHARDS · EDITOR MOLLY MAHAN · GROUP EDITOR JAMIE S. RICH

SHAZAM! CREATED BY BILL PARKER & C.C. BECK

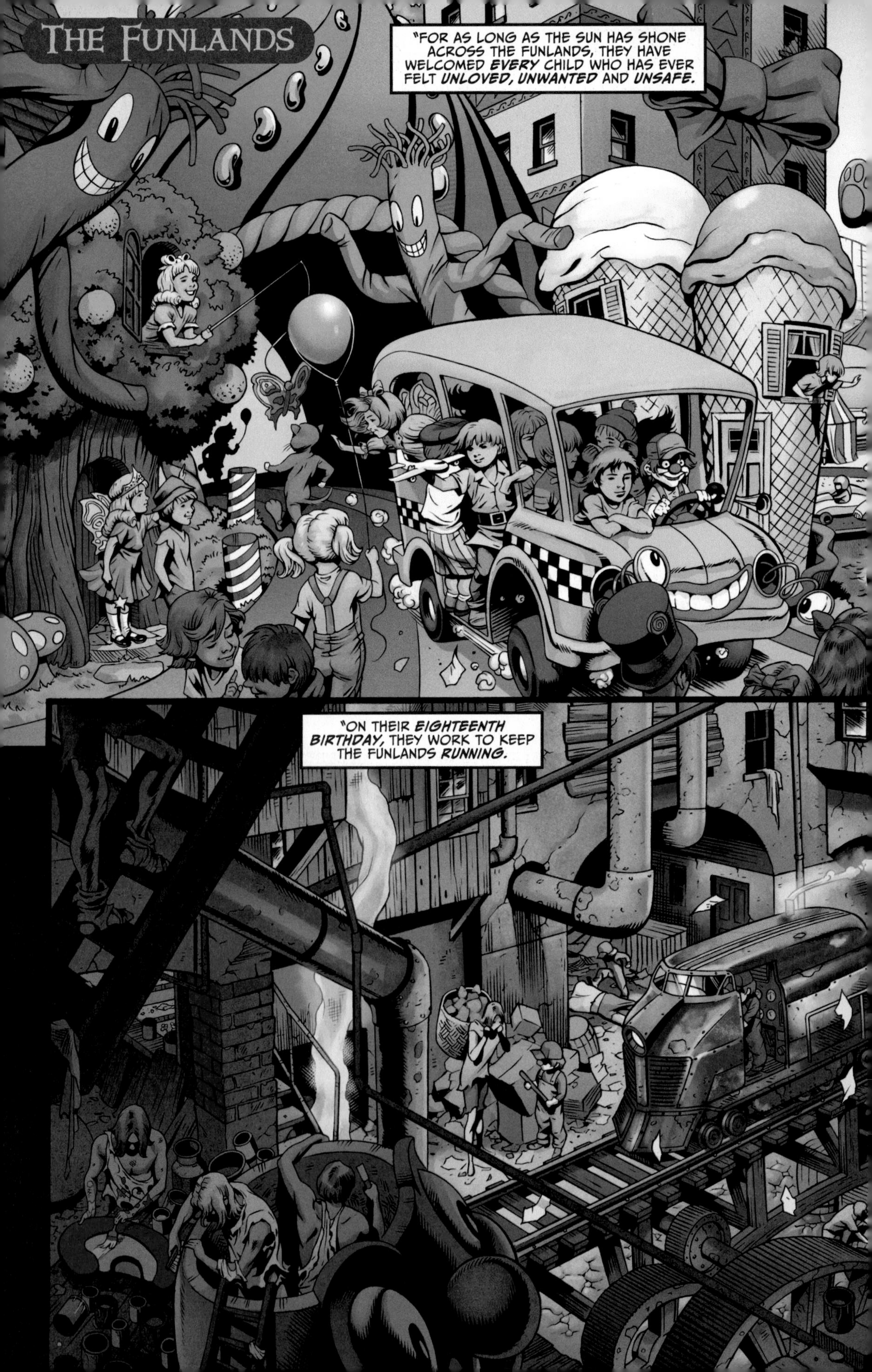
THE FUNLANDS
"FOR AS LONG AS THE SUN HAS SHONE ACROSS THE FUNLANDS, THEY HAVE WELCOMED EVERY CHILD WHO HAS EVER FELT UNLOVED, UNWANTED AND UNSAFE.
"ON THEIR EIGHTEENTH BIRTHDAY, THEY WORK TO KEEP THE FUNLANDS RUNNING.

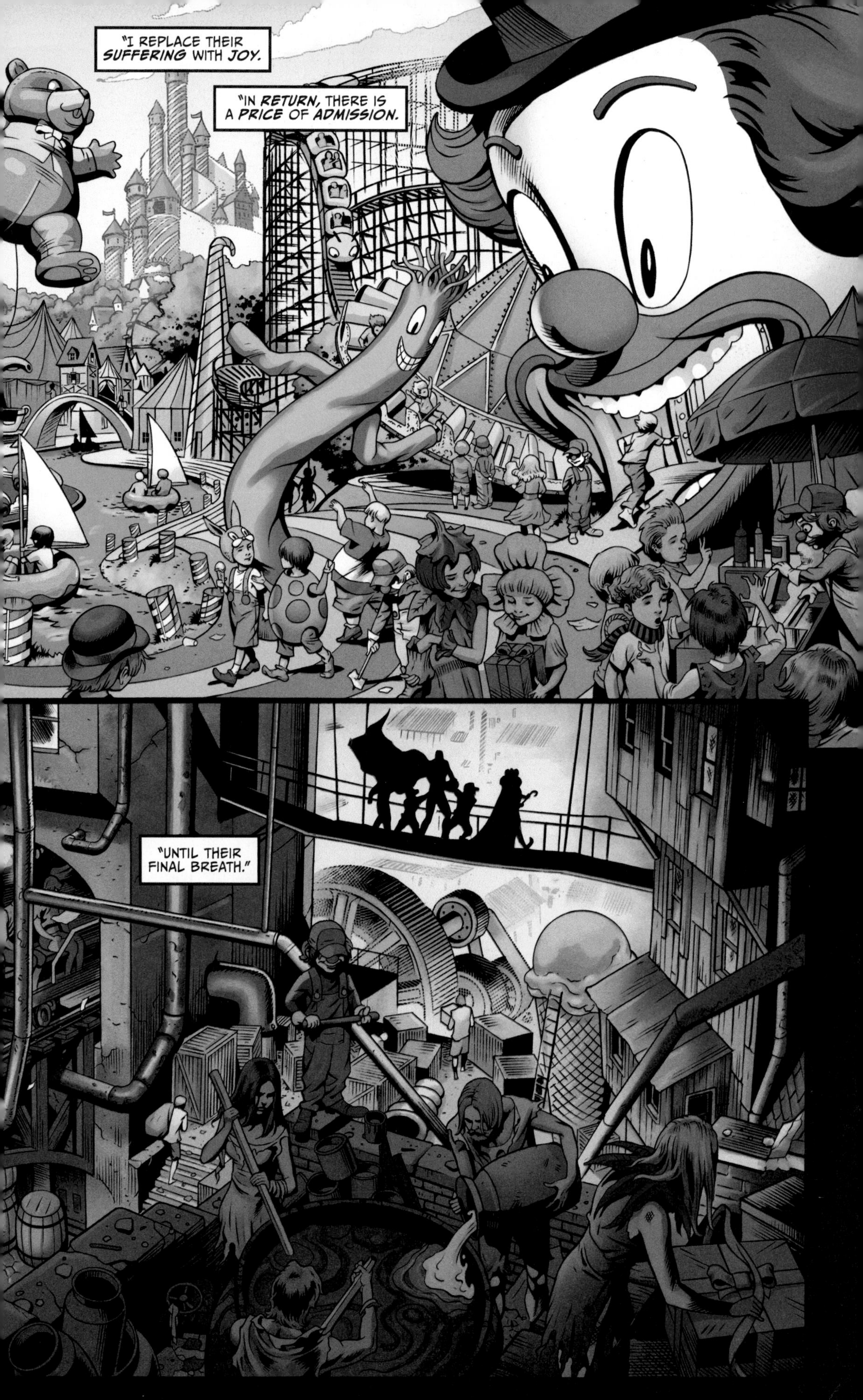
"I REPLACE THEIR SUFFERING WITH JOY.
"IN RETURN, THERE IS A PRICE OF ADMISSION.
"UNTIL THEIR FINAL BREATH."

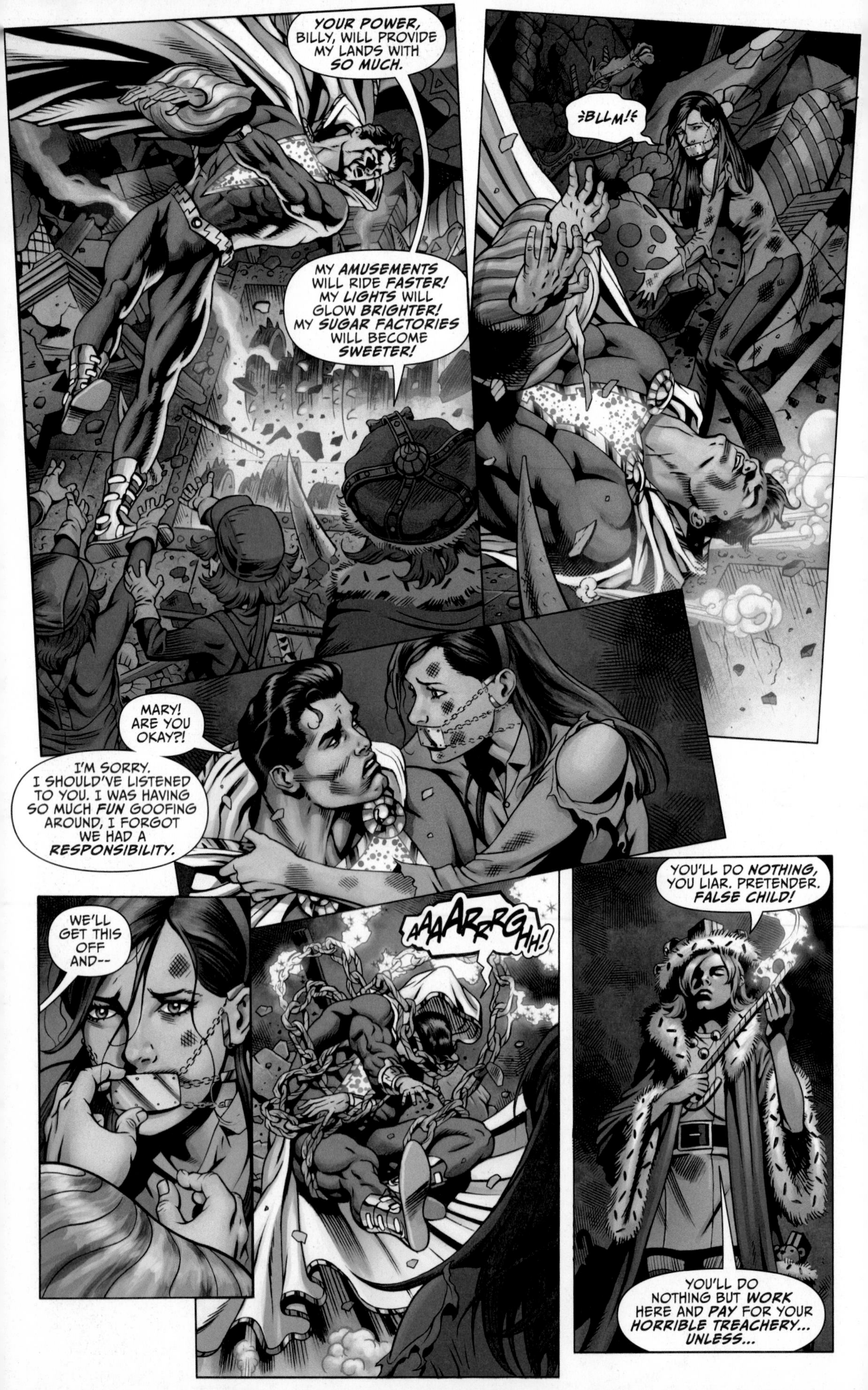
YOUR POWER, BILLY, WILL PROVIDE MY LANDS WITH SO MUCH.
MY AMUSEMENTS WILL RIDE FASTER! MY LIGHTS WILL GLOW BRIGHTER! MY SUGAR FACTORIES WILL BECOME SWEETER!
=BLLM!=
MARY! ARE YOU OKAY?!
I'M SORRY. I SHOULD'VE LISTENED TO YOU. I WAS HAVING SO MUCH FUN GOOFING AROUND, I FORGOT WE HAD A RESPONSIBILITY.
WE'LL GET THIS OFF AND--
AAAARRRGHH!
YOU'LL DO NOTHING, YOU LIAR. PRETENDER. FALSE CHILD!
YOU'LL DO NOTHING BUT WORK HERE AND PAY FOR YOUR HORRIBLE TREACHERY... UNLESS...

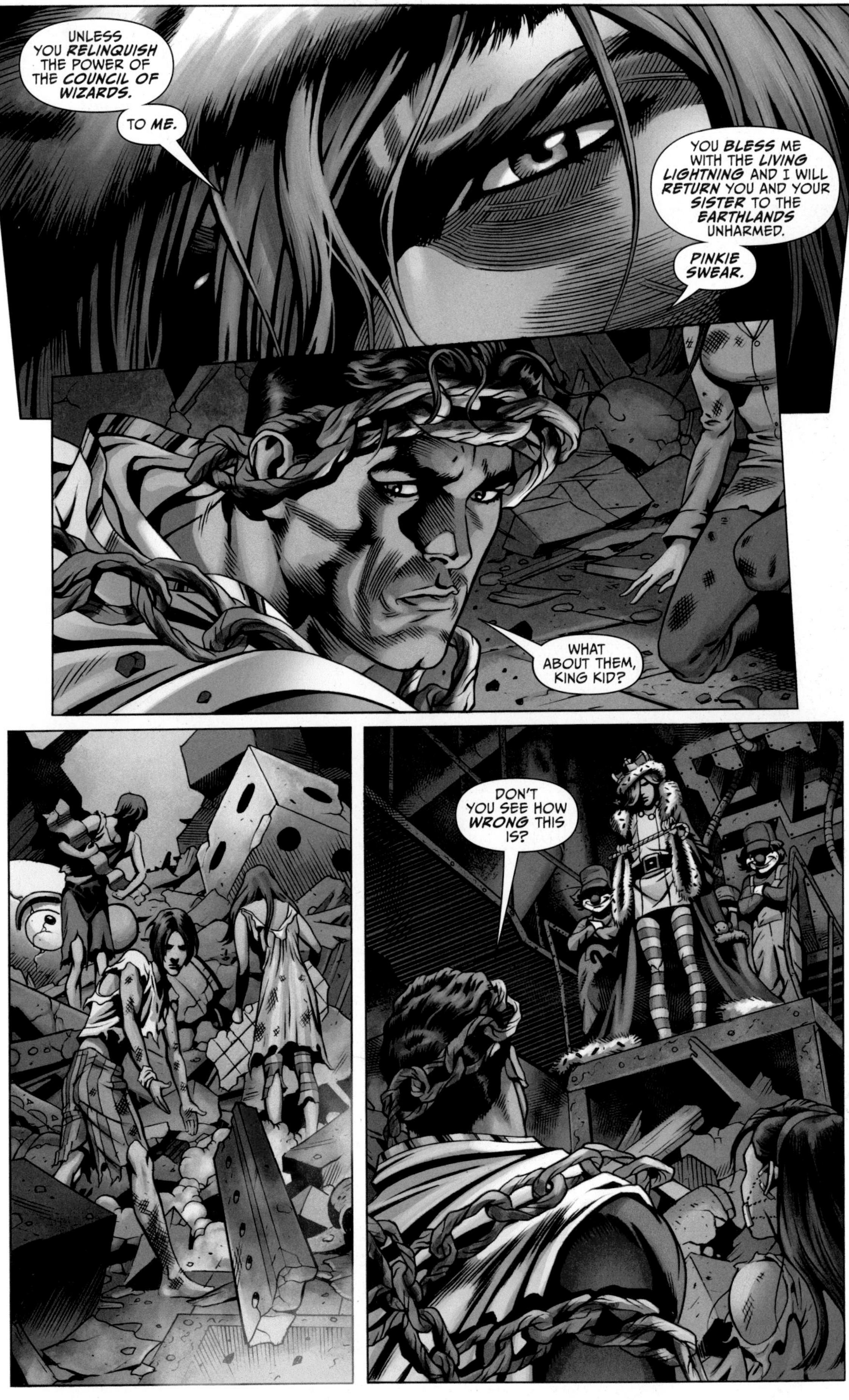
UNLESS YOU RELINQUISH THE POWER OF THE COUNCIL OF WIZARDS.
TO ME.
YOU BLESS ME WITH THE LIVING LIGHTNING AND I WILL RETURN YOU AND YOUR SISTER TO THE EARTHLANDS UNHARMED.
PINKIE SWEAR.
WHAT ABOUT THEM, KING KID?
DON'T YOU SEE HOW WRONG THIS IS?

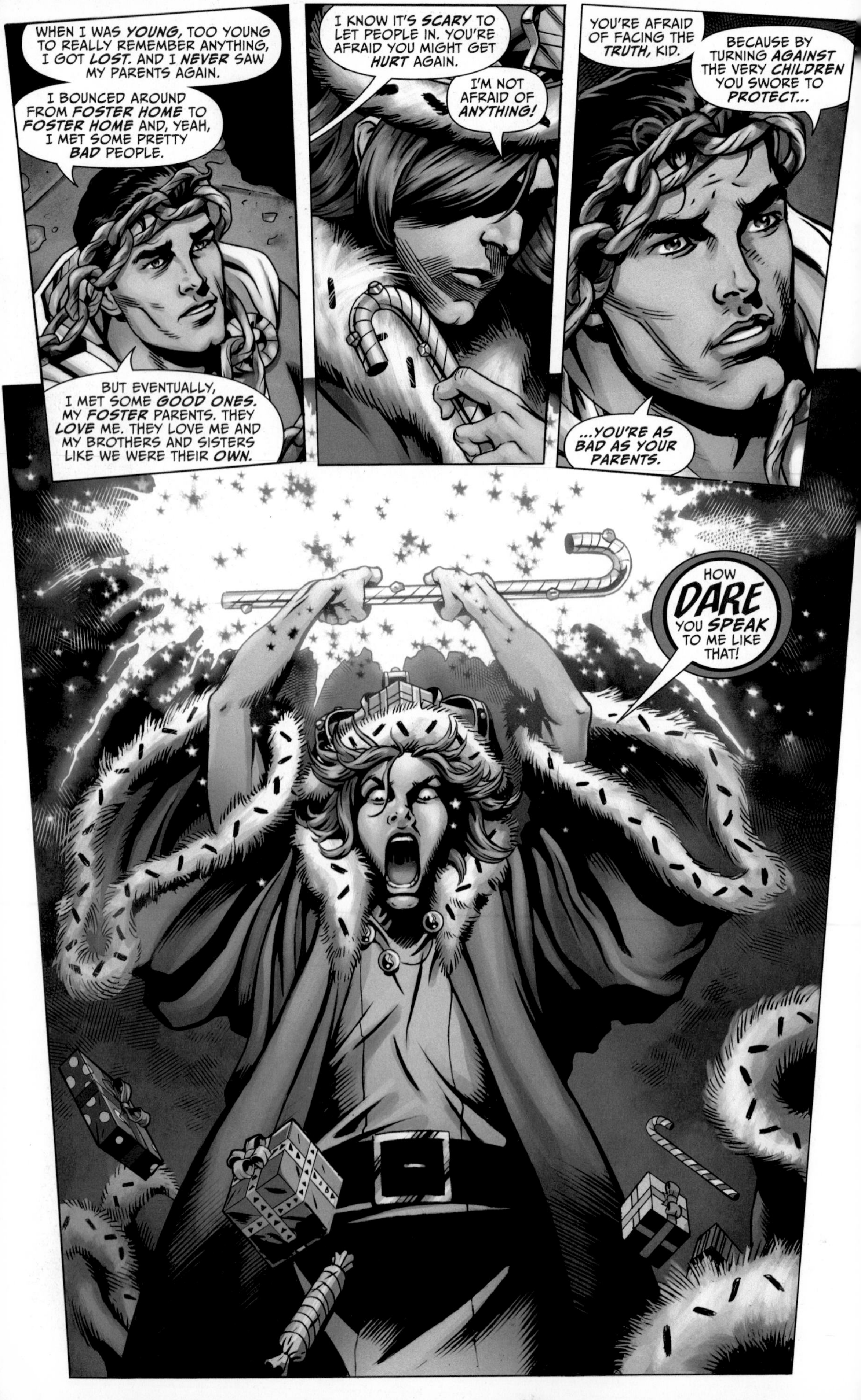

WHEN I WAS YOUNG, TOO YOUNG TO REALLY REMEMBER ANYTHING, I GOT LOST. AND I NEVER SAW MY PARENTS AGAIN.
I BOUNCED AROUND FROM FOSTER HOME TO FOSTER HOME AND, YEAH, I MET SOME PRETTY BAD PEOPLE.
BUT EVENTUALLY, I MET SOME GOOD ONES. MY FOSTER PARENTS. THEY LOVE ME. THEY LOVE ME AND MY BROTHERS AND SISTERS LIKE WE WERE THEIR OWN.
I KNOW IT'S SCARY TO LET PEOPLE IN. YOU'RE AFRAID YOU MIGHT GET HURT AGAIN.
I'M NOT AFRAID OF ANYTHING!
YOU'RE AFRAID OF FACING THE TRUTH, KID.
BECAUSE BY TURNING AGAINST THE VERY CHILDREN YOU SWORE TO PROTECT...
...YOU'RE AS BAD AS YOUR PARENTS.
HOW DARE YOU SPEAK TO ME LIKE THAT!

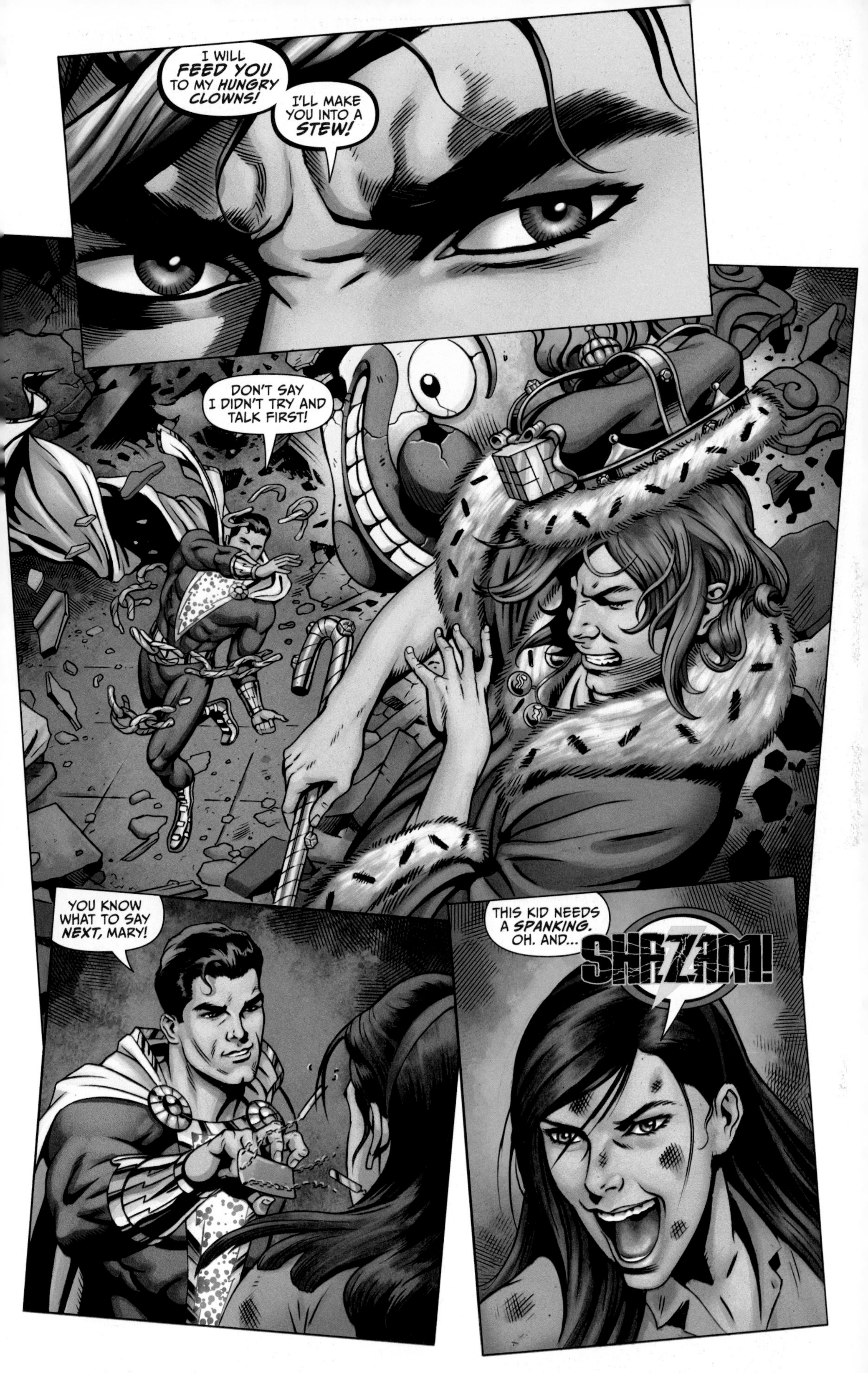
I WILL FEED YOU TO MY HUNGRY CLOWNS!
I'LL MAKE YOU INTO A STEW!
DON'T SAY I DIDN'T TRY AND TALK FIRST!
YOU KNOW WHAT TO SAY NEXT, MARY!
THIS KID NEEDS A SPANKING. OH. AND...
SHAZAM!

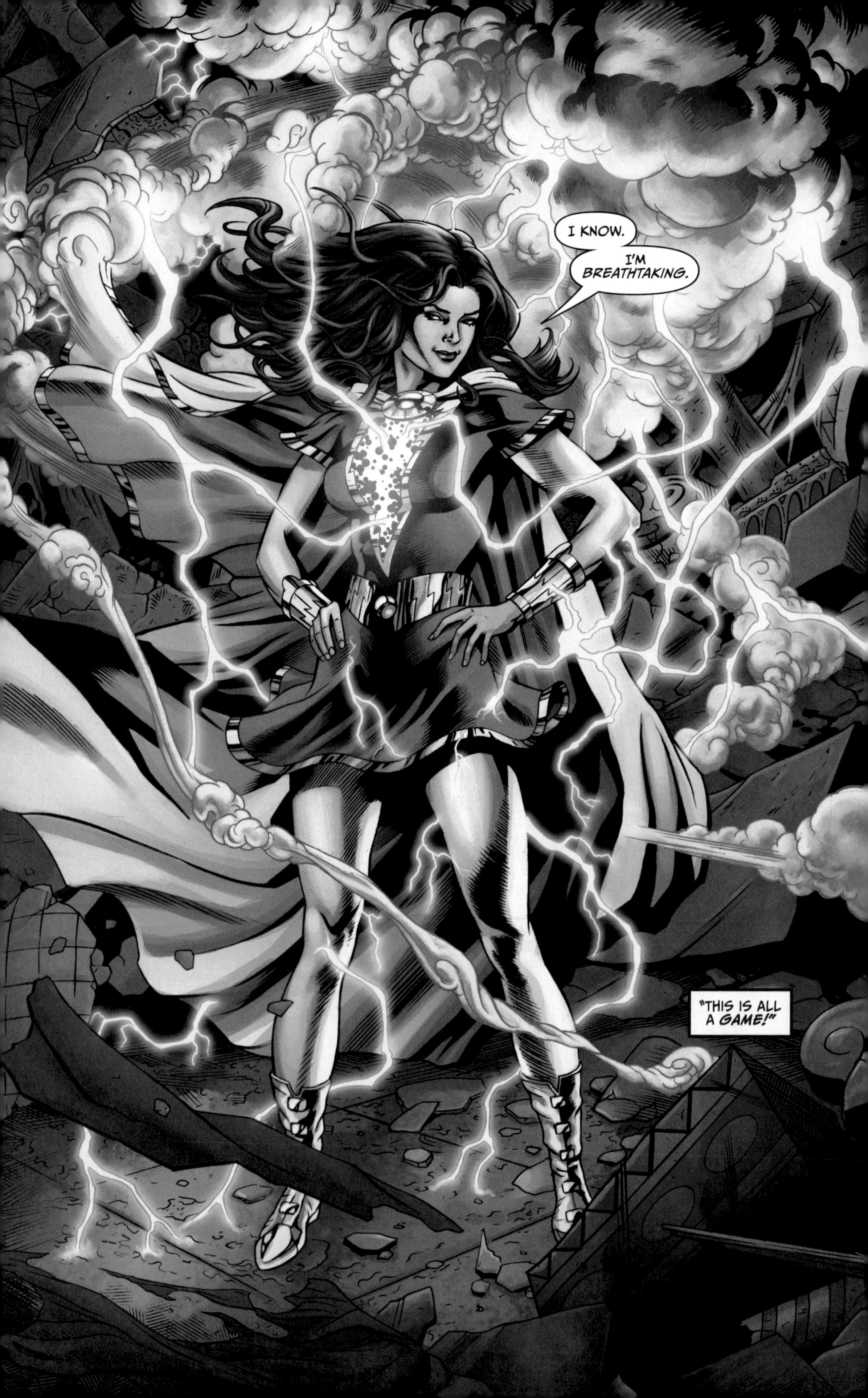
I KNOW.
I'M BREATHTAKING.
"THIS IS ALL A GAME!"

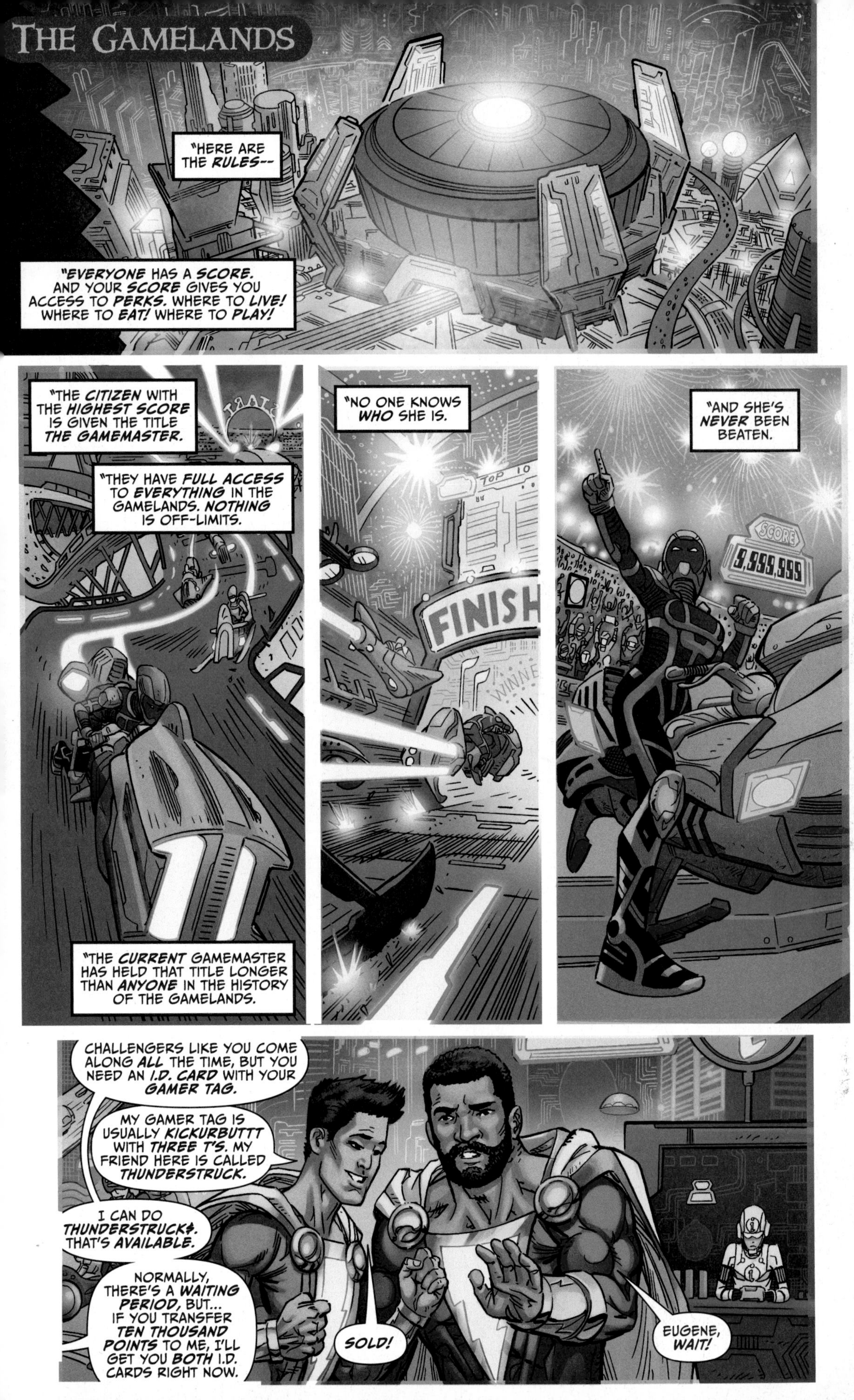
THE GAMELANDS
"HERE ARE THE *RULES*--
"*EVERYONE* HAS A *SCORE*. AND YOUR *SCORE* GIVES YOU ACCESS TO *PERKS*. WHERE TO *LIVE*! WHERE TO *EAT*! WHERE TO *PLAY*!
"THE *CITIZEN* WITH THE *HIGHEST SCORE* IS GIVEN THE TITLE *THE GAMEMASTER*.
"THEY HAVE *FULL ACCESS* TO *EVERYTHING* IN THE GAMELANDS. *NOTHING* IS OFF-LIMITS.
"THE *CURRENT* GAMEMASTER HAS HELD THAT TITLE LONGER THAN *ANYONE* IN THE HISTORY OF THE GAMELANDS.
"NO ONE KNOWS *WHO* SHE IS.
TOP 10
FINISH
"AND SHE'S *NEVER* BEEN BEATEN.
SCORE
9,999,999
CHALLENGERS LIKE YOU COME ALONG *ALL* THE TIME, BUT YOU NEED AN *I.D. CARD* WITH YOUR *GAMER TAG*.
MY GAMER TAG IS USUALLY *KICKURBUTTT* WITH *THREE T'S*. MY FRIEND HERE IS CALLED *THUNDERSTRUCK*.
I CAN DO *THUNDERSTRUCK$*. THAT'S *AVAILABLE*.
NORMALLY, THERE'S A *WAITING PERIOD*, BUT... IF YOU TRANSFER *TEN THOUSAND POINTS* TO ME, I'LL GET YOU *BOTH* I.D. CARDS RIGHT NOW.
*SOLD!*
EUGENE, *WAIT!*

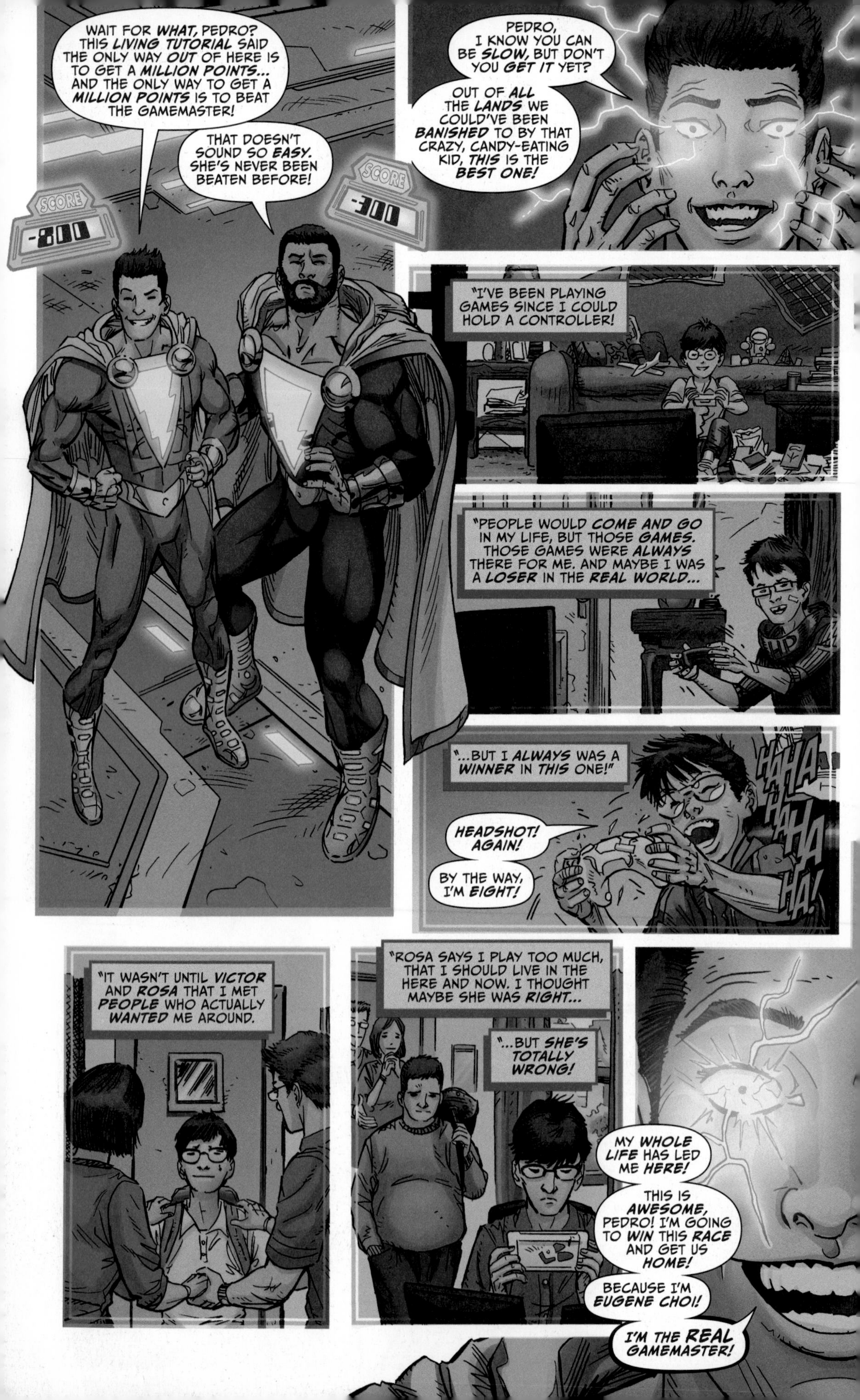
WAIT FOR WHAT, PEDRO? THIS LIVING TUTORIAL SAID THE ONLY WAY OUT OF HERE IS TO GET A MILLION POINTS... AND THE ONLY WAY TO GET A MILLION POINTS IS TO BEAT THE GAMEMASTER!
THAT DOESN'T SOUND SO EASY. SHE'S NEVER BEEN BEATEN BEFORE!
SCORE
-800
SCORE
-300
PEDRO, I KNOW YOU CAN BE SLOW, BUT DON'T YOU GET IT YET?
OUT OF ALL THE LANDS WE COULD'VE BEEN BANISHED TO BY THAT CRAZY, CANDY-EATING KID, THIS IS THE BEST ONE!
"I'VE BEEN PLAYING GAMES SINCE I COULD HOLD A CONTROLLER!
"PEOPLE WOULD COME AND GO IN MY LIFE, BUT THOSE GAMES. THOSE GAMES WERE ALWAYS THERE FOR ME. AND MAYBE I WAS A LOSER IN THE REAL WORLD...
"...BUT I ALWAYS WAS A WINNER IN THIS ONE!"
HEADSHOT! AGAIN!
BY THE WAY, I'M EIGHT!
HAHAHAHAHA!
"IT WASN'T UNTIL VICTOR AND ROSA THAT I MET PEOPLE WHO ACTUALLY WANTED ME AROUND.
"ROSA SAYS I PLAY TOO MUCH, THAT I SHOULD LIVE IN THE HERE AND NOW. I THOUGHT MAYBE SHE WAS RIGHT...
"...BUT SHE'S TOTALLY WRONG!
MY WHOLE LIFE HAS LED ME HERE!
THIS IS AWESOME, PEDRO! I'M GOING TO WIN THIS RACE AND GET US HOME!
BECAUSE I'M EUGENE CHOI!
I'M THE REAL GAMEMASTER!

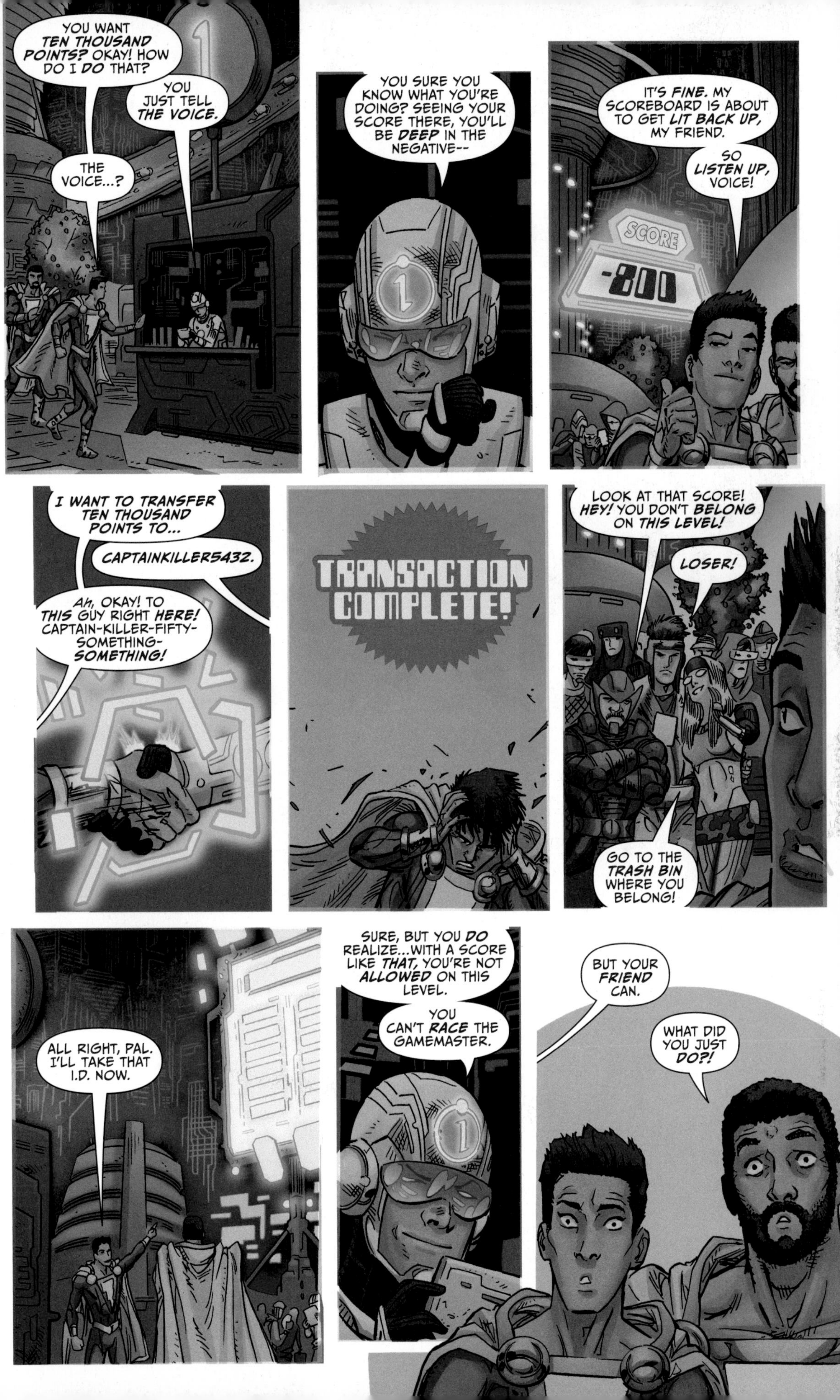
YOU WANT TEN THOUSAND POINTS? OKAY! HOW DO I DO THAT?
YOU JUST TELL THE VOICE.
THE VOICE...?
YOU SURE YOU KNOW WHAT YOU'RE DOING? SEEING YOUR SCORE THERE, YOU'LL BE DEEP IN THE NEGATIVE--
IT'S FINE. MY SCOREBOARD IS ABOUT TO GET LIT BACK UP, MY FRIEND.
SO LISTEN UP, VOICE!
SCORE
-800
I WANT TO TRANSFER TEN THOUSAND POINTS TO...
CAPTAINKILLER5432.
Ah, OKAY! TO THIS GUY RIGHT HERE! CAPTAIN-KILLER-FIFTY-SOMETHING-SOMETHING!
TRANSACTION COMPLETE!
LOOK AT THAT SCORE! HEY! YOU DON'T BELONG ON THIS LEVEL!
LOSER!
GO TO THE TRASH BIN WHERE YOU BELONG!
ALL RIGHT, PAL. I'LL TAKE THAT I.D. NOW.
SURE, BUT YOU DO REALIZE...WITH A SCORE LIKE THAT, YOU'RE NOT ALLOWED ON THIS LEVEL.
YOU CAN'T RACE THE GAMEMASTER.
BUT YOUR FRIEND CAN.
WHAT DID YOU JUST DO?!

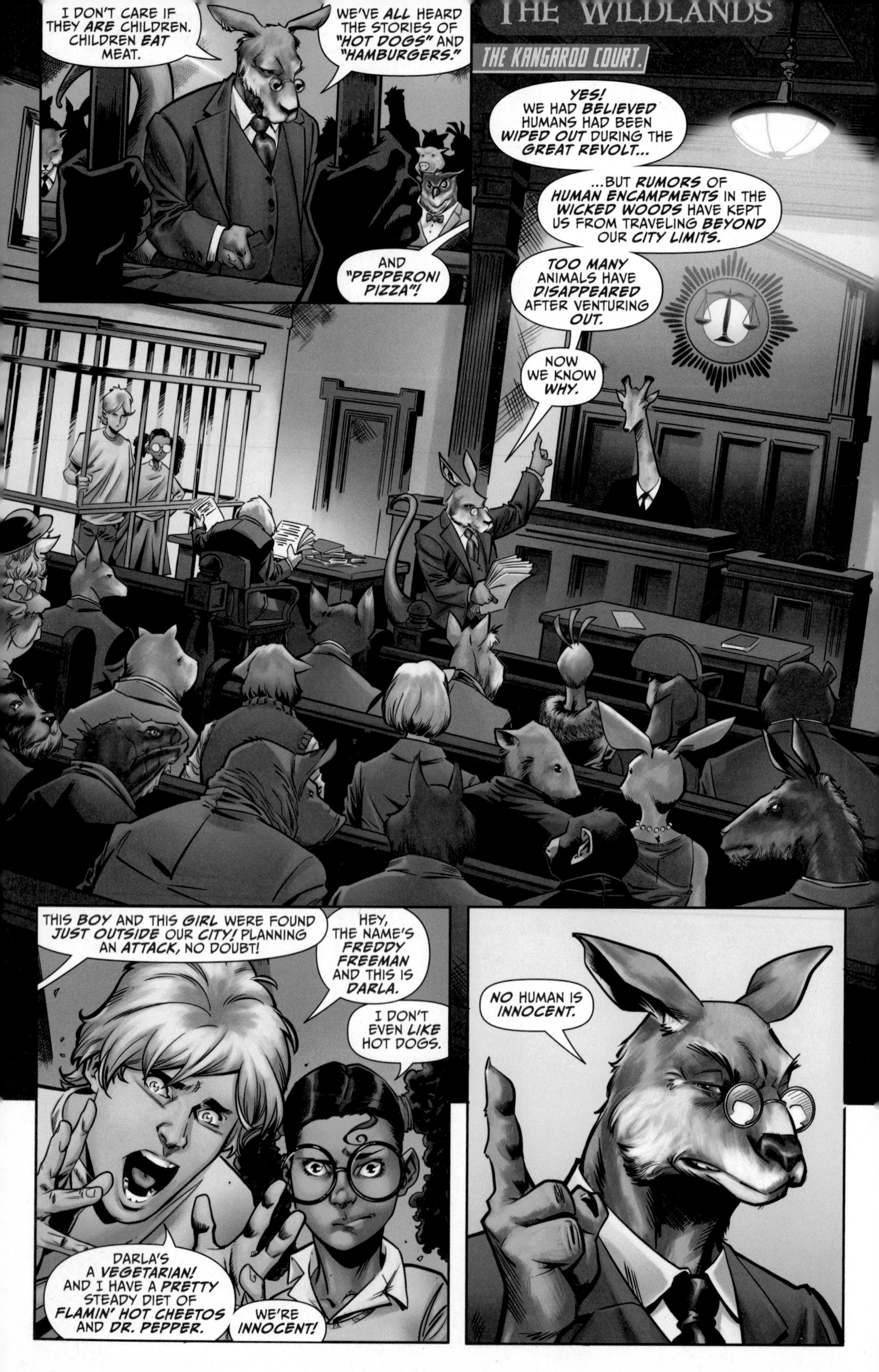
I DON'T CARE IF THEY ARE CHILDREN. CHILDREN EAT MEAT.
WE'VE ALL HEARD THE STORIES OF "HOT DOGS" AND "HAMBURGERS."
AND "PEPPERONI PIZZA"!
THE WILDLANDS
THE KANGAROO COURT.
YES! WE HAD BELIEVED HUMANS HAD BEEN WIPED OUT DURING THE GREAT REVOLT...
...BUT RUMORS OF HUMAN ENCAMPMENTS IN THE WICKED WOODS HAVE KEPT US FROM TRAVELING BEYOND OUR CITY LIMITS.
TOO MANY ANIMALS HAVE DISAPPEARED AFTER VENTURING OUT.
NOW WE KNOW WHY.
THIS BOY AND THIS GIRL WERE FOUND JUST OUTSIDE OUR CITY! PLANNING AN ATTACK, NO DOUBT!
HEY, THE NAME'S FREDDY FREEMAN AND THIS IS DARLA.
I DON'T EVEN LIKE HOT DOGS.
DARLA'S A VEGETARIAN! AND I HAVE A PRETTY STEADY DIET OF FLAMIN' HOT CHEETOS AND DR. PEPPER.
WE'RE INNOCENT!
NO HUMAN IS INNOCENT.

I'VE HEARD *ENOUGH* FROM THE PROSECUTION.

IS THERE *ANYTHING* THE *DEFENSE* FEELS THE *NEED* TO SAY?

THAT'S *YOU*, RIGHT?

HEY! SHEEP-DOG!

I, *uh*, HAD A *STATEMENT* PREPARED, BUT...OH, *WHO* AM I KIDDING?

HOW CAN *ANYONE* POSSIBLY *DEFEND* A *HUMAN?*

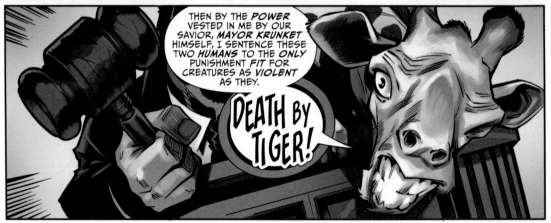

THEN BY THE *POWER* VESTED IN ME BY OUR *SAVIOR, MAYOR KRUNKET* HIMSELF, I SENTENCE THESE TWO *HUMANS* TO THE *ONLY* PUNISHMENT *FIT* FOR CREATURES AS *VIOLENT* AS THEY.

DEATH BY TIGER!

DEATH BY *WHAT?*

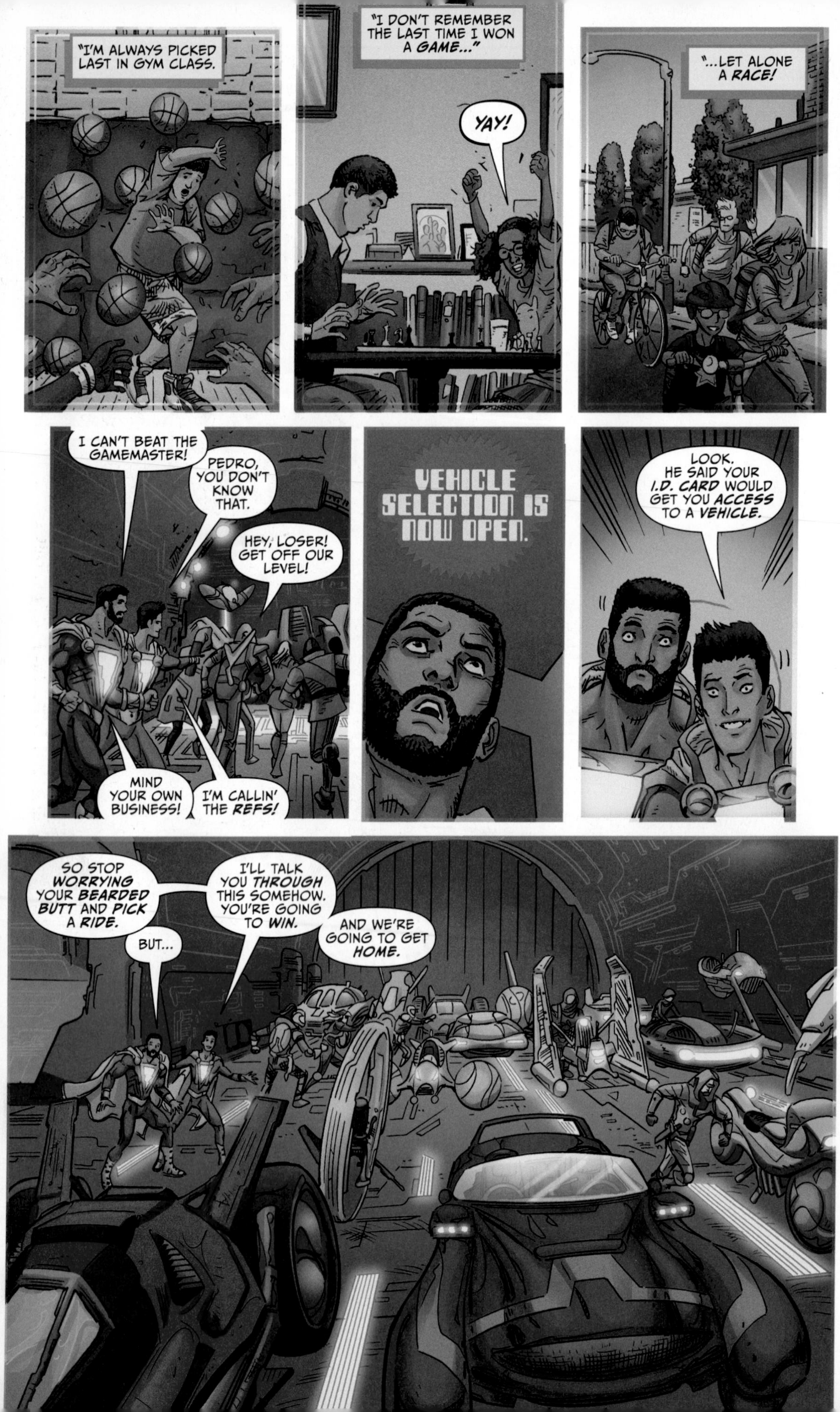
"I'M ALWAYS PICKED LAST IN GYM CLASS.
"I DON'T REMEMBER THE LAST TIME I WON A GAME..."
YAY!
"...LET ALONE A RACE!
I CAN'T BEAT THE GAMEMASTER!
PEDRO, YOU DON'T KNOW THAT.
HEY, LOSER! GET OFF OUR LEVEL!
MIND YOUR OWN BUSINESS!
I'M CALLIN' THE REFS!
VEHICLE SELECTION IS NOW OPEN.
LOOK. HE SAID YOUR I.D. CARD WOULD GET YOU ACCESS TO A VEHICLE.
SO STOP WORRYING YOUR BEARDED BUTT AND PICK A RIDE.
BUT...
I'LL TALK YOU THROUGH THIS SOMEHOW. YOU'RE GOING TO WIN.
AND WE'RE GOING TO GET HOME.

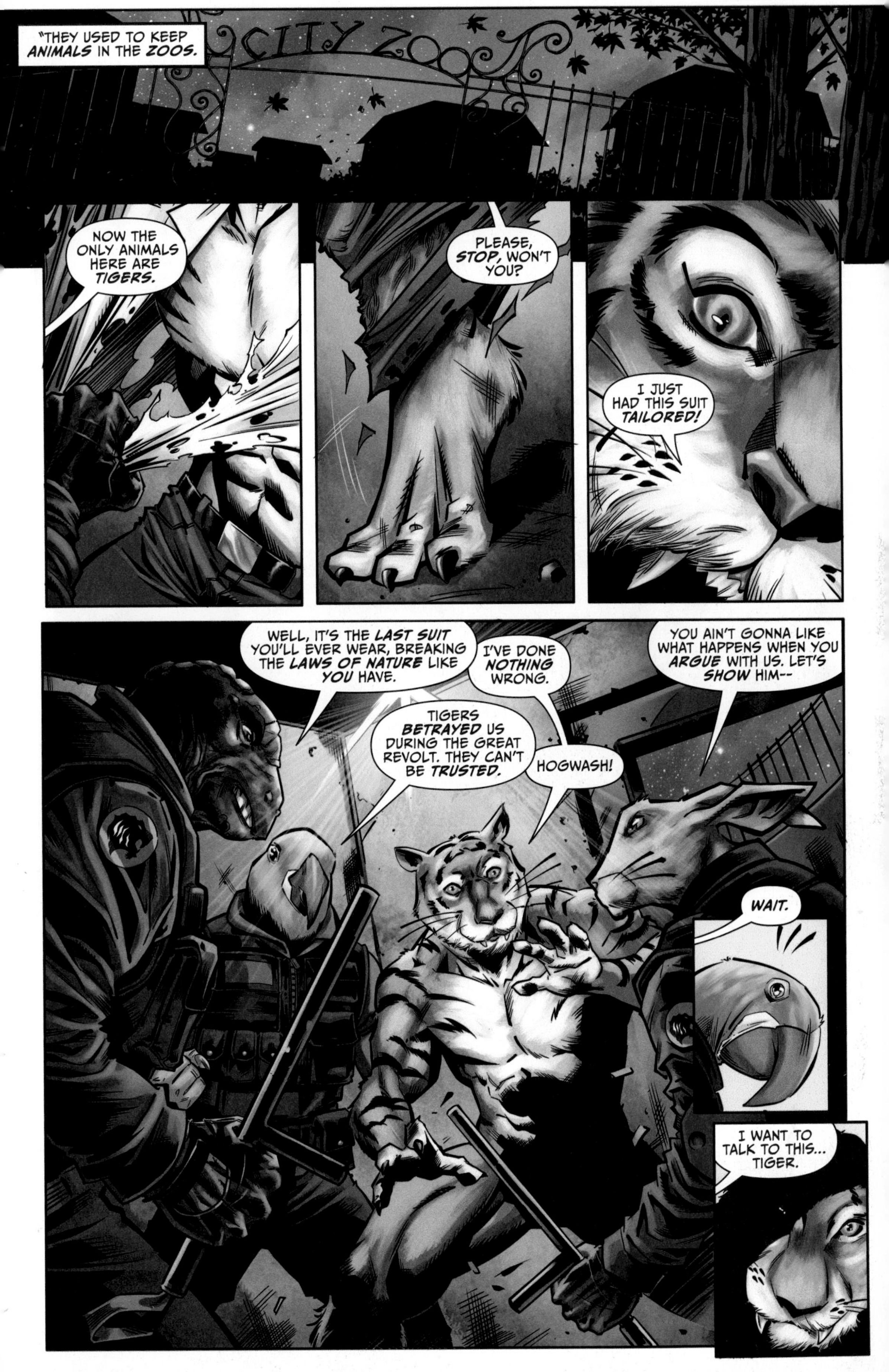
"THEY USED TO KEEP ANIMALS IN THE ZOOS.
CITY ZOO
NOW THE ONLY ANIMALS HERE ARE TIGERS.
PLEASE, STOP, WON'T YOU?
I JUST HAD THIS SUIT TAILORED!
WELL, IT'S THE LAST SUIT YOU'LL EVER WEAR, BREAKING THE LAWS OF NATURE LIKE YOU HAVE.
I'VE DONE NOTHING WRONG.
TIGERS BETRAYED US DURING THE GREAT REVOLT. THEY CAN'T BE TRUSTED.
HOGWASH!
YOU AIN'T GONNA LIKE WHAT HAPPENS WHEN YOU ARGUE WITH US. LET'S SHOW HIM--
WAIT.
I WANT TO TALK TO THIS... TIGER.

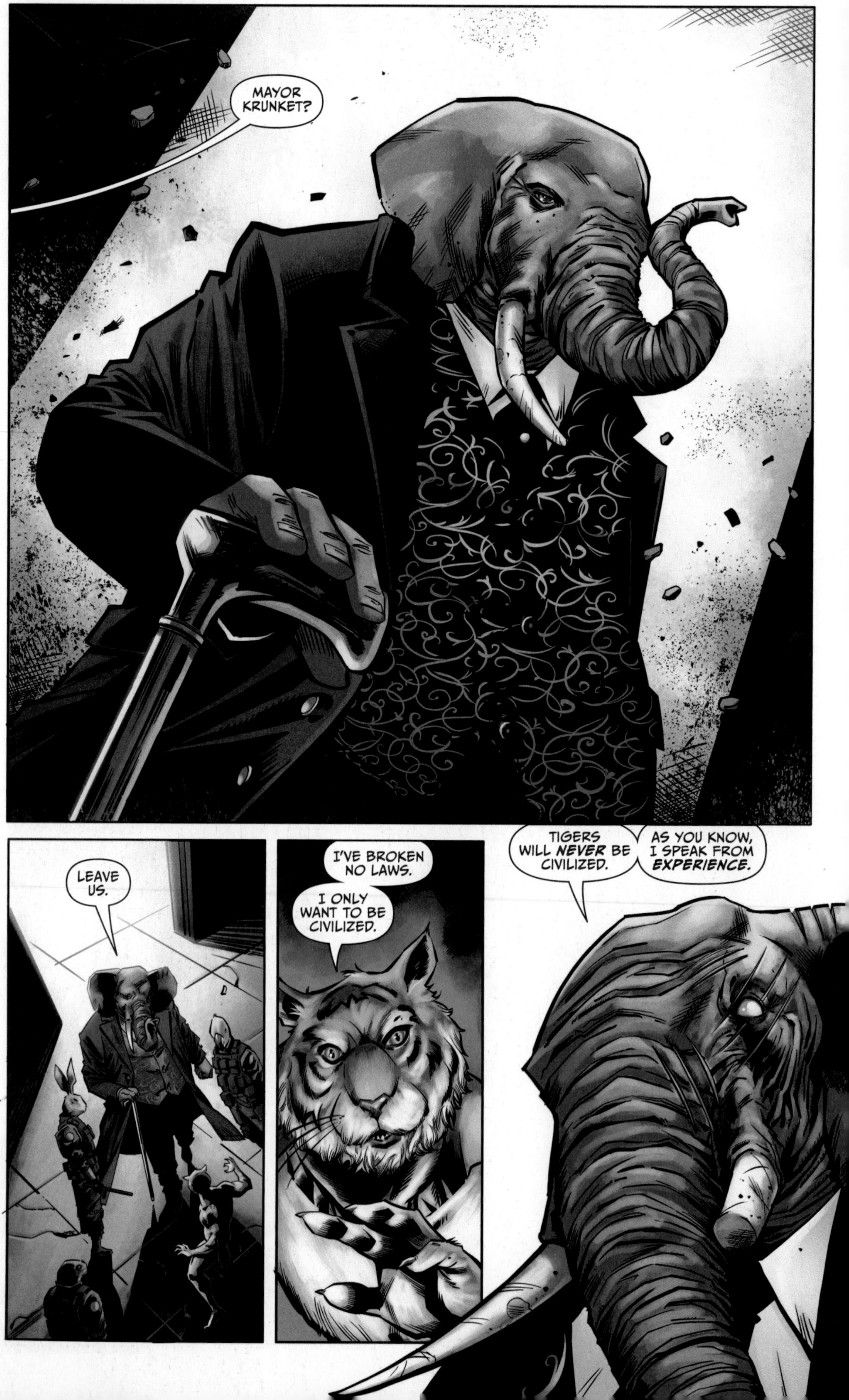
MAYOR KRUNKET?
LEAVE US.
I'VE BROKEN NO LAWS.
I ONLY WANT TO BE CIVILIZED.
TIGERS WILL NEVER BE CIVILIZED.
AS YOU KNOW, I SPEAK FROM EXPERIENCE.

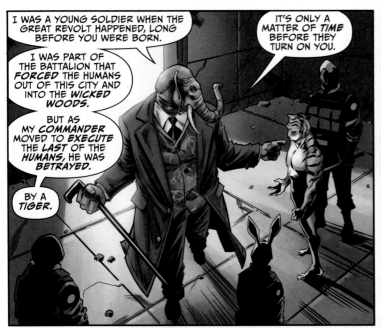

I WAS A YOUNG SOLDIER WHEN THE GREAT REVOLT HAPPENED, LONG BEFORE YOU WERE BORN.

I WAS PART OF THE BATTALION THAT *FORCED* THE HUMANS OUT OF THIS CITY AND INTO THE *WICKED WOODS.*

BUT AS MY *COMMANDER* MOVED TO *EXECUTE* THE *LAST* OF THE *HUMANS,* HE WAS *BETRAYED.*

BY A *TIGER.*

IT'S ONLY A MATTER OF *TIME* BEFORE THEY TURN ON YOU.

NOT *ALL* TIGERS ARE LIKE THAT.

THEY ARE *SAVAGES!*

WORSE THAN HUMANS!

YOU *WANT TO ATTACK* ME *NOW,* DON'T YOU? Hm?

I *KNOW* YOU'RE *HUNGRY.* WE'VE KEPT YOU WITHOUT *FOOD* FOR *QUITE* SOME TIME.

YOU OBVIOUSLY CAN *READ* GIVEN THE *FORBIDDEN LITERATURE* THAT WAS FOUND IN YOUR POSSESSION...

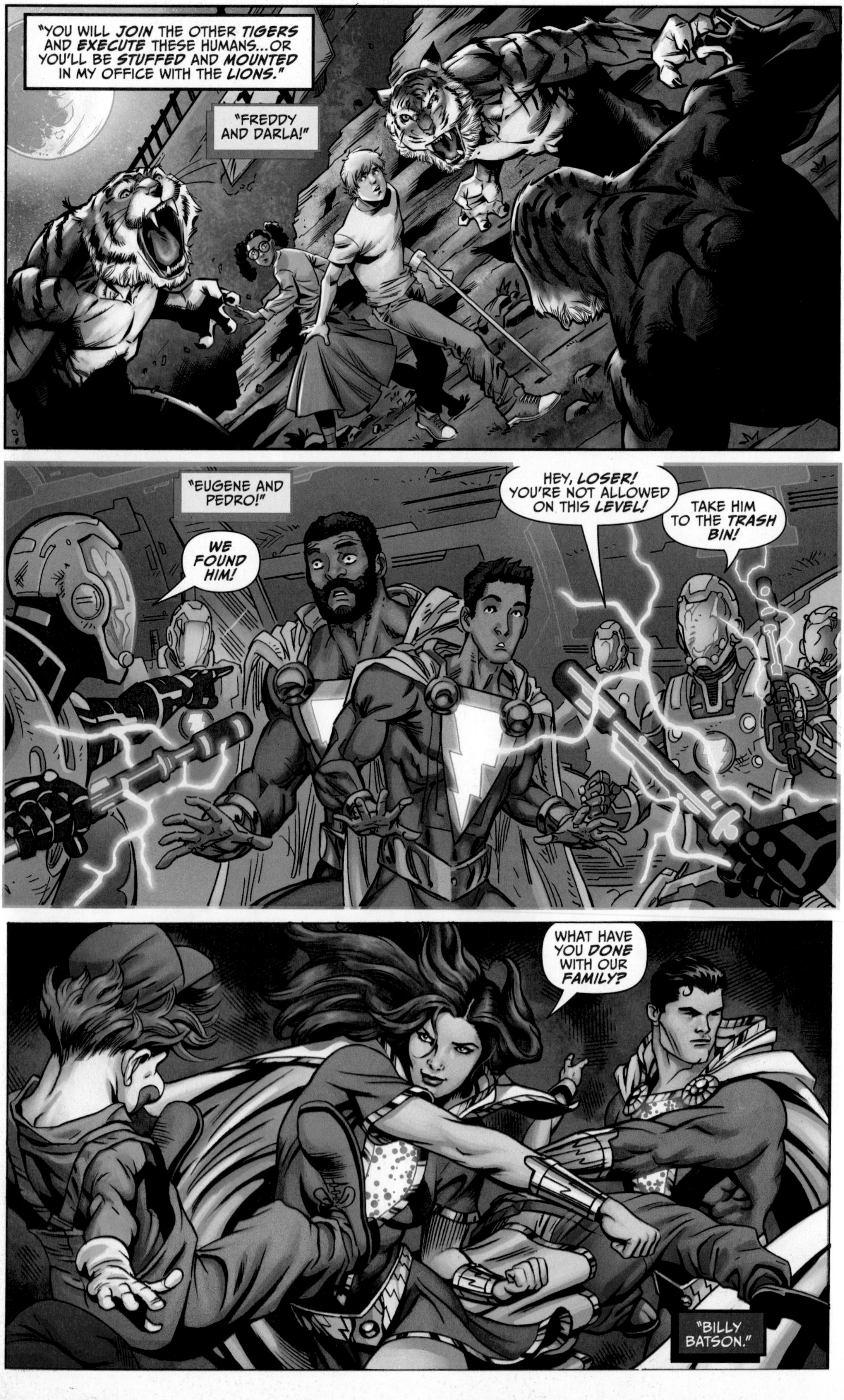
"YOU WILL JOIN THE OTHER TIGERS AND EXECUTE THESE HUMANS...OR YOU'LL BE STUFFED AND MOUNTED IN MY OFFICE WITH THE LIONS."
"FREDDY AND DARLA!"
"EUGENE AND PEDRO!"
WE FOUND HIM!
HEY, LOSER! YOU'RE NOT ALLOWED ON THIS LEVEL!
TAKE HIM TO THE TRASH BIN!
WHAT HAVE YOU DONE WITH OUR FAMILY?
"BILLY BATSON."

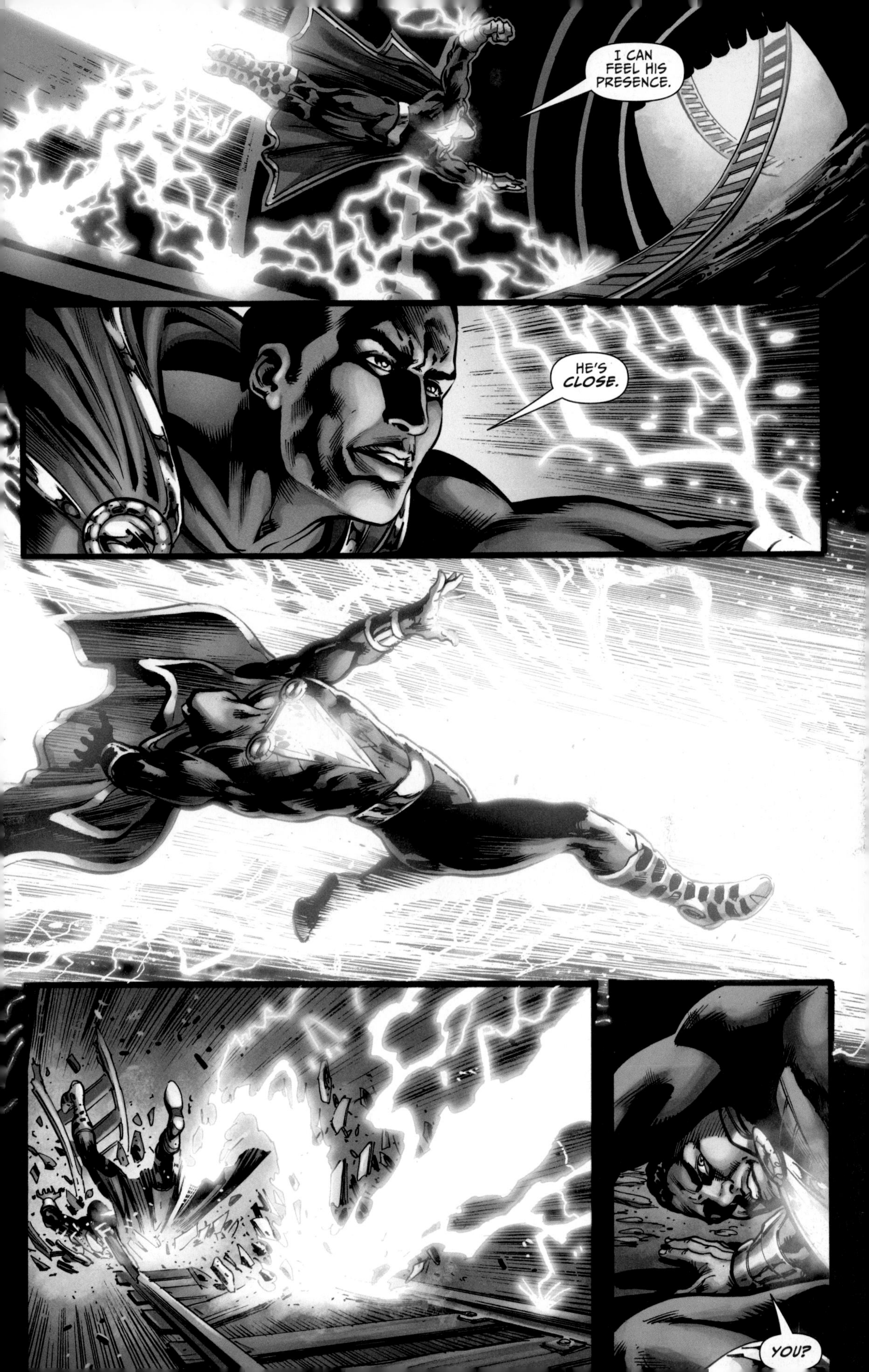
I CAN FEEL HIS PRESENCE.
HE'S CLOSE.
YOU?

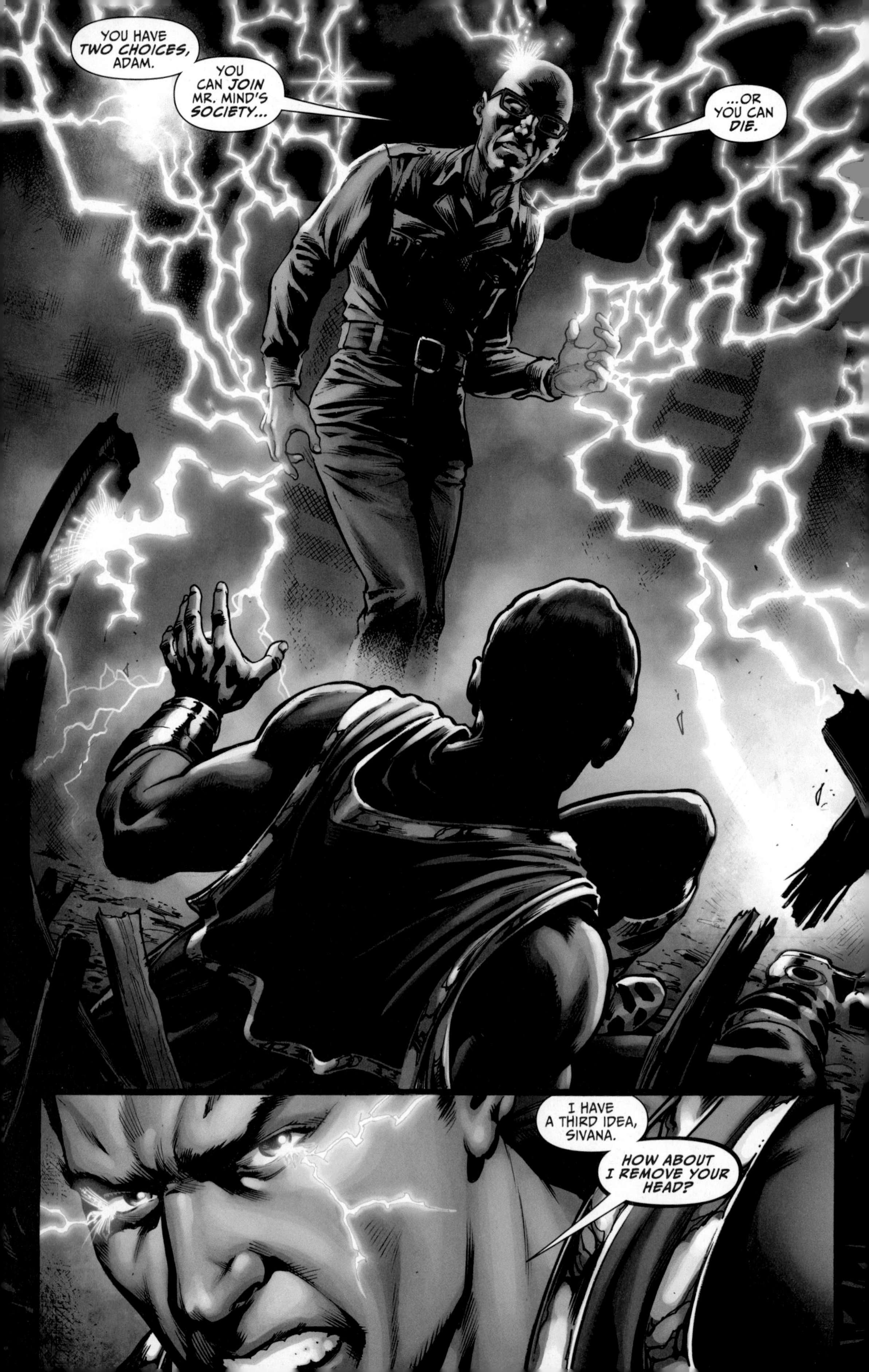
YOU HAVE TWO CHOICES, ADAM.
YOU CAN JOIN MR. MIND'S SOCIETY...
...OR YOU CAN DIE.
I HAVE A THIRD IDEA, SIVANA.
HOW ABOUT I REMOVE YOUR HEAD?

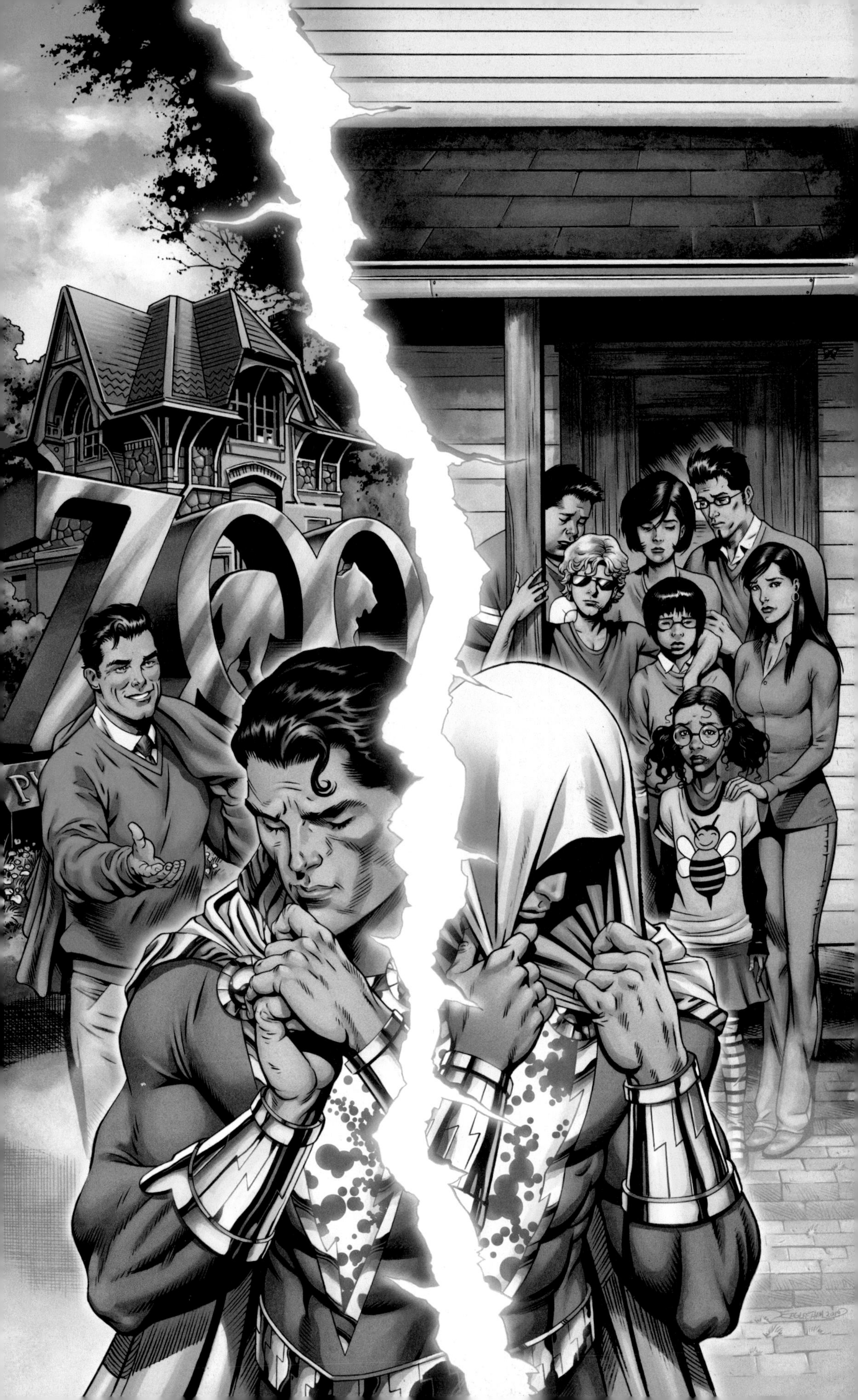

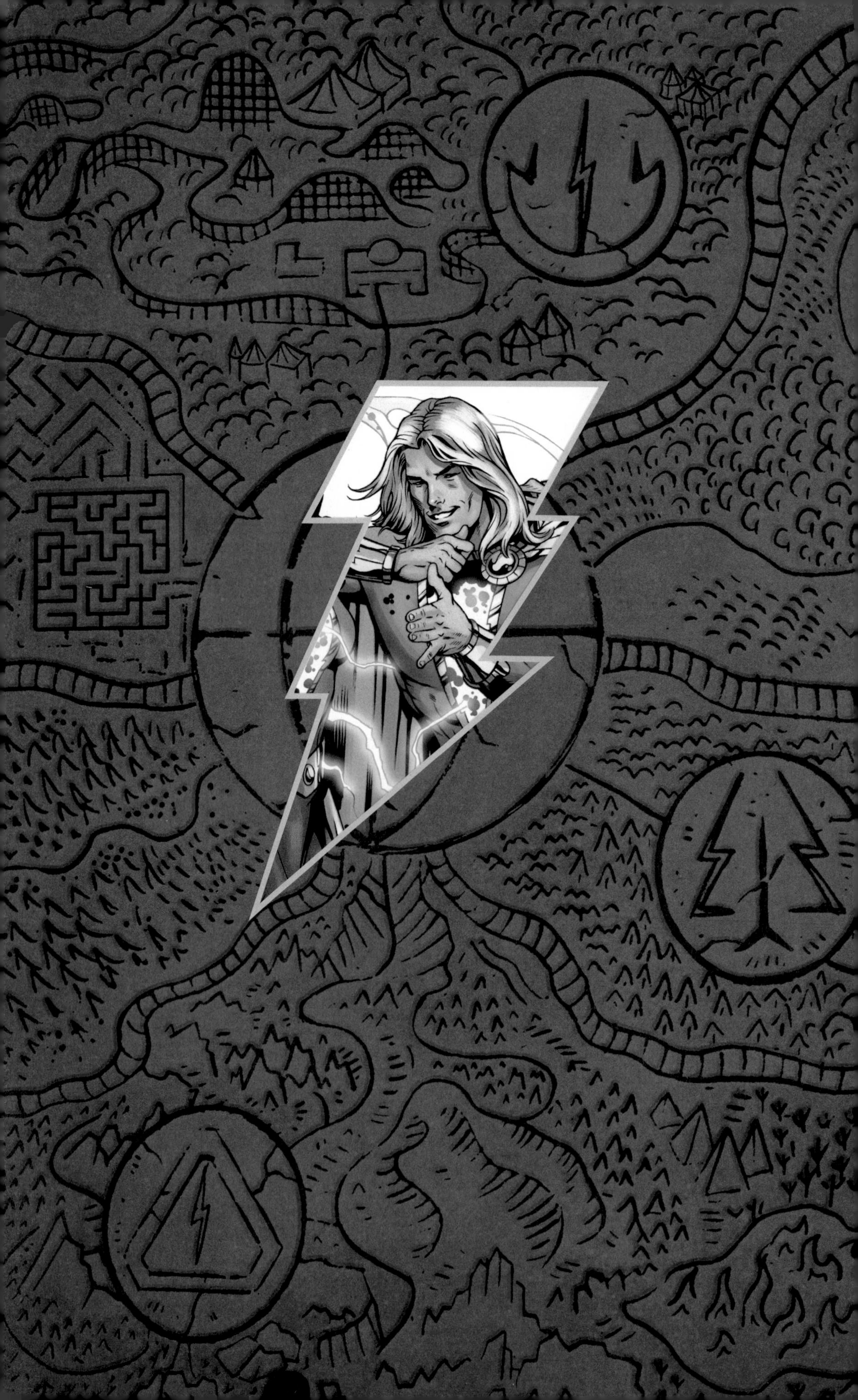

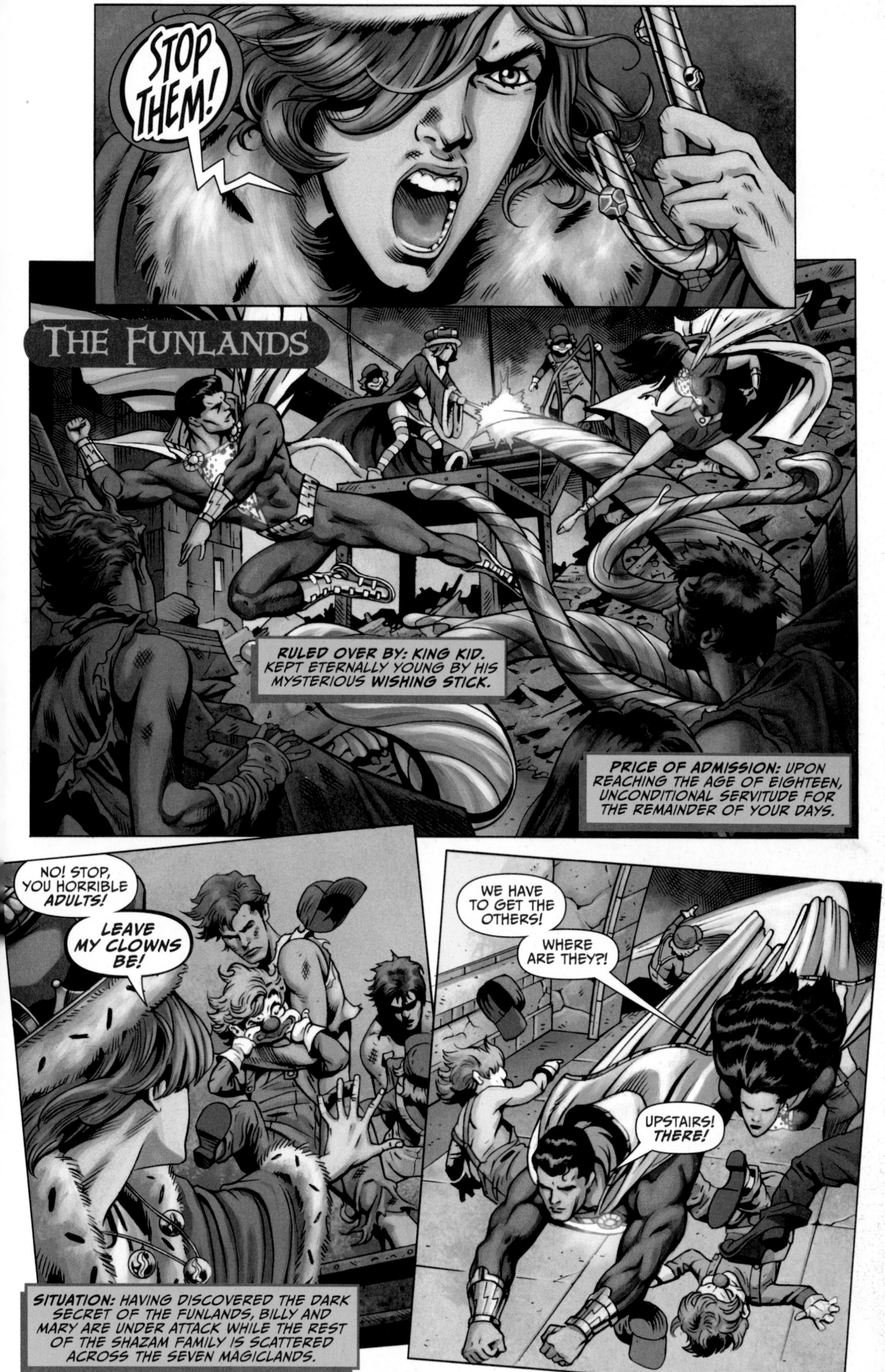
STOP THEM!
THE FUNLANDS
RULED OVER BY: KING KID. KEPT ETERNALLY YOUNG BY HIS MYSTERIOUS WISHING STICK.
PRICE OF ADMISSION: UPON REACHING THE AGE OF EIGHTEEN, UNCONDITIONAL SERVITUDE FOR THE REMAINDER OF YOUR DAYS.
NO! STOP, YOU HORRIBLE ADULTS!
LEAVE MY CLOWNS BE!
SITUATION: HAVING DISCOVERED THE DARK SECRET OF THE FUNLANDS, BILLY AND MARY ARE UNDER ATTACK WHILE THE REST OF THE SHAZAM FAMILY IS SCATTERED ACROSS THE SEVEN MAGICLANDS.
WE HAVE TO GET THE OTHERS!
WHERE ARE THEY?!
UPSTAIRS! THERE!

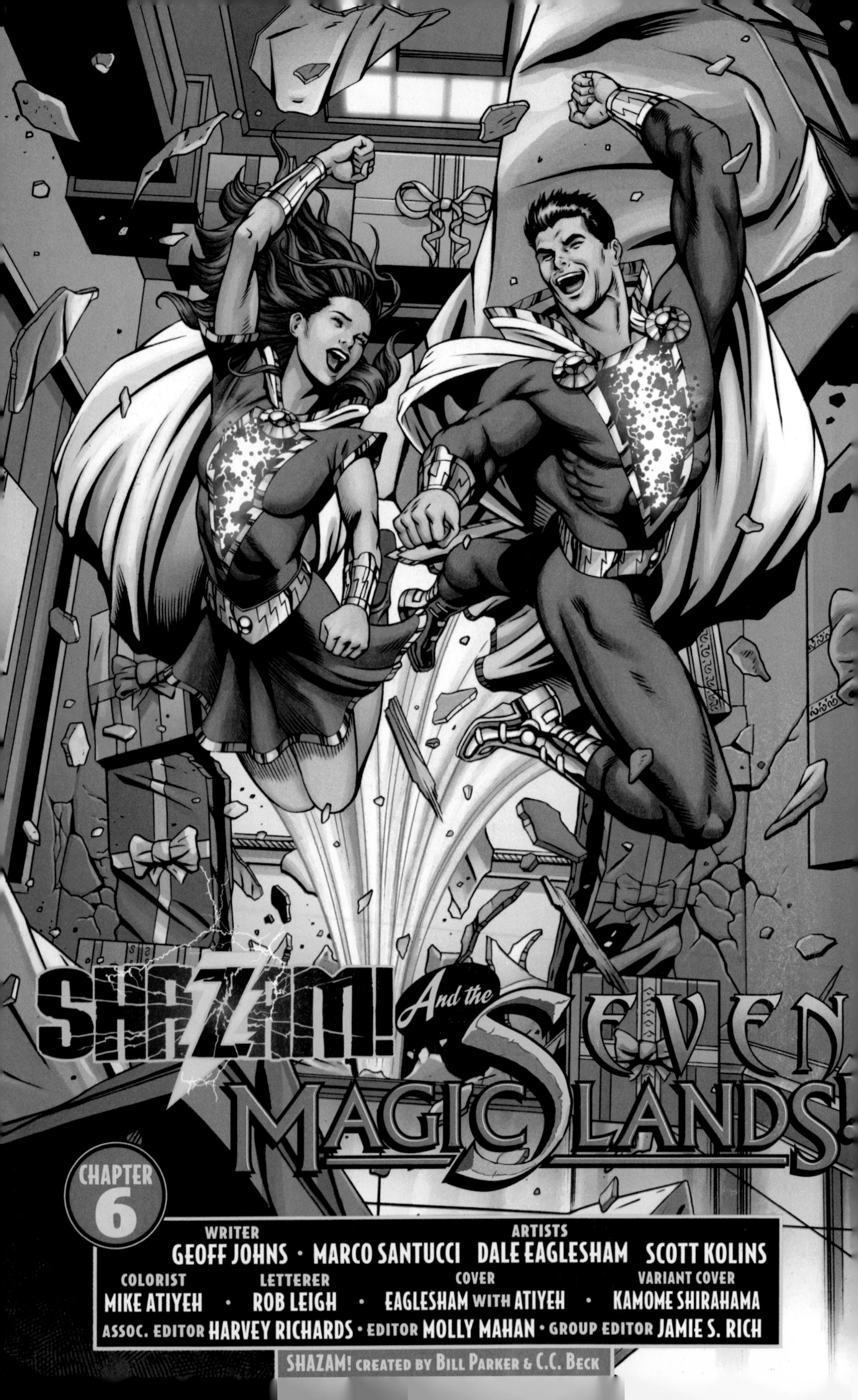
SHAZAM! And the SEVEN MAGIC LANDS!
CHAPTER 6
WRITER
GEOFF JOHNS
ARTISTS
MARCO SANTUCCI · DALE EAGLESHAM · SCOTT KOLINS
COLORIST
MIKE ATIYEH
LETTERER
ROB LEIGH
COVER
EAGLESHAM WITH ATIYEH
VARIANT COVER
KAMOME SHIRAHAMA
ASSOC. EDITOR HARVEY RICHARDS · EDITOR MOLLY MAHAN · GROUP EDITOR JAMIE S. RICH
SHAZAM! CREATED BY BILL PARKER & C.C. BECK

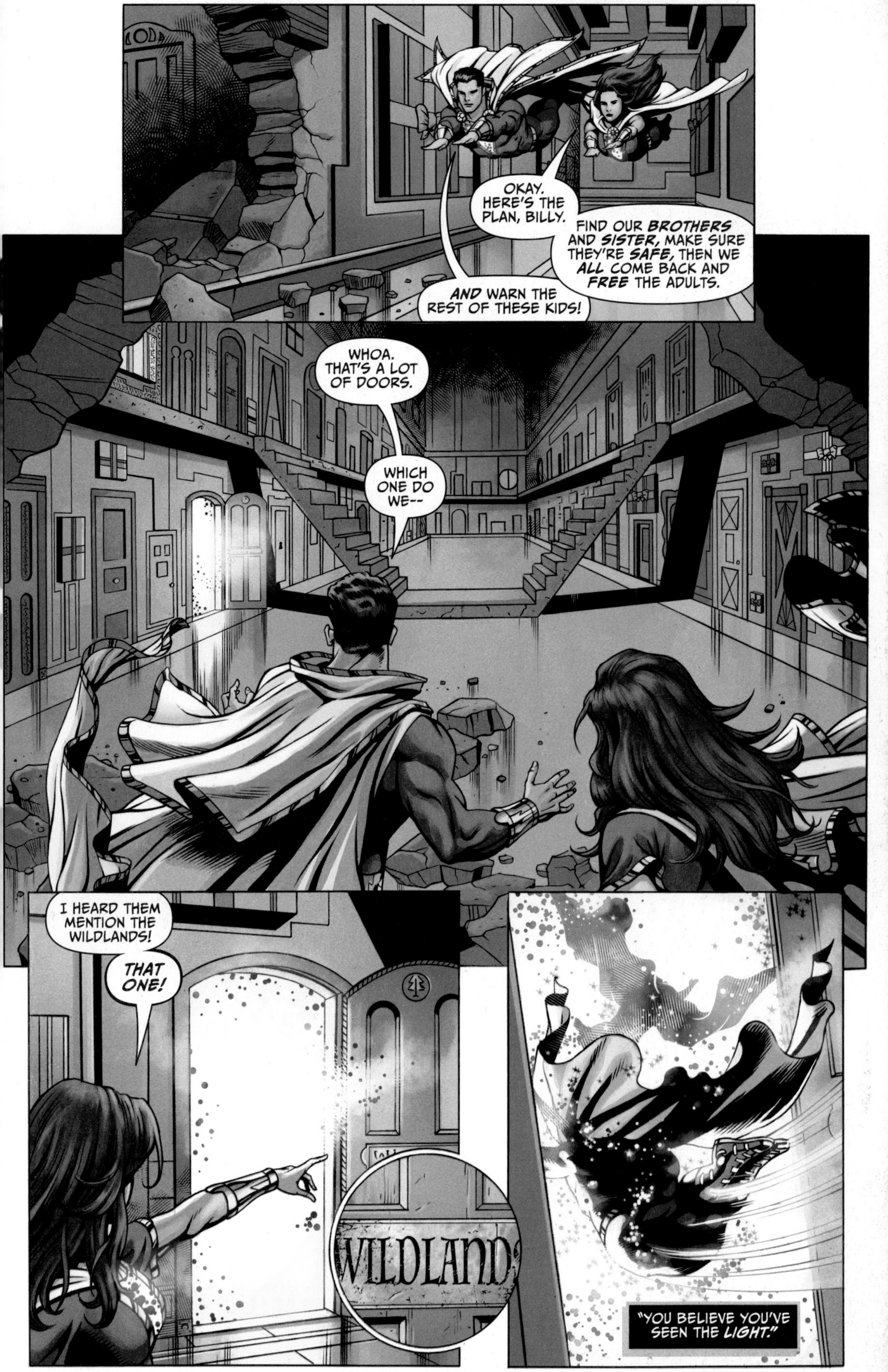
OKAY. HERE'S THE PLAN, BILLY.
FIND OUR BROTHERS AND SISTER, MAKE SURE THEY'RE SAFE, THEN WE ALL COME BACK AND FREE THE ADULTS.
AND WARN THE REST OF THESE KIDS!
WHOA. THAT'S A LOT OF DOORS.
WHICH ONE DO WE--
I HEARD THEM MENTION THE WILDLANDS!
THAT ONE!
WILDLANDS
"YOU BELIEVE YOU'VE SEEN THE LIGHT."

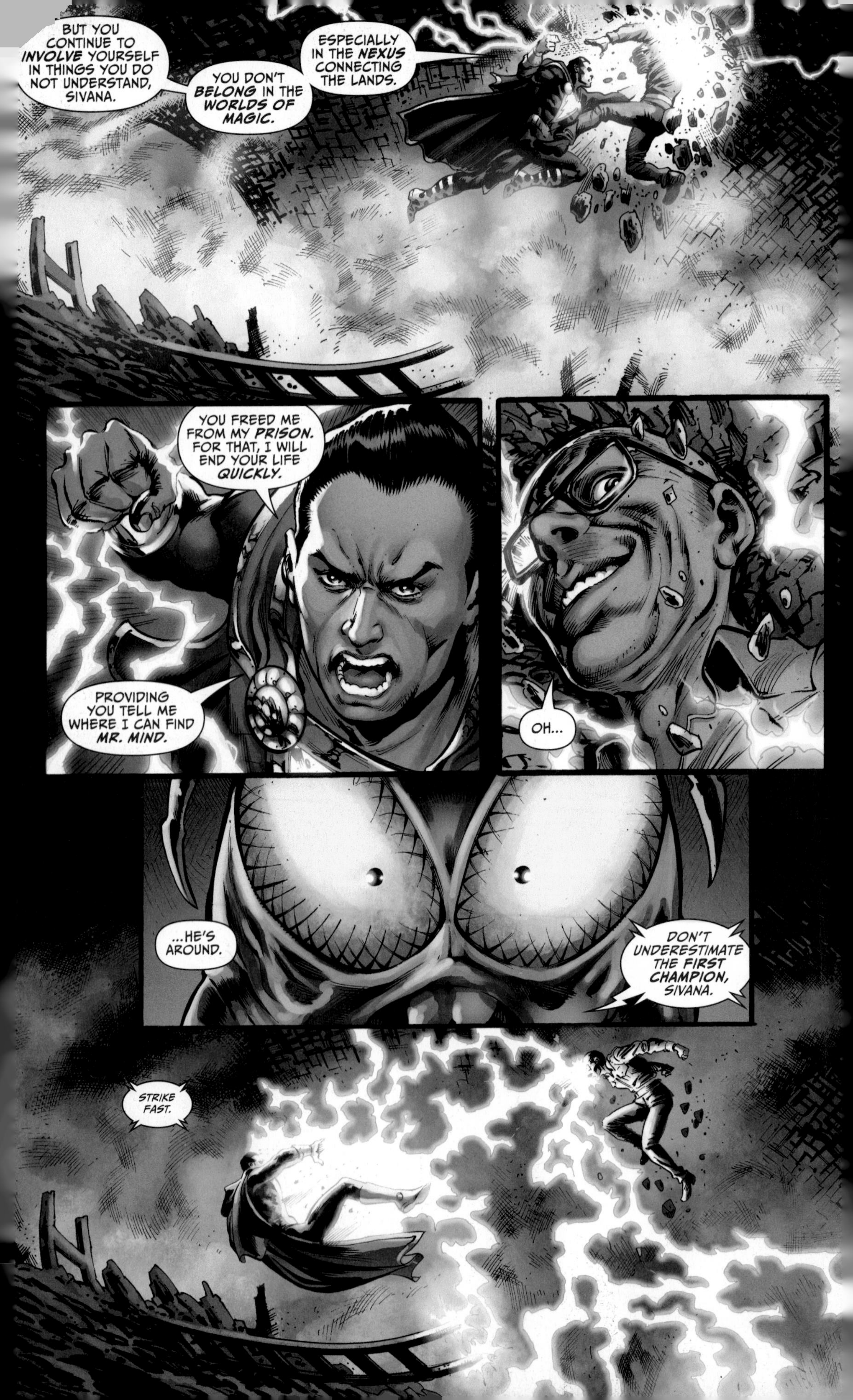
BUT YOU CONTINUE TO INVOLVE YOURSELF IN THINGS YOU DO NOT UNDERSTAND, SIVANA.
YOU DON'T BELONG IN THE WORLDS OF MAGIC.
ESPECIALLY IN THE NEXUS CONNECTING THE LANDS.
YOU FREED ME FROM MY PRISON. FOR THAT, I WILL END YOUR LIFE QUICKLY.
PROVIDING YOU TELL ME WHERE I CAN FIND MR. MIND.
OH...
...HE'S AROUND.
DON'T UNDERESTIMATE THE FIRST CHAMPION, SIVANA.
STRIKE FAST.

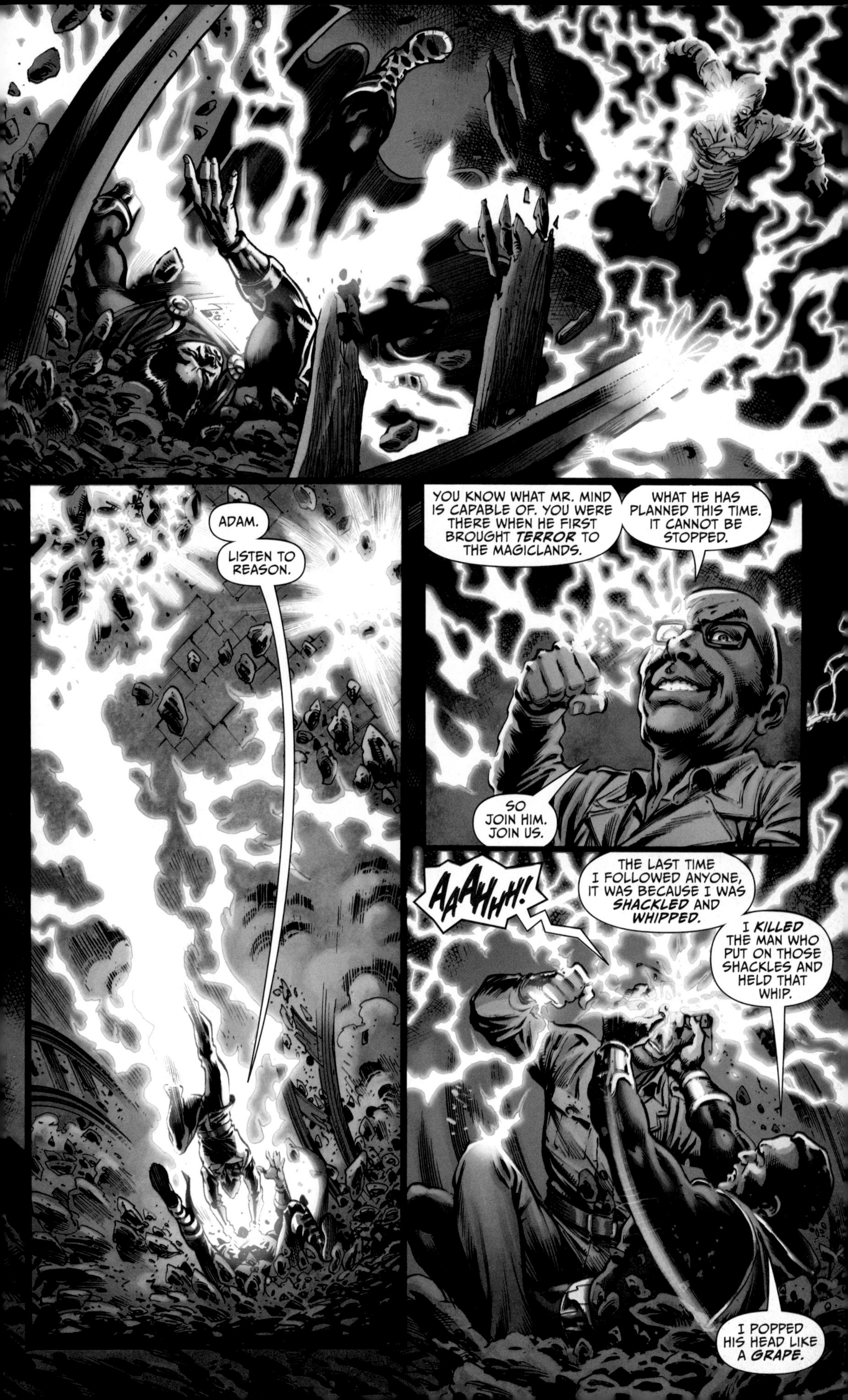
ADAM.
LISTEN TO REASON.
YOU KNOW WHAT MR. MIND IS CAPABLE OF. YOU WERE THERE WHEN HE FIRST BROUGHT TERROR TO THE MAGICLANDS.
WHAT HE HAS PLANNED THIS TIME. IT CANNOT BE STOPPED.
SO JOIN HIM. JOIN US.
AAAHHH!
THE LAST TIME I FOLLOWED ANYONE, IT WAS BECAUSE I WAS SHACKLED AND WHIPPED.
I KILLED THE MAN WHO PUT ON THOSE SHACKLES AND HELD THAT WHIP.
I POPPED HIS HEAD LIKE A GRAPE.

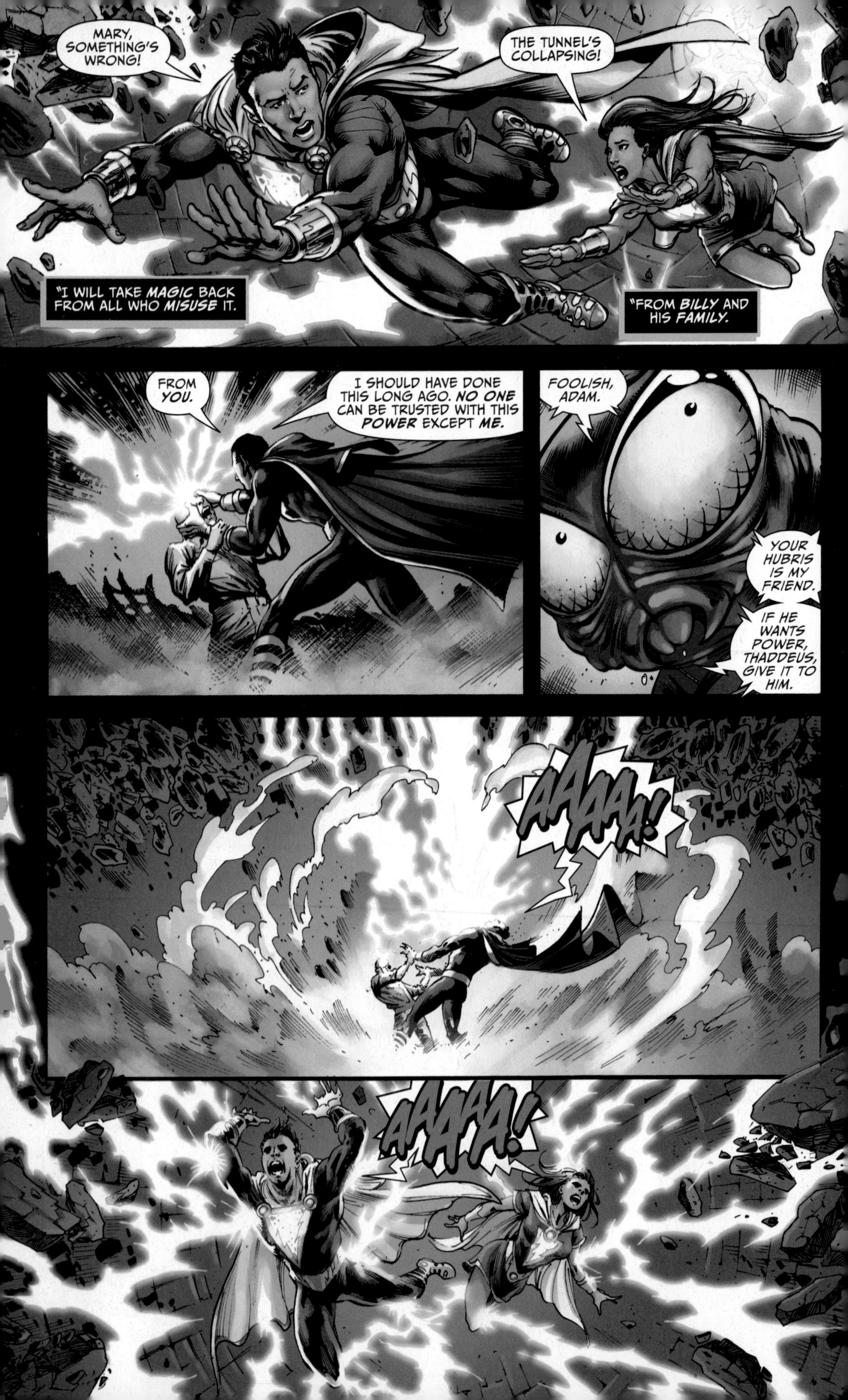
MARY, SOMETHING'S WRONG!
THE TUNNEL'S COLLAPSING!
"I WILL TAKE MAGIC BACK FROM ALL WHO MISUSE IT.
"FROM BILLY AND HIS FAMILY.
FROM YOU.
I SHOULD HAVE DONE THIS LONG AGO. NO ONE CAN BE TRUSTED WITH THIS POWER EXCEPT ME.
FOOLISH, ADAM.
YOUR HUBRIS IS MY FRIEND.
IF HE WANTS POWER, THADDEUS, GIVE IT TO HIM.
AAAAA!
AAAAA!

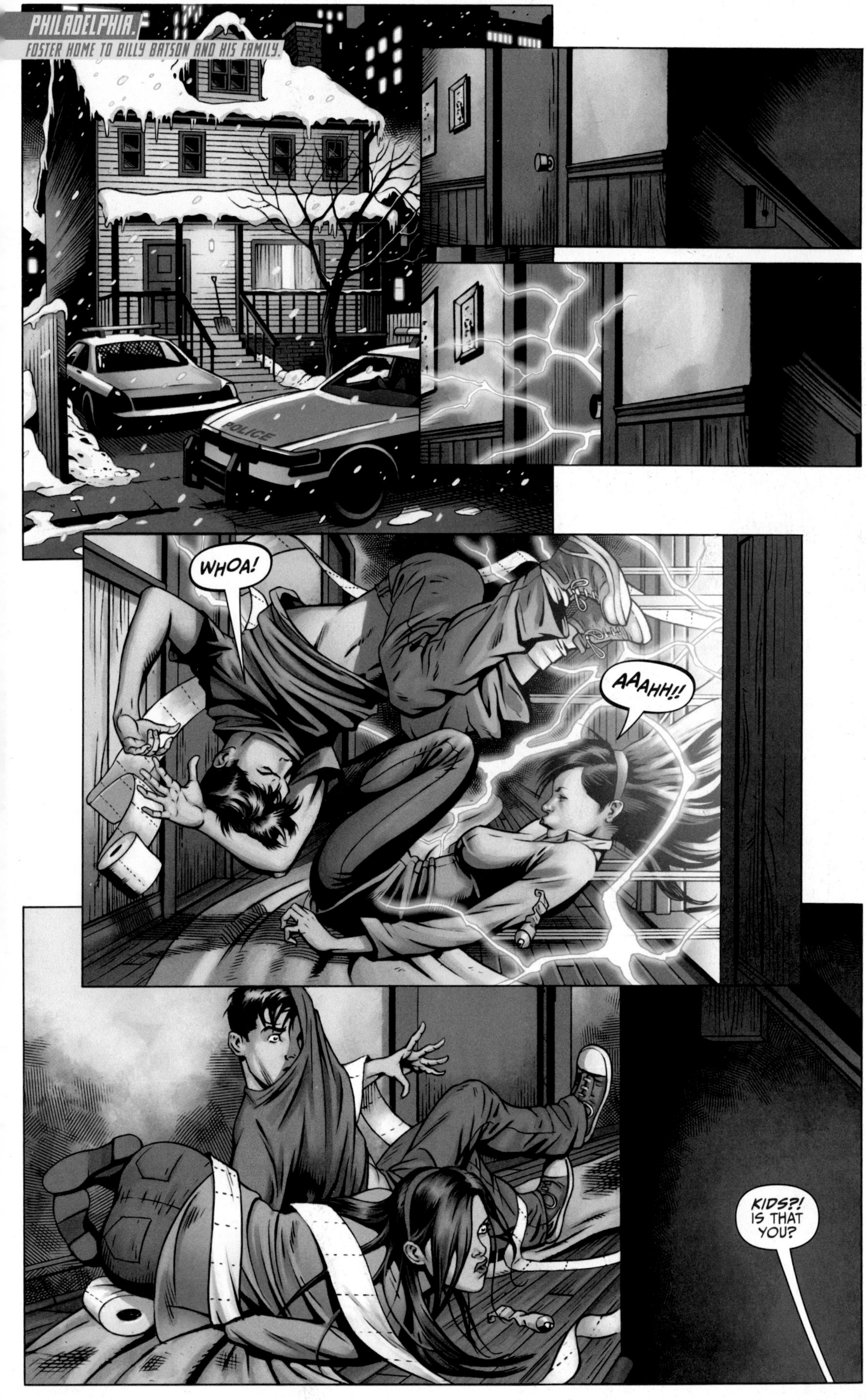
PHILADELPHIA.
FOSTER HOME TO BILLY BATSON AND HIS FAMILY.
POLICE
WHOA!
AAAHH!!
KIDS?! IS THAT YOU?

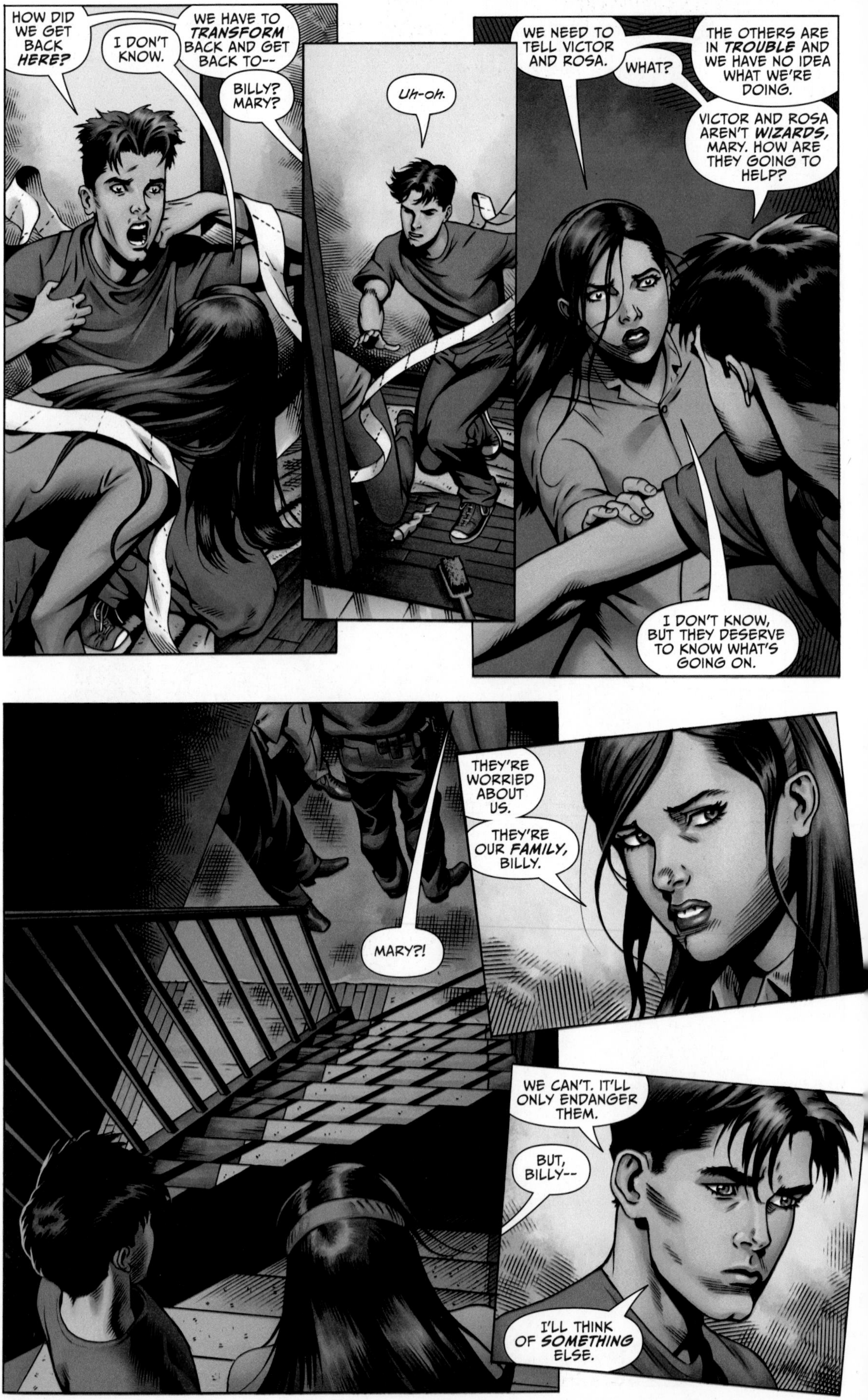
HOW DID WE GET BACK HERE?
I DON'T KNOW.
WE HAVE TO TRANSFORM BACK AND GET BACK TO--
BILLY? MARY?
Uh-oh.
WE NEED TO TELL VICTOR AND ROSA.
WHAT?
THE OTHERS ARE IN TROUBLE AND WE HAVE NO IDEA WHAT WE'RE DOING.
VICTOR AND ROSA AREN'T WIZARDS, MARY. HOW ARE THEY GOING TO HELP?
I DON'T KNOW, BUT THEY DESERVE TO KNOW WHAT'S GOING ON.
MARY?!
THEY'RE WORRIED ABOUT US.
THEY'RE OUR FAMILY, BILLY.
WE CAN'T. IT'LL ONLY ENDANGER THEM.
BUT, BILLY--
I'LL THINK OF SOMETHING ELSE.

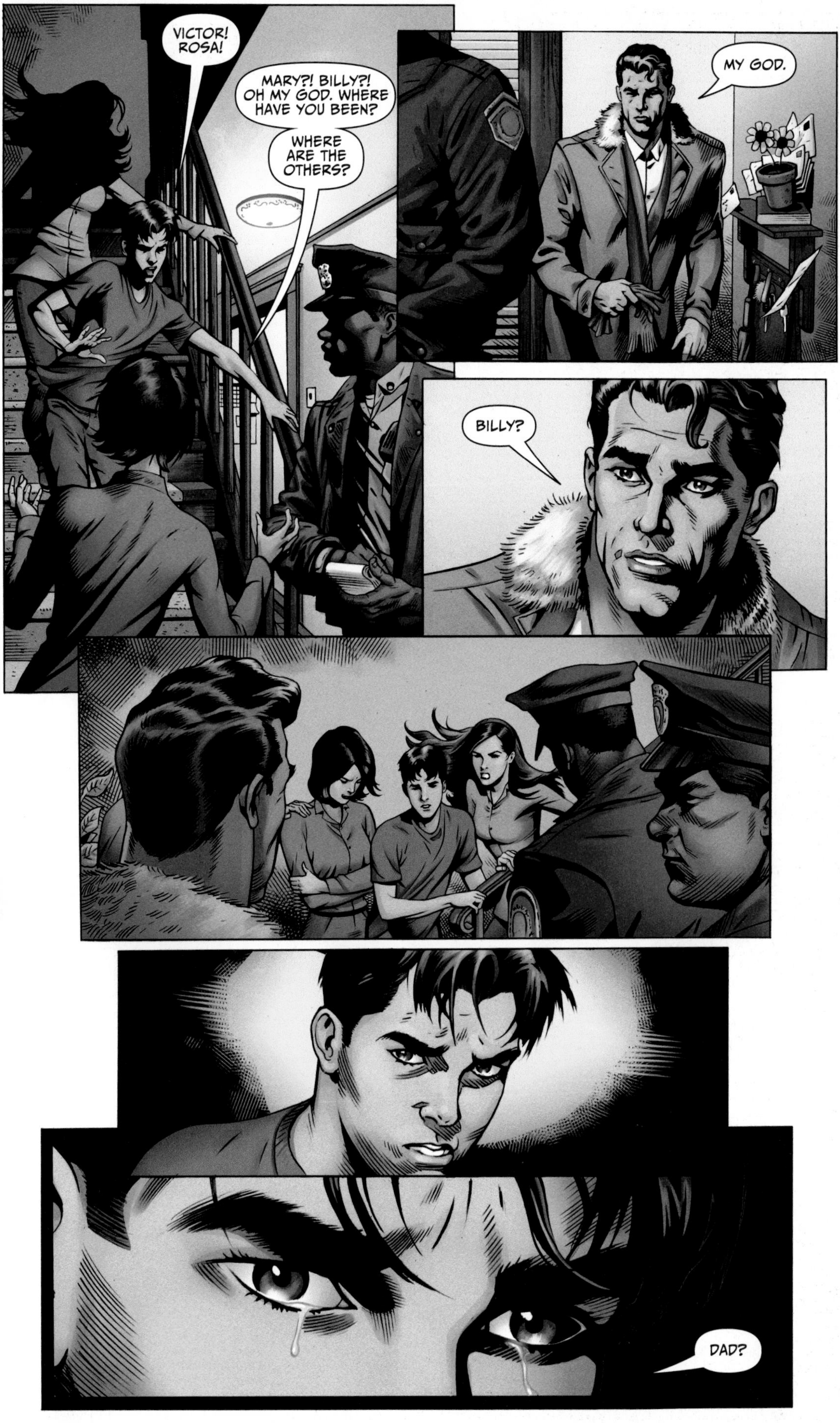
VICTOR! ROSA!
MARY?! BILLY?! OH MY GOD. WHERE HAVE YOU BEEN?
WHERE ARE THE OTHERS?
MY GOD.
BILLY?
DAD?

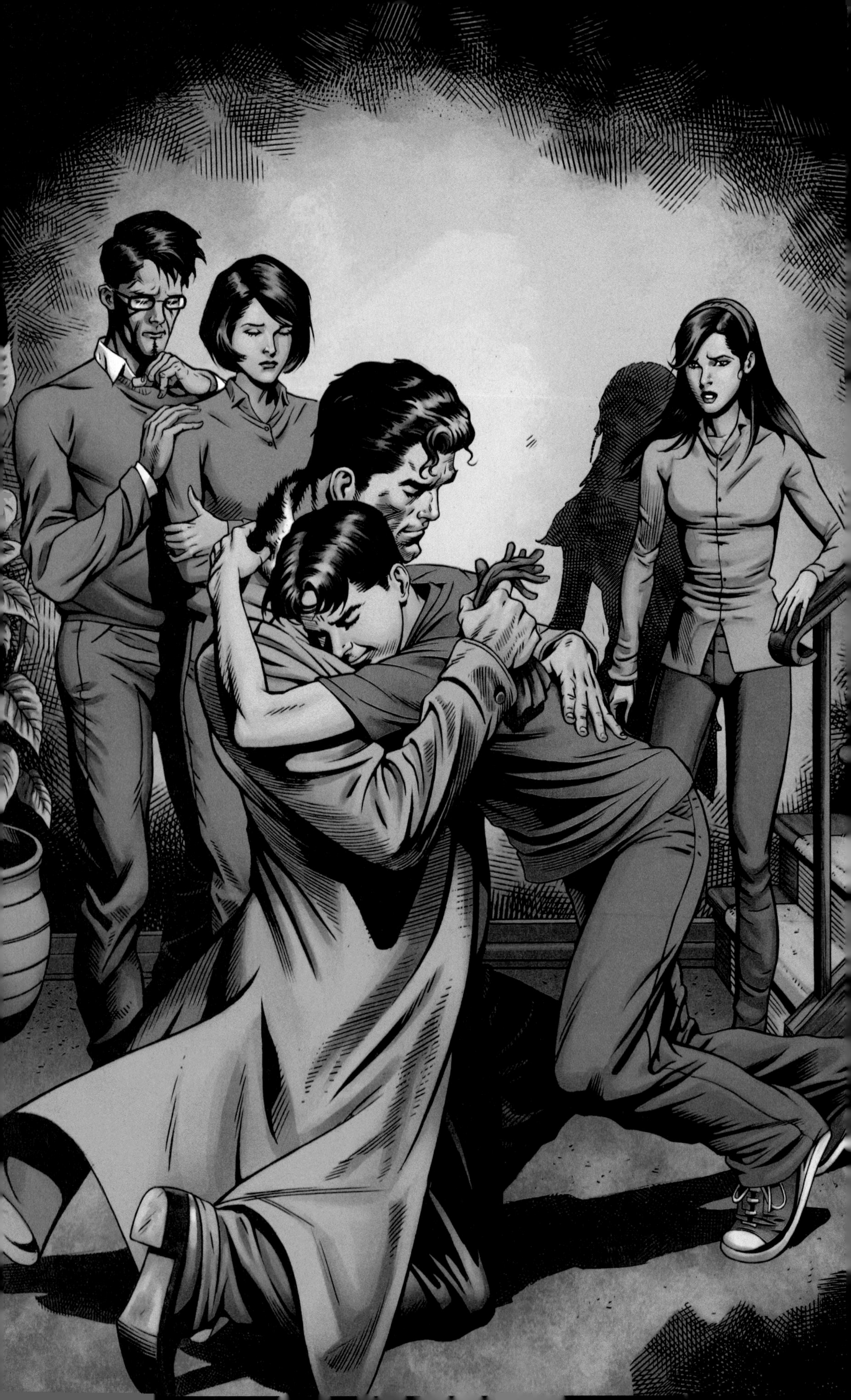

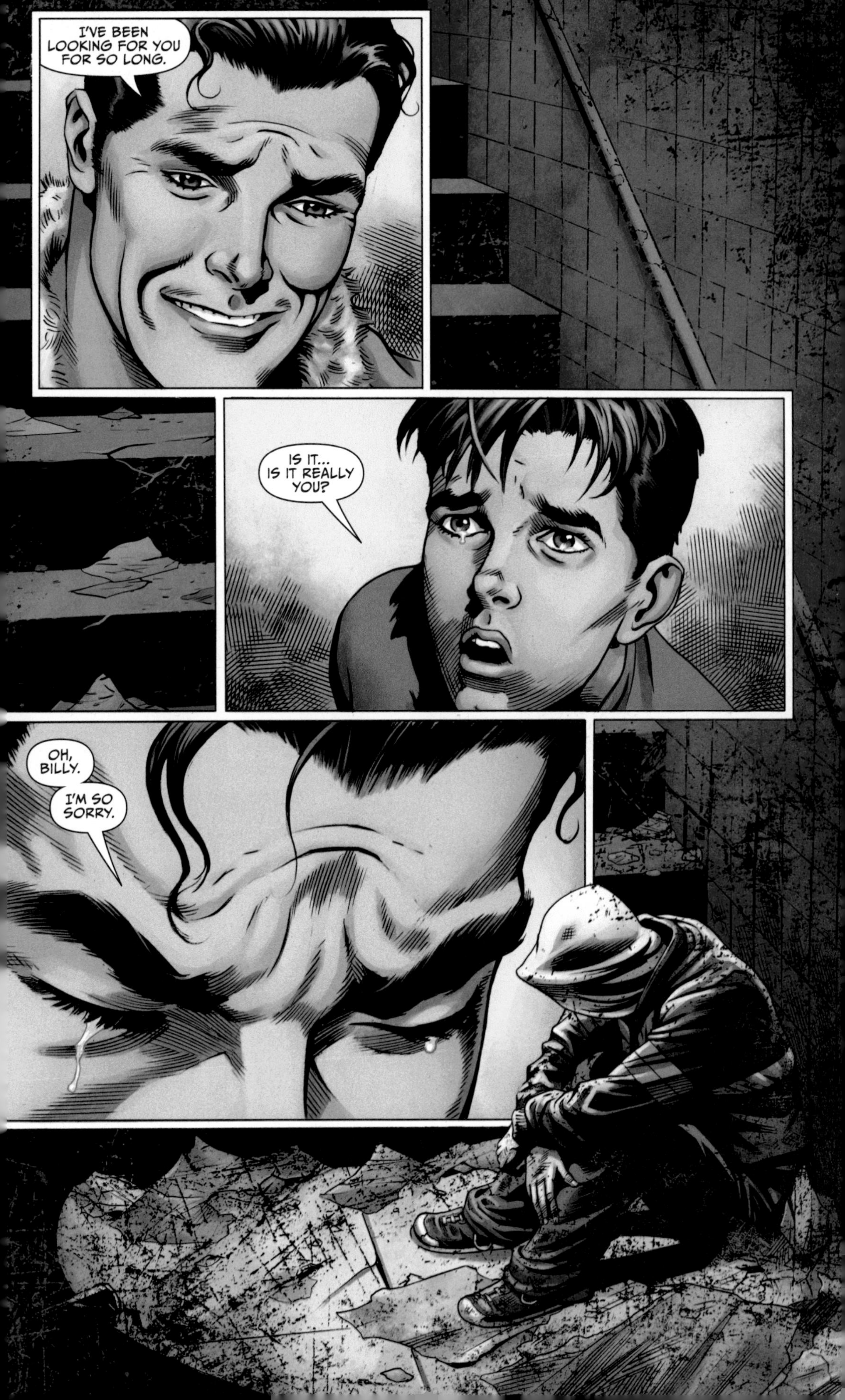
I'VE BEEN LOOKING FOR YOU FOR SO LONG.
IS IT... IS IT REALLY YOU?
OH, BILLY.
I'M SO SORRY.

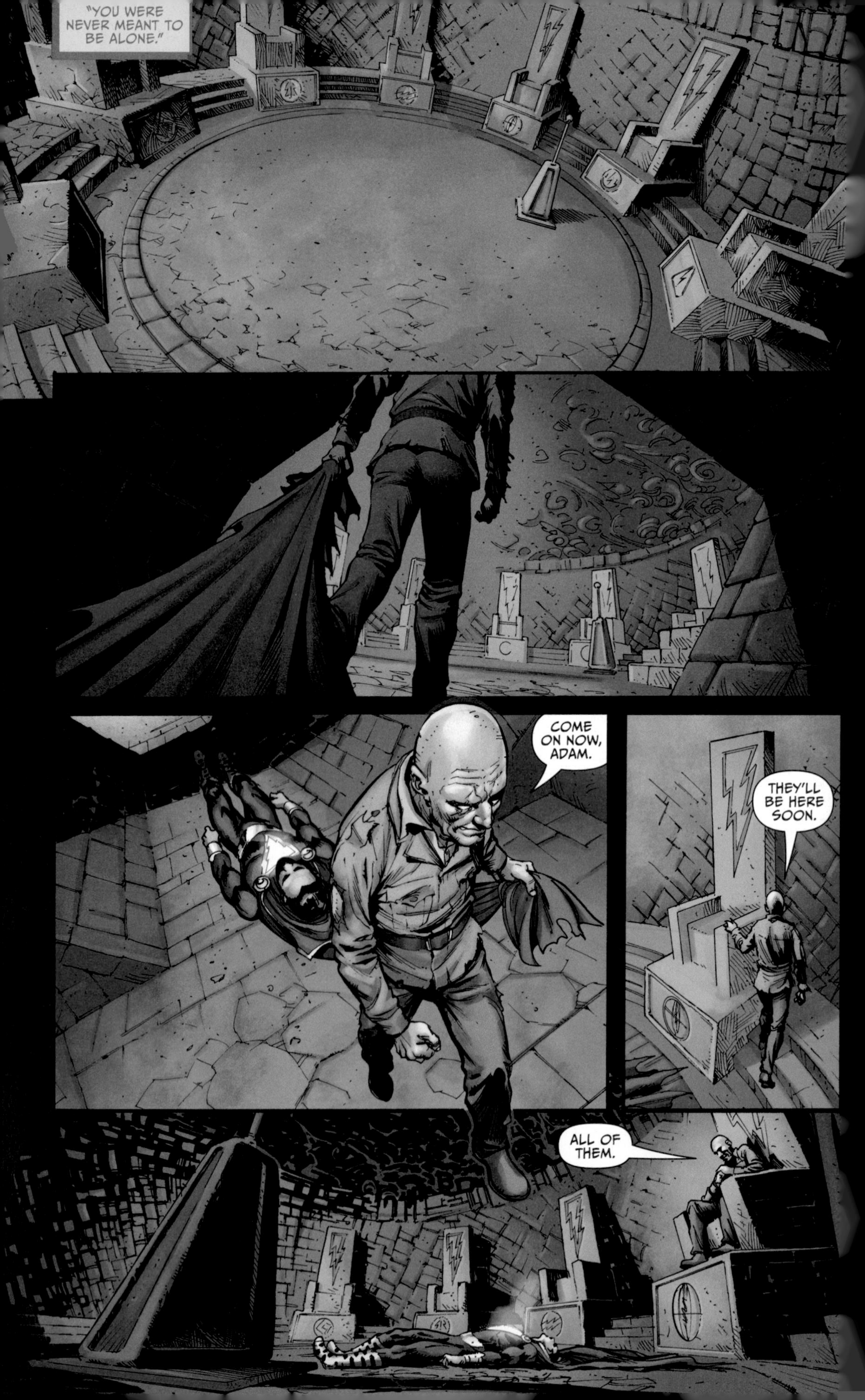
"YOU WERE NEVER MEANT TO BE ALONE."
COME ON NOW, ADAM.
THEY'LL BE HERE SOON.
ALL OF THEM.

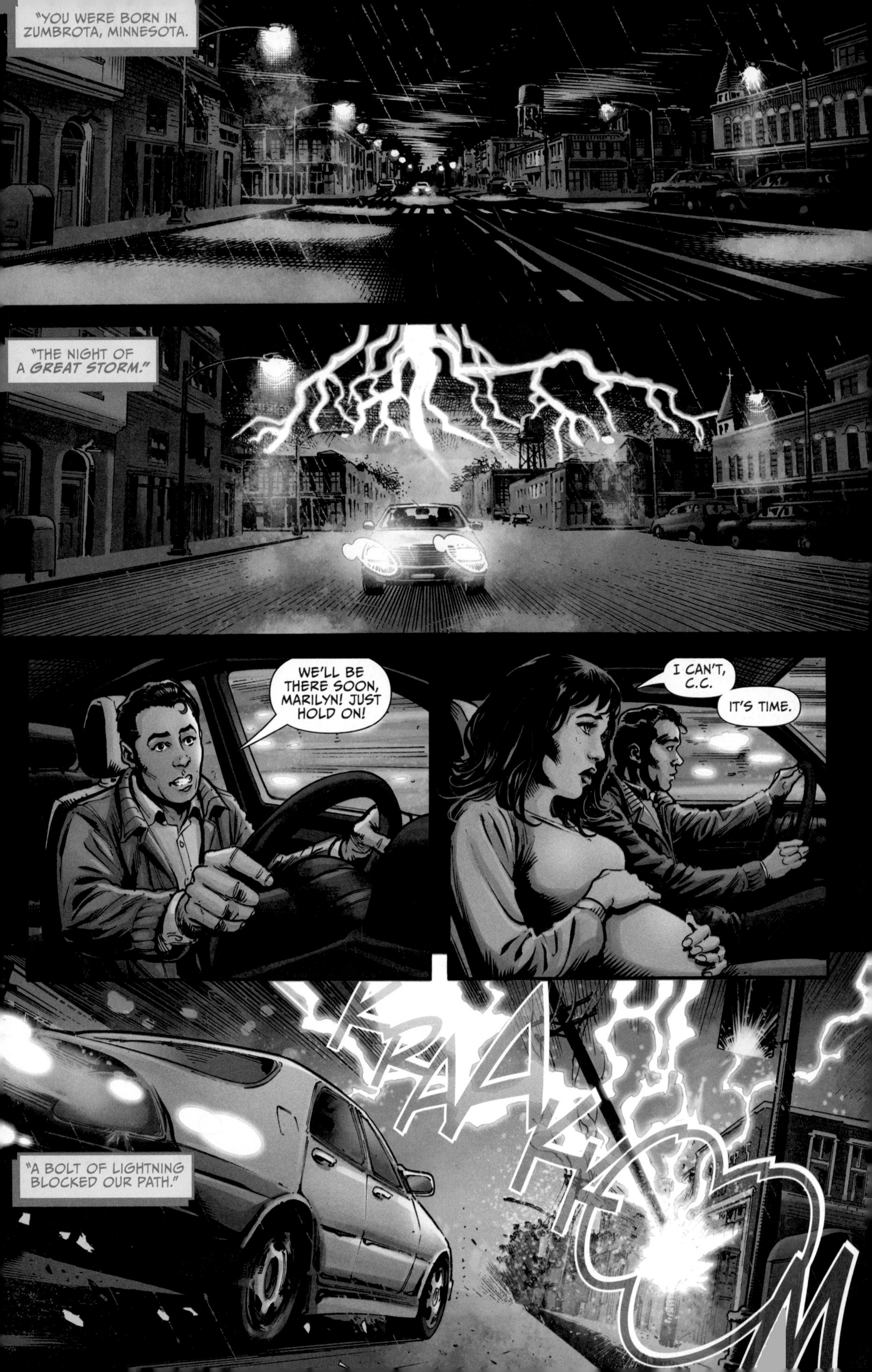
"YOU WERE BORN IN ZUMBROTA, MINNESOTA.
"THE NIGHT OF A GREAT STORM."
WE'LL BE THERE SOON, MARILYN! JUST HOLD ON!
I CAN'T, C.C.
IT'S TIME.
KRAAKOOM
"A BOLT OF LIGHTNING BLOCKED OUR PATH."

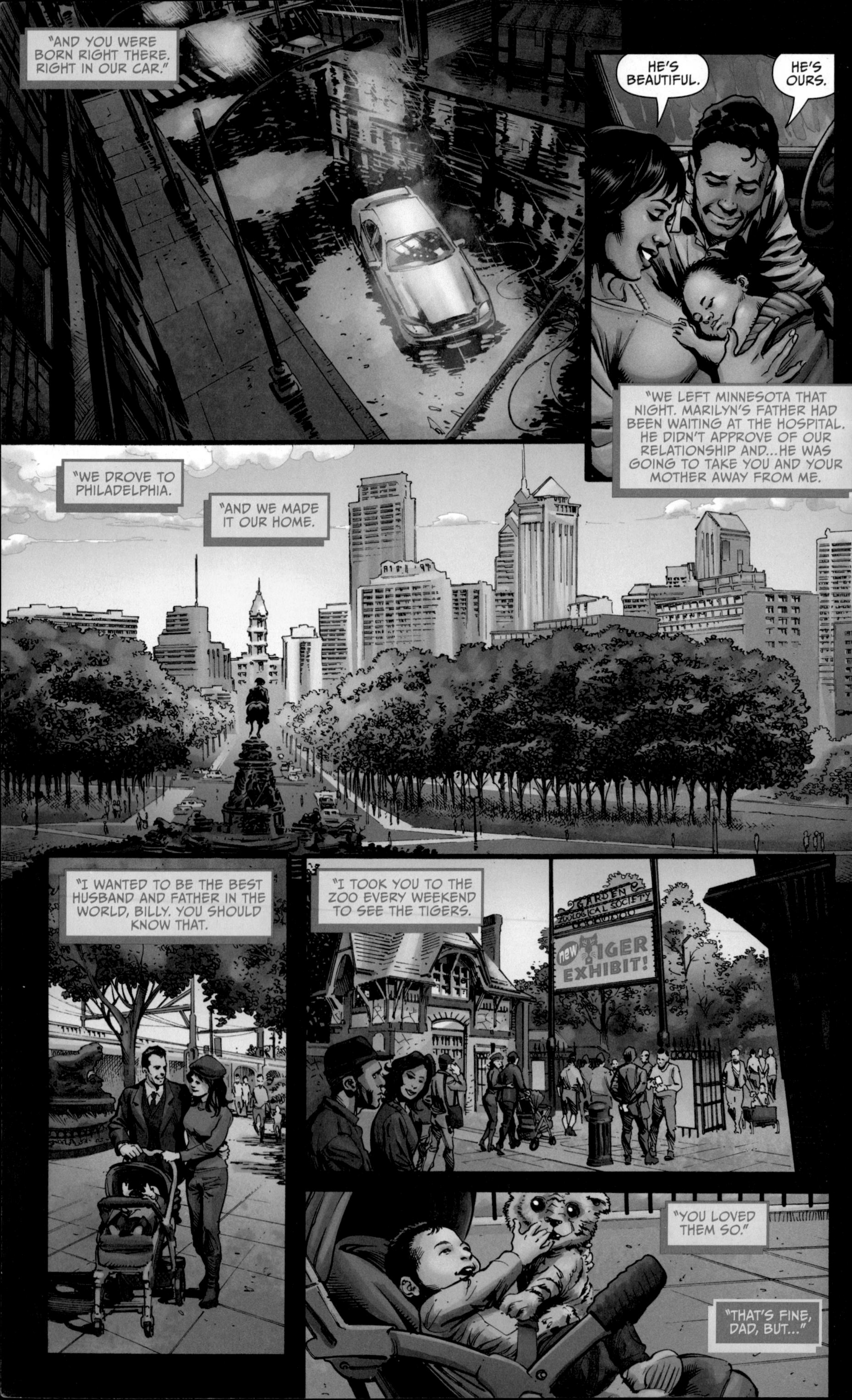

"AND YOU WERE BORN RIGHT THERE. RIGHT IN OUR CAR."
HE'S BEAUTIFUL.
HE'S OURS.
"WE LEFT MINNESOTA THAT NIGHT. MARILYN'S FATHER HAD BEEN WAITING AT THE HOSPITAL. HE DIDN'T APPROVE OF OUR RELATIONSHIP AND...HE WAS GOING TO TAKE YOU AND YOUR MOTHER AWAY FROM ME.
"WE DROVE TO PHILADELPHIA.
"AND WE MADE IT OUR HOME.
"I WANTED TO BE THE BEST HUSBAND AND FATHER IN THE WORLD, BILLY. YOU SHOULD KNOW THAT.
"I TOOK YOU TO THE ZOO EVERY WEEKEND TO SEE THE TIGERS.
GARDEN
ZOOLOGICAL SOCIETY
new TIGER EXHIBIT!
"YOU LOVED THEM SO."
"THAT'S FINE, DAD, BUT..."

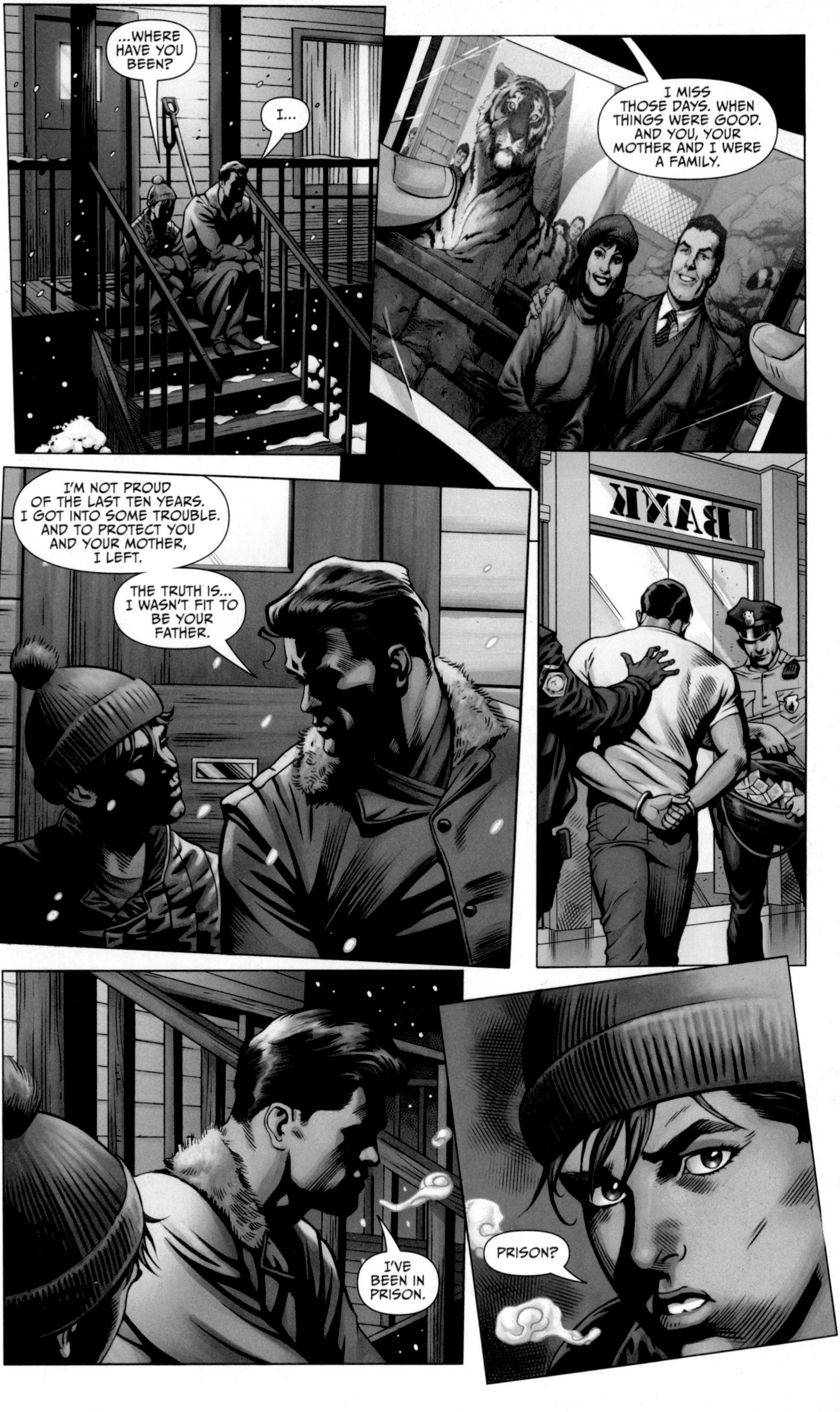
...WHERE HAVE YOU BEEN?
I...
I MISS THOSE DAYS. WHEN THINGS WERE GOOD. AND YOU, YOUR MOTHER AND I WERE A FAMILY.
I'M NOT PROUD OF THE LAST TEN YEARS. I GOT INTO SOME TROUBLE. AND TO PROTECT YOU AND YOUR MOTHER, I LEFT.
THE TRUTH IS... I WASN'T FIT TO BE YOUR FATHER.
BANK
I'VE BEEN IN PRISON.
PRISON?

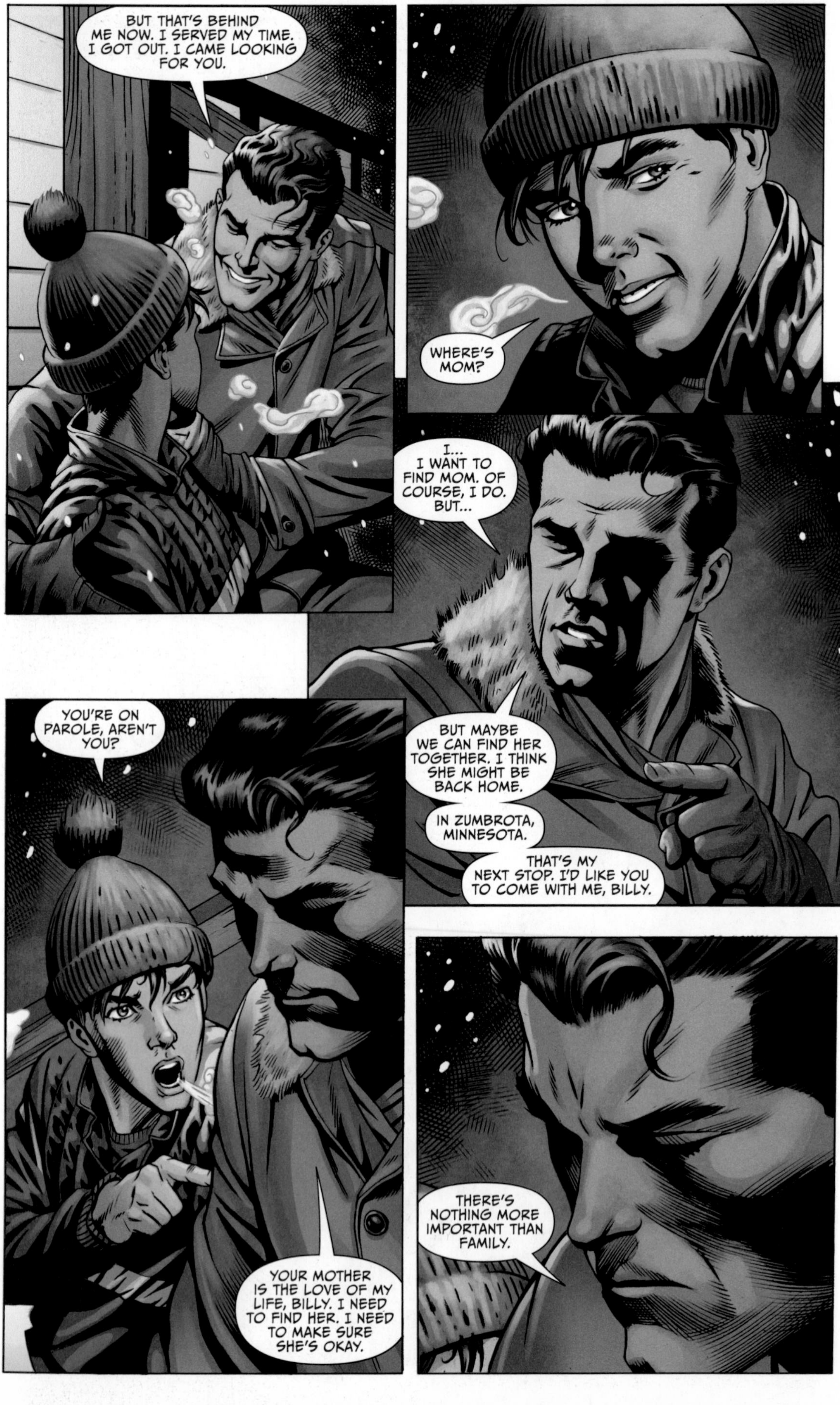

BUT THAT'S BEHIND ME NOW. I SERVED MY TIME. I GOT OUT. I CAME LOOKING FOR YOU.
WHERE'S MOM?
I... I WANT TO FIND MOM. OF COURSE, I DO. BUT...
BUT MAYBE WE CAN FIND HER TOGETHER. I THINK SHE MIGHT BE BACK HOME.
IN ZUMBROTA, MINNESOTA.
THAT'S MY NEXT STOP. I'D LIKE YOU TO COME WITH ME, BILLY.
YOU'RE ON PAROLE, AREN'T YOU?
YOUR MOTHER IS THE LOVE OF MY LIFE, BILLY. I NEED TO FIND HER. I NEED TO MAKE SURE SHE'S OKAY.
THERE'S NOTHING MORE IMPORTANT THAN FAMILY.

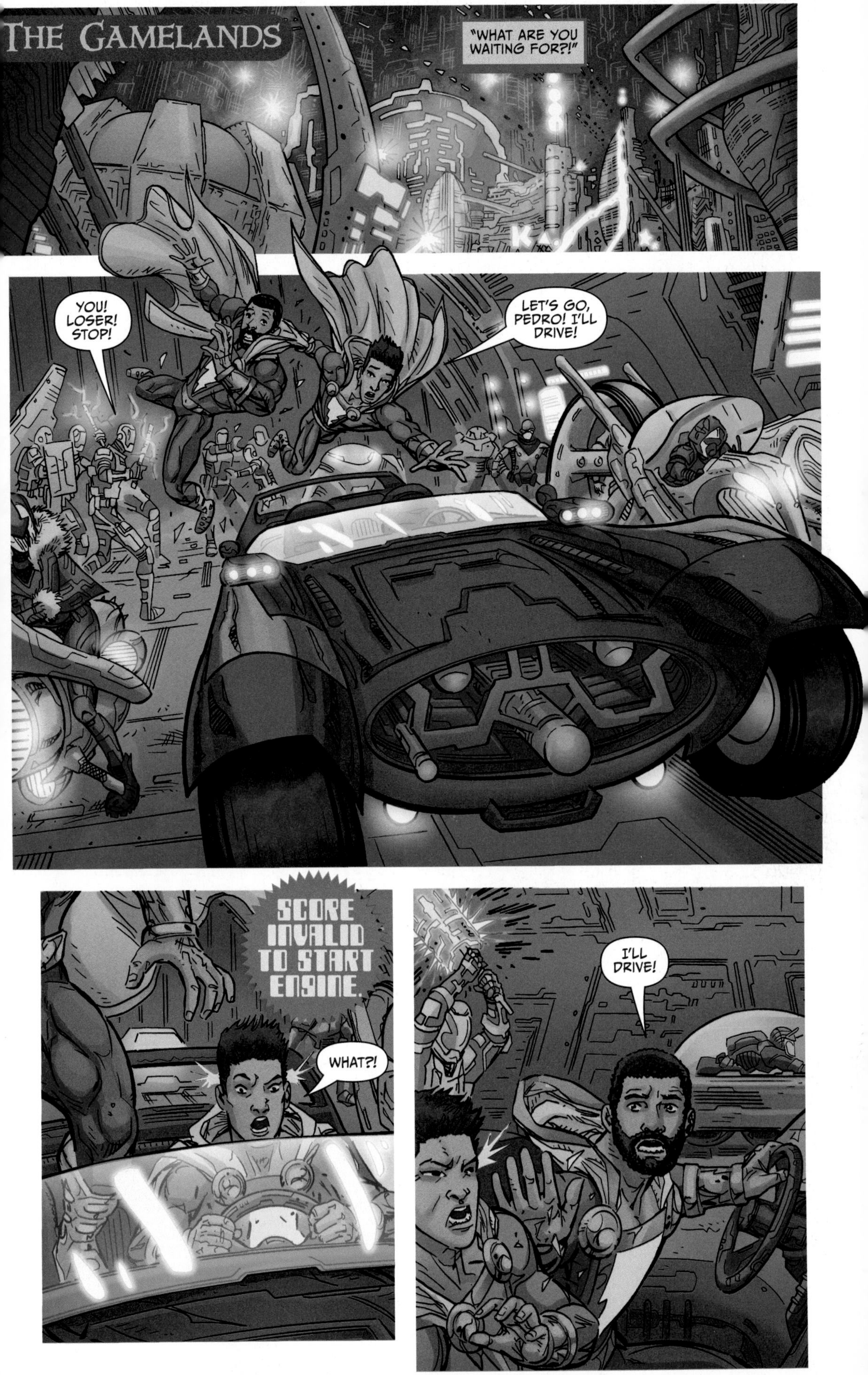
THE GAMELANDS
"WHAT ARE YOU WAITING FOR?!"
YOU! LOSER! STOP!
LET'S GO, PEDRO! I'LL DRIVE!
SCORE INVALID TO START ENGINE.
WHAT?!
I'LL DRIVE!

SCORE -300

RACERS, ON YOUR MARK!

GET SET.

LOOK OUT!

FOR WHAT?!

EVERYTHING! GO LEFT, PEDRO! LEFT, NOT RIGHT!

ZRRR KOOOMM

GO!

STOP YELLING AT ME! I'VE NEVER DRIVEN BEFORE!

ME EITHER, BUT I'VE PLAYED ENOUGH *GRAND THEFT AUTO* TO KNOW THE BASICS!

ROSA AND VICTOR LET YOU PLAY THAT?

NO, BUT I BORROWED ONE OF VICTOR'S COATS, SAID THE MAGIC WORD AND BOUGHT IT! *HA HA!*

HOW CAN YOU GOOF AROUND AT A TIME LIKE THIS?

WE'RE *LOST!* WE DON'T KNOW WHERE ANYONE ELSE IS!

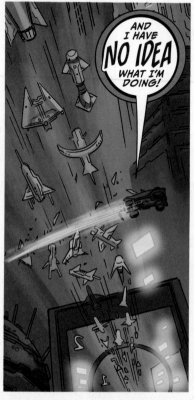

AND I HAVE NO IDEA WHAT I'M DOING!

A NEW PLAYER HAS ENTERED THE GAME!

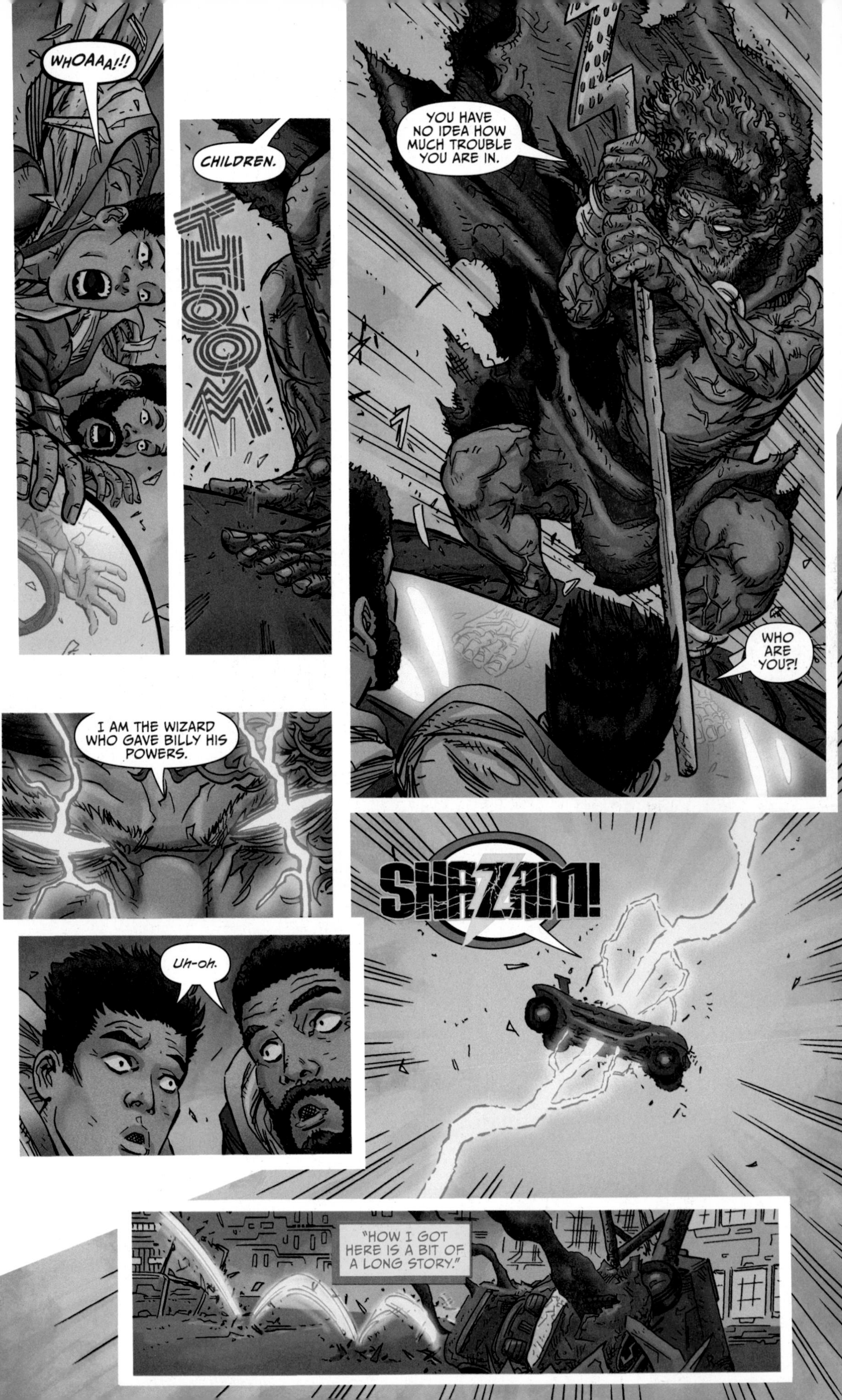
WHOAAA!!!
CHILDREN.
THOOM
YOU HAVE NO IDEA HOW MUCH TROUBLE YOU ARE IN.
WHO ARE YOU?!
I AM THE WIZARD WHO GAVE BILLY HIS POWERS.
Uh-oh.
SHAZAM!
"HOW I GOT HERE IS A BIT OF A LONG STORY."

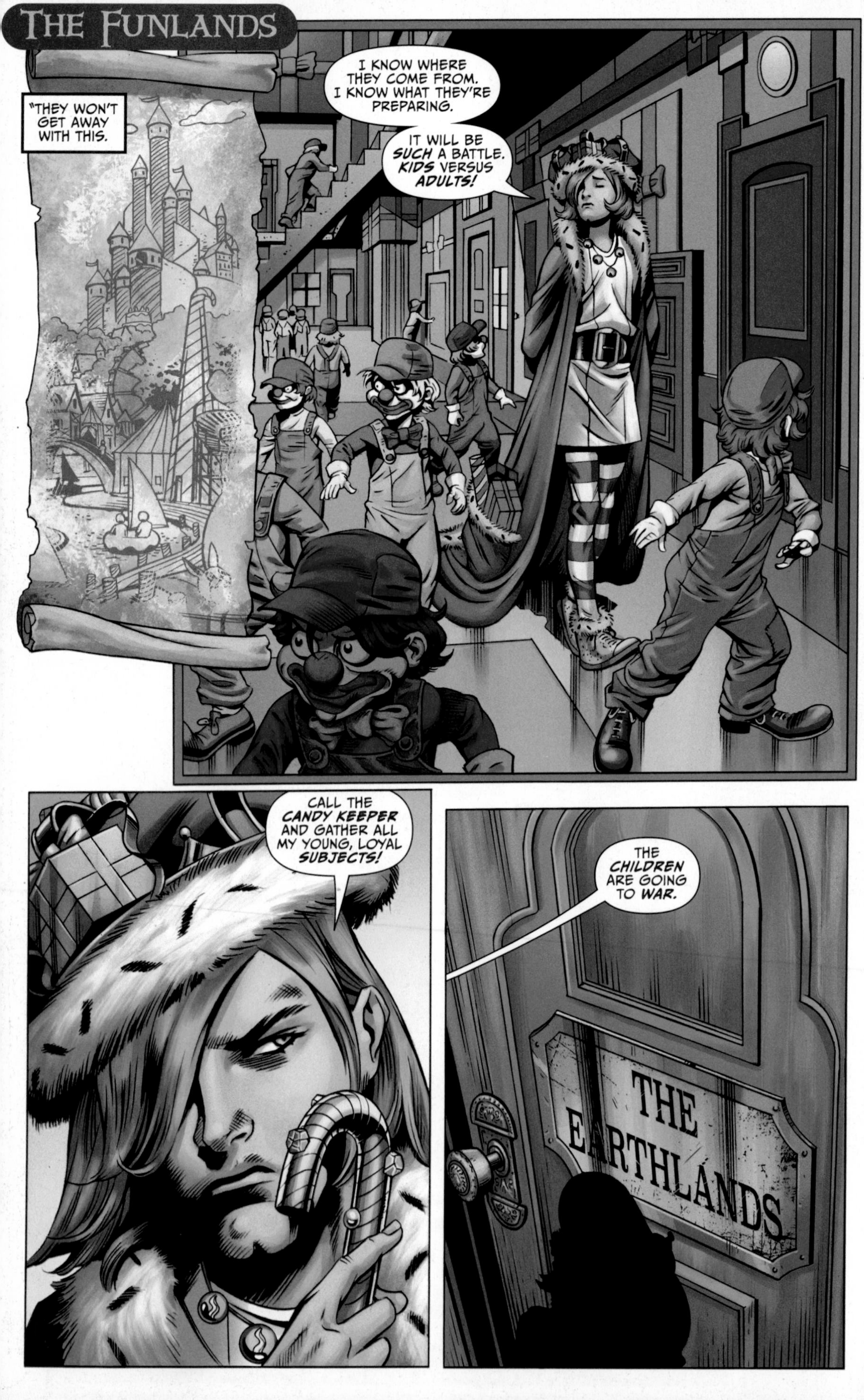

THE FUNLANDS
"THEY WON'T GET AWAY WITH THIS.
I KNOW WHERE THEY COME FROM. I KNOW WHAT THEY'RE PREPARING.
IT WILL BE SUCH A BATTLE. KIDS VERSUS ADULTS!
CALL THE CANDY KEEPER AND GATHER ALL MY YOUNG, LOYAL SUBJECTS!
THE CHILDREN ARE GOING TO WAR.
THE EARTHLANDS

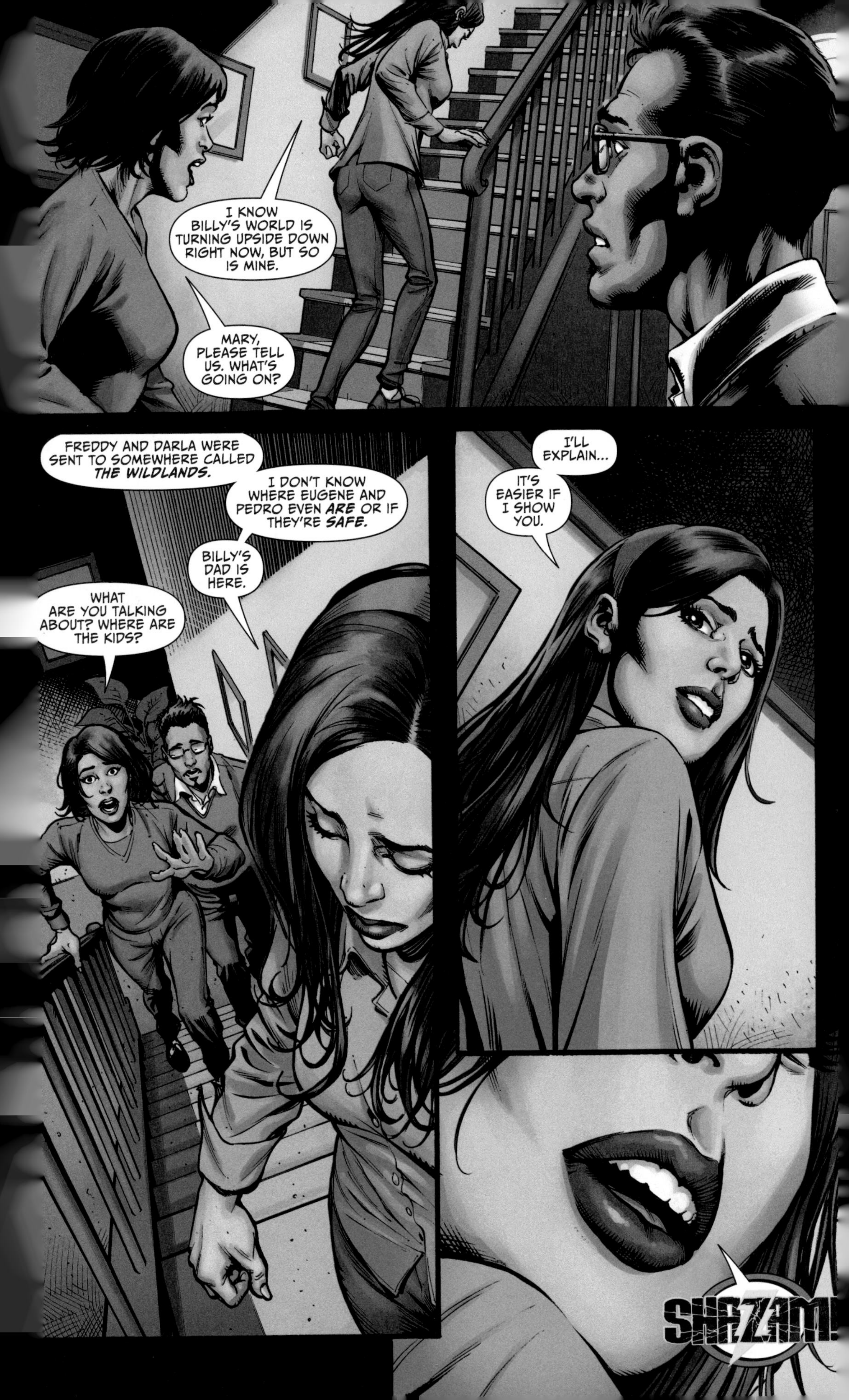
I KNOW BILLY'S WORLD IS TURNING UPSIDE DOWN RIGHT NOW, BUT SO IS MINE.
MARY, PLEASE TELL US. WHAT'S GOING ON?
FREDDY AND DARLA WERE SENT TO SOMEWHERE CALLED THE WILDLANDS.
I DON'T KNOW WHERE EUGENE AND PEDRO EVEN ARE OR IF THEY'RE SAFE.
BILLY'S DAD IS HERE.
WHAT ARE YOU TALKING ABOUT? WHERE ARE THE KIDS?
I'LL EXPLAIN...
IT'S EASIER IF I SHOW YOU.
SHAZAM!

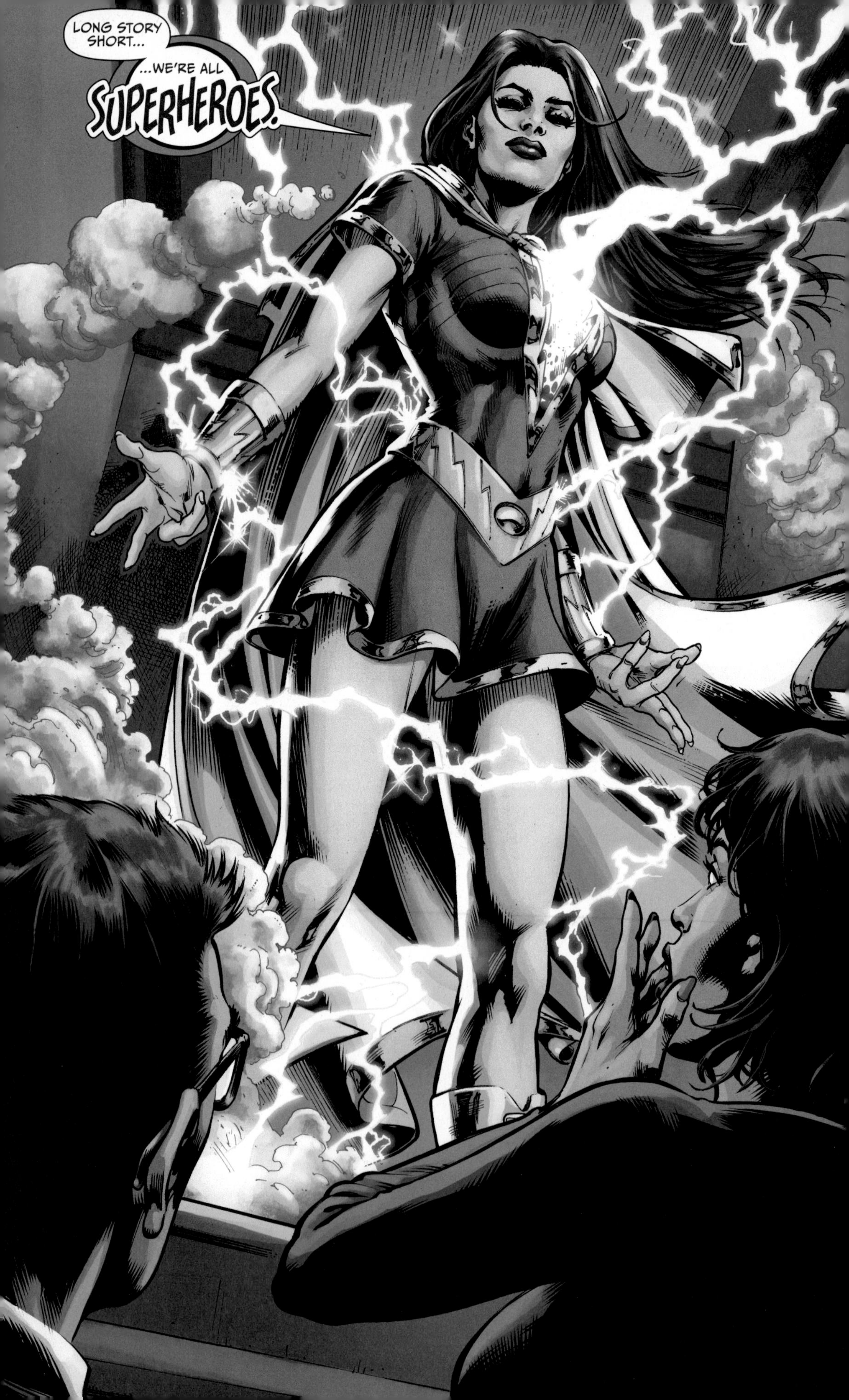
LONG STORY SHORT...
...WE'RE ALL SUPERHEROES.

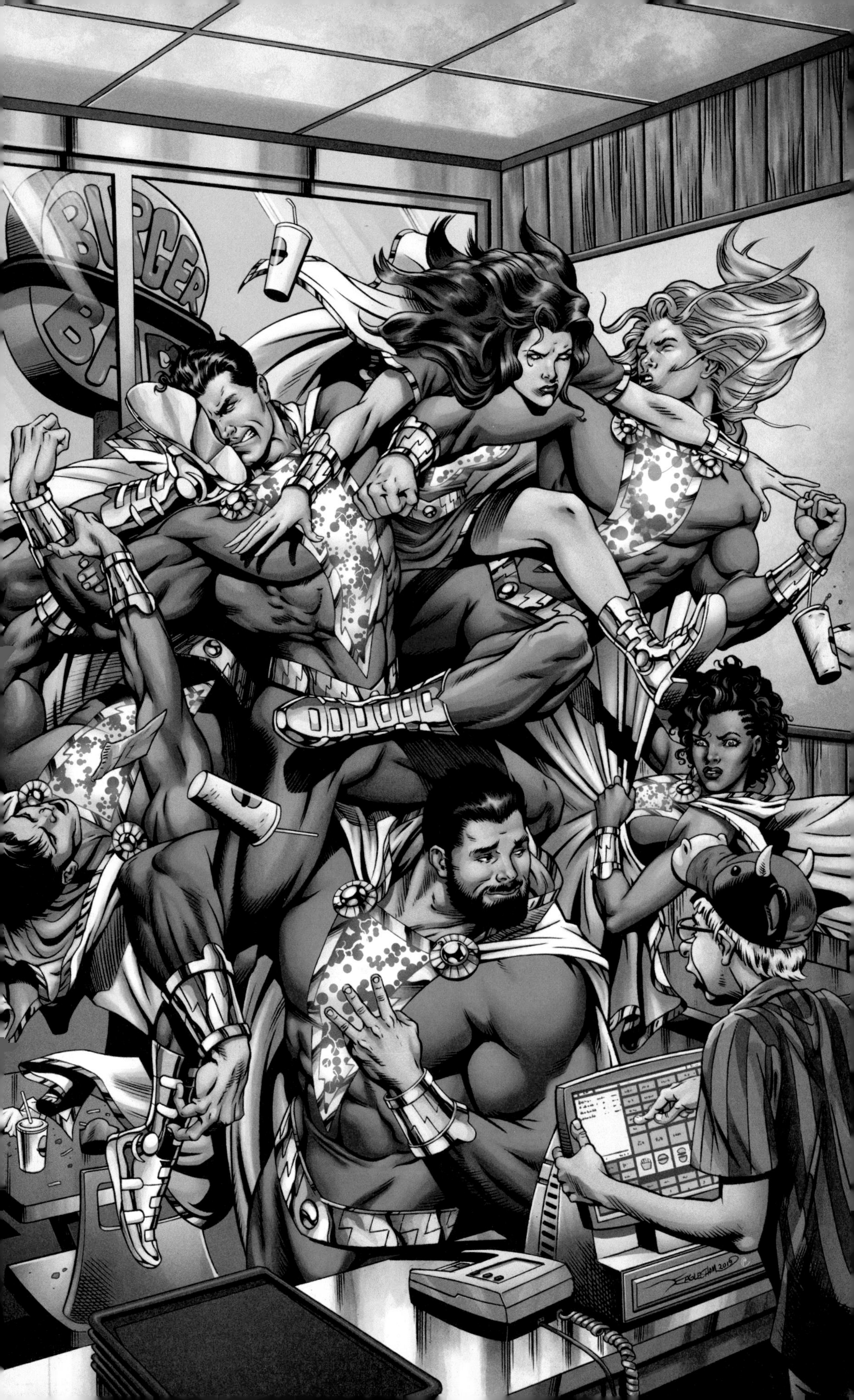
BURGER

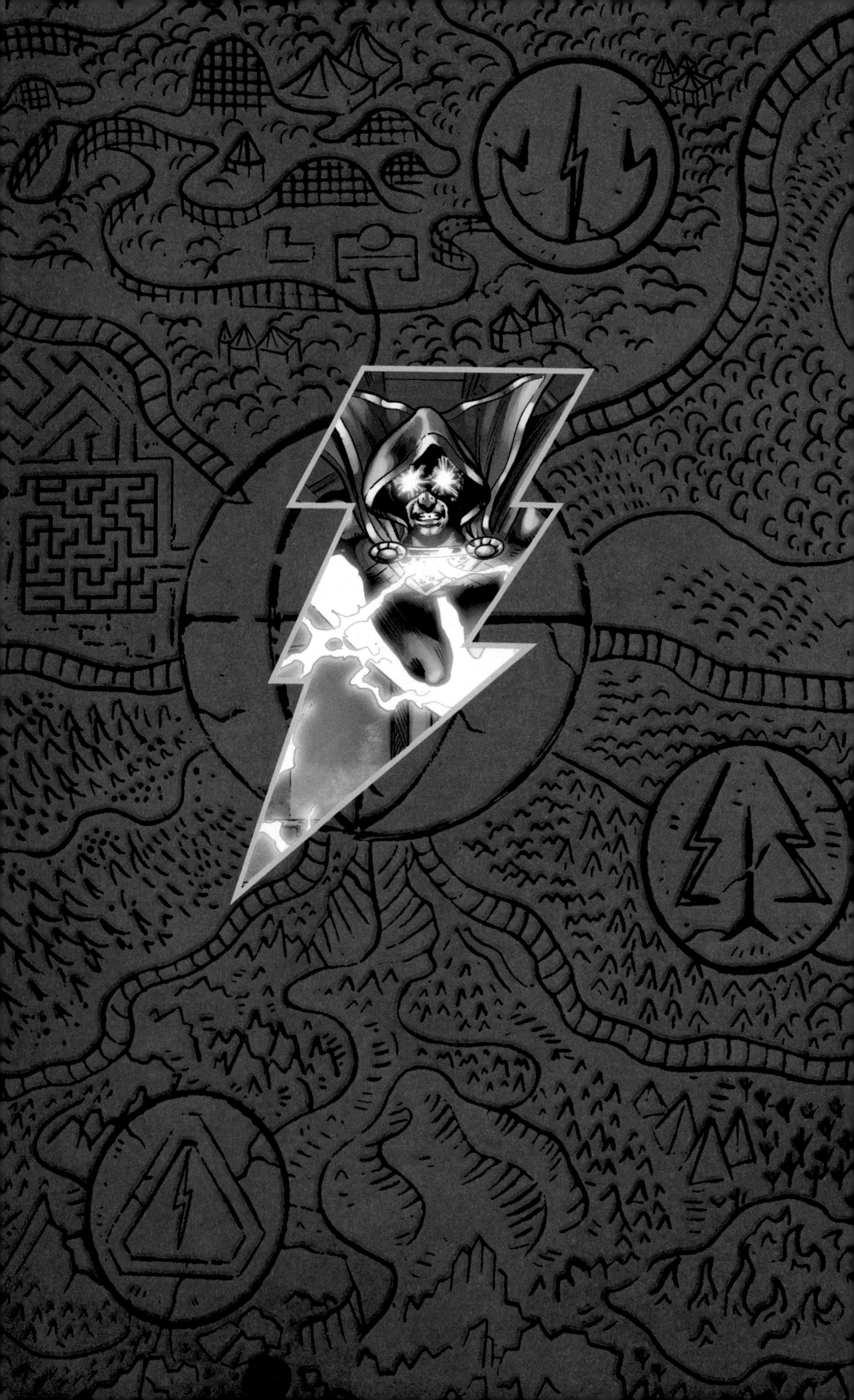

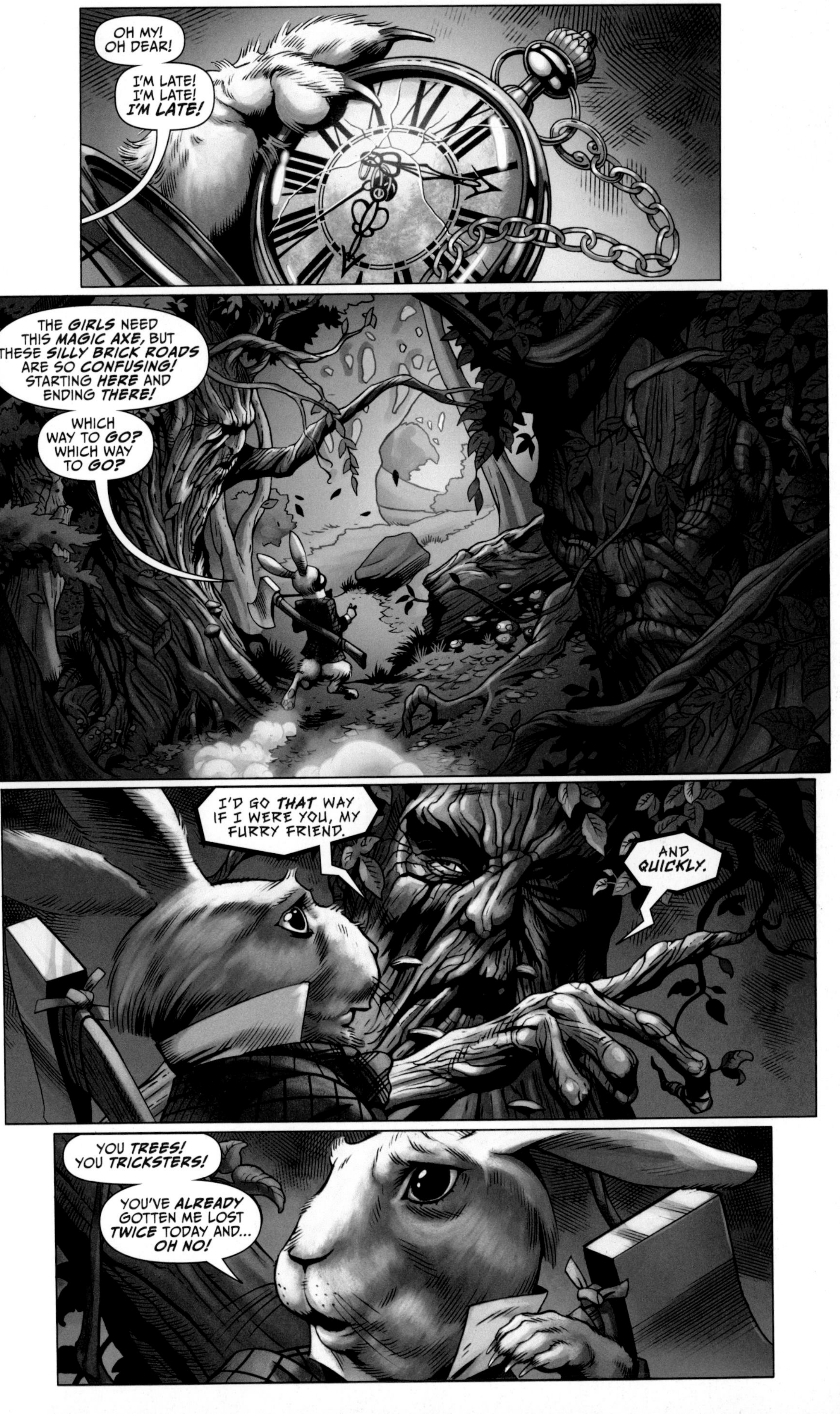
OH MY! OH DEAR!
I'M LATE! I'M LATE! I'M LATE!
THE GIRLS NEED THIS MAGIC AXE, BUT THESE SILLY BRICK ROADS ARE SO CONFUSING! STARTING HERE AND ENDING THERE!
WHICH WAY TO GO? WHICH WAY TO GO?
I'D GO THAT WAY IF I WERE YOU, MY FURRY FRIEND.
AND QUICKLY.
YOU TREES! YOU TRICKSTERS!
YOU'VE ALREADY GOTTEN ME LOST TWICE TODAY AND... OH NO!

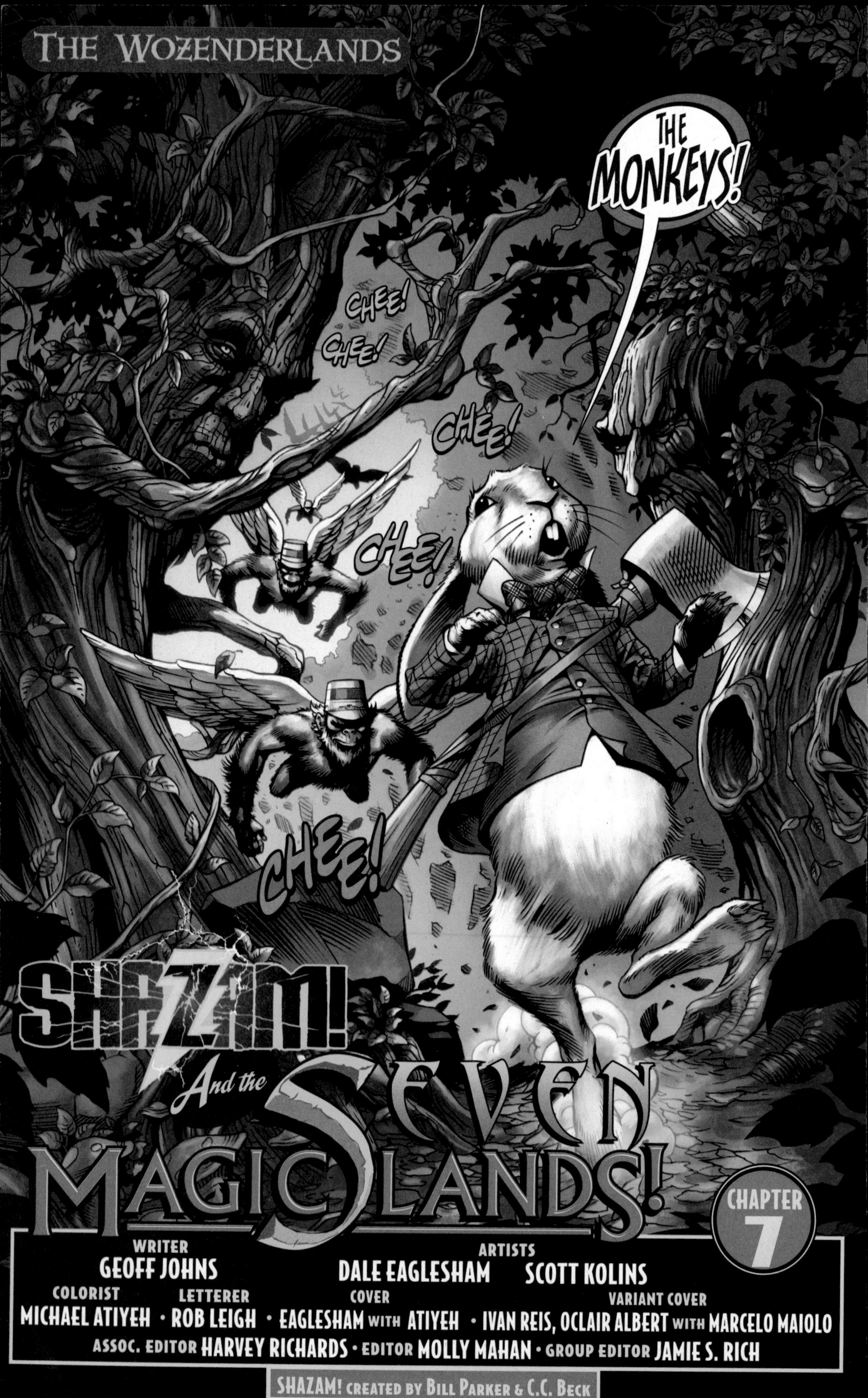
THE WOZENDERLANDS
THE MONKEYS!
CHEE! CHEE!
CHEE!
CHEE!
CHEE!
SHAZAM! And the SEVEN MAGIC LANDS!
CHAPTER 7
WRITER GEOFF JOHNS
ARTISTS DALE EAGLESHAM SCOTT KOLINS
COLORIST MICHAEL ATIYEH · LETTERER ROB LEIGH · COVER EAGLESHAM WITH ATIYEH · VARIANT COVER IVAN REIS, OCLAIR ALBERT WITH MARCELO MAIOLO
ASSOC. EDITOR HARVEY RICHARDS · EDITOR MOLLY MAHAN · GROUP EDITOR JAMIE S. RICH
SHAZAM! CREATED BY BILL PARKER & C.C. BECK

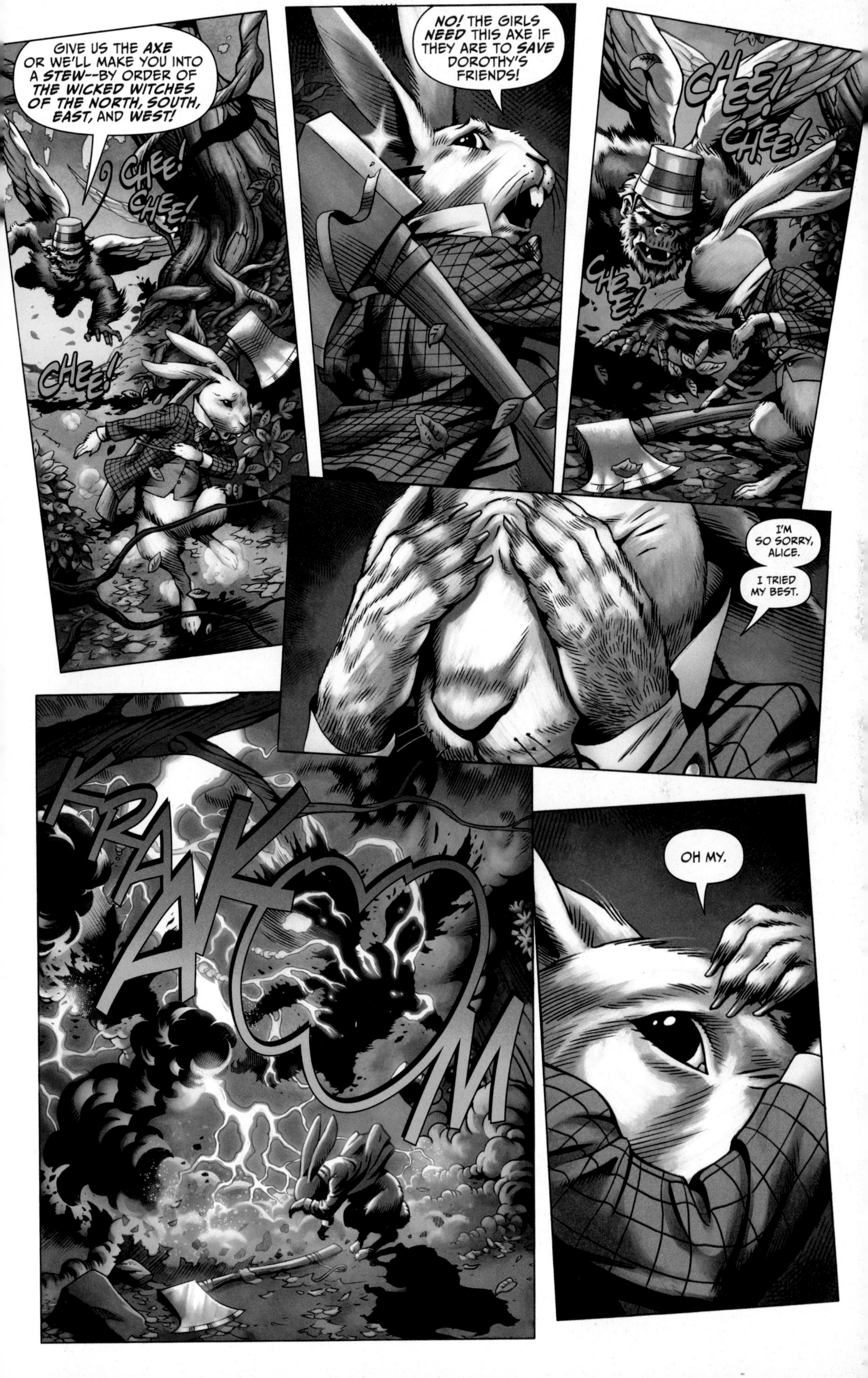
GIVE US THE AXE OR WE'LL MAKE YOU INTO A STEW--BY ORDER OF THE WICKED WITCHES OF THE NORTH, SOUTH, EAST, AND WEST!
CHEE! CHEE!
CHEE!
NO! THE GIRLS NEED THIS AXE IF THEY ARE TO SAVE DOROTHY'S FRIENDS!
CHEE! CHEE!
CHEE!
I'M SO SORRY, ALICE.
I TRIED MY BEST.
KRAKAKOOM
OH MY.

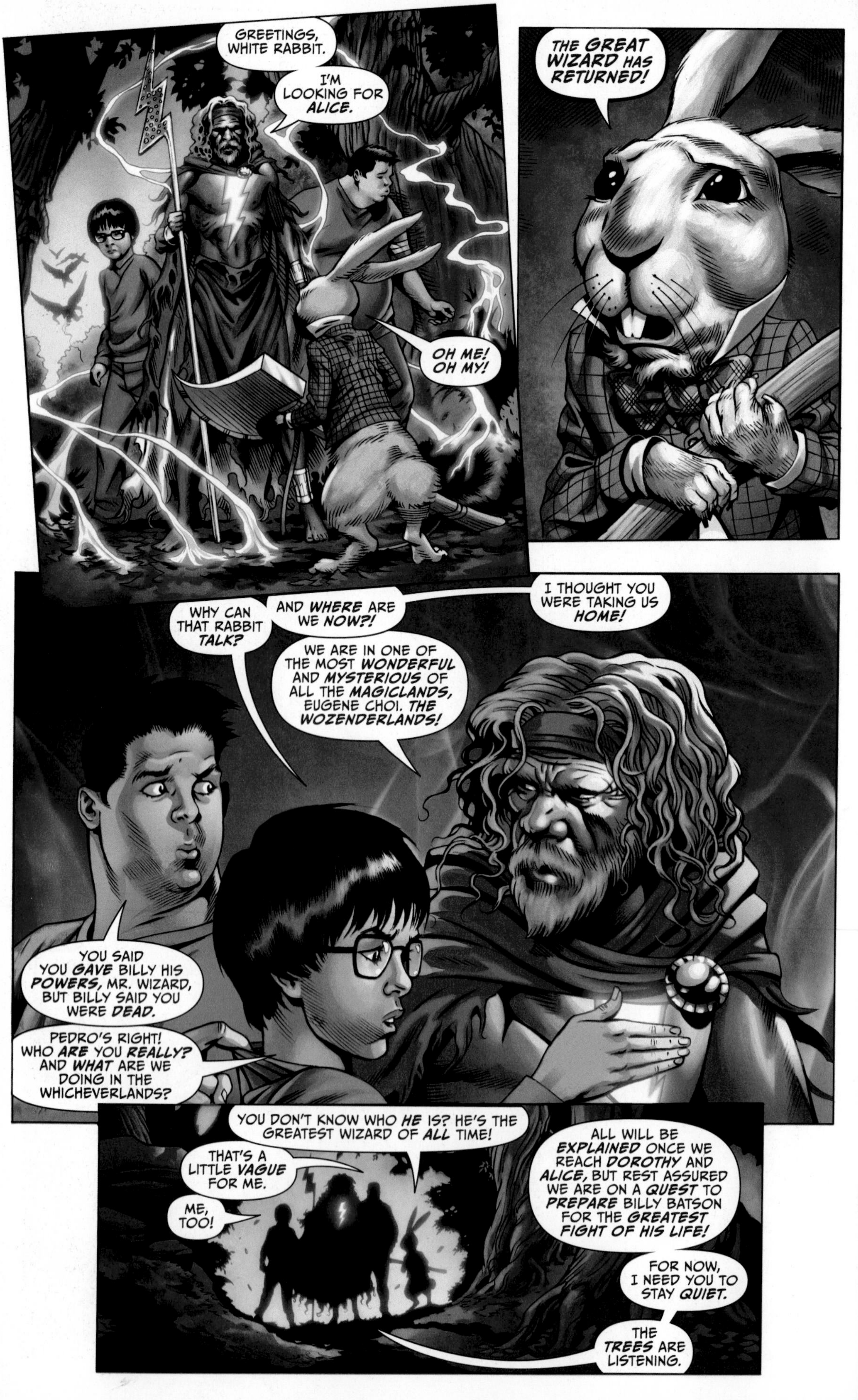
GREETINGS, WHITE RABBIT.
I'M LOOKING FOR ALICE.
OH ME! OH MY!
THE GREAT WIZARD HAS RETURNED!
WHY CAN THAT RABBIT TALK?
AND WHERE ARE WE NOW?!
I THOUGHT YOU WERE TAKING US HOME!
WE ARE IN ONE OF THE MOST WONDERFUL AND MYSTERIOUS OF ALL THE MAGICLANDS, EUGENE CHOI. THE WOZENDERLANDS!
YOU SAID YOU GAVE BILLY HIS POWERS, MR. WIZARD, BUT BILLY SAID YOU WERE DEAD.
PEDRO'S RIGHT! WHO ARE YOU REALLY? AND WHAT ARE WE DOING IN THE WHICHEVERLANDS?
YOU DON'T KNOW WHO HE IS? HE'S THE GREATEST WIZARD OF ALL TIME!
THAT'S A LITTLE VAGUE FOR ME.
ME, TOO!
ALL WILL BE EXPLAINED ONCE WE REACH DOROTHY AND ALICE, BUT REST ASSURED WE ARE ON A QUEST TO PREPARE BILLY BATSON FOR THE GREATEST FIGHT OF HIS LIFE!
FOR NOW, I NEED YOU TO STAY QUIET.
THE TREES ARE LISTENING.

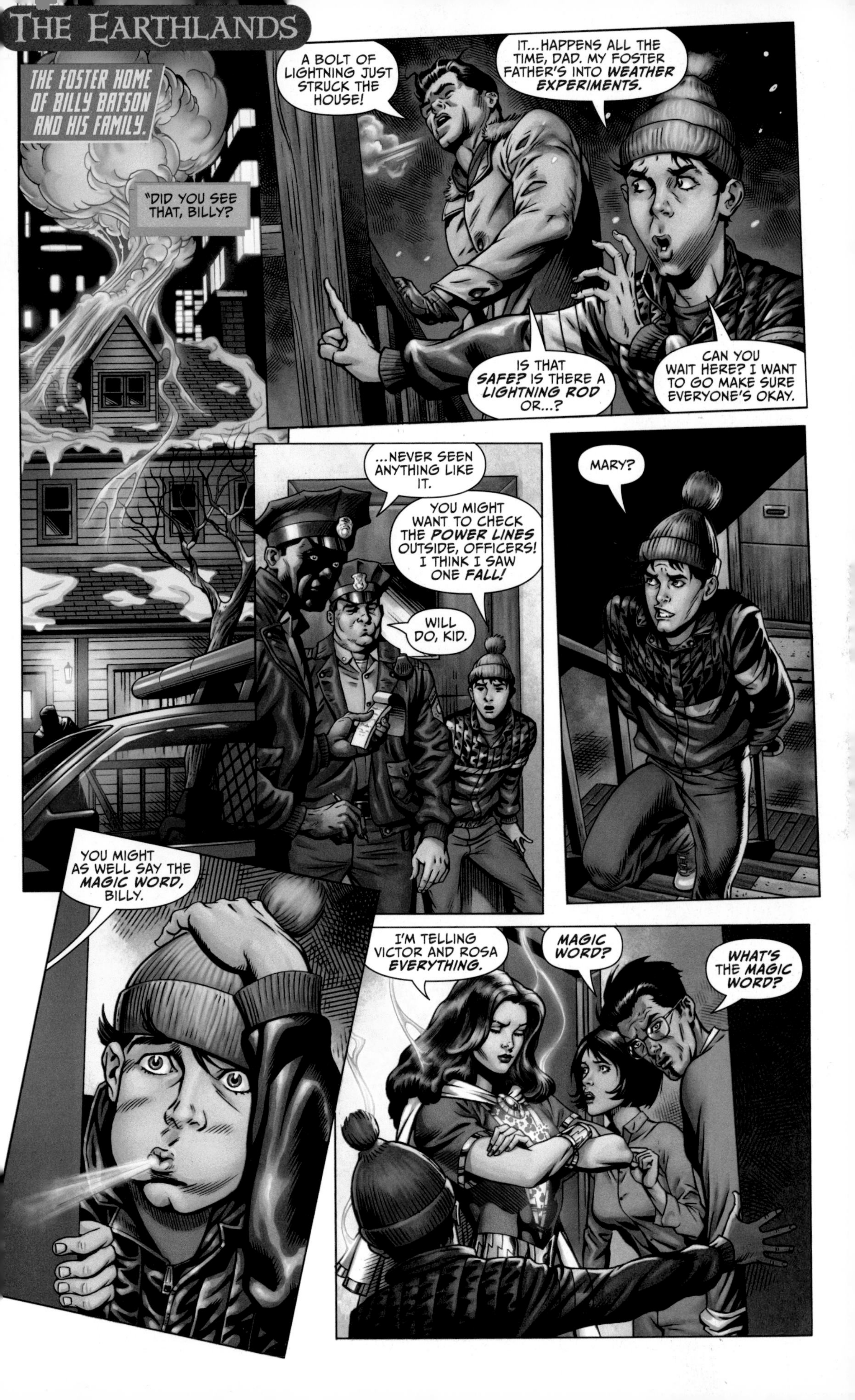
THE EARTHLANDS
THE FOSTER HOME OF BILLY BATSON AND HIS FAMILY.
"DID YOU SEE THAT, BILLY?
A BOLT OF LIGHTNING JUST STRUCK THE HOUSE!
IT...HAPPENS ALL THE TIME, DAD. MY FOSTER FATHER'S INTO WEATHER EXPERIMENTS.
IS THAT SAFE? IS THERE A LIGHTNING ROD OR...?
CAN YOU WAIT HERE? I WANT TO GO MAKE SURE EVERYONE'S OKAY.
...NEVER SEEN ANYTHING LIKE IT.
YOU MIGHT WANT TO CHECK THE POWER LINES OUTSIDE, OFFICERS! I THINK I SAW ONE FALL!
WILL DO, KID.
MARY?
YOU MIGHT AS WELL SAY THE MAGIC WORD, BILLY.
I'M TELLING VICTOR AND ROSA EVERYTHING.
MAGIC WORD?
WHAT'S THE MAGIC WORD?

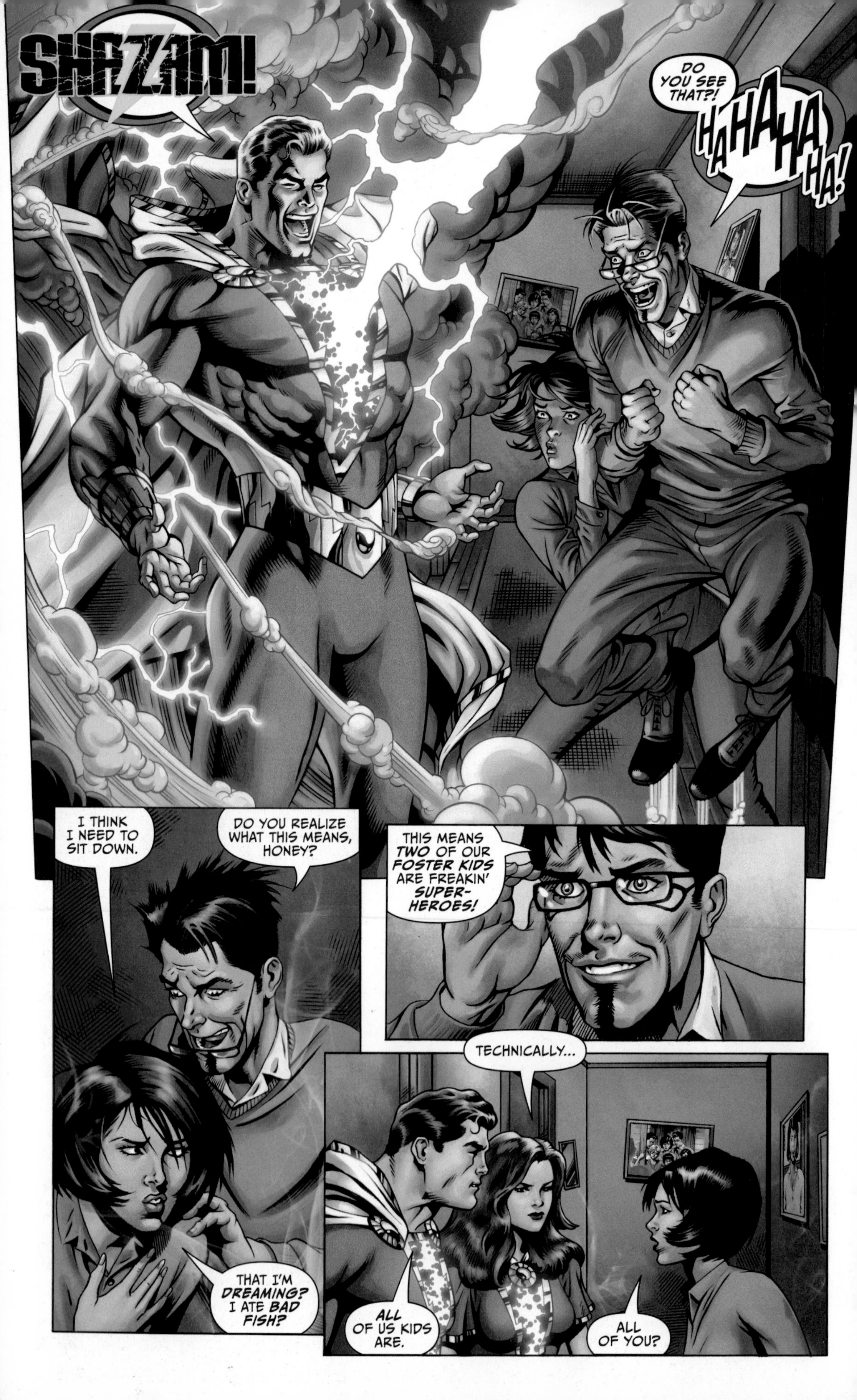
SHAZAM!
DO YOU SEE THAT?!
HAHAHAHA!
I THINK I NEED TO SIT DOWN.
DO YOU REALIZE WHAT THIS MEANS, HONEY?
THAT I'M *DREAMING?* I ATE *BAD FISH?*
THIS MEANS *TWO* OF OUR *FOSTER KIDS* ARE FREAKIN' *SUPER-HEROES!*
TECHNICALLY...
*ALL* OF US KIDS ARE.
ALL OF YOU?

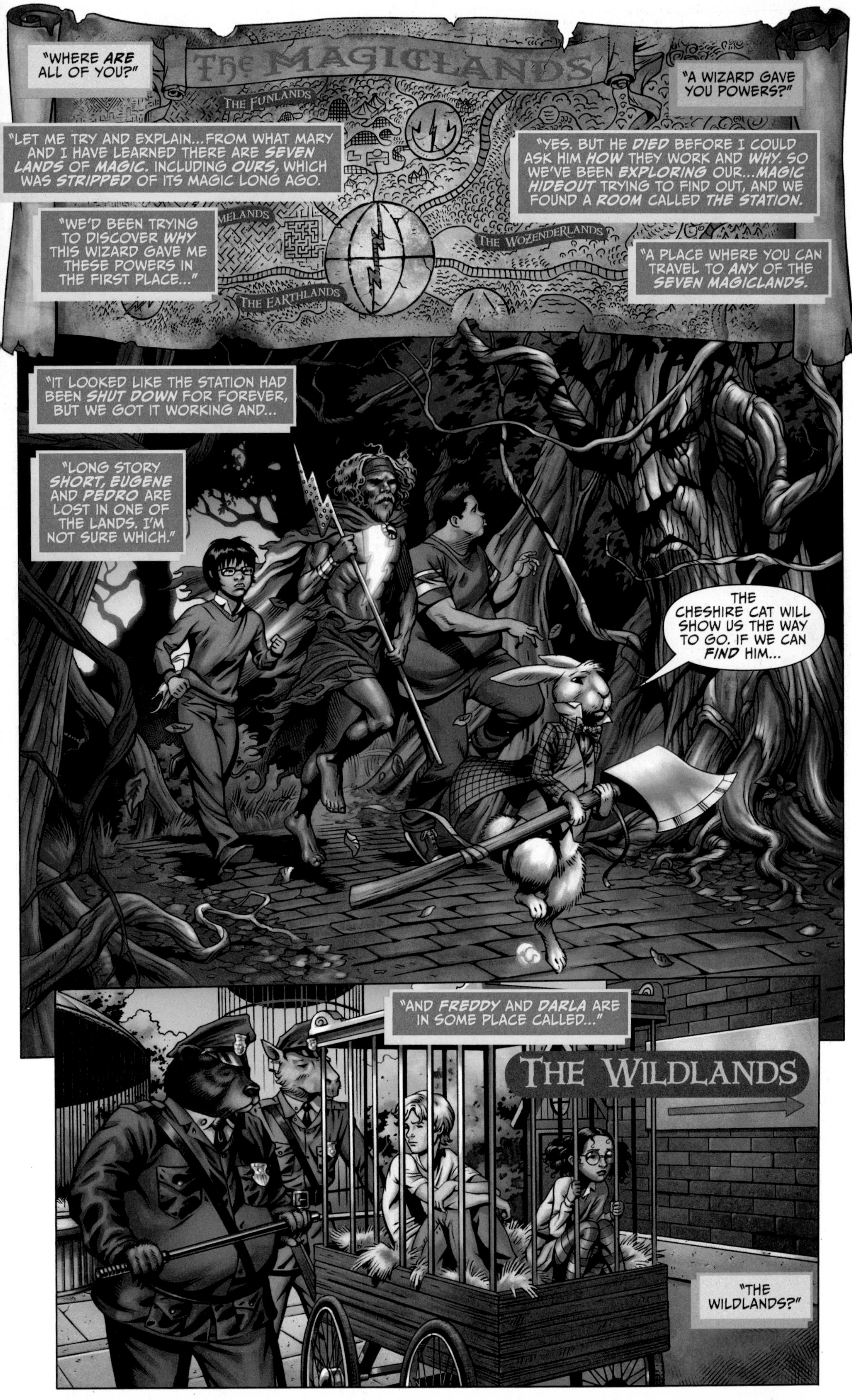
THE MAGICLANDS
THE FUNLANDS
THE WOZENDERLANDS
THE EARTHLANDS
"WHERE ARE ALL OF YOU?"
"LET ME TRY AND EXPLAIN...FROM WHAT MARY AND I HAVE LEARNED THERE ARE SEVEN LANDS OF MAGIC. INCLUDING OURS, WHICH WAS STRIPPED OF ITS MAGIC LONG AGO.
"WE'D BEEN TRYING TO DISCOVER WHY THIS WIZARD GAVE ME THESE POWERS IN THE FIRST PLACE..."
"A WIZARD GAVE YOU POWERS?"
"YES. BUT HE DIED BEFORE I COULD ASK HIM HOW THEY WORK AND WHY. SO WE'VE BEEN EXPLORING OUR...MAGIC HIDEOUT TRYING TO FIND OUT, AND WE FOUND A ROOM CALLED THE STATION.
"A PLACE WHERE YOU CAN TRAVEL TO ANY OF THE SEVEN MAGICLANDS.
"IT LOOKED LIKE THE STATION HAD BEEN SHUT DOWN FOR FOREVER, BUT WE GOT IT WORKING AND...
"LONG STORY SHORT, EUGENE AND PEDRO ARE LOST IN ONE OF THE LANDS. I'M NOT SURE WHICH."
THE CHESHIRE CAT WILL SHOW US THE WAY TO GO. IF WE CAN FIND HIM...
"AND FREDDY AND DARLA ARE IN SOME PLACE CALLED..."
THE WILDLANDS
"THE WILDLANDS?"

"THAT DOESN'T SOUND VERY SAFE!"

BEWARE OF TIGERS

LISTEN TO REASON, GENTLEMEN...

WE SHOULDN'T BE *FORCED* INTO THIS SIMPLY BECAUSE WE WERE *BORN* WITH *SHARP TEETH* AND *CLAWS.*

IT'S *RIGHTEOUS SERVITUDE,* TAWNY, FOR WHAT *OUR* KIND DID TO THE MAYOR DURING THE *WAR.*

I HATE THE *TASTE* OF HUMANS AS MUCH AS *ANYONE,* BUT IT'S NOT LIKE WE HAVE A *CHOICE* HERE.

IF WE DON'T DO WHAT THE MAYOR ORDERS...

THE TIGERS *SIDED* WITH HUMANS.

IT'S OUR *DUTY* TO BE THEIR *EXECUTIONERS.*

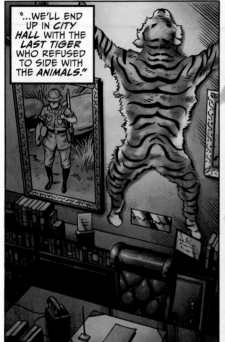

"...WE'LL END UP IN *CITY HALL* WITH THE *LAST TIGER* WHO REFUSED TO SIDE WITH THE *ANIMALS."*

BUT THOSE *HUMANS* UP THERE HAD *NO PART* IN THE WAR.

THEY WEREN'T EVEN *BORN* YET! THEY'RE *CHILDREN.*

LOOK ON THE BRIGHT SIDE, TAWNY.

I HEAR *CHILDREN* TASTE BETTER.

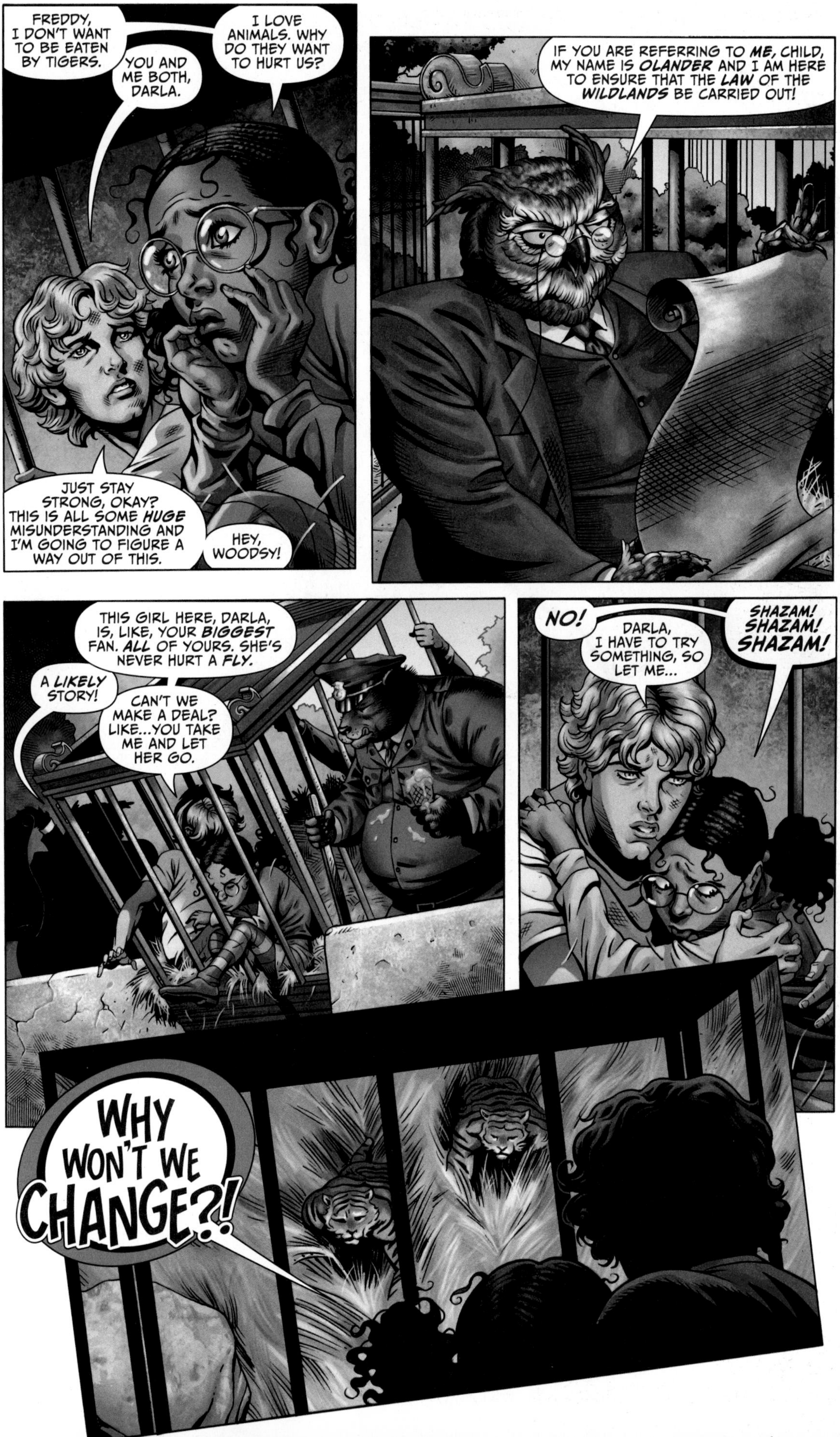
FREDDY, I DON'T WANT TO BE EATEN BY TIGERS.
I LOVE ANIMALS. WHY DO THEY WANT TO HURT US?
YOU AND ME BOTH, DARLA.
JUST STAY STRONG, OKAY? THIS IS ALL SOME HUGE MISUNDERSTANDING AND I'M GOING TO FIGURE A WAY OUT OF THIS.
HEY, WOODSY!
IF YOU ARE REFERRING TO ME, CHILD, MY NAME IS OLANDER AND I AM HERE TO ENSURE THAT THE LAW OF THE WILDLANDS BE CARRIED OUT!
THIS GIRL HERE, DARLA, IS, LIKE, YOUR BIGGEST FAN. ALL OF YOURS. SHE'S NEVER HURT A FLY.
A LIKELY STORY!
CAN'T WE MAKE A DEAL? LIKE...YOU TAKE ME AND LET HER GO.
NO!
DARLA, I HAVE TO TRY SOMETHING, SO LET ME...
SHAZAM! SHAZAM! SHAZAM!
WHY WON'T WE CHANGE?!

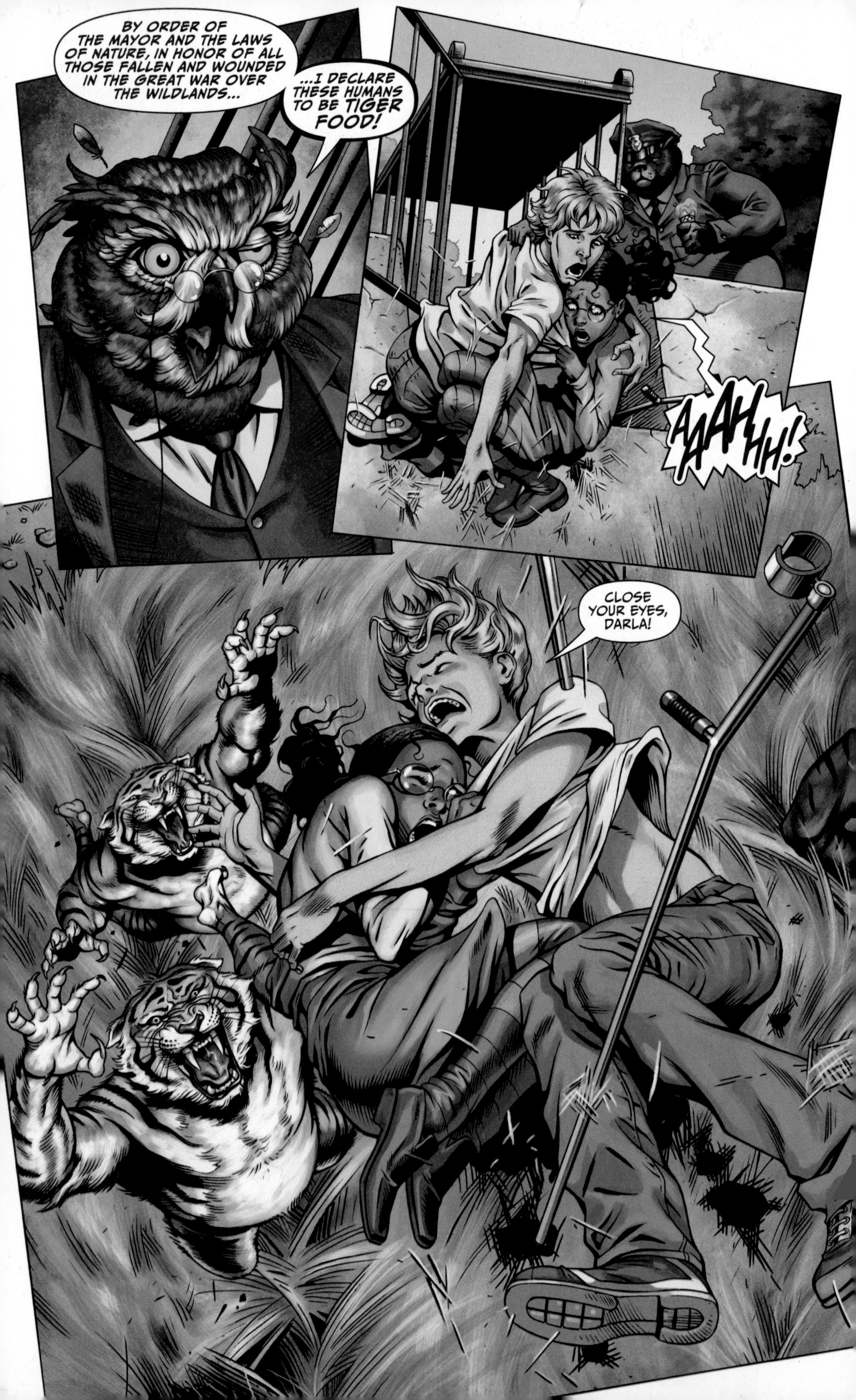
BY ORDER OF THE MAYOR AND THE LAWS OF NATURE, IN HONOR OF ALL THOSE FALLEN AND WOUNDED IN THE GREAT WAR OVER THE WILDLANDS...
...I DECLARE THESE HUMANS TO BE TIGER FOOD!
AAAHHH!
CLOSE YOUR EYES, DARLA!

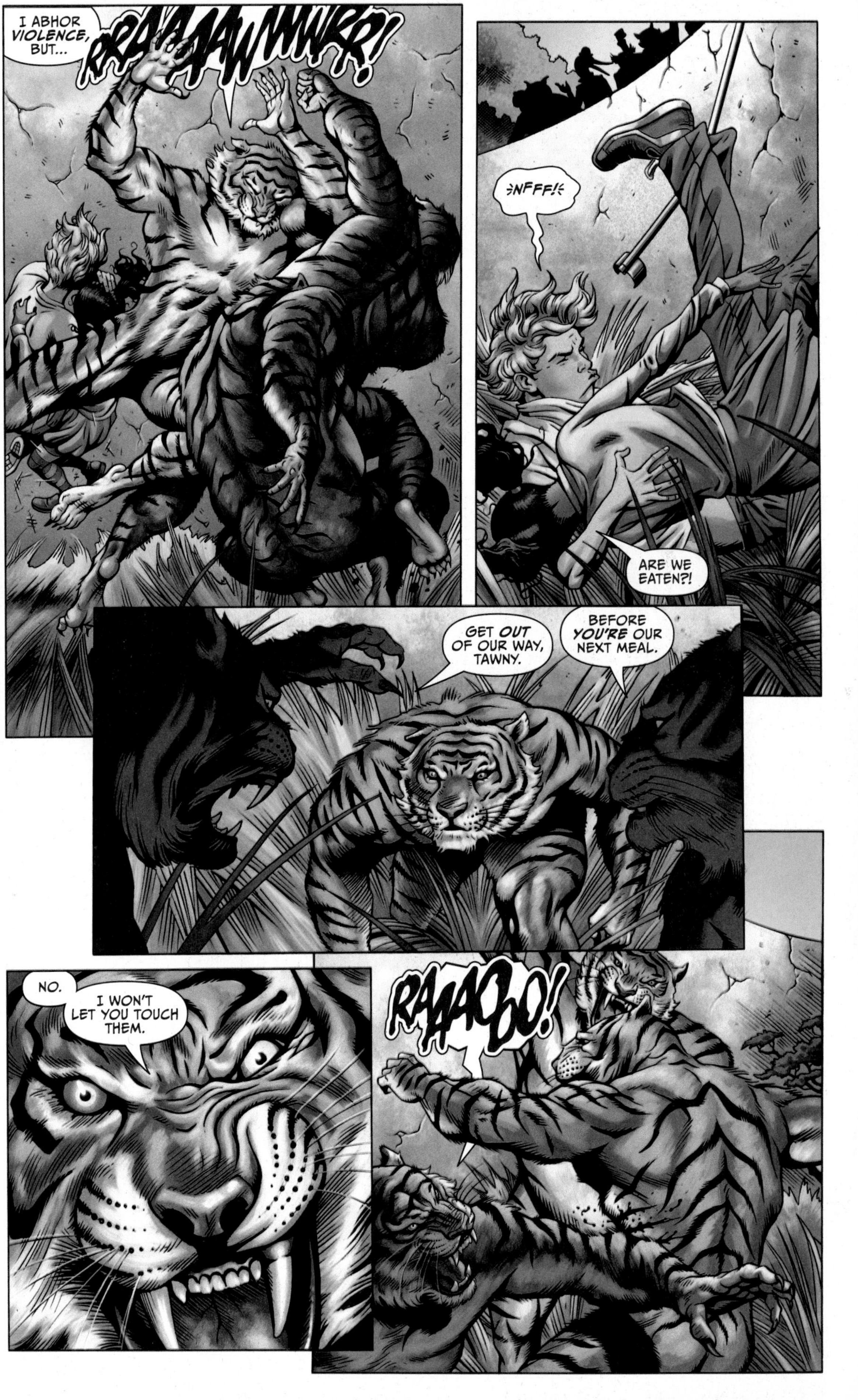
I ABHOR VIOLENCE, BUT...
RRAAAAAWWWR!
¬NFFF!¬
ARE WE EATEN?!
GET OUT OF OUR WAY, TAWNY.
BEFORE YOU'RE OUR NEXT MEAL.
NO.
I WON'T LET YOU TOUCH THEM.
RAAAOOO!

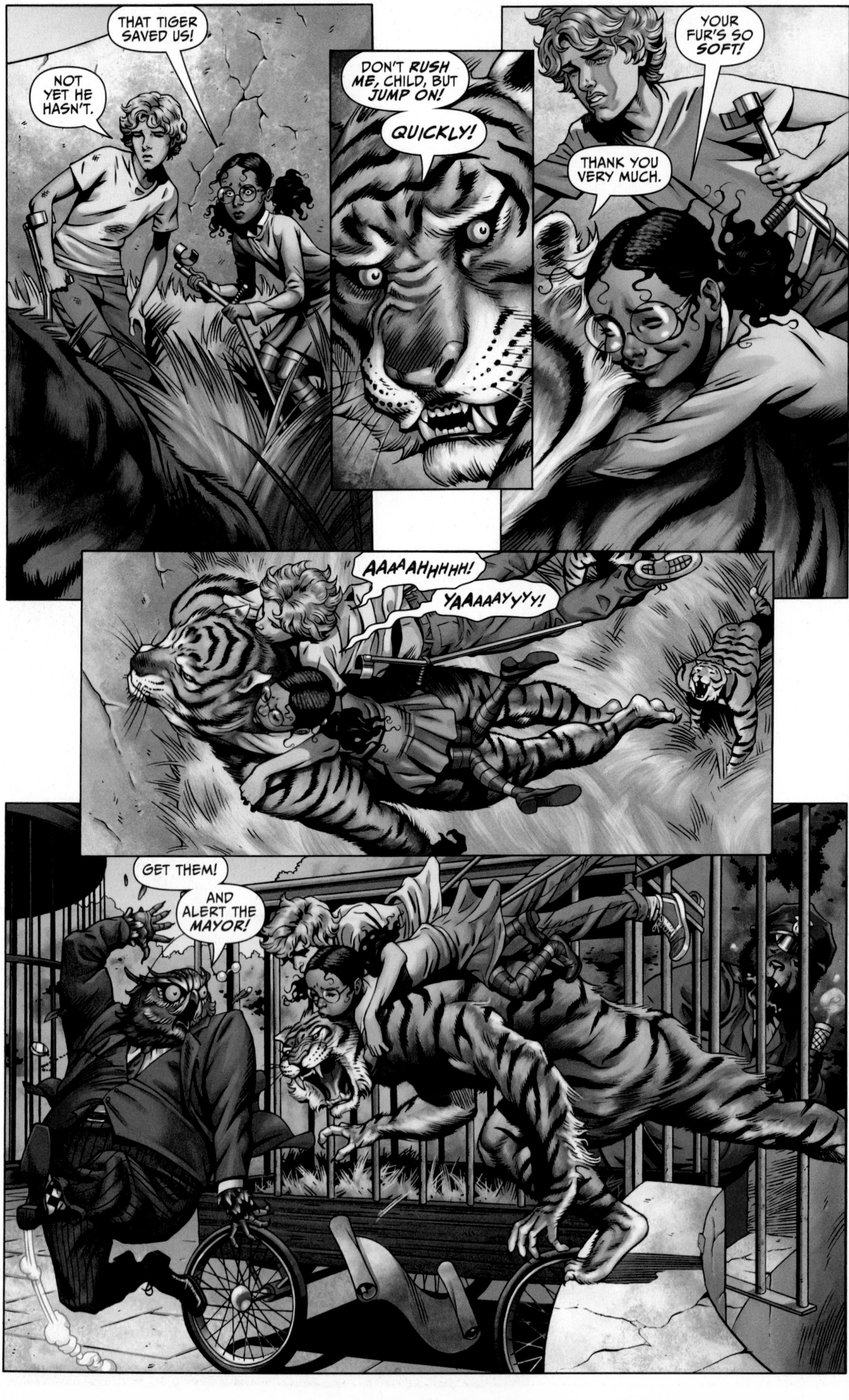
THAT TIGER SAVED US!
NOT YET HE HASN'T.
DON'T RUSH ME, CHILD, BUT JUMP ON!
QUICKLY!
YOUR FUR'S SO SOFT!
THANK YOU VERY MUCH.
AAAAAHHHHH!
YAAAAAYYYY!
GET THEM!
AND ALERT THE MAYOR!

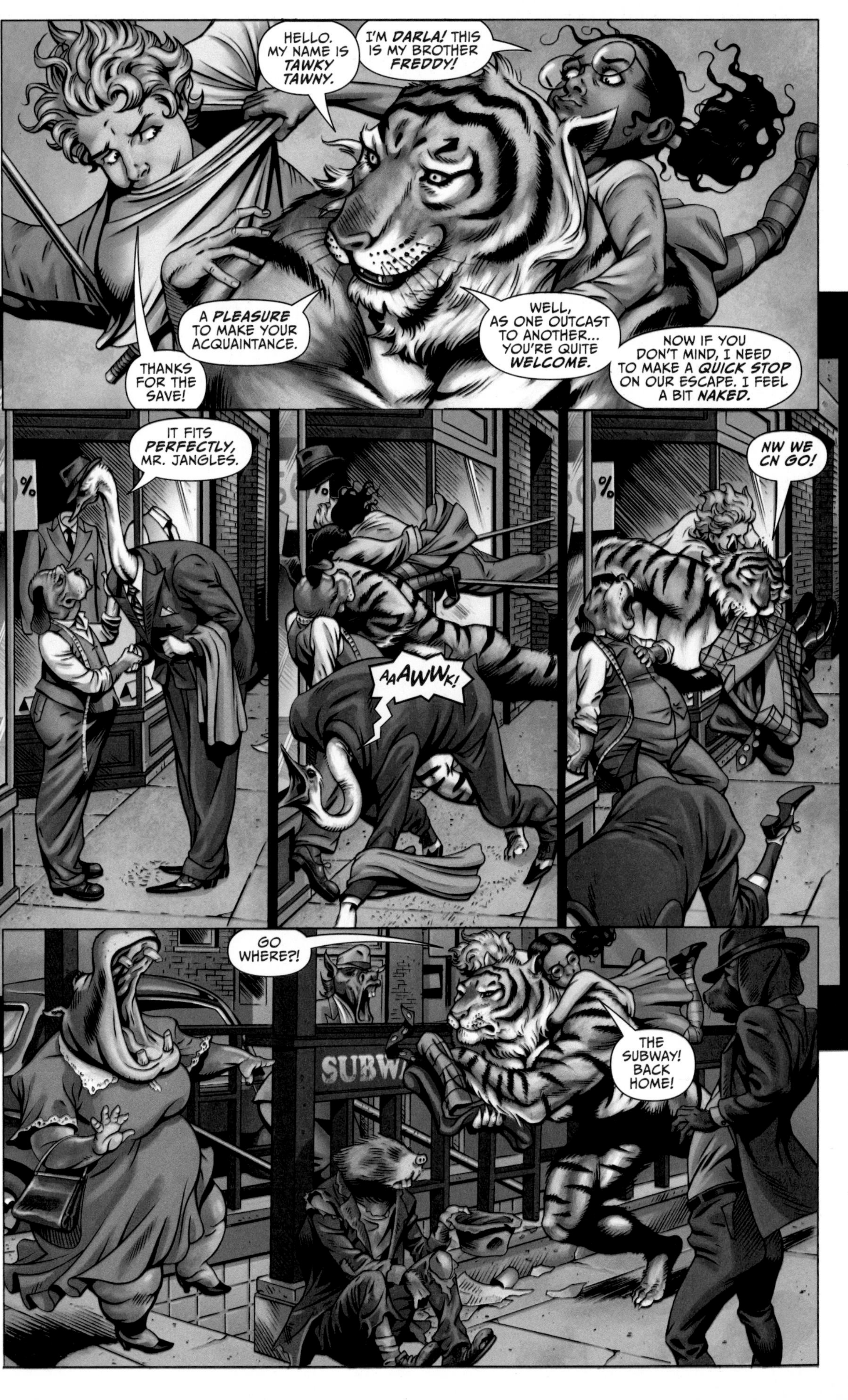
HELLO. MY NAME IS TAWKY TAWNY.
I'M DARLA! THIS IS MY BROTHER FREDDY!
A PLEASURE TO MAKE YOUR ACQUAINTANCE.
THANKS FOR THE SAVE!
WELL, AS ONE OUTCAST TO ANOTHER... YOU'RE QUITE WELCOME.
NOW IF YOU DON'T MIND, I NEED TO MAKE A QUICK STOP ON OUR ESCAPE. I FEEL A BIT NAKED.
IT FITS PERFECTLY, MR. JANGLES.
AAAWWK!
NW WE CN GO!
GO WHERE?!
THE SUBWAY! BACK HOME!
SUBW

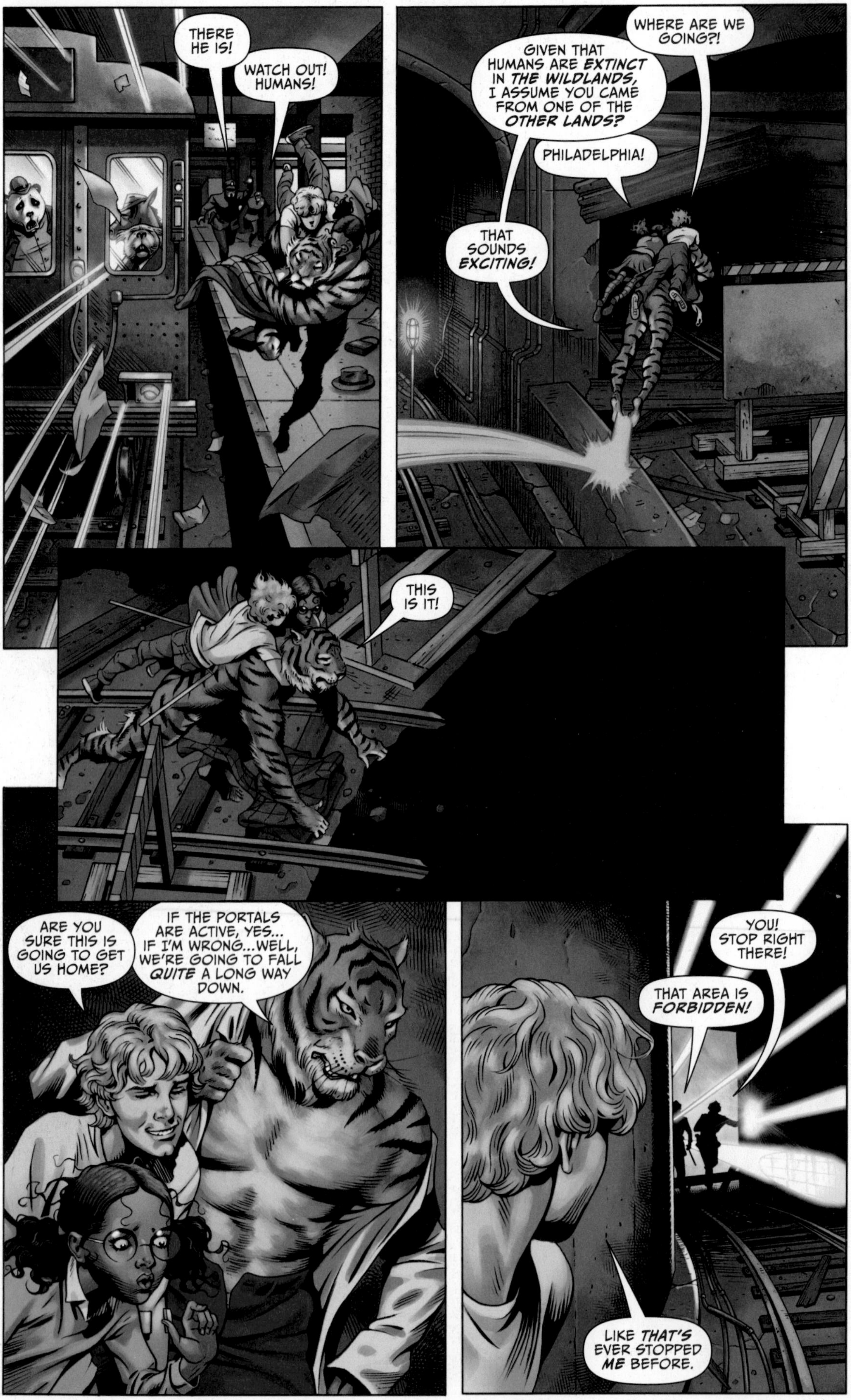
THERE HE IS!
WATCH OUT! HUMANS!
WHERE ARE WE GOING?!
GIVEN THAT HUMANS ARE EXTINCT IN THE WILDLANDS, I ASSUME YOU CAME FROM ONE OF THE OTHER LANDS?
PHILADELPHIA!
THAT SOUNDS EXCITING!
THIS IS IT!
ARE YOU SURE THIS IS GOING TO GET US HOME?
IF THE PORTALS ARE ACTIVE, YES... IF I'M WRONG...WELL, WE'RE GOING TO FALL QUITE A LONG WAY DOWN.
YOU! STOP RIGHT THERE!
THAT AREA IS FORBIDDEN!
LIKE THAT'S EVER STOPPED ME BEFORE.

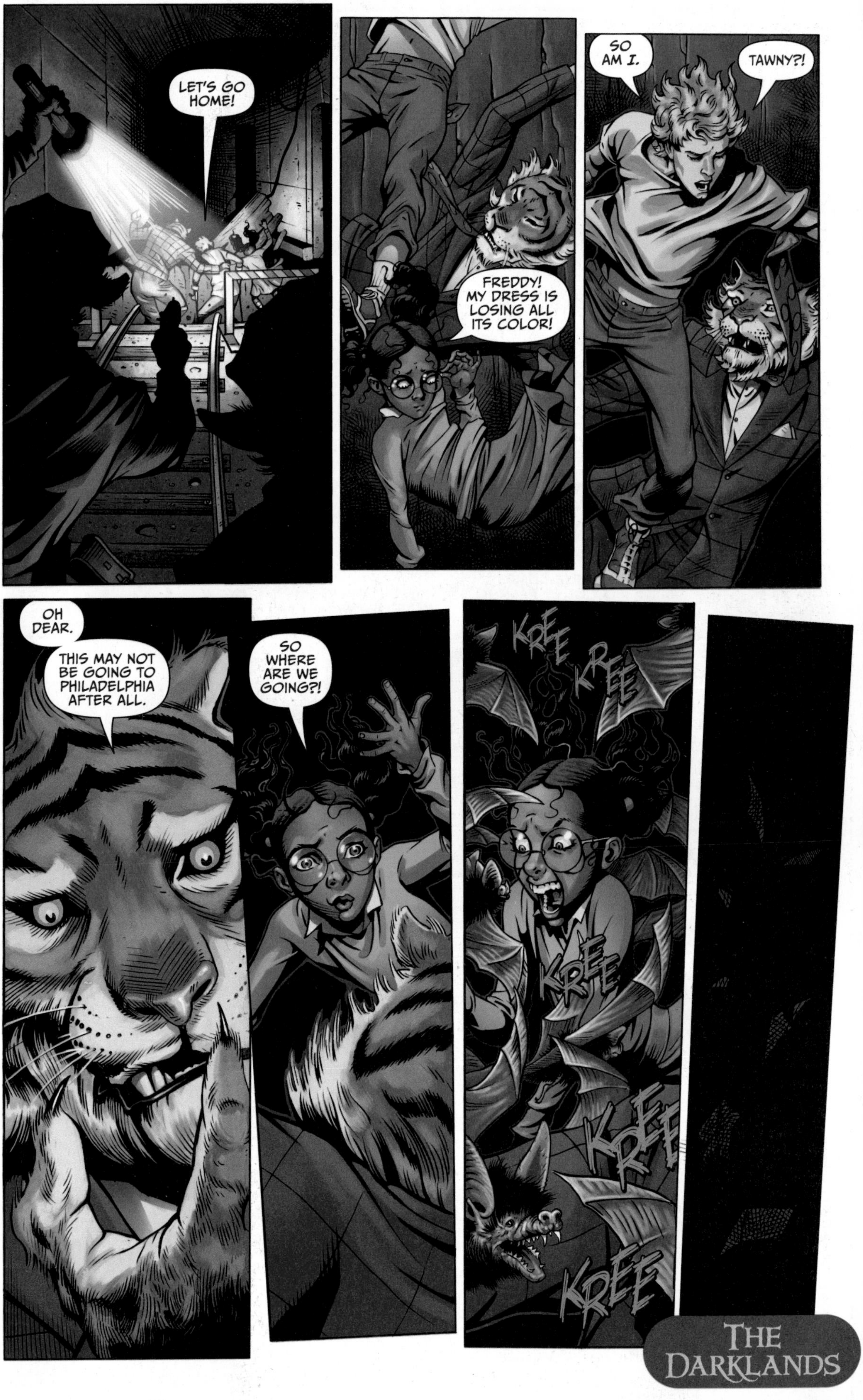
LET'S GO HOME!
FREDDY! MY DRESS IS LOSING ALL ITS COLOR!
SO AM I.
TAWNY?!
OH DEAR.
THIS MAY NOT BE GOING TO PHILADELPHIA AFTER ALL.
SO WHERE ARE WE GOING?!
KREE KREE
KREE
KREE KREE
KREE
THE DARKLANDS

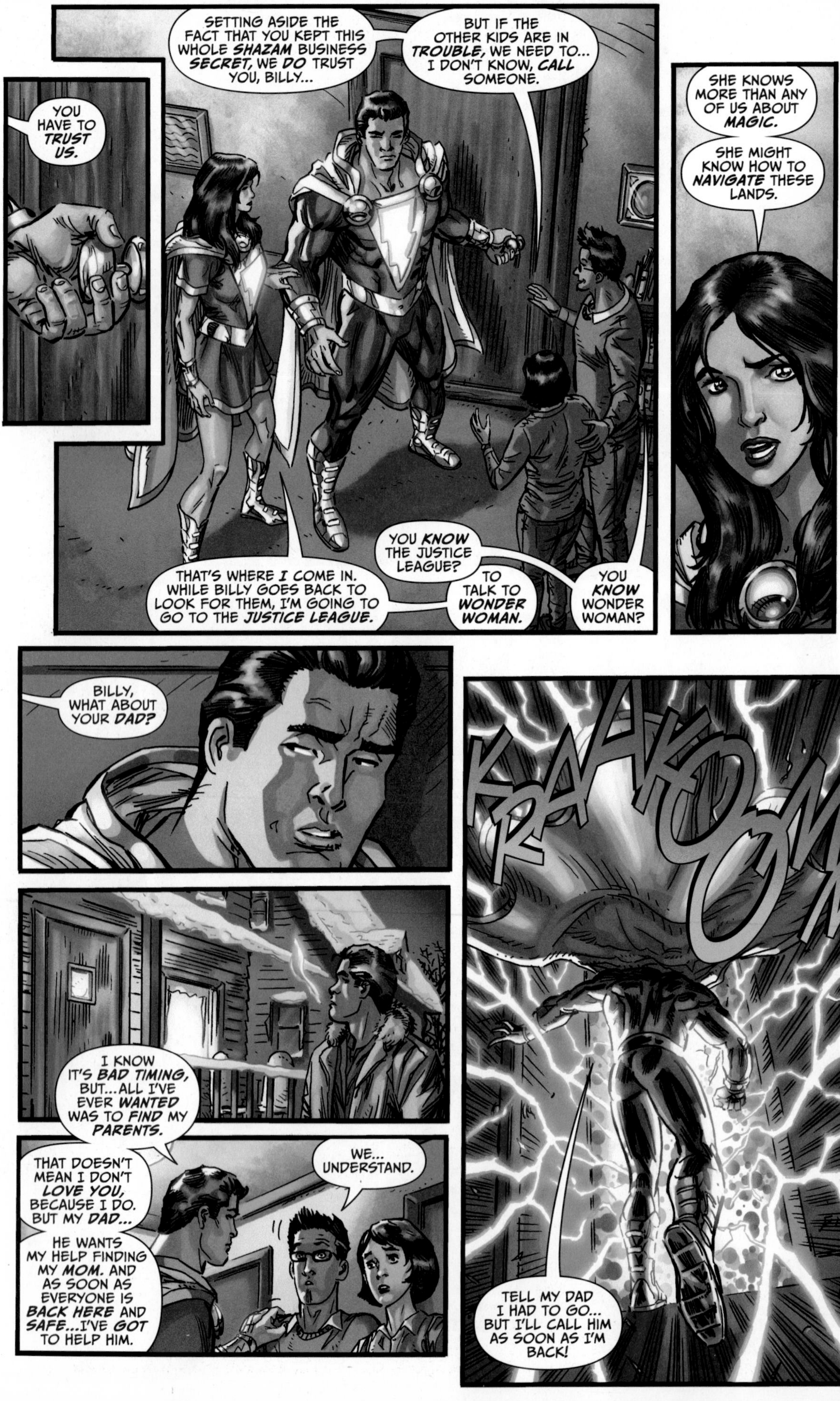
YOU HAVE TO TRUST US.
SETTING ASIDE THE FACT THAT YOU KEPT THIS WHOLE SHAZAM BUSINESS SECRET, WE DO TRUST YOU, BILLY...
BUT IF THE OTHER KIDS ARE IN TROUBLE, WE NEED TO... I DON'T KNOW, CALL SOMEONE.
THAT'S WHERE I COME IN. WHILE BILLY GOES BACK TO LOOK FOR THEM, I'M GOING TO GO TO THE JUSTICE LEAGUE.
YOU KNOW THE JUSTICE LEAGUE?
TO TALK TO WONDER WOMAN.
YOU KNOW WONDER WOMAN?
SHE KNOWS MORE THAN ANY OF US ABOUT MAGIC.
SHE MIGHT KNOW HOW TO NAVIGATE THESE LANDS.
BILLY, WHAT ABOUT YOUR DAD?
I KNOW IT'S BAD TIMING, BUT...ALL I'VE EVER WANTED WAS TO FIND MY PARENTS.
THAT DOESN'T MEAN I DON'T LOVE YOU, BECAUSE I DO. BUT MY DAD...
HE WANTS MY HELP FINDING MY MOM. AND AS SOON AS EVERYONE IS BACK HERE AND SAFE...I'VE GOT TO HELP HIM.
WE... UNDERSTAND.
KRAAKOOM
TELL MY DAD I HAD TO GO... BUT I'LL CALL HIM AS SOON AS I'M BACK!

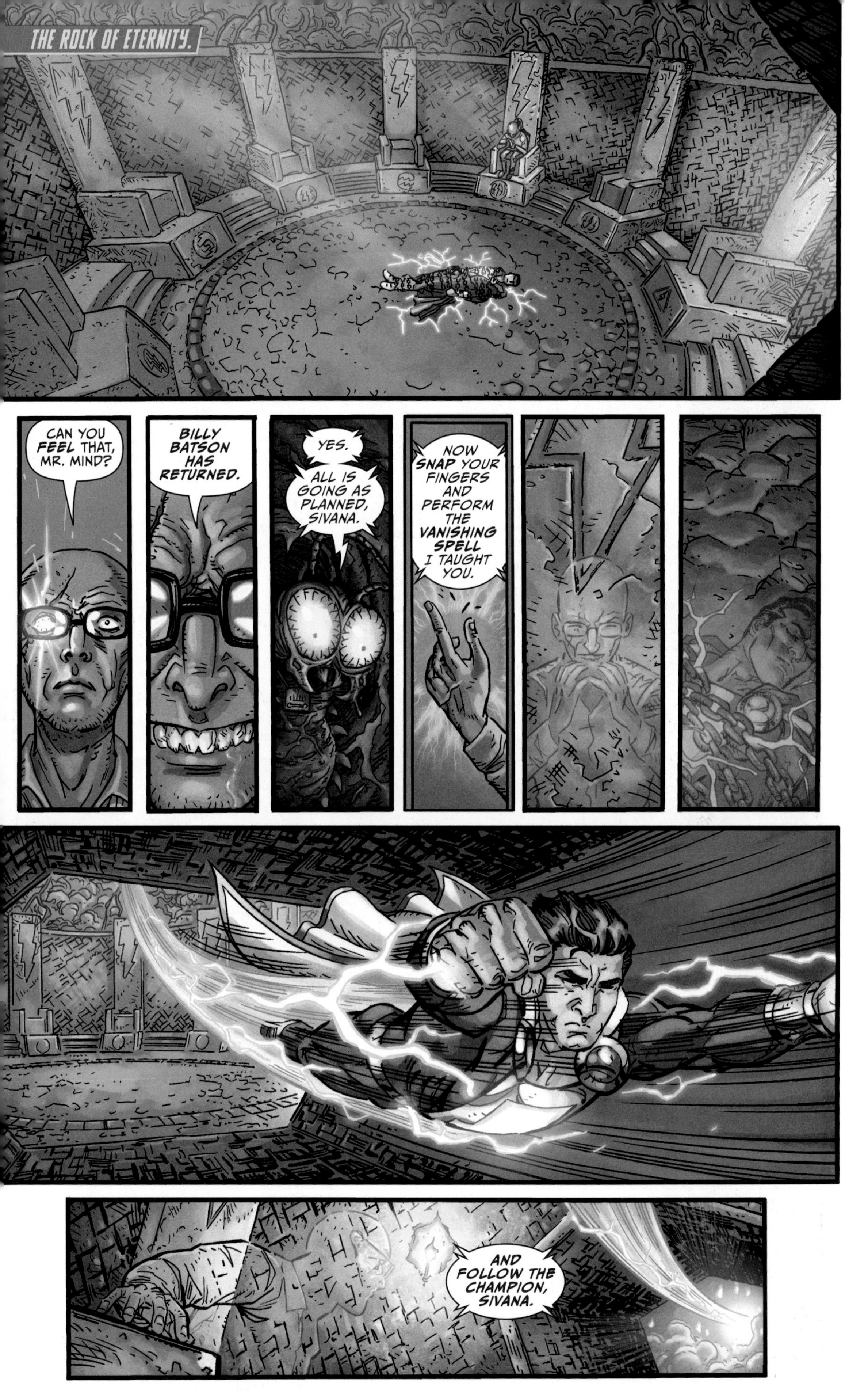
THE ROCK OF ETERNITY.
CAN YOU FEEL THAT, MR. MIND?
BILLY BATSON HAS RETURNED.
YES. ALL IS GOING AS PLANNED, SIVANA.
NOW SNAP YOUR FINGERS AND PERFORM THE VANISHING SPELL I TAUGHT YOU.
AND FOLLOW THE CHAMPION, SIVANA.

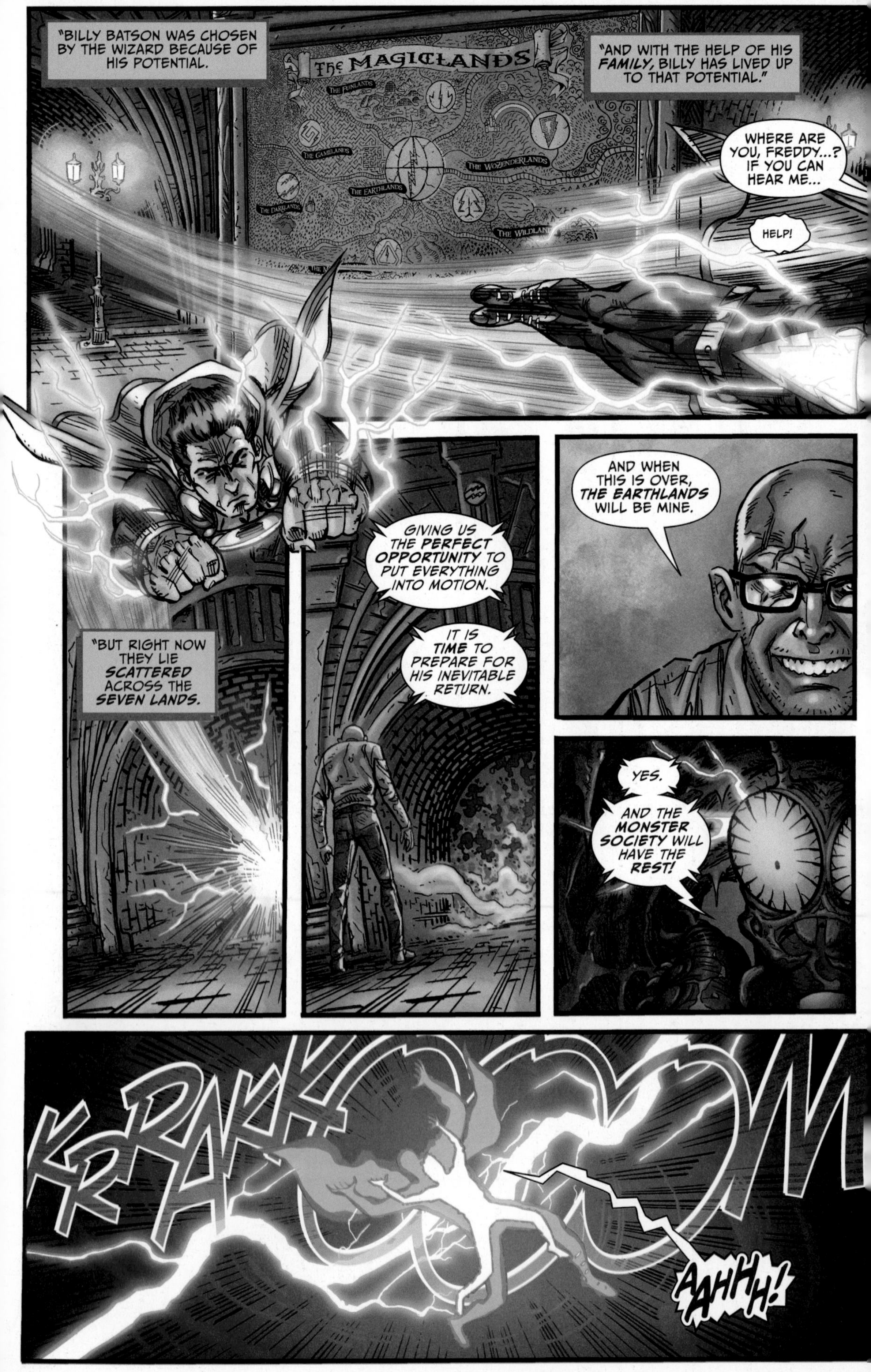
"BILLY BATSON WAS CHOSEN BY THE WIZARD BECAUSE OF HIS POTENTIAL.
The MAGICLANDS
THE FUNLANDS
THE GAMELANDS
THE WOZENDERLANDS
THE EARTHLANDS
THE DARKLANDS
THE WILDLANDS
"AND WITH THE HELP OF HIS FAMILY, BILLY HAS LIVED UP TO THAT POTENTIAL."
WHERE ARE YOU, FREDDY...? IF YOU CAN HEAR ME...
HELP!
"BUT RIGHT NOW THEY LIE SCATTERED ACROSS THE SEVEN LANDS.
GIVING US THE PERFECT OPPORTUNITY TO PUT EVERYTHING INTO MOTION.
IT IS TIME TO PREPARE FOR HIS INEVITABLE RETURN.
AND WHEN THIS IS OVER, THE EARTHLANDS WILL BE MINE.
YES.
AND THE MONSTER SOCIETY WILL HAVE THE REST!
KRAKKOOOM
AAHHH!

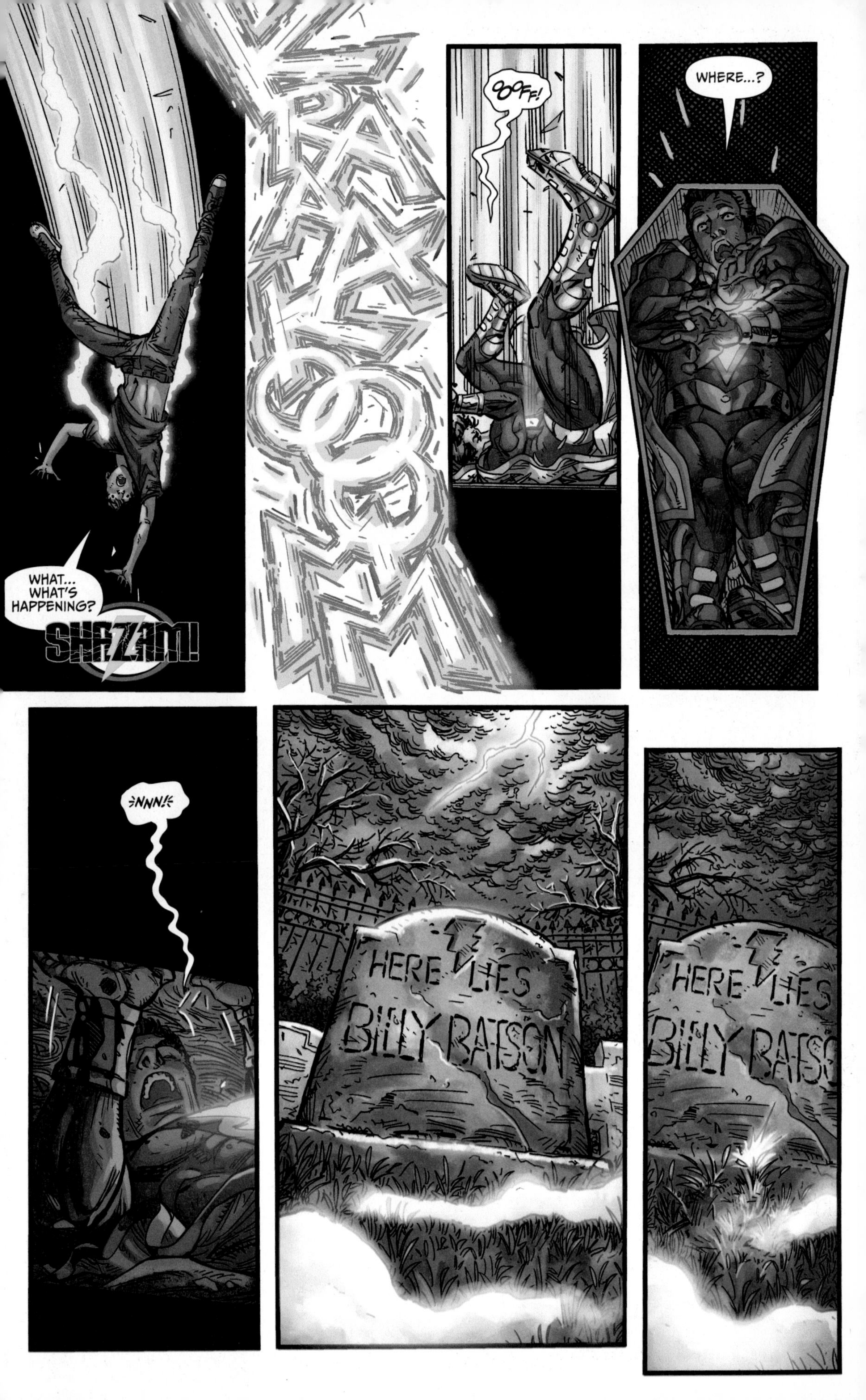
WHAT... WHAT'S HAPPENING?
SHAZAM!
KRAKA-BOOM
OOOFF!
WHERE...?
NNN!
HERE LIES BILLY BATSON
HERE LIES BILLY BATSO

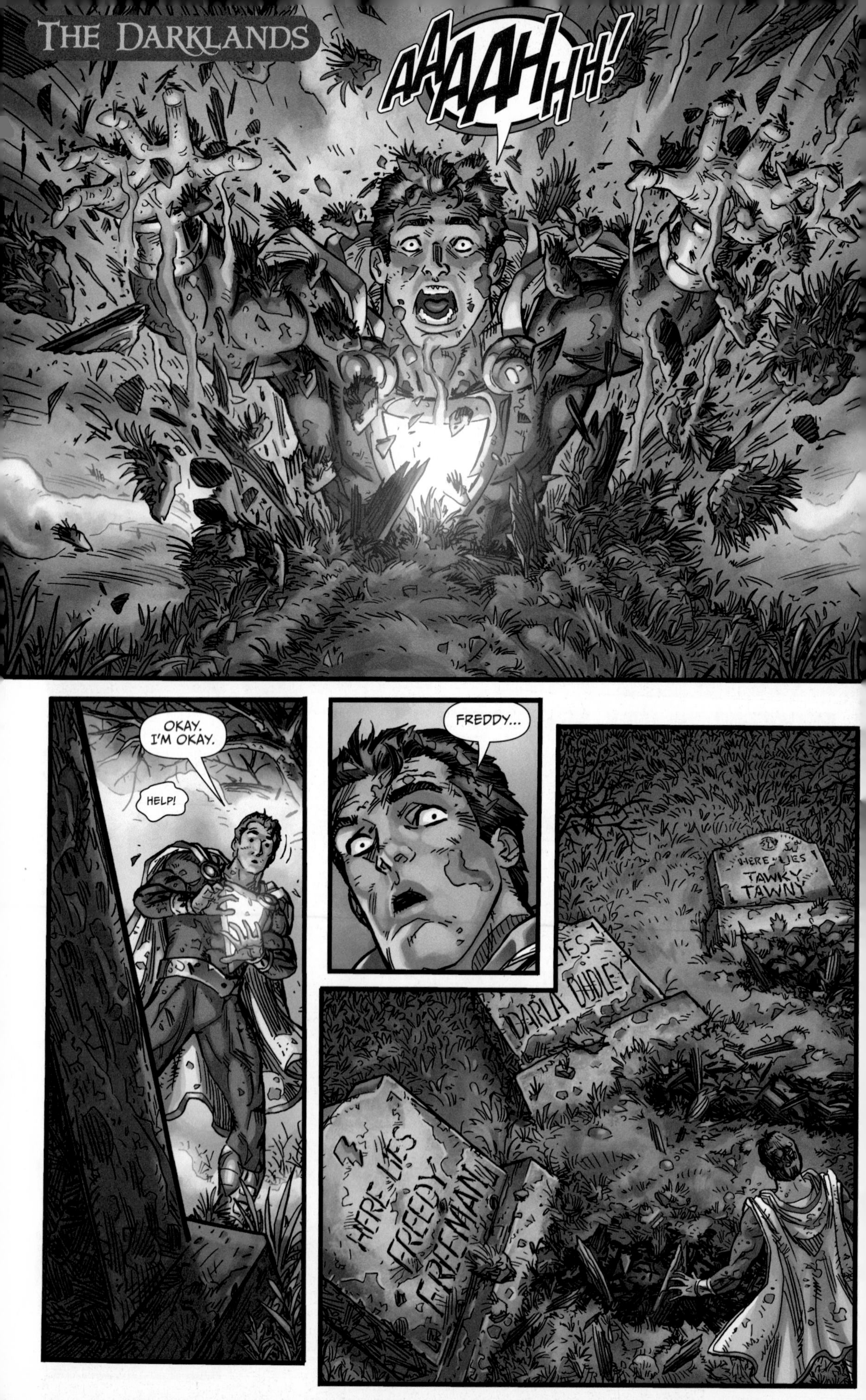
THE DARKLANDS
AAAAHHH!
OKAY. I'M OKAY.
HELP!
FREDDY...
HERE LIES TAWKY TAWNY
DARLA DUDLEY
HERE LIES FREDDY FREEMAN

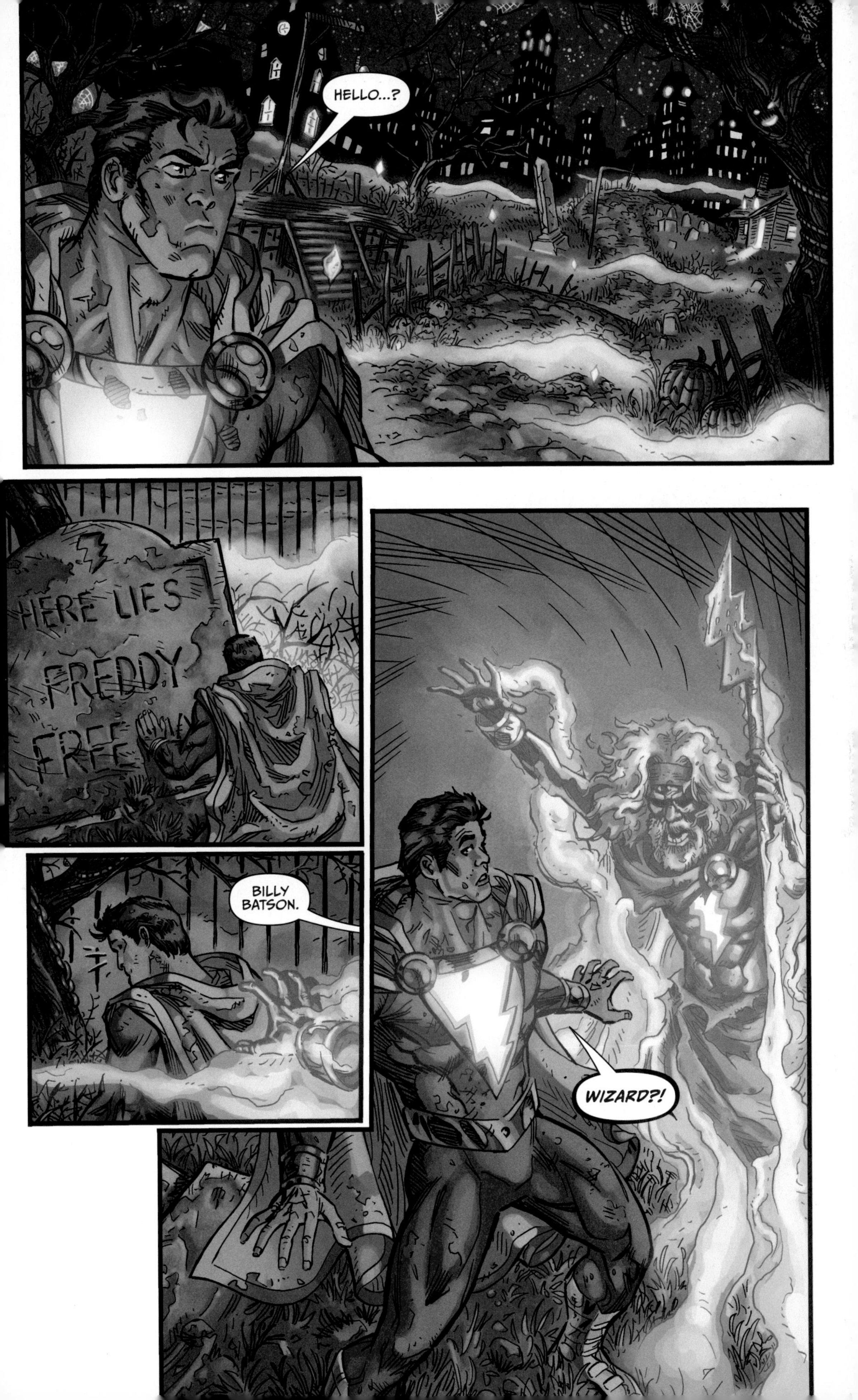
HELLO...?
HERE LIES
FREDDY
FREE
BILLY BATSON.
WIZARD?!

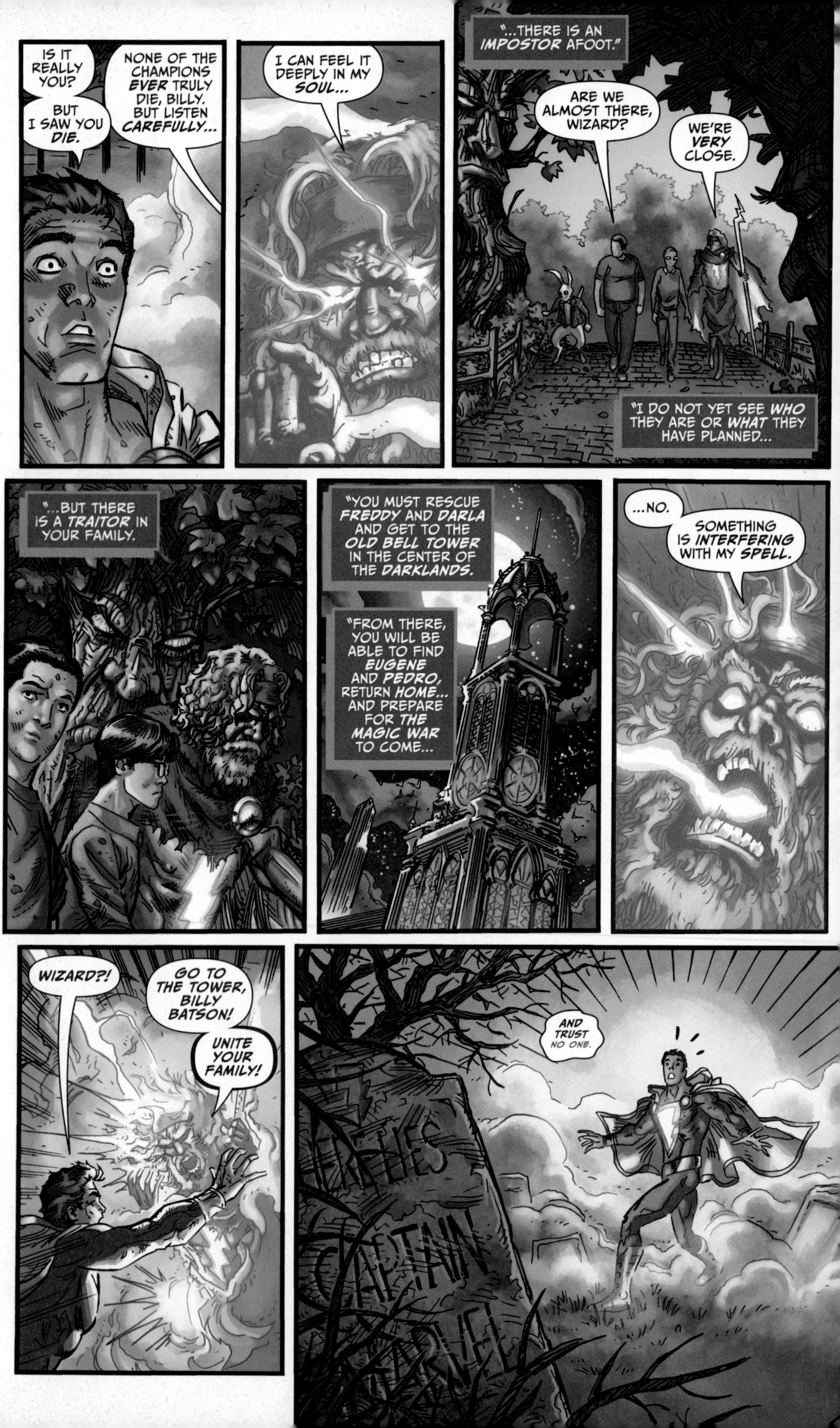
IS IT REALLY YOU?
BUT I SAW YOU DIE.
NONE OF THE CHAMPIONS EVER TRULY DIE, BILLY. BUT LISTEN CAREFULLY...
I CAN FEEL IT DEEPLY IN MY SOUL...
"...THERE IS AN IMPOSTOR AFOOT."
ARE WE ALMOST THERE, WIZARD?
WE'RE VERY CLOSE.
"I DO NOT YET SEE WHO THEY ARE OR WHAT THEY HAVE PLANNED...
"...BUT THERE IS A TRAITOR IN YOUR FAMILY.
"YOU MUST RESCUE FREDDY AND DARLA AND GET TO THE OLD BELL TOWER IN THE CENTER OF THE DARKLANDS.
"FROM THERE, YOU WILL BE ABLE TO FIND EUGENE AND PEDRO, RETURN HOME... AND PREPARE FOR THE MAGIC WAR TO COME...
...NO.
SOMETHING IS INTERFERING WITH MY SPELL.
WIZARD?!
GO TO THE TOWER, BILLY BATSON!
UNITE YOUR FAMILY!
AND TRUST NO ONE.
HERE LIES CAPTAIN MARVEL

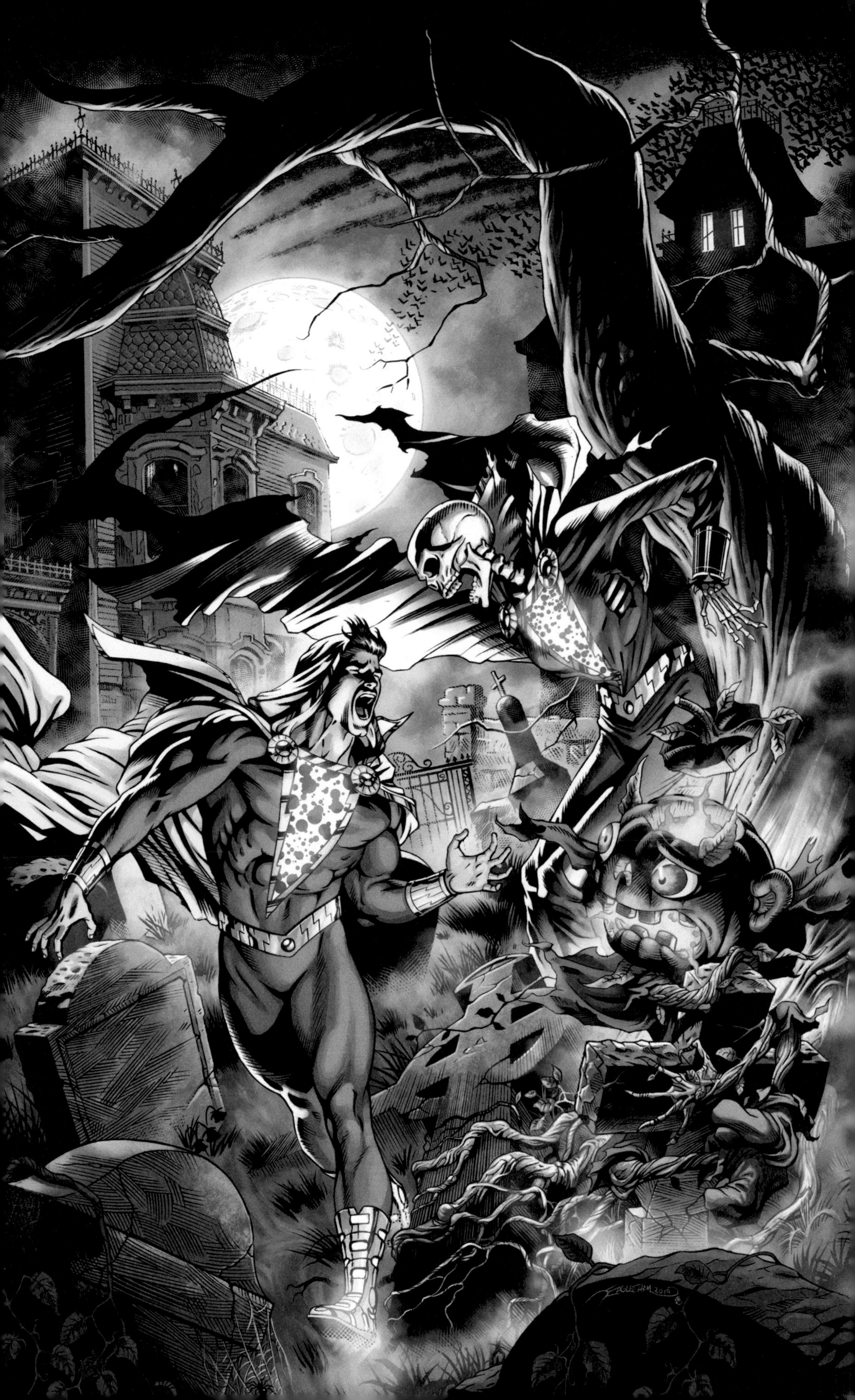

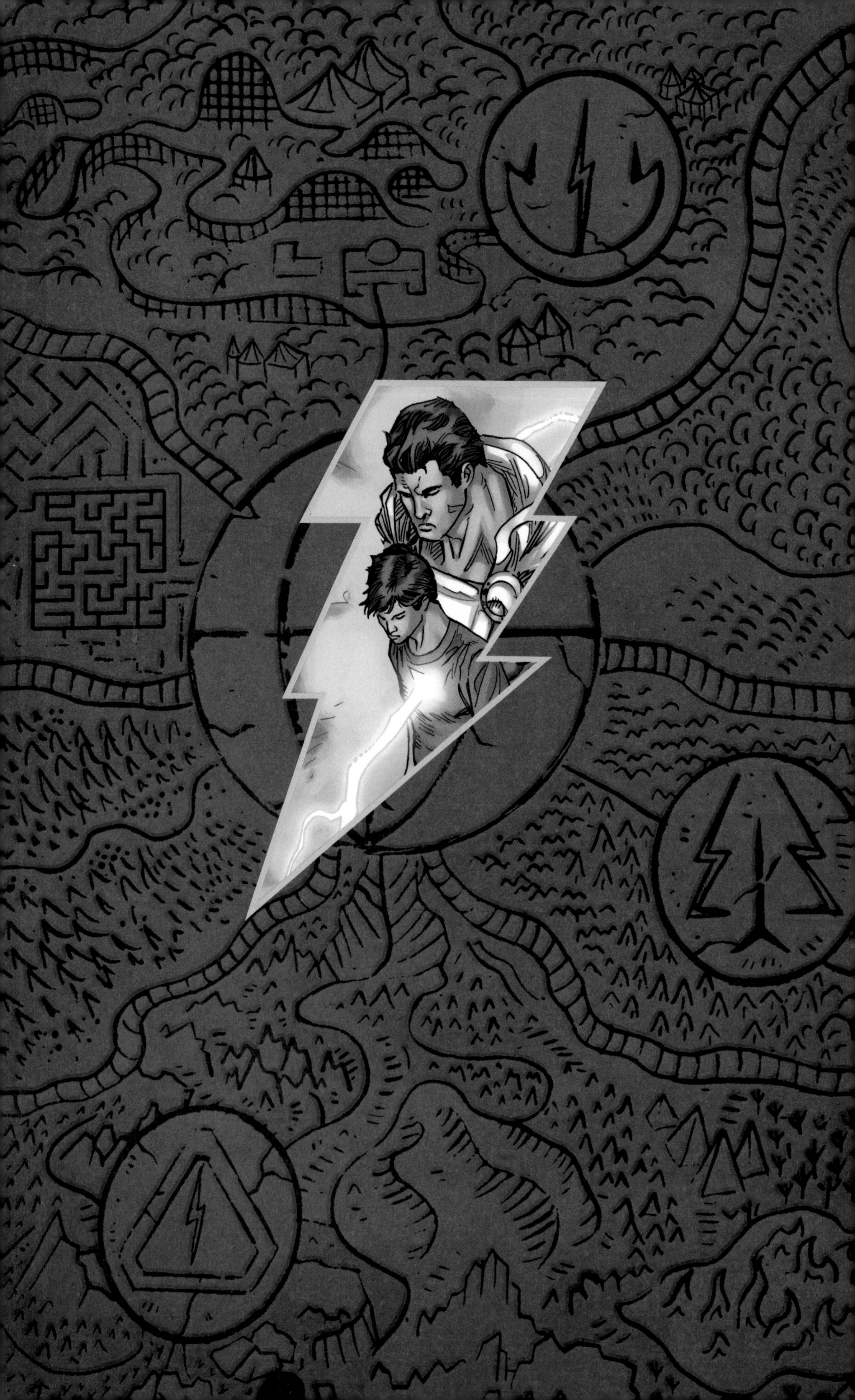

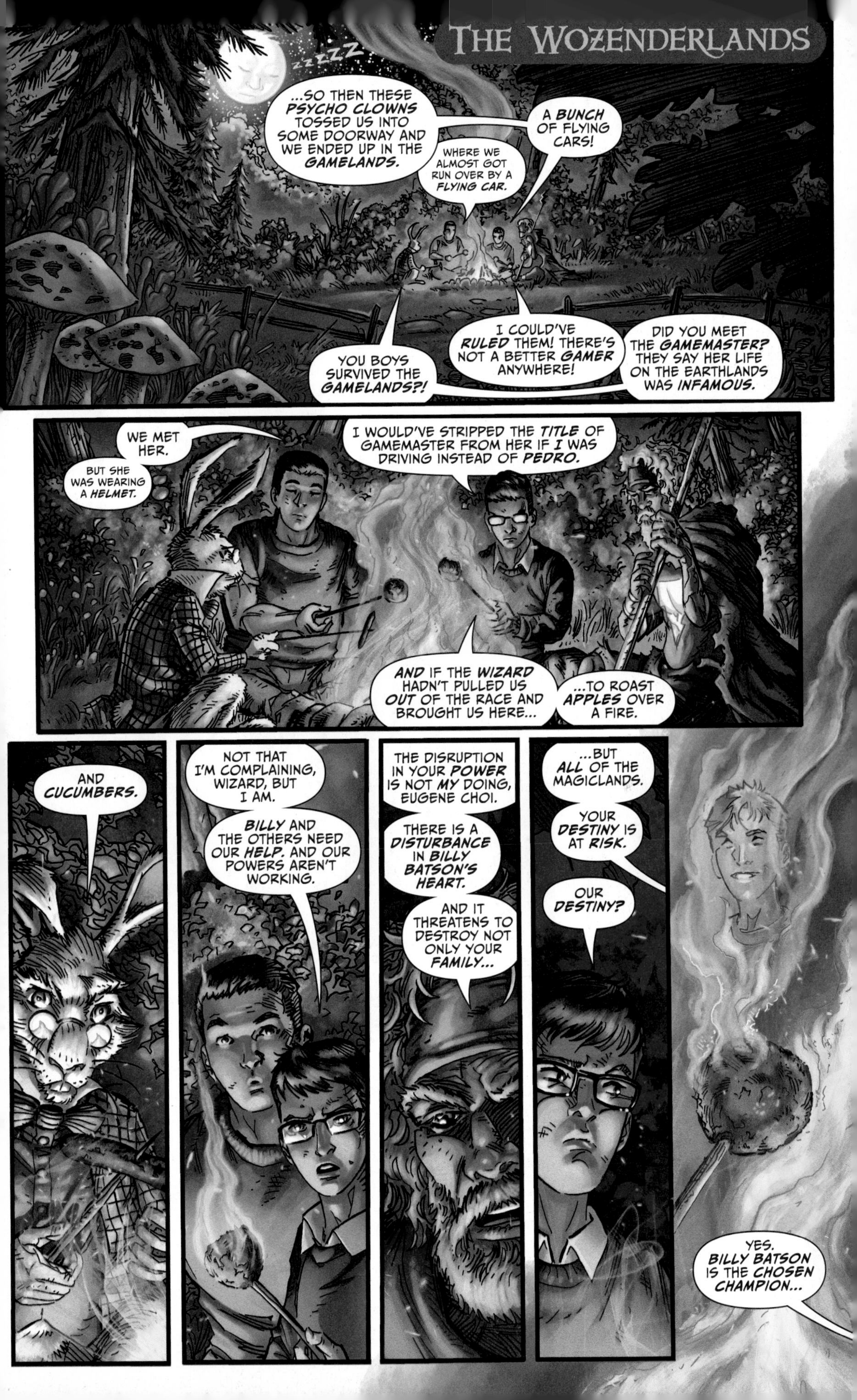
THE WOZENDERLANDS
ZZZZZ
...SO THEN THESE PSYCHO CLOWNS TOSSED US INTO SOME DOORWAY AND WE ENDED UP IN THE GAMELANDS.
WHERE WE ALMOST GOT RUN OVER BY A FLYING CAR.
A BUNCH OF FLYING CARS!
YOU BOYS SURVIVED THE GAMELANDS?!
I COULD'VE RULED THEM! THERE'S NOT A BETTER GAMER ANYWHERE!
DID YOU MEET THE GAMEMASTER? THEY SAY HER LIFE ON THE EARTHLANDS WAS INFAMOUS.
WE MET HER.
BUT SHE WAS WEARING A HELMET.
I WOULD'VE STRIPPED THE TITLE OF GAMEMASTER FROM HER IF I WAS DRIVING INSTEAD OF PEDRO.
AND IF THE WIZARD HADN'T PULLED US OUT OF THE RACE AND BROUGHT US HERE...
...TO ROAST APPLES OVER A FIRE.
AND CUCUMBERS.
NOT THAT I'M COMPLAINING, WIZARD, BUT I AM.
BILLY AND THE OTHERS NEED OUR HELP. AND OUR POWERS AREN'T WORKING.
THE DISRUPTION IN YOUR POWER IS NOT MY DOING, EUGENE CHOI.
THERE IS A DISTURBANCE IN BILLY BATSON'S HEART.
AND IT THREATENS TO DESTROY NOT ONLY YOUR FAMILY...
...BUT ALL OF THE MAGICLANDS.
YOUR DESTINY IS AT RISK.
OUR DESTINY?
YES. BILLY BATSON IS THE CHOSEN CHAMPION...

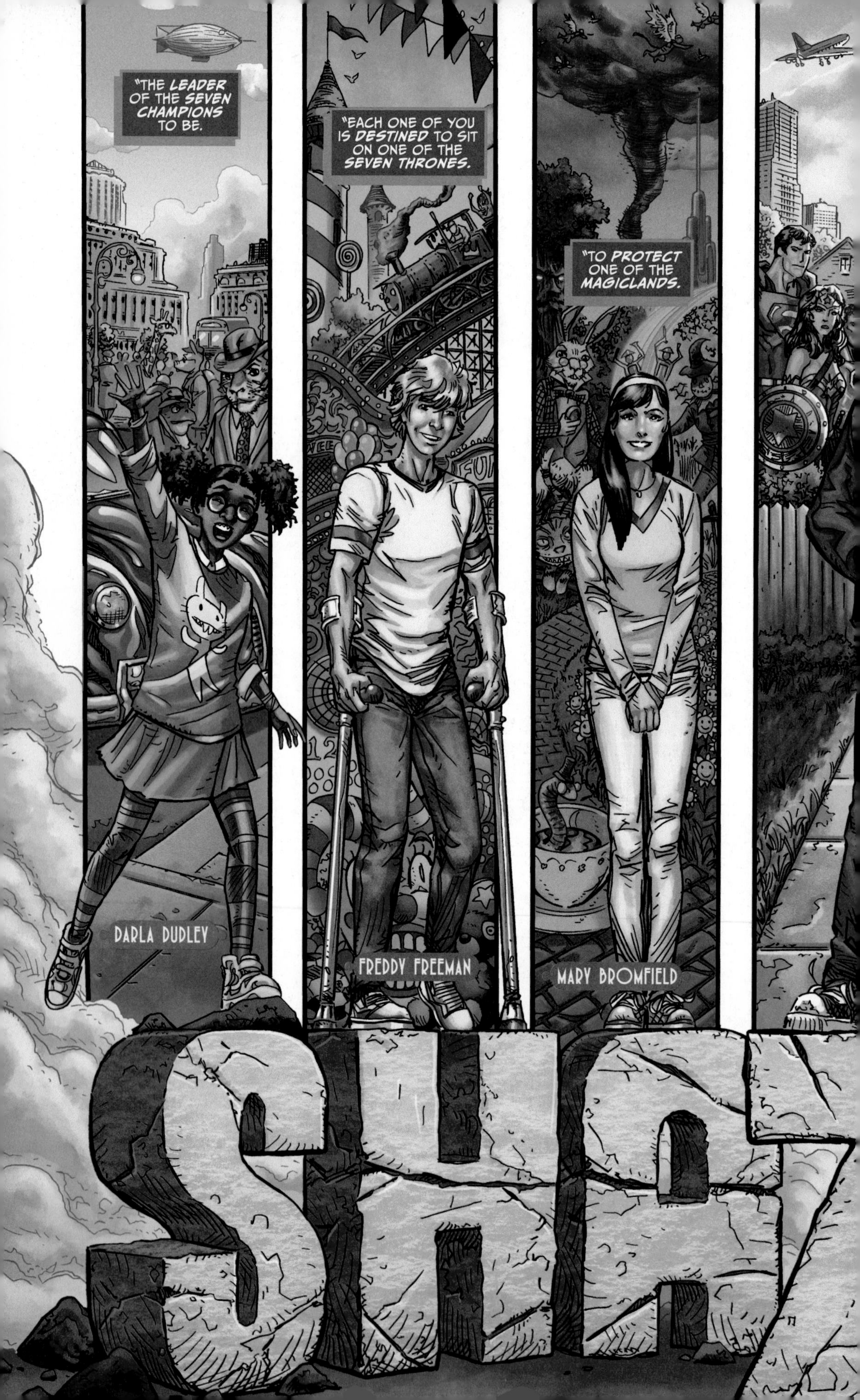

"THE LEADER OF THE SEVEN CHAMPIONS TO BE.
"EACH ONE OF YOU IS DESTINED TO SIT ON ONE OF THE SEVEN THRONES.
"TO PROTECT ONE OF THE MAGICLANDS.
DARLA DUDLEY
FREDDY FREEMAN
MARY BROMFIELD

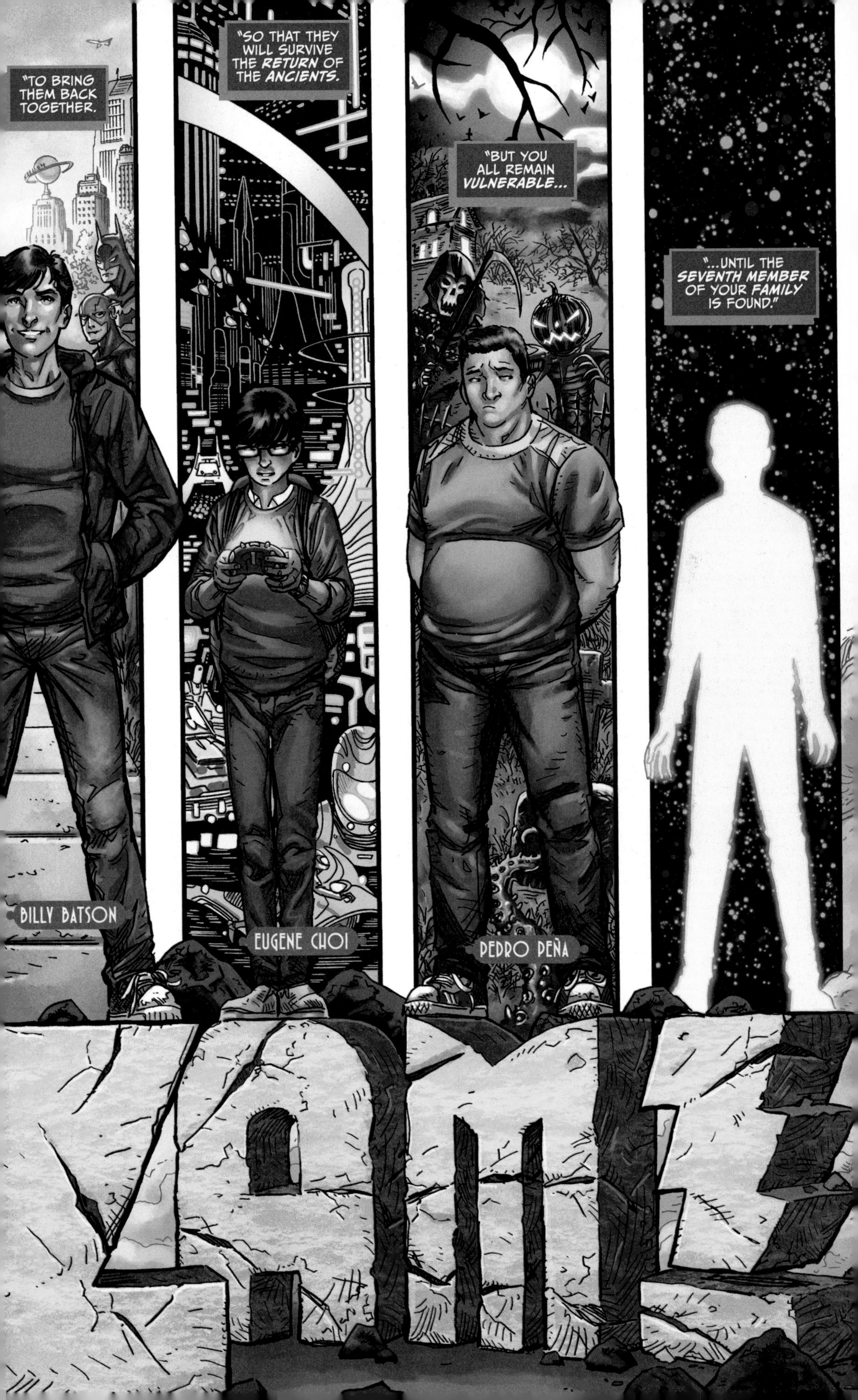
"TO BRING THEM BACK TOGETHER.
"SO THAT THEY WILL SURVIVE THE RETURN OF THE ANCIENTS.
"BUT YOU ALL REMAIN VULNERABLE...
"...UNTIL THE SEVENTH MEMBER OF YOUR FAMILY IS FOUND."
BILLY BATSON
EUGENE CHOI
PEDRO PEÑA

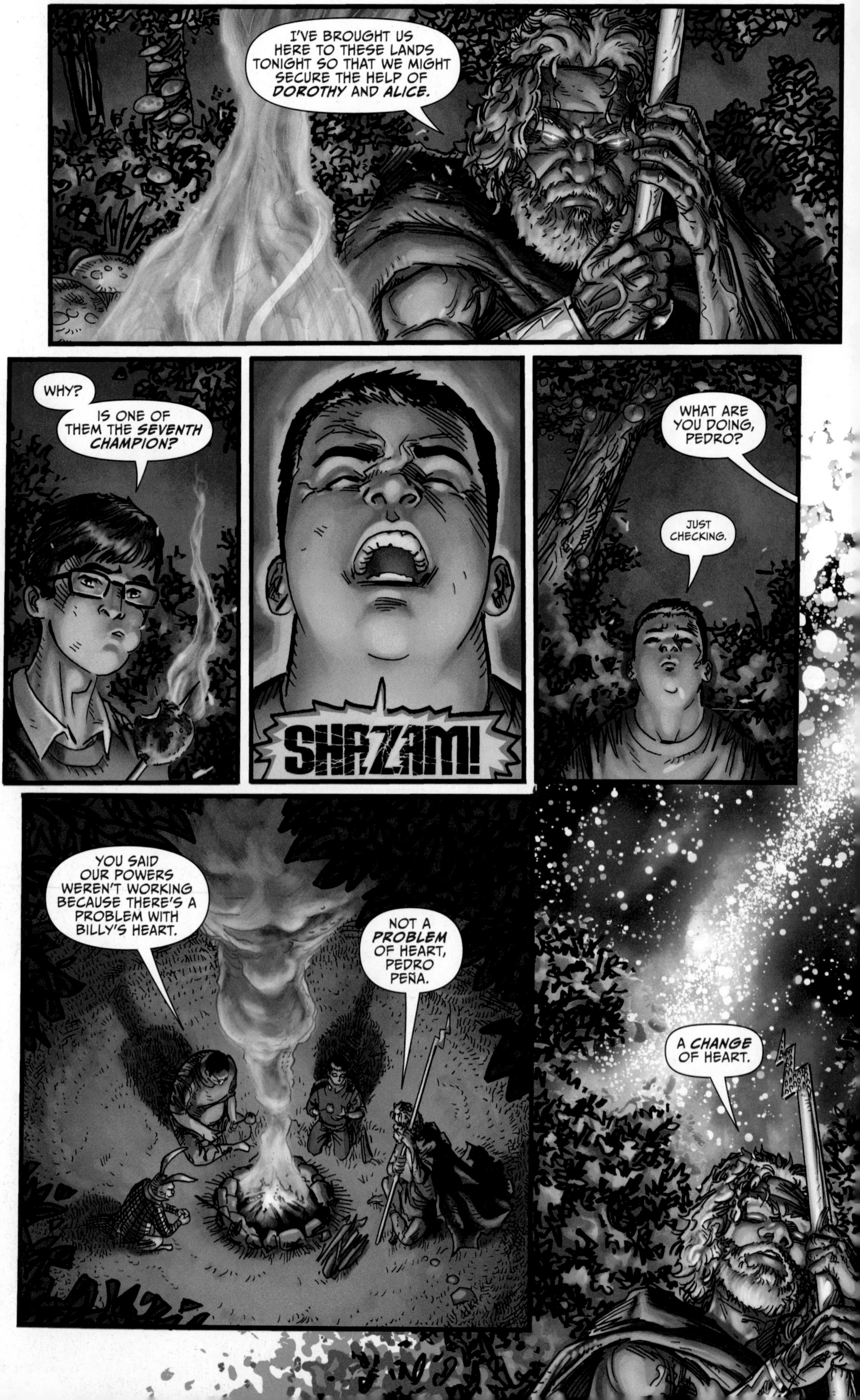
I'VE BROUGHT US HERE TO THESE LANDS TONIGHT SO THAT WE MIGHT SECURE THE HELP OF DOROTHY AND ALICE.
WHY?
IS ONE OF THEM THE SEVENTH CHAMPION?
SHAZAM!
WHAT ARE YOU DOING, PEDRO?
JUST CHECKING.
YOU SAID OUR POWERS WEREN'T WORKING BECAUSE THERE'S A PROBLEM WITH BILLY'S HEART.
NOT A PROBLEM OF HEART, PEDRO PEÑA.
A CHANGE OF HEART.

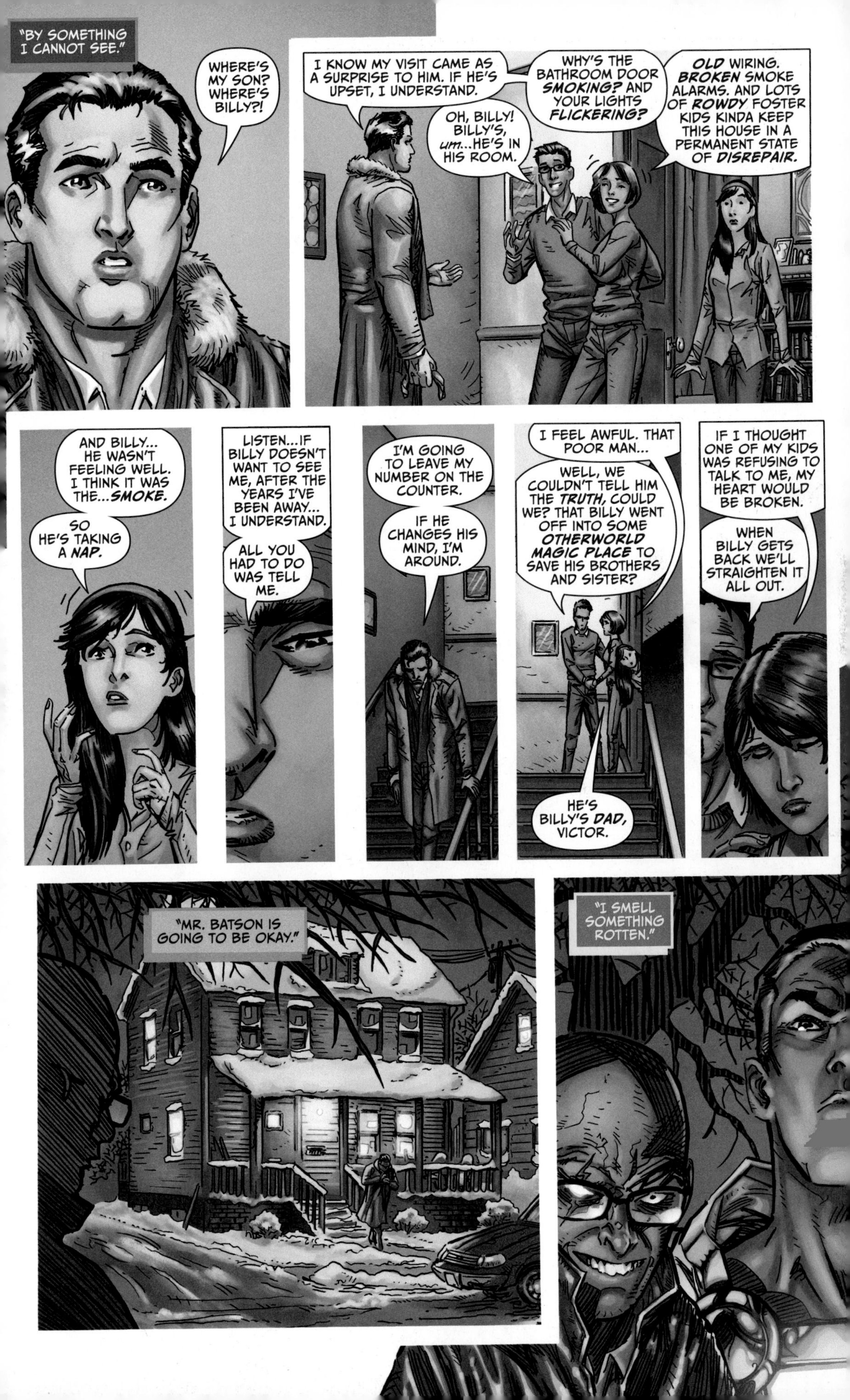
"BY SOMETHING I CANNOT SEE."
WHERE'S MY SON? WHERE'S BILLY?!
I KNOW MY VISIT CAME AS A SURPRISE TO HIM. IF HE'S UPSET, I UNDERSTAND.
OH, BILLY! BILLY'S, *um*...HE'S IN HIS ROOM.
WHY'S THE BATHROOM DOOR **SMOKING?** AND YOUR LIGHTS **FLICKERING?**
**OLD** WIRING. **BROKEN** SMOKE ALARMS. AND LOTS OF **ROWDY** FOSTER KIDS KINDA KEEP THIS HOUSE IN A PERMANENT STATE OF **DISREPAIR.**
AND BILLY... HE WASN'T FEELING WELL. I THINK IT WAS THE...**SMOKE.**
SO HE'S TAKING A **NAP.**
LISTEN...IF BILLY DOESN'T WANT TO SEE ME, AFTER THE YEARS I'VE BEEN AWAY... I UNDERSTAND.
ALL YOU HAD TO DO WAS TELL ME.
I'M GOING TO LEAVE MY NUMBER ON THE COUNTER.
IF HE CHANGES HIS MIND, I'M AROUND.
I FEEL AWFUL. THAT POOR MAN...
WELL, WE COULDN'T TELL HIM THE **TRUTH,** COULD WE? THAT BILLY WENT OFF INTO SOME **OTHERWORLD MAGIC PLACE** TO SAVE HIS BROTHERS AND SISTER?
HE'S BILLY'S **DAD,** VICTOR.
IF I THOUGHT ONE OF MY KIDS WAS REFUSING TO TALK TO ME, MY HEART WOULD BE BROKEN.
WHEN BILLY GETS BACK WE'LL STRAIGHTEN IT ALL OUT.
"MR. BATSON IS GOING TO BE OKAY."
"I SMELL SOMETHING ROTTEN."

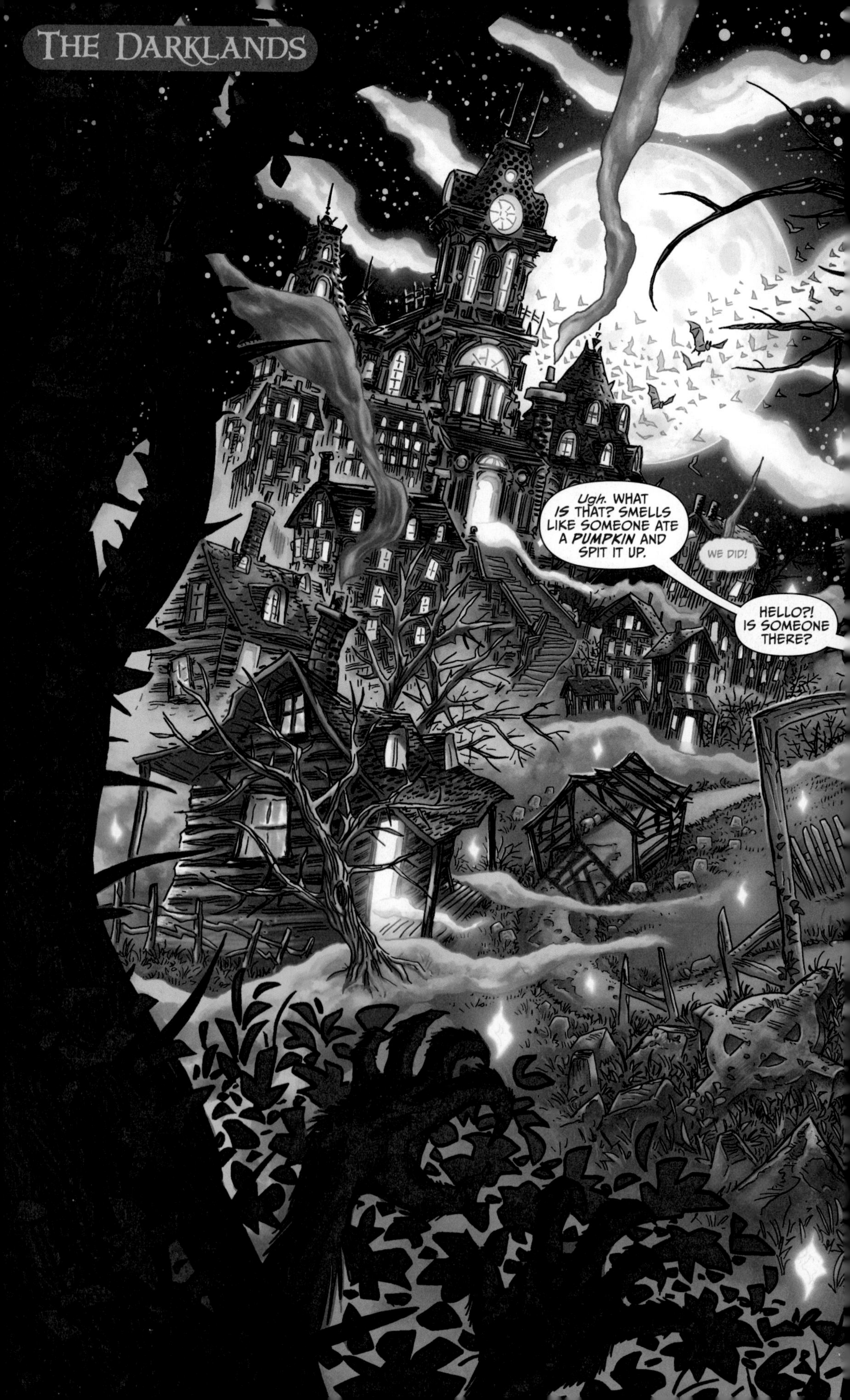
THE DARKLANDS
Ugh. WHAT IS THAT? SMELLS LIKE SOMEONE ATE A PUMPKIN AND SPIT IT UP.
WE DID!
HELLO?! IS SOMEONE THERE?

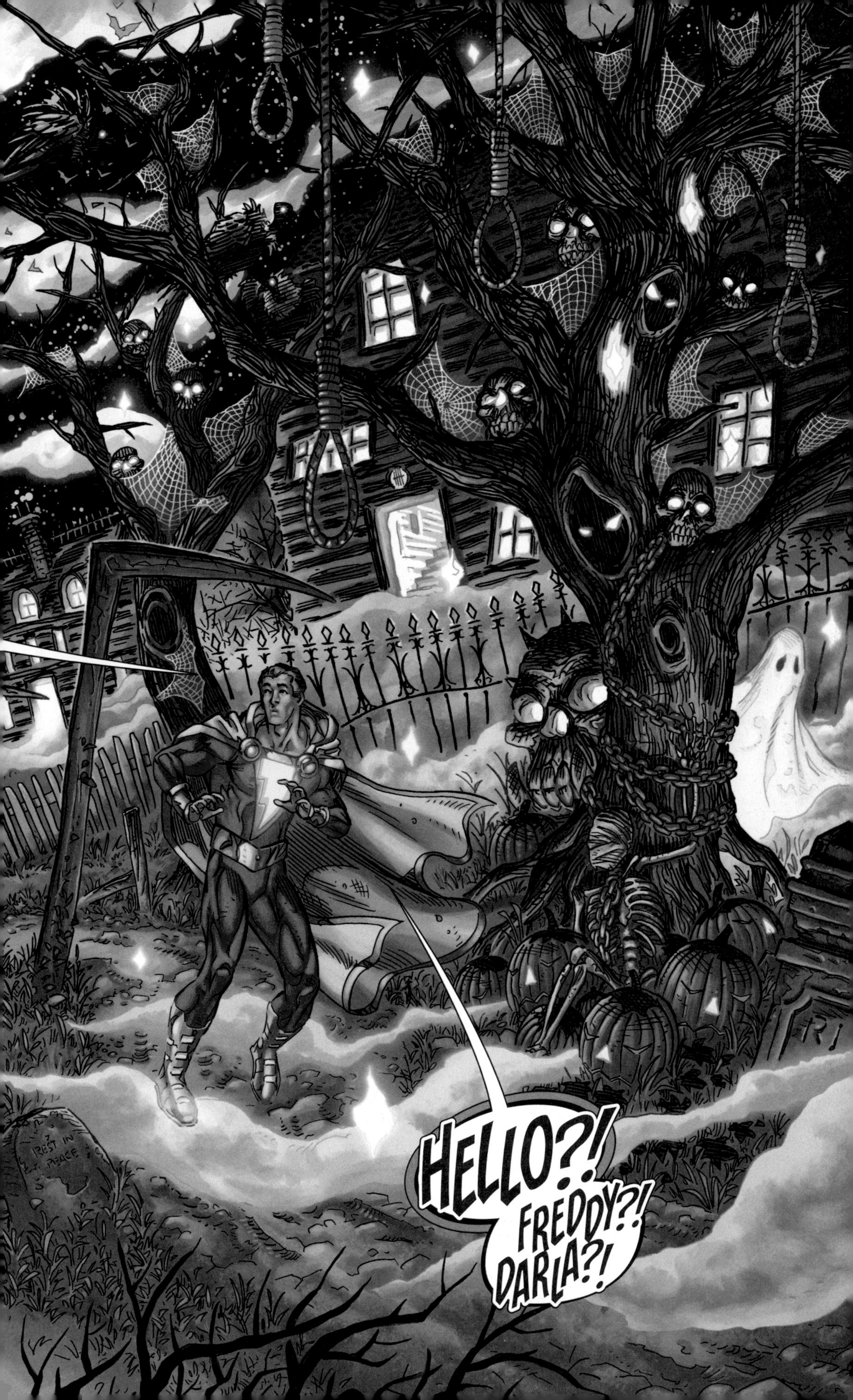
HELLO?! FREDDY?! DARLA?!
REST IN PEACE

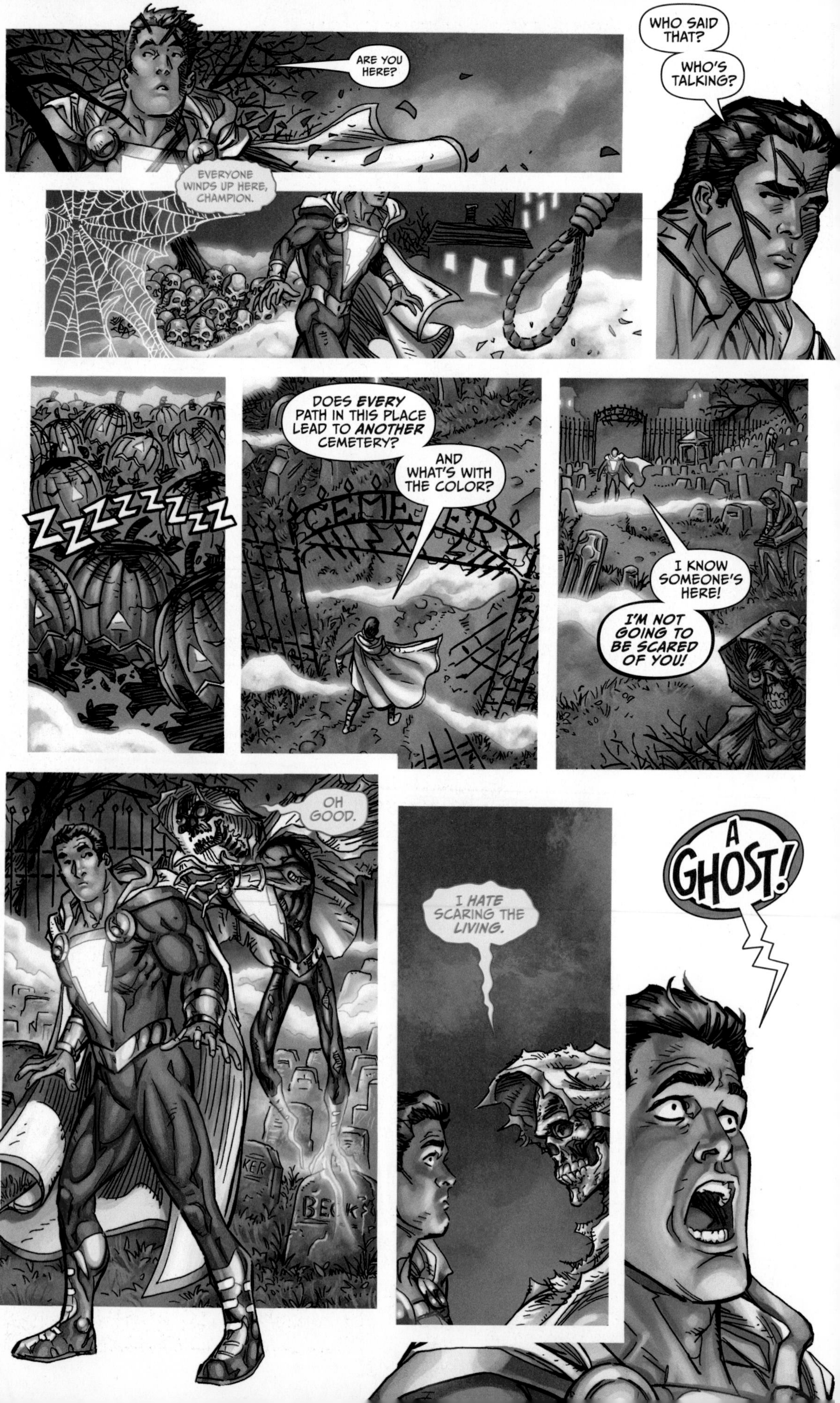
ARE YOU HERE?
WHO SAID THAT?
WHO'S TALKING?
EVERYONE WINDS UP HERE, CHAMPION.
ZZZZZZZZZZ
DOES EVERY PATH IN THIS PLACE LEAD TO ANOTHER CEMETERY?
AND WHAT'S WITH THE COLOR?
CEMETERY
I KNOW SOMEONE'S HERE!
I'M NOT GOING TO BE SCARED OF YOU!
OH GOOD.
I HATE SCARING THE LIVING.
A GHOST!

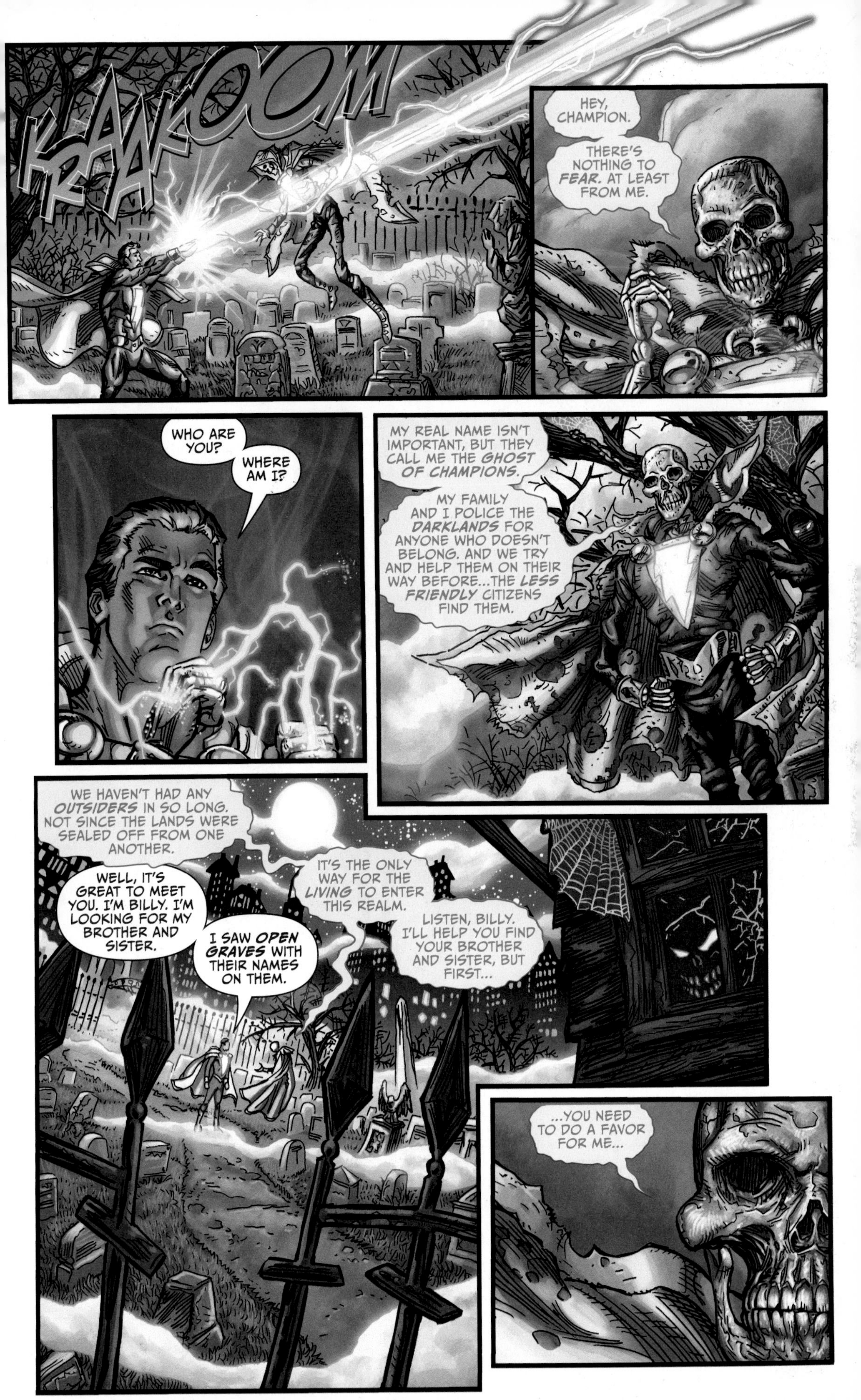
KRAKOOM
HEY, CHAMPION.
THERE'S NOTHING TO FEAR. AT LEAST FROM ME.
WHO ARE YOU?
WHERE AM I?
MY REAL NAME ISN'T IMPORTANT, BUT THEY CALL ME THE GHOST OF CHAMPIONS.
MY FAMILY AND I POLICE THE DARKLANDS FOR ANYONE WHO DOESN'T BELONG. AND WE TRY AND HELP THEM ON THEIR WAY BEFORE...THE LESS FRIENDLY CITIZENS FIND THEM.
WE HAVEN'T HAD ANY OUTSIDERS IN SO LONG. NOT SINCE THE LANDS WERE SEALED OFF FROM ONE ANOTHER.
WELL, IT'S GREAT TO MEET YOU. I'M BILLY. I'M LOOKING FOR MY BROTHER AND SISTER.
I SAW OPEN GRAVES WITH THEIR NAMES ON THEM.
IT'S THE ONLY WAY FOR THE LIVING TO ENTER THIS REALM.
LISTEN, BILLY. I'LL HELP YOU FIND YOUR BROTHER AND SISTER, BUT FIRST...
...YOU NEED TO DO A FAVOR FOR ME...

"...IF YOU WANT TO FIND YOUR FAMILY."

HE'S THE KEY TO BILLY BATSON, ADAM.

ONCE WE HAVE BILLY'S FATHER, HE'LL DO ANYTHING WE ASK.

INCLUDING HANDING OVER HIS POWER.

I'VE TOLERATED YOU LONG ENOUGH, SIVANA.

I SHOULD'VE REMOVED YOUR HEAD FROM YOUR SHOULDERS LONG AGO.

AAAAAARR?!

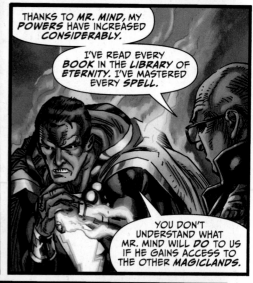

THANKS TO MR. MIND, MY POWERS HAVE INCREASED CONSIDERABLY.

I'VE READ EVERY BOOK IN THE LIBRARY OF ETERNITY. I'VE MASTERED EVERY SPELL.

YOU DON'T UNDERSTAND WHAT MR. MIND WILL DO TO US IF HE GAINS ACCESS TO THE OTHER MAGICLANDS.

OH, BUT HE DOES, MY DEAR OLD FRIEND.

I'VE TOLD HIM MY PLAN.

TO RELEASE MY MONSTER SOCIETY FROM THEIR PRISON AND CLAIM THE SEVEN LANDS FOR MYSELF.

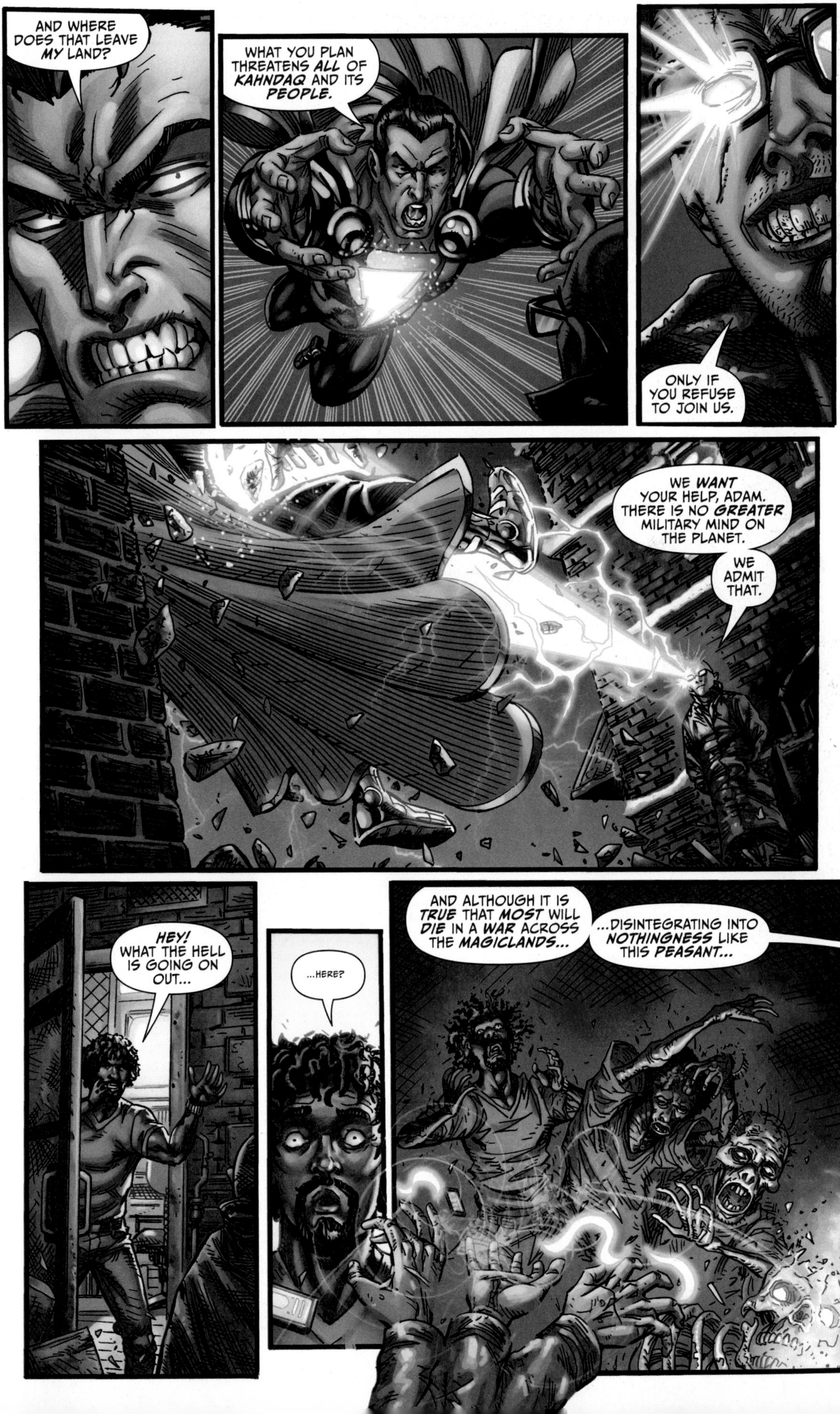
AND WHERE DOES THAT LEAVE *MY* LAND?
WHAT YOU PLAN THREATENS *ALL* OF *KAHNDAQ* AND ITS *PEOPLE.*
ONLY IF YOU REFUSE TO JOIN US.
WE *WANT* YOUR HELP, ADAM. THERE IS NO *GREATER* MILITARY MIND ON THE PLANET.
WE ADMIT THAT.
*HEY!* WHAT THE HELL IS GOING ON OUT...
...HERE?
AND ALTHOUGH IT IS *TRUE* THAT *MOST* WILL *DIE* IN A *WAR* ACROSS THE *MAGICLANDS...*
...DISINTEGRATING INTO *NOTHINGNESS* LIKE THIS *PEASANT...*

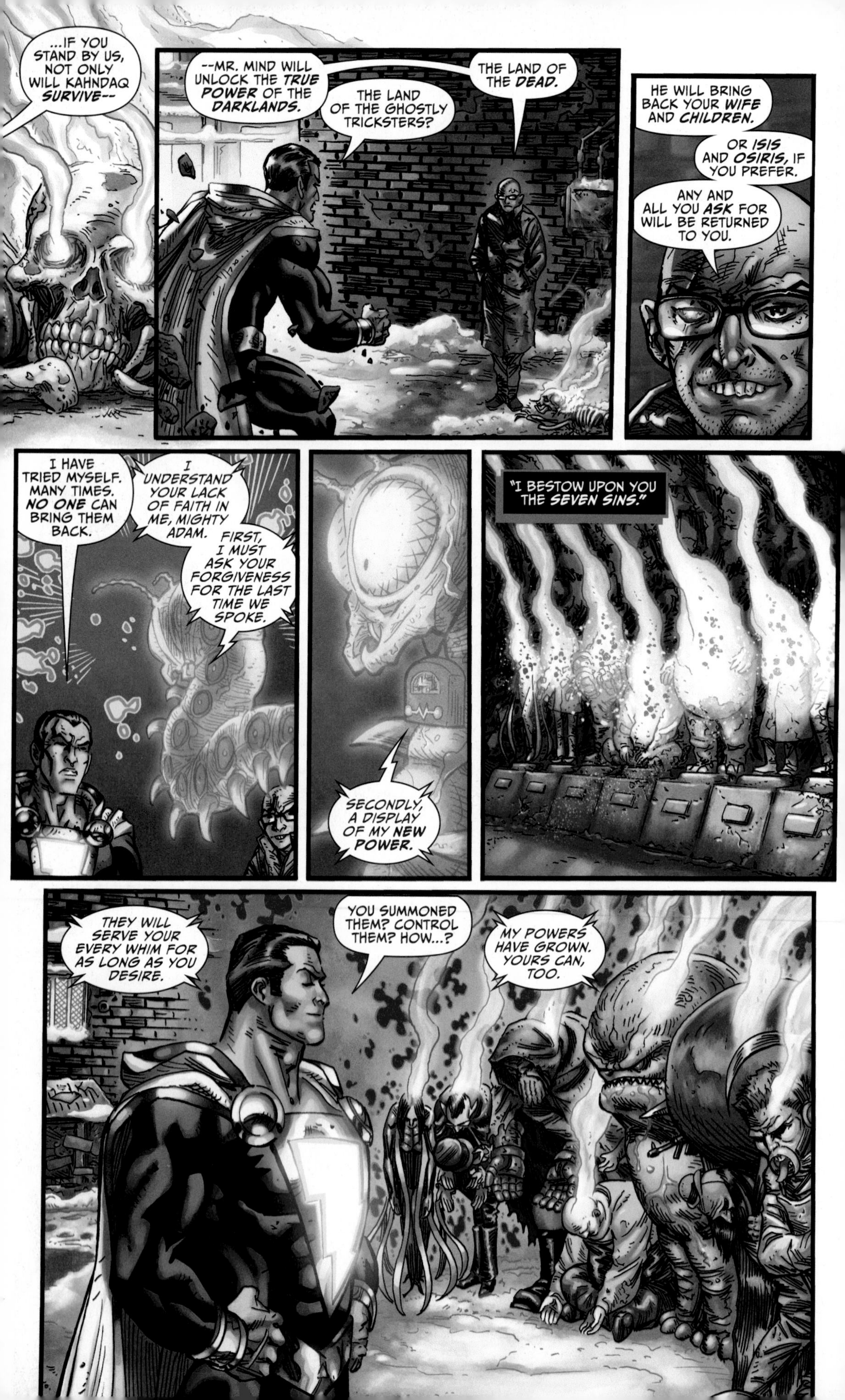
...IF YOU STAND BY US, NOT ONLY WILL KAHNDAQ SURVIVE--
--MR. MIND WILL UNLOCK THE TRUE POWER OF THE DARKLANDS.
THE LAND OF THE GHOSTLY TRICKSTERS?
THE LAND OF THE DEAD.
HE WILL BRING BACK YOUR WIFE AND CHILDREN.
OR ISIS AND OSIRIS, IF YOU PREFER.
ANY AND ALL YOU ASK FOR WILL BE RETURNED TO YOU.
I HAVE TRIED MYSELF. MANY TIMES. NO ONE CAN BRING THEM BACK.
I UNDERSTAND YOUR LACK OF FAITH IN ME, MIGHTY ADAM.
FIRST, I MUST ASK YOUR FORGIVENESS FOR THE LAST TIME WE SPOKE.
SECONDLY, A DISPLAY OF MY NEW POWER.
"I BESTOW UPON YOU THE SEVEN SINS."
THEY WILL SERVE YOUR EVERY WHIM FOR AS LONG AS YOU DESIRE.
YOU SUMMONED THEM? CONTROL THEM? HOW...?
MY POWERS HAVE GROWN. YOURS CAN, TOO.

I WANT TO COME BACK.

TO THE LAND OF THE LIVING.

COME BACK WHERE?

I DIED WELL BEFORE MY TIME. AND I HAD SO MANY THINGS LEFT TO DO. PEOPLE I LEFT BEHIND.

A GIRL.

"AND THE DEAD WILL RETURN."

WHAT FAVOR?

THE DEAD CAN'T COME BACK.

THEY CAN. YOU HAVE THAT POWER. IF WE WORK TOGETHER.

YOUR FATHER COULD DIE TODAY. DID YOU KNOW THAT? I'LL TELL YOU WHAT I SEE IF YOU GIVE ME YOUR WORD.

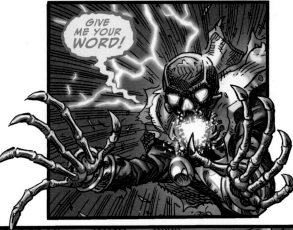

GIVE ME YOUR WORD!

SON?

HERE LIES CAPTAIN MARVEL SR.

HEY! DON'T YELL AT ME.

WHAT DID YOU SAY ABOUT MY DAD?

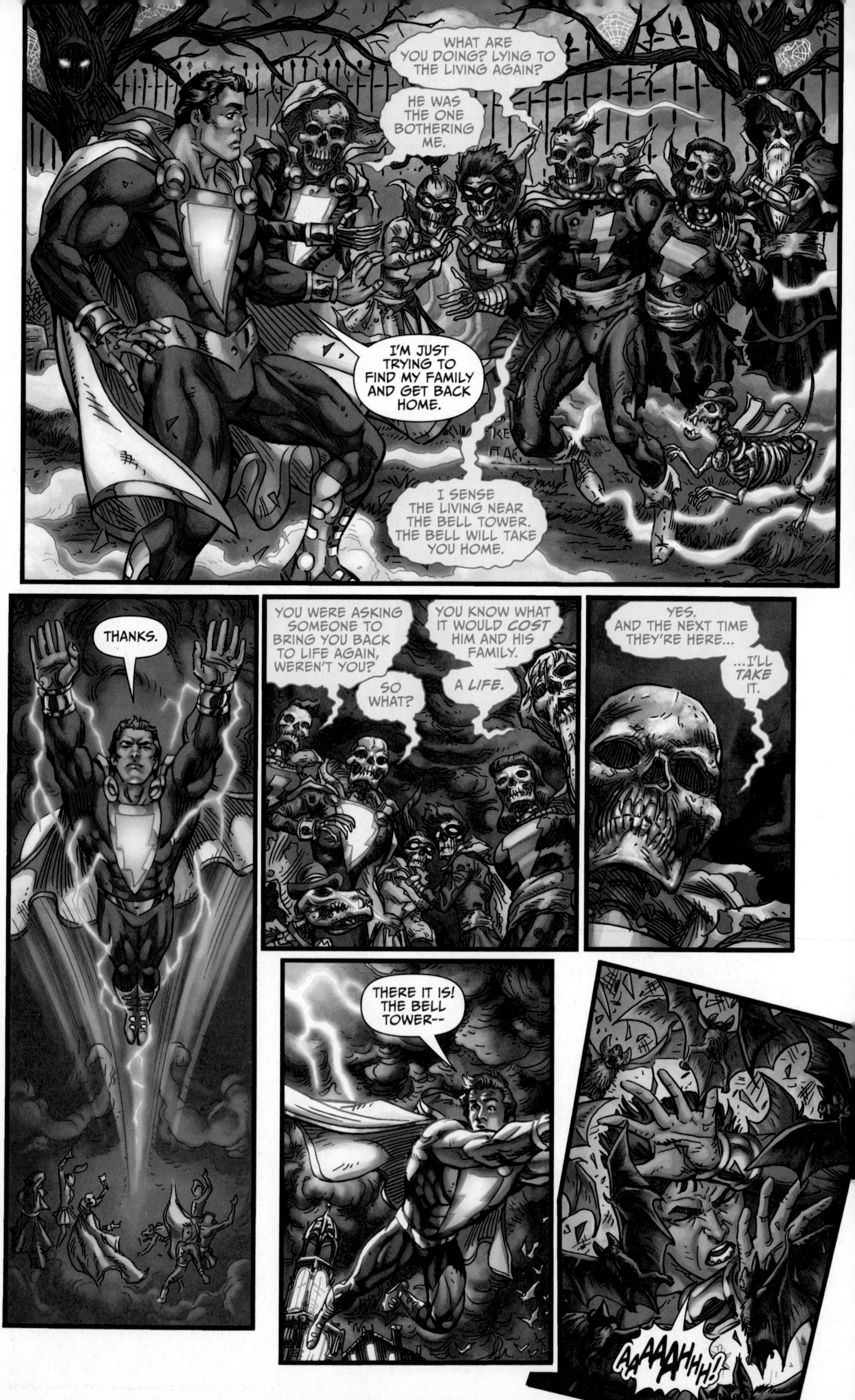
WHAT ARE YOU DOING? LYING TO THE LIVING AGAIN?
HE WAS THE ONE BOTHERING ME.
I'M JUST TRYING TO FIND MY FAMILY AND GET BACK HOME.
I SENSE THE LIVING NEAR THE BELL TOWER. THE BELL WILL TAKE YOU HOME.
THANKS.
YOU WERE ASKING SOMEONE TO BRING YOU BACK TO LIFE AGAIN, WEREN'T YOU?
SO WHAT?
YOU KNOW WHAT IT WOULD *COST* HIM AND HIS FAMILY.
A *LIFE*.
YES. AND THE NEXT TIME THEY'RE HERE...
...I'LL *TAKE* IT.
THERE IT IS! THE BELL TOWER--
AAAAAHHHH!

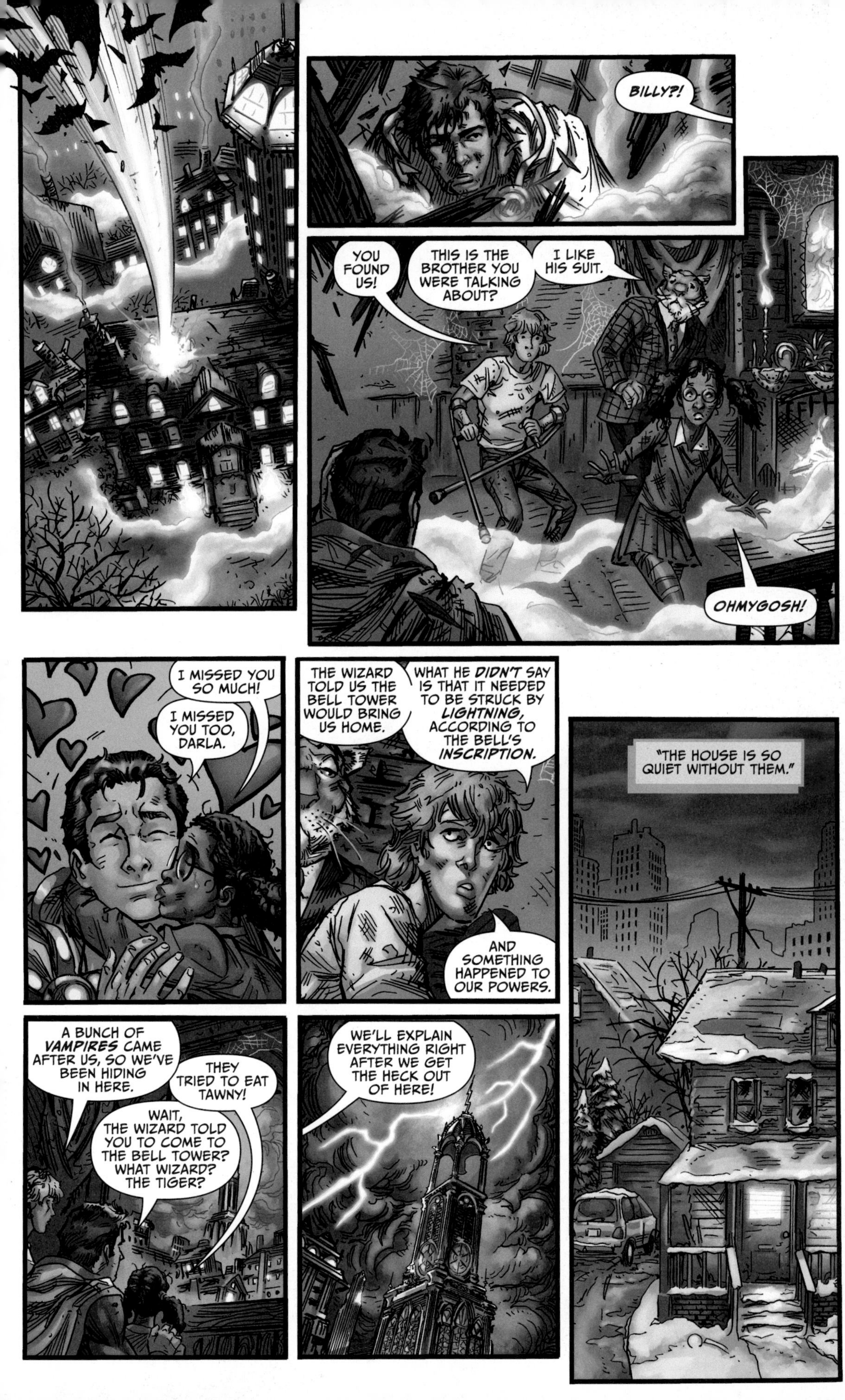
BILLY?!
YOU FOUND US!
THIS IS THE BROTHER YOU WERE TALKING ABOUT?
I LIKE HIS SUIT.
OHMYGOSH!
I MISSED YOU SO MUCH!
I MISSED YOU TOO, DARLA.
THE WIZARD TOLD US THE BELL TOWER WOULD BRING US HOME.
WHAT HE *DIDN'T* SAY IS THAT IT NEEDED TO BE STRUCK BY *LIGHTNING*, ACCORDING TO THE BELL'S *INSCRIPTION*.
AND SOMETHING HAPPENED TO OUR POWERS.
A BUNCH OF *VAMPIRES* CAME AFTER US, SO WE'VE BEEN HIDING IN HERE.
THEY TRIED TO EAT TAWNY!
WAIT, THE WIZARD TOLD YOU TO COME TO THE BELL TOWER? WHAT WIZARD? THE TIGER?
WE'LL EXPLAIN EVERYTHING RIGHT AFTER WE GET THE HECK OUT OF HERE!
"THE HOUSE IS SO QUIET WITHOUT THEM."

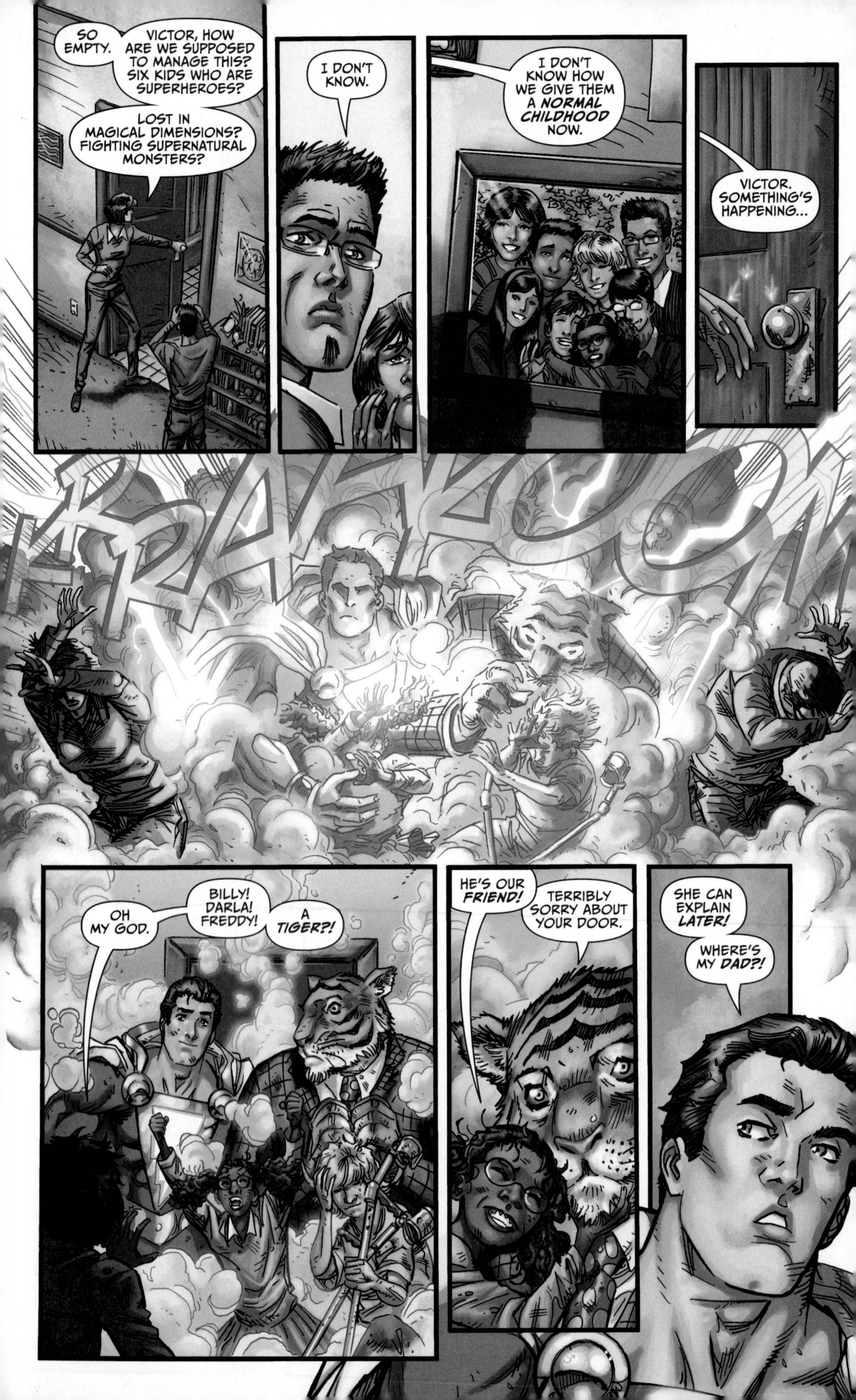
SO EMPTY.
VICTOR, HOW ARE WE SUPPOSED TO MANAGE THIS? SIX KIDS WHO ARE SUPERHEROES?
LOST IN MAGICAL DIMENSIONS? FIGHTING SUPERNATURAL MONSTERS?
I DON'T KNOW.
I DON'T KNOW HOW WE GIVE THEM A NORMAL CHILDHOOD NOW.
VICTOR. SOMETHING'S HAPPENING...
KRAKOOM
OH MY GOD.
BILLY! DARLA! FREDDY!
A TIGER?!
HE'S OUR FRIEND!
TERRIBLY SORRY ABOUT YOUR DOOR.
SHE CAN EXPLAIN LATER!
WHERE'S MY DAD?!

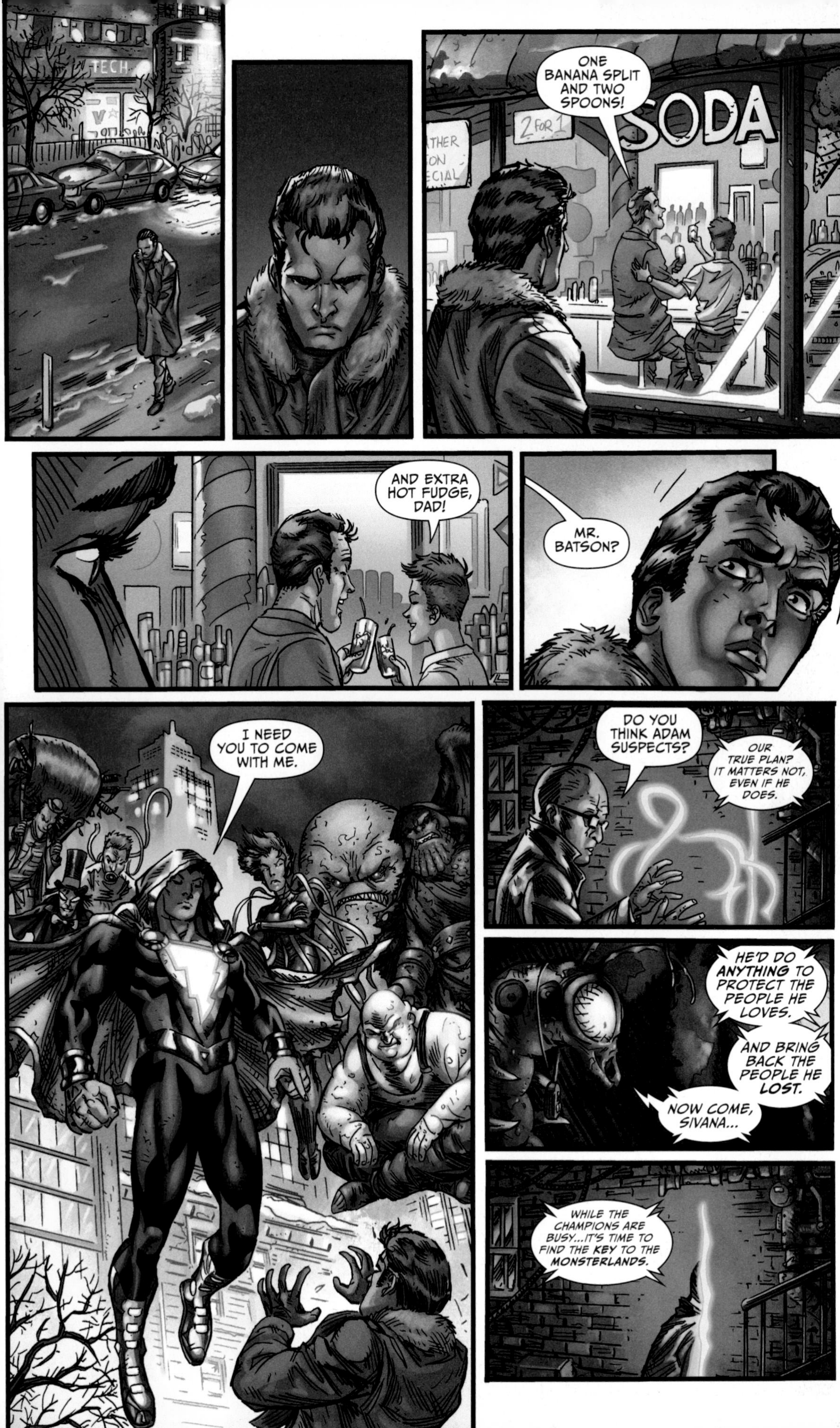
TECH
ONE BANANA SPLIT AND TWO SPOONS!
2 FOR 1
SODA
AND EXTRA HOT FUDGE, DAD!
MR. BATSON?
I NEED YOU TO COME WITH ME.
DO YOU THINK ADAM SUSPECTS?
OUR TRUE PLAN? IT MATTERS NOT, EVEN IF HE DOES.
HE'D DO ANYTHING TO PROTECT THE PEOPLE HE LOVES.
AND BRING BACK THE PEOPLE HE LOST.
NOW COME, SIVANA...
WHILE THE CHAMPIONS ARE BUSY...IT'S TIME TO FIND THE KEY TO THE MONSTERLANDS.

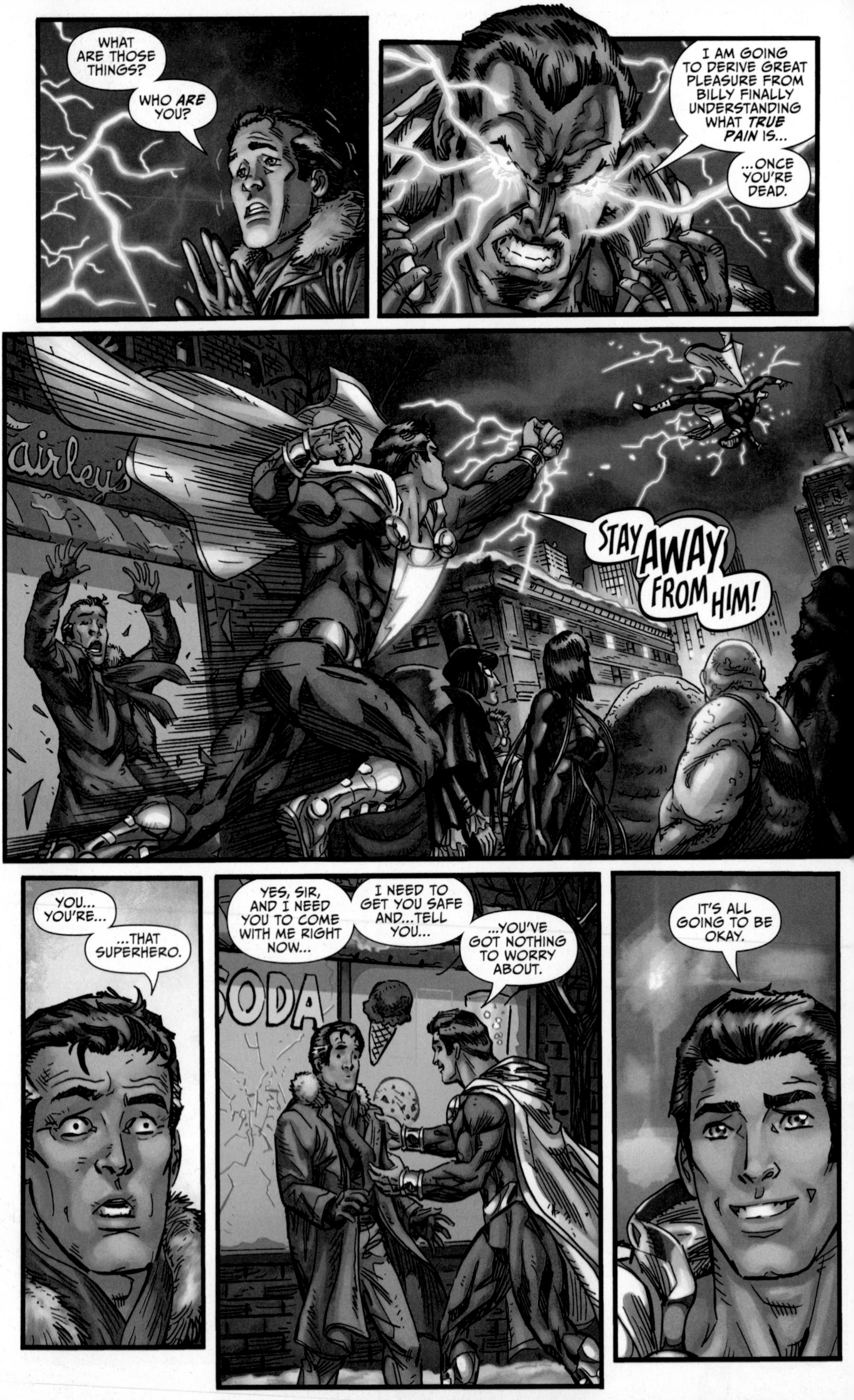
WHAT ARE THOSE THINGS?
WHO *ARE* YOU?
I AM GOING TO DERIVE GREAT PLEASURE FROM BILLY FINALLY UNDERSTANDING WHAT *TRUE PAIN* IS...
...ONCE YOU'RE DEAD.
Fairley's
STAY AWAY FROM HIM!
YOU... YOU'RE...
...THAT SUPERHERO.
YES, SIR, AND I NEED YOU TO COME WITH ME RIGHT NOW...
I NEED TO GET YOU SAFE AND...TELL YOU...
...YOU'VE GOT NOTHING TO WORRY ABOUT.
SODA
IT'S ALL GOING TO BE OKAY.

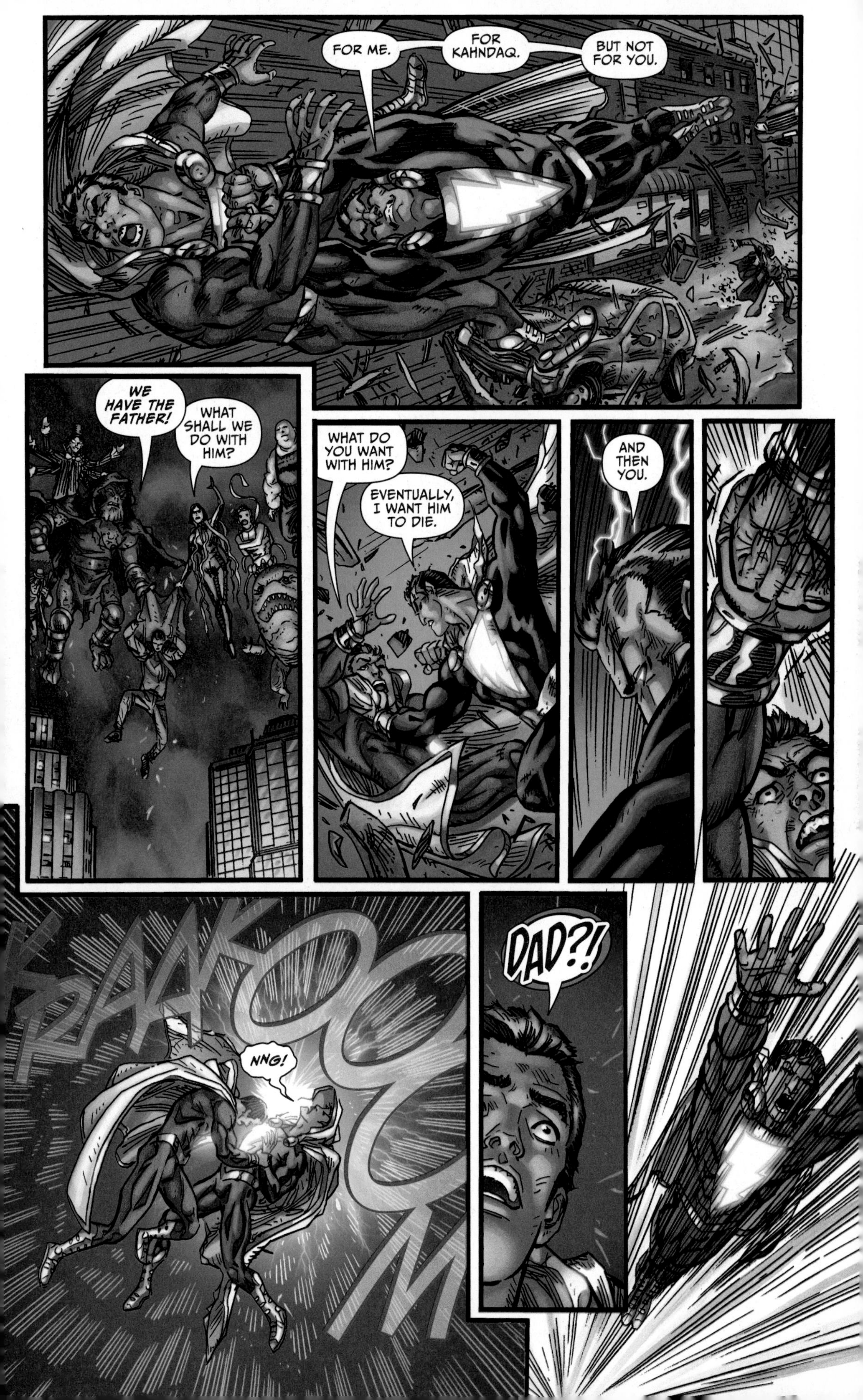
FOR ME.
FOR KAHNDAQ.
BUT NOT FOR YOU.
WE HAVE THE FATHER!
WHAT SHALL WE DO WITH HIM?
WHAT DO YOU WANT WITH HIM?
EVENTUALLY, I WANT HIM TO DIE.
AND THEN YOU.
KRAKOOOOM
NNG!
DAD?!

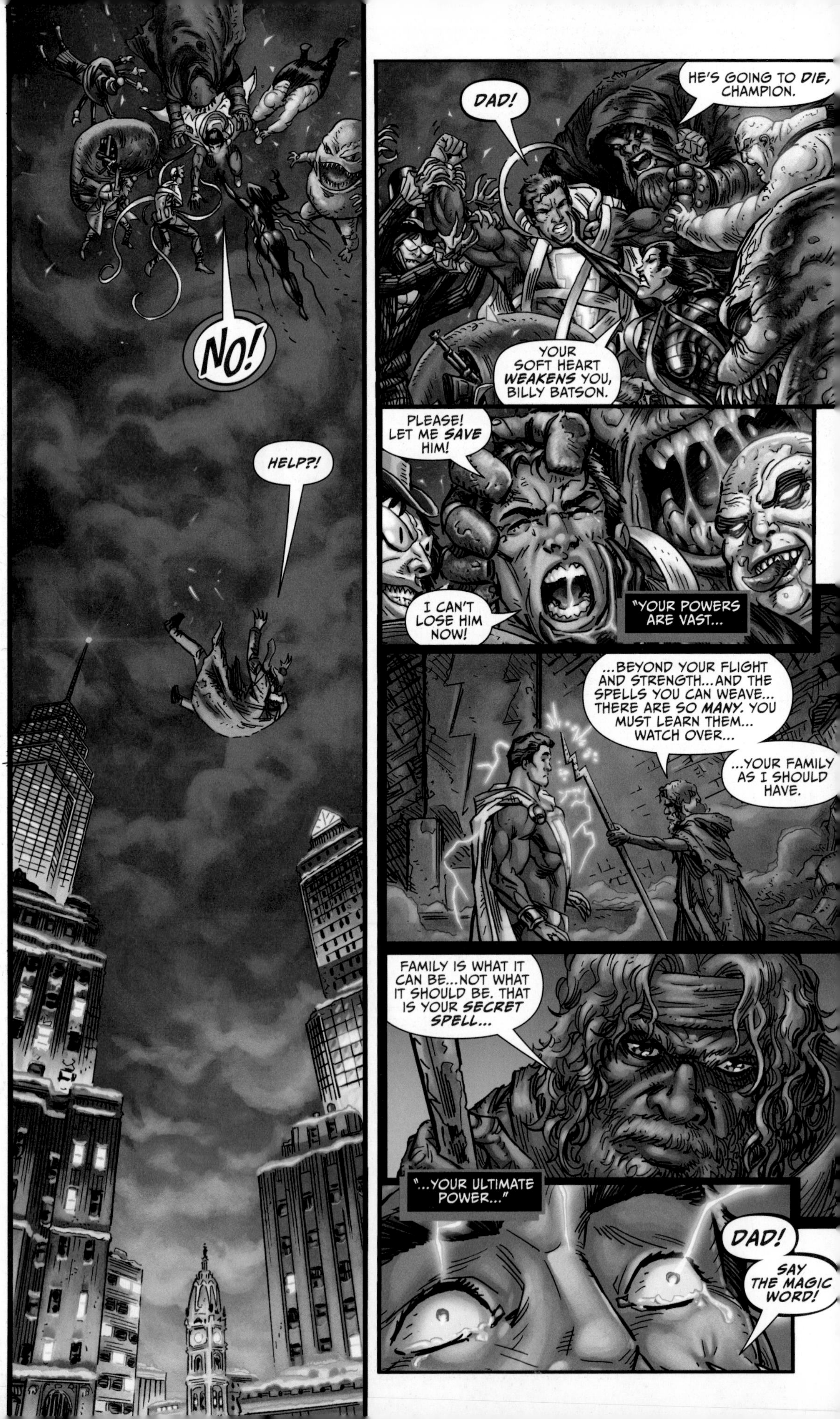
NO!
HELP?!
DAD!
HE'S GOING TO DIE, CHAMPION.
YOUR SOFT HEART WEAKENS YOU, BILLY BATSON.
PLEASE! LET ME SAVE HIM!
I CAN'T LOSE HIM NOW!
"YOUR POWERS ARE VAST...
...BEYOND YOUR FLIGHT AND STRENGTH...AND THE SPELLS YOU CAN WEAVE... THERE ARE SO MANY. YOU MUST LEARN THEM... WATCH OVER...
...YOUR FAMILY AS I SHOULD HAVE.
FAMILY IS WHAT IT CAN BE...NOT WHAT IT SHOULD BE. THAT IS YOUR SECRET SPELL...
"...YOUR ULTIMATE POWER..."
DAD!
SAY THE MAGIC WORD!

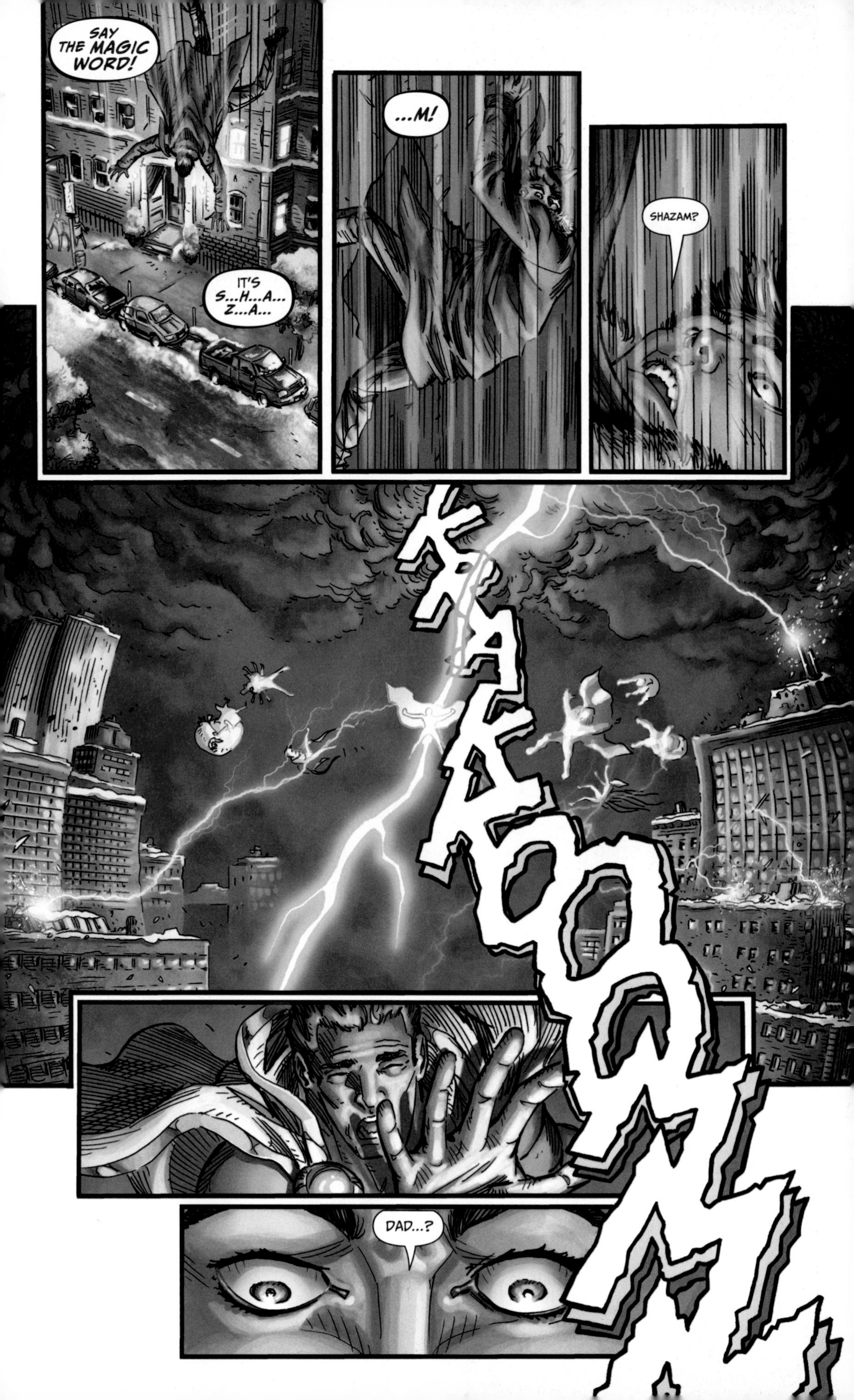
SAY THE MAGIC WORD!
IT'S S...H...A... Z...A...
...M!
SHAZAM?
KRAKOOOM!
DAD...?

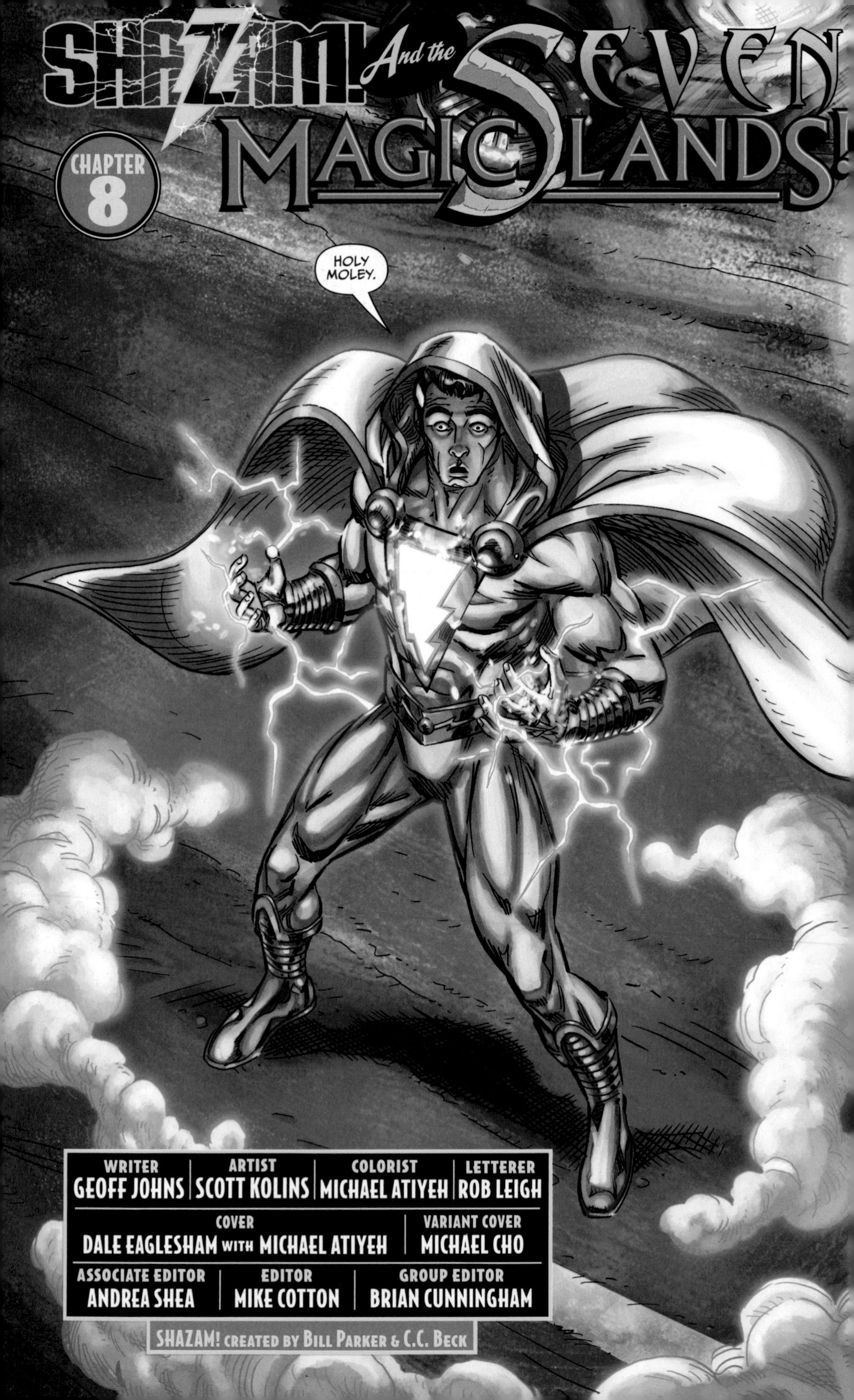
SHAZAM! And the SEVEN MAGIC LANDS!
CHAPTER 8
HOLY MOLEY.
WRITER GEOFF JOHNS
ARTIST SCOTT KOLINS
COLORIST MICHAEL ATIYEH
LETTERER ROB LEIGH
COVER DALE EAGLESHAM WITH MICHAEL ATIYEH
VARIANT COVER MICHAEL CHO
ASSOCIATE EDITOR ANDREA SHEA
EDITOR MIKE COTTON
GROUP EDITOR BRIAN CUNNINGHAM
SHAZAM! CREATED BY BILL PARKER & C.C. BECK

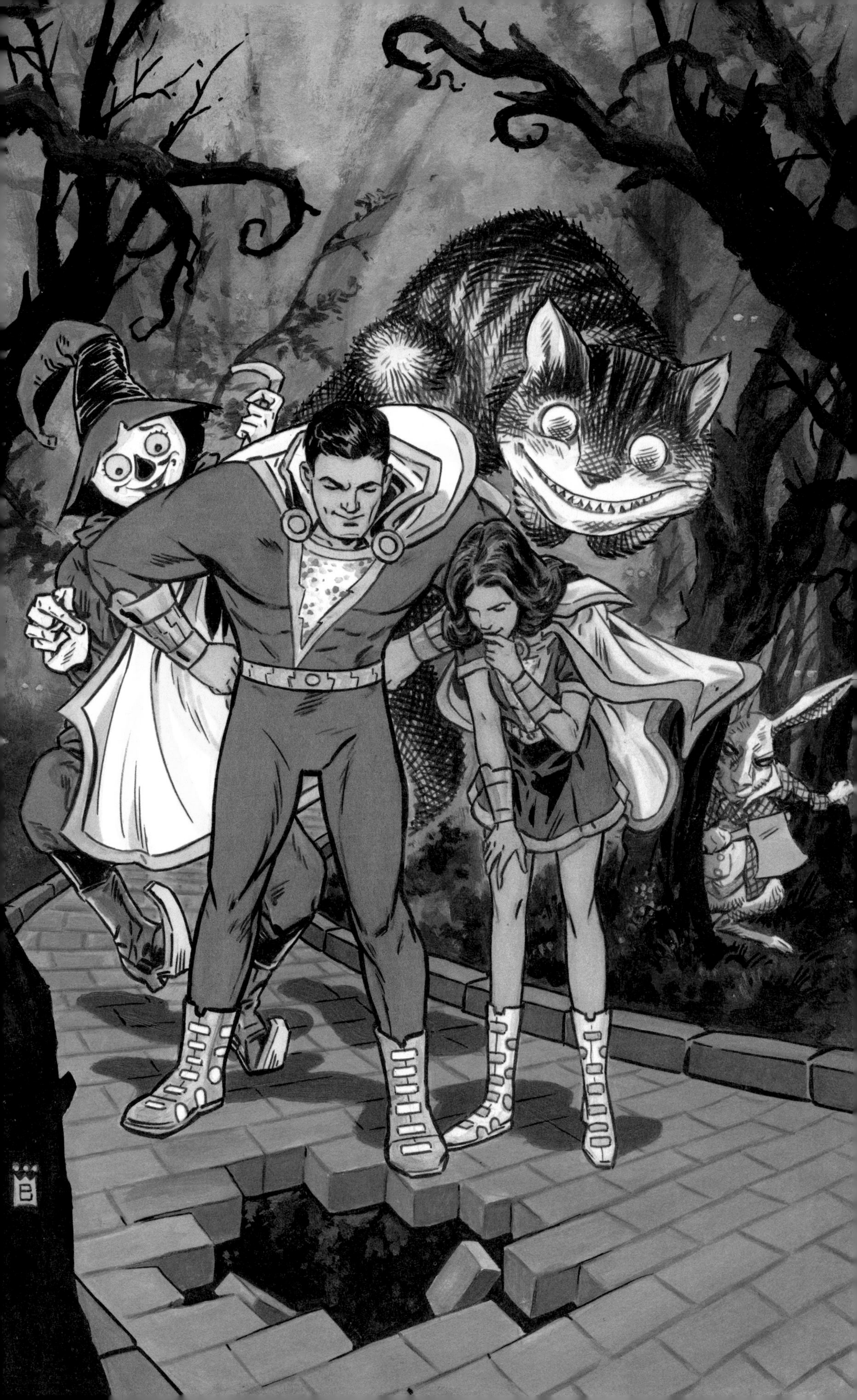

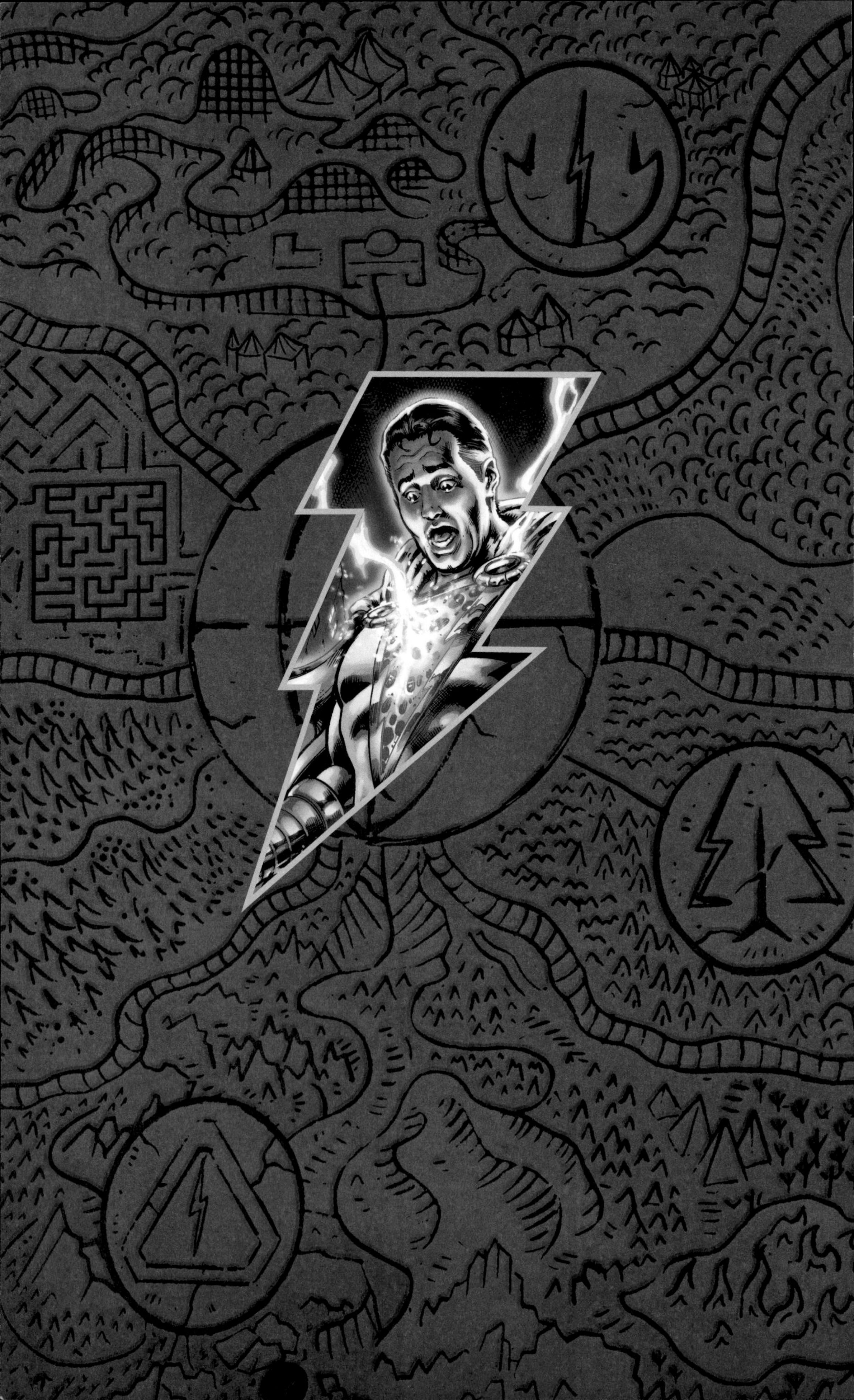

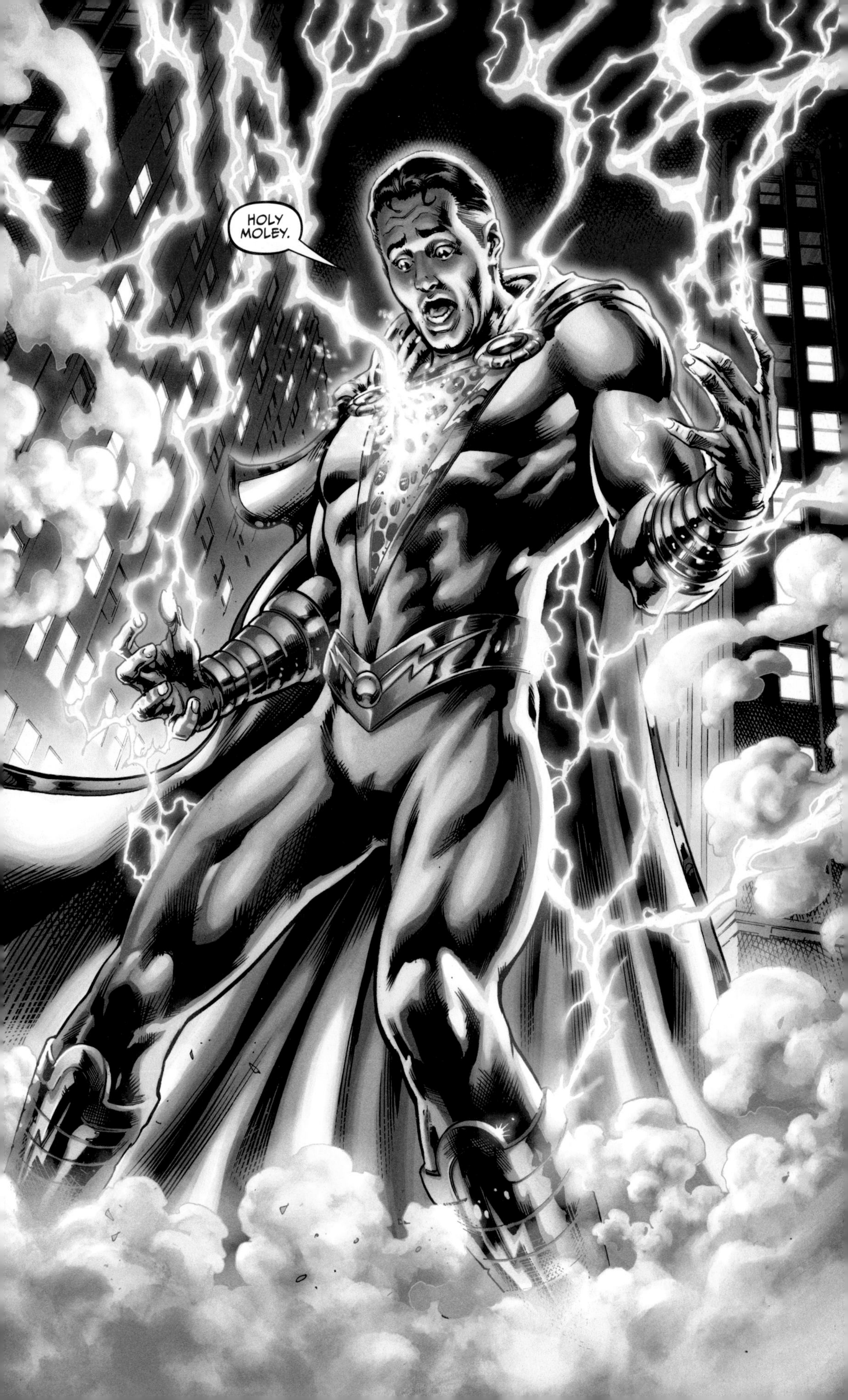
HOLY MOLEY.

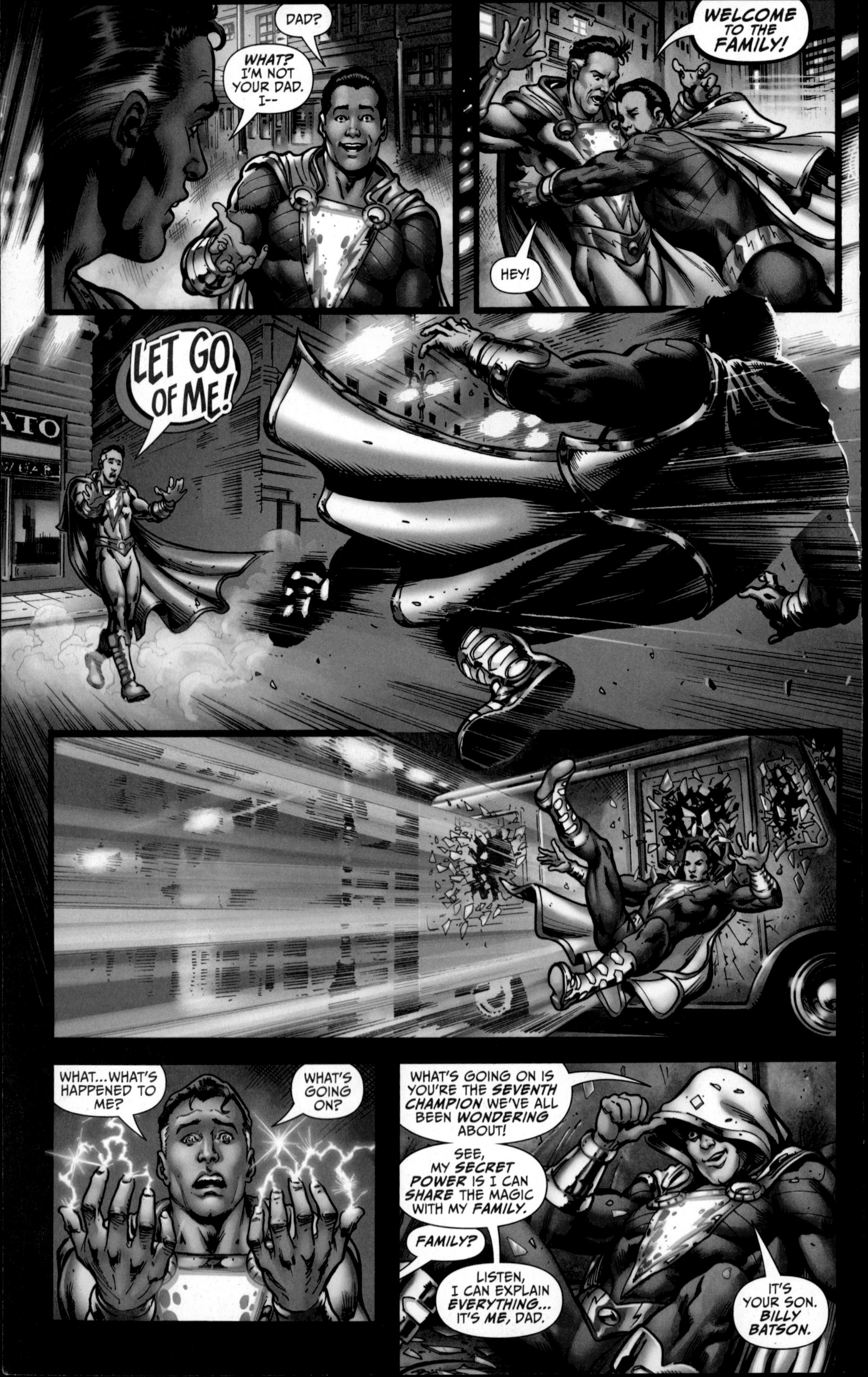
DAD?
WHAT? I'M NOT YOUR DAD. I--
WELCOME TO THE FAMILY!
HEY!
LET GO OF ME!
WHAT...WHAT'S HAPPENED TO ME?
WHAT'S GOING ON?
WHAT'S GOING ON IS YOU'RE THE SEVENTH CHAMPION WE'VE ALL BEEN WONDERING ABOUT!
SEE, MY SECRET POWER IS I CAN SHARE THE MAGIC WITH MY FAMILY.
FAMILY?
LISTEN, I CAN EXPLAIN EVERYTHING... IT'S ME, DAD.
IT'S YOUR SON. BILLY BATSON.

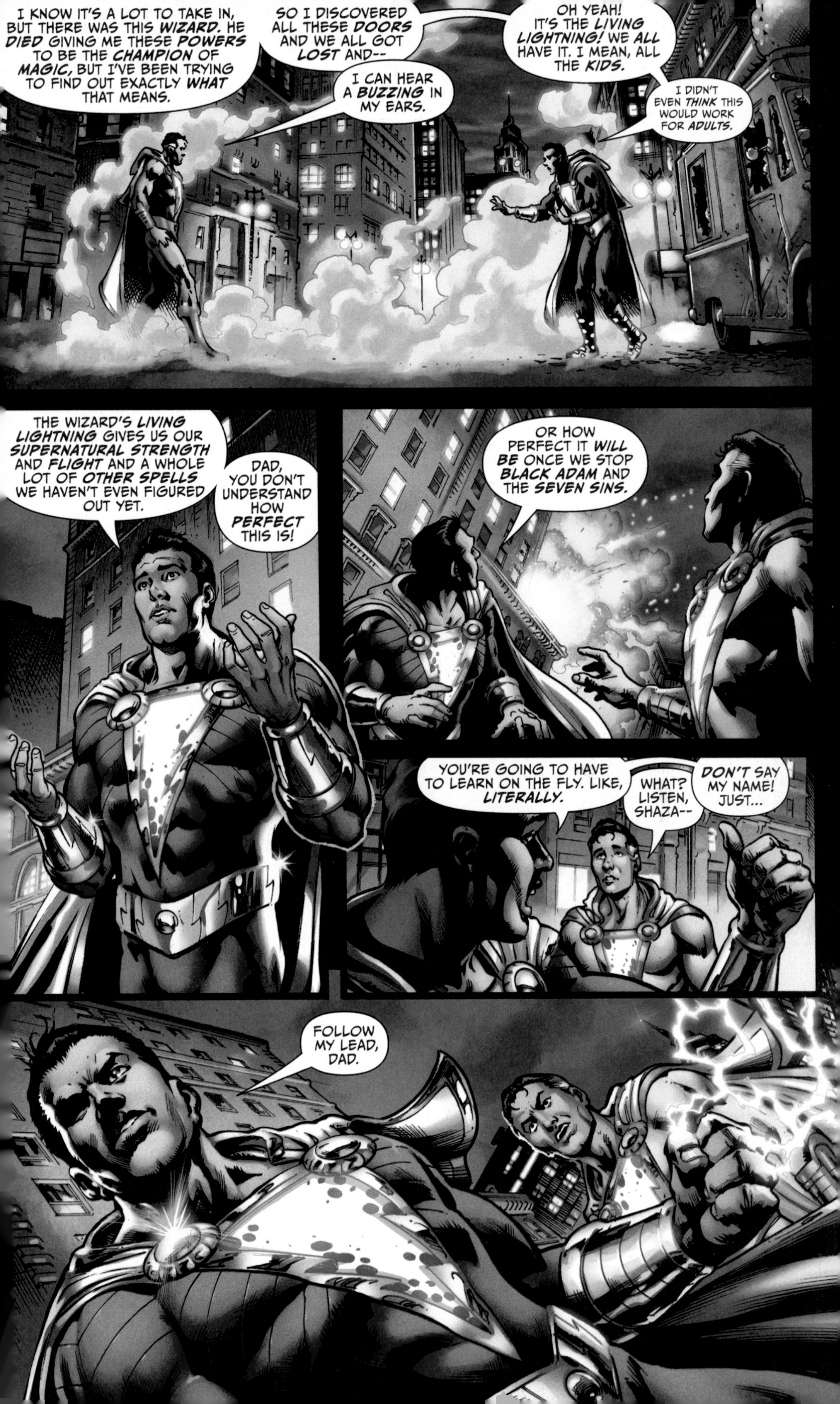
I KNOW IT'S A LOT TO TAKE IN, BUT THERE WAS THIS WIZARD. HE DIED GIVING ME THESE POWERS TO BE THE CHAMPION OF MAGIC, BUT I'VE BEEN TRYING TO FIND OUT EXACTLY WHAT THAT MEANS.
SO I DISCOVERED ALL THESE DOORS AND WE ALL GOT LOST AND--
I CAN HEAR A BUZZING IN MY EARS.
OH YEAH! IT'S THE LIVING LIGHTNING! WE ALL HAVE IT. I MEAN, ALL THE KIDS.
I DIDN'T EVEN THINK THIS WOULD WORK FOR ADULTS.
THE WIZARD'S LIVING LIGHTNING GIVES US OUR SUPERNATURAL STRENGTH AND FLIGHT AND A WHOLE LOT OF OTHER SPELLS WE HAVEN'T EVEN FIGURED OUT YET.
DAD, YOU DON'T UNDERSTAND HOW PERFECT THIS IS!
OR HOW PERFECT IT WILL BE ONCE WE STOP BLACK ADAM AND THE SEVEN SINS.
YOU'RE GOING TO HAVE TO LEARN ON THE FLY. LIKE, LITERALLY.
WHAT? LISTEN, SHAZA--
DON'T SAY MY NAME! JUST...
FOLLOW MY LEAD, DAD.

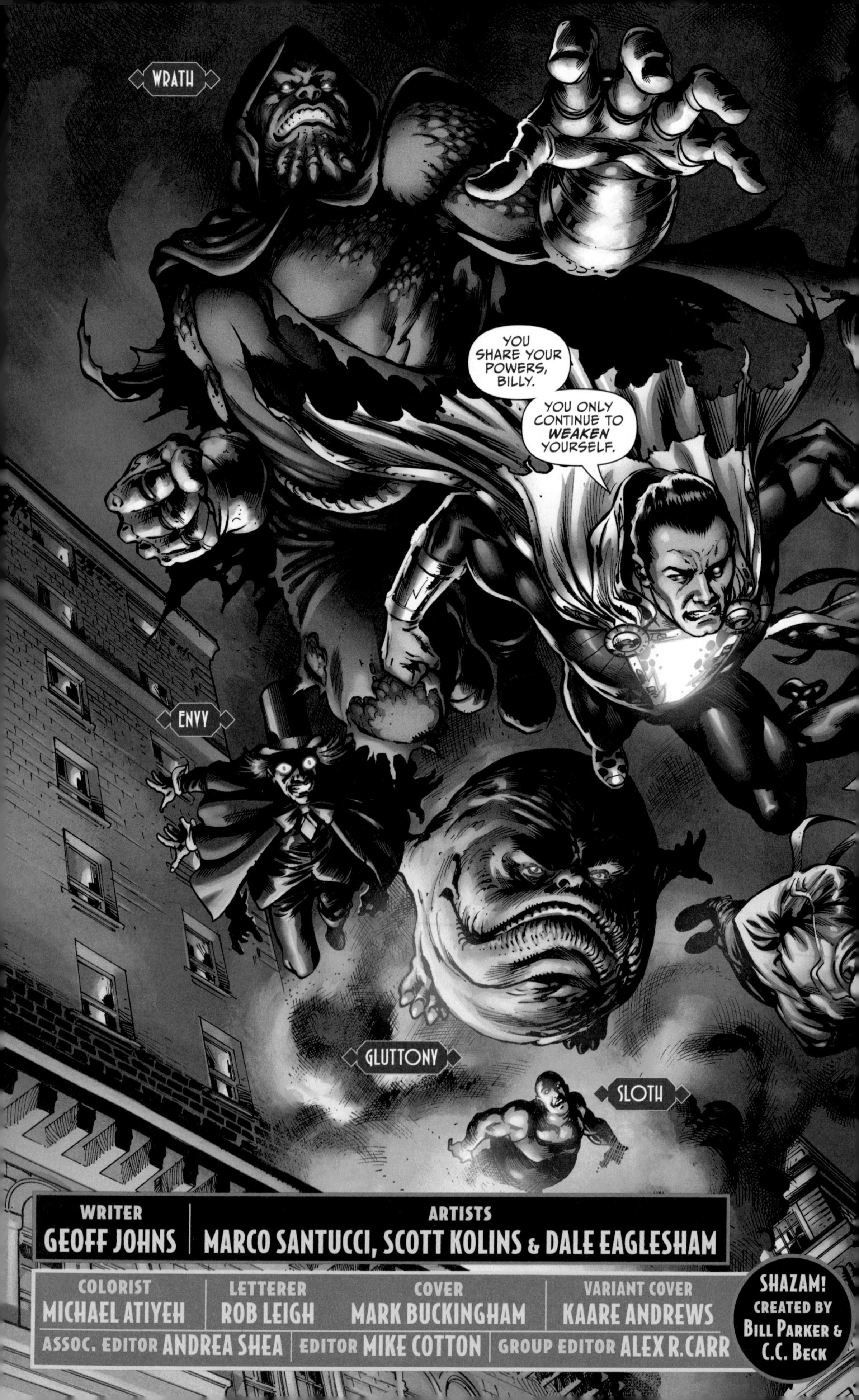
WRATH
YOU SHARE YOUR POWERS, BILLY.
YOU ONLY CONTINUE TO **WEAKEN** YOURSELF.
ENVY
GLUTTONY
SLOTH
WRITER GEOFF JOHNS
ARTISTS MARCO SANTUCCI, SCOTT KOLINS & DALE EAGLESHAM
COLORIST MICHAEL ATIYEH
LETTERER ROB LEIGH
COVER MARK BUCKINGHAM
VARIANT COVER KAARE ANDREWS
ASSOC. EDITOR ANDREA SHEA
EDITOR MIKE COTTON
GROUP EDITOR ALEX R.CARR
SHAZAM! CREATED BY BILL PARKER & C.C. BECK

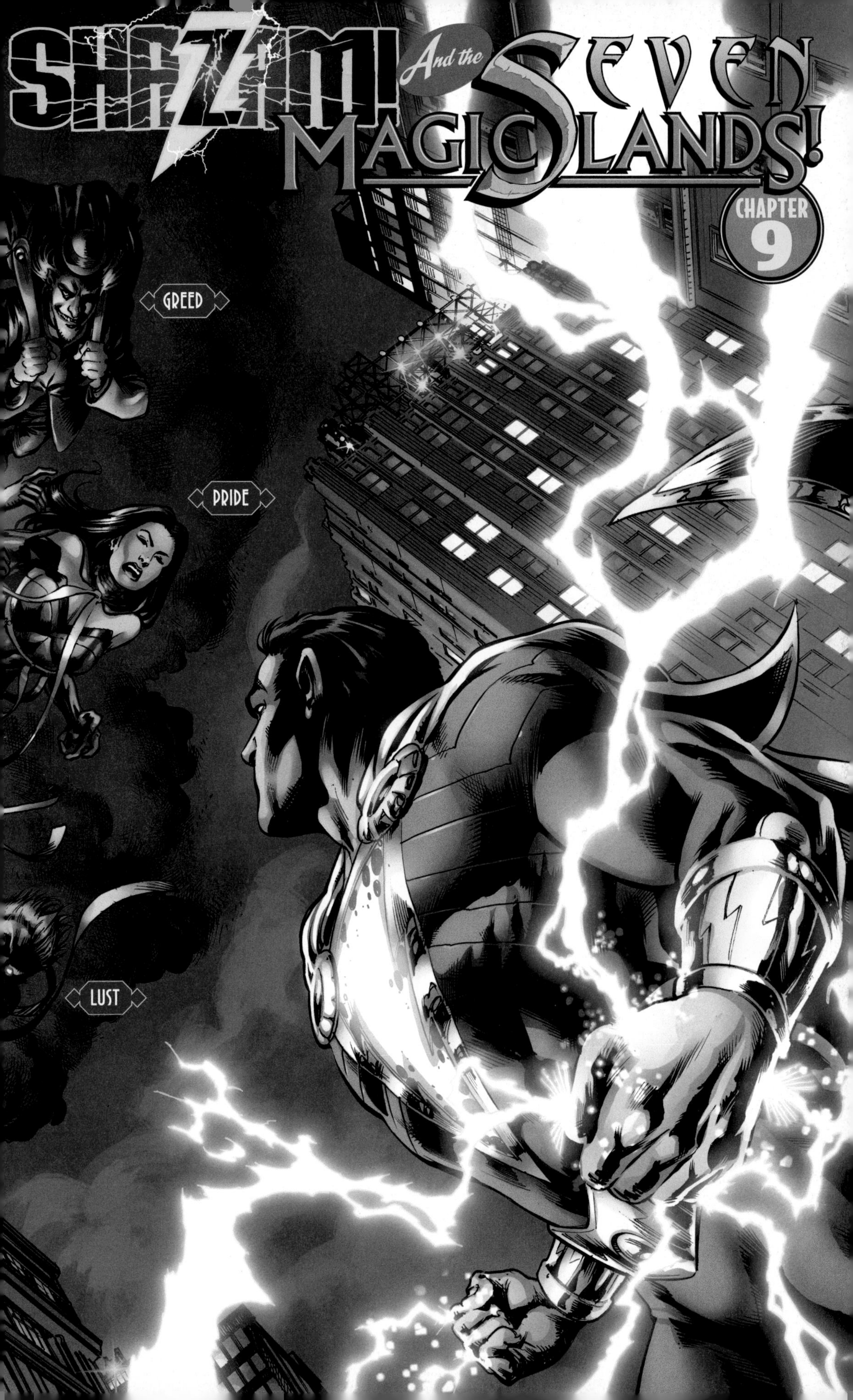
SHAZAM! And the SEVEN MAGIC LANDS!
CHAPTER 9
GREED
PRIDE
LUST

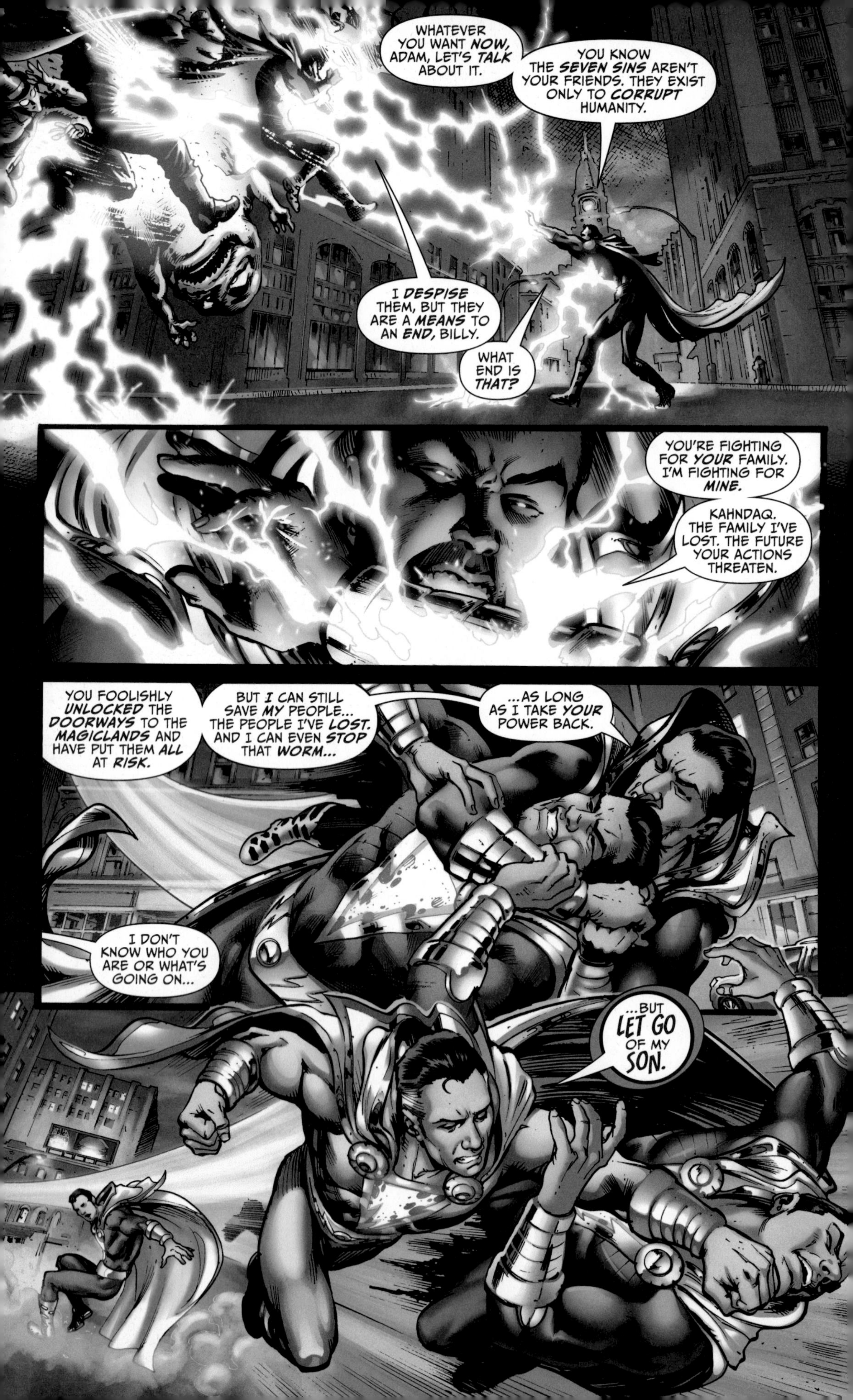
WHATEVER YOU WANT NOW, ADAM, LET'S TALK ABOUT IT.
YOU KNOW THE SEVEN SINS AREN'T YOUR FRIENDS. THEY EXIST ONLY TO CORRUPT HUMANITY.
I DESPISE THEM, BUT THEY ARE A MEANS TO AN END, BILLY.
WHAT END IS THAT?
YOU'RE FIGHTING FOR YOUR FAMILY. I'M FIGHTING FOR MINE.
KAHNDAQ. THE FAMILY I'VE LOST. THE FUTURE YOUR ACTIONS THREATEN.
YOU FOOLISHLY UNLOCKED THE DOORWAYS TO THE MAGICLANDS AND HAVE PUT THEM ALL AT RISK.
BUT I CAN STILL SAVE MY PEOPLE... THE PEOPLE I'VE LOST. AND I CAN EVEN STOP THAT WORM...
...AS LONG AS I TAKE YOUR POWER BACK.
I DON'T KNOW WHO YOU ARE OR WHAT'S GOING ON...
...BUT LET GO OF MY SON.

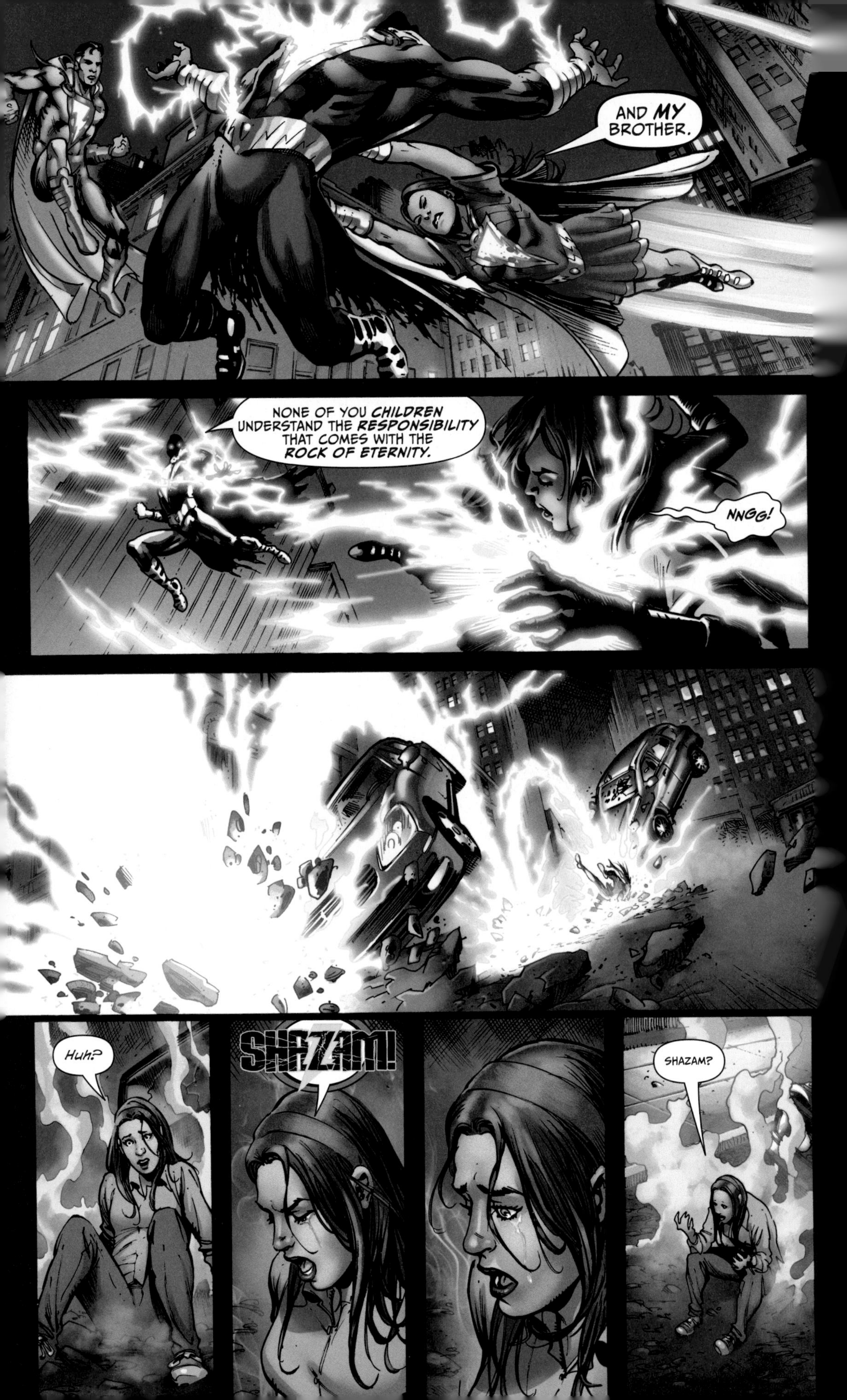
AND MY BROTHER.
NONE OF YOU CHILDREN UNDERSTAND THE RESPONSIBILITY THAT COMES WITH THE ROCK OF ETERNITY.
NNGG!
Huh?
SHAZAM!
SHAZAM?

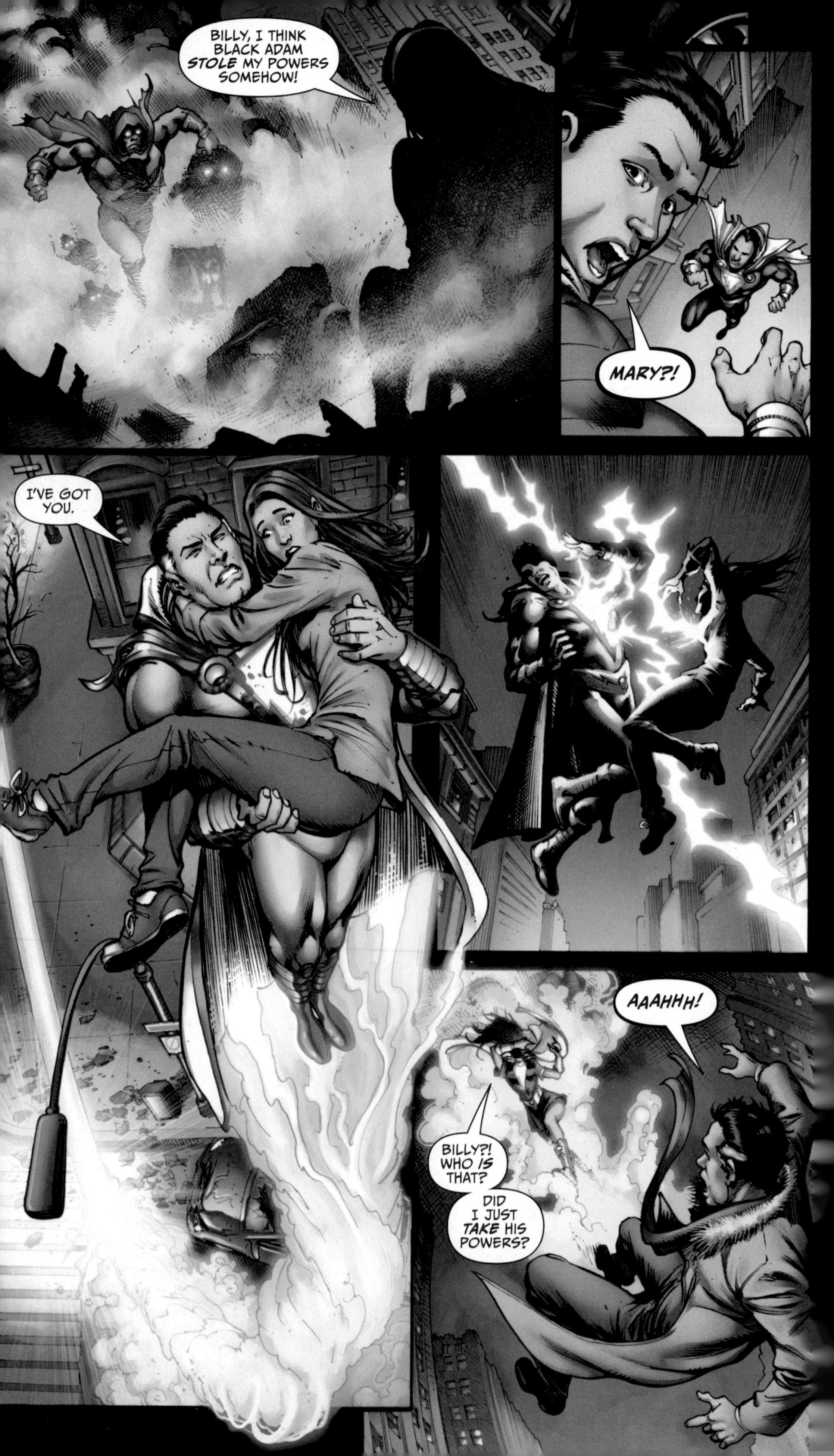

BILLY, I THINK BLACK ADAM STOLE MY POWERS SOMEHOW!
MARY?!
I'VE GOT YOU.
AAAHHH!
BILLY?! WHO IS THAT?
DID I JUST TAKE HIS POWERS?

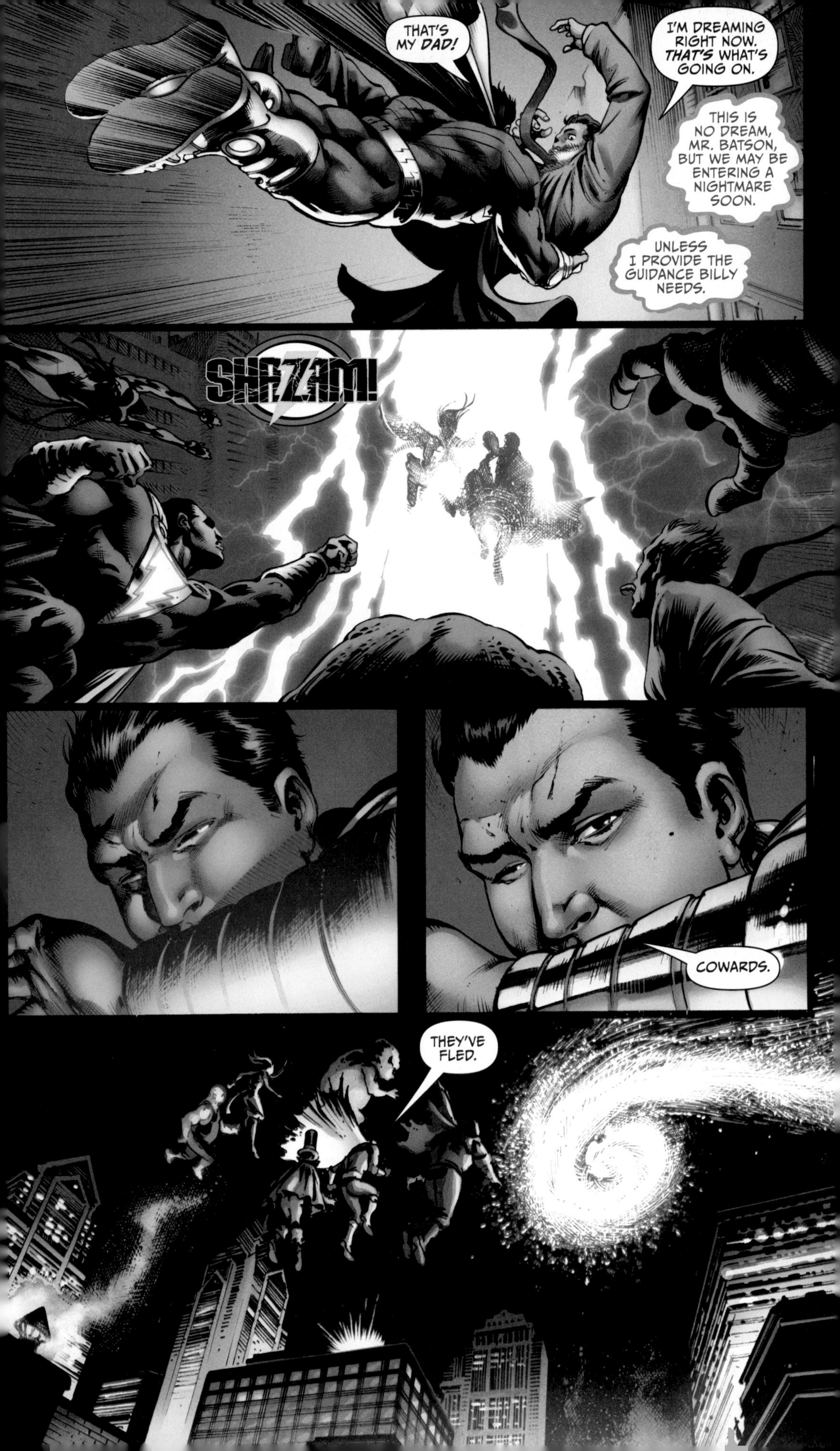
THAT'S MY DAD!
I'M DREAMING RIGHT NOW. THAT'S WHAT'S GOING ON.
THIS IS NO DREAM, MR. BATSON, BUT WE MAY BE ENTERING A NIGHTMARE SOON.
UNLESS I PROVIDE THE GUIDANCE BILLY NEEDS.
SHAZAM!
COWARDS.
THEY'VE FLED.

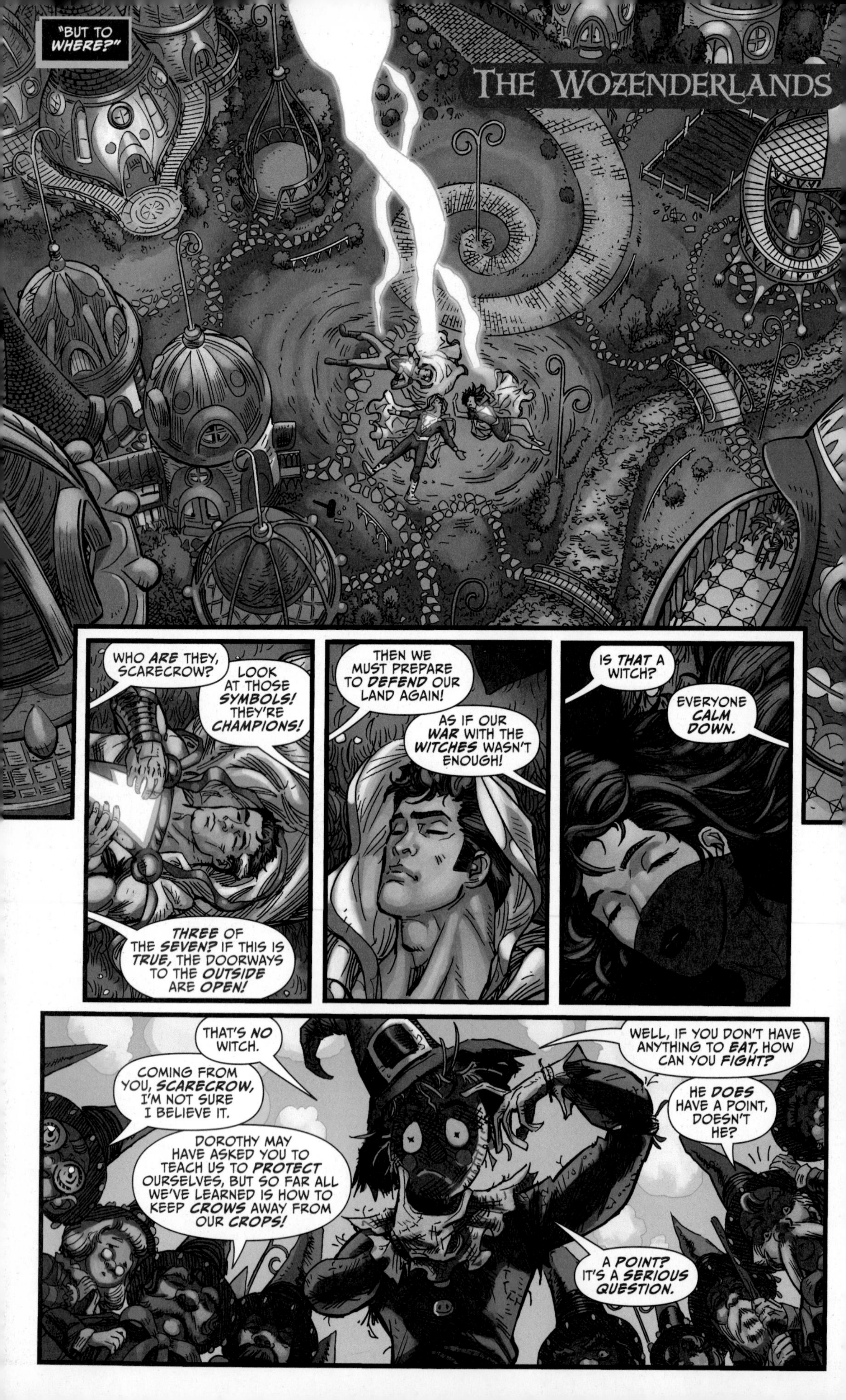
"BUT TO WHERE?"
THE WOZENDERLANDS
WHO ARE THEY, SCARECROW?
LOOK AT THOSE SYMBOLS! THEY'RE CHAMPIONS!
THREE OF THE SEVEN? IF THIS IS TRUE, THE DOORWAYS TO THE OUTSIDE ARE OPEN!
THEN WE MUST PREPARE TO DEFEND OUR LAND AGAIN!
AS IF OUR WAR WITH THE WITCHES WASN'T ENOUGH!
IS THAT A WITCH?
EVERYONE CALM DOWN.
THAT'S NO WITCH.
COMING FROM YOU, SCARECROW, I'M NOT SURE I BELIEVE IT.
DOROTHY MAY HAVE ASKED YOU TO TEACH US TO PROTECT OURSELVES, BUT SO FAR ALL WE'VE LEARNED IS HOW TO KEEP CROWS AWAY FROM OUR CROPS!
WELL, IF YOU DON'T HAVE ANYTHING TO EAT, HOW CAN YOU FIGHT?
HE DOES HAVE A POINT, DOESN'T HE?
A POINT? IT'S A SERIOUS QUESTION.

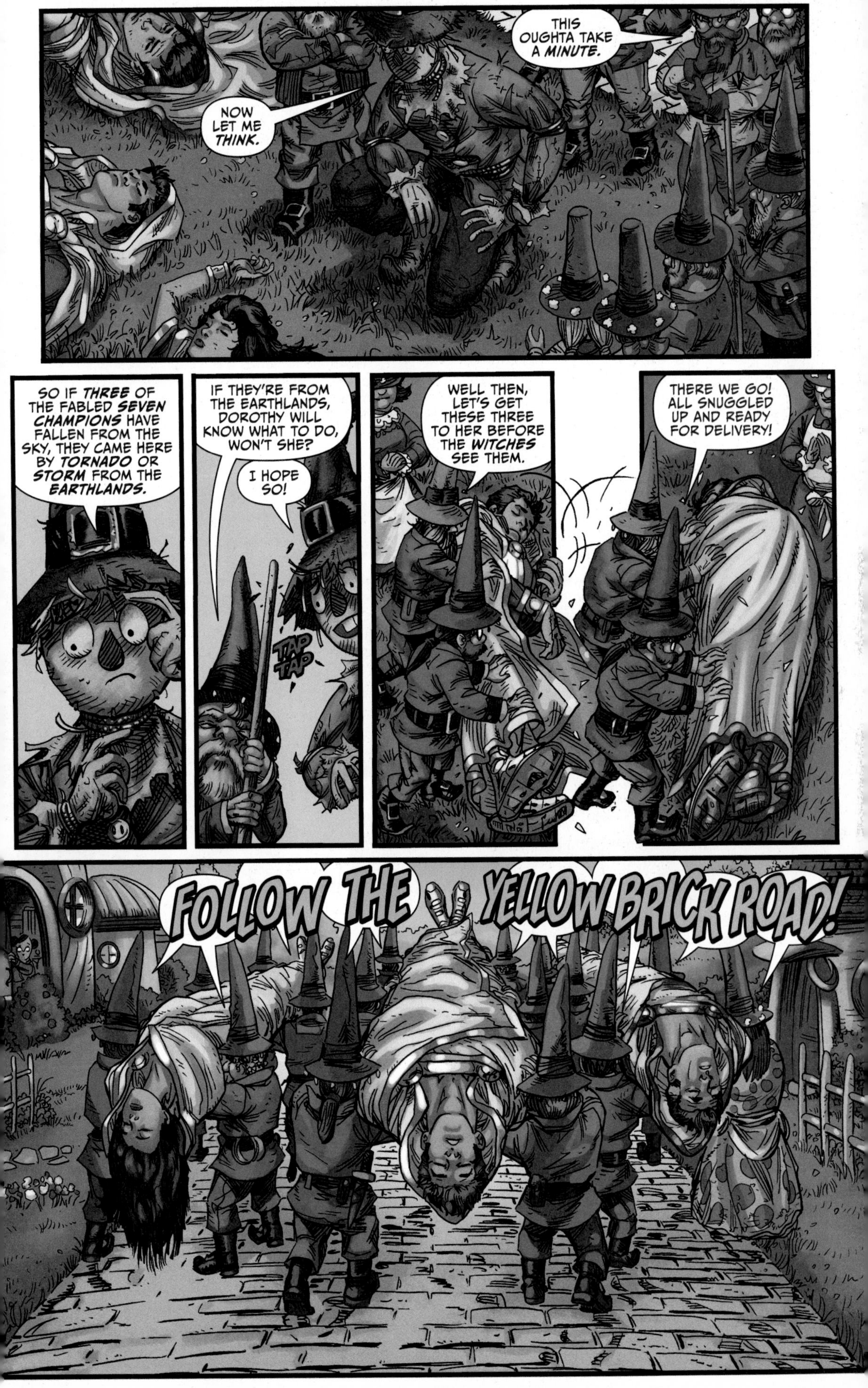
THIS OUGHTA TAKE A MINUTE.
NOW LET ME THINK.
SO IF THREE OF THE FABLED SEVEN CHAMPIONS HAVE FALLEN FROM THE SKY, THEY CAME HERE BY TORNADO OR STORM FROM THE EARTHLANDS.
IF THEY'RE FROM THE EARTHLANDS, DOROTHY WILL KNOW WHAT TO DO, WON'T SHE?
I HOPE SO!
TAP TAP
WELL THEN, LET'S GET THESE THREE TO HER BEFORE THE WITCHES SEE THEM.
THERE WE GO! ALL SNUGGLED UP AND READY FOR DELIVERY!
FOLLOW THE YELLOW BRICK ROAD!

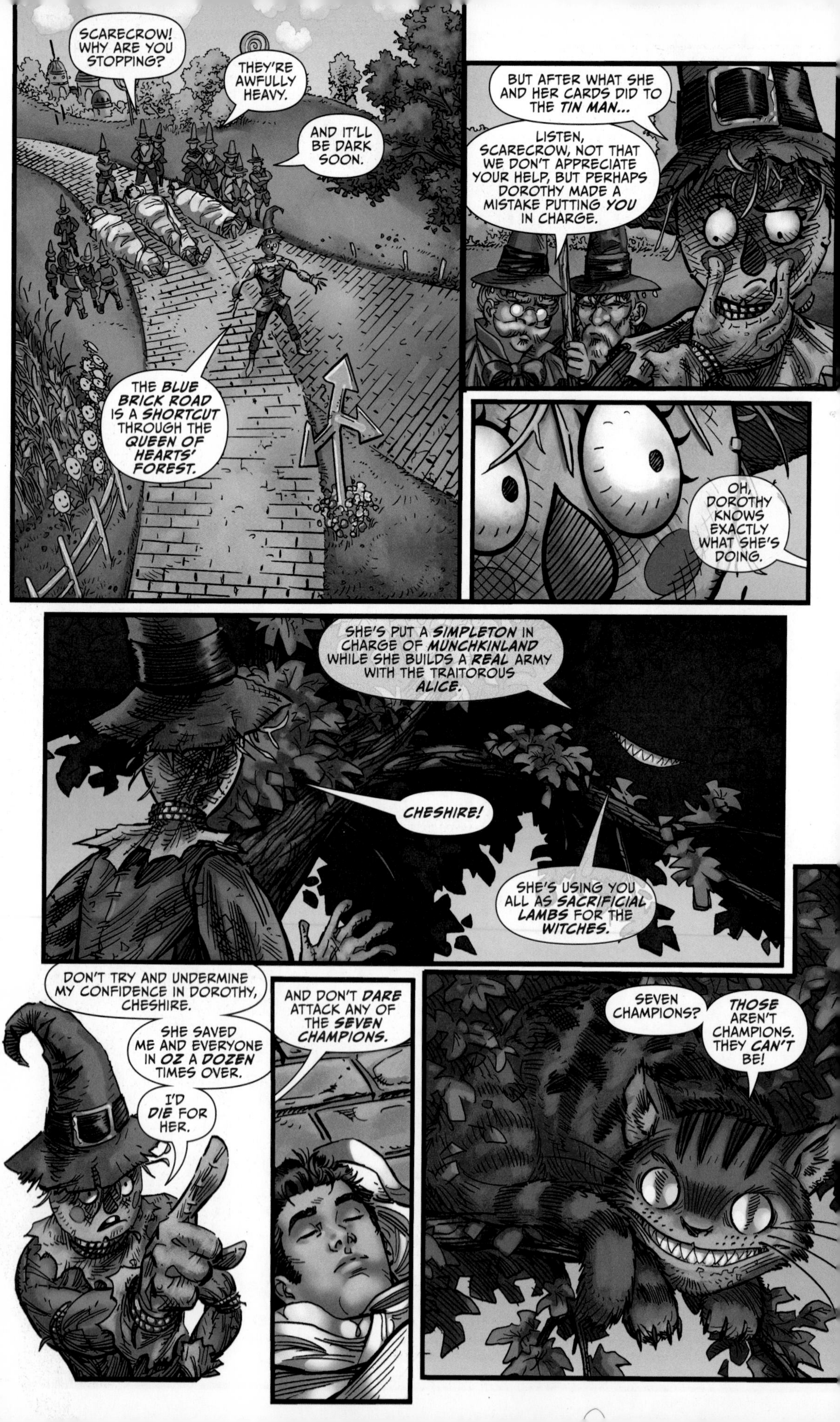
SCARECROW! WHY ARE YOU STOPPING?
THEY'RE AWFULLY HEAVY.
AND IT'LL BE DARK SOON.
THE BLUE BRICK ROAD IS A SHORTCUT THROUGH THE QUEEN OF HEARTS' FOREST.
BUT AFTER WHAT SHE AND HER CARDS DID TO THE TIN MAN...
LISTEN, SCARECROW, NOT THAT WE DON'T APPRECIATE YOUR HELP, BUT PERHAPS DOROTHY MADE A MISTAKE PUTTING YOU IN CHARGE.
OH, DOROTHY KNOWS EXACTLY WHAT SHE'S DOING.
SHE'S PUT A SIMPLETON IN CHARGE OF MUNCHKINLAND WHILE SHE BUILDS A REAL ARMY WITH THE TRAITOROUS ALICE.
CHESHIRE!
SHE'S USING YOU ALL AS SACRIFICIAL LAMBS FOR THE WITCHES.
DON'T TRY AND UNDERMINE MY CONFIDENCE IN DOROTHY, CHESHIRE.
SHE SAVED ME AND EVERYONE IN OZ A DOZEN TIMES OVER.
I'D DIE FOR HER.
AND DON'T DARE ATTACK ANY OF THE SEVEN CHAMPIONS.
SEVEN CHAMPIONS?
THOSE AREN'T CHAMPIONS. THEY CAN'T BE!

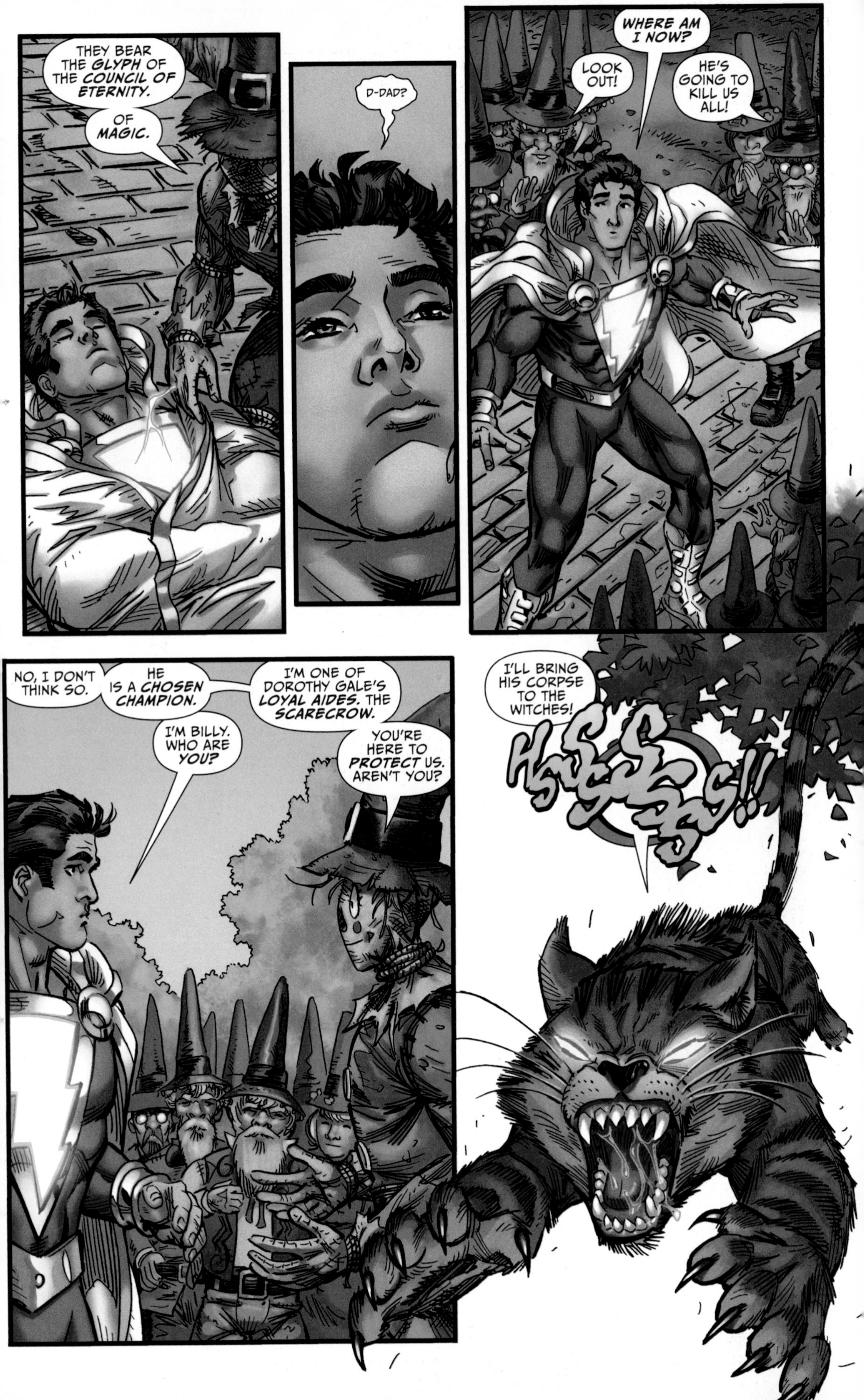
THEY BEAR THE GLYPH OF THE COUNCIL OF ETERNITY.
OF MAGIC.
D-DAD?
WHERE AM I NOW?
LOOK OUT!
HE'S GOING TO KILL US ALL!
NO, I DON'T THINK SO.
HE IS A CHOSEN CHAMPION.
I'M ONE OF DOROTHY GALE'S LOYAL AIDES. THE SCARECROW.
I'M BILLY. WHO ARE YOU?
YOU'RE HERE TO PROTECT US. AREN'T YOU?
I'LL BRING HIS CORPSE TO THE WITCHES!
HSSSSS!!

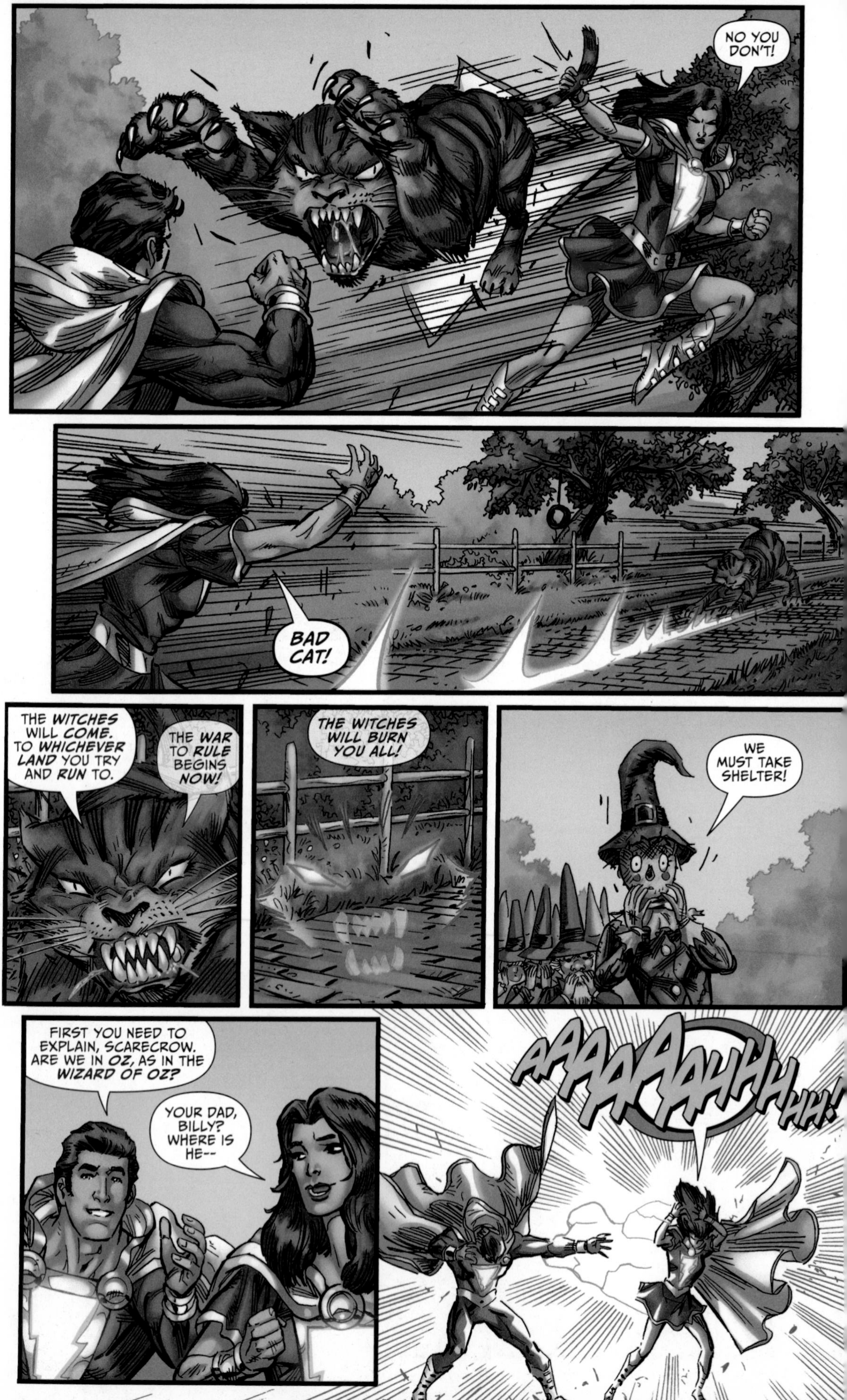
NO YOU DON'T!
BAD CAT!
THE WITCHES WILL COME. TO WHICHEVER LAND YOU TRY AND RUN TO.
THE WAR TO RULE BEGINS NOW!
THE WITCHES WILL BURN YOU ALL!
WE MUST TAKE SHELTER!
FIRST YOU NEED TO EXPLAIN, SCARECROW. ARE WE IN OZ, AS IN THE WIZARD OF OZ?
YOUR DAD, BILLY? WHERE IS HE--
AAAAAAAHHHHHH!

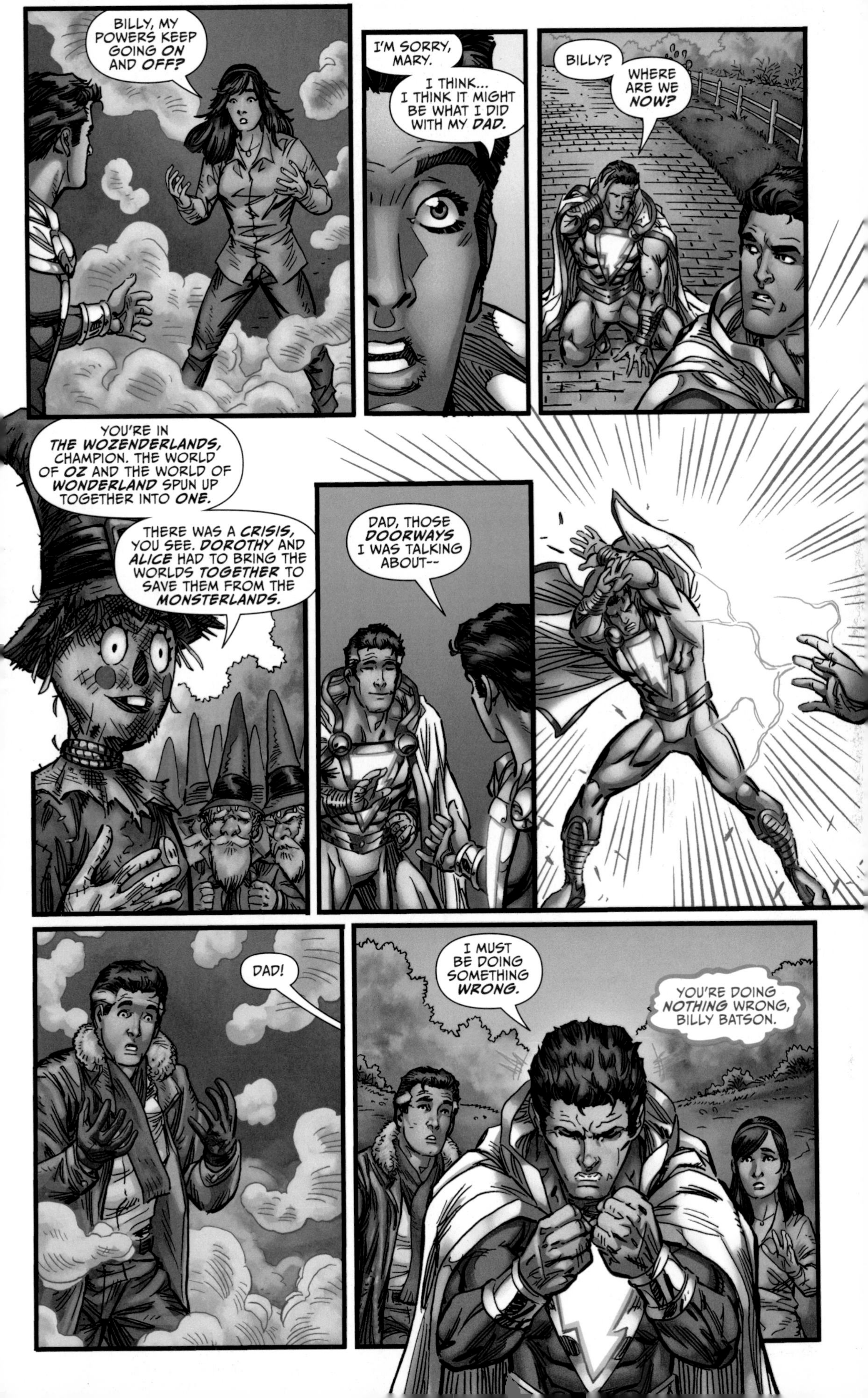
BILLY, MY POWERS KEEP GOING ON AND OFF?
I'M SORRY, MARY.
I THINK... I THINK IT MIGHT BE WHAT I DID WITH MY DAD.
BILLY?
WHERE ARE WE NOW?
YOU'RE IN THE WOZENDERLANDS, CHAMPION. THE WORLD OF OZ AND THE WORLD OF WONDERLAND SPUN UP TOGETHER INTO ONE.
THERE WAS A CRISIS, YOU SEE. DOROTHY AND ALICE HAD TO BRING THE WORLDS TOGETHER TO SAVE THEM FROM THE MONSTERLANDS.
DAD, THOSE DOORWAYS I WAS TALKING ABOUT--
DAD!
I MUST BE DOING SOMETHING WRONG.
YOU'RE DOING NOTHING WRONG, BILLY BATSON.

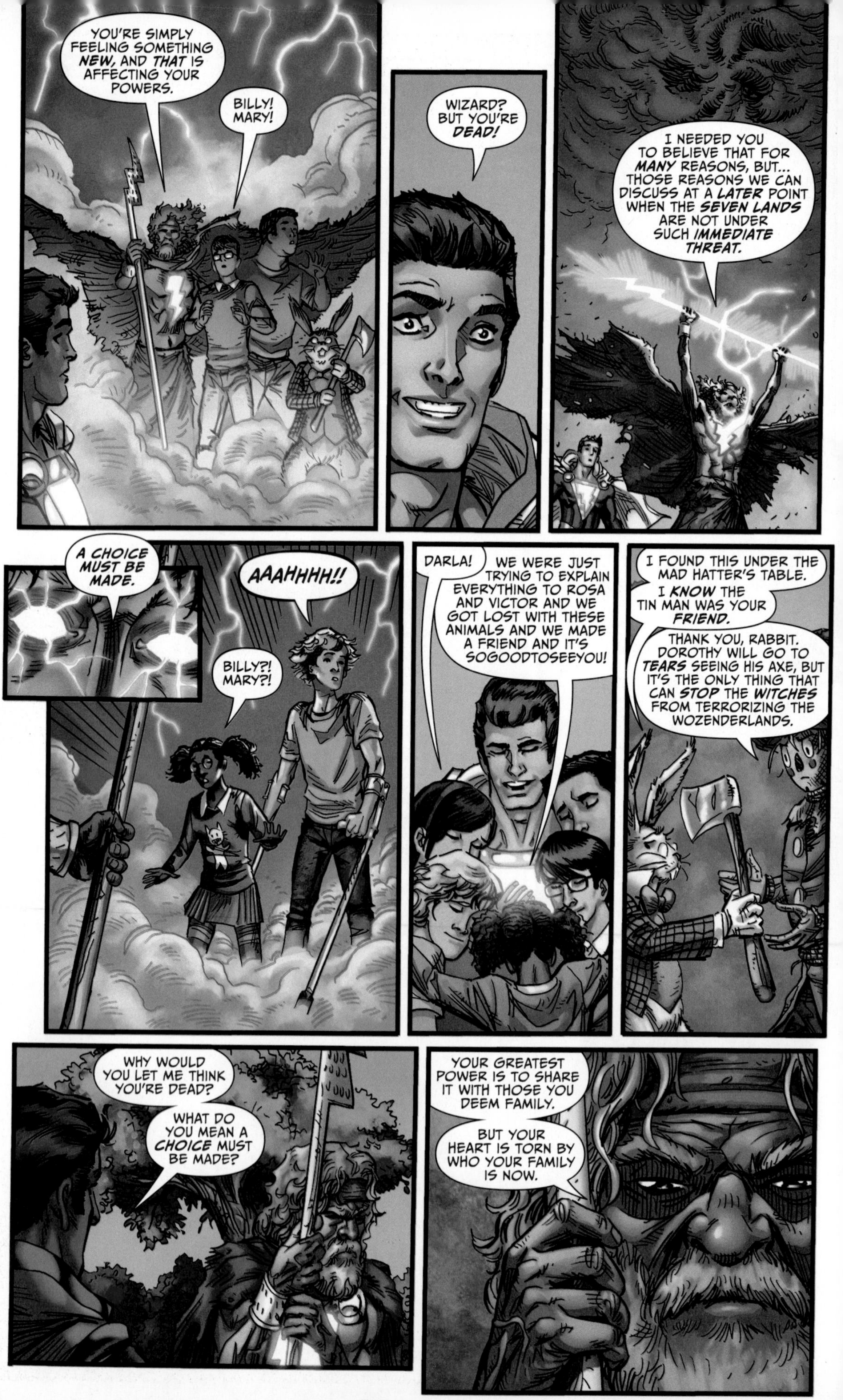
YOU'RE SIMPLY FEELING SOMETHING NEW, AND THAT IS AFFECTING YOUR POWERS.
BILLY! MARY!
WIZARD? BUT YOU'RE DEAD!
I NEEDED YOU TO BELIEVE THAT FOR MANY REASONS, BUT... THOSE REASONS WE CAN DISCUSS AT A LATER POINT WHEN THE SEVEN LANDS ARE NOT UNDER SUCH IMMEDIATE THREAT.
A CHOICE MUST BE MADE.
AAAHHHH!!
BILLY?! MARY?!
DARLA!
WE WERE JUST TRYING TO EXPLAIN EVERYTHING TO ROSA AND VICTOR AND WE GOT LOST WITH THESE ANIMALS AND WE MADE A FRIEND AND IT'S SOGOODTOSEEYOU!
I FOUND THIS UNDER THE MAD HATTER'S TABLE.
I KNOW THE TIN MAN WAS YOUR FRIEND.
THANK YOU, RABBIT. DOROTHY WILL GO TO TEARS SEEING HIS AXE, BUT IT'S THE ONLY THING THAT CAN STOP THE WITCHES FROM TERRORIZING THE WOZENDERLANDS.
WHY WOULD YOU LET ME THINK YOU'RE DEAD?
WHAT DO YOU MEAN A CHOICE MUST BE MADE?
YOUR GREATEST POWER IS TO SHARE IT WITH THOSE YOU DEEM FAMILY.
BUT YOUR HEART IS TORN BY WHO YOUR FAMILY IS NOW.

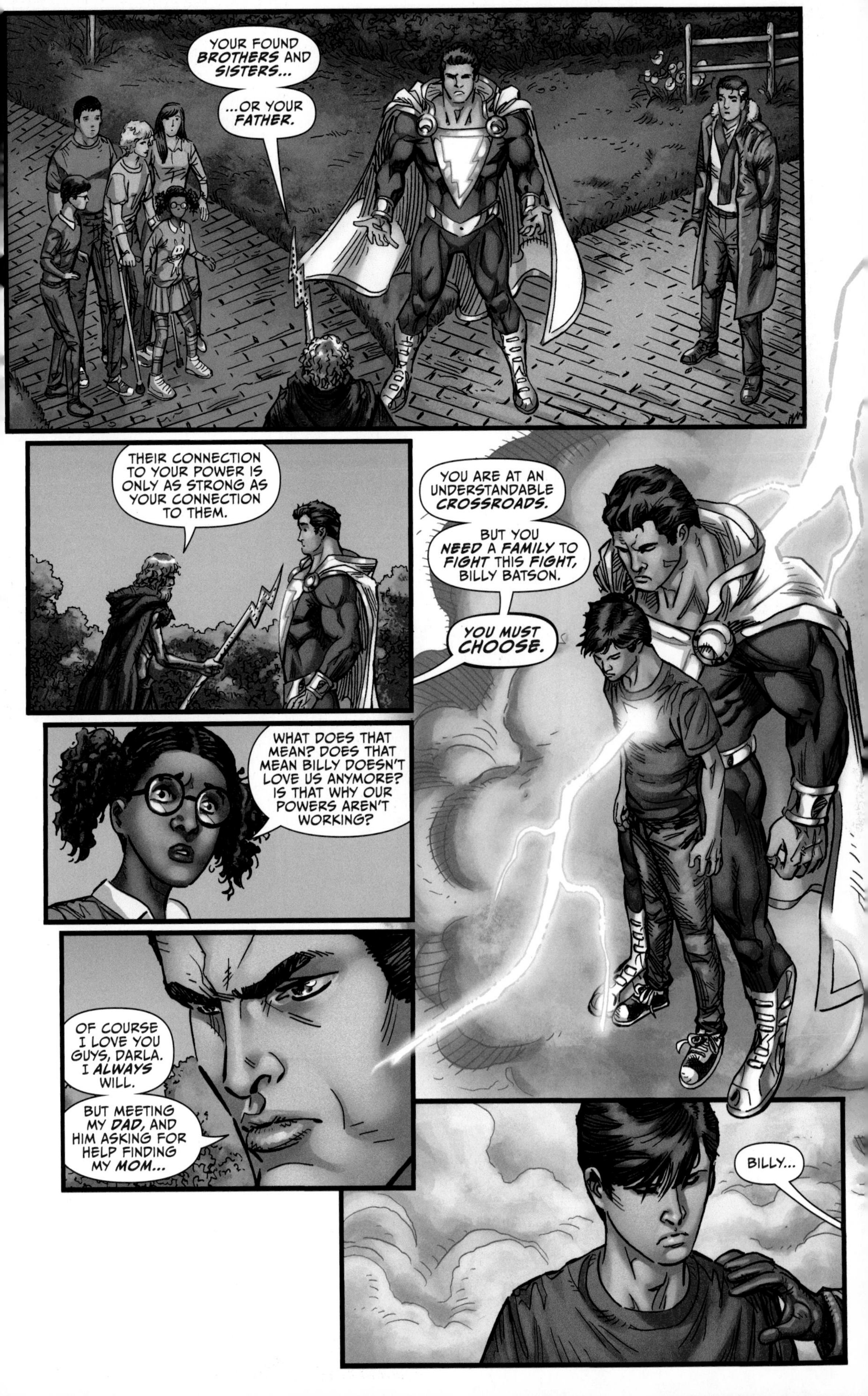
YOUR FOUND BROTHERS AND SISTERS...
...OR YOUR FATHER.
THEIR CONNECTION TO YOUR POWER IS ONLY AS STRONG AS YOUR CONNECTION TO THEM.
YOU ARE AT AN UNDERSTANDABLE CROSSROADS.
BUT YOU NEED A FAMILY TO FIGHT THIS FIGHT, BILLY BATSON.
YOU MUST CHOOSE.
WHAT DOES THAT MEAN? DOES THAT MEAN BILLY DOESN'T LOVE US ANYMORE? IS THAT WHY OUR POWERS AREN'T WORKING?
OF COURSE I LOVE YOU GUYS, DARLA. I ALWAYS WILL.
BUT MEETING MY DAD, AND HIM ASKING FOR HELP FINDING MY MOM...
BILLY...

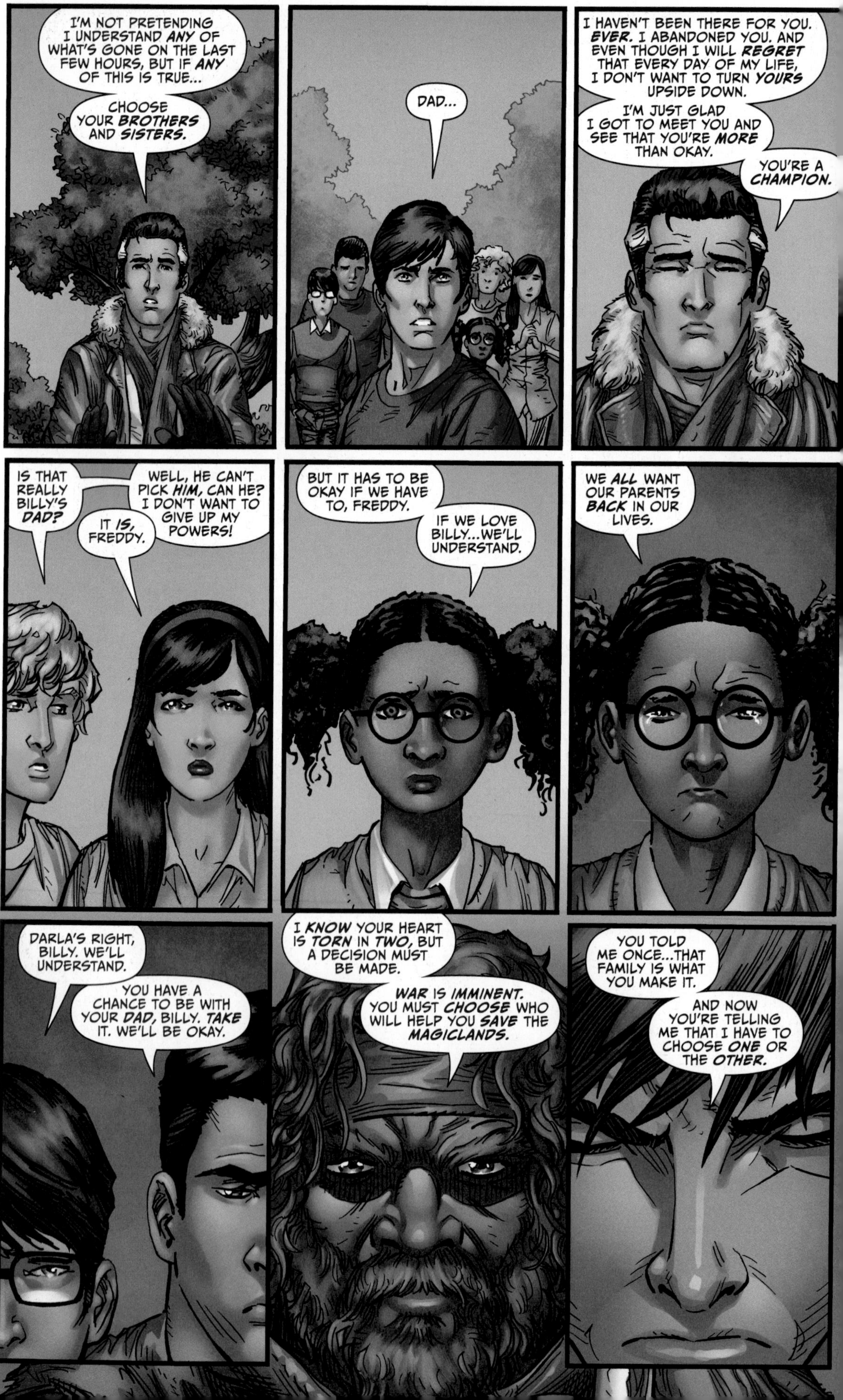

I'M NOT PRETENDING I UNDERSTAND ANY OF WHAT'S GONE ON THE LAST FEW HOURS, BUT IF ANY OF THIS IS TRUE...
CHOOSE YOUR BROTHERS AND SISTERS.
DAD...
I HAVEN'T BEEN THERE FOR YOU. EVER. I ABANDONED YOU. AND EVEN THOUGH I WILL REGRET THAT EVERY DAY OF MY LIFE, I DON'T WANT TO TURN YOURS UPSIDE DOWN.
I'M JUST GLAD I GOT TO MEET YOU AND SEE THAT YOU'RE MORE THAN OKAY.
YOU'RE A CHAMPION.
IS THAT REALLY BILLY'S DAD?
IT IS, FREDDY.
WELL, HE CAN'T PICK HIM, CAN HE? I DON'T WANT TO GIVE UP MY POWERS!
BUT IT HAS TO BE OKAY IF WE HAVE TO, FREDDY.
IF WE LOVE BILLY...WE'LL UNDERSTAND.
WE ALL WANT OUR PARENTS BACK IN OUR LIVES.
DARLA'S RIGHT, BILLY. WE'LL UNDERSTAND.
YOU HAVE A CHANCE TO BE WITH YOUR DAD, BILLY. TAKE IT. WE'LL BE OKAY.
I KNOW YOUR HEART IS TORN IN TWO, BUT A DECISION MUST BE MADE.
WAR IS IMMINENT. YOU MUST CHOOSE WHO WILL HELP YOU SAVE THE MAGICLANDS.
YOU TOLD ME ONCE...THAT FAMILY IS WHAT YOU MAKE IT.
AND NOW YOU'RE TELLING ME THAT I HAVE TO CHOOSE ONE OR THE OTHER.

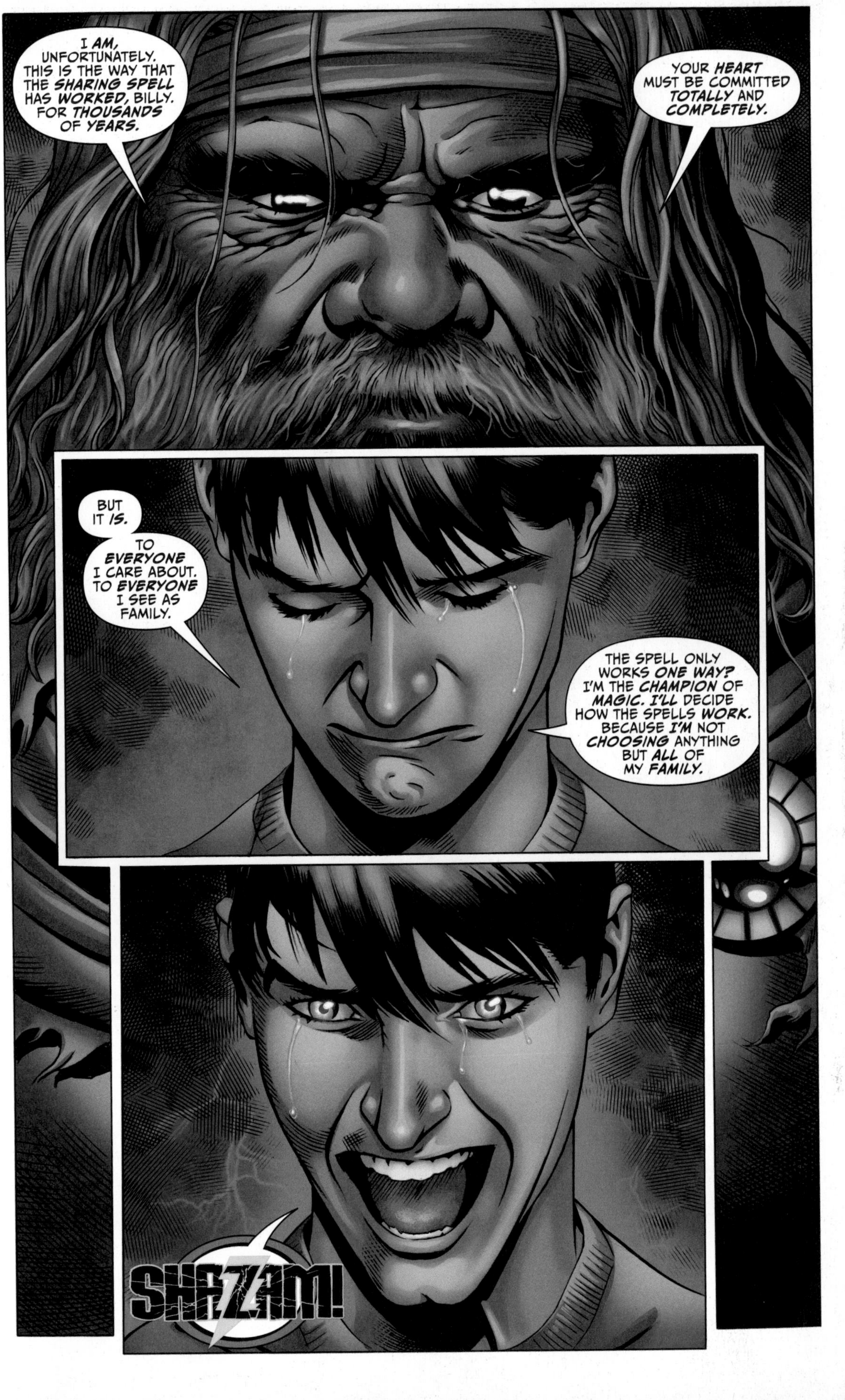
I AM, UNFORTUNATELY. THIS IS THE WAY THAT THE SHARING SPELL HAS WORKED, BILLY. FOR THOUSANDS OF YEARS.
YOUR HEART MUST BE COMMITTED TOTALLY AND COMPLETELY.
BUT IT IS.
TO EVERYONE I CARE ABOUT. TO EVERYONE I SEE AS FAMILY.
THE SPELL ONLY WORKS ONE WAY? I'M THE CHAMPION OF MAGIC. I'LL DECIDE HOW THE SPELLS WORK. BECAUSE I'M NOT CHOOSING ANYTHING BUT ALL OF MY FAMILY.
SHAZAM!

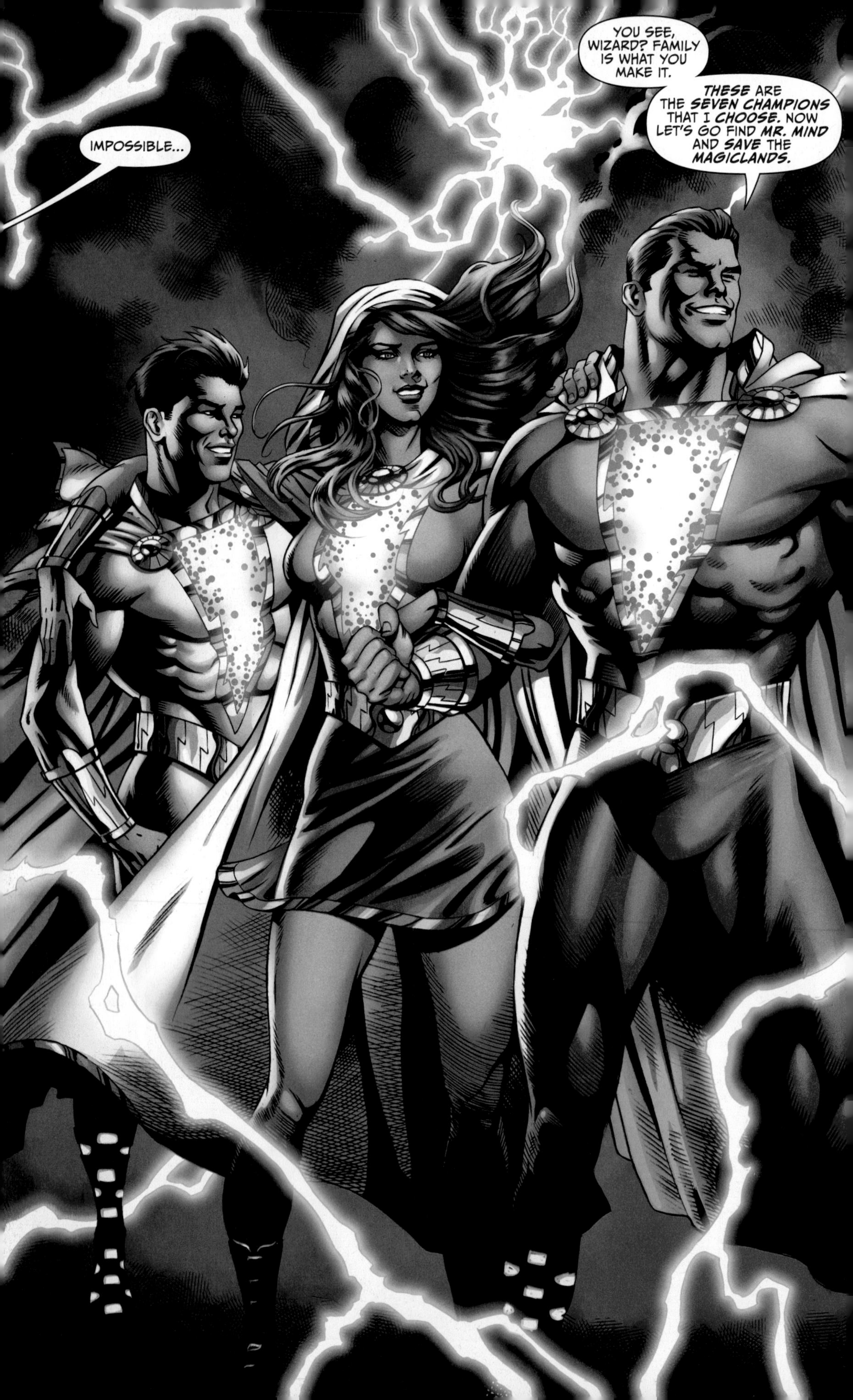
IMPOSSIBLE...
YOU SEE, WIZARD? FAMILY IS WHAT YOU MAKE IT.
THESE ARE THE SEVEN CHAMPIONS THAT I CHOOSE. NOW LET'S GO FIND MR. MIND AND SAVE THE MAGICLANDS.

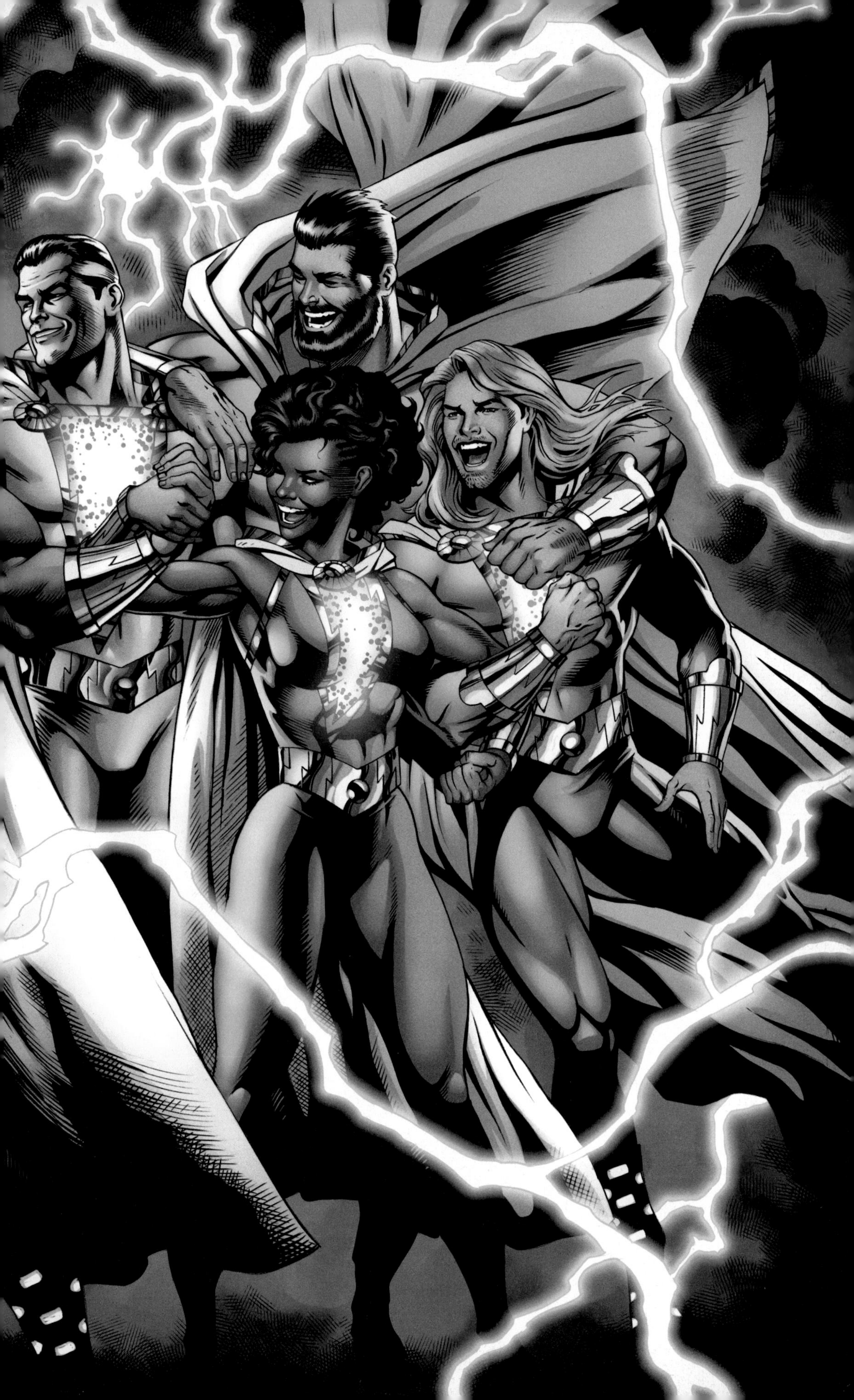

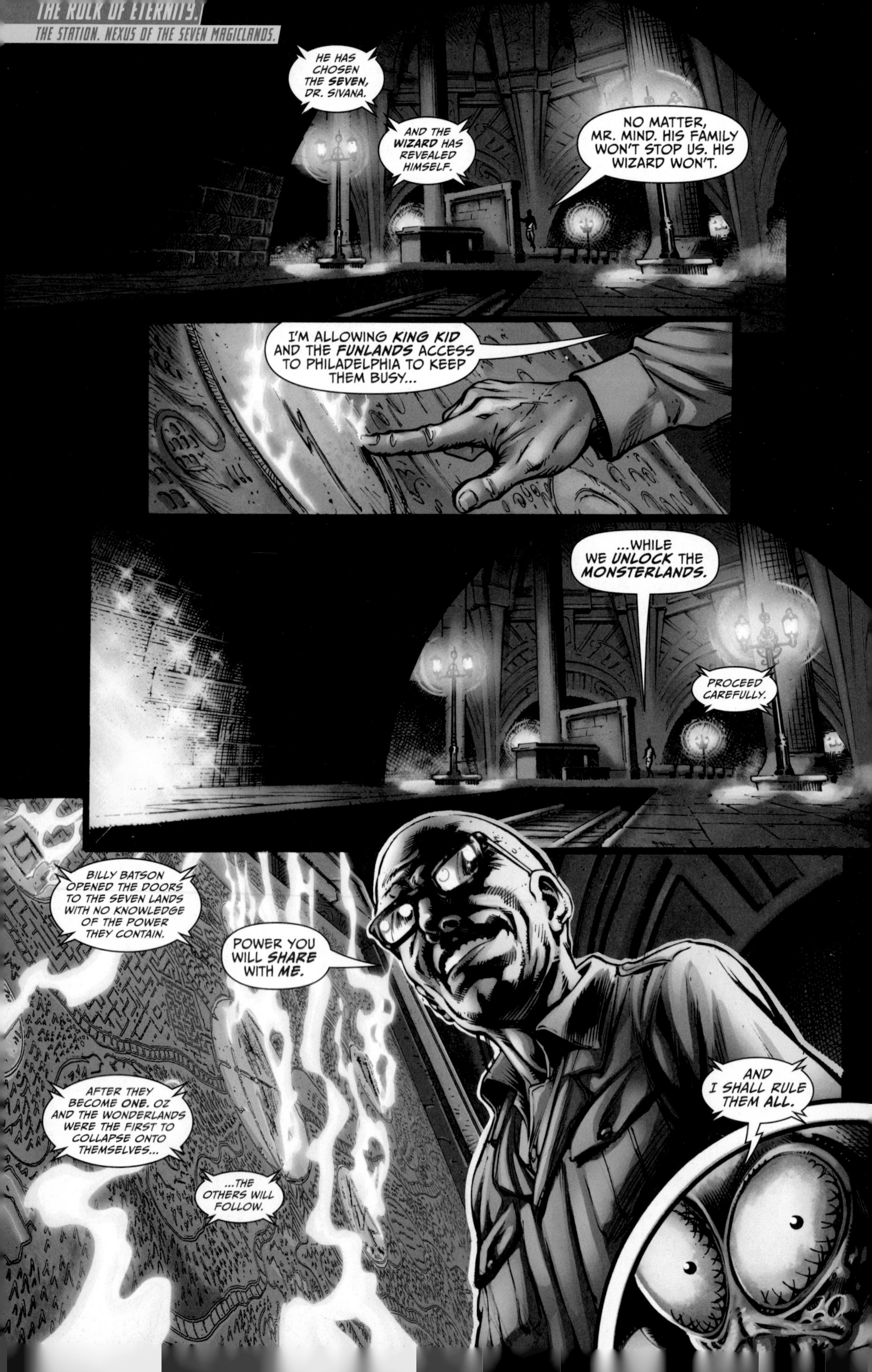
THE ROCK OF ETERNITY.
THE STATION. NEXUS OF THE SEVEN MAGICLANDS.
HE HAS CHOSEN THE SEVEN, DR. SIVANA.
AND THE WIZARD HAS REVEALED HIMSELF.
NO MATTER, MR. MIND. HIS FAMILY WON'T STOP US. HIS WIZARD WON'T.
I'M ALLOWING KING KID AND THE FUNLANDS ACCESS TO PHILADELPHIA TO KEEP THEM BUSY...
...WHILE WE UNLOCK THE MONSTERLANDS.
PROCEED CAREFULLY.
BILLY BATSON OPENED THE DOORS TO THE SEVEN LANDS WITH NO KNOWLEDGE OF THE POWER THEY CONTAIN.
POWER YOU WILL SHARE WITH ME.
AFTER THEY BECOME ONE. OZ AND THE WONDERLANDS WERE THE FIRST TO COLLAPSE ONTO THEMSELVES...
...THE OTHERS WILL FOLLOW.
AND I SHALL RULE THEM ALL.

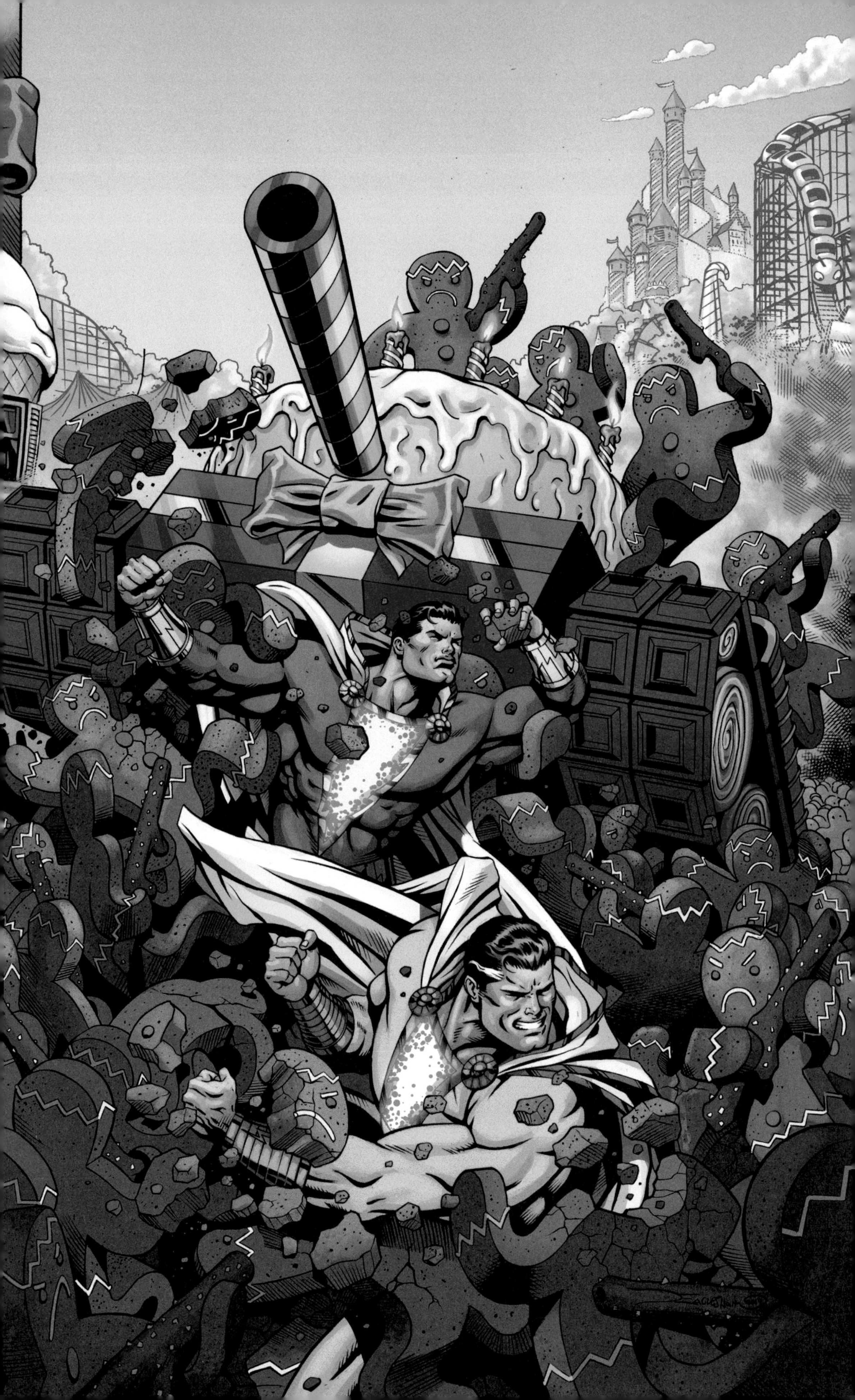

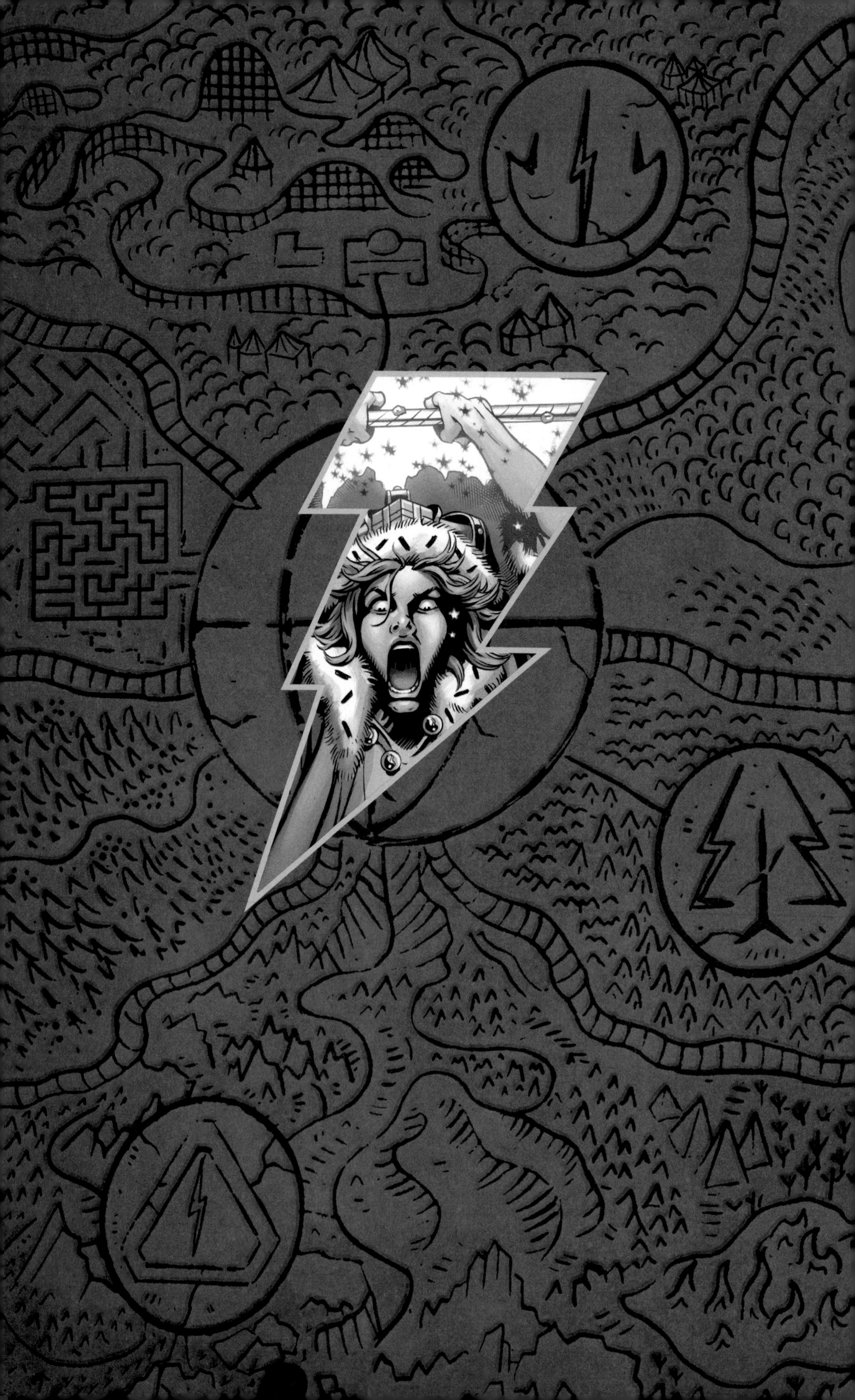

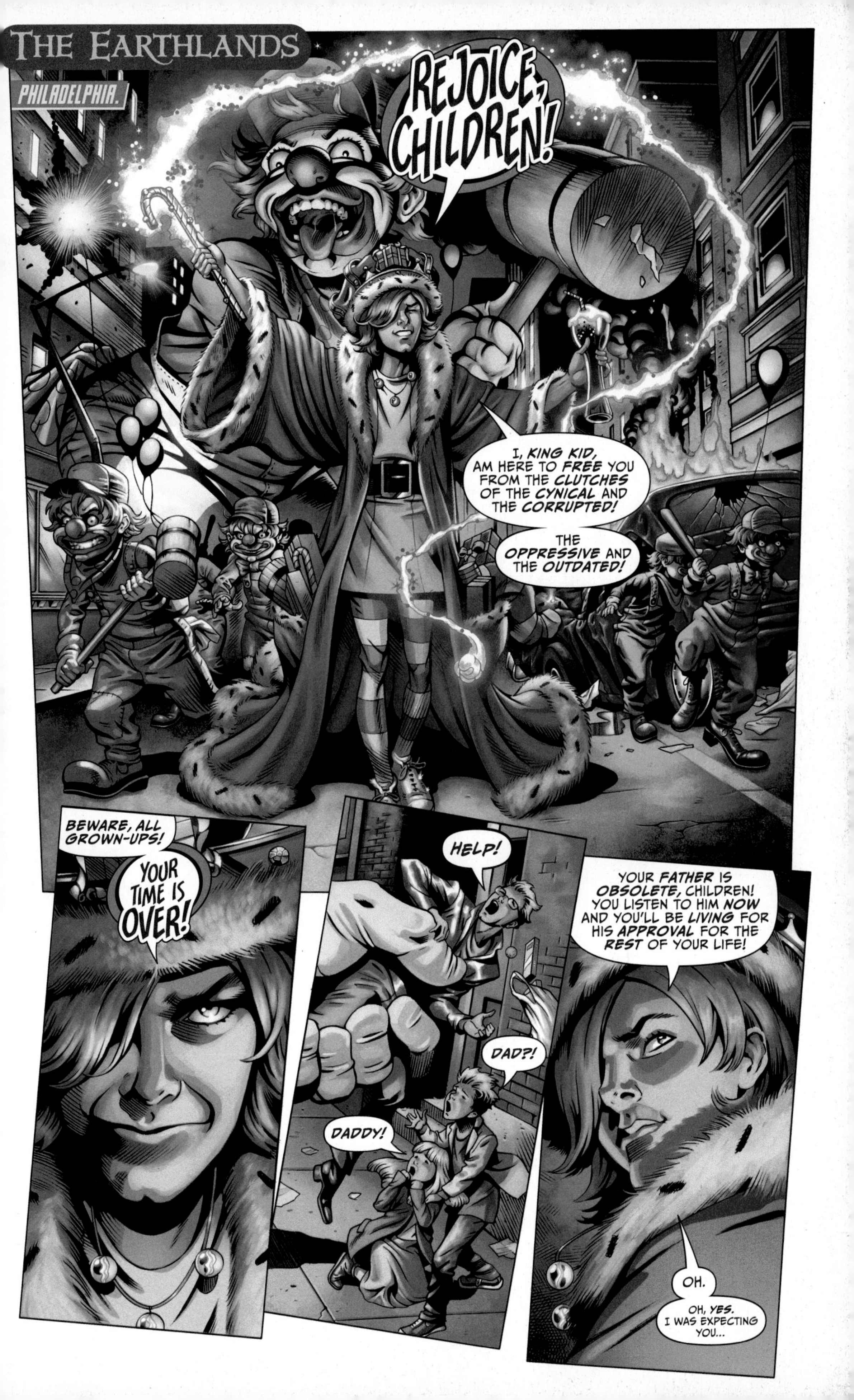
THE EARTHLANDS
PHILADELPHIA.
REJOICE, CHILDREN!
I, KING KID, AM HERE TO FREE YOU FROM THE CLUTCHES OF THE CYNICAL AND THE CORRUPTED!
THE OPPRESSIVE AND THE OUTDATED!
BEWARE, ALL GROWN-UPS!
YOUR TIME IS OVER!
HELP!
DAD?!
DADDY!
YOUR FATHER IS OBSOLETE, CHILDREN! YOU LISTEN TO HIM NOW AND YOU'LL BE LIVING FOR HIS APPROVAL FOR THE REST OF YOUR LIFE!
OH.
OH, YES. I WAS EXPECTING YOU...

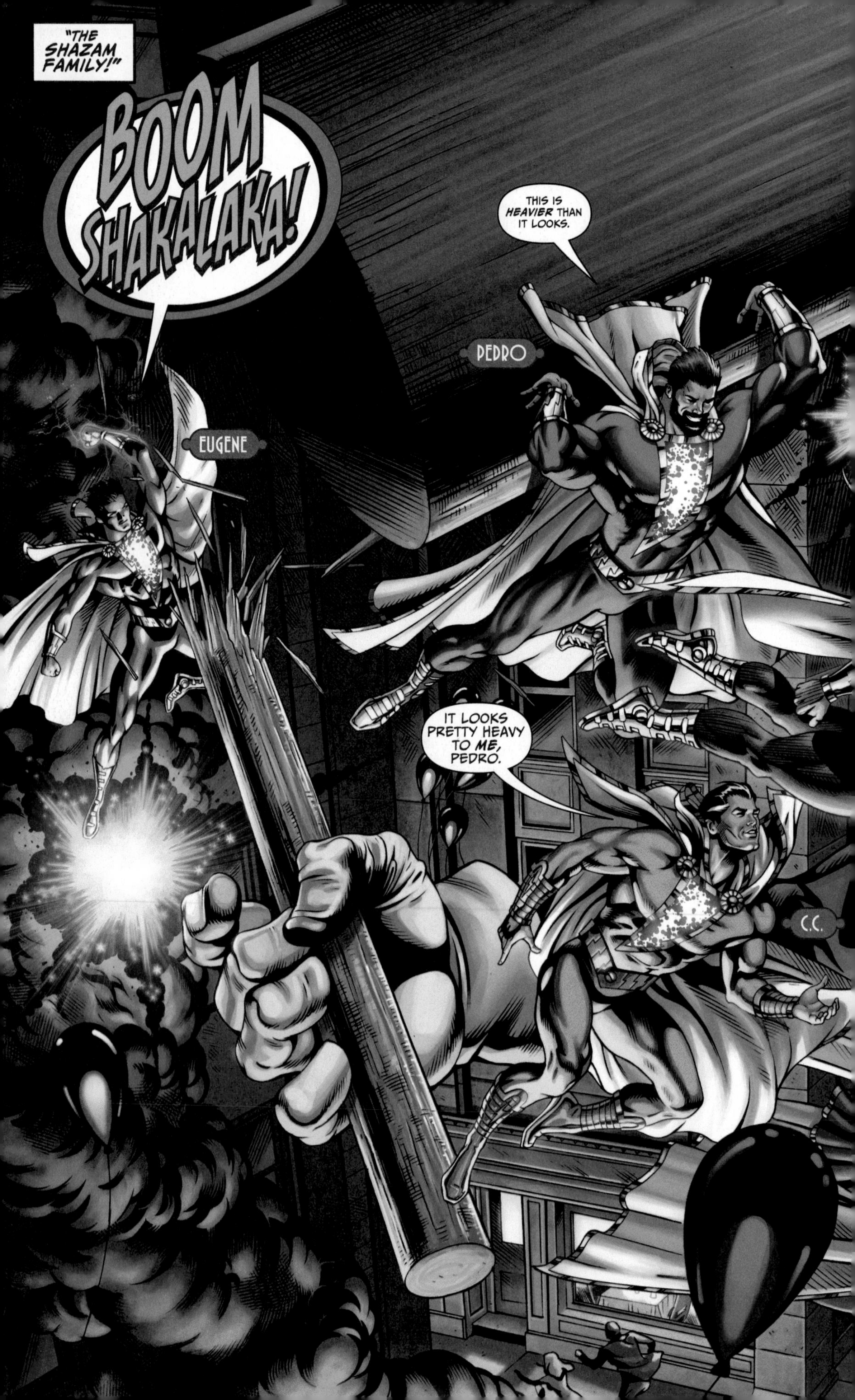
"THE SHAZAM FAMILY!"
BOOM SHAKALAKA!
THIS IS HEAVIER THAN IT LOOKS.
PEDRO
EUGENE
IT LOOKS PRETTY HEAVY TO ME, PEDRO.
C.C.

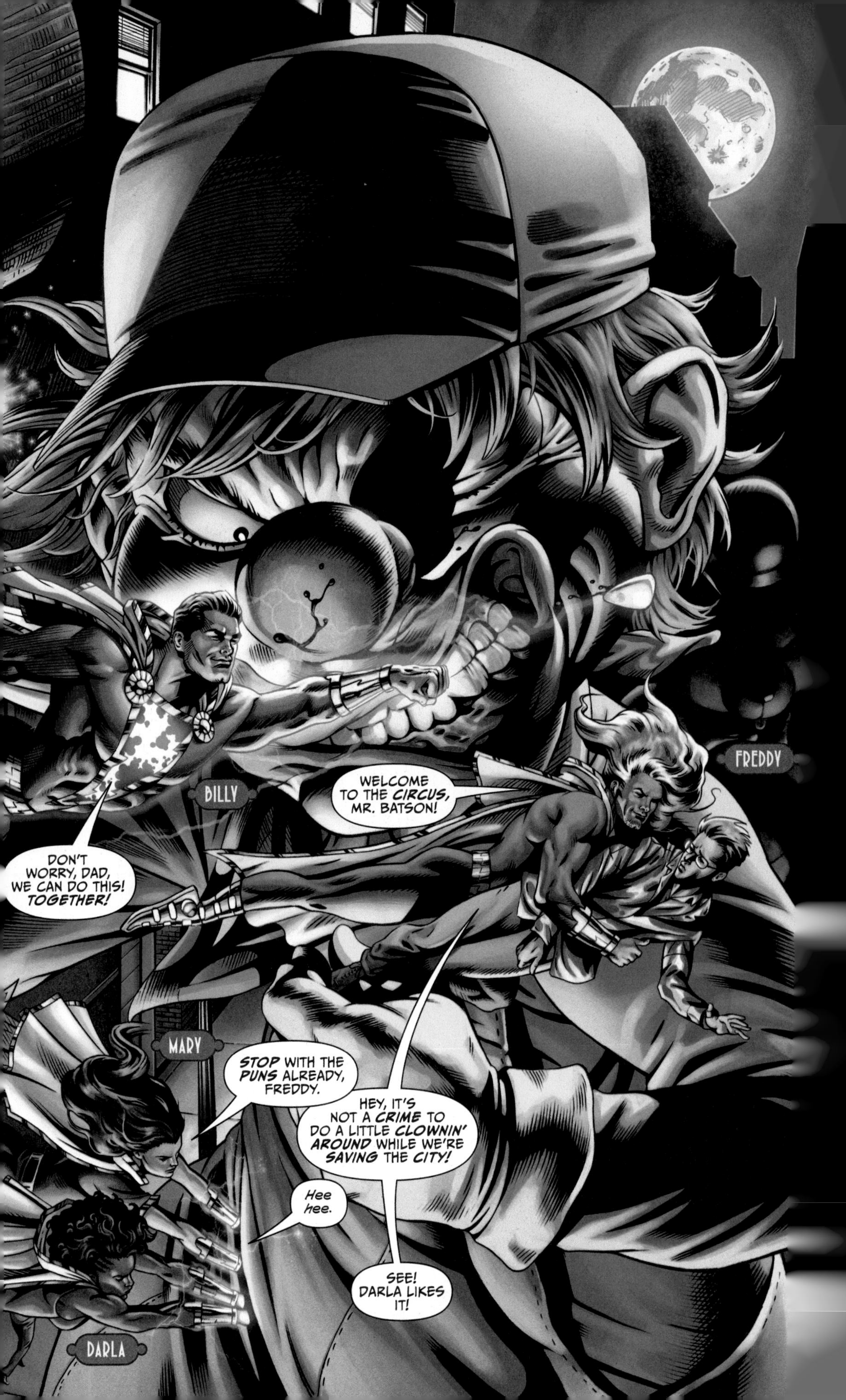
BILLY
FREDDY
WELCOME TO THE CIRCUS, MR. BATSON!
DON'T WORRY, DAD, WE CAN DO THIS! TOGETHER!
MARY
STOP WITH THE PUNS ALREADY, FREDDY.
HEY, IT'S NOT A CRIME TO DO A LITTLE CLOWNIN' AROUND WHILE WE'RE SAVING THE CITY!
Hee hee.
SEE! DARLA LIKES IT!
DARLA

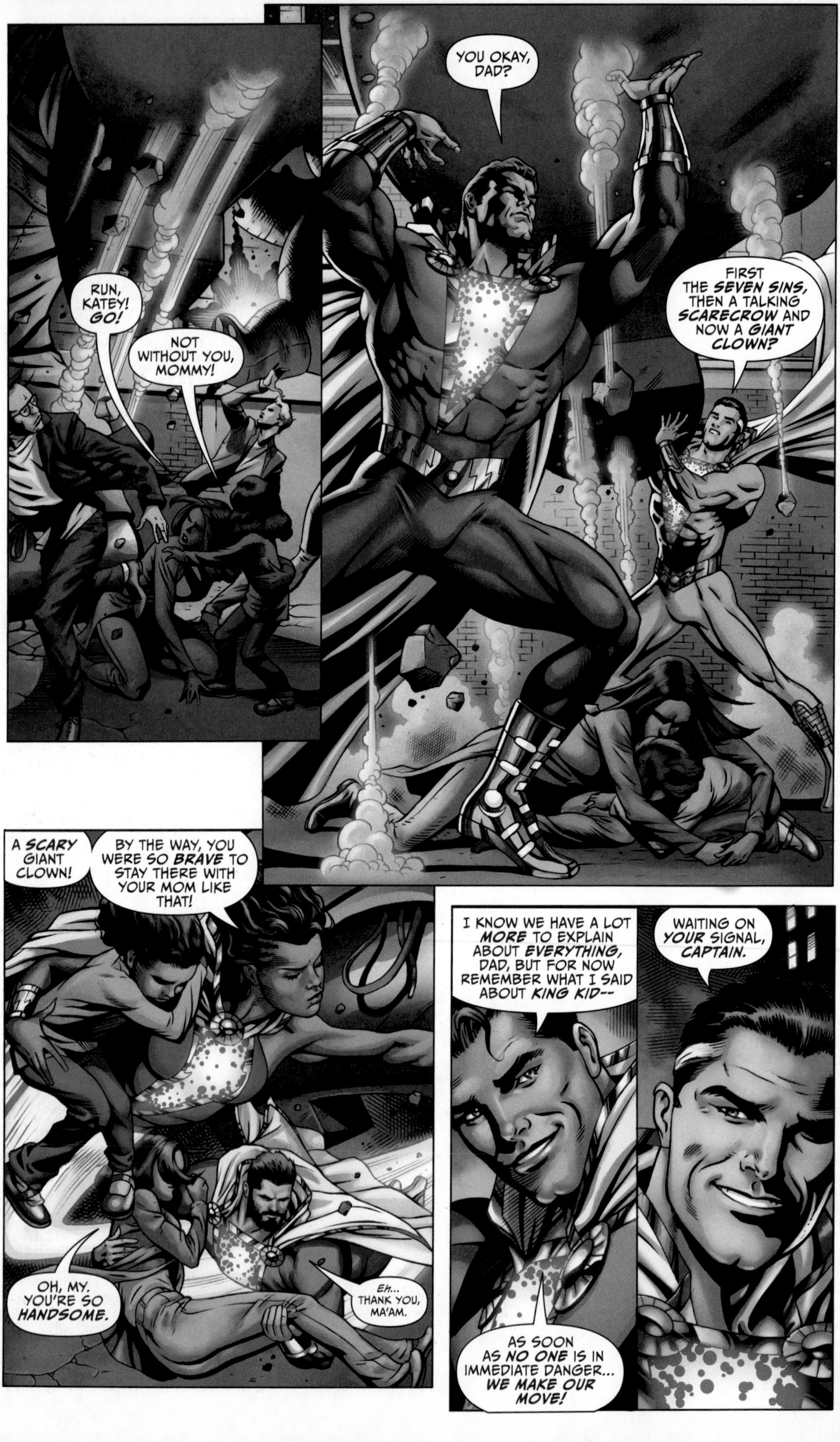
RUN, KATEY! GO!
NOT WITHOUT YOU, MOMMY!
YOU OKAY, DAD?
FIRST THE SEVEN SINS, THEN A TALKING SCARECROW AND NOW A GIANT CLOWN?
A SCARY GIANT CLOWN!
BY THE WAY, YOU WERE SO BRAVE TO STAY THERE WITH YOUR MOM LIKE THAT!
OH, MY. YOU'RE SO HANDSOME.
Eh... THANK YOU, MA'AM.
I KNOW WE HAVE A LOT MORE TO EXPLAIN ABOUT EVERYTHING, DAD, BUT FOR NOW REMEMBER WHAT I SAID ABOUT KING KID--
AS SOON AS NO ONE IS IN IMMEDIATE DANGER... WE MAKE OUR MOVE!
WAITING ON YOUR SIGNAL, CAPTAIN.

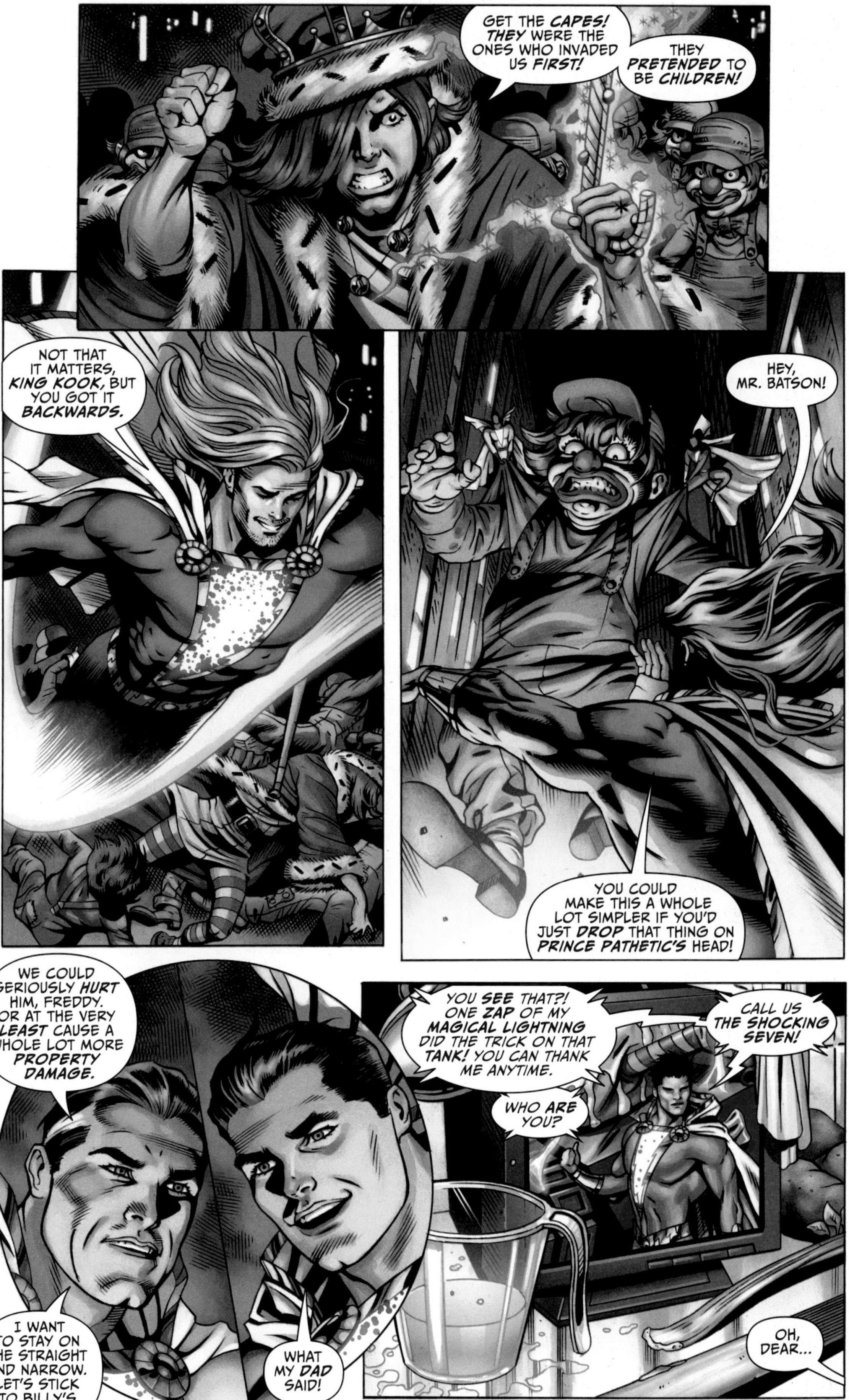
GET THE CAPES! THEY WERE THE ONES WHO INVADED US FIRST!
THEY PRETENDED TO BE CHILDREN!
NOT THAT IT MATTERS, KING KOOK, BUT YOU GOT IT BACKWARDS.
HEY, MR. BATSON!
YOU COULD MAKE THIS A WHOLE LOT SIMPLER IF YOU'D JUST DROP THAT THING ON PRINCE PATHETIC'S HEAD!
WE COULD SERIOUSLY HURT HIM, FREDDY. OR AT THE VERY LEAST CAUSE A WHOLE LOT MORE PROPERTY DAMAGE.
I WANT TO STAY ON THE STRAIGHT AND NARROW. LET'S STICK TO BILLY'S PLAN.
WHAT MY DAD SAID!
YOU SEE THAT?! ONE ZAP OF MY MAGICAL LIGHTNING DID THE TRICK ON THAT TANK! YOU CAN THANK ME ANYTIME.
CALL US THE SHOCKING SEVEN!
WHO ARE YOU?
OH, DEAR...

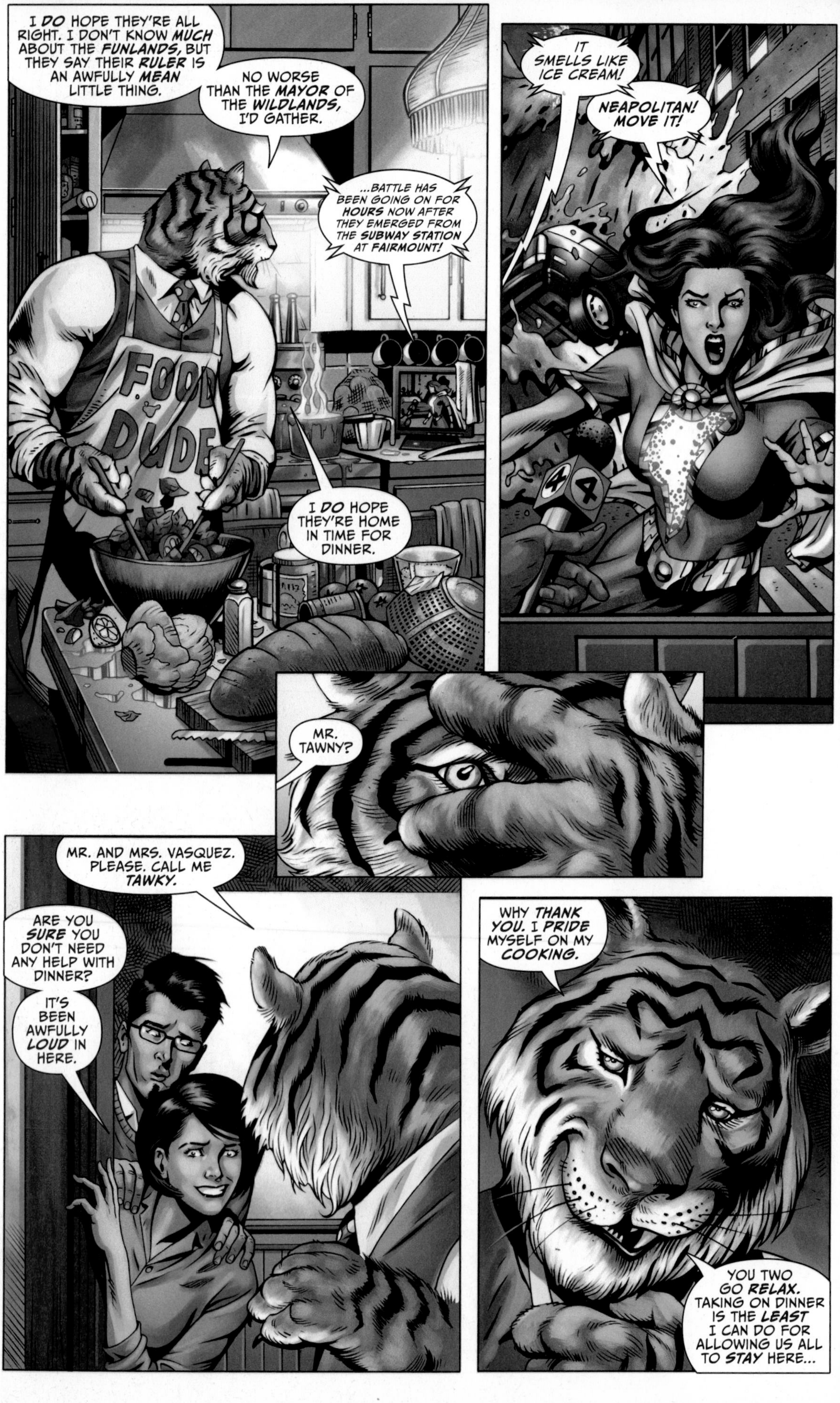

I DO HOPE THEY'RE ALL RIGHT. I DON'T KNOW MUCH ABOUT THE FUNLANDS, BUT THEY SAY THEIR RULER IS AN AWFULLY MEAN LITTLE THING.
NO WORSE THAN THE MAYOR OF THE WILDLANDS, I'D GATHER.
...BATTLE HAS BEEN GOING ON FOR HOURS NOW AFTER THEY EMERGED FROM THE SUBWAY STATION AT FAIRMOUNT!
I DO HOPE THEY'RE HOME IN TIME FOR DINNER.
FOOD DUDE
IT SMELLS LIKE ICE CREAM!
NEAPOLITAN! MOVE IT!
4
MR. TAWNY?
MR. AND MRS. VASQUEZ. PLEASE. CALL ME TAWKY.
ARE YOU SURE YOU DON'T NEED ANY HELP WITH DINNER?
IT'S BEEN AWFULLY LOUD IN HERE.
WHY THANK YOU. I PRIDE MYSELF ON MY COOKING.
YOU TWO GO RELAX. TAKING ON DINNER IS THE LEAST I CAN DO FOR ALLOWING US ALL TO STAY HERE...

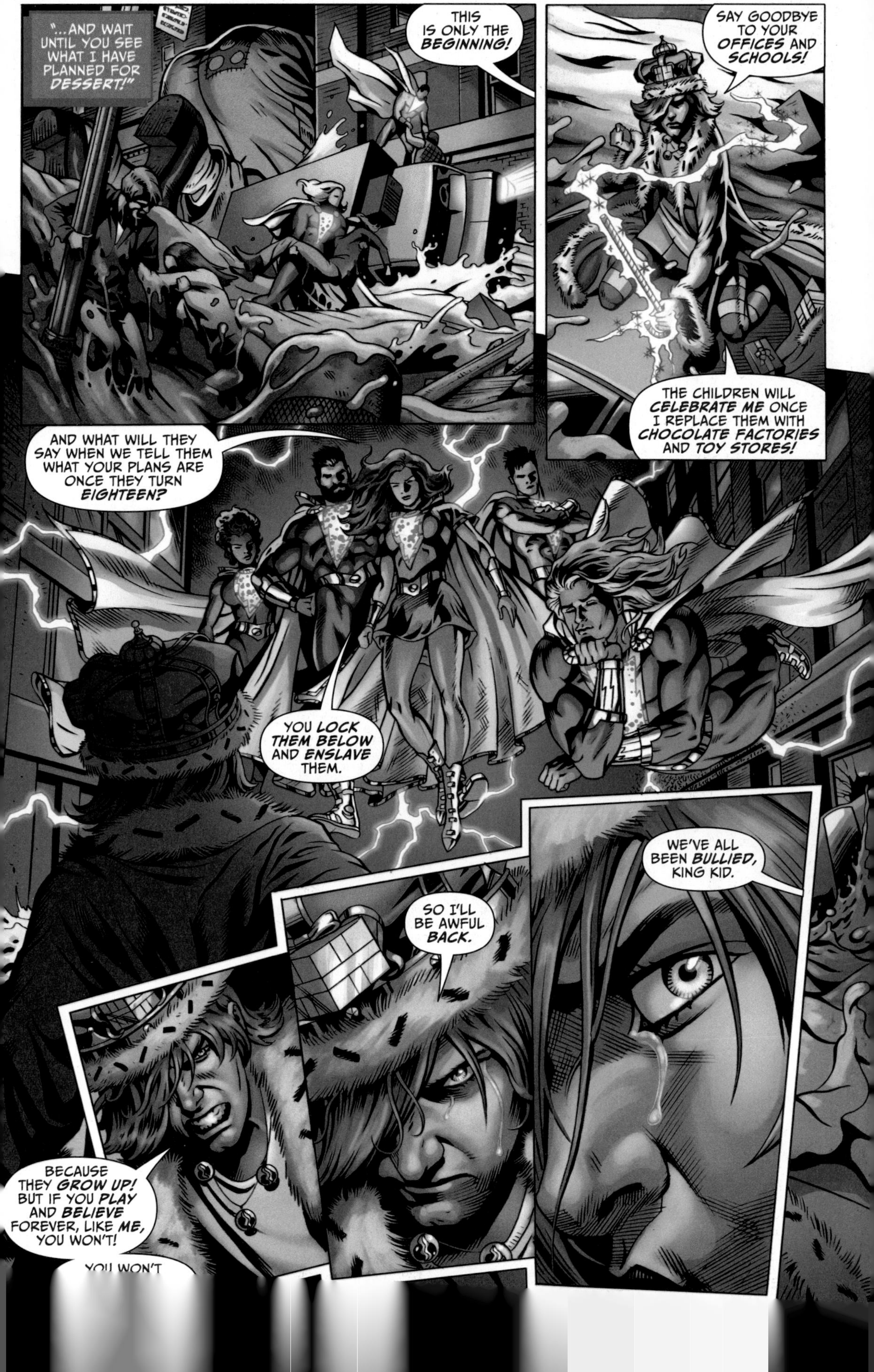
"...AND WAIT UNTIL YOU SEE WHAT I HAVE PLANNED FOR DESSERT!"
THIS IS ONLY THE BEGINNING!
SAY GOODBYE TO YOUR OFFICES AND SCHOOLS!
THE CHILDREN WILL CELEBRATE ME ONCE I REPLACE THEM WITH CHOCOLATE FACTORIES AND TOY STORES!
AND WHAT WILL THEY SAY WHEN WE TELL THEM WHAT YOUR PLANS ARE ONCE THEY TURN EIGHTEEN?
YOU LOCK THEM BELOW AND ENSLAVE THEM.
BECAUSE THEY GROW UP! BUT IF YOU PLAY AND BELIEVE FOREVER, LIKE ME, YOU WON'T!
YOU WON'T
SO I'LL BE AWFUL BACK.
WE'VE ALL BEEN BULLIED, KING KID.

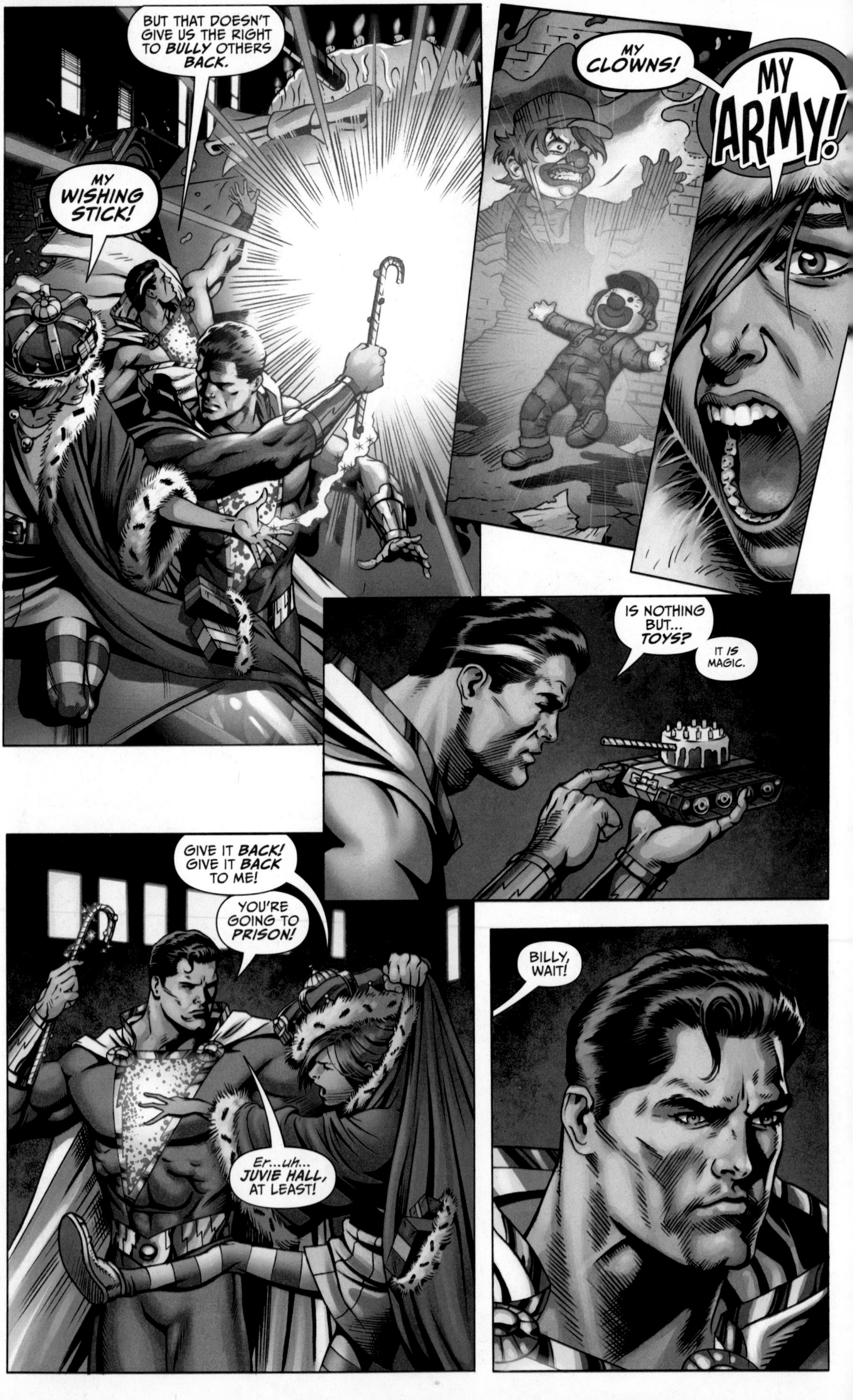
BUT THAT DOESN'T GIVE US THE RIGHT TO BULLY OTHERS BACK.
MY WISHING STICK!
MY CLOWNS!
MY ARMY!
IS NOTHING BUT... TOYS?
IT IS MAGIC.
GIVE IT BACK! GIVE IT BACK TO ME!
YOU'RE GOING TO PRISON!
Er...uh... JUVIE HALL, AT LEAST!
BILLY, WAIT!

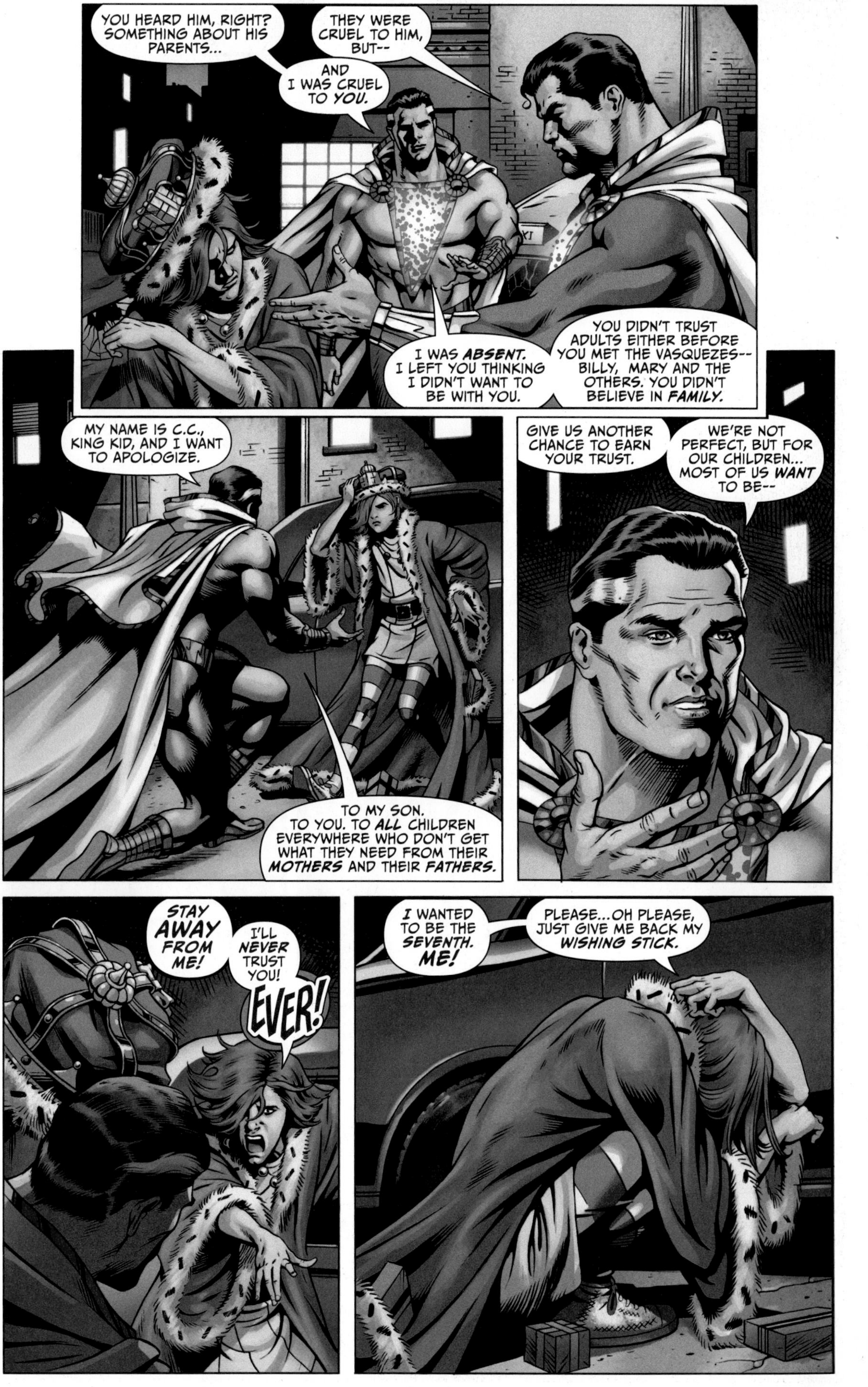
YOU HEARD HIM, RIGHT? SOMETHING ABOUT HIS PARENTS...
THEY WERE CRUEL TO HIM, BUT--
AND I WAS CRUEL TO *YOU.*
I WAS ***ABSENT.*** I LEFT YOU THINKING I DIDN'T WANT TO BE WITH YOU.
YOU DIDN'T TRUST ADULTS EITHER BEFORE YOU MET THE VASQUEZES-- BILLY, MARY AND THE OTHERS. YOU DIDN'T BELIEVE IN *FAMILY.*
MY NAME IS C.C., KING KID, AND I WANT TO APOLOGIZE.
TO MY SON. TO YOU. TO *ALL* CHILDREN EVERYWHERE WHO DON'T GET WHAT THEY NEED FROM THEIR *MOTHERS* AND THEIR *FATHERS.*
GIVE US ANOTHER CHANCE TO EARN YOUR TRUST.
WE'RE NOT PERFECT, BUT FOR OUR CHILDREN... MOST OF US *WANT* TO BE--
STAY AWAY FROM ME!
I'LL NEVER TRUST YOU!
EVER!
I WANTED TO BE THE SEVENTH. ME!
PLEASE...OH PLEASE, JUST GIVE ME BACK MY *WISHING STICK.*

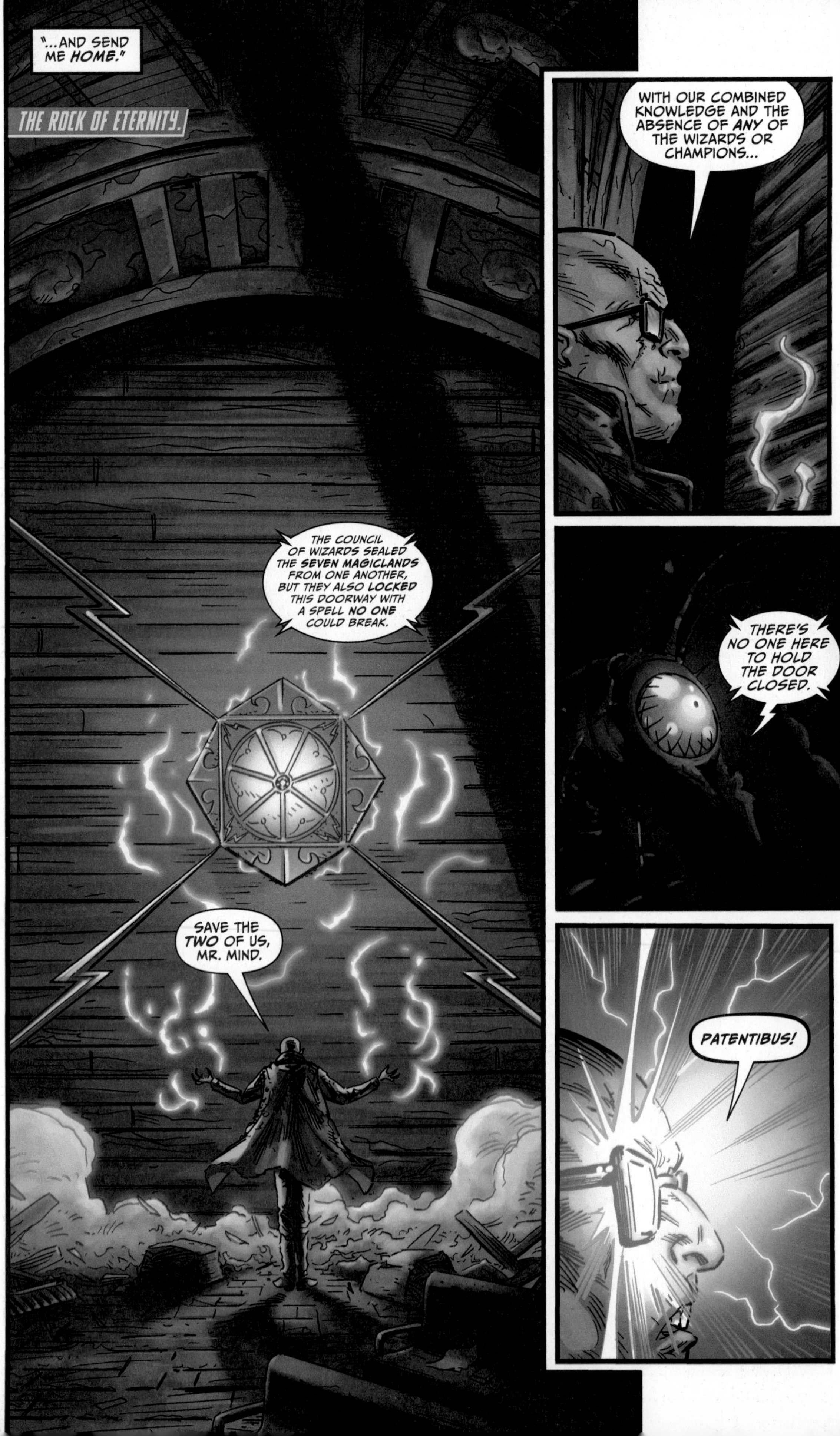
"...AND SEND ME HOME."
THE ROCK OF ETERNITY.
THE COUNCIL OF WIZARDS SEALED THE SEVEN MAGICLANDS FROM ONE ANOTHER, BUT THEY ALSO LOCKED THIS DOORWAY WITH A SPELL NO ONE COULD BREAK.
SAVE THE TWO OF US, MR. MIND.
WITH OUR COMBINED KNOWLEDGE AND THE ABSENCE OF ANY OF THE WIZARDS OR CHAMPIONS...
THERE'S NO ONE HERE TO HOLD THE DOOR CLOSED.
PATENTIBUS!

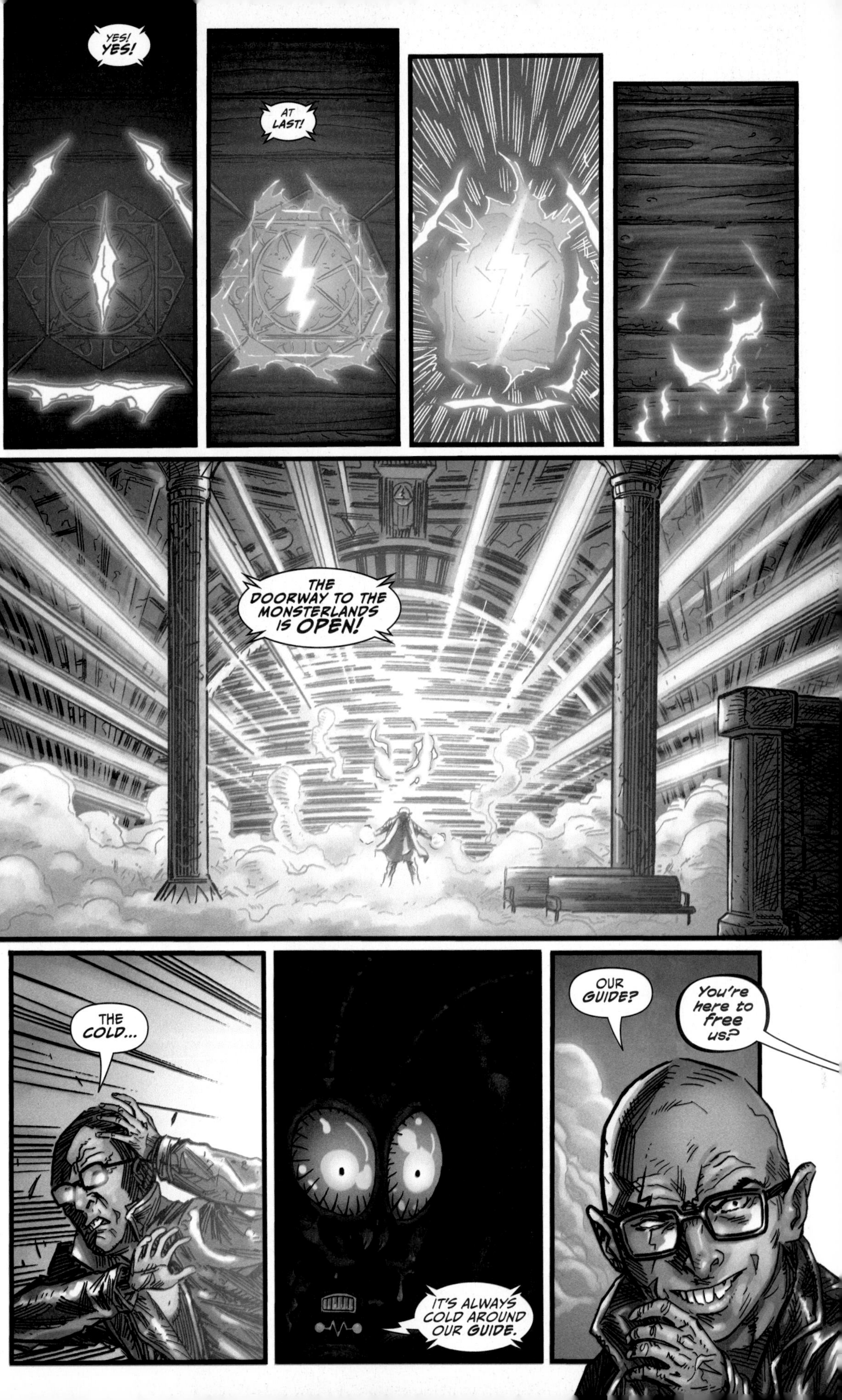
YES! YES!
AT LAST!
THE DOORWAY TO THE MONSTERLANDS IS OPEN!
THE COLD...
IT'S ALWAYS COLD AROUND OUR GUIDE.
OUR GUIDE?
You're here to free us?

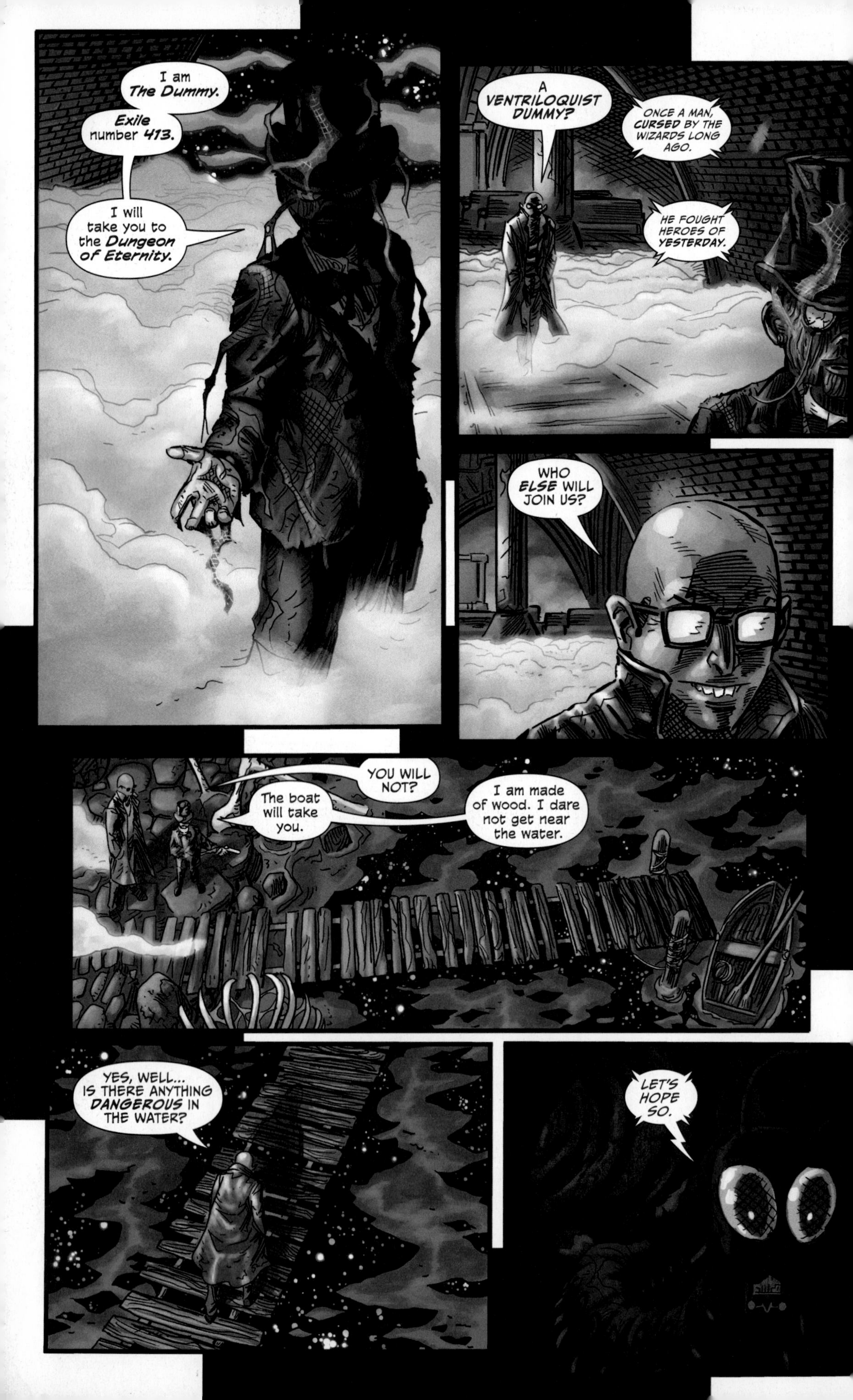

I am The Dummy.
Exile number 413.
I will take you to the Dungeon of Eternity.
A VENTRILOQUIST DUMMY?
ONCE A MAN, CURSED BY THE WIZARDS LONG AGO.
HE FOUGHT HEROES OF YESTERDAY.
WHO ELSE WILL JOIN US?
The boat will take you.
YOU WILL NOT?
I am made of wood. I dare not get near the water.
YES, WELL... IS THERE ANYTHING DANGEROUS IN THE WATER?
LET'S HOPE SO.

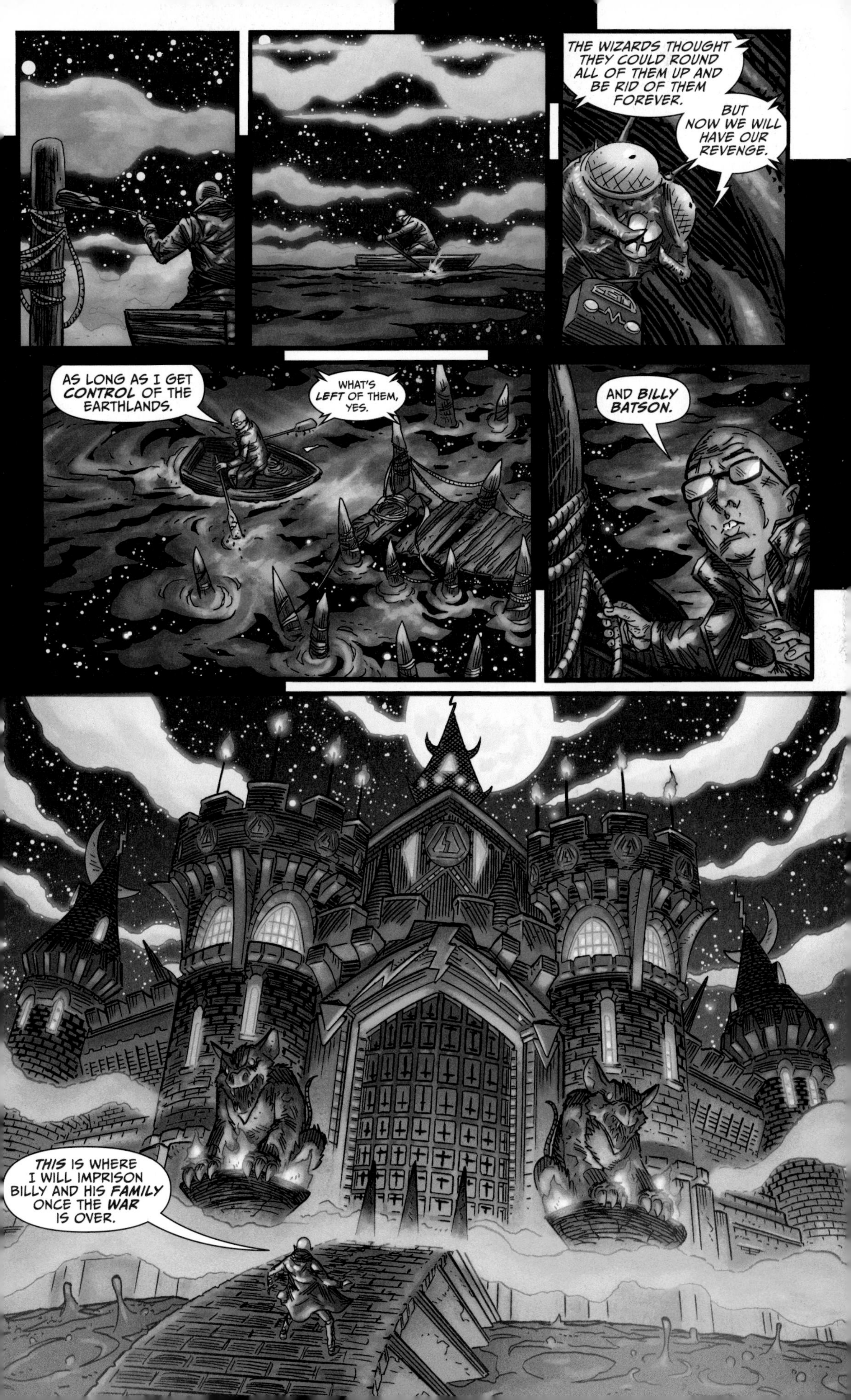
THE WIZARDS THOUGHT THEY COULD ROUND ALL OF THEM UP AND BE RID OF THEM FOREVER.
BUT NOW WE WILL HAVE OUR REVENGE.
AS LONG AS I GET *CONTROL* OF THE EARTHLANDS.
WHAT'S *LEFT* OF THEM, YES.
AND *BILLY BATSON.*
*THIS* IS WHERE I WILL IMPRISON BILLY AND HIS *FAMILY* ONCE THE *WAR* IS OVER.

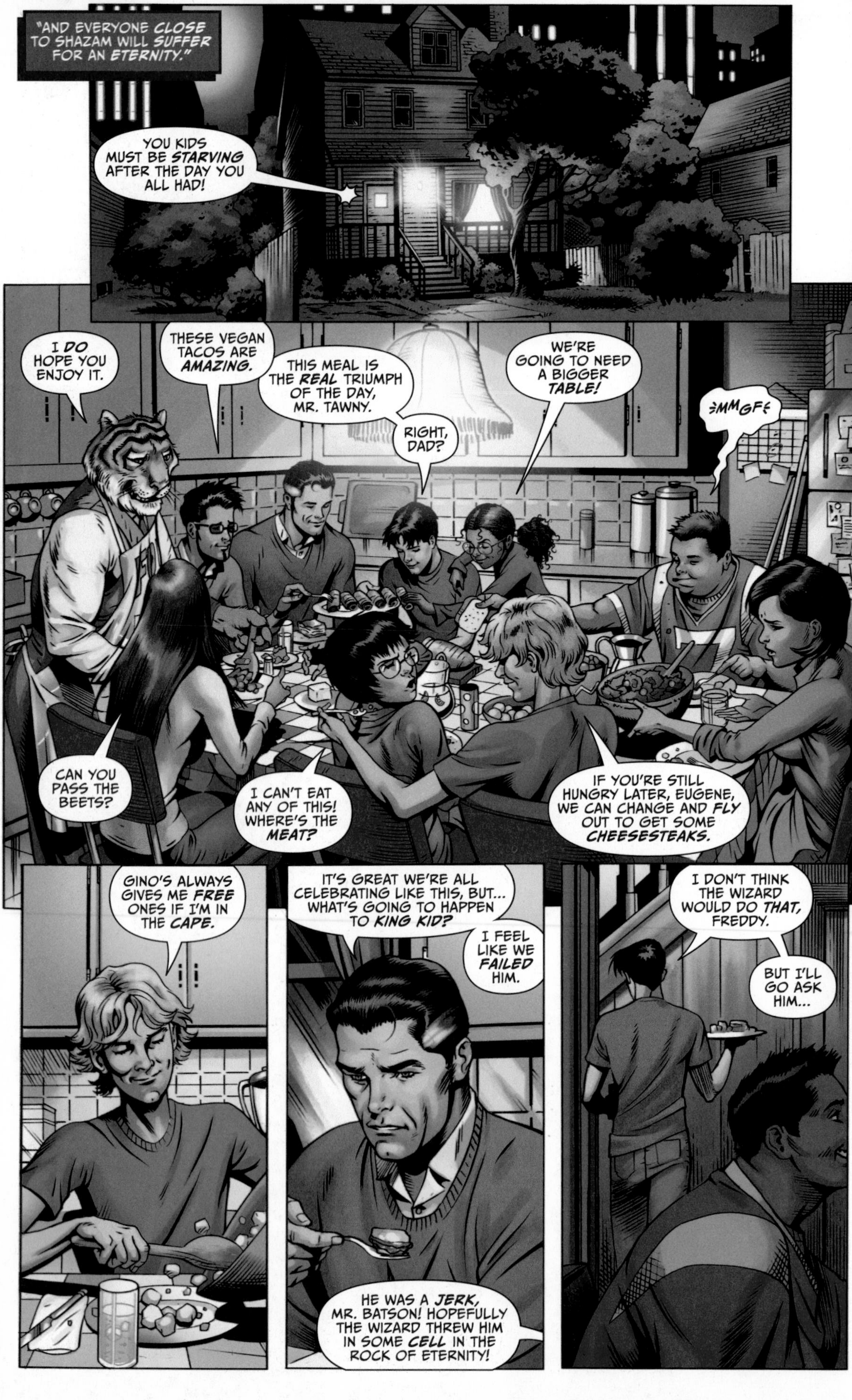

"AND EVERYONE CLOSE TO SHAZAM WILL SUFFER FOR AN ETERNITY."
YOU KIDS MUST BE STARVING AFTER THE DAY YOU ALL HAD!
I DO HOPE YOU ENJOY IT.
THESE VEGAN TACOS ARE AMAZING.
THIS MEAL IS THE REAL TRIUMPH OF THE DAY, MR. TAWNY.
RIGHT, DAD?
WE'RE GOING TO NEED A BIGGER TABLE!
MMGF
CAN YOU PASS THE BEETS?
I CAN'T EAT ANY OF THIS! WHERE'S THE MEAT?
IF YOU'RE STILL HUNGRY LATER, EUGENE, WE CAN CHANGE AND FLY OUT TO GET SOME CHEESESTEAKS.
GINO'S ALWAYS GIVES ME FREE ONES IF I'M IN THE CAPE.
IT'S GREAT WE'RE ALL CELEBRATING LIKE THIS, BUT... WHAT'S GOING TO HAPPEN TO KING KID?
I FEEL LIKE WE FAILED HIM.
HE WAS A JERK, MR. BATSON! HOPEFULLY THE WIZARD THREW HIM IN SOME CELL IN THE ROCK OF ETERNITY!
I DON'T THINK THE WIZARD WOULD DO THAT, FREDDY.
BUT I'LL GO ASK HIM...

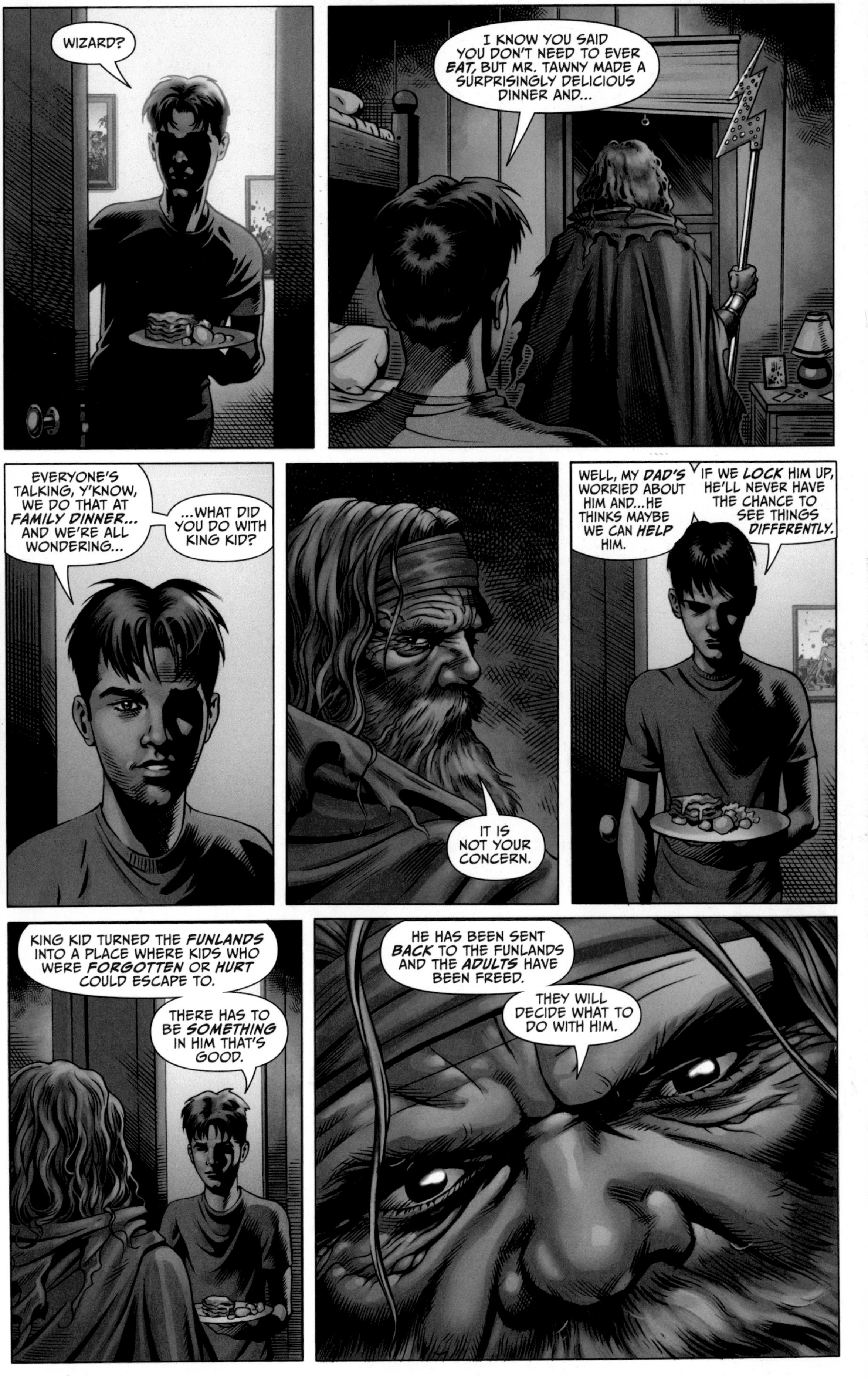
WIZARD?
I KNOW YOU SAID YOU DON'T NEED TO EVER EAT, BUT MR. TAWNY MADE A SURPRISINGLY DELICIOUS DINNER AND...
EVERYONE'S TALKING, Y'KNOW, WE DO THAT AT FAMILY DINNER... AND WE'RE ALL WONDERING...
...WHAT DID YOU DO WITH KING KID?
IT IS NOT YOUR CONCERN.
WELL, MY DAD'S WORRIED ABOUT HIM AND...HE THINKS MAYBE WE CAN HELP HIM.
IF WE LOCK HIM UP, HE'LL NEVER HAVE THE CHANCE TO SEE THINGS DIFFERENTLY.
KING KID TURNED THE FUNLANDS INTO A PLACE WHERE KIDS WHO WERE FORGOTTEN OR HURT COULD ESCAPE TO.
THERE HAS TO BE SOMETHING IN HIM THAT'S GOOD.
HE HAS BEEN SENT BACK TO THE FUNLANDS AND THE ADULTS HAVE BEEN FREED.
THEY WILL DECIDE WHAT TO DO WITH HIM.

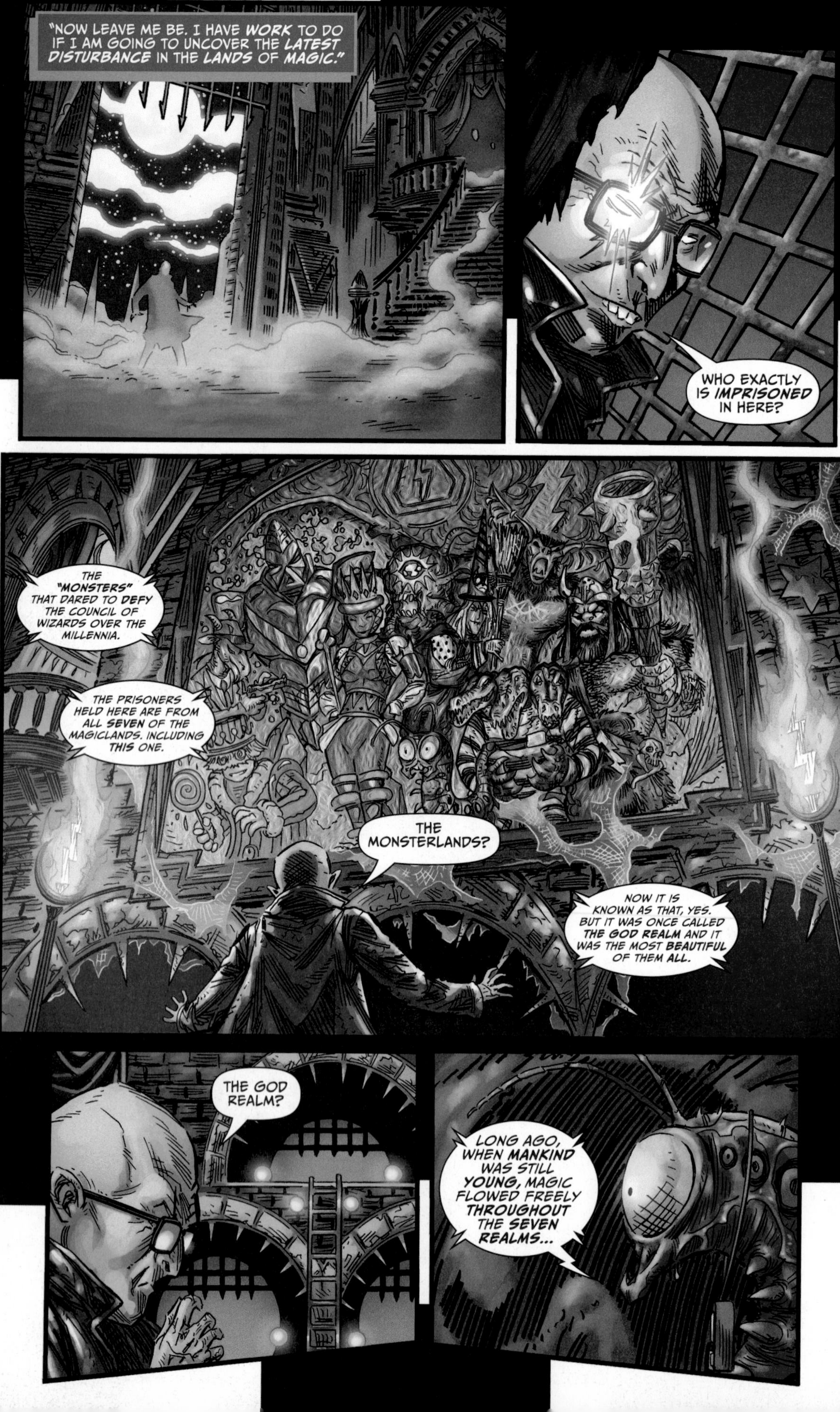
"NOW LEAVE ME BE. I HAVE WORK TO DO IF I AM GOING TO UNCOVER THE LATEST DISTURBANCE IN THE LANDS OF MAGIC."
WHO EXACTLY IS IMPRISONED IN HERE?
THE "MONSTERS" THAT DARED TO DEFY THE COUNCIL OF WIZARDS OVER THE MILLENNIA.
THE PRISONERS HELD HERE ARE FROM ALL SEVEN OF THE MAGICLANDS. INCLUDING THIS ONE.
THE MONSTERLANDS?
NOW IT IS KNOWN AS THAT, YES. BUT IT WAS ONCE CALLED THE GOD REALM AND IT WAS THE MOST BEAUTIFUL OF THEM ALL.
THE GOD REALM?
LONG AGO, WHEN MANKIND WAS STILL YOUNG, MAGIC FLOWED FREELY THROUGHOUT THE SEVEN REALMS...

"A COUNCIL OF WIZARDS FROM THROUGHOUT THE LANDS CAME TOGETHER AND CREATED A *MAGICAL CASTLE* DEDICATED TO *PEACE* AND *PROSPERITY*.

"THE *ROCK OF ETERNITY* BECAME THE PLACE OF *PILGRIMAGE* FOR *ALL* MAGICIANS AND THE *NEXUS* TO THE *SEVEN LANDS*.

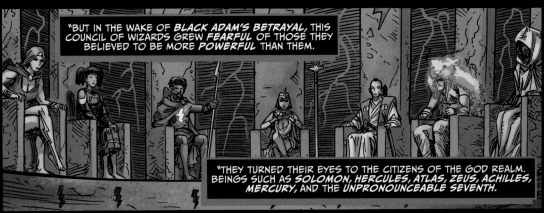

"BUT IN THE WAKE OF *BLACK ADAM'S BETRAYAL*, THIS COUNCIL OF WIZARDS GREW *FEARFUL* OF THOSE THEY BELIEVED TO BE MORE *POWERFUL* THAN THEM.

"THEY TURNED THEIR EYES TO THE CITIZENS OF THE GOD REALM. BEINGS SUCH AS *SOLOMON, HERCULES, ATLAS, ZEUS, ACHILLES, MERCURY,* AND THE *UNPRONOUNCEABLE SEVENTH*.

"AND THE WIZARDS MADE A *PLAN*.

"THEN THEY *HID* THE ROCK OF ETERNITY FROM THE WORLD, KEEPING *ALL MAGIC* FOR THEMSELVES."

THEY STRIPPED THE *GODS* OF THEIR POWERS AND THEY *SEALED OFF* THE DOORWAYS TO THE *MAGICLANDS.*

I'M *CURIOUS,* MR. MIND...

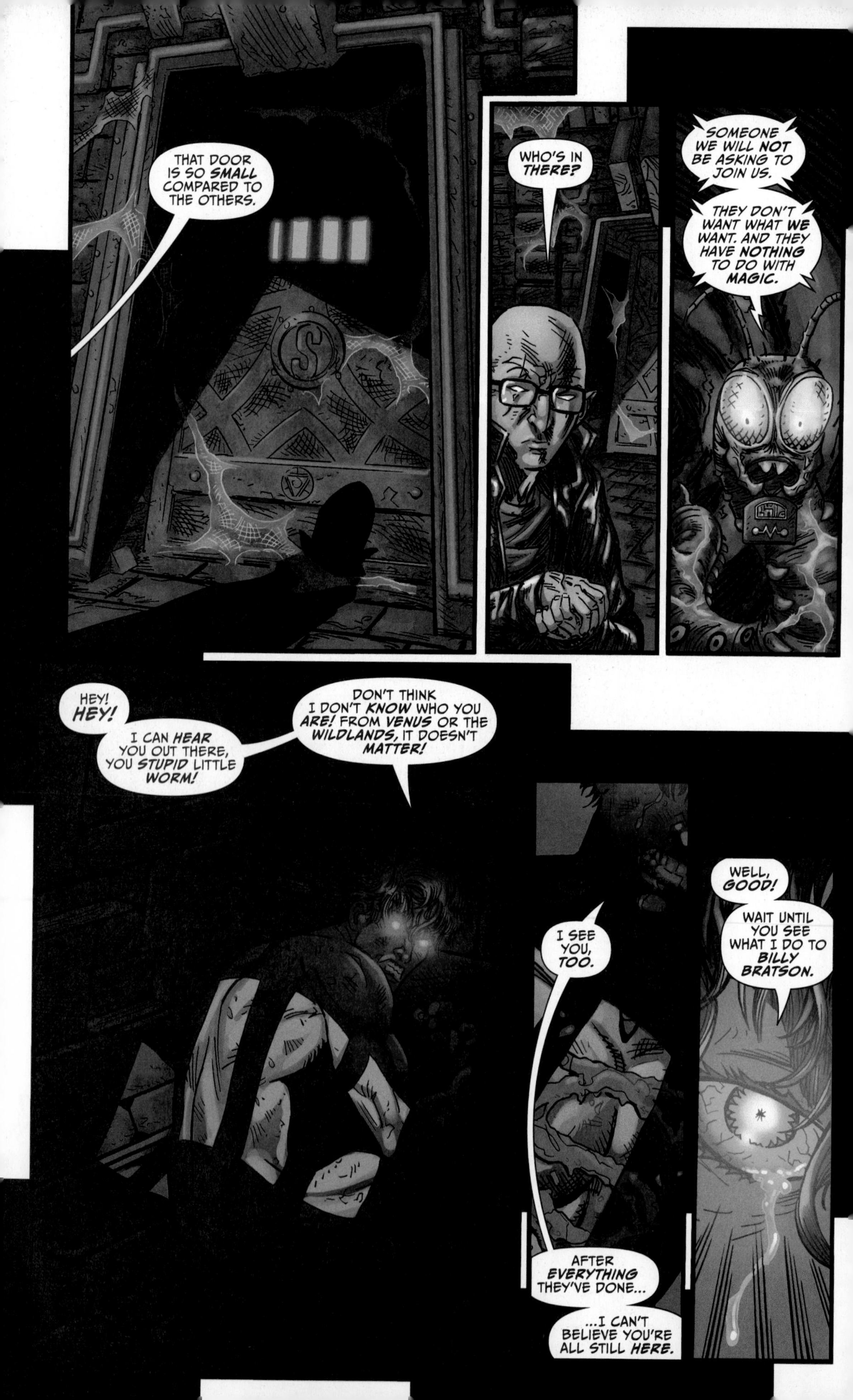
THAT DOOR IS SO SMALL COMPARED TO THE OTHERS.
WHO'S IN THERE?
SOMEONE WE WILL NOT BE ASKING TO JOIN US.
THEY DON'T WANT WHAT WE WANT. AND THEY HAVE NOTHING TO DO WITH MAGIC.
HEY! HEY!
I CAN HEAR YOU OUT THERE, YOU STUPID LITTLE WORM!
DON'T THINK I DON'T KNOW WHO YOU ARE! FROM VENUS OR THE WILDLANDS, IT DOESN'T MATTER!
I SEE YOU, TOO.
AFTER EVERYTHING THEY'VE DONE...
...I CAN'T BELIEVE YOU'RE ALL STILL HERE.
WELL, GOOD!
WAIT UNTIL YOU SEE WHAT I DO TO BILLY BRATSON.

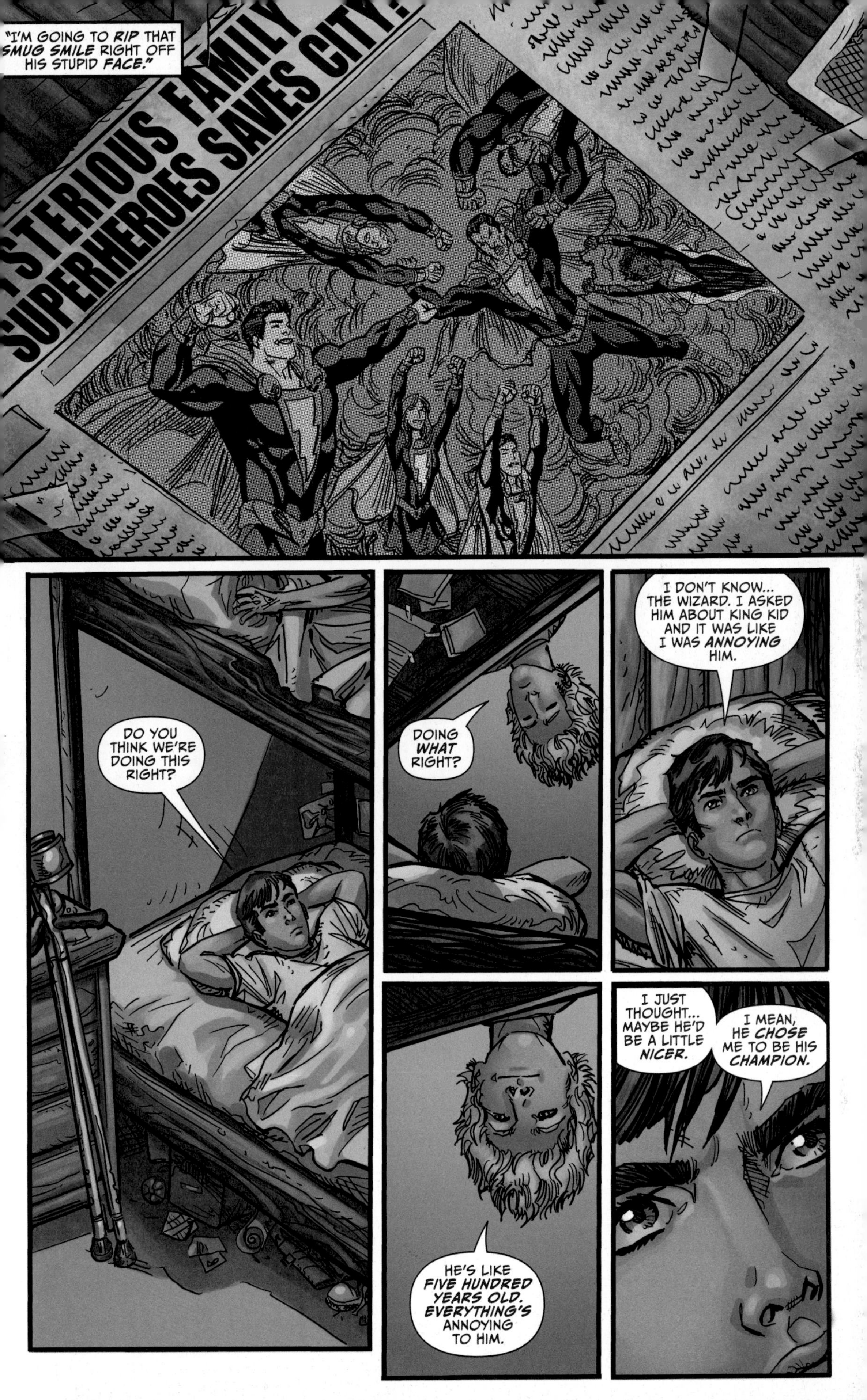
"I'M GOING TO RIP THAT SMUG SMILE RIGHT OFF HIS STUPID FACE."
STERIOUS FAMILY SUPERHEROES SAVES CITY!
DO YOU THINK WE'RE DOING THIS RIGHT?
DOING WHAT RIGHT?
I DON'T KNOW... THE WIZARD. I ASKED HIM ABOUT KING KID AND IT WAS LIKE I WAS ANNOYING HIM.
HE'S LIKE FIVE HUNDRED YEARS OLD. EVERYTHING'S ANNOYING TO HIM.
I JUST THOUGHT... MAYBE HE'D BE A LITTLE NICER.
I MEAN, HE CHOSE ME TO BE HIS CHAMPION.

"HE SAYS THAT IT'S *OUR* FAULT THE *DOORWAYS* WERE OPENED, BUT SO FAR...THE ONLY *BAD THING* THAT'S REALLY HAPPENED OUTSIDE OF TODAY IS THAT *YOU* AND *DARLA* MADE FRIENDS WITH A *TALKING TIGER*."

I REALLY APPRECIATE THIS, ROSA AND VICTOR. I KNOW THE HOUSE IS *FULL*--

YOU STAY AS LONG AS YOU LIKE, C.C.

YOU'RE A MEMBER OF THE *FAMILY* NOW.

ALTHOUGH WE *SHOULD* TALK ABOUT SOME *GROUND RULES* FOR THESE KIDS...

...I'M GLAD YOU'RE THERE TO *CHAPERONE* THEM NOW, BUT--

I'M DEFINITELY NOT THE ONE LEADING THEM. IT'S BILLY.

"HE'S THE *REAL* CHAMPION."

I SEE WHAT I NEED TO DO.

THEY ARE JUST BEYOND THESE GATES, SIVANA.

THE MONSTER SOCIETY.

YOU NEED ONLY TO *REACH* INTO THAT *KEYHOLE*.

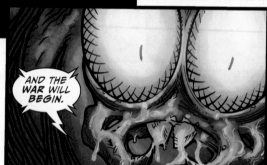

AND THE WAR WILL BEGIN.

I GUESS SO.

LISTEN, THE WIZARD IS REALLY *WORRIED* ABOUT *SOMETHING*, BILLY.

AND IF HE ISN'T READY TO TELL US WHAT THAT IS OR HE DOESN'T KNOW YET, MAYBE THAT'S OKAY.

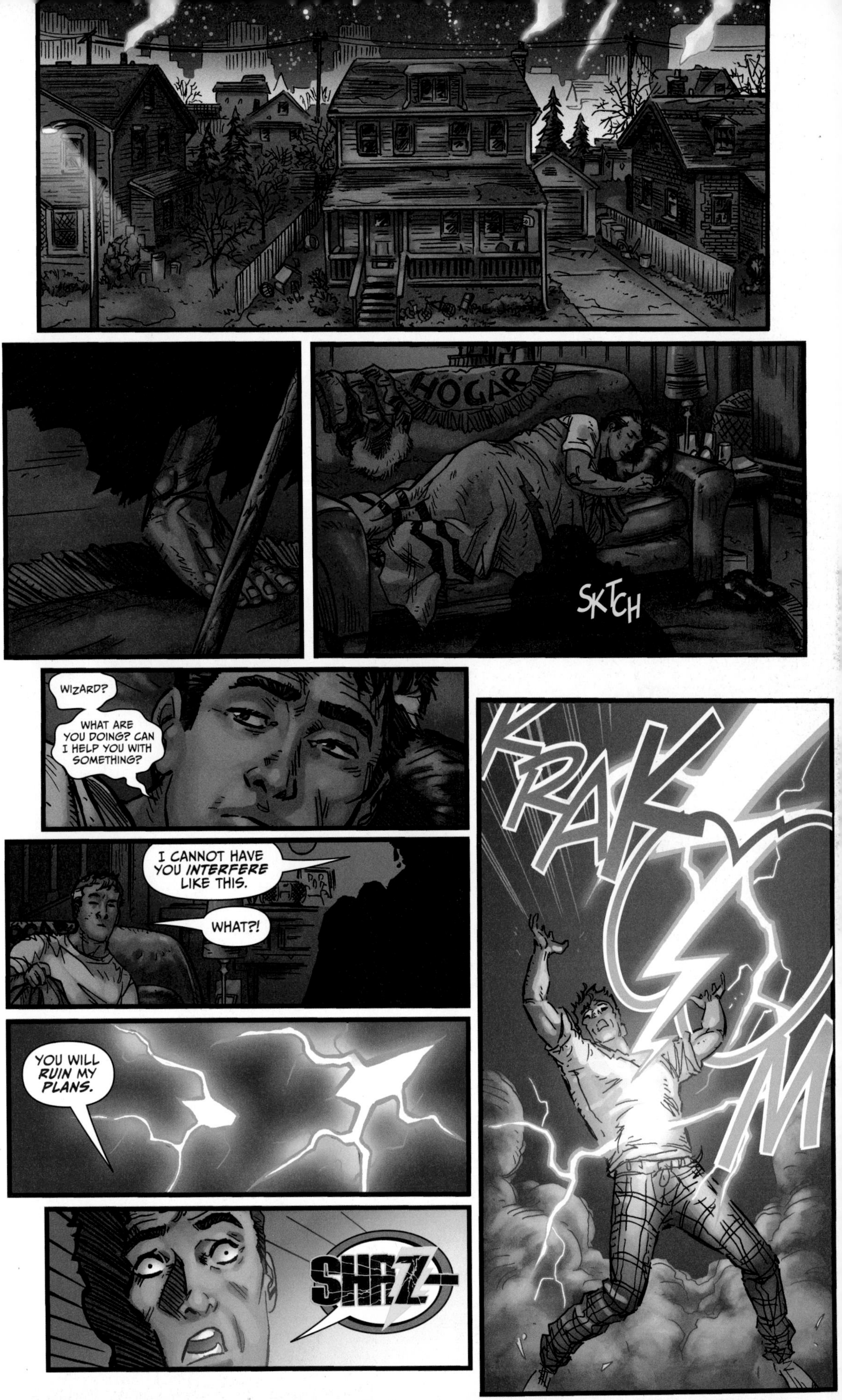
HOGAR
SKTCH
WIZARD?
WHAT ARE YOU DOING? CAN I HELP YOU WITH SOMETHING?
I CANNOT HAVE YOU *INTERFERE* LIKE THIS.
WHAT?!
YOU WILL *RUIN* MY *PLANS.*
SHAZ-
KRAKOOM

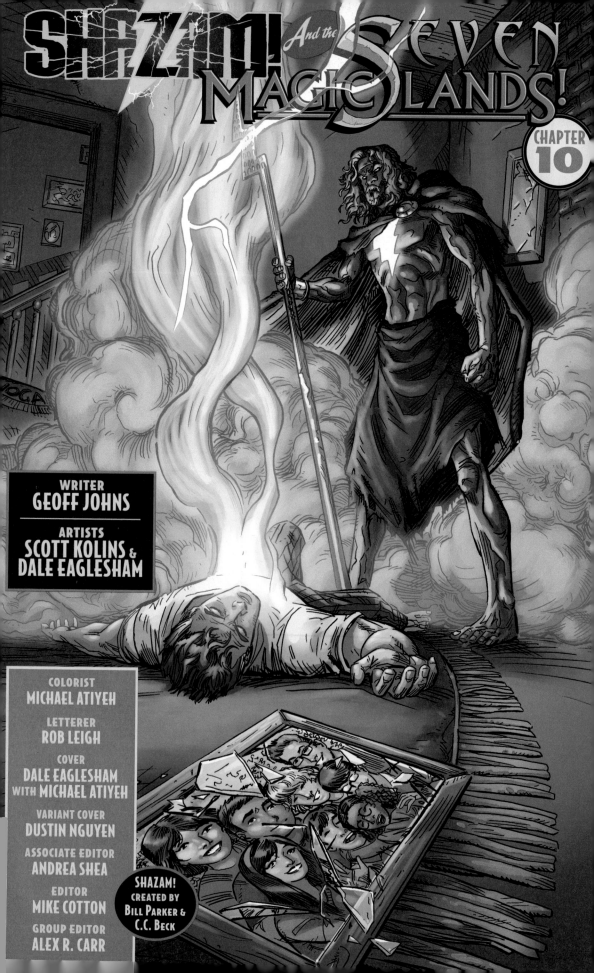

# SHAZAM! AND THE SEVEN MAGIC LANDS!

CHAPTER 10

WRITER
GEOFF JOHNS

ARTISTS
SCOTT KOLINS &
DALE EAGLESHAM

COLORIST
MICHAEL ATIYEH

LETTERER
ROB LEIGH

COVER
DALE EAGLESHAM
WITH MICHAEL ATIYEH

VARIANT COVER
DUSTIN NGUYEN

ASSOCIATE EDITOR
ANDREA SHEA

EDITOR
MIKE COTTON

GROUP EDITOR
ALEX R. CARR

SHAZAM!
CREATED BY
Bill Parker &
C.C. Beck

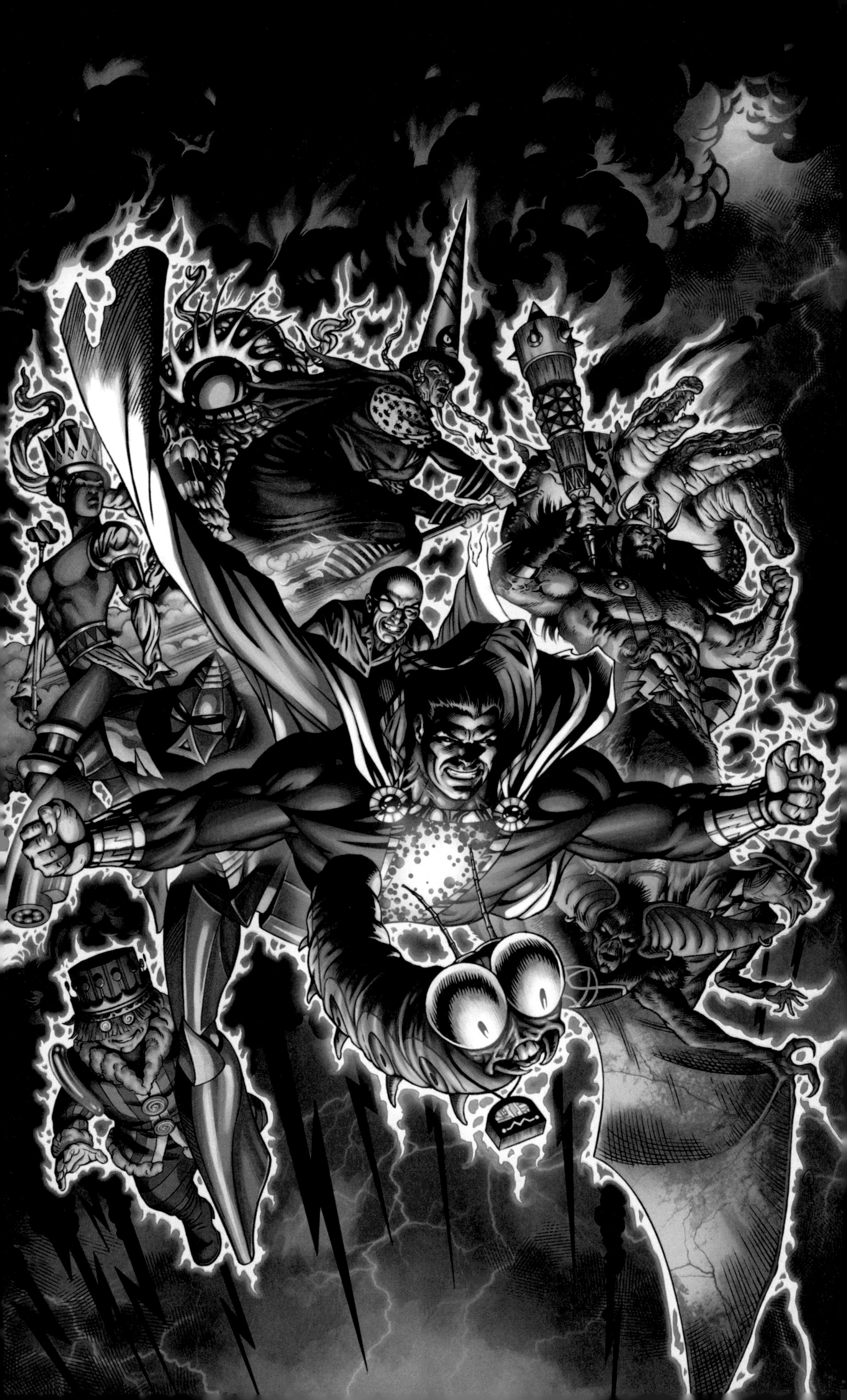

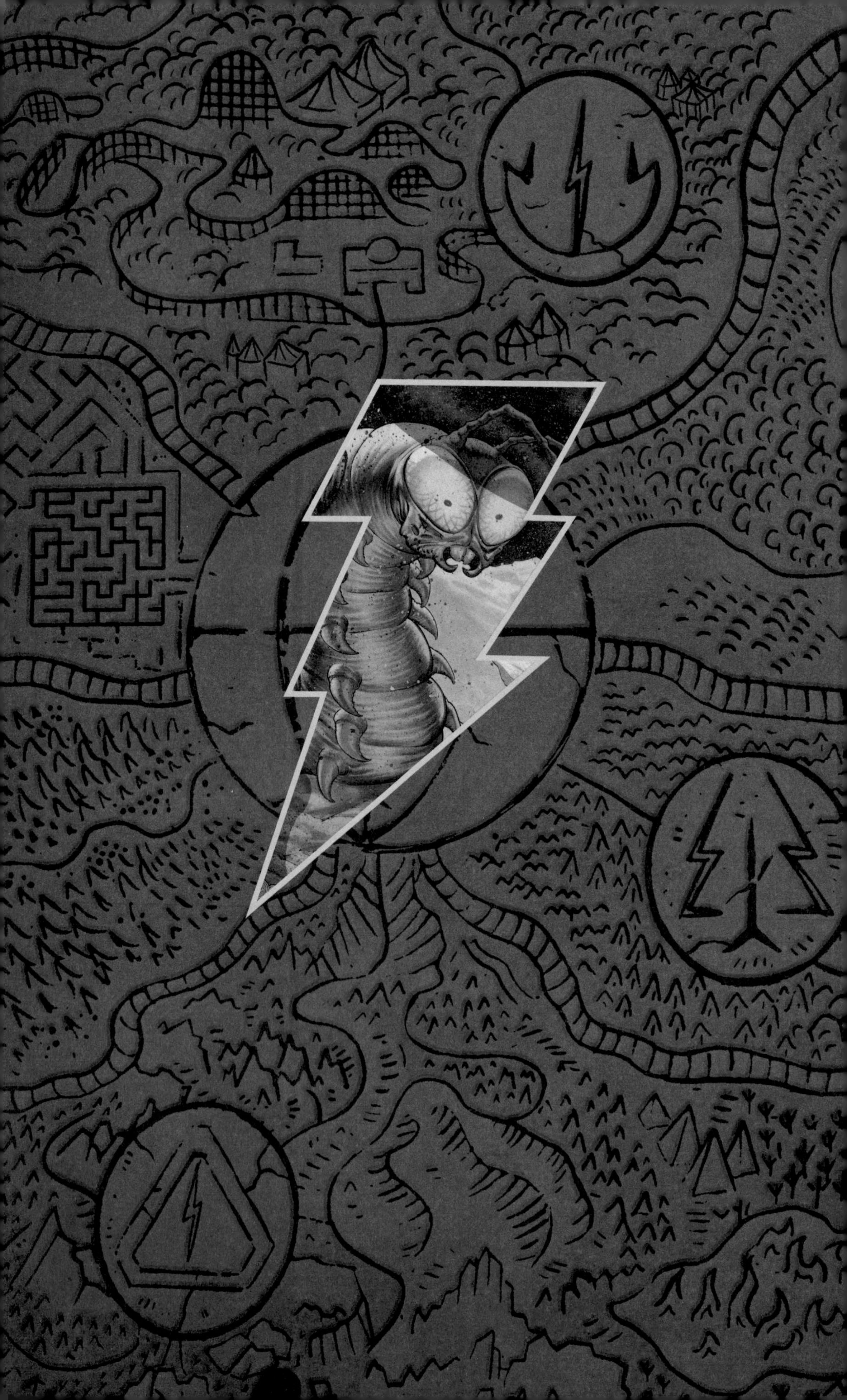

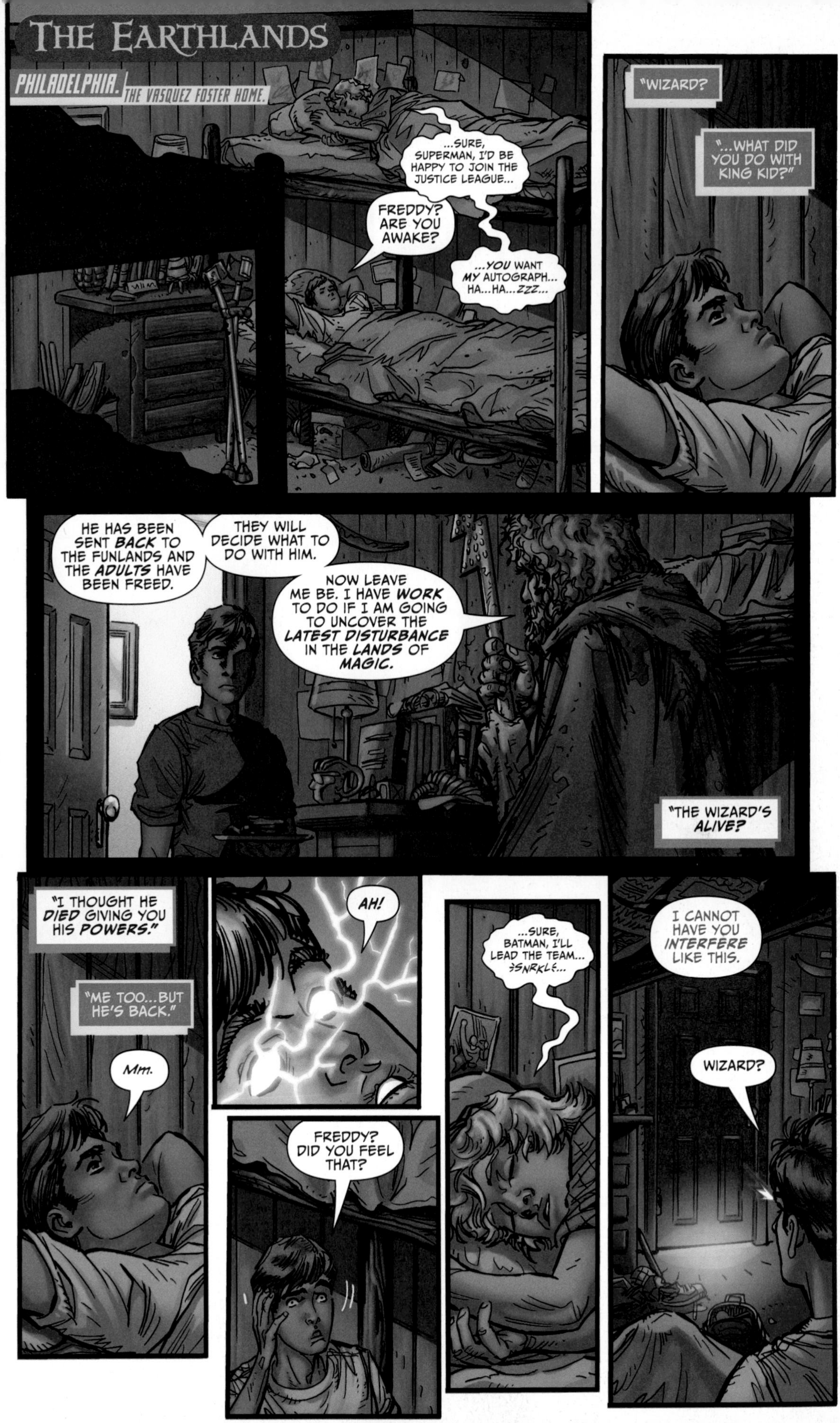
THE EARTHLANDS
PHILADELPHIA. THE VASQUEZ FOSTER HOME.
...SURE, SUPERMAN, I'D BE HAPPY TO JOIN THE JUSTICE LEAGUE...
FREDDY? ARE YOU AWAKE?
...YOU WANT MY AUTOGRAPH... HA...HA...ZZZ...
"WIZARD?
"...WHAT DID YOU DO WITH KING KID?"
HE HAS BEEN SENT BACK TO THE FUNLANDS AND THE ADULTS HAVE BEEN FREED.
THEY WILL DECIDE WHAT TO DO WITH HIM.
NOW LEAVE ME BE. I HAVE WORK TO DO IF I AM GOING TO UNCOVER THE LATEST DISTURBANCE IN THE LANDS OF MAGIC.
"THE WIZARD'S ALIVE?
"I THOUGHT HE DIED GIVING YOU HIS POWERS."
"ME TOO...BUT HE'S BACK."
Mm.
AH!
FREDDY? DID YOU FEEL THAT?
...SURE, BATMAN, I'LL LEAD THE TEAM... SNRKL...
I CANNOT HAVE YOU INTERFERE LIKE THIS.
WIZARD?

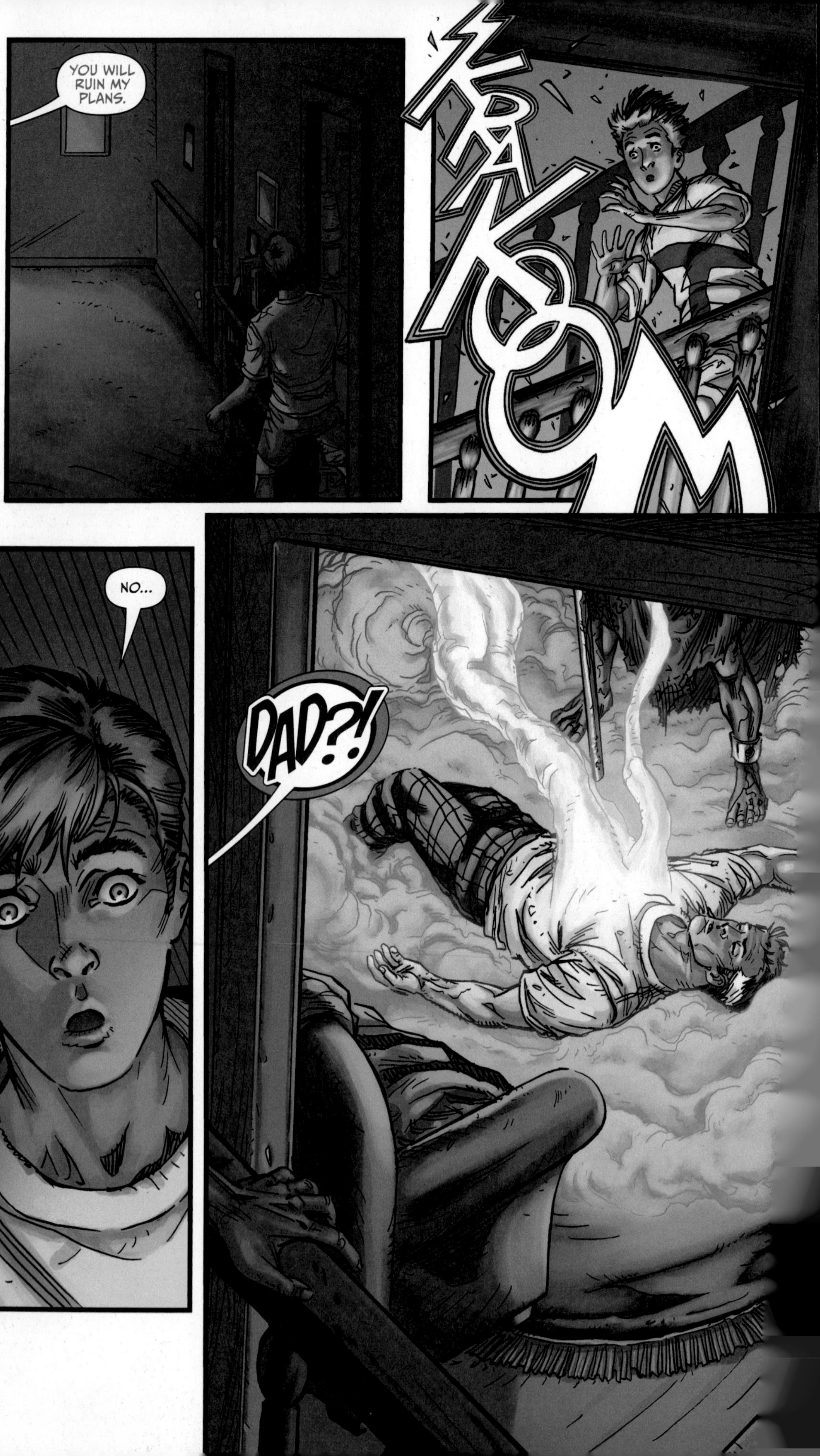
YOU WILL RUIN MY PLANS.
KRAKOOM
NO...
DAD?!

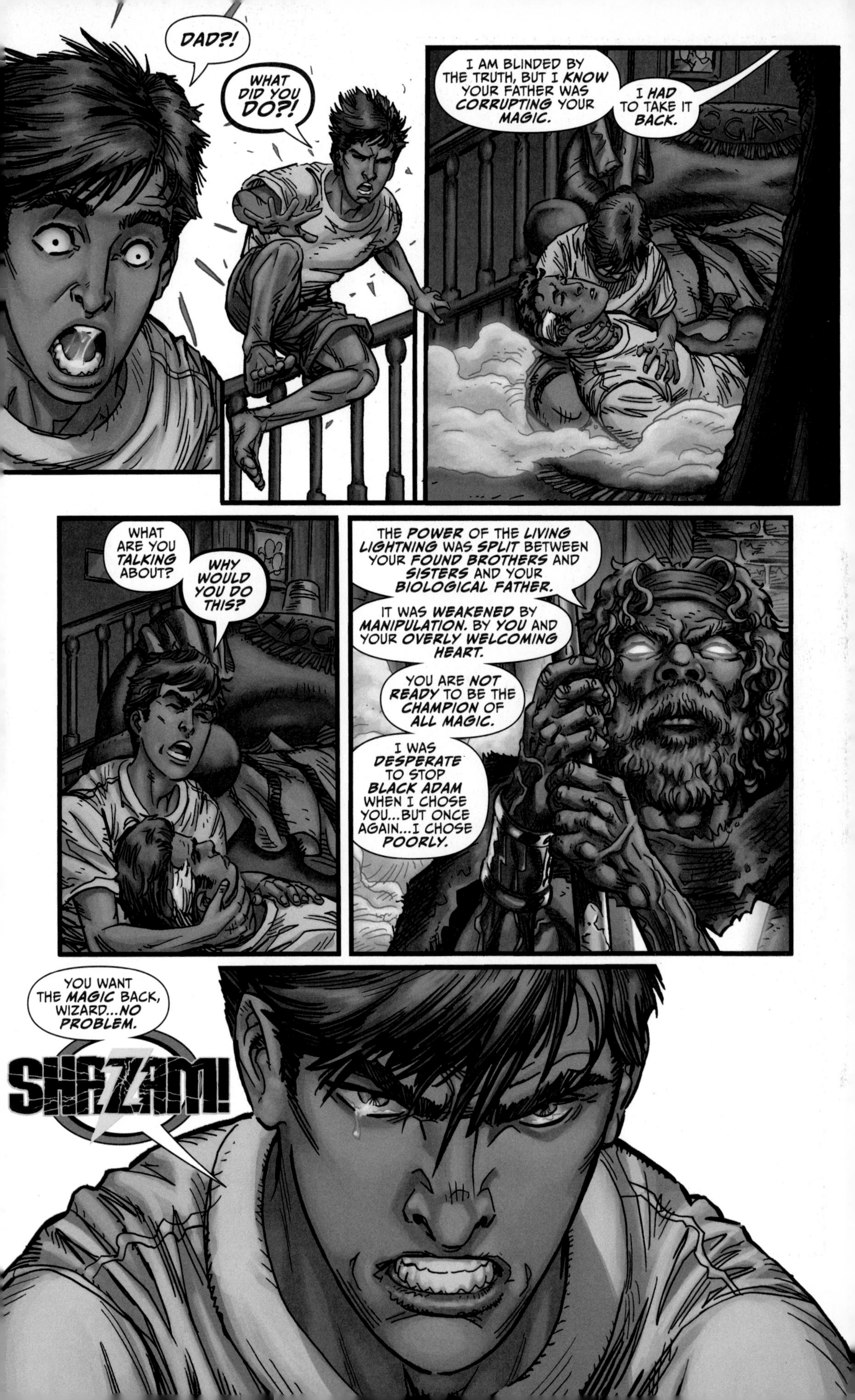
DAD?!
WHAT DID YOU DO?!
I AM BLINDED BY THE TRUTH, BUT I KNOW YOUR FATHER WAS CORRUPTING YOUR MAGIC.
I HAD TO TAKE IT BACK.
WHAT ARE YOU TALKING ABOUT?
WHY WOULD YOU DO THIS?
THE POWER OF THE LIVING LIGHTNING WAS SPLIT BETWEEN YOUR FOUND BROTHERS AND SISTERS AND YOUR BIOLOGICAL FATHER.
IT WAS WEAKENED BY MANIPULATION. BY YOU AND YOUR OVERLY WELCOMING HEART.
YOU ARE NOT READY TO BE THE CHAMPION OF ALL MAGIC.
I WAS DESPERATE TO STOP BLACK ADAM WHEN I CHOSE YOU...BUT ONCE AGAIN...I CHOSE POORLY.
YOU WANT THE MAGIC BACK, WIZARD...NO PROBLEM.
SHAZAM!

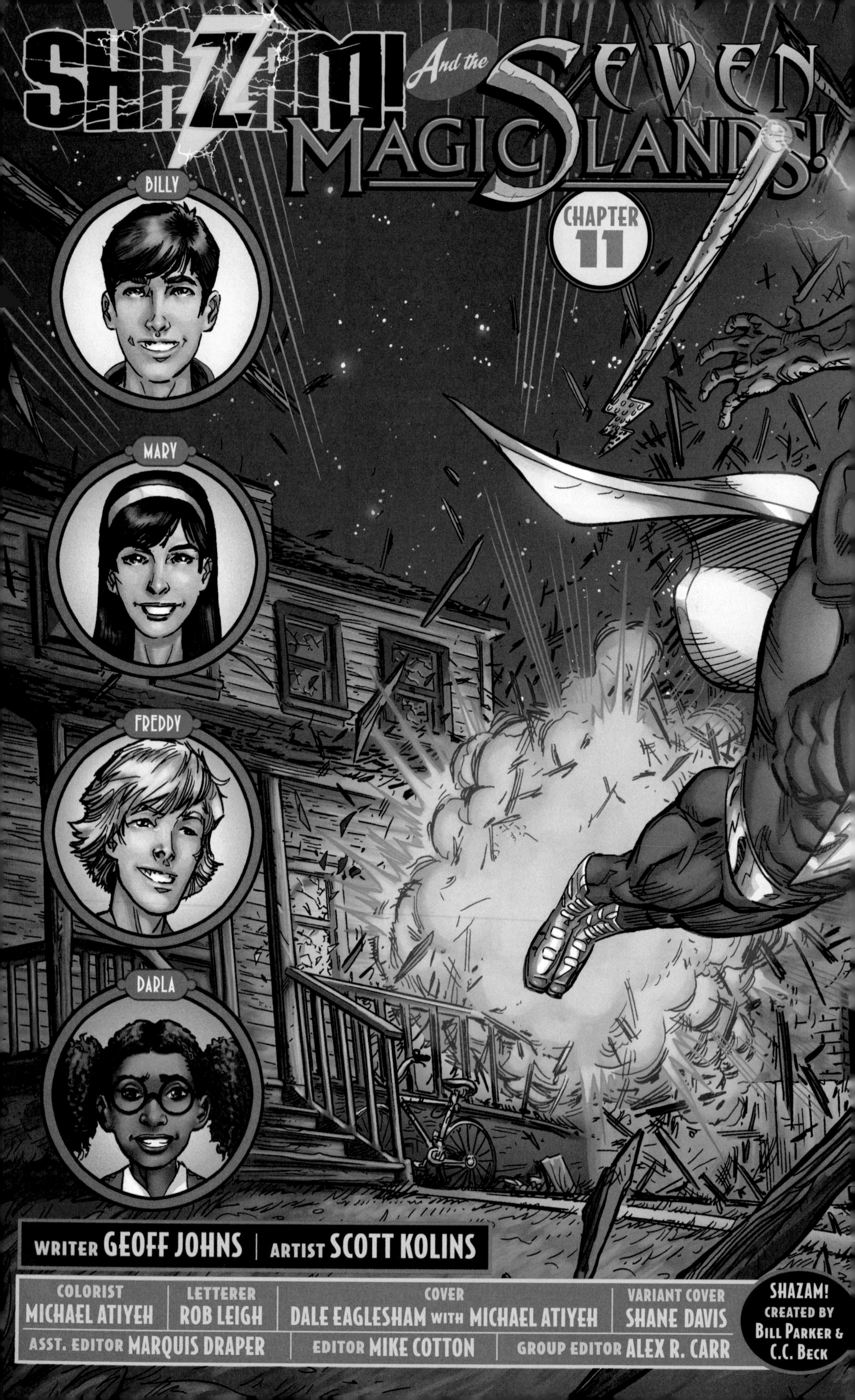
SHAZAM! And the SEVEN MAGIC LANDS!
CHAPTER 11
BILLY
MARY
FREDDY
DARLA
WRITER GEOFF JOHNS | ARTIST SCOTT KOLINS
COLORIST MICHAEL ATIYEH
LETTERER ROB LEIGH
COVER DALE EAGLESHAM WITH MICHAEL ATIYEH
VARIANT COVER SHANE DAVIS
ASST. EDITOR MARQUIS DRAPER
EDITOR MIKE COTTON
GROUP EDITOR ALEX R. CARR
SHAZAM! CREATED BY BILL PARKER & C.C. BECK

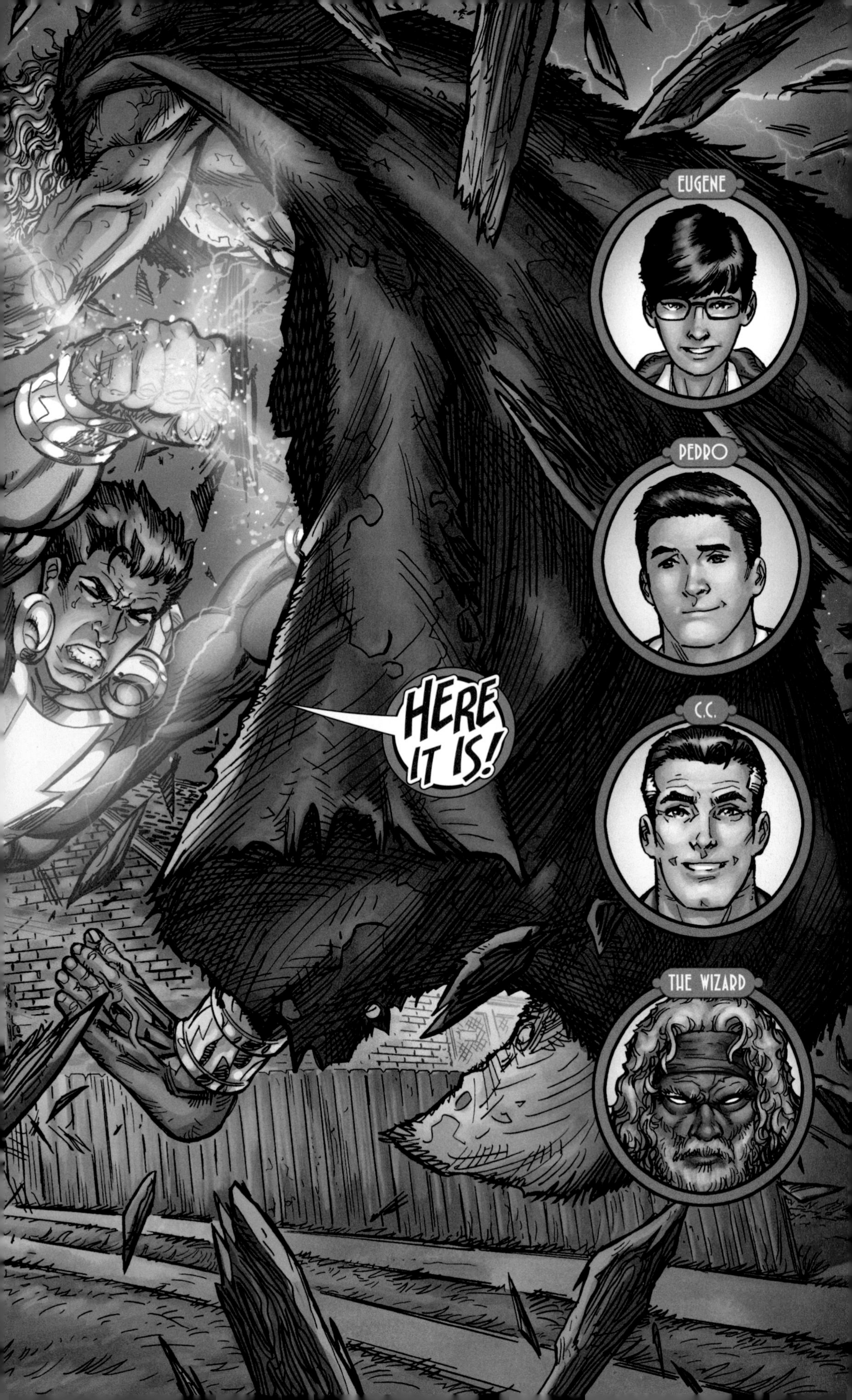
EUGENE
PEDRO
HERE IT IS!
C.C.
THE WIZARD

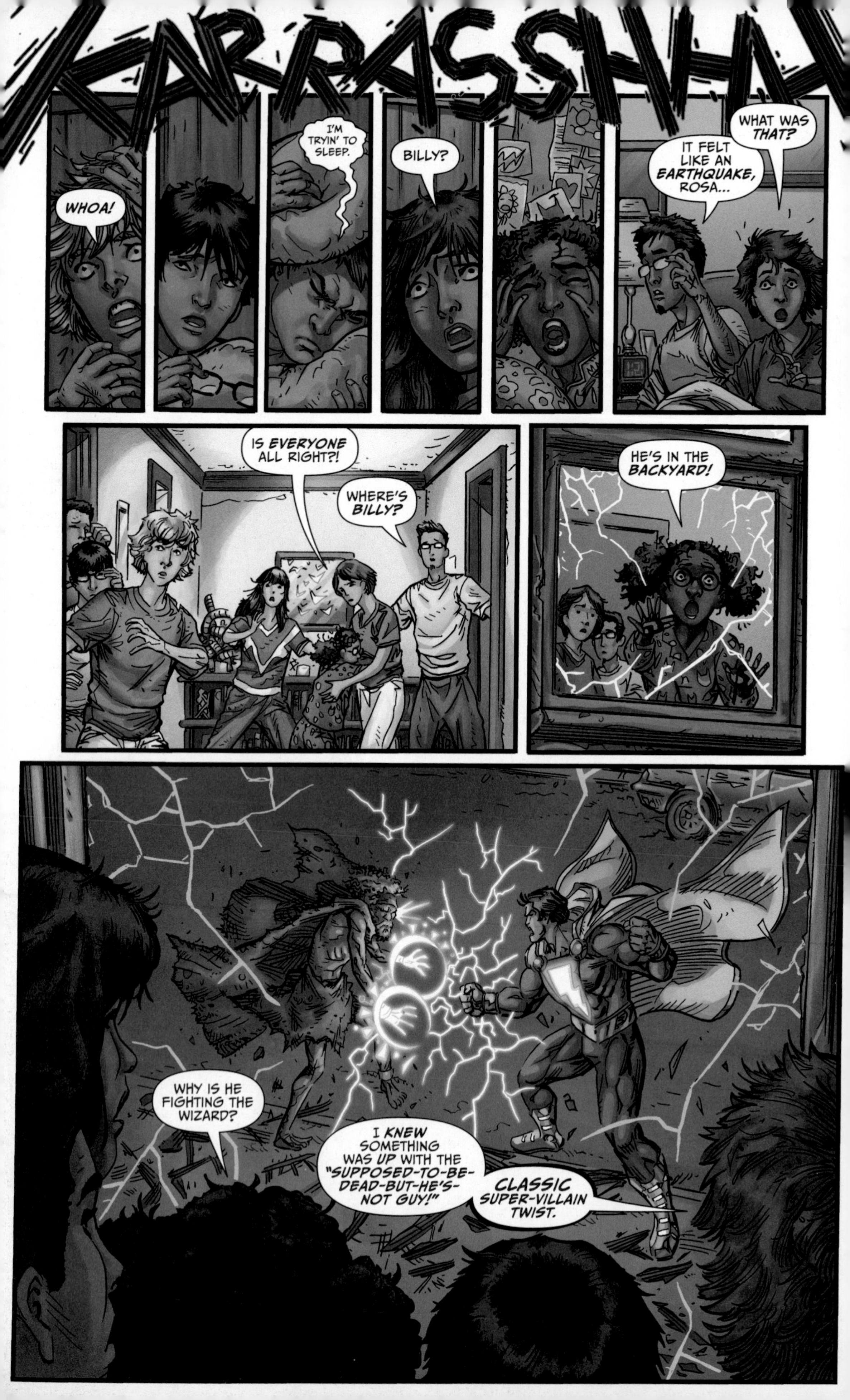
KARASSHHH
WHOA!
I'M TRYIN' TO SLEEP.
BILLY?
WHAT WAS THAT?
IT FELT LIKE AN EARTHQUAKE, ROSA...
IS EVERYONE ALL RIGHT?!
WHERE'S BILLY?
HE'S IN THE BACKYARD!
WHY IS HE FIGHTING THE WIZARD?
I KNEW SOMETHING WAS UP WITH THE "SUPPOSED-TO-BE-DEAD-BUT-HE'S-NOT GUY!"
CLASSIC SUPER-VILLAIN TWIST.

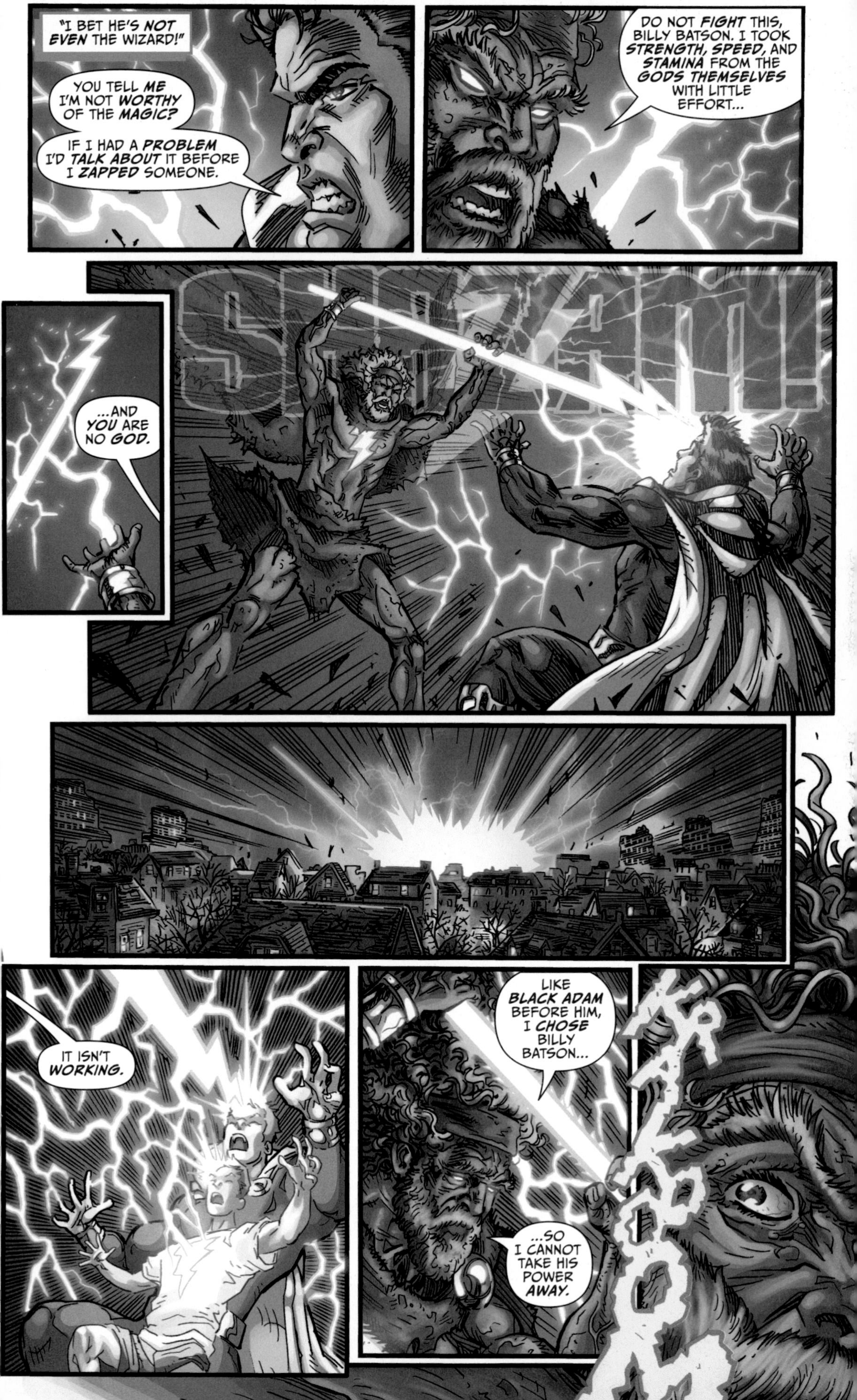
"I BET HE'S NOT EVEN THE WIZARD!"
YOU TELL ME I'M NOT WORTHY OF THE MAGIC?
IF I HAD A PROBLEM I'D TALK ABOUT IT BEFORE I ZAPPED SOMEONE.
DO NOT FIGHT THIS, BILLY BATSON. I TOOK STRENGTH, SPEED, AND STAMINA FROM THE GODS THEMSELVES WITH LITTLE EFFORT...
...AND YOU ARE NO GOD.
SHAZAM!
IT ISN'T WORKING.
LIKE BLACK ADAM BEFORE HIM, I CHOSE BILLY BATSON...
...SO I CANNOT TAKE HIS POWER AWAY.

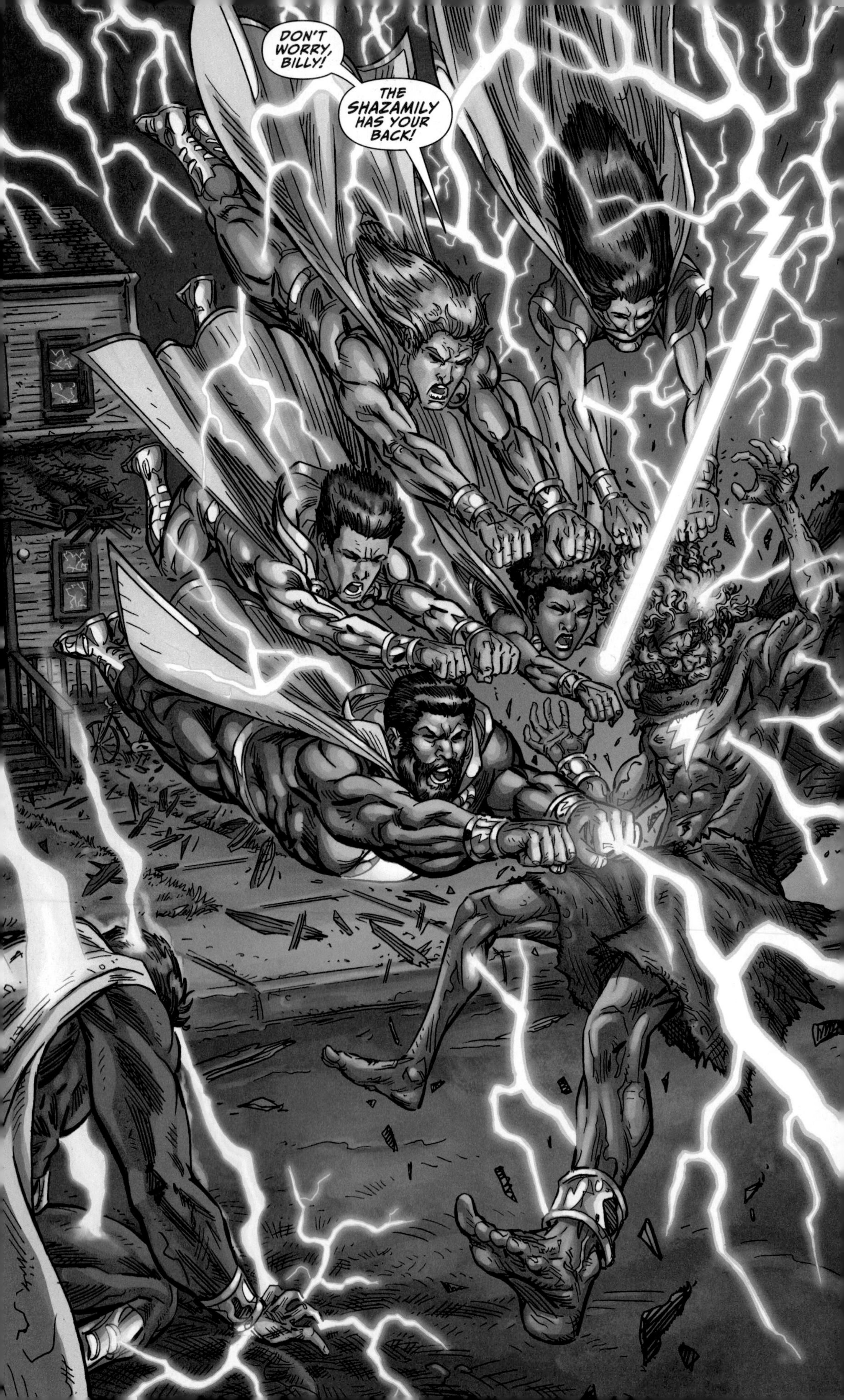
DON'T WORRY, BILLY!
THE SHAZAMILY HAS YOUR BACK!

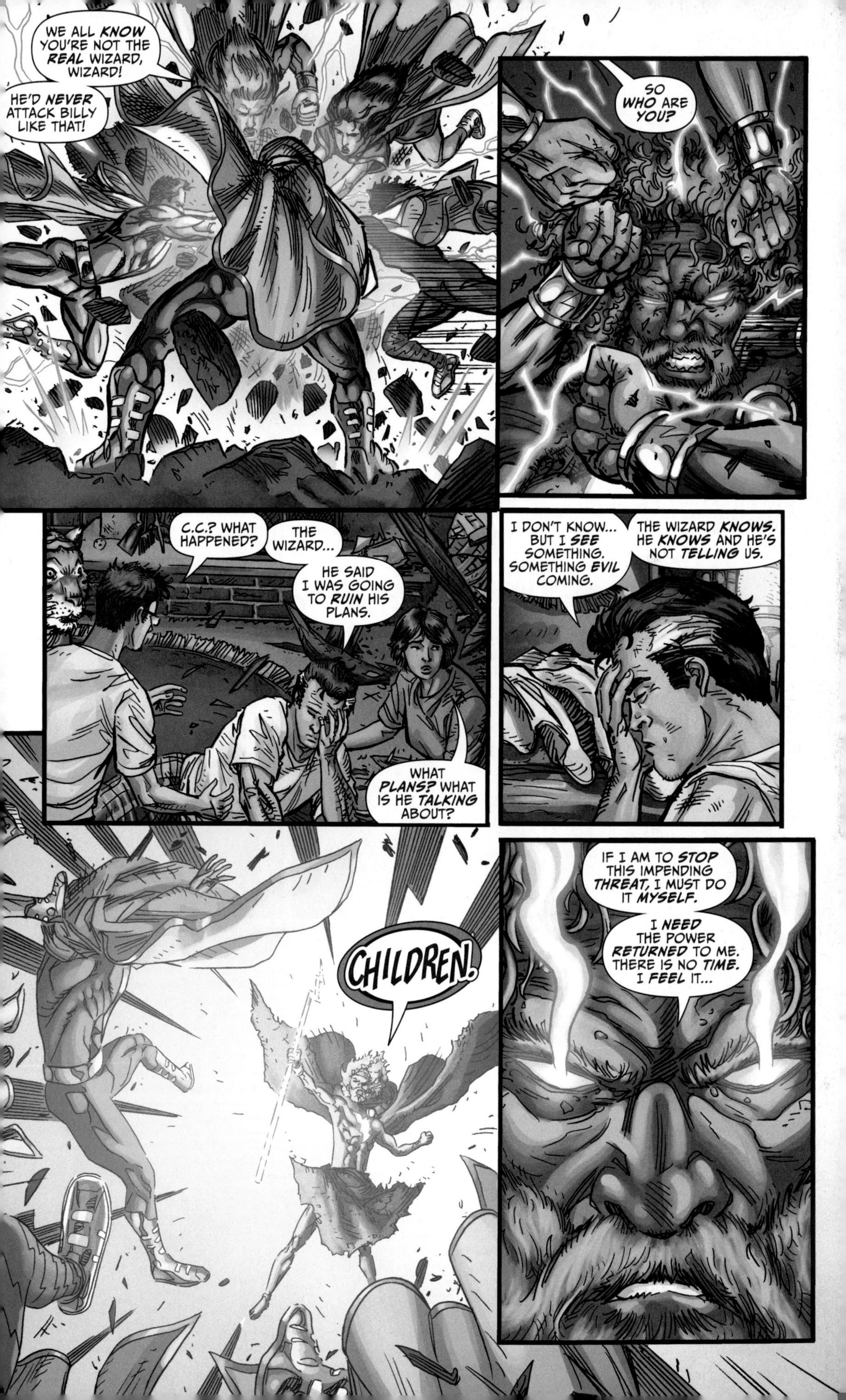
WE ALL KNOW YOU'RE NOT THE REAL WIZARD, WIZARD!
HE'D NEVER ATTACK BILLY LIKE THAT!
SO WHO ARE YOU?
C.C.? WHAT HAPPENED?
THE WIZARD...
HE SAID I WAS GOING TO RUIN HIS PLANS.
WHAT PLANS? WHAT IS HE TALKING ABOUT?
I DON'T KNOW... BUT I SEE SOMETHING. SOMETHING EVIL COMING.
THE WIZARD KNOWS. HE KNOWS AND HE'S NOT TELLING US.
CHILDREN.
IF I AM TO STOP THIS IMPENDING THREAT, I MUST DO IT MYSELF.
I NEED THE POWER RETURNED TO ME. THERE IS NO TIME. I FEEL IT...

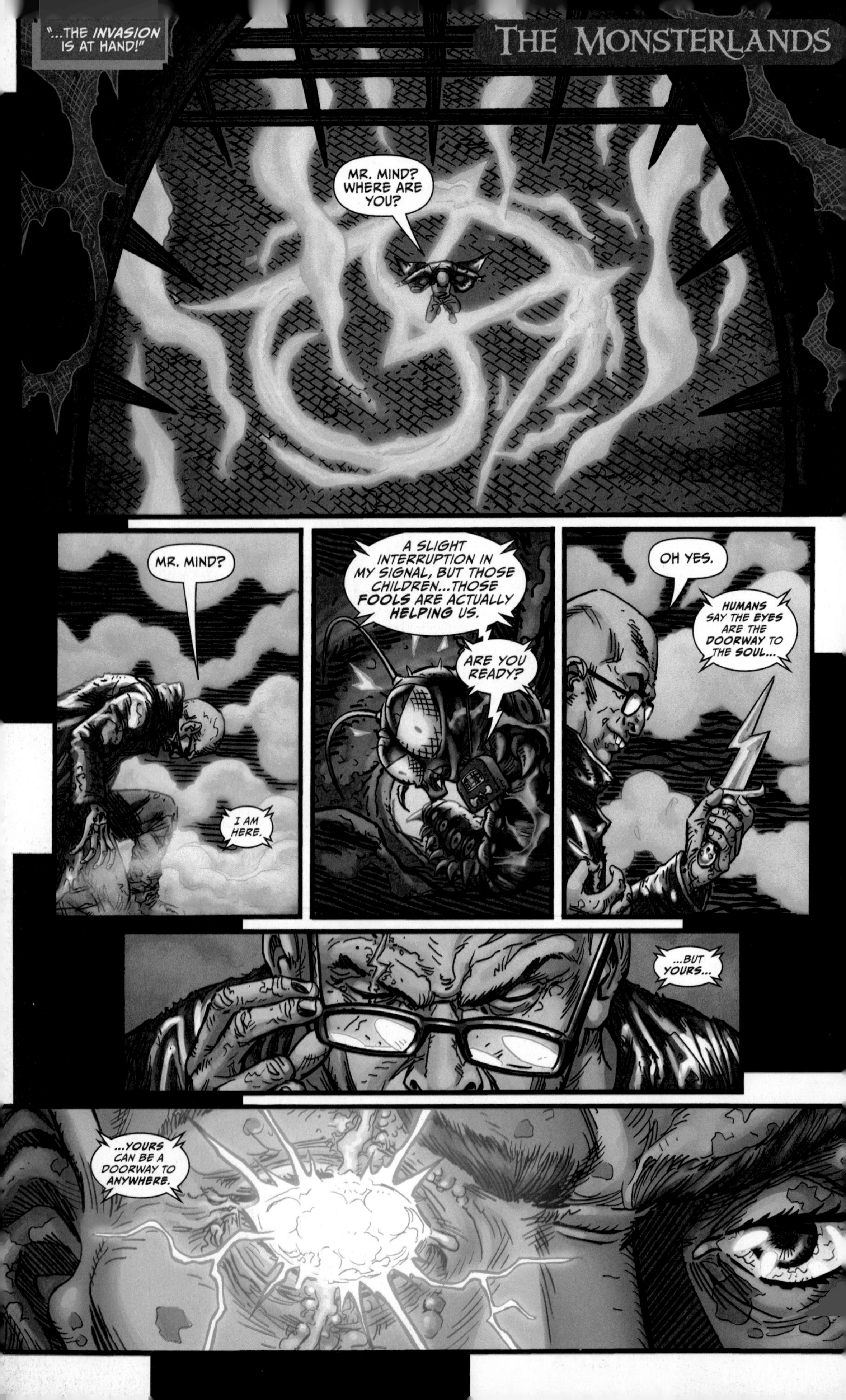
"...THE INVASION IS AT HAND!"
THE MONSTERLANDS
MR. MIND? WHERE ARE YOU?
MR. MIND?
I AM HERE.
A SLIGHT INTERRUPTION IN MY SIGNAL, BUT THOSE CHILDREN...THOSE FOOLS ARE ACTUALLY HELPING US.
ARE YOU READY?
OH YES.
HUMANS SAY THE EYES ARE THE DOORWAY TO THE SOUL...
...BUT YOURS...
...YOURS CAN BE A DOORWAY TO ANYWHERE.

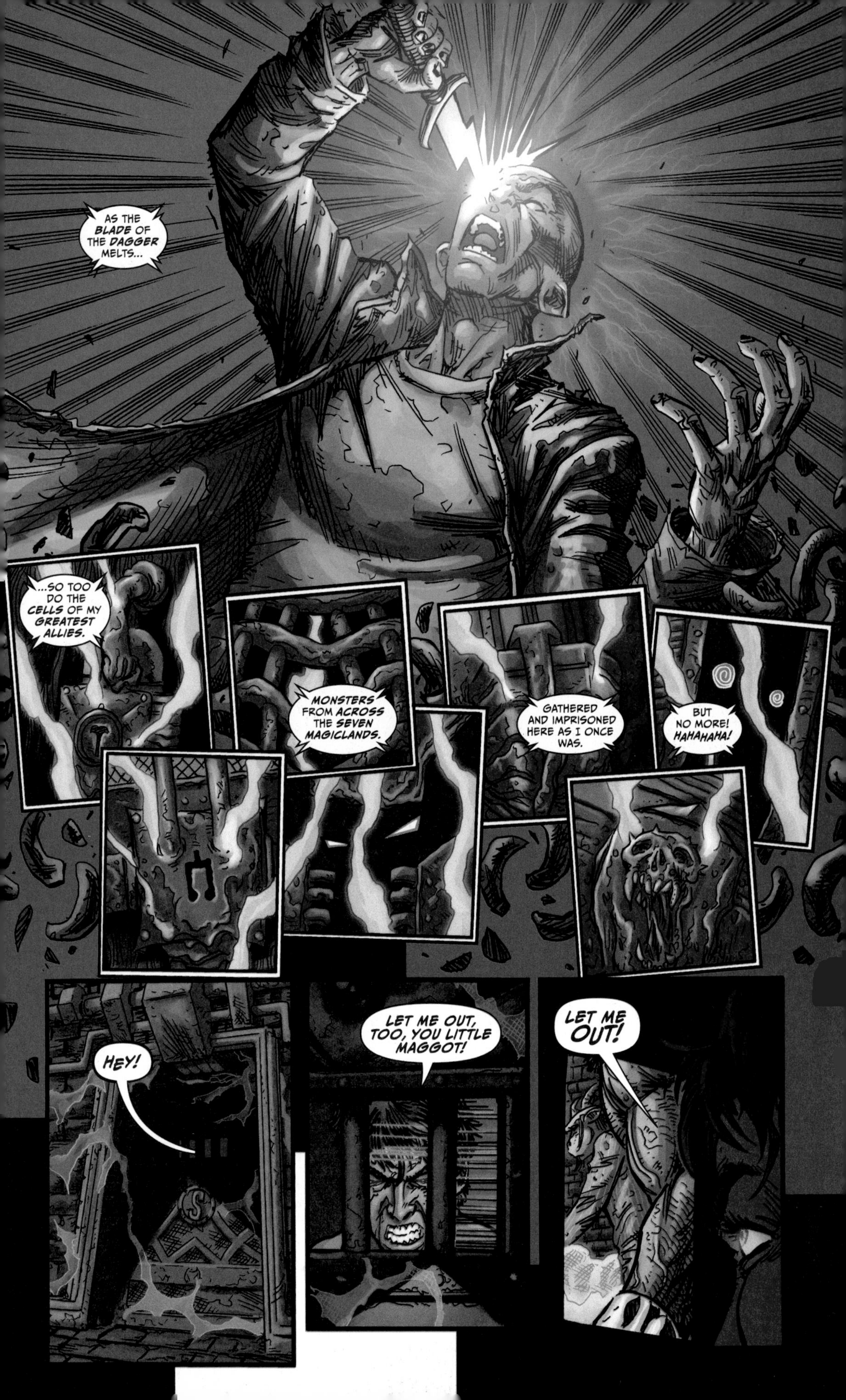
AS THE BLADE OF THE DAGGER MELTS...
...SO TOO DO THE CELLS OF MY GREATEST ALLIES.
MONSTERS FROM ACROSS THE SEVEN MAGICLANDS.
GATHERED AND IMPRISONED HERE AS I ONCE WAS.
BUT NO MORE! HAHAHAHA!
HEY!
LET ME OUT, TOO, YOU LITTLE MAGGOT!
LET ME OUT!

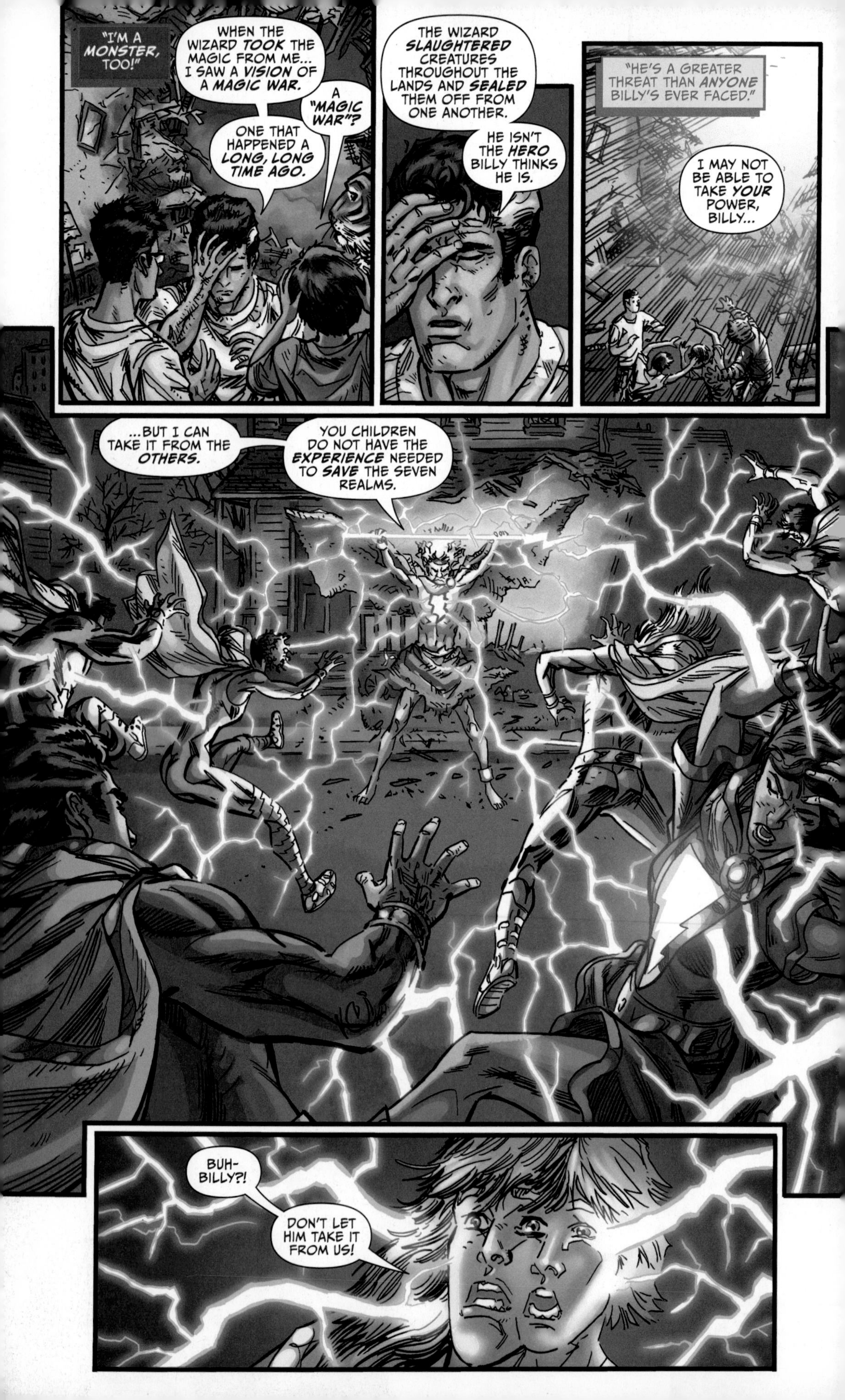
"I'M A MONSTER, TOO!"
WHEN THE WIZARD TOOK THE MAGIC FROM ME... I SAW A VISION OF A MAGIC WAR.
ONE THAT HAPPENED A LONG, LONG TIME AGO.
A "MAGIC WAR"?
THE WIZARD SLAUGHTERED CREATURES THROUGHOUT THE LANDS AND SEALED THEM OFF FROM ONE ANOTHER.
HE ISN'T THE HERO BILLY THINKS HE IS.
"HE'S A GREATER THREAT THAN ANYONE BILLY'S EVER FACED."
I MAY NOT BE ABLE TO TAKE YOUR POWER, BILLY...
...BUT I CAN TAKE IT FROM THE OTHERS.
YOU CHILDREN DO NOT HAVE THE EXPERIENCE NEEDED TO SAVE THE SEVEN REALMS.
BUH-BILLY?!
DON'T LET HIM TAKE IT FROM US!

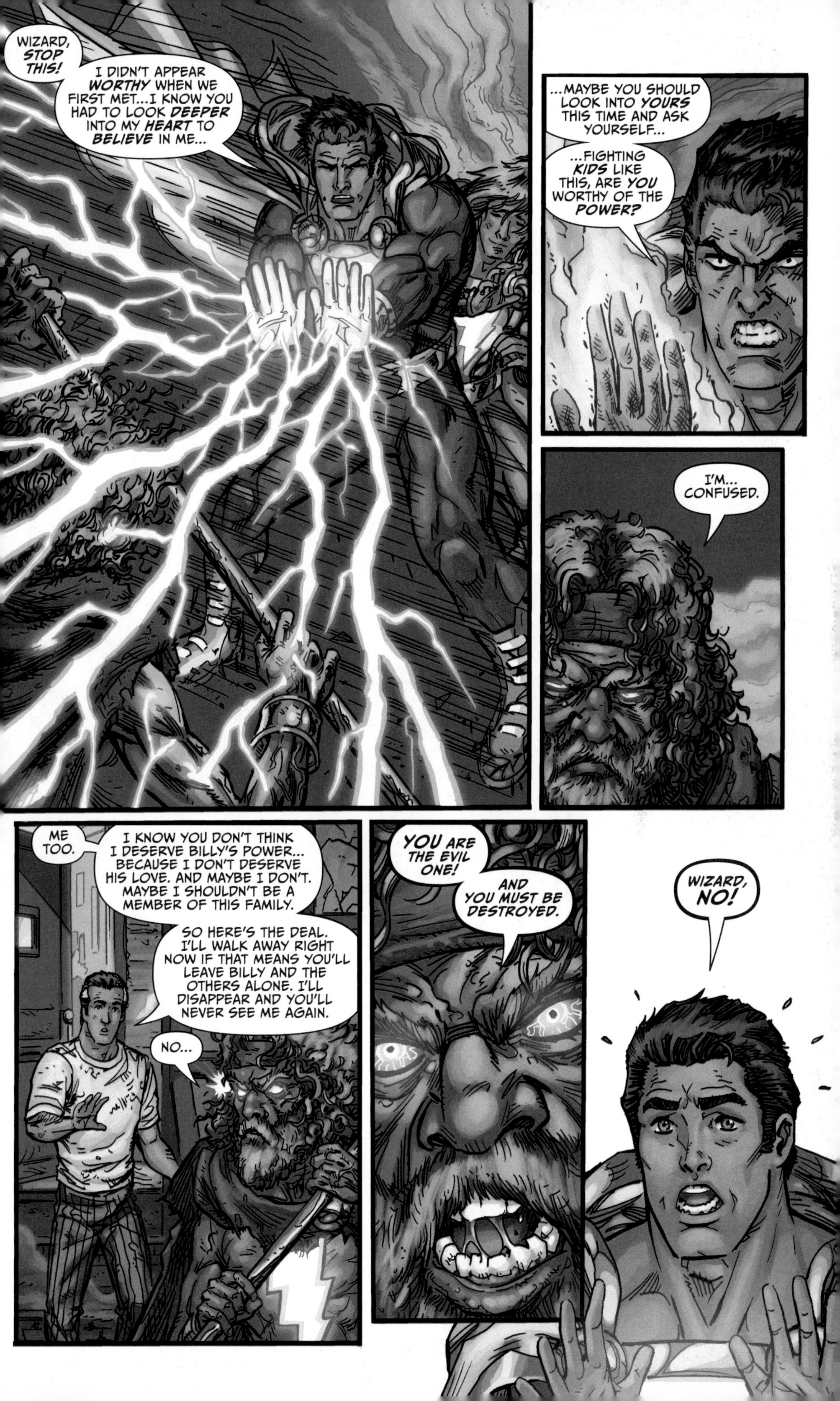
WIZARD, STOP THIS!
I DIDN'T APPEAR WORTHY WHEN WE FIRST MET...I KNOW YOU HAD TO LOOK DEEPER INTO MY HEART TO BELIEVE IN ME...
...MAYBE YOU SHOULD LOOK INTO YOURS THIS TIME AND ASK YOURSELF...
...FIGHTING KIDS LIKE THIS, ARE YOU WORTHY OF THE POWER?
I'M... CONFUSED.
ME TOO.
I KNOW YOU DON'T THINK I DESERVE BILLY'S POWER... BECAUSE I DON'T DESERVE HIS LOVE. AND MAYBE I DON'T. MAYBE I SHOULDN'T BE A MEMBER OF THIS FAMILY.
SO HERE'S THE DEAL. I'LL WALK AWAY RIGHT NOW IF THAT MEANS YOU'LL LEAVE BILLY AND THE OTHERS ALONE. I'LL DISAPPEAR AND YOU'LL NEVER SEE ME AGAIN.
NO...
YOU ARE THE EVIL ONE!
AND YOU MUST BE DESTROYED.
WIZARD, NO!

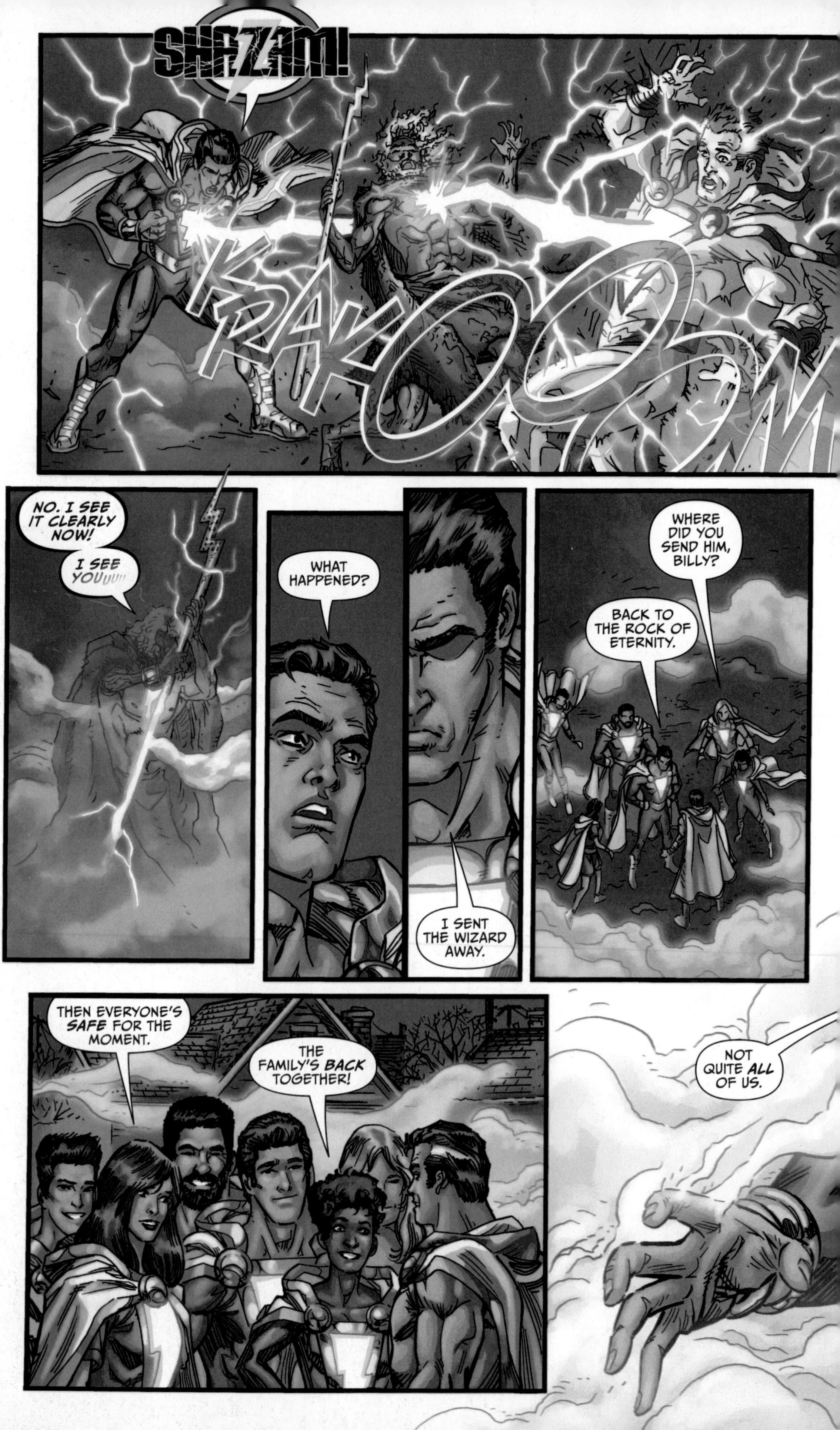
SHAZAM!
KRAKOOOM
NO. I SEE IT CLEARLY NOW!
I SEE YOUUU!!
WHAT HAPPENED?
I SENT THE WIZARD AWAY.
WHERE DID YOU SEND HIM, BILLY?
BACK TO THE ROCK OF ETERNITY.
THEN EVERYONE'S SAFE FOR THE MOMENT.
THE FAMILY'S BACK TOGETHER!
NOT QUITE ALL OF US.

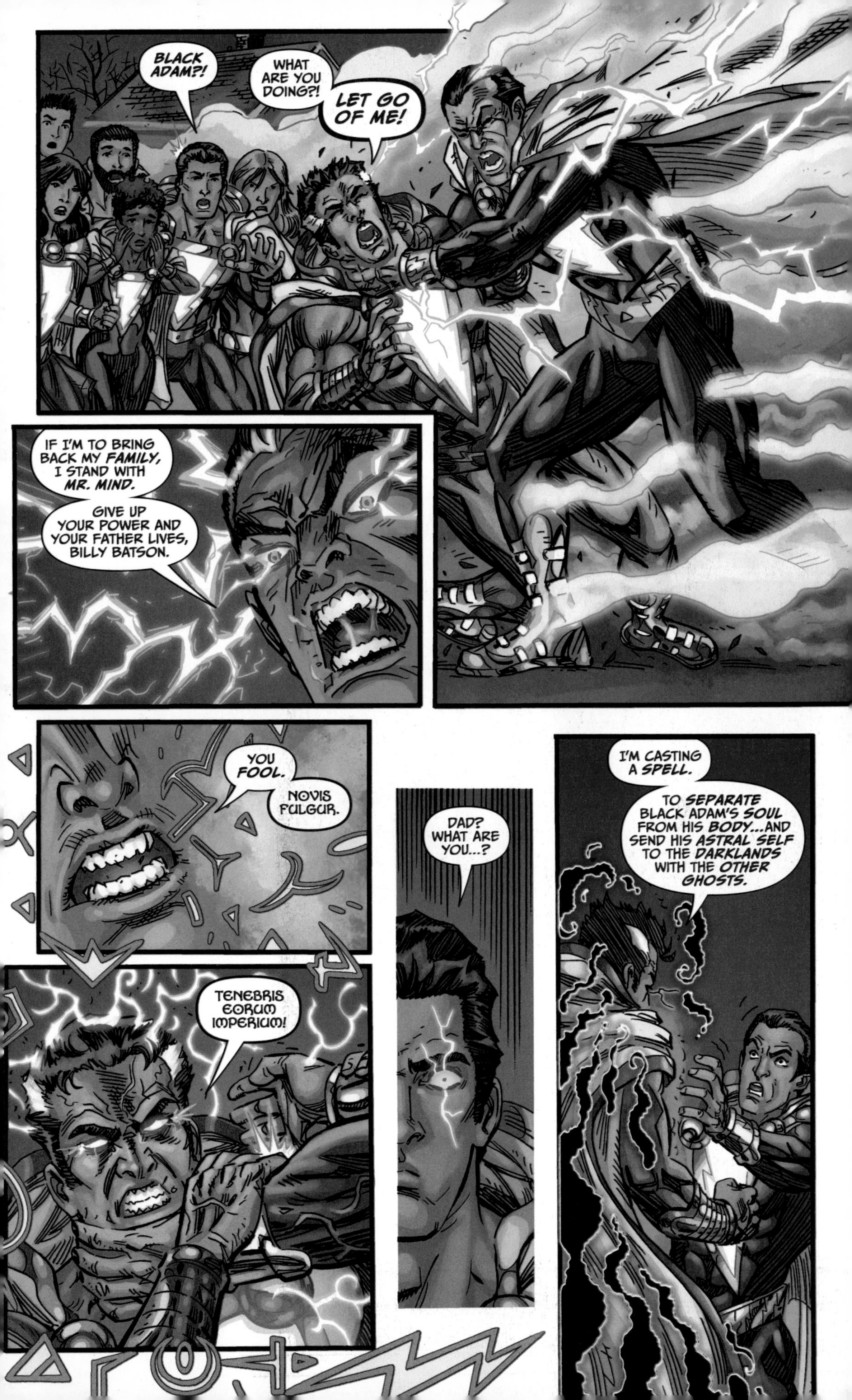
BLACK ADAM?!
WHAT ARE YOU DOING?!
LET GO OF ME!
IF I'M TO BRING BACK MY FAMILY, I STAND WITH MR. MIND.
GIVE UP YOUR POWER AND YOUR FATHER LIVES, BILLY BATSON.
YOU FOOL.
NOVIS FULGUR.
TENEBRIS EORUM IMPERIUM!
DAD? WHAT ARE YOU...?
I'M CASTING A SPELL.
TO SEPARATE BLACK ADAM'S SOUL FROM HIS BODY...AND SEND HIS ASTRAL SELF TO THE DARKLANDS WITH THE OTHER GHOSTS.

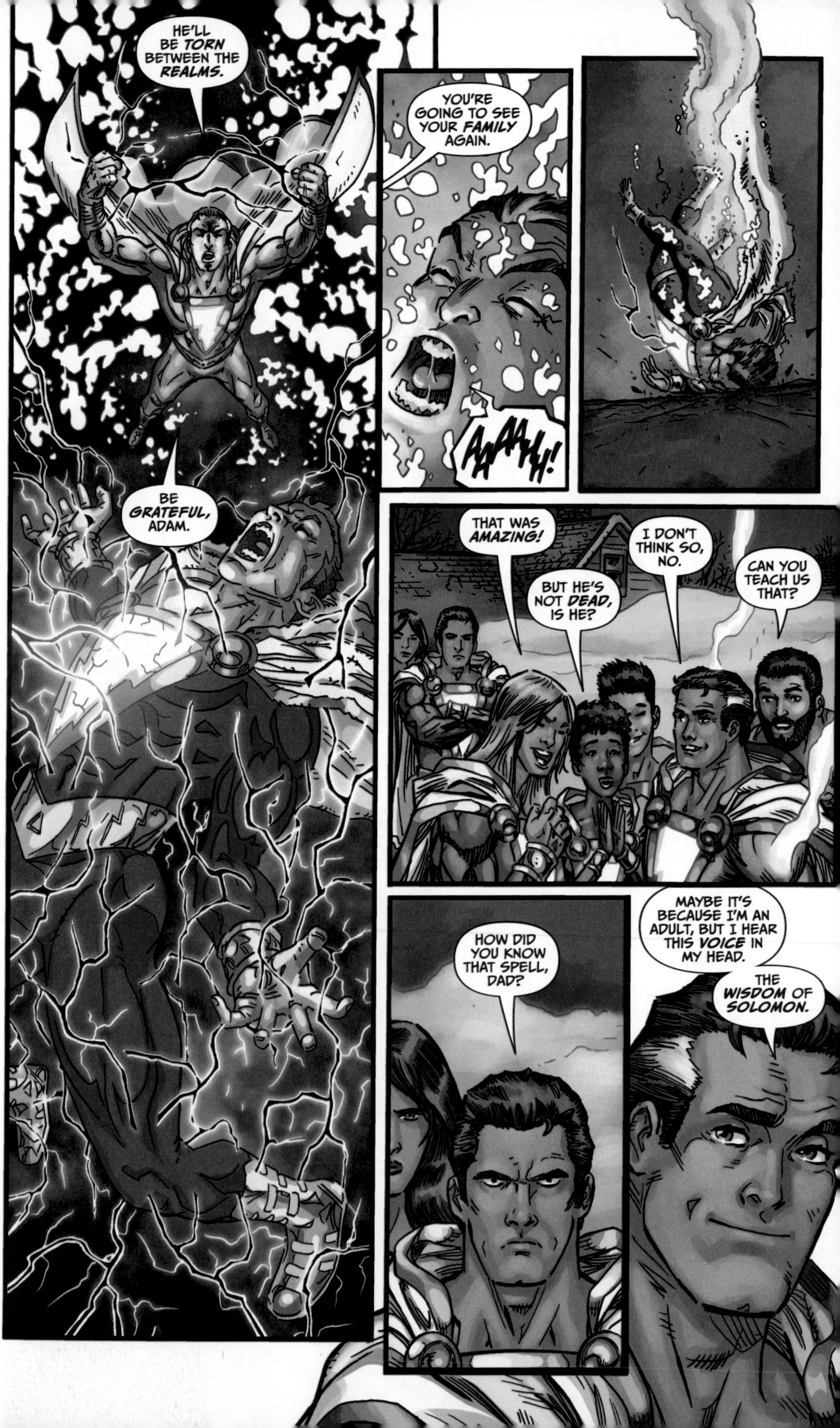
HE'LL BE *TORN* BETWEEN THE *REALMS.*
BE *GRATEFUL,* ADAM.
YOU'RE GOING TO SEE YOUR *FAMILY* AGAIN.
AAAAHH!
THAT WAS *AMAZING!*
BUT HE'S NOT *DEAD,* IS HE?
I DON'T THINK SO, NO.
CAN YOU TEACH US THAT?
HOW DID YOU KNOW THAT SPELL, DAD?
MAYBE IT'S BECAUSE I'M AN ADULT, BUT I HEAR THIS *VOICE* IN MY HEAD.
THE *WISDOM* OF *SOLOMON.*

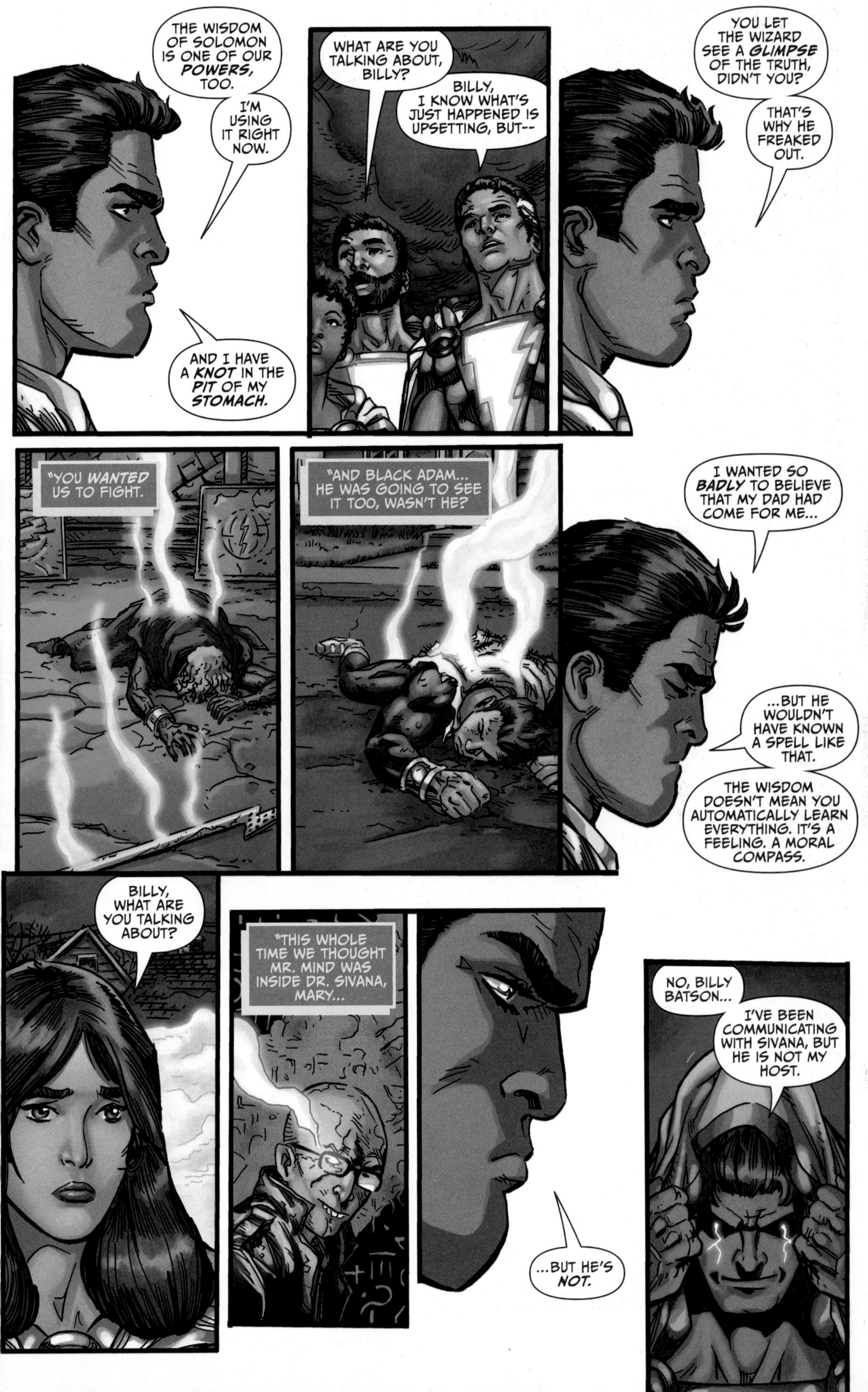

THE WISDOM OF SOLOMON IS ONE OF OUR POWERS, TOO.
I'M USING IT RIGHT NOW.
AND I HAVE A KNOT IN THE PIT OF MY STOMACH.
WHAT ARE YOU TALKING ABOUT, BILLY?
BILLY, I KNOW WHAT'S JUST HAPPENED IS UPSETTING, BUT--
YOU LET THE WIZARD SEE A GLIMPSE OF THE TRUTH, DIDN'T YOU?
THAT'S WHY HE FREAKED OUT.
"YOU WANTED US TO FIGHT.
"AND BLACK ADAM... HE WAS GOING TO SEE IT TOO, WASN'T HE?
I WANTED SO BADLY TO BELIEVE THAT MY DAD HAD COME FOR ME...
...BUT HE WOULDN'T HAVE KNOWN A SPELL LIKE THAT.
THE WISDOM DOESN'T MEAN YOU AUTOMATICALLY LEARN EVERYTHING. IT'S A FEELING. A MORAL COMPASS.
BILLY, WHAT ARE YOU TALKING ABOUT?
"THIS WHOLE TIME WE THOUGHT MR. MIND WAS INSIDE DR. SIVANA, MARY...
...BUT HE'S NOT.
NO, BILLY BATSON...
I'VE BEEN COMMUNICATING WITH SIVANA, BUT HE IS NOT MY HOST.

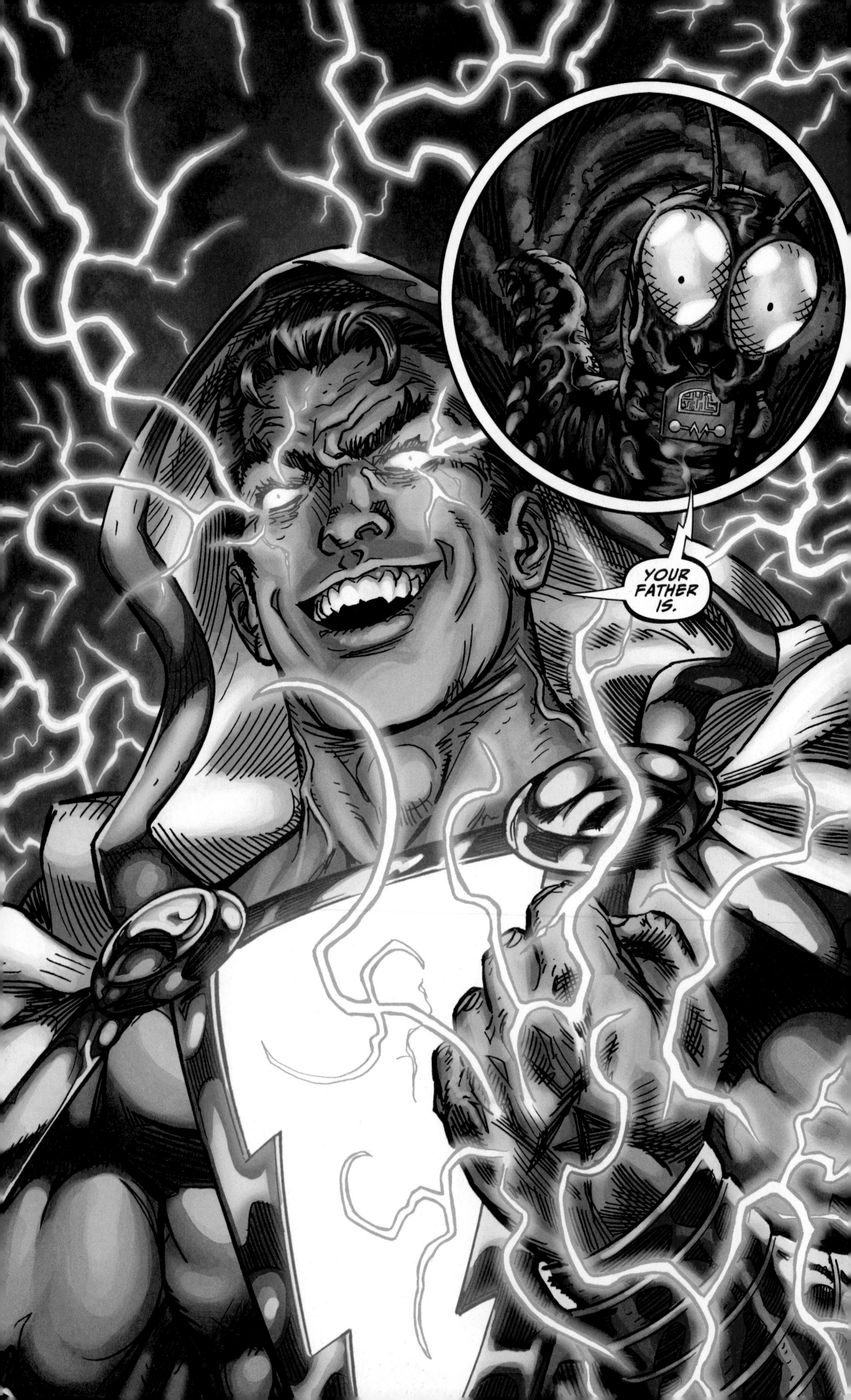
YOUR FATHER IS.

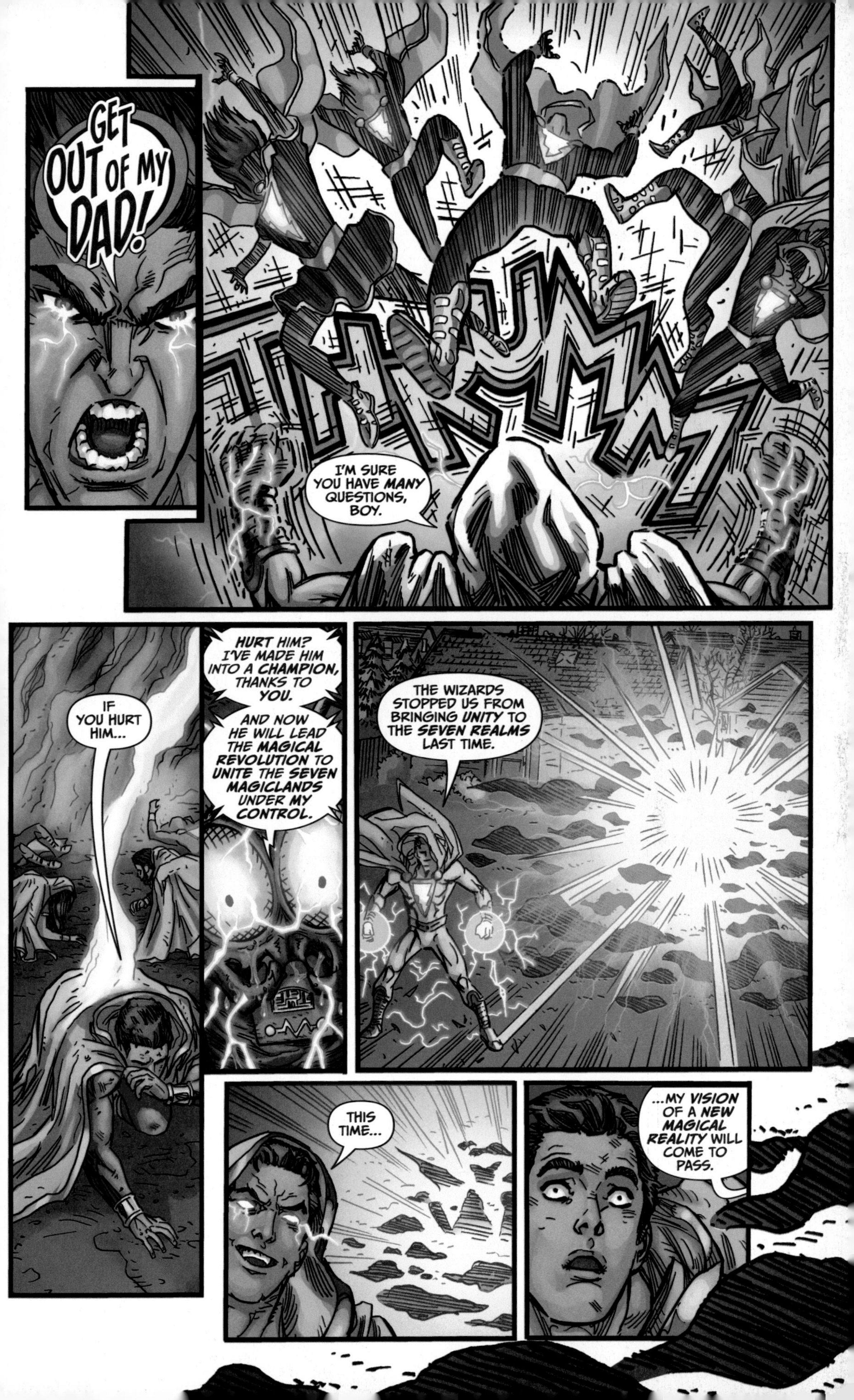
GET OUT OF MY DAD!
I'M SURE YOU HAVE MANY QUESTIONS, BOY.
IF YOU HURT HIM...
HURT HIM? I'VE MADE HIM INTO A CHAMPION, THANKS TO YOU.
AND NOW HE WILL LEAD THE MAGICAL REVOLUTION TO UNITE THE SEVEN MAGICLANDS UNDER MY CONTROL.
THE WIZARDS STOPPED US FROM BRINGING UNITY TO THE SEVEN REALMS LAST TIME.
THIS TIME...
...MY VISION OF A NEW MAGICAL REALITY WILL COME TO PASS.

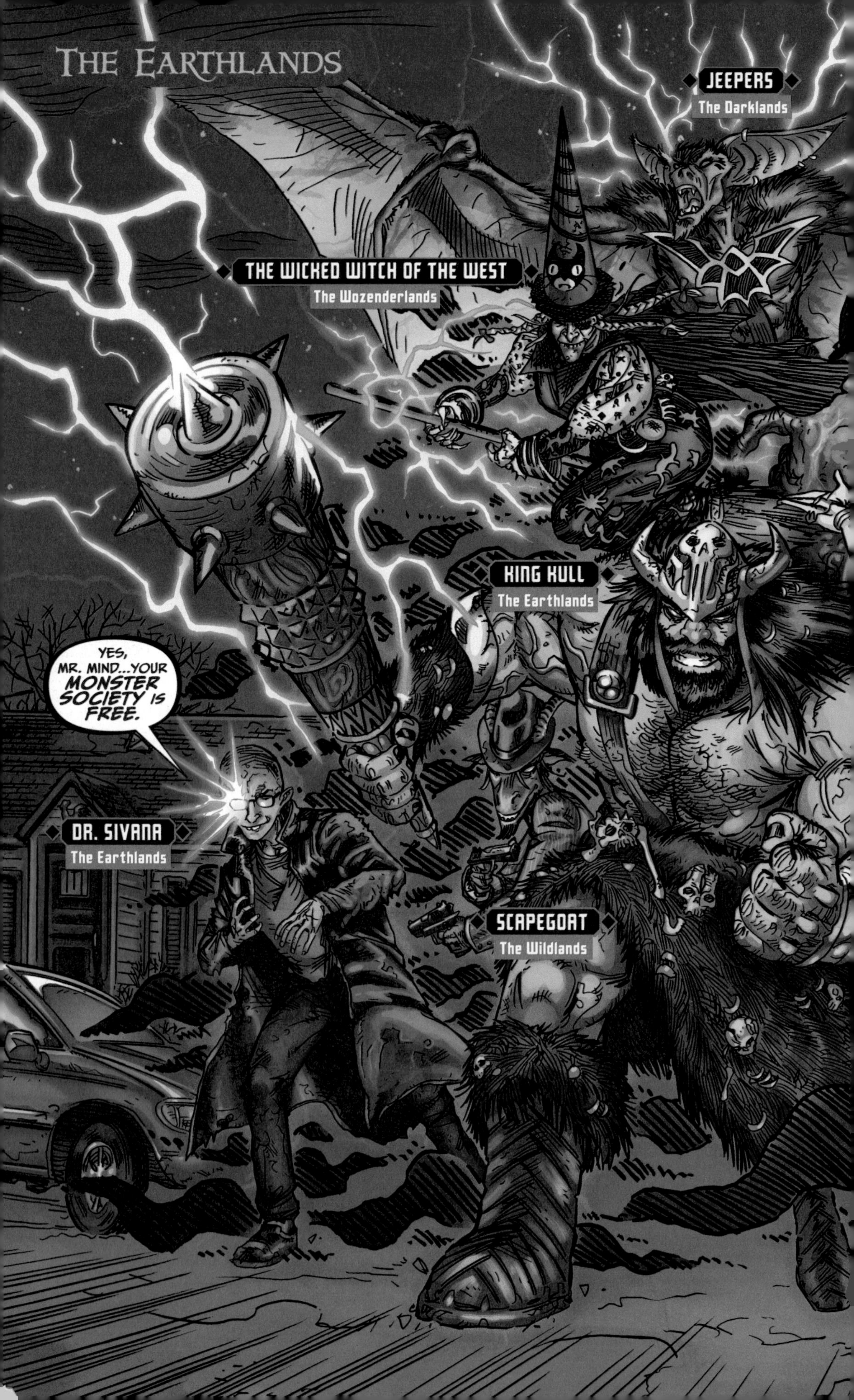
THE EARTHLANDS
JEEPERS
The Darklands
THE WICKED WITCH OF THE WEST
The Wozenderlands
KING KULL
The Earthlands
YES, MR. MIND...YOUR MONSTER SOCIETY IS FREE.
DR. SIVANA
The Earthlands
SCAPEGOAT
The Wildlands

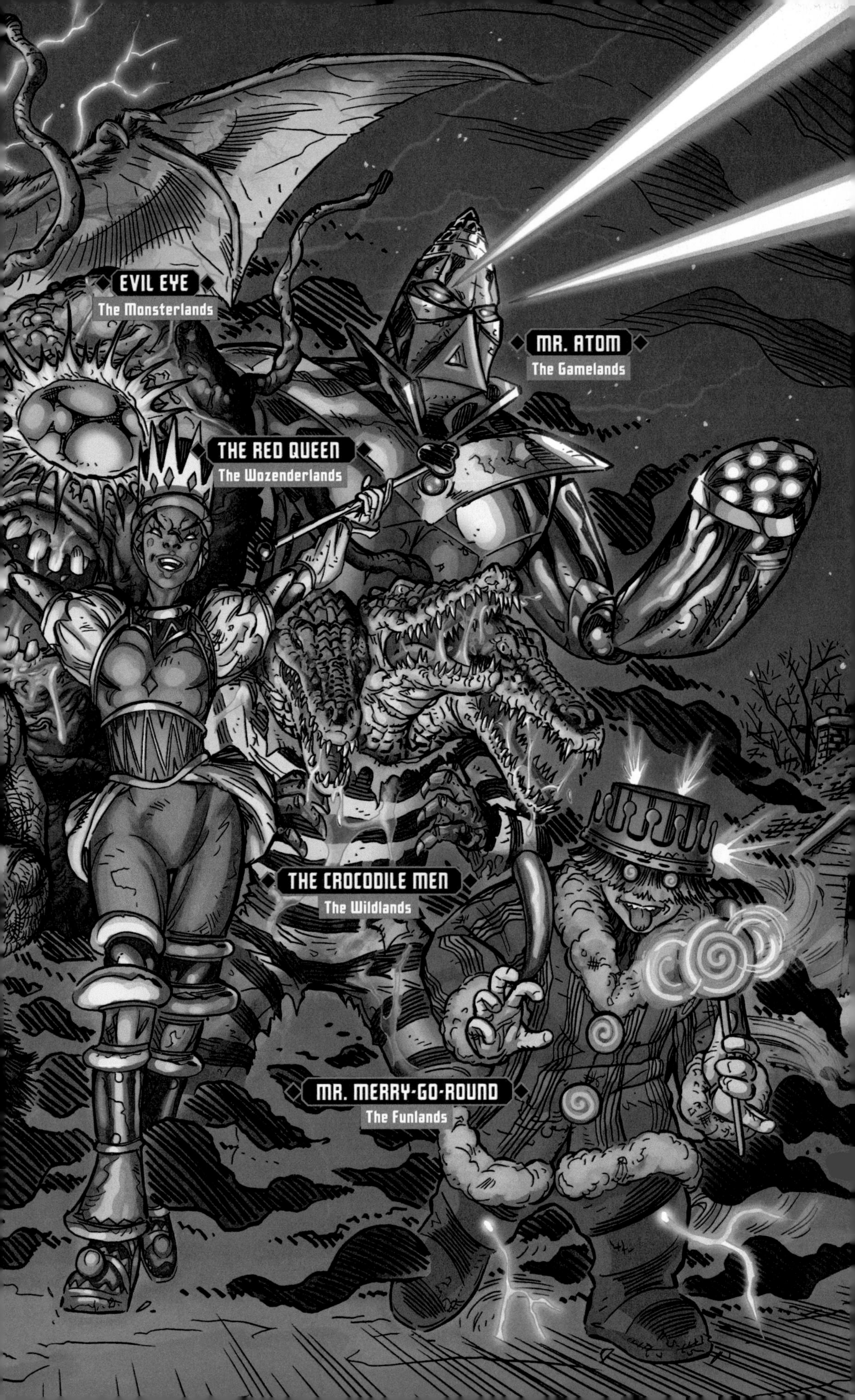
EVIL EYE
The Monsterlands
MR. ATOM
The Gamelands
THE RED QUEEN
The Wozenderlands
THE CROCODILE MEN
The Wildlands
MR. MERRY-GO-ROUND
The Funlands

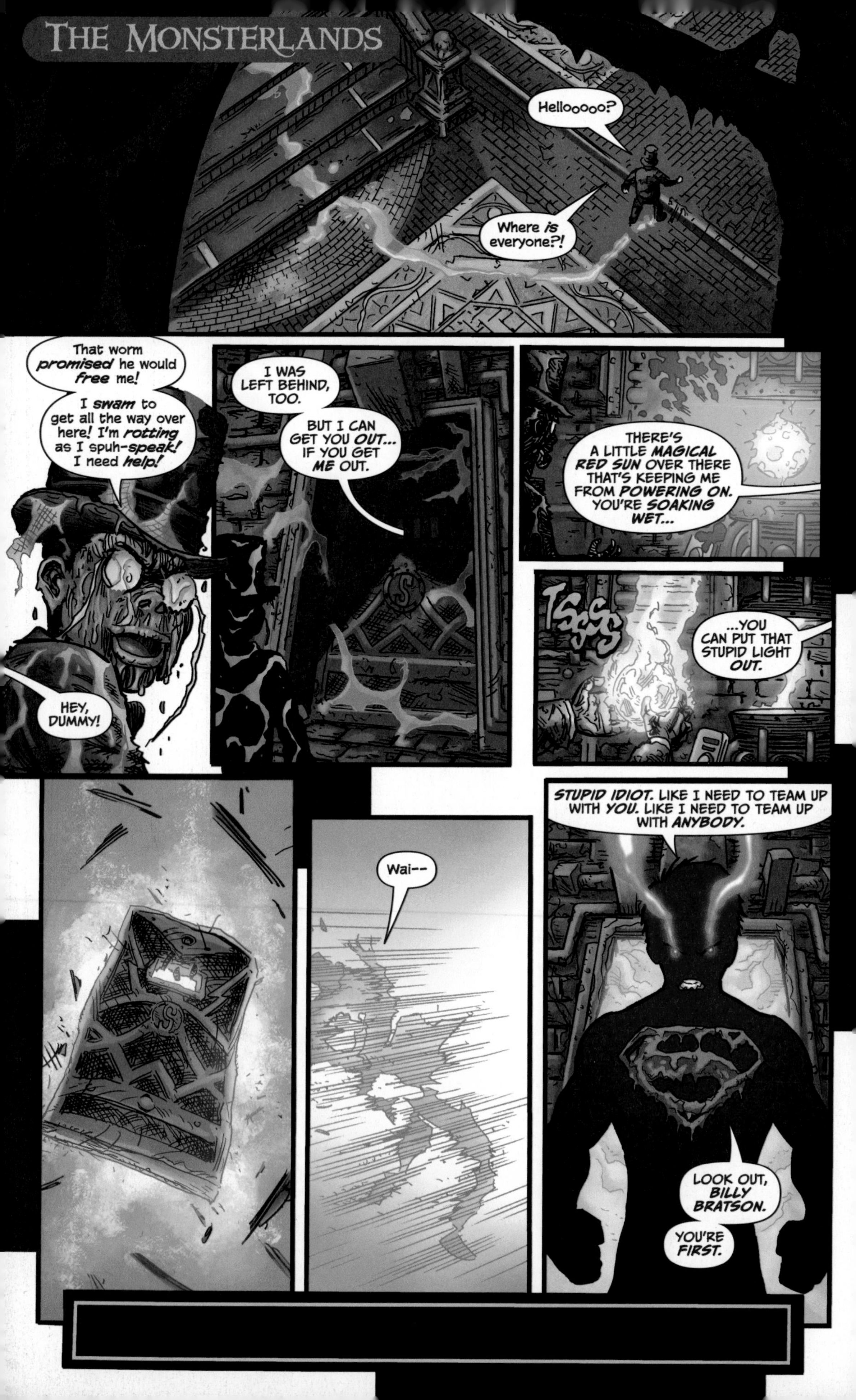
THE MONSTERLANDS
Hellooooo?
Where *is* everyone?!
That worm *promised* he would *free* me!
I *swam* to get all the way over here! I'm *rotting* as I spuh-*speak!* I need *help!*
HEY, DUMMY!
I WAS LEFT BEHIND, TOO.
BUT I CAN GET YOU *OUT*... IF YOU GET *ME* OUT.
THERE'S A LITTLE *MAGICAL RED SUN* OVER THERE THAT'S KEEPING ME FROM *POWERING ON.* YOU'RE *SOAKING WET*...
TSSSS
...YOU CAN PUT THAT STUPID LIGHT *OUT.*
Wai--
*STUPID IDIOT.* LIKE I NEED TO TEAM UP WITH *YOU.* LIKE I NEED TO TEAM UP WITH *ANYBODY.*
LOOK OUT, *BILLY BRATSON.*
YOU'RE *FIRST.*

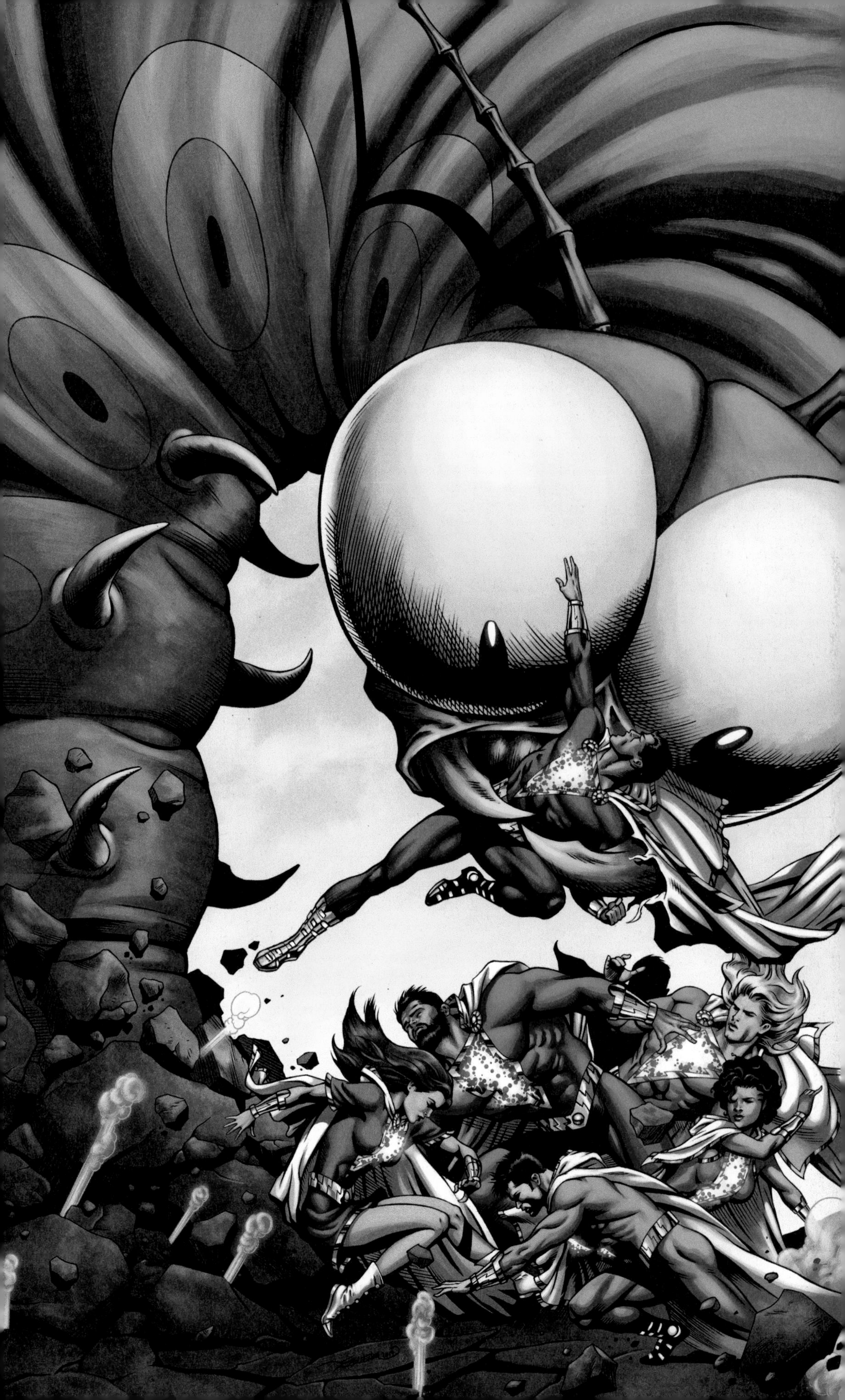

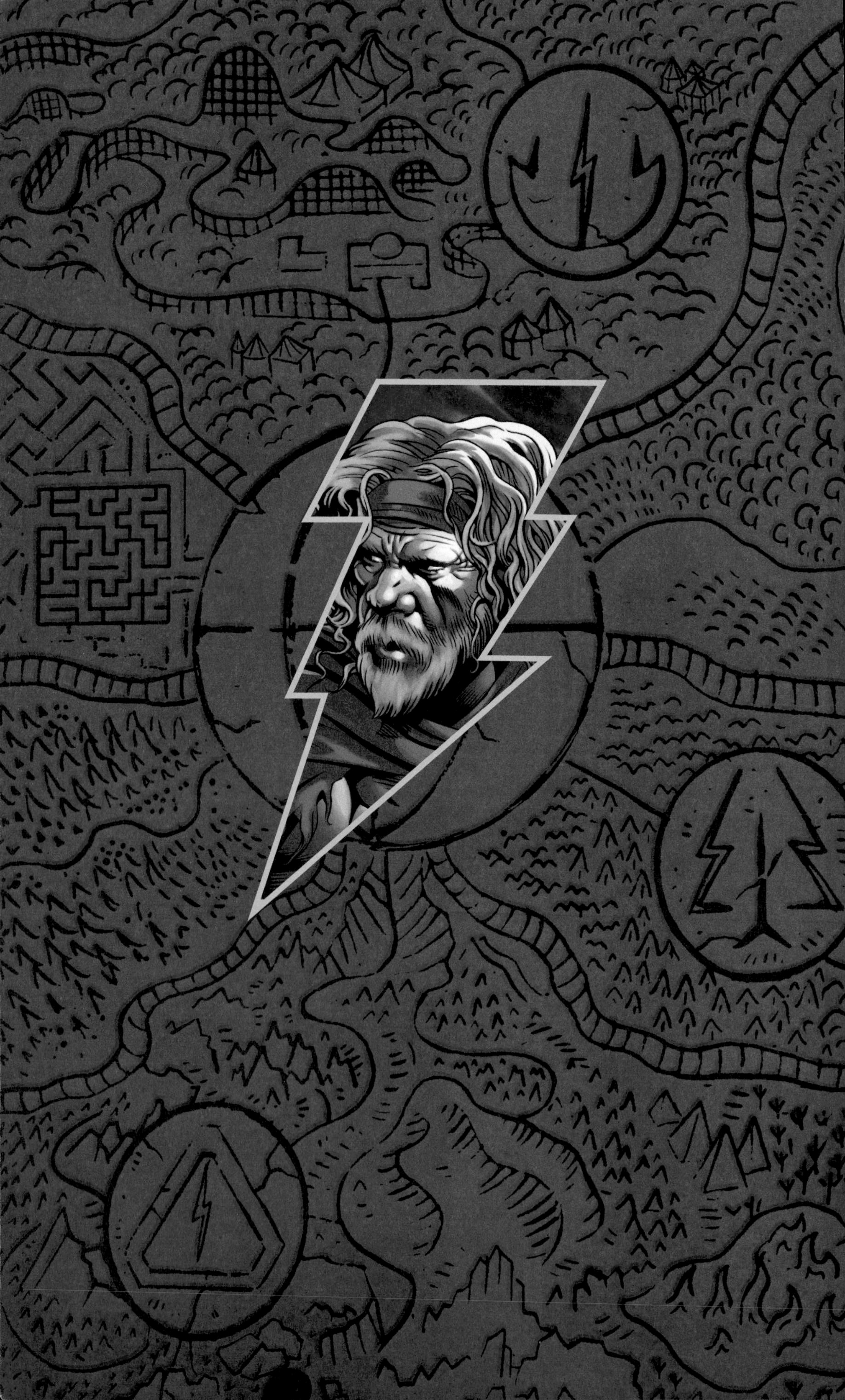

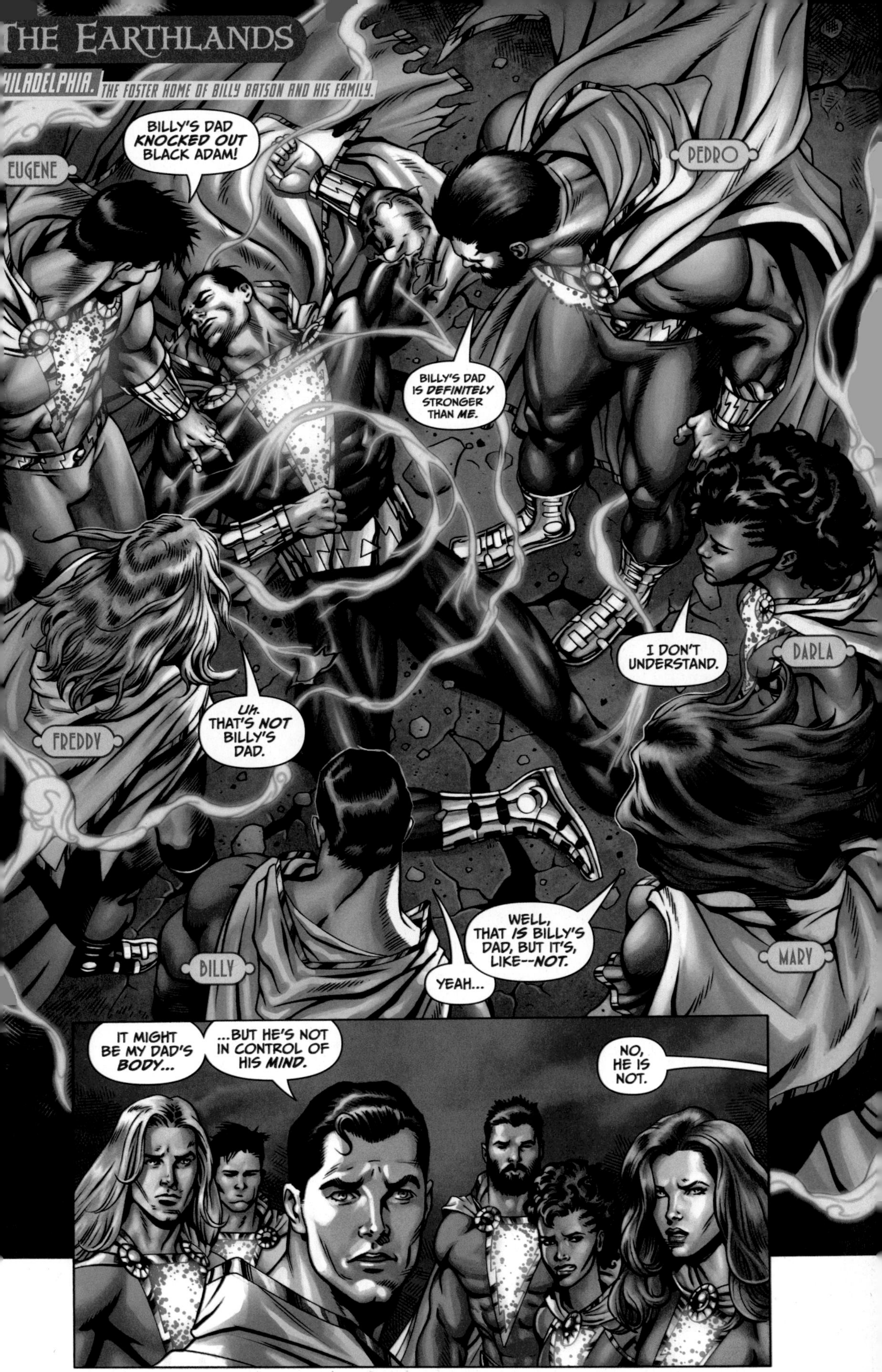
THE EARTHLANDS
PHILADELPHIA. THE FOSTER HOME OF BILLY BATSON AND HIS FAMILY.
EUGENE
BILLY'S DAD KNOCKED OUT BLACK ADAM!
PEDRO
BILLY'S DAD IS DEFINITELY STRONGER THAN ME.
DARLA
I DON'T UNDERSTAND.
FREDDY
Uh. THAT'S NOT BILLY'S DAD.
MARY
WELL, THAT IS BILLY'S DAD, BUT IT'S, LIKE--NOT.
BILLY
YEAH...
IT MIGHT BE MY DAD'S BODY...
...BUT HE'S NOT IN CONTROL OF HIS MIND.
NO, HE IS NOT.

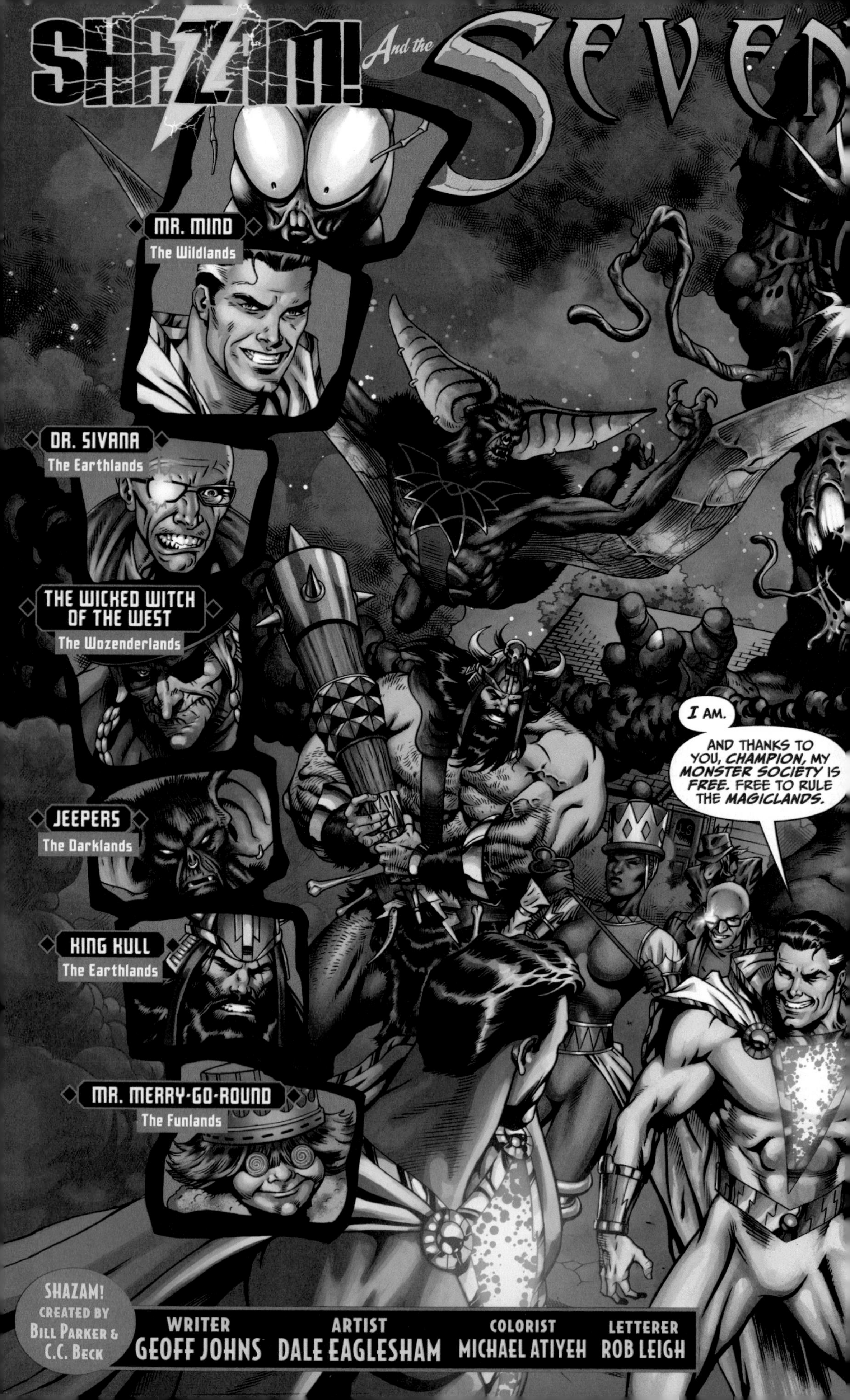
SHAZAM! And the SEVEN
MR. MIND
The Wildlands
DR. SIVANA
The Earthlands
THE WICKED WITCH OF THE WEST
The Wozenderlands
JEEPERS
The Darklands
KING KULL
The Earthlands
MR. MERRY-GO-ROUND
The Funlands
I AM.
AND THANKS TO YOU, CHAMPION, MY MONSTER SOCIETY IS FREE. FREE TO RULE THE MAGICLANDS.
SHAZAM! CREATED BY BILL PARKER & C.C. BECK
WRITER GEOFF JOHNS
ARTIST DALE EAGLESHAM
COLORIST MICHAEL ATIYEH
LETTERER ROB LEIGH

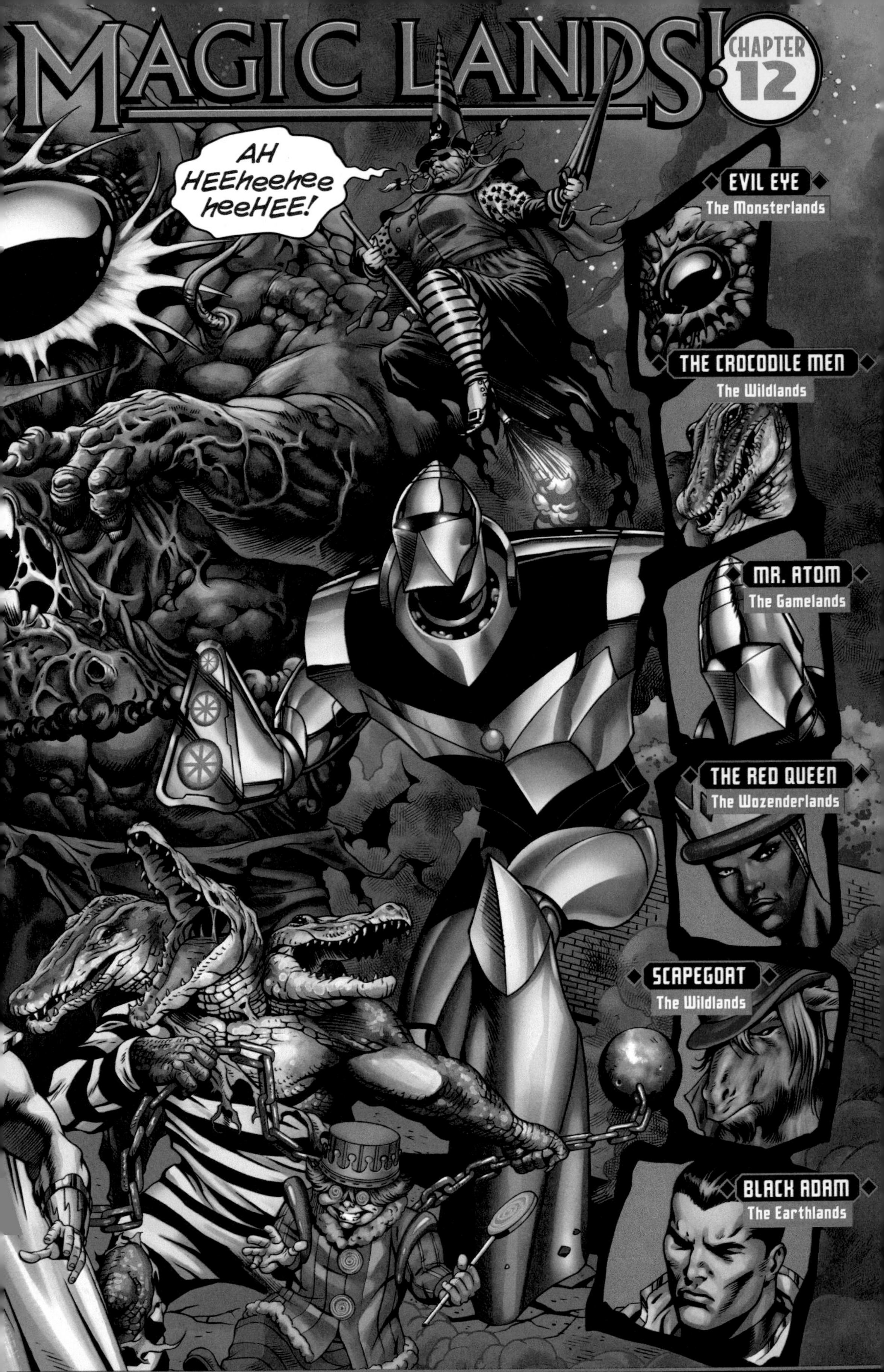


COVER DALE EAGLESHAM WITH MICHAEL ATIYEH · VARIANT COVER JULIAN TOTINO TEDESCO · ASST. EDITOR MARQUIS DRAPER · EDITOR MIKE COTTON · GROUP EDITOR ALEX R. CARR

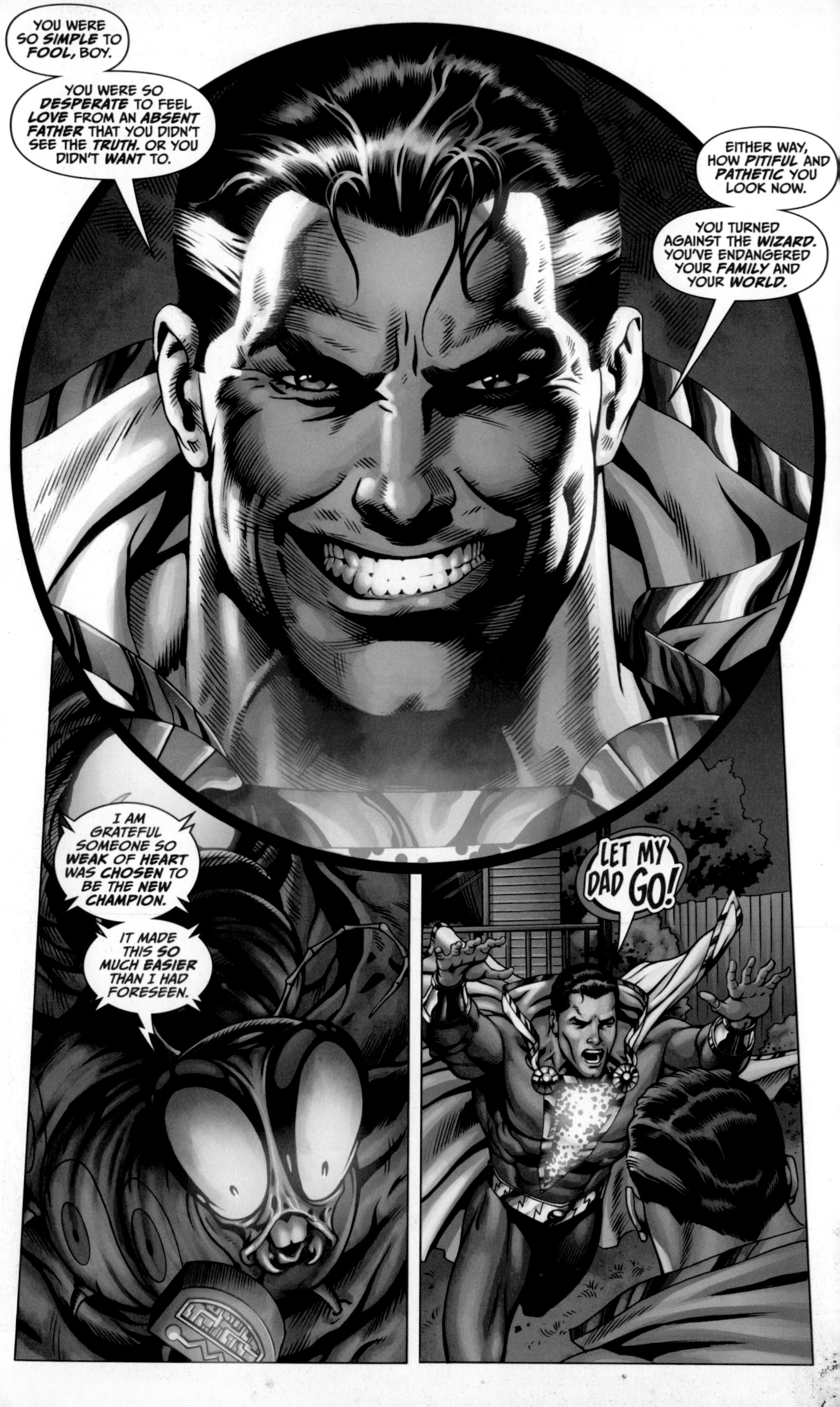
YOU WERE SO SIMPLE TO FOOL, BOY.
YOU WERE SO DESPERATE TO FEEL LOVE FROM AN ABSENT FATHER THAT YOU DIDN'T SEE THE TRUTH. OR YOU DIDN'T WANT TO.
EITHER WAY, HOW PITIFUL AND PATHETIC YOU LOOK NOW.
YOU TURNED AGAINST THE WIZARD. YOU'VE ENDANGERED YOUR FAMILY AND YOUR WORLD.
I AM GRATEFUL SOMEONE SO WEAK OF HEART WAS CHOSEN TO BE THE NEW CHAMPION.
IT MADE THIS SO MUCH EASIER THAN I HAD FORESEEN.
LET MY DAD GO!

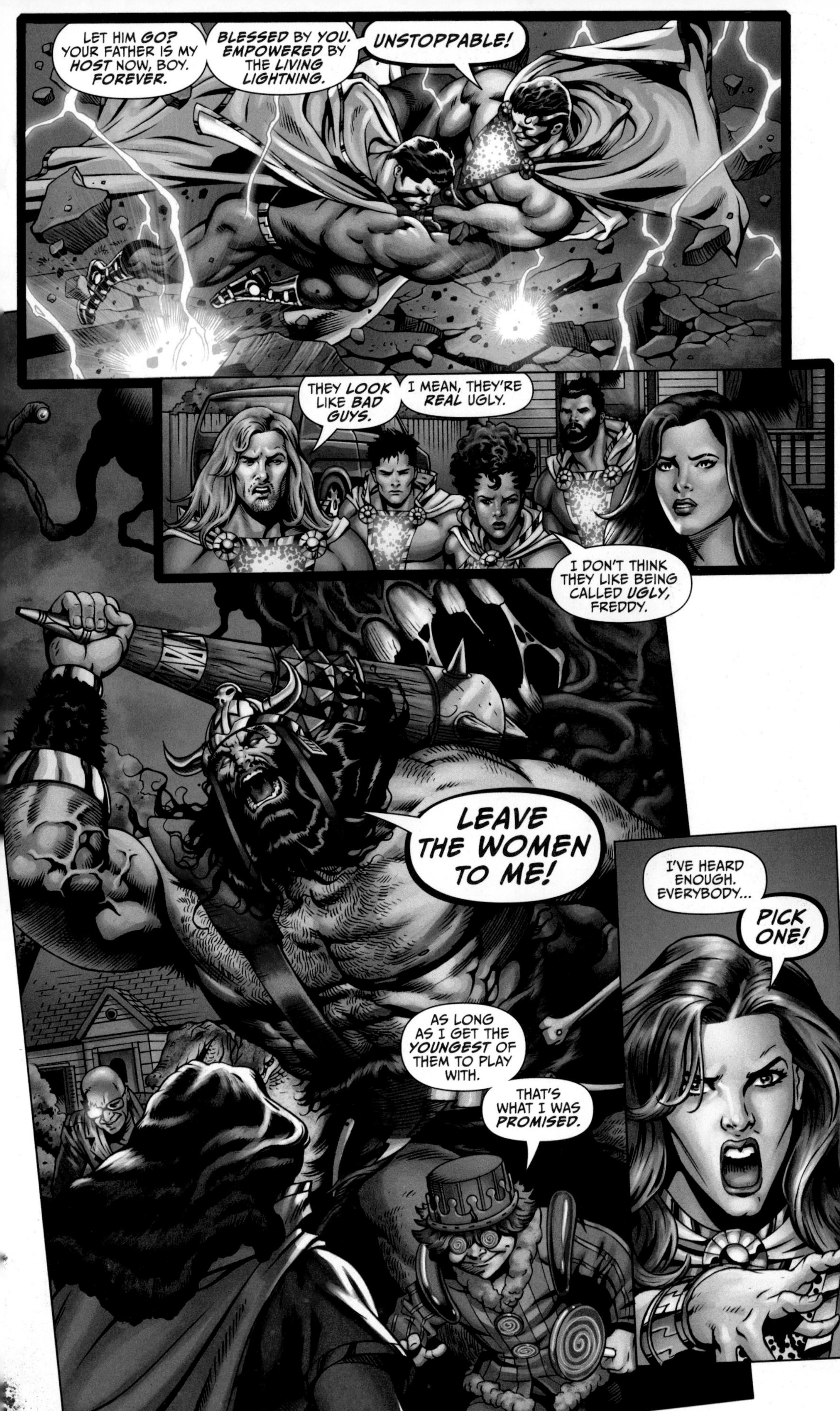
LET HIM GO? YOUR FATHER IS MY HOST NOW, BOY. FOREVER.
BLESSED BY YOU. EMPOWERED BY THE LIVING LIGHTNING.
UNSTOPPABLE!
THEY LOOK LIKE BAD GUYS.
I MEAN, THEY'RE REAL UGLY.
I DON'T THINK THEY LIKE BEING CALLED UGLY, FREDDY.
LEAVE THE WOMEN TO ME!
AS LONG AS I GET THE YOUNGEST OF THEM TO PLAY WITH.
THAT'S WHAT I WAS PROMISED.
I'VE HEARD ENOUGH. EVERYBODY...
PICK ONE!

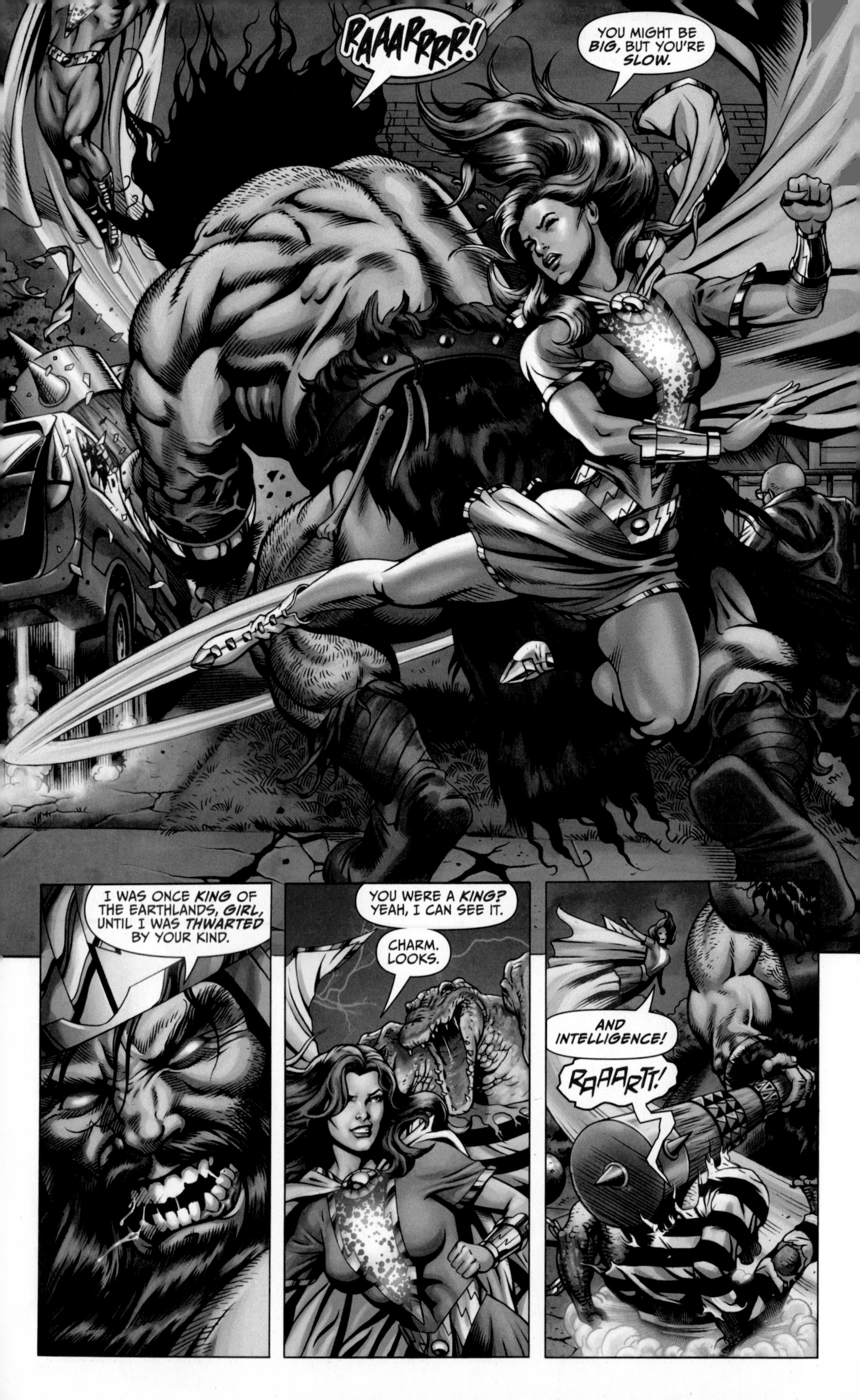
RAAARRRR!
YOU MIGHT BE BIG, BUT YOU'RE SLOW.
I WAS ONCE KING OF THE EARTHLANDS, GIRL, UNTIL I WAS THWARTED BY YOUR KIND.
YOU WERE A KING? YEAH, I CAN SEE IT.
CHARM. LOOKS.
AND INTELLIGENCE!
RAAARTT!

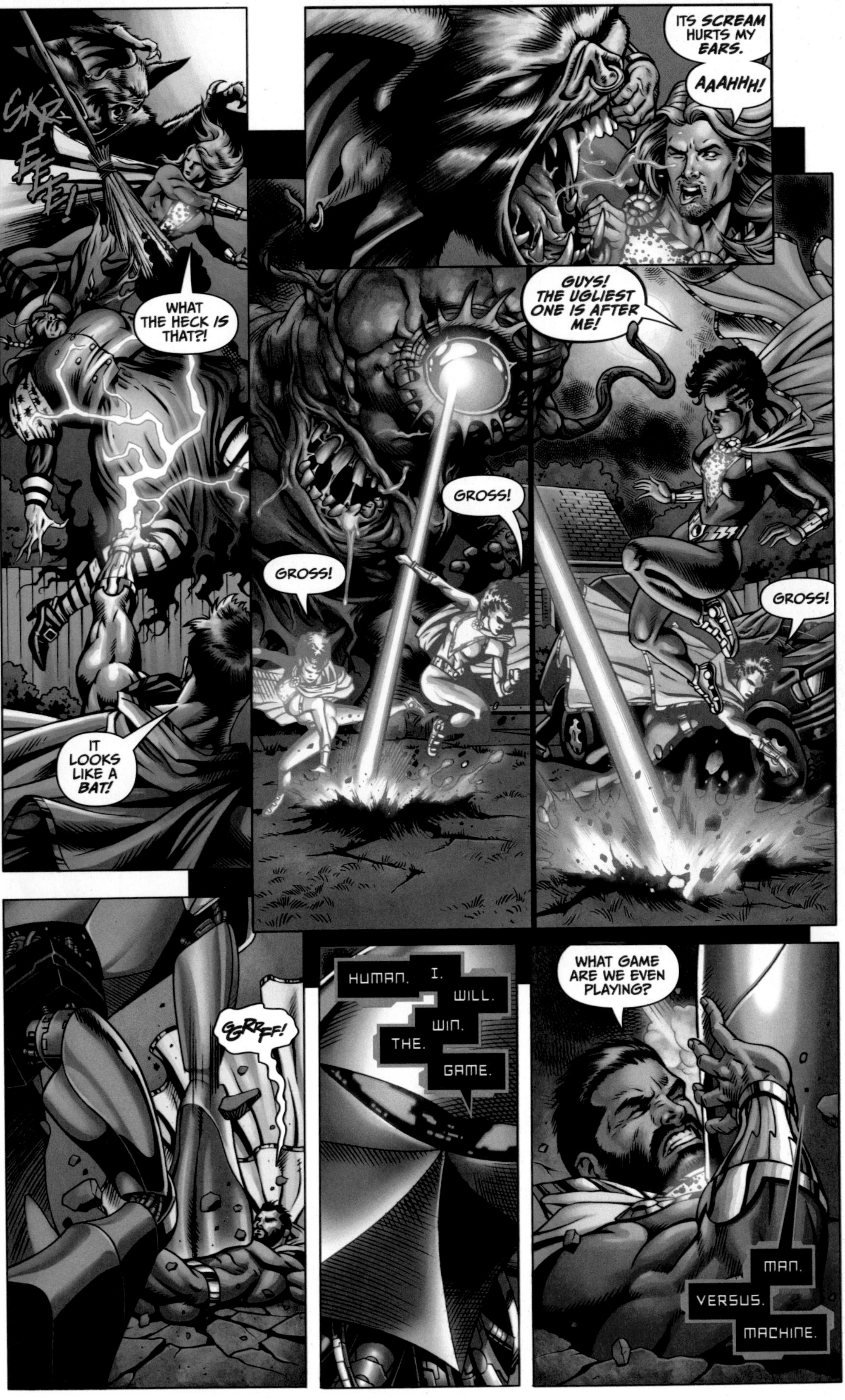
SKREEEE!
ITS SCREAM HURTS MY EARS.
AAAHHH!
WHAT THE HECK IS THAT?!
IT LOOKS LIKE A BAT!
GUYS! THE UGLIEST ONE IS AFTER ME!
GROSS!
GROSS!
GROSS!
GSRRFF!
HUMAN. I. WILL. WIN. THE. GAME.
WHAT GAME ARE WE EVEN PLAYING?
MAN. VERSUS. MACHINE.

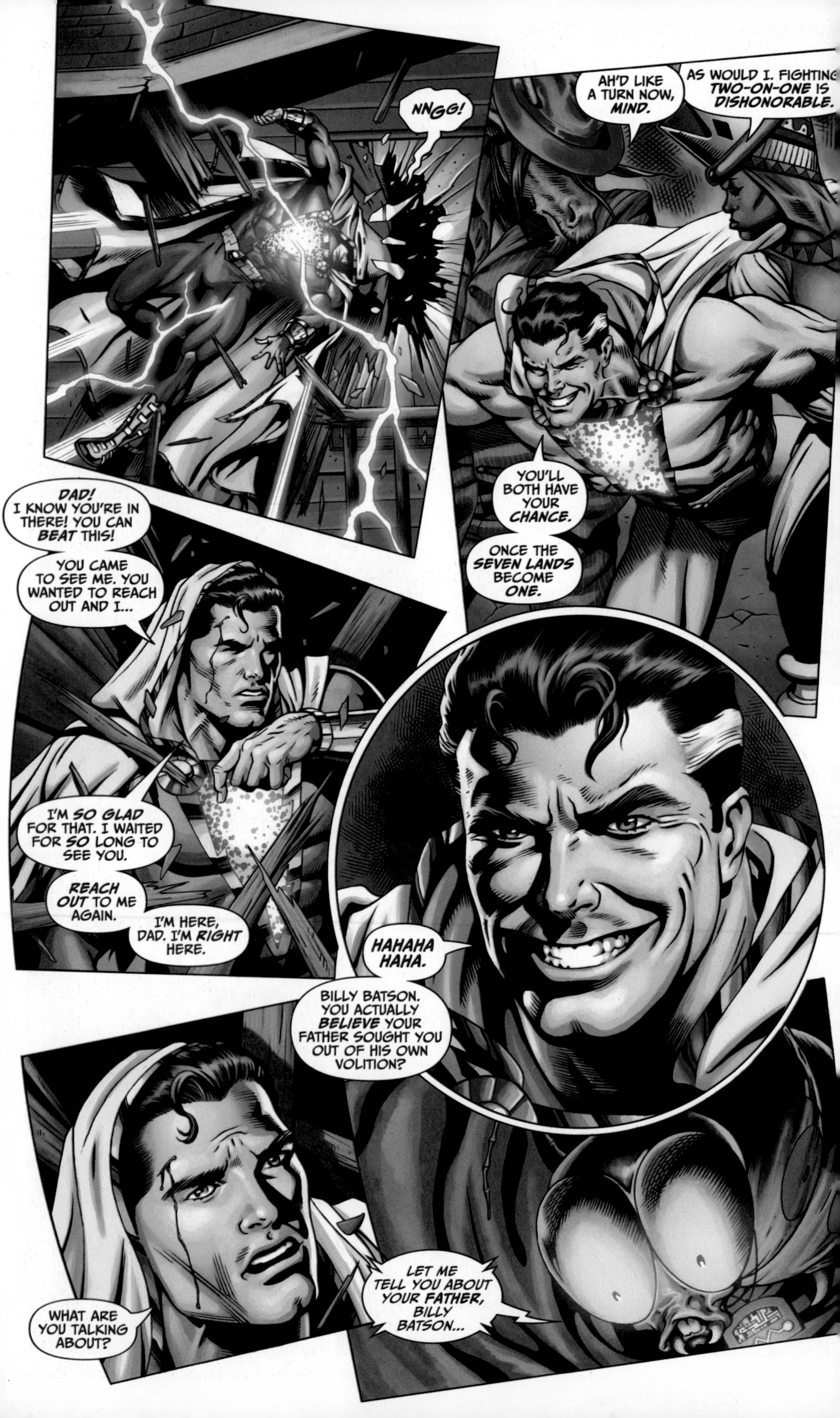
NNGG!
AH'D LIKE A TURN NOW, MIND.
AS WOULD I. FIGHTING TWO-ON-ONE IS DISHONORABLE.
YOU'LL BOTH HAVE YOUR CHANCE.
ONCE THE SEVEN LANDS BECOME ONE.
DAD! I KNOW YOU'RE IN THERE! YOU CAN BEAT THIS!
YOU CAME TO SEE ME. YOU WANTED TO REACH OUT AND I...
I'M SO GLAD FOR THAT. I WAITED FOR SO LONG TO SEE YOU.
REACH OUT TO ME AGAIN.
I'M HERE, DAD. I'M RIGHT HERE.
HAHAHA HAHA.
BILLY BATSON. YOU ACTUALLY BELIEVE YOUR FATHER SOUGHT YOU OUT OF HIS OWN VOLITION?
WHAT ARE YOU TALKING ABOUT?
LET ME TELL YOU ABOUT YOUR FATHER, BILLY BATSON...

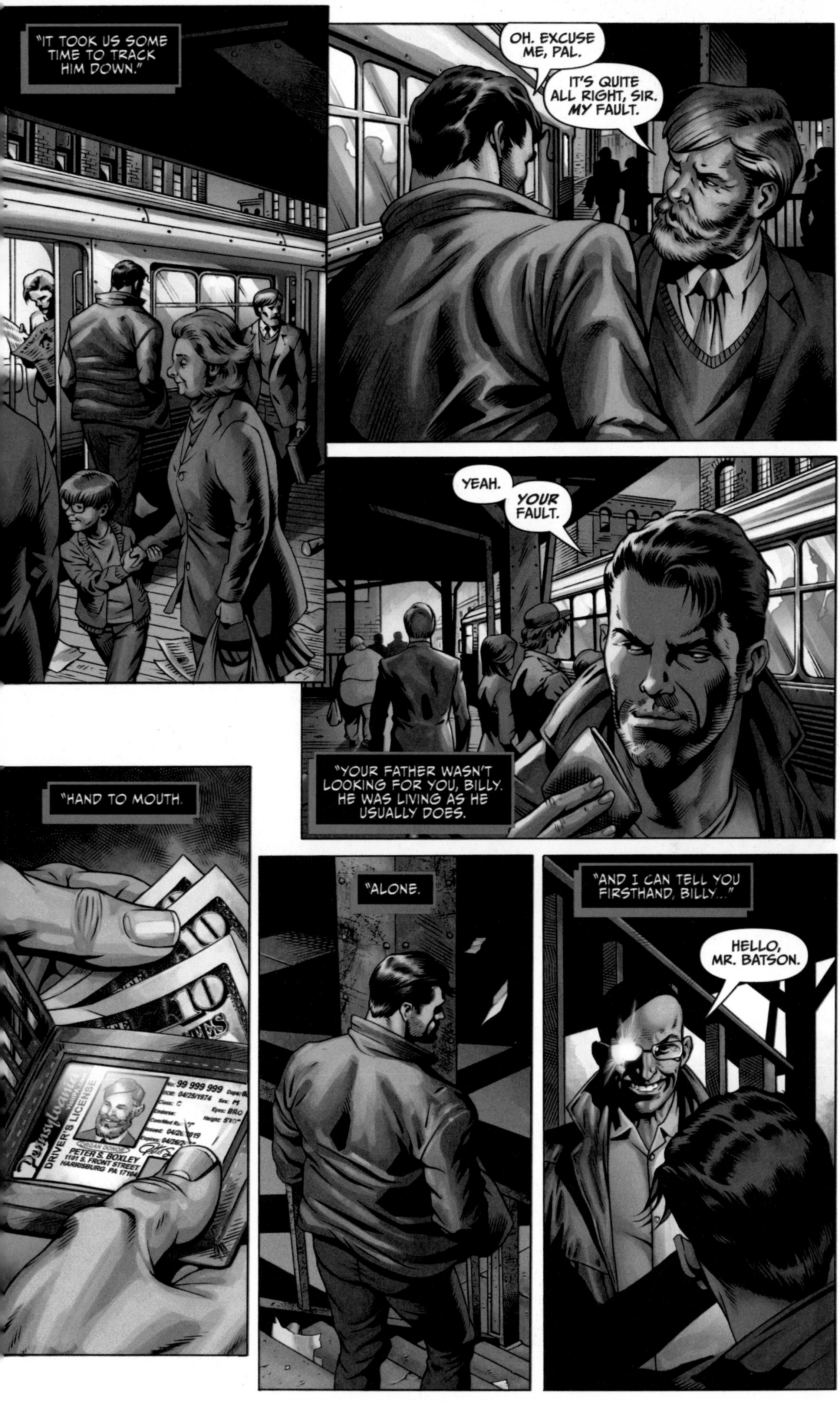
"IT TOOK US SOME TIME TO TRACK HIM DOWN."
OH. EXCUSE ME, PAL.
IT'S QUITE ALL RIGHT, SIR. MY FAULT.
YEAH.
YOUR FAULT.
"YOUR FATHER WASN'T LOOKING FOR YOU, BILLY. HE WAS LIVING AS HE USUALLY DOES.
"HAND TO MOUTH.
DRIVER'S LICENSE
PETER S. BOXLEY
1101 S. FRONT STREET
HARRISBURG PA 17104
"ALONE.
"AND I CAN TELL YOU FIRSTHAND, BILLY..."
HELLO, MR. BATSON.

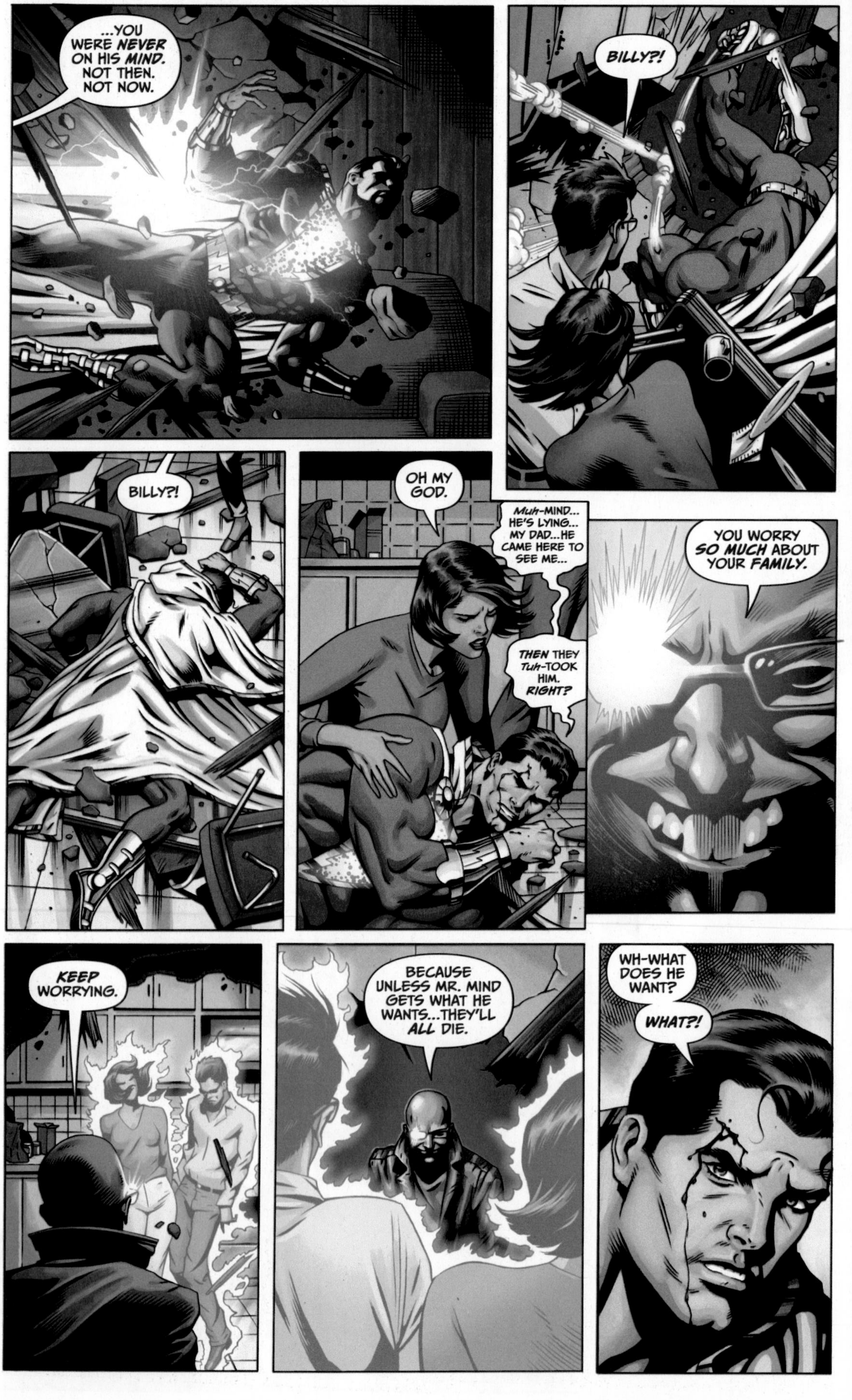
...YOU WERE *NEVER* ON HIS *MIND*. NOT THEN. NOT NOW.
*BILLY?!*
BILLY?!
OH MY GOD.
*Muh*-MIND... HE'S LYING... MY DAD...HE CAME HERE TO SEE ME...
*THEN* THEY *Tuh*-TOOK HIM. *RIGHT?*
YOU WORRY *SO MUCH* ABOUT YOUR *FAMILY.*
*KEEP* WORRYING.
BECAUSE UNLESS MR. MIND GETS WHAT HE WANTS...THEY'LL *ALL* DIE.
WH-WHAT DOES HE WANT?
*WHAT?!*

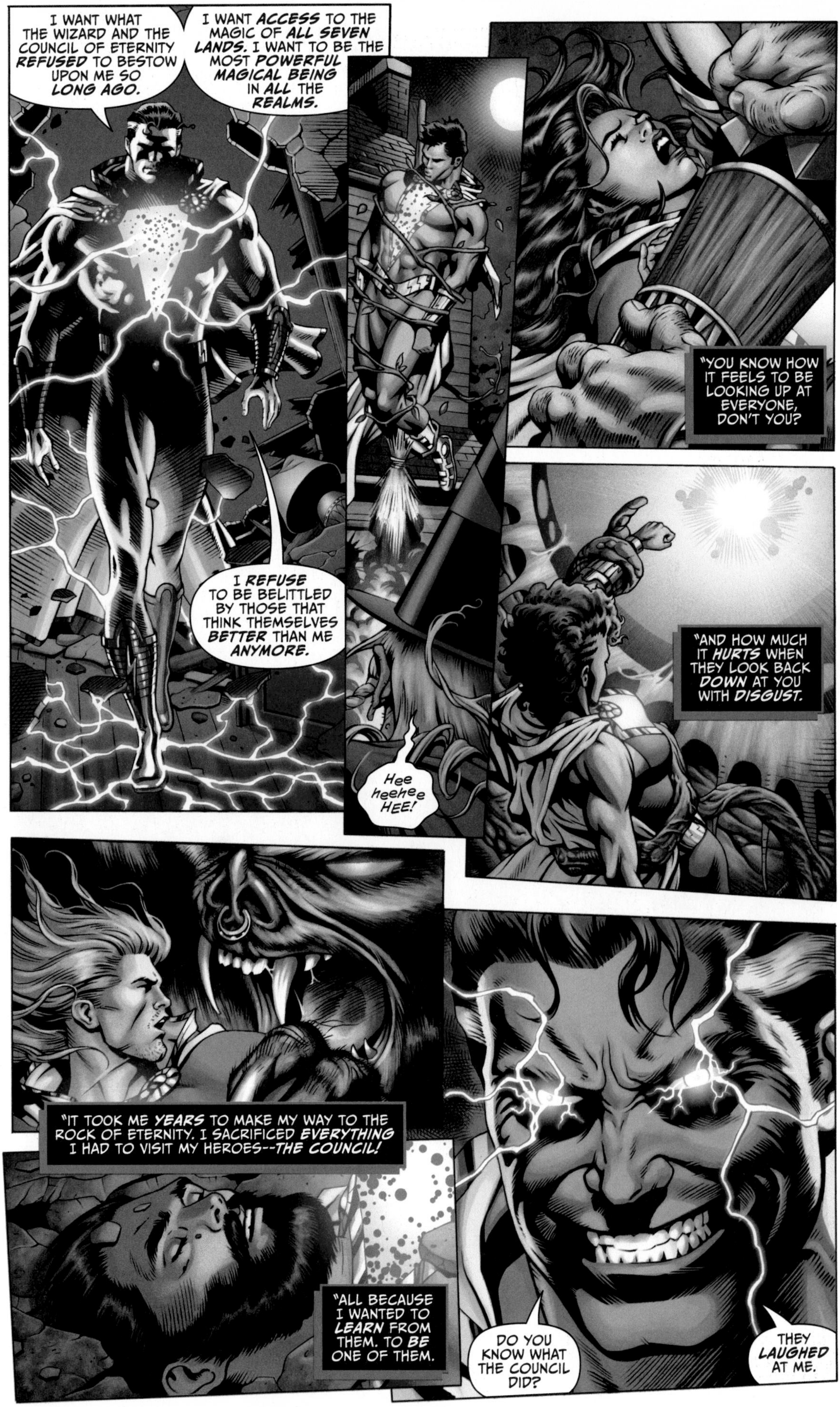
I WANT WHAT THE WIZARD AND THE COUNCIL OF ETERNITY REFUSED TO BESTOW UPON ME SO LONG AGO.
I WANT ACCESS TO THE MAGIC OF ALL SEVEN LANDS. I WANT TO BE THE MOST POWERFUL MAGICAL BEING IN ALL THE REALMS.
I REFUSE TO BE BELITTLED BY THOSE THAT THINK THEMSELVES BETTER THAN ME ANYMORE.
"YOU KNOW HOW IT FEELS TO BE LOOKING UP AT EVERYONE, DON'T YOU?
Hee heehee HEE!
"AND HOW MUCH IT HURTS WHEN THEY LOOK BACK DOWN AT YOU WITH DISGUST.
"IT TOOK ME YEARS TO MAKE MY WAY TO THE ROCK OF ETERNITY. I SACRIFICED EVERYTHING I HAD TO VISIT MY HEROES--THE COUNCIL!
"ALL BECAUSE I WANTED TO LEARN FROM THEM. TO BE ONE OF THEM.
DO YOU KNOW WHAT THE COUNCIL DID?
THEY LAUGHED AT ME.

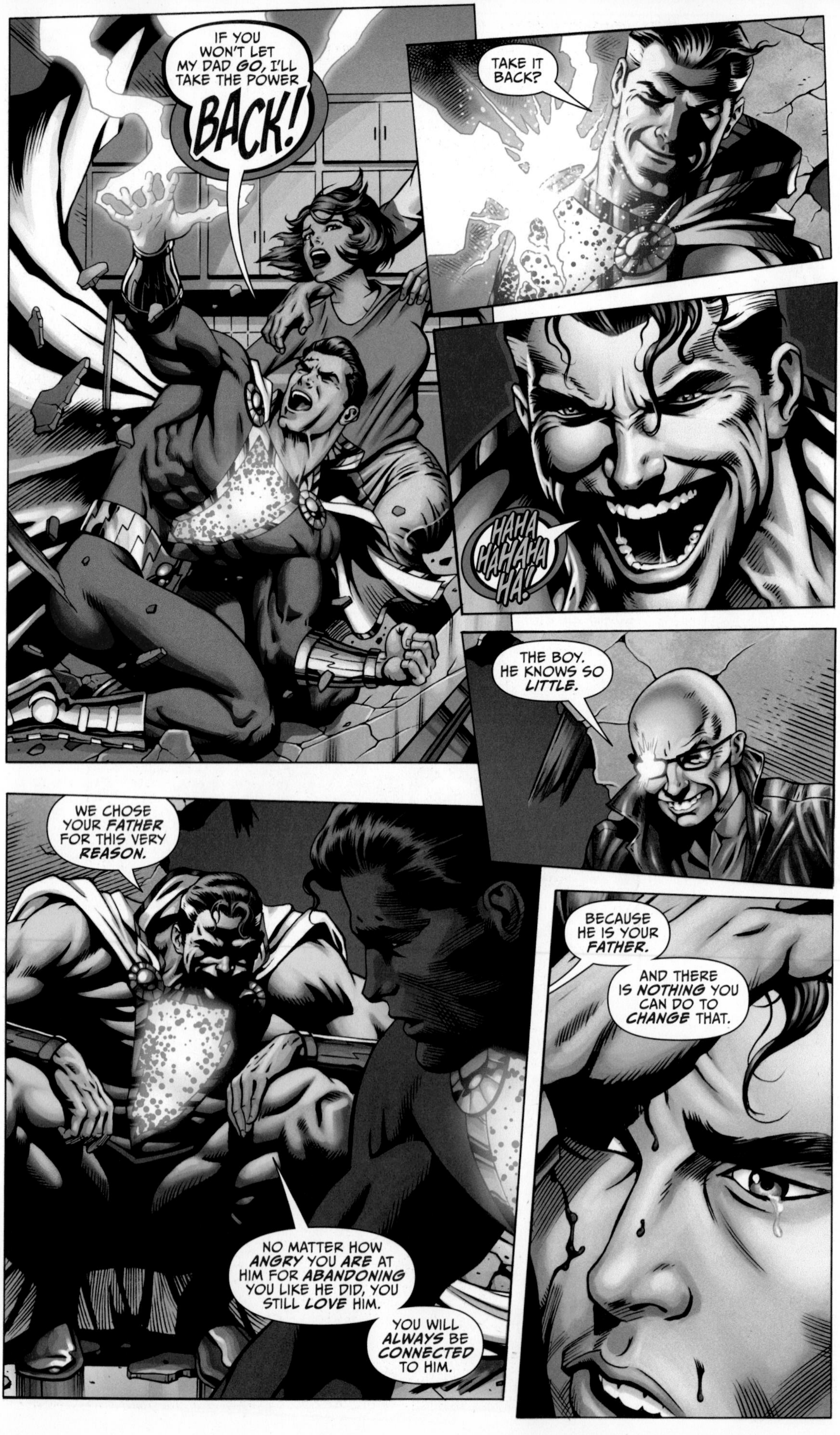
IF YOU WON'T LET MY DAD GO, I'LL TAKE THE POWER BACK!
TAKE IT BACK?
HAHA HAHAHA HA!
THE BOY. HE KNOWS SO LITTLE.
WE CHOSE YOUR FATHER FOR THIS VERY REASON.
BECAUSE HE IS YOUR FATHER.
AND THERE IS NOTHING YOU CAN DO TO CHANGE THAT.
NO MATTER HOW ANGRY YOU ARE AT HIM FOR ABANDONING YOU LIKE HE DID, YOU STILL LOVE HIM.
YOU WILL ALWAYS BE CONNECTED TO HIM.

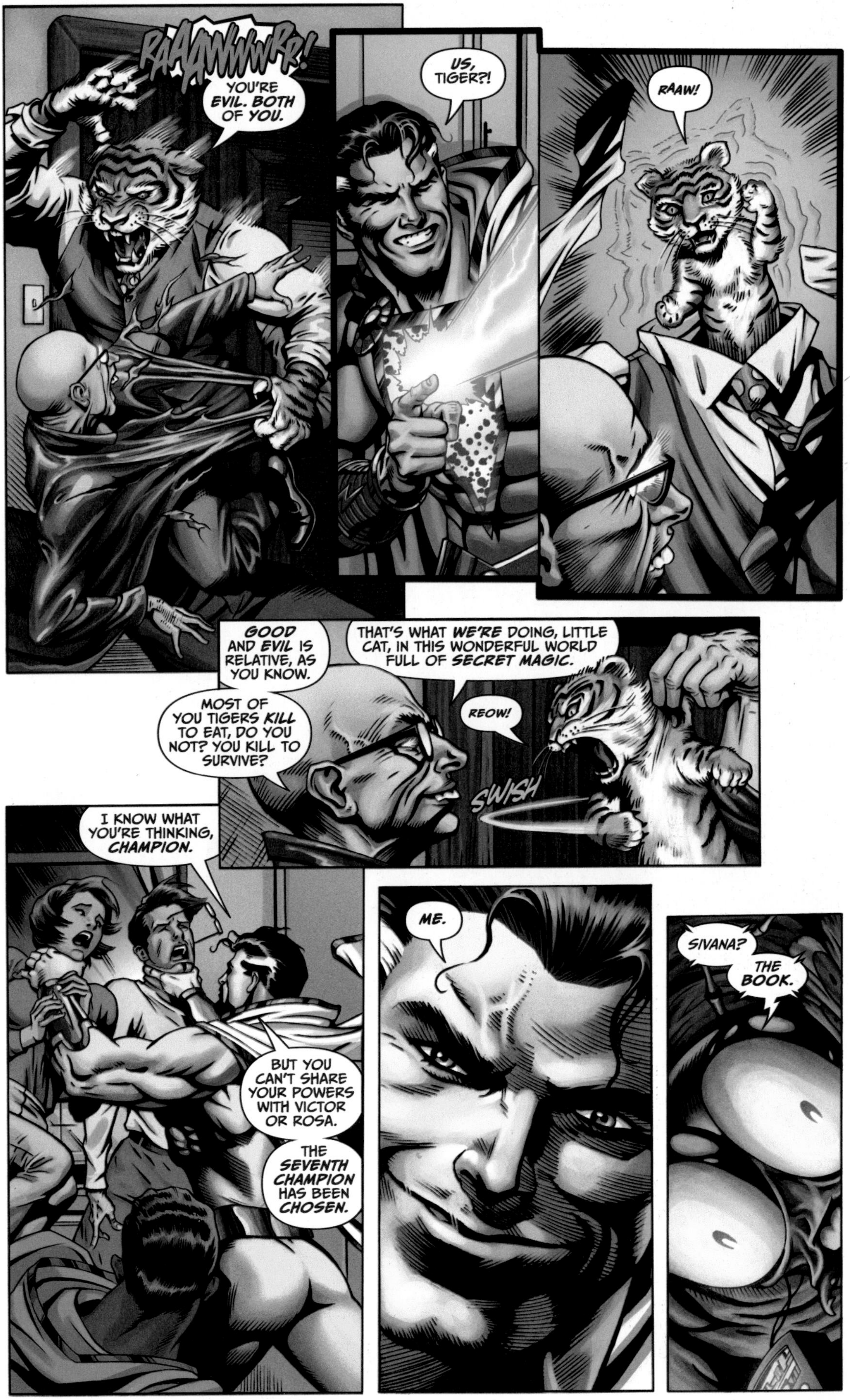

RAAGWWWRR!
YOU'RE EVIL. BOTH OF YOU.
US, TIGER?!
RAAW!
GOOD AND EVIL IS RELATIVE, AS YOU KNOW.
THAT'S WHAT WE'RE DOING, LITTLE CAT, IN THIS WONDERFUL WORLD FULL OF SECRET MAGIC.
MOST OF YOU TIGERS KILL TO EAT, DO YOU NOT? YOU KILL TO SURVIVE?
REOW!
SWISH
I KNOW WHAT YOU'RE THINKING, CHAMPION.
BUT YOU CAN'T SHARE YOUR POWERS WITH VICTOR OR ROSA.
THE SEVENTH CHAMPION HAS BEEN CHOSEN.
ME.
SIVANA?
THE BOOK.

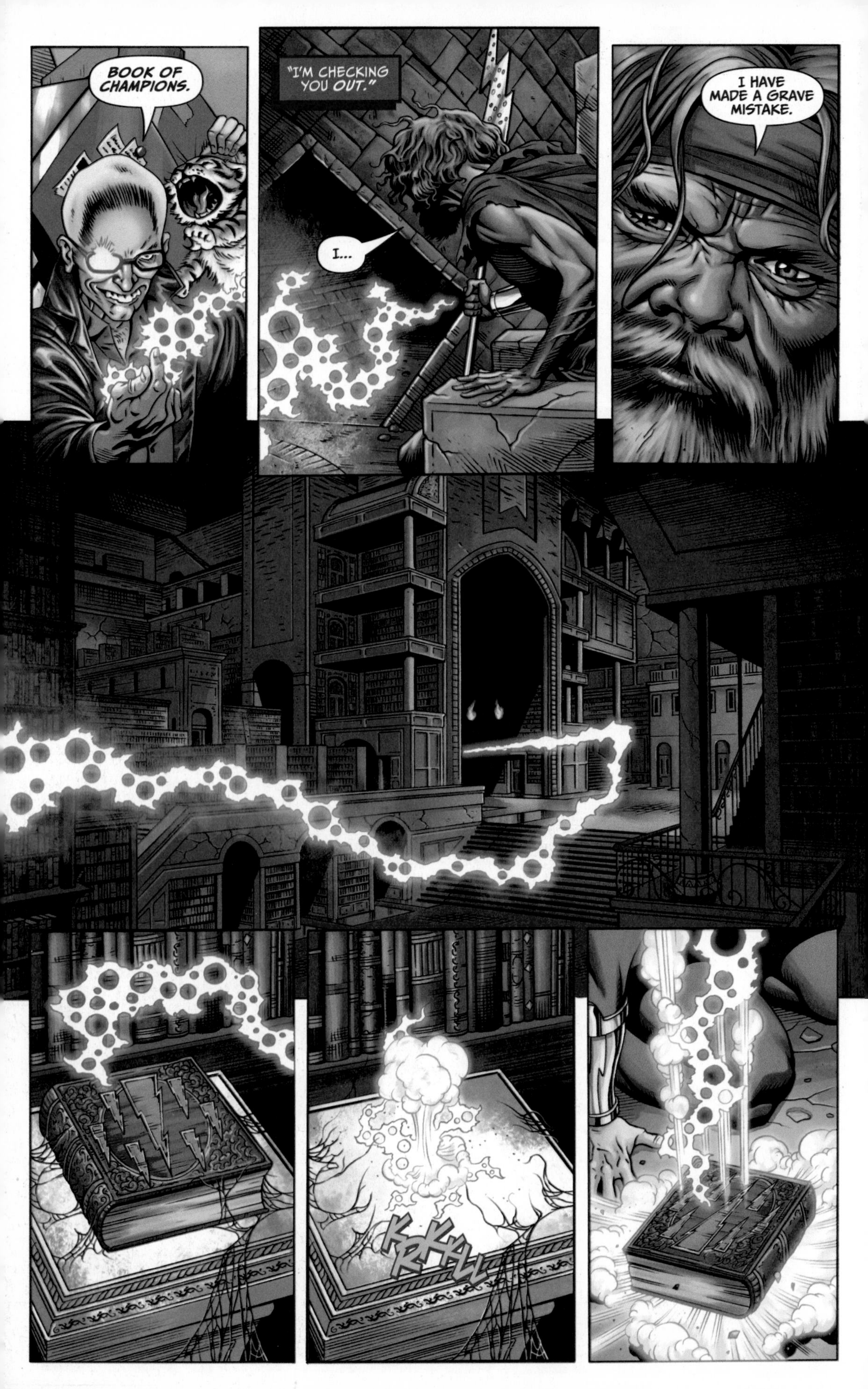
BOOK OF CHAMPIONS.
"I'M CHECKING YOU OUT."
I...
I HAVE MADE A GRAVE MISTAKE.
KRKKLL

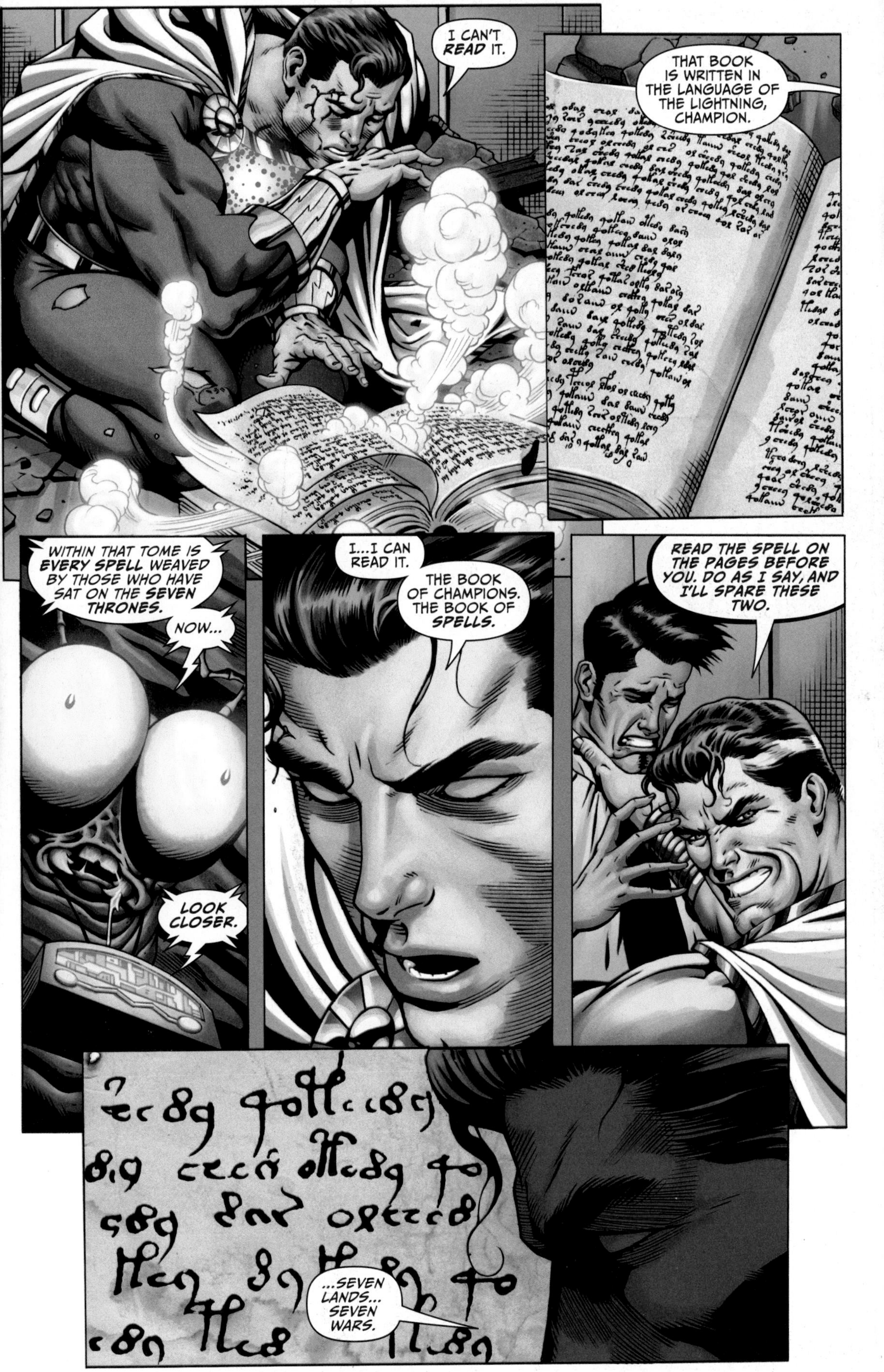

I CAN'T READ IT.
THAT BOOK IS WRITTEN IN THE LANGUAGE OF THE LIGHTNING, CHAMPION.
WITHIN THAT TOME IS EVERY SPELL WEAVED BY THOSE WHO HAVE SAT ON THE SEVEN THRONES.
NOW...
LOOK CLOSER.
I...I CAN READ IT.
THE BOOK OF CHAMPIONS. THE BOOK OF SPELLS.
READ THE SPELL ON THE PAGES BEFORE YOU. DO AS I SAY, AND I'LL SPARE THESE TWO.
...SEVEN LANDS... SEVEN WARS.

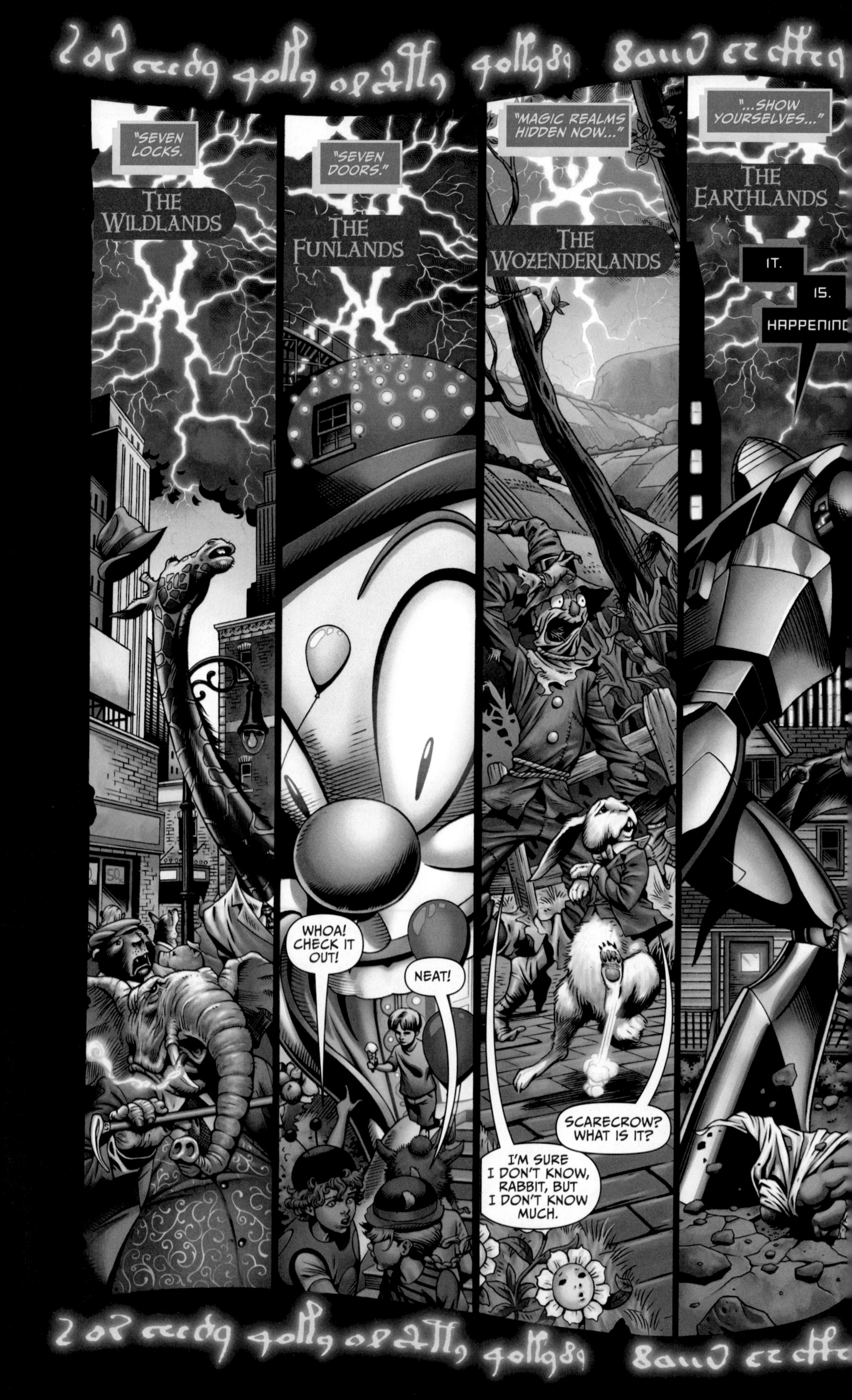
"SEVEN LOCKS.
THE WILDLANDS
"SEVEN DOORS."
THE FUNLANDS
"MAGIC REALMS HIDDEN NOW..."
THE WOZENDERLANDS
"...SHOW YOURSELVES..."
THE EARTHLANDS
IT.
IS.
HAPPENING
WHOA! CHECK IT OUT!
NEAT!
SCARECROW? WHAT IS IT?
I'M SURE I DON'T KNOW, RABBIT, BUT I DON'T KNOW MUCH.

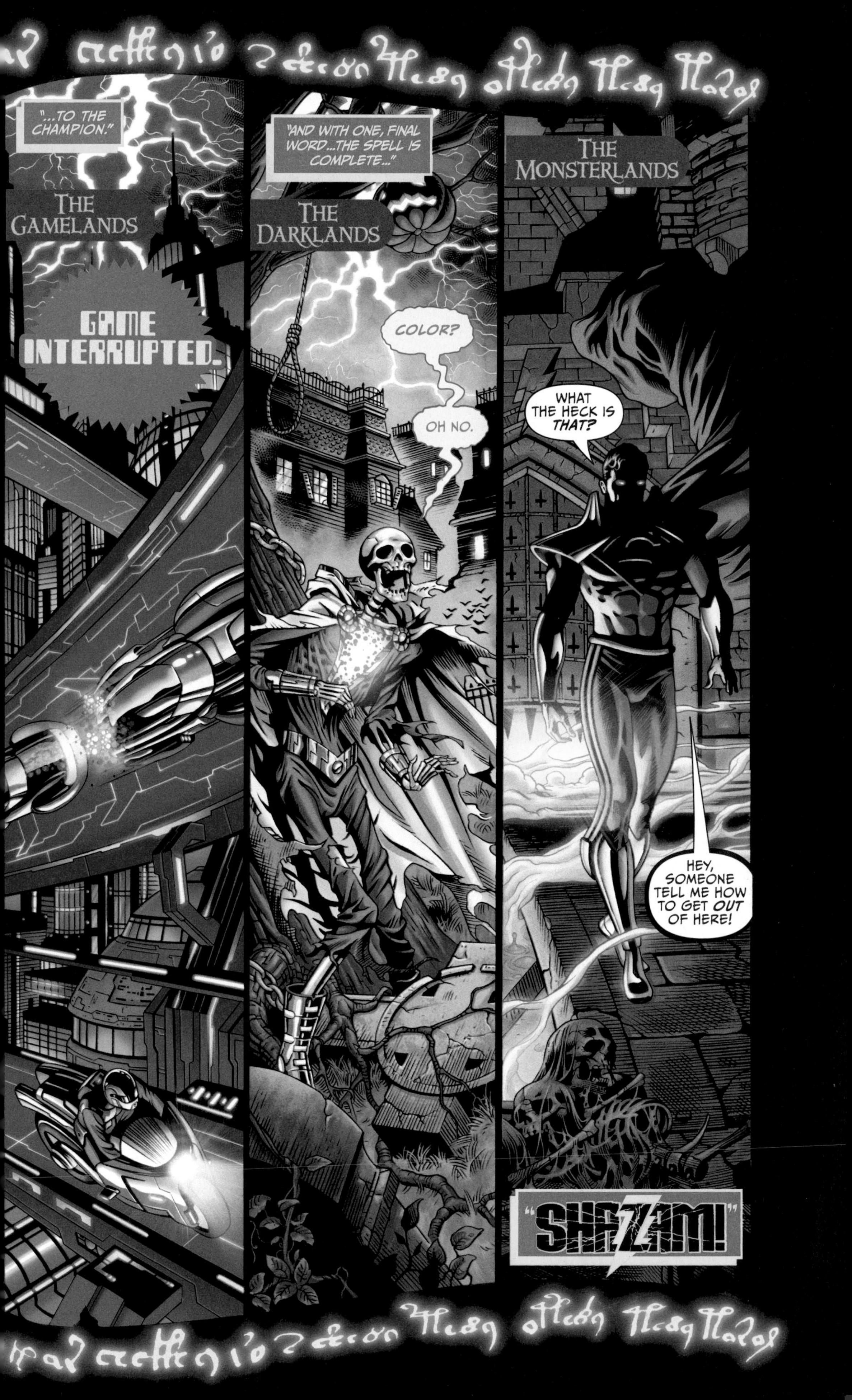
"...TO THE CHAMPION."
THE GAMELANDS
GAME INTERRUPTED.
"AND WITH ONE, FINAL WORD...THE SPELL IS COMPLETE..."
THE DARKLANDS
COLOR?
OH NO.
THE MONSTERLANDS
WHAT THE HECK IS THAT?
HEY, SOMEONE TELL ME HOW TO GET OUT OF HERE!
"SHAZAM!"

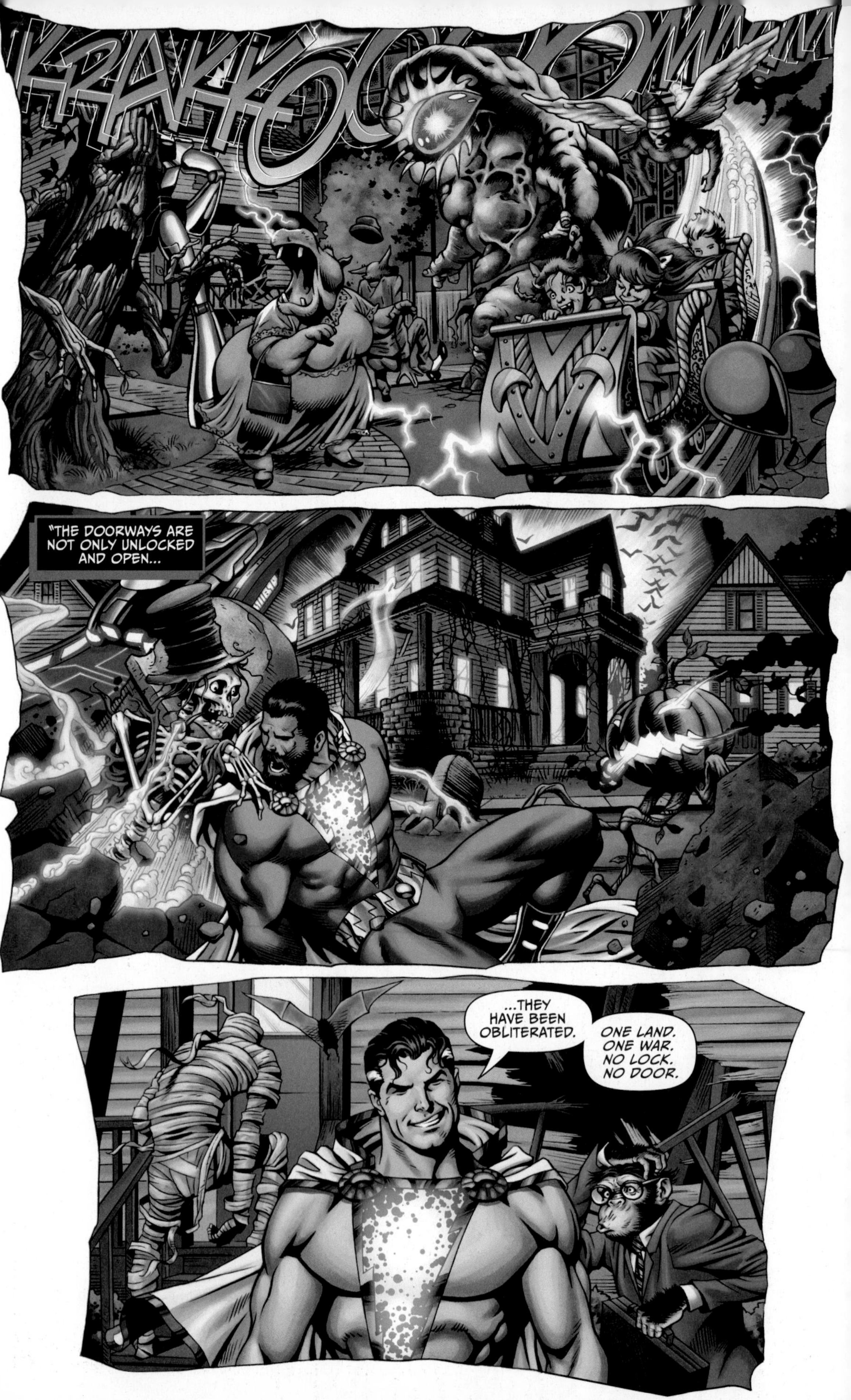
"THE DOORWAYS ARE NOT ONLY UNLOCKED AND OPEN...
...THEY HAVE BEEN OBLITERATED.
ONE LAND. ONE WAR. NO LOCK. NO DOOR.

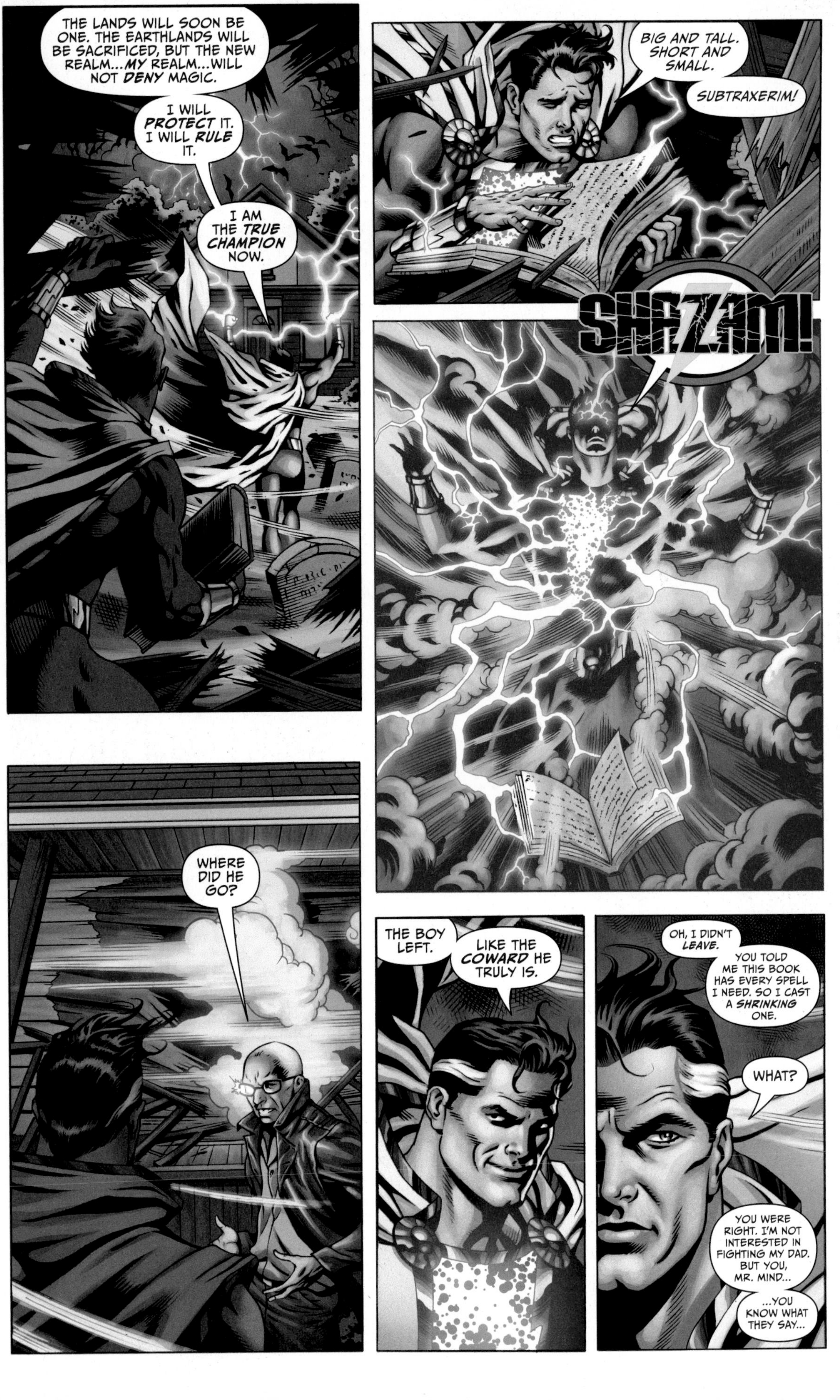

THE LANDS WILL SOON BE ONE. THE EARTHLANDS WILL BE SACRIFICED, BUT THE NEW REALM...MY REALM...WILL NOT DENY MAGIC.
I WILL PROTECT IT. I WILL RULE IT.
I AM THE TRUE CHAMPION NOW.
BIG AND TALL. SHORT AND SMALL.
SUBTRAXERIM!
SHAZAM!
WHERE DID HE GO?
THE BOY LEFT.
LIKE THE COWARD HE TRULY IS.
OH, I DIDN'T LEAVE.
YOU TOLD ME THIS BOOK HAS EVERY SPELL I NEED. SO I CAST A SHRINKING ONE.
WHAT?
YOU WERE RIGHT. I'M NOT INTERESTED IN FIGHTING MY DAD. BUT YOU, MR. MIND...
...YOU KNOW WHAT THEY SAY...

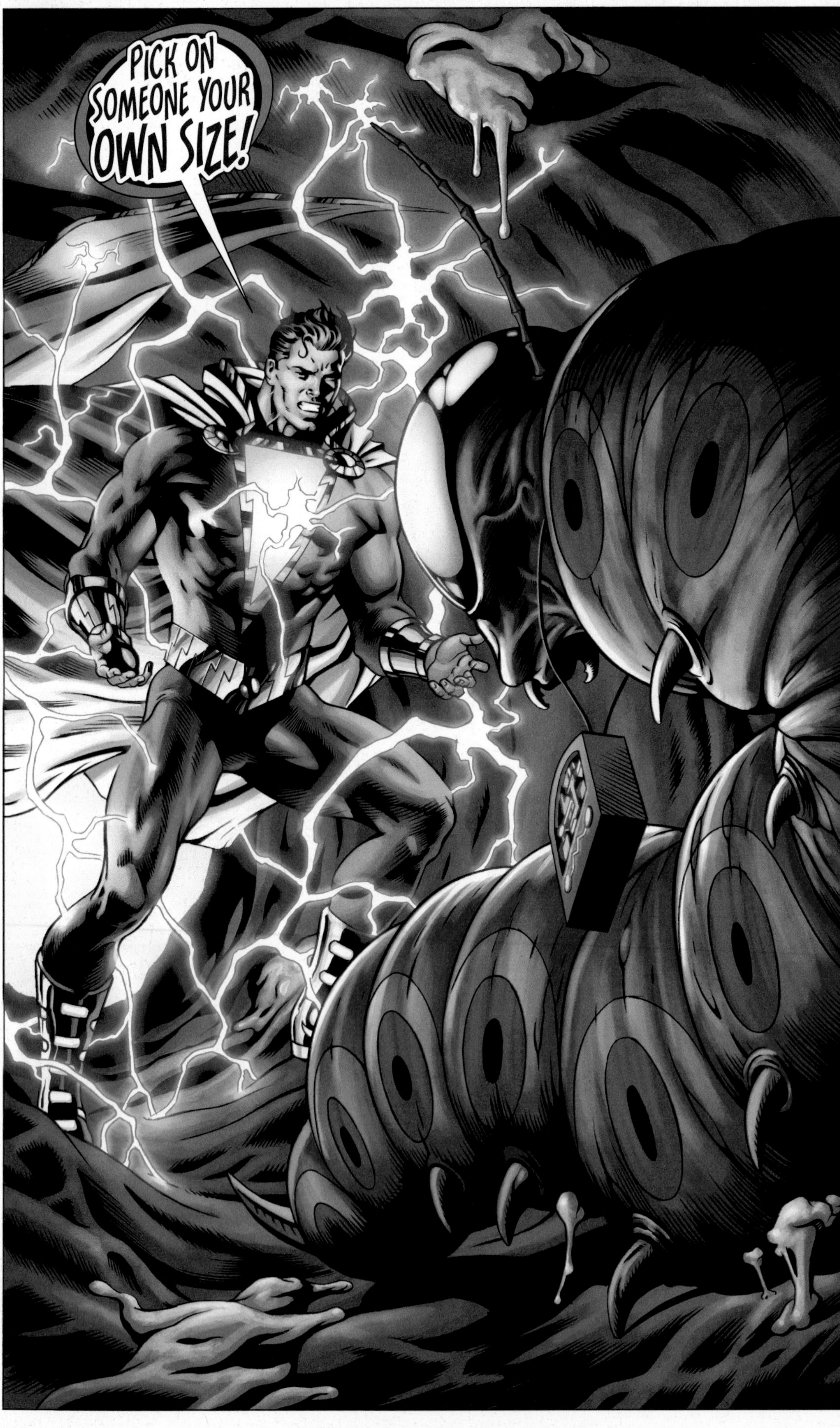
PICK ON SOMEONE YOUR OWN SIZE!

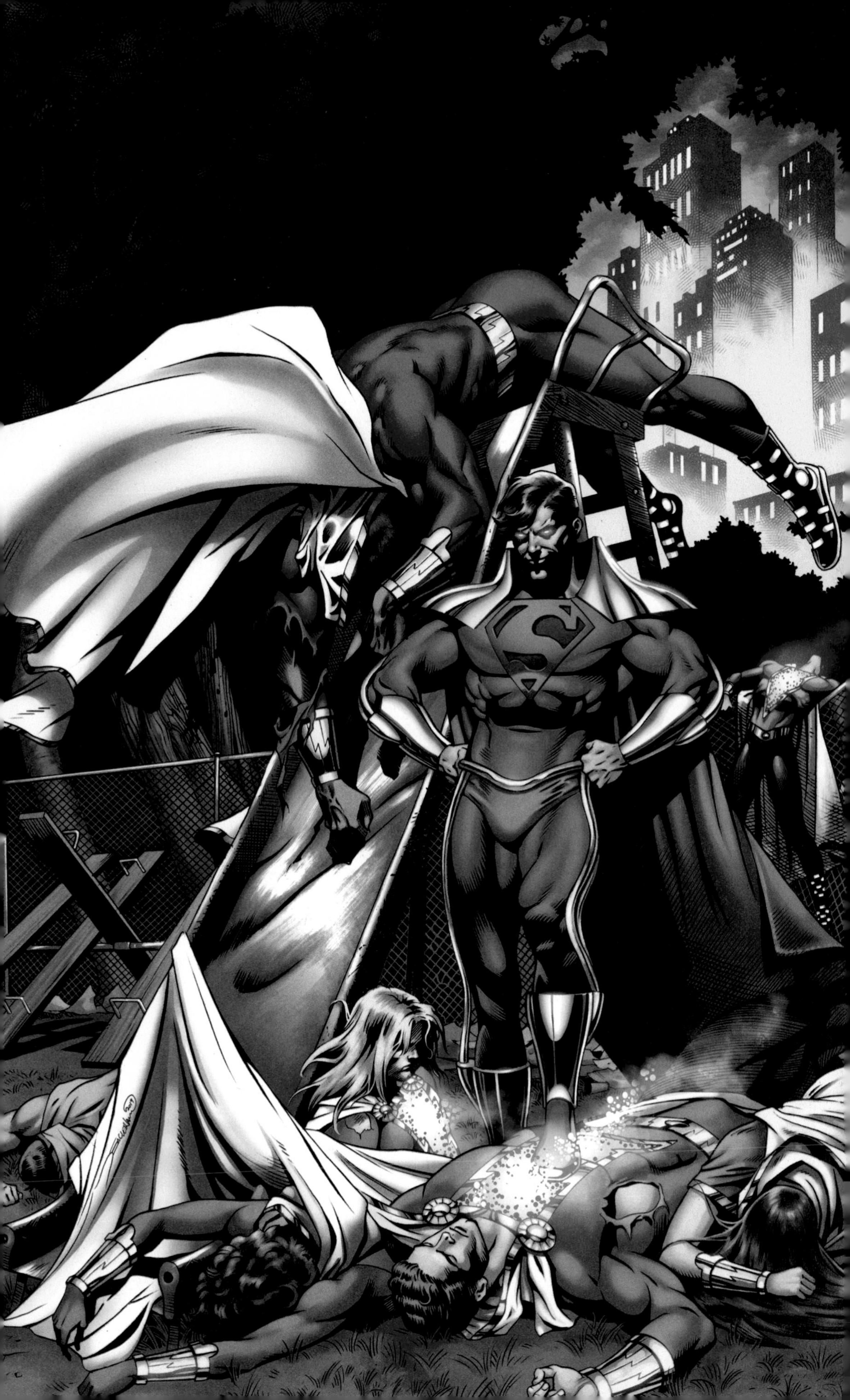

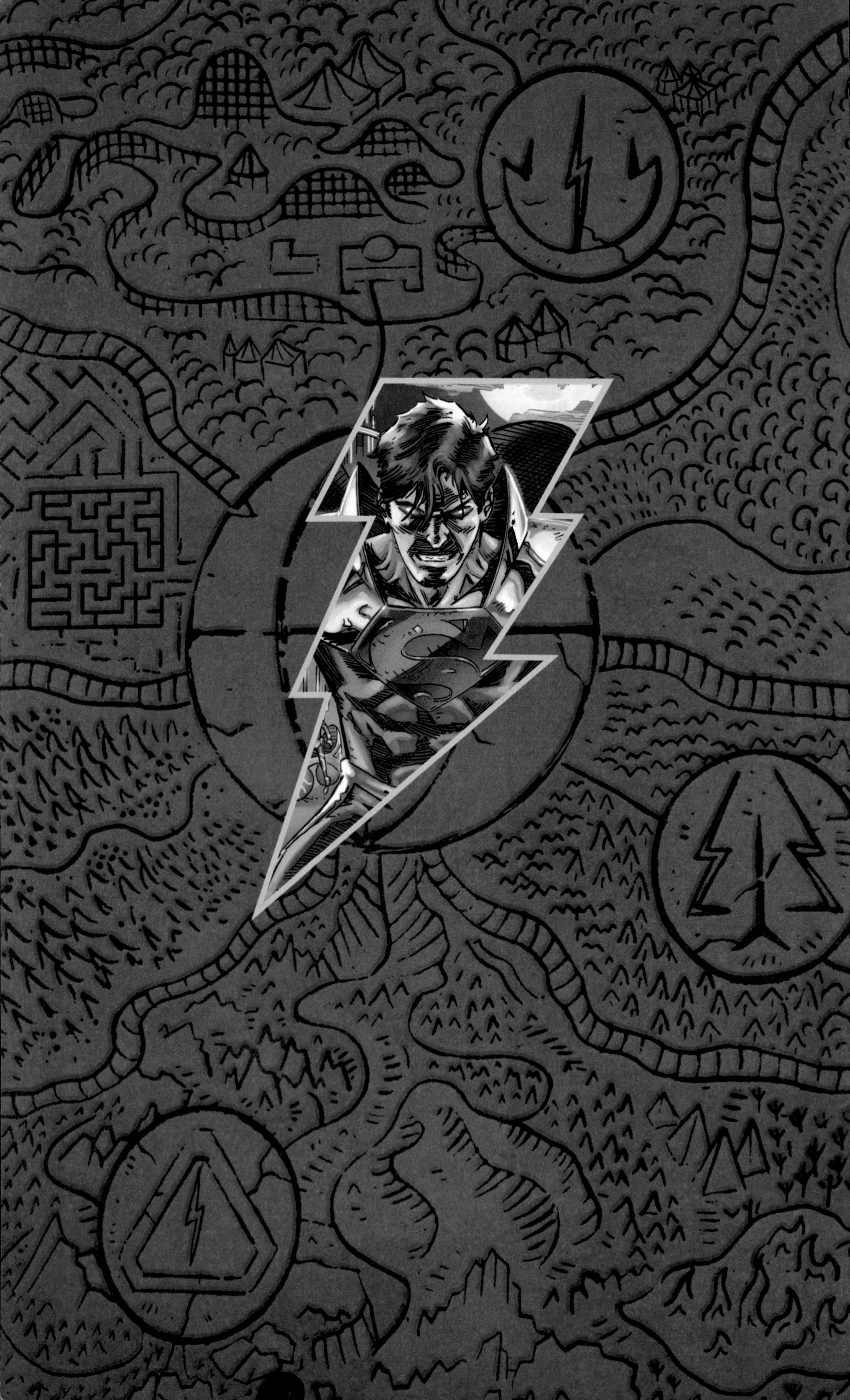

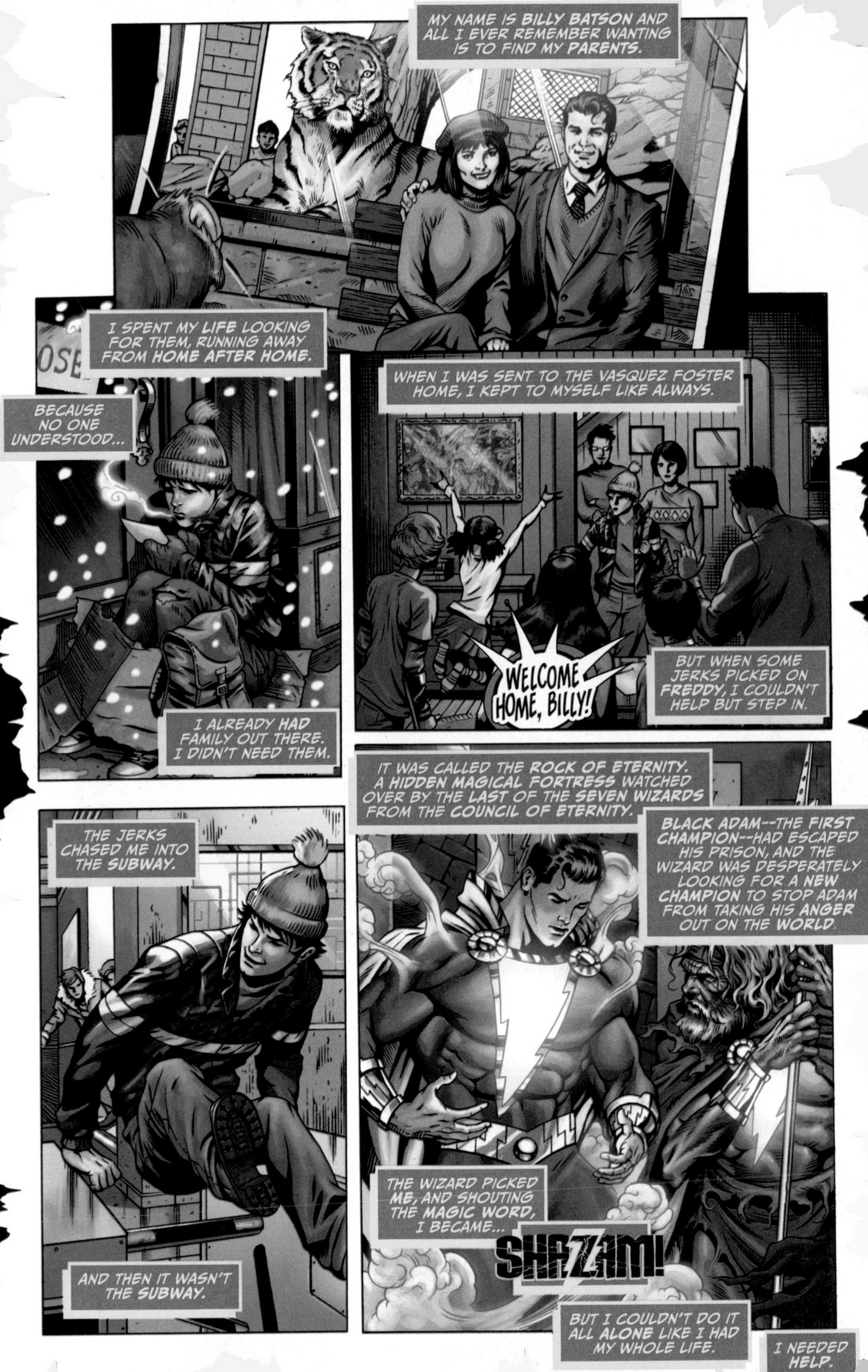
MY NAME IS BILLY BATSON AND ALL I EVER REMEMBER WANTING IS TO FIND MY PARENTS.
I SPENT MY LIFE LOOKING FOR THEM, RUNNING AWAY FROM HOME AFTER HOME.
BECAUSE NO ONE UNDERSTOOD...
I ALREADY HAD FAMILY OUT THERE. I DIDN'T NEED THEM.
WHEN I WAS SENT TO THE VASQUEZ FOSTER HOME, I KEPT TO MYSELF LIKE ALWAYS.
WELCOME HOME, BILLY!
BUT WHEN SOME JERKS PICKED ON FREDDY, I COULDN'T HELP BUT STEP IN.
THE JERKS CHASED ME INTO THE SUBWAY.
AND THEN IT WASN'T THE SUBWAY.
IT WAS CALLED THE ROCK OF ETERNITY. A HIDDEN MAGICAL FORTRESS WATCHED OVER BY THE LAST OF THE SEVEN WIZARDS FROM THE COUNCIL OF ETERNITY.
BLACK ADAM--THE FIRST CHAMPION--HAD ESCAPED HIS PRISON, AND THE WIZARD WAS DESPERATELY LOOKING FOR A NEW CHAMPION TO STOP ADAM FROM TAKING HIS ANGER OUT ON THE WORLD.
THE WIZARD PICKED ME, AND SHOUTING THE MAGIC WORD, I BECAME...
SHAZAM!
BUT I COULDN'T DO IT ALL ALONE LIKE I HAD MY WHOLE LIFE.
I NEEDED HELP.

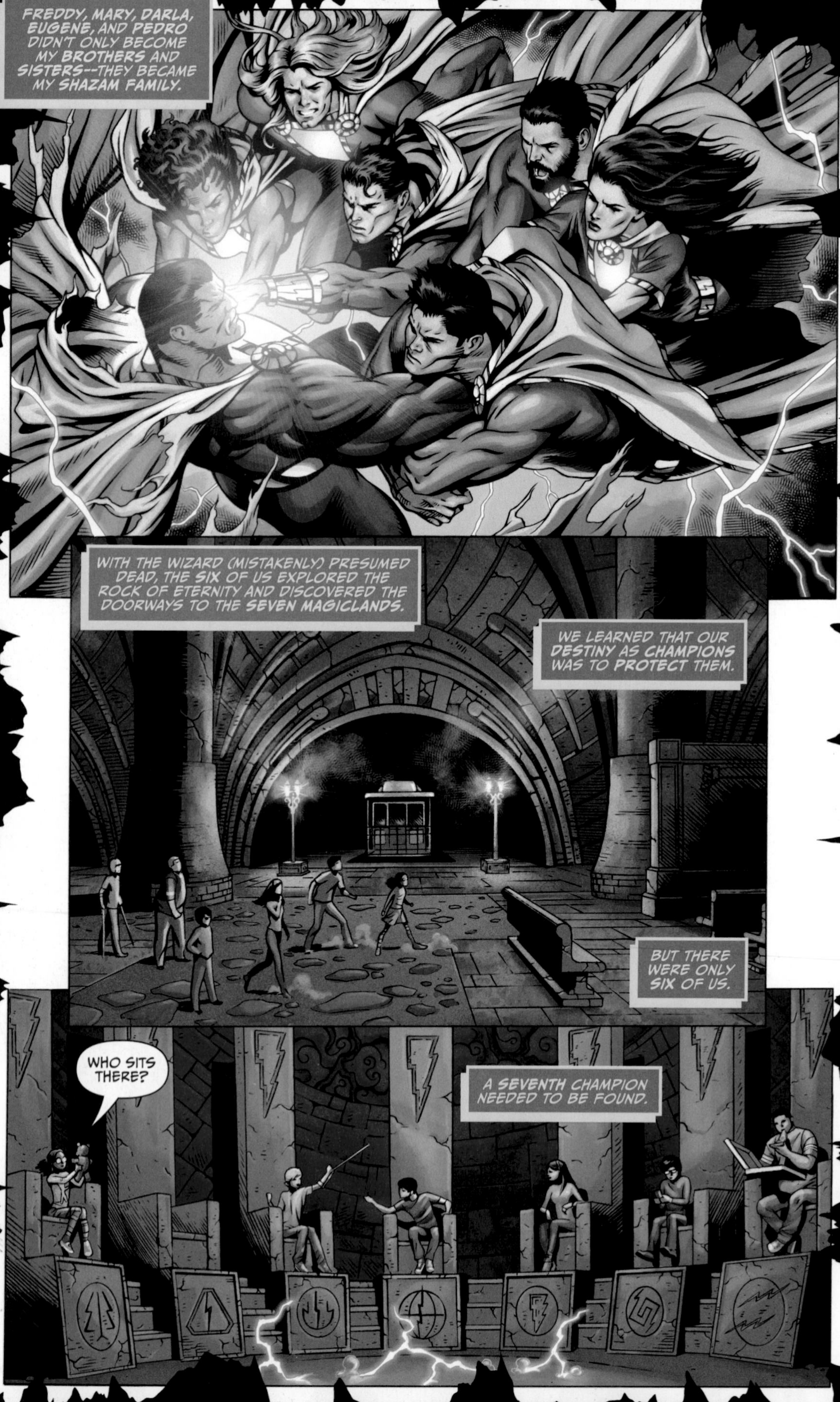

FREDDY, MARY, DARLA, EUGENE, AND PEDRO DIDN'T ONLY BECOME MY BROTHERS AND SISTERS--THEY BECAME MY SHAZAM FAMILY.
WITH THE WIZARD (MISTAKENLY) PRESUMED DEAD, THE SIX OF US EXPLORED THE ROCK OF ETERNITY AND DISCOVERED THE DOORWAYS TO THE SEVEN MAGICLANDS.
WE LEARNED THAT OUR DESTINY AS CHAMPIONS WAS TO PROTECT THEM.
BUT THERE WERE ONLY SIX OF US.
WHO SITS THERE?
A SEVENTH CHAMPION NEEDED TO BE FOUND.

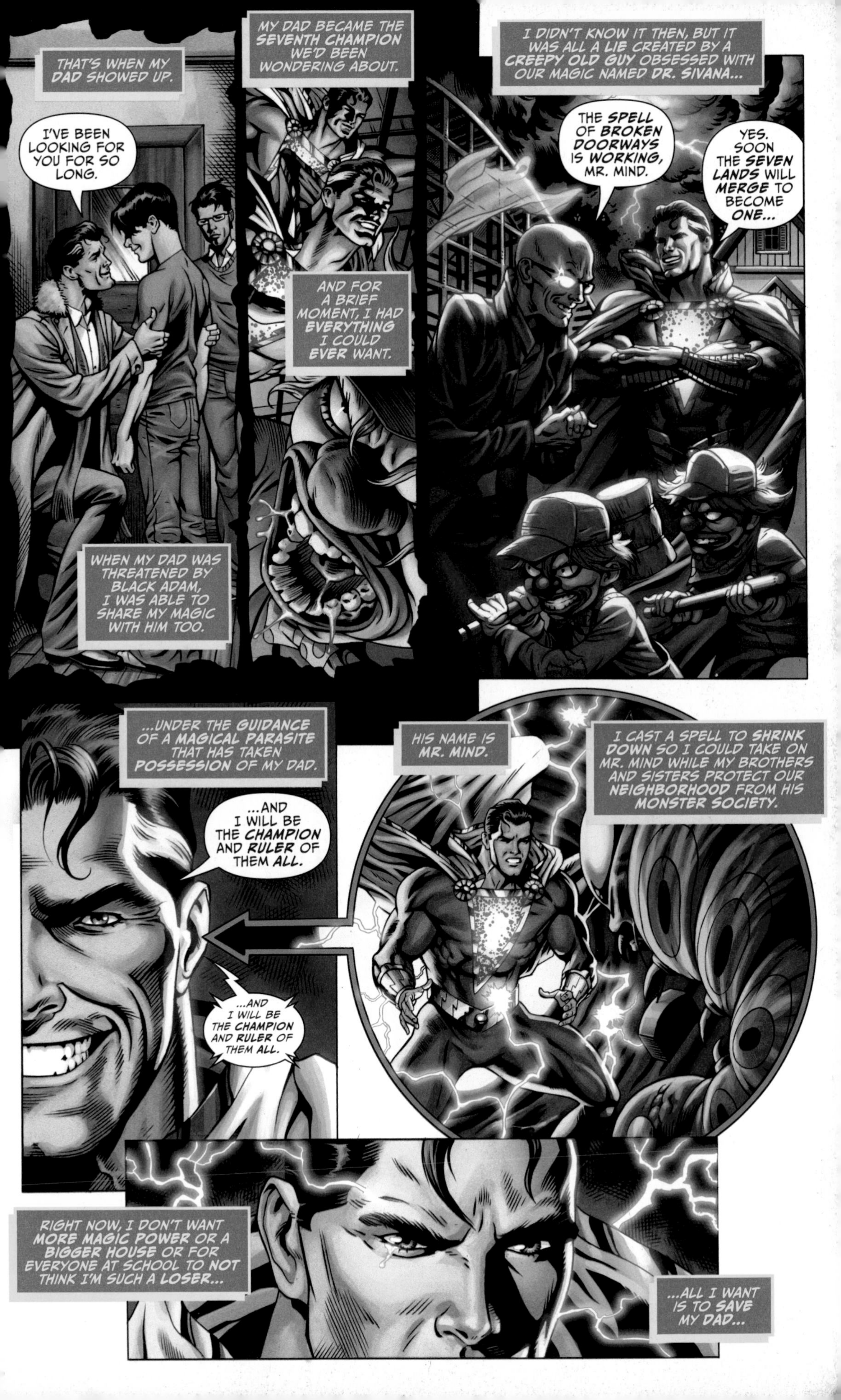

THAT'S WHEN MY DAD SHOWED UP.
I'VE BEEN LOOKING FOR YOU FOR SO LONG.
WHEN MY DAD WAS THREATENED BY BLACK ADAM, I WAS ABLE TO SHARE MY MAGIC WITH HIM TOO.
MY DAD BECAME THE SEVENTH CHAMPION WE'D BEEN WONDERING ABOUT.
AND FOR A BRIEF MOMENT, I HAD EVERYTHING I COULD EVER WANT.
I DIDN'T KNOW IT THEN, BUT IT WAS ALL A LIE CREATED BY A CREEPY OLD GUY OBSESSED WITH OUR MAGIC NAMED DR. SIVANA...
THE SPELL OF BROKEN DOORWAYS IS WORKING, MR. MIND.
YES. SOON THE SEVEN LANDS WILL MERGE TO BECOME ONE...
...UNDER THE GUIDANCE OF A MAGICAL PARASITE THAT HAS TAKEN POSSESSION OF MY DAD.
...AND I WILL BE THE CHAMPION AND RULER OF THEM ALL.
...AND I WILL BE THE CHAMPION AND RULER OF THEM ALL.
HIS NAME IS MR. MIND.
I CAST A SPELL TO SHRINK DOWN SO I COULD TAKE ON MR. MIND WHILE MY BROTHERS AND SISTERS PROTECT OUR NEIGHBORHOOD FROM HIS MONSTER SOCIETY.
RIGHT NOW, I DON'T WANT MORE MAGIC POWER OR A BIGGER HOUSE OR FOR EVERYONE AT SCHOOL TO NOT THINK I'M SUCH A LOSER...
...ALL I WANT IS TO SAVE MY DAD...

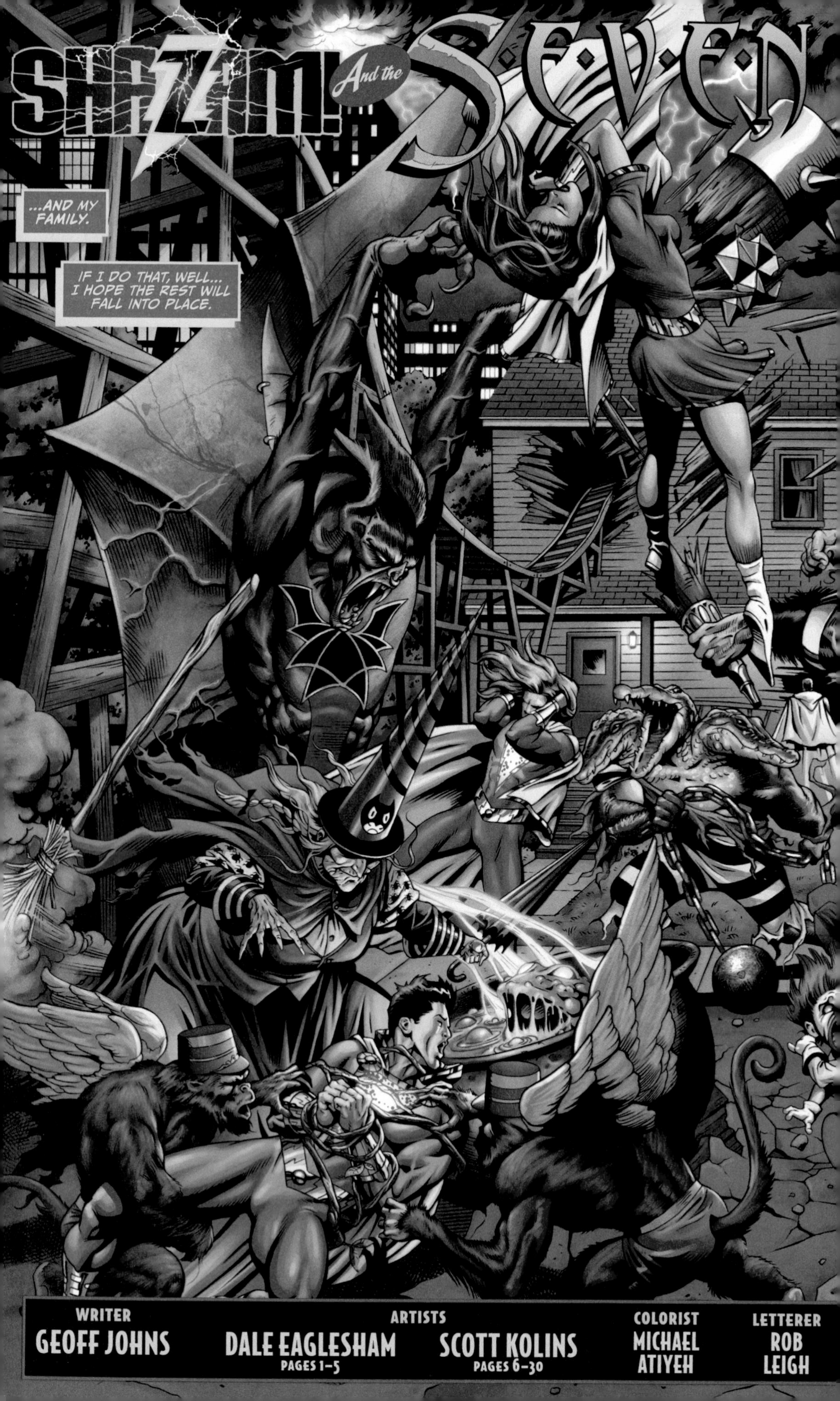

SHAZAM! And the SEVEN
...AND MY FAMILY.
IF I DO THAT, WELL... I HOPE THE REST WILL FALL INTO PLACE.
WRITER GEOFF JOHNS
ARTISTS DALE EAGLESHAM PAGES 1–5 SCOTT KOLINS PAGES 6–30
COLORIST MICHAEL ATIYEH
LETTERER ROB LEIGH

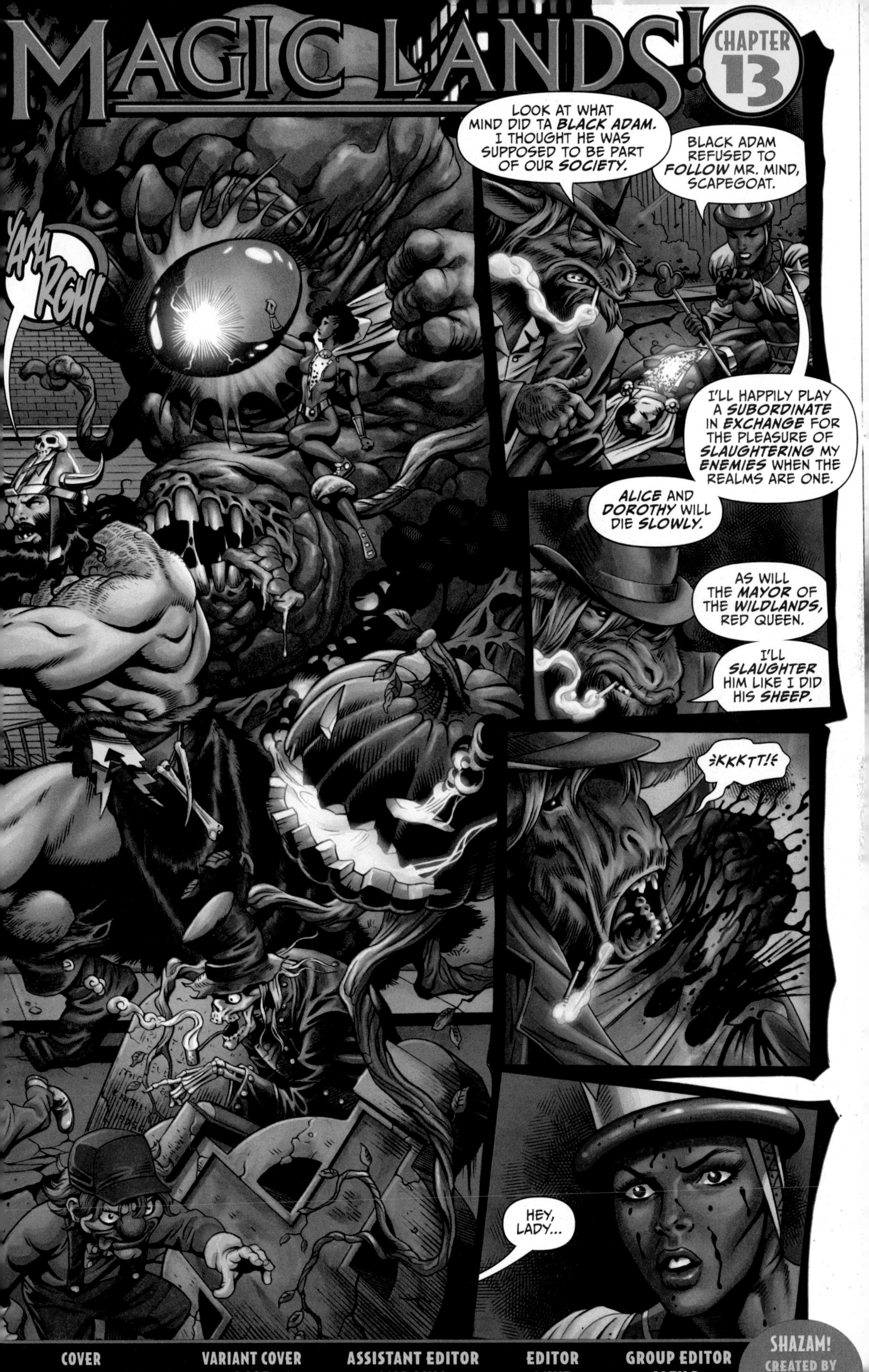
MAGIC LANDS!
CHAPTER 13
YAAARGH!
LOOK AT WHAT MIND DID TA BLACK ADAM. I THOUGHT HE WAS SUPPOSED TO BE PART OF OUR SOCIETY.
BLACK ADAM REFUSED TO FOLLOW MR. MIND, SCAPEGOAT.
I'LL HAPPILY PLAY A SUBORDINATE IN EXCHANGE FOR THE PLEASURE OF SLAUGHTERING MY ENEMIES WHEN THE REALMS ARE ONE.
ALICE AND DOROTHY WILL DIE SLOWLY.
AS WILL THE MAYOR OF THE WILDLANDS, RED QUEEN.
I'LL SLAUGHTER HIM LIKE I DID HIS SHEEP.
KKKTT!
HEY, LADY...

COVER DALE EAGLESHAM WITH MICHAEL ATIYEH | VARIANT COVER DALE KEOWN | ASSISTANT EDITOR MARQUIS DRAPER | EDITOR MIKE COTTON | GROUP EDITOR ALEX R. CARR | SHAZAM! CREATED BY BILL PARKER & C.C. BECK

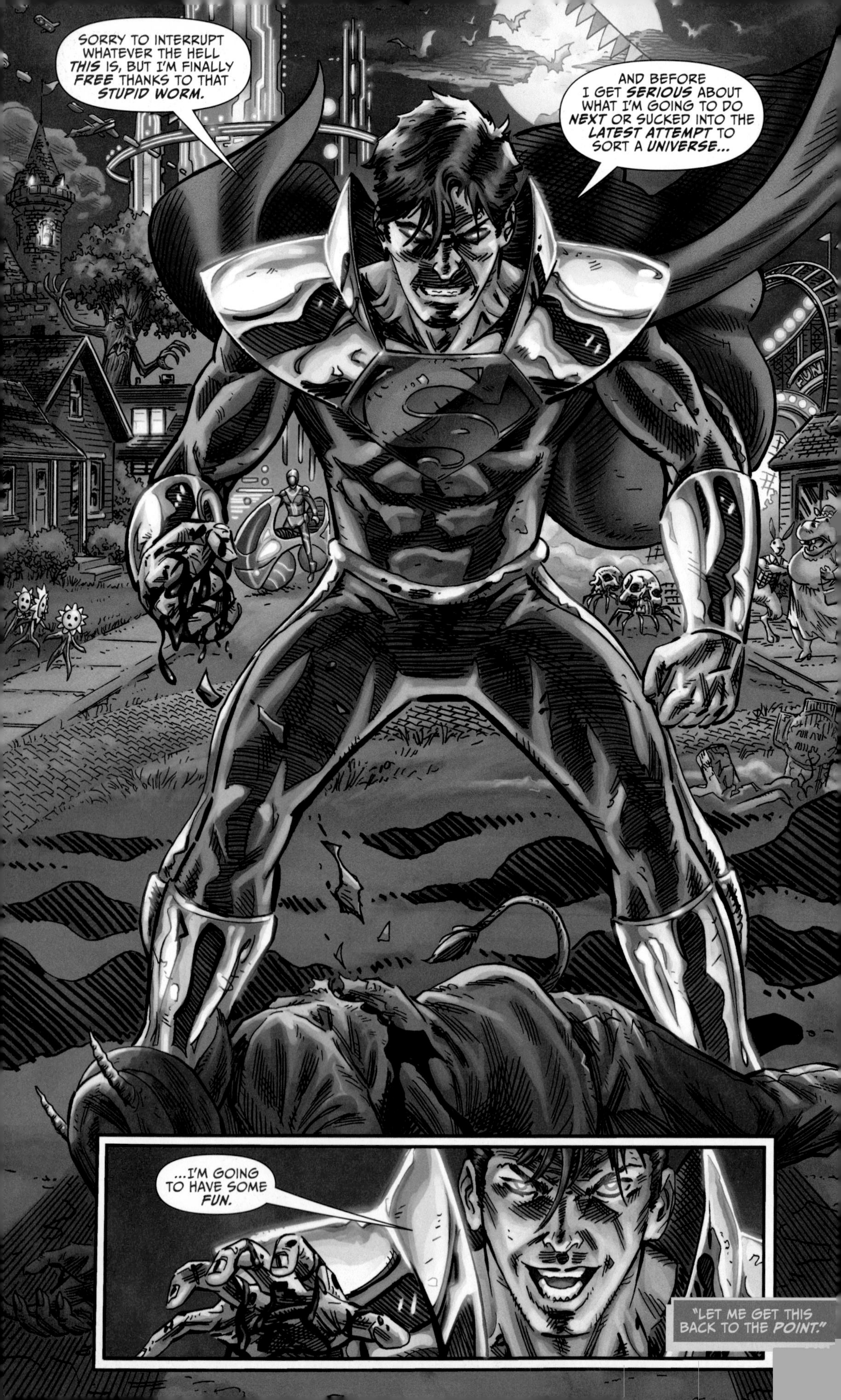
SORRY TO INTERRUPT WHATEVER THE HELL *THIS* IS, BUT I'M FINALLY *FREE* THANKS TO THAT *STUPID WORM.*
AND BEFORE I GET *SERIOUS* ABOUT WHAT I'M GOING TO DO *NEXT* OR SUCKED INTO THE *LATEST ATTEMPT* TO SORT A *UNIVERSE*...
...I'M GOING TO HAVE SOME *FUN.*
"LET ME GET THIS BACK TO THE *POINT.*"

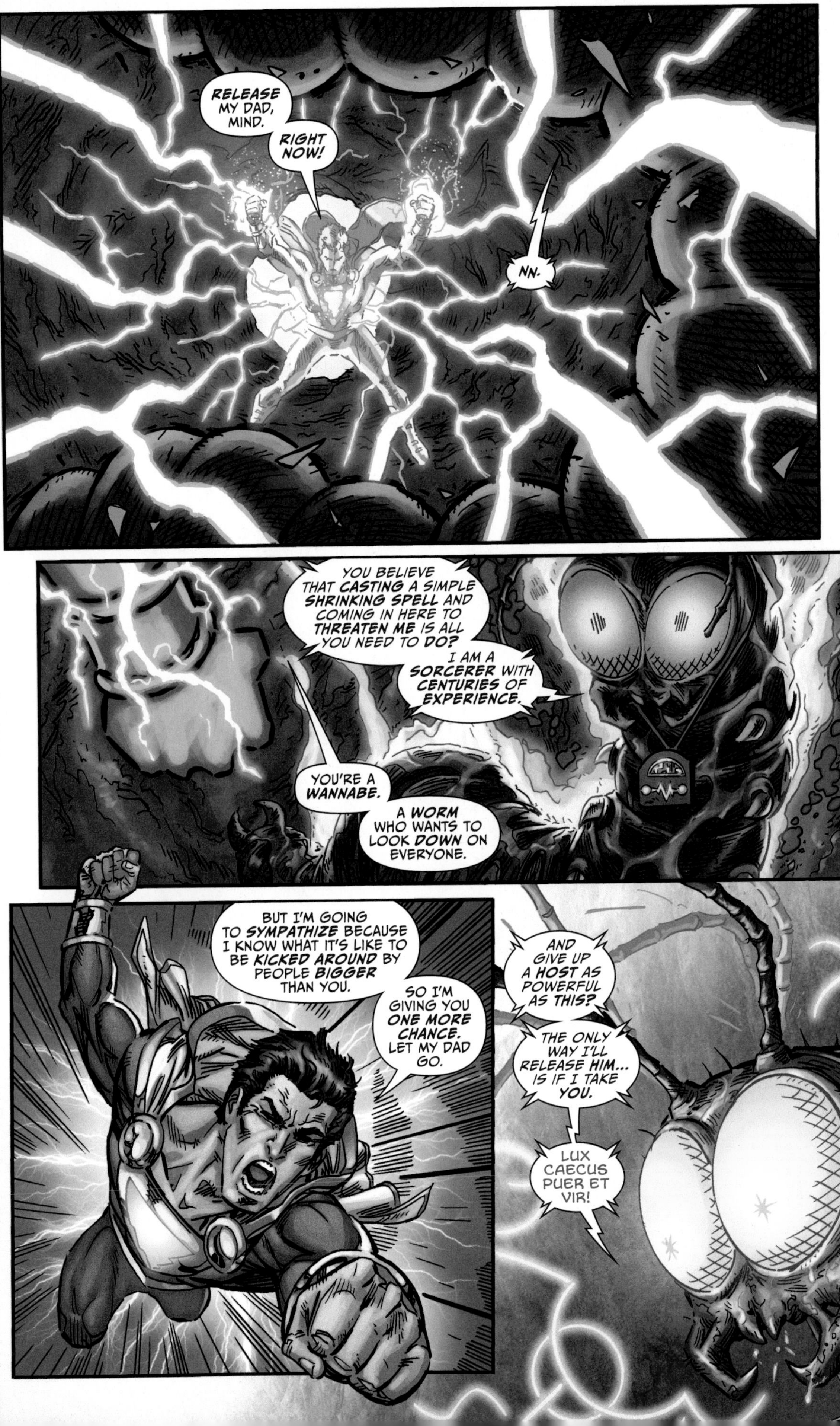
RELEASE MY DAD, MIND.
RIGHT NOW!
NN.
YOU BELIEVE THAT CASTING A SIMPLE SHRINKING SPELL AND COMING IN HERE TO THREATEN ME IS ALL YOU NEED TO DO?
I AM A SORCERER WITH CENTURIES OF EXPERIENCE.
YOU'RE A WANNABE.
A WORM WHO WANTS TO LOOK DOWN ON EVERYONE.
BUT I'M GOING TO SYMPATHIZE BECAUSE I KNOW WHAT IT'S LIKE TO BE KICKED AROUND BY PEOPLE BIGGER THAN YOU.
SO I'M GIVING YOU ONE MORE CHANCE. LET MY DAD GO.
AND GIVE UP A HOST AS POWERFUL AS THIS?
THE ONLY WAY I'LL RELEASE HIM... IS IF I TAKE YOU.
LUX CAECUS PUER ET VIR!

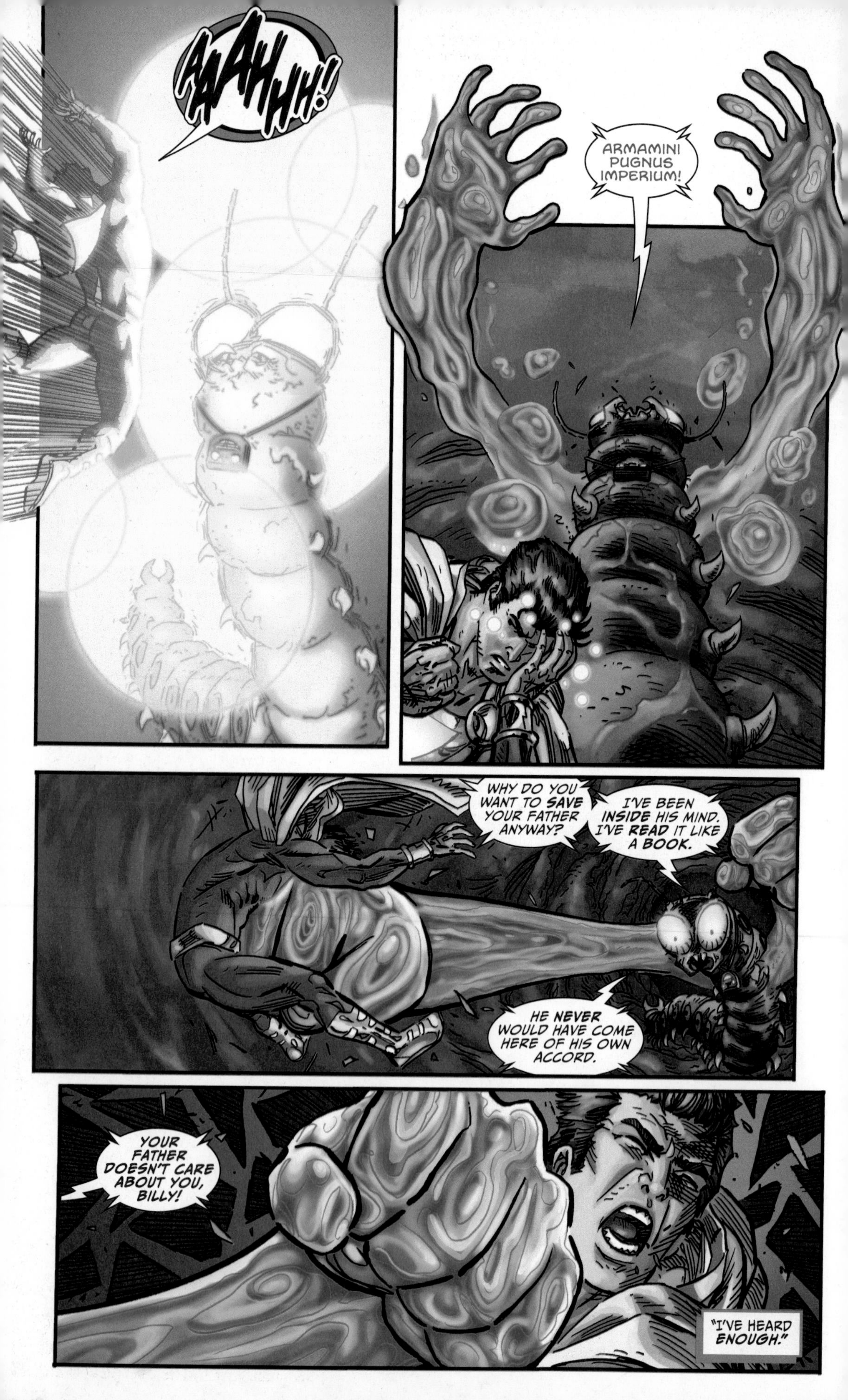
AAAHHH!
ARMAMINI PUGNUS IMPERIUM!
WHY DO YOU WANT TO SAVE YOUR FATHER ANYWAY?
I'VE BEEN INSIDE HIS MIND. I'VE READ IT LIKE A BOOK.
HE NEVER WOULD HAVE COME HERE OF HIS OWN ACCORD.
YOUR FATHER DOESN'T CARE ABOUT YOU, BILLY!
"I'VE HEARD ENOUGH."

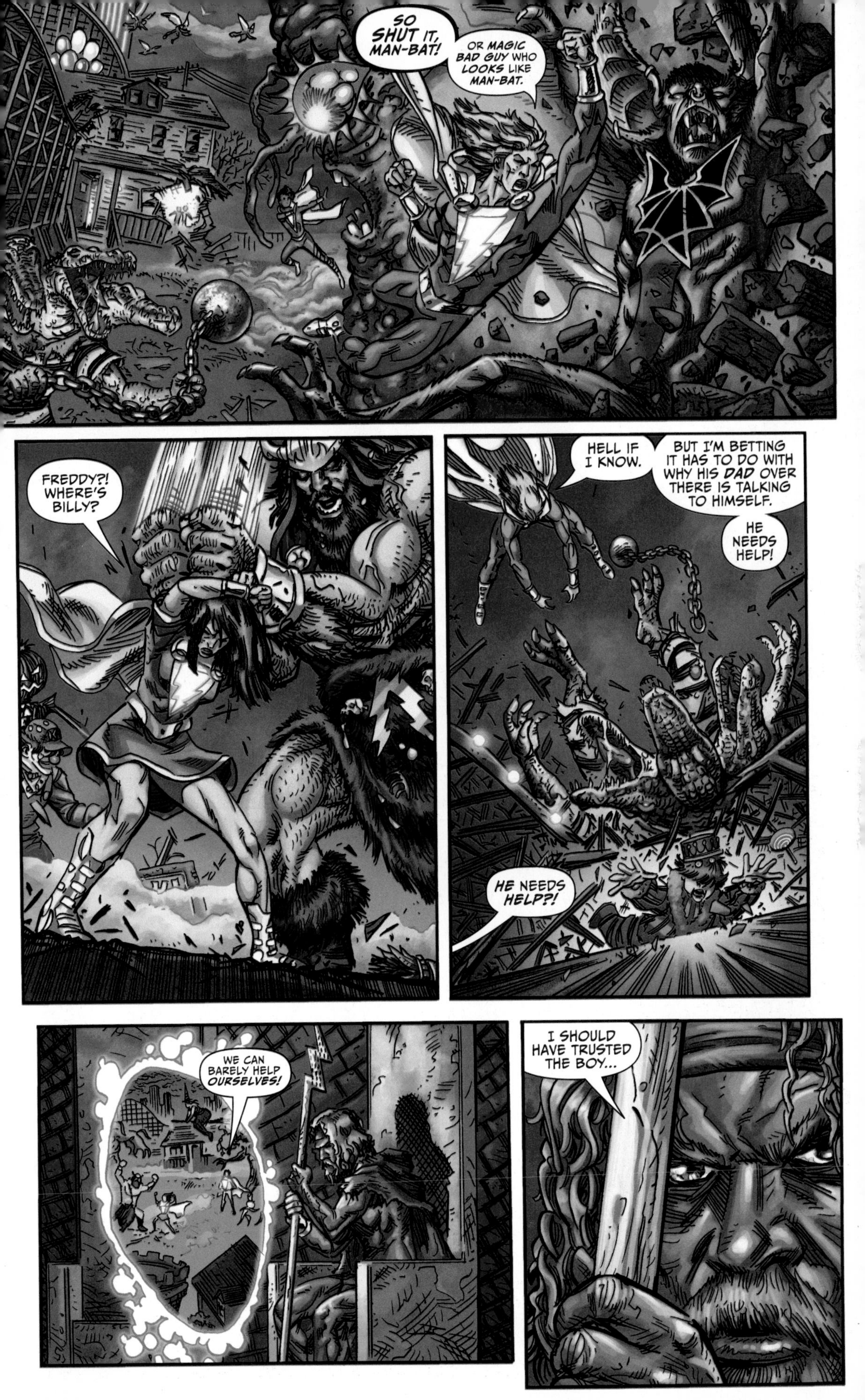
SO SHUT IT, MAN-BAT!
OR MAGIC BAD GUY WHO LOOKS LIKE MAN-BAT.
FREDDY?! WHERE'S BILLY?
HELL IF I KNOW.
BUT I'M BETTING IT HAS TO DO WITH WHY HIS DAD OVER THERE IS TALKING TO HIMSELF.
HE NEEDS HELP!
HE NEEDS HELP?!
WE CAN BARELY HELP OURSELVES!
I SHOULD HAVE TRUSTED THE BOY...

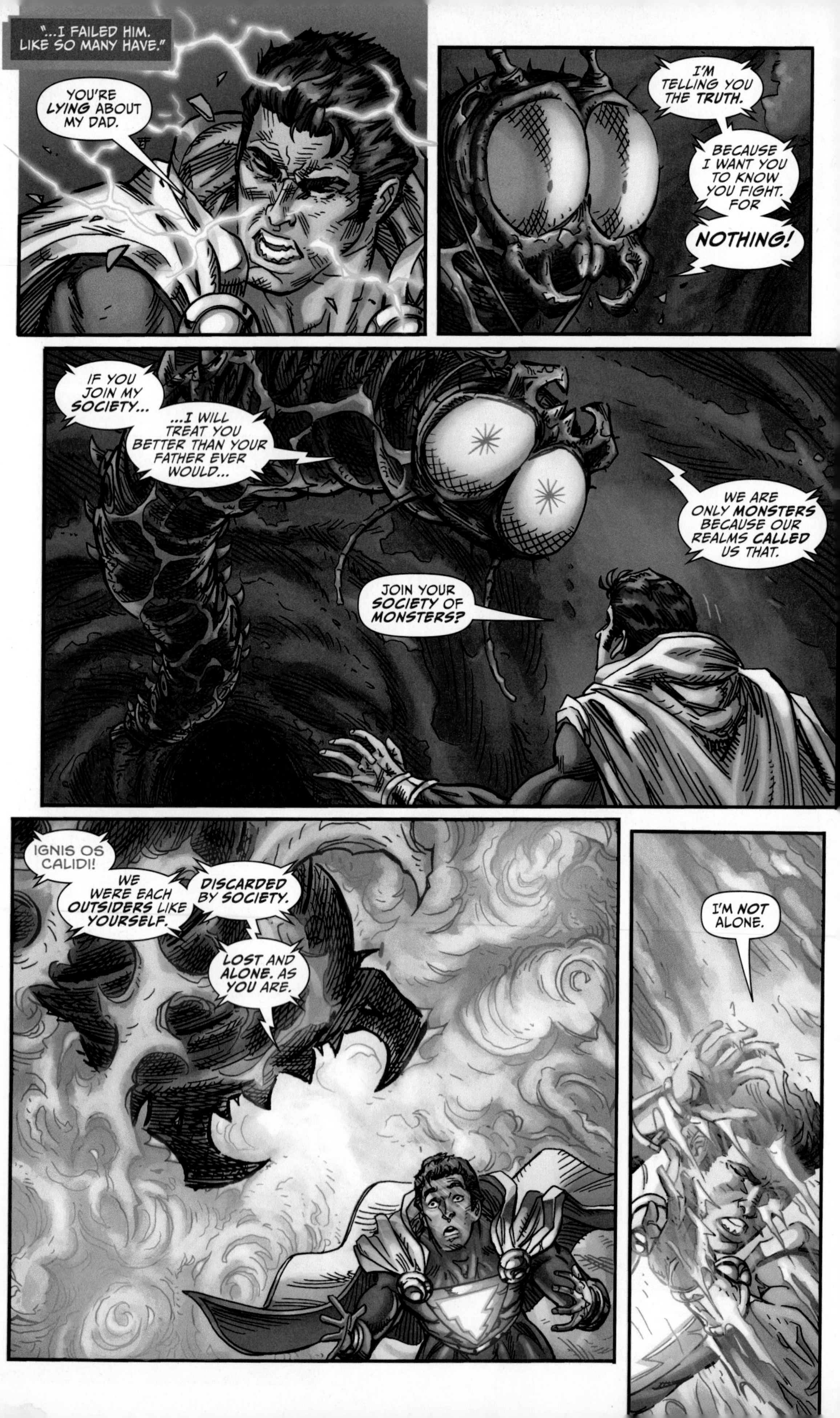
"...I FAILED HIM. LIKE SO MANY HAVE."
YOU'RE LYING ABOUT MY DAD.
I'M TELLING YOU THE TRUTH.
BECAUSE I WANT YOU TO KNOW YOU FIGHT. FOR
NOTHING!
IF YOU JOIN MY SOCIETY...
...I WILL TREAT YOU BETTER THAN YOUR FATHER EVER WOULD...
WE ARE ONLY MONSTERS BECAUSE OUR REALMS CALLED US THAT.
JOIN YOUR SOCIETY OF MONSTERS?
IGNIS OS CALIDI!
WE WERE EACH OUTSIDERS LIKE YOURSELF.
DISCARDED BY SOCIETY.
LOST AND ALONE. AS YOU ARE.
I'M NOT ALONE.

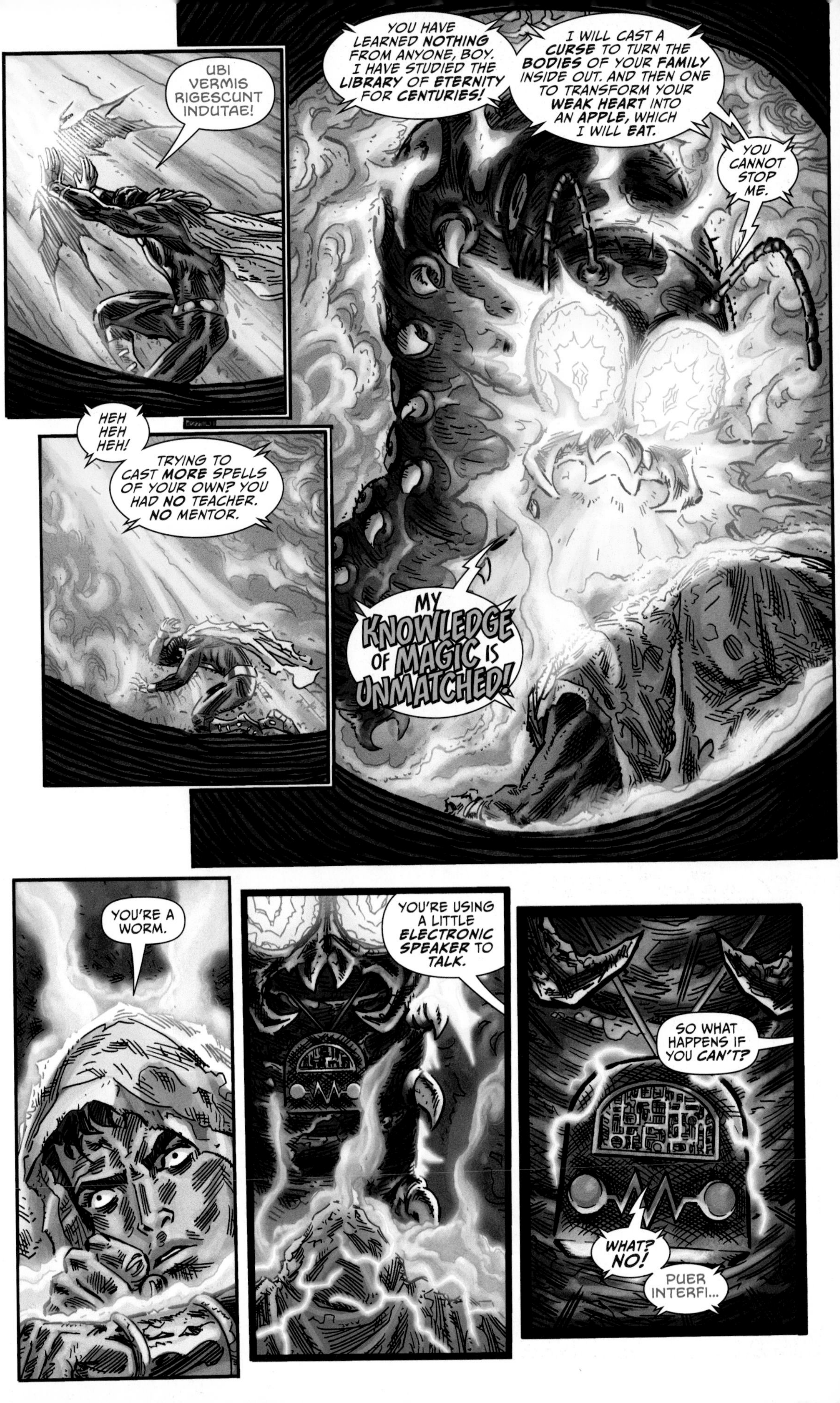
UBI VERMIS RIGESCUNT INDUTAE!
HEH HEH HEH!
TRYING TO CAST MORE SPELLS OF YOUR OWN? YOU HAD NO TEACHER. NO MENTOR.
YOU HAVE LEARNED NOTHING FROM ANYONE, BOY. I HAVE STUDIED THE LIBRARY OF ETERNITY FOR CENTURIES!
I WILL CAST A CURSE TO TURN THE BODIES OF YOUR FAMILY INSIDE OUT. AND THEN ONE TO TRANSFORM YOUR WEAK HEART INTO AN APPLE, WHICH I WILL EAT.
YOU CANNOT STOP ME.
MY KNOWLEDGE OF MAGIC IS UNMATCHED!
YOU'RE A WORM.
YOU'RE USING A LITTLE ELECTRONIC SPEAKER TO TALK.
SO WHAT HAPPENS IF YOU CAN'T?
WHAT? NO!
PUER INTERFI...

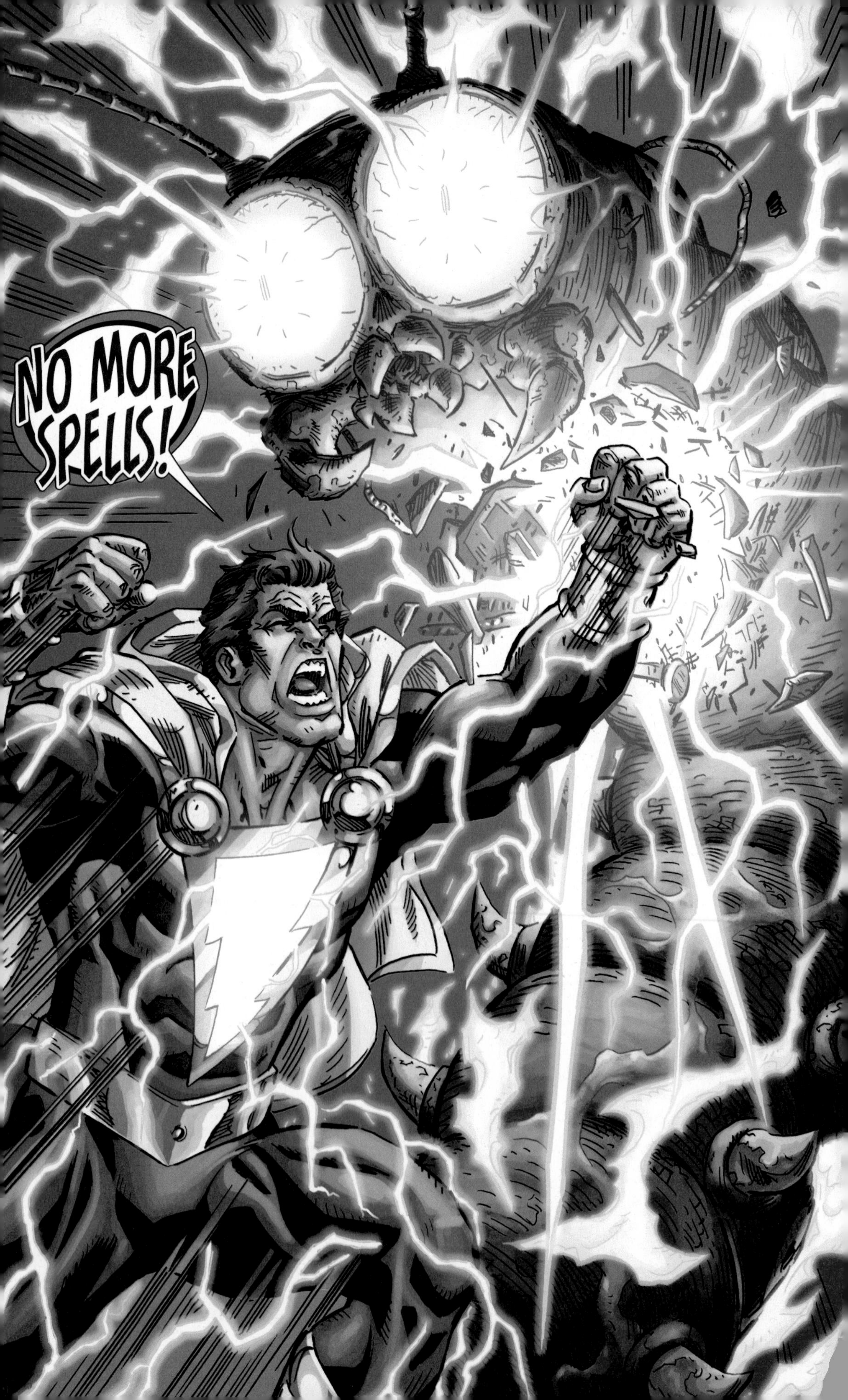
NO MORE SPELLS!

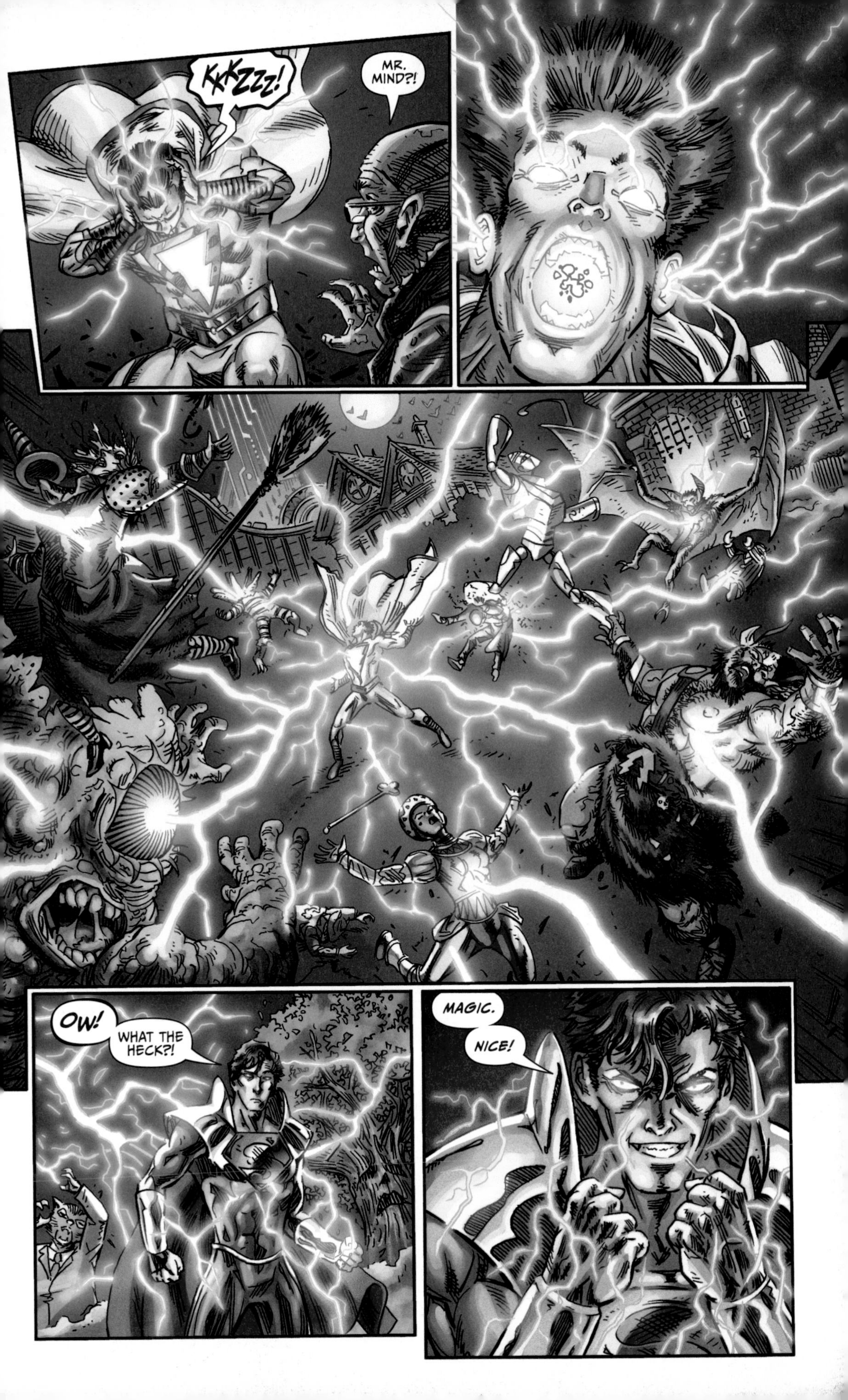
KKKZZZ!
MR. MIND?!
OW!
WHAT THE HECK?!
MAGIC.
NICE!

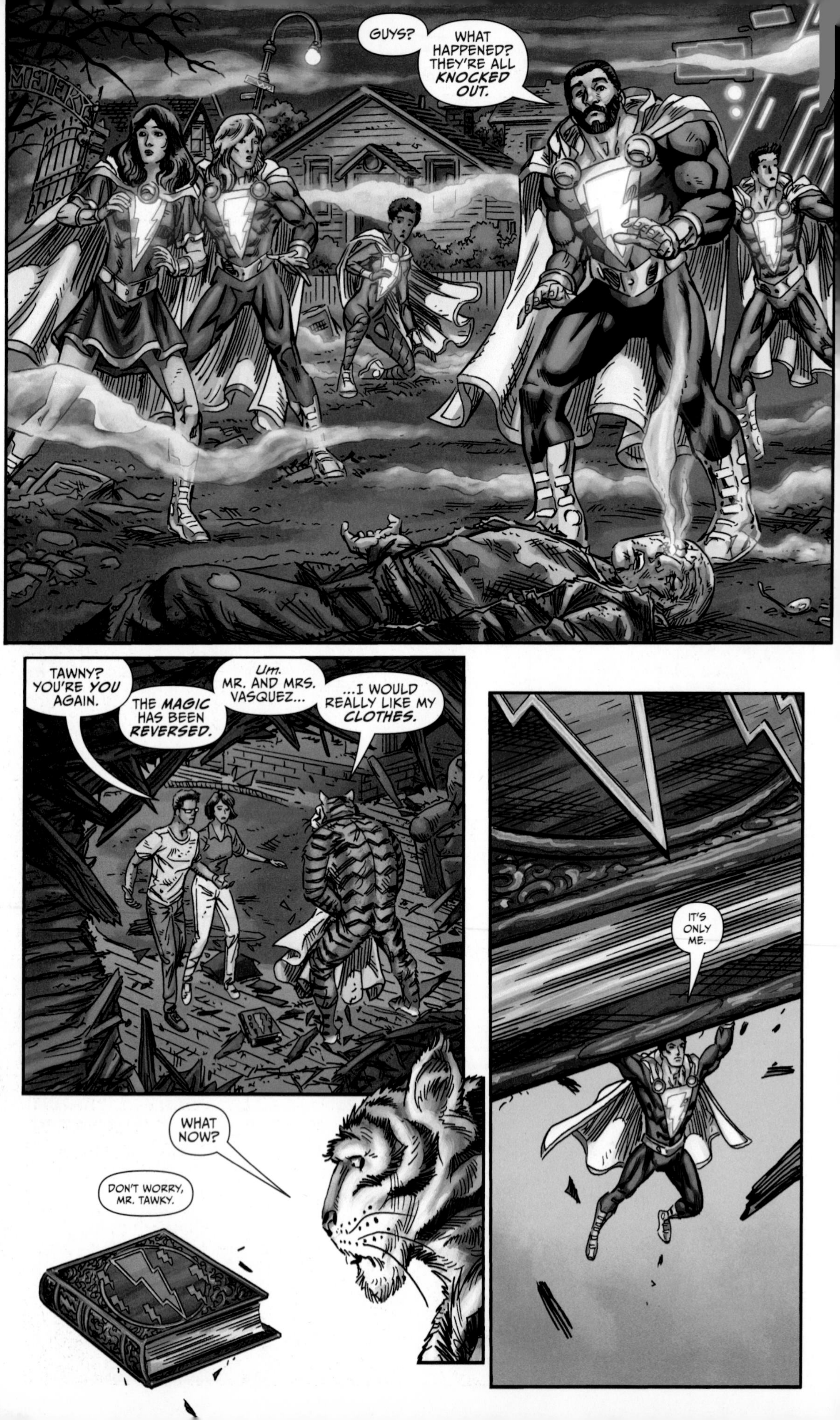
GUYS?
WHAT HAPPENED? THEY'RE ALL KNOCKED OUT.
TAWNY? YOU'RE YOU AGAIN.
THE MAGIC HAS BEEN REVERSED.
Um. MR. AND MRS. VASQUEZ...
...I WOULD REALLY LIKE MY CLOTHES.
IT'S ONLY ME.
WHAT NOW?
DON'T WORRY, MR. TAWKY.

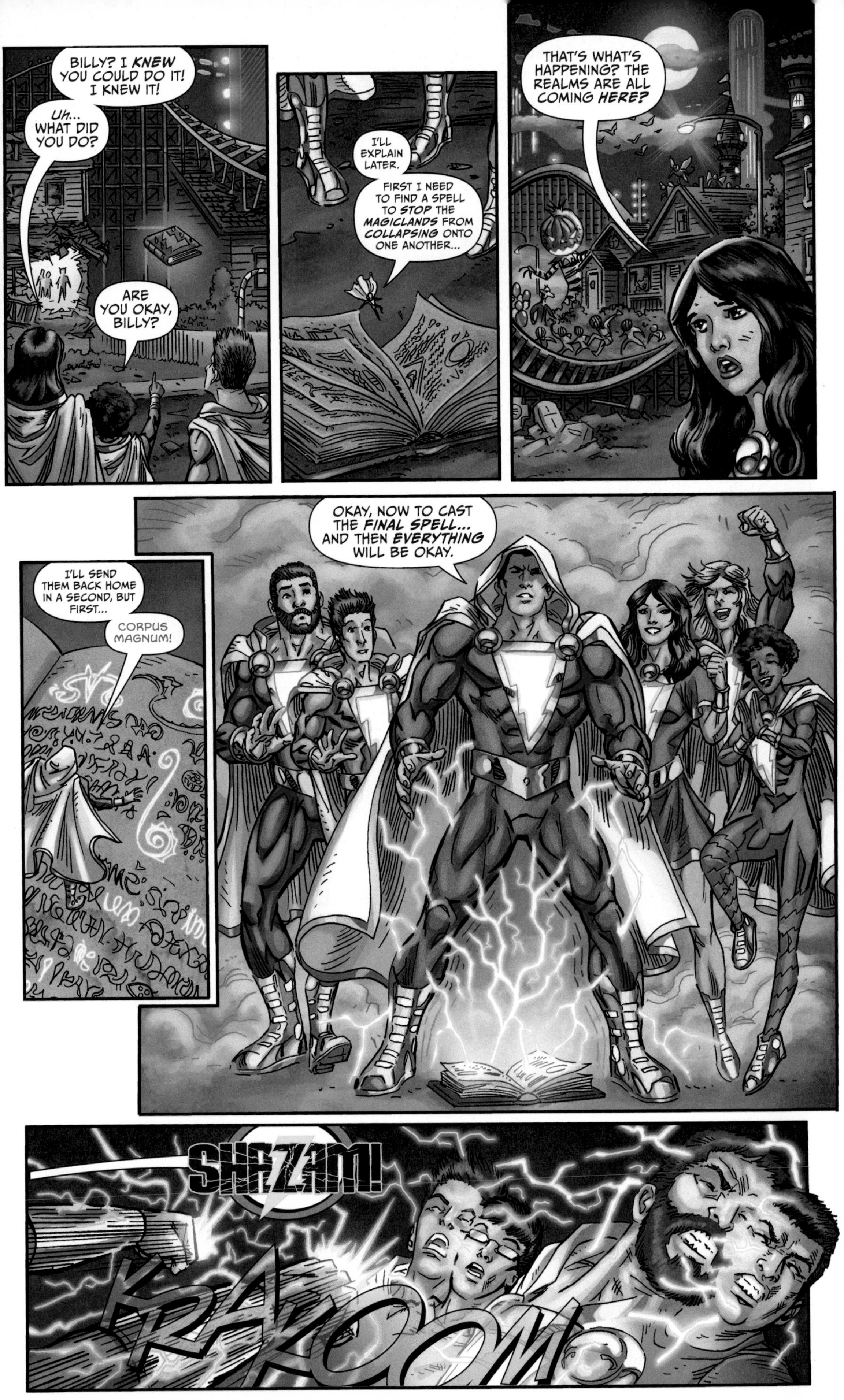

BILLY? I KNEW YOU COULD DO IT! I KNEW IT!
Uh... WHAT DID YOU DO?
ARE YOU OKAY, BILLY?
I'LL EXPLAIN LATER.
FIRST I NEED TO FIND A SPELL TO STOP THE MAGICLANDS FROM COLLAPSING ONTO ONE ANOTHER...
THAT'S WHAT'S HAPPENING? THE REALMS ARE ALL COMING HERE?
I'LL SEND THEM BACK HOME IN A SECOND, BUT FIRST...
CORPUS MAGNUM!
OKAY, NOW TO CAST THE FINAL SPELL... AND THEN EVERYTHING WILL BE OKAY.
SHAZAM!
KRAKOOM!

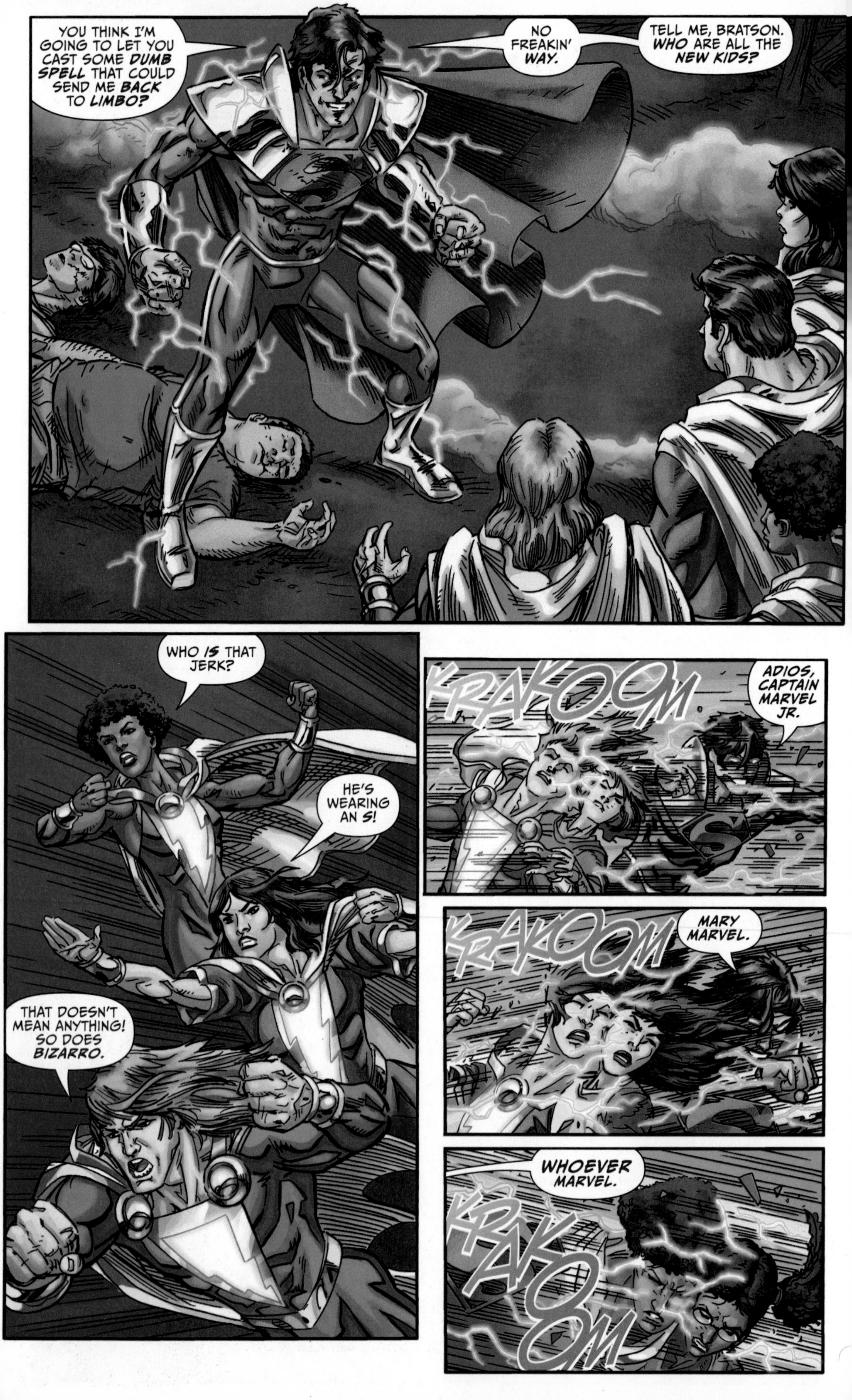

YOU THINK I'M GOING TO LET YOU CAST SOME DUMB SPELL THAT COULD SEND ME BACK TO LIMBO?
NO FREAKIN' WAY.
TELL ME, BRATSON. WHO ARE ALL THE NEW KIDS?
WHO IS THAT JERK?
HE'S WEARING AN S!
THAT DOESN'T MEAN ANYTHING! SO DOES BIZARRO.
KRAKOOM
ADIOS, CAPTAIN MARVEL JR.
KRAKOOM
MARY MARVEL.
WHOEVER MARVEL.
KRAKAKOOM

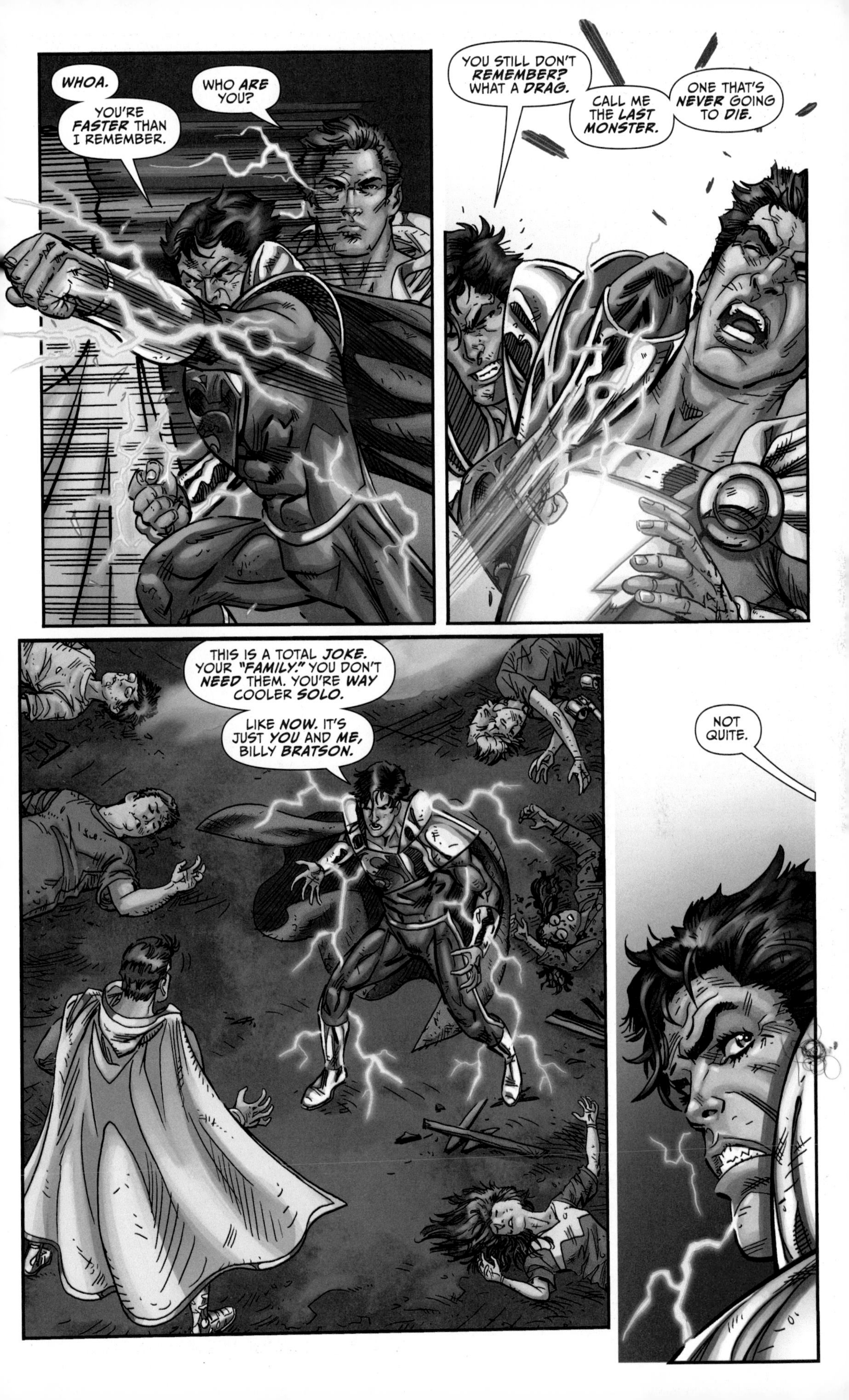
WHOA.
YOU'RE FASTER THAN I REMEMBER.
WHO ARE YOU?
YOU STILL DON'T REMEMBER? WHAT A DRAG.
CALL ME THE LAST MONSTER.
ONE THAT'S NEVER GOING TO DIE.
THIS IS A TOTAL JOKE. YOUR "FAMILY." YOU DON'T NEED THEM. YOU'RE WAY COOLER SOLO.
LIKE NOW. IT'S JUST YOU AND ME, BILLY BRATSON.
NOT QUITE.

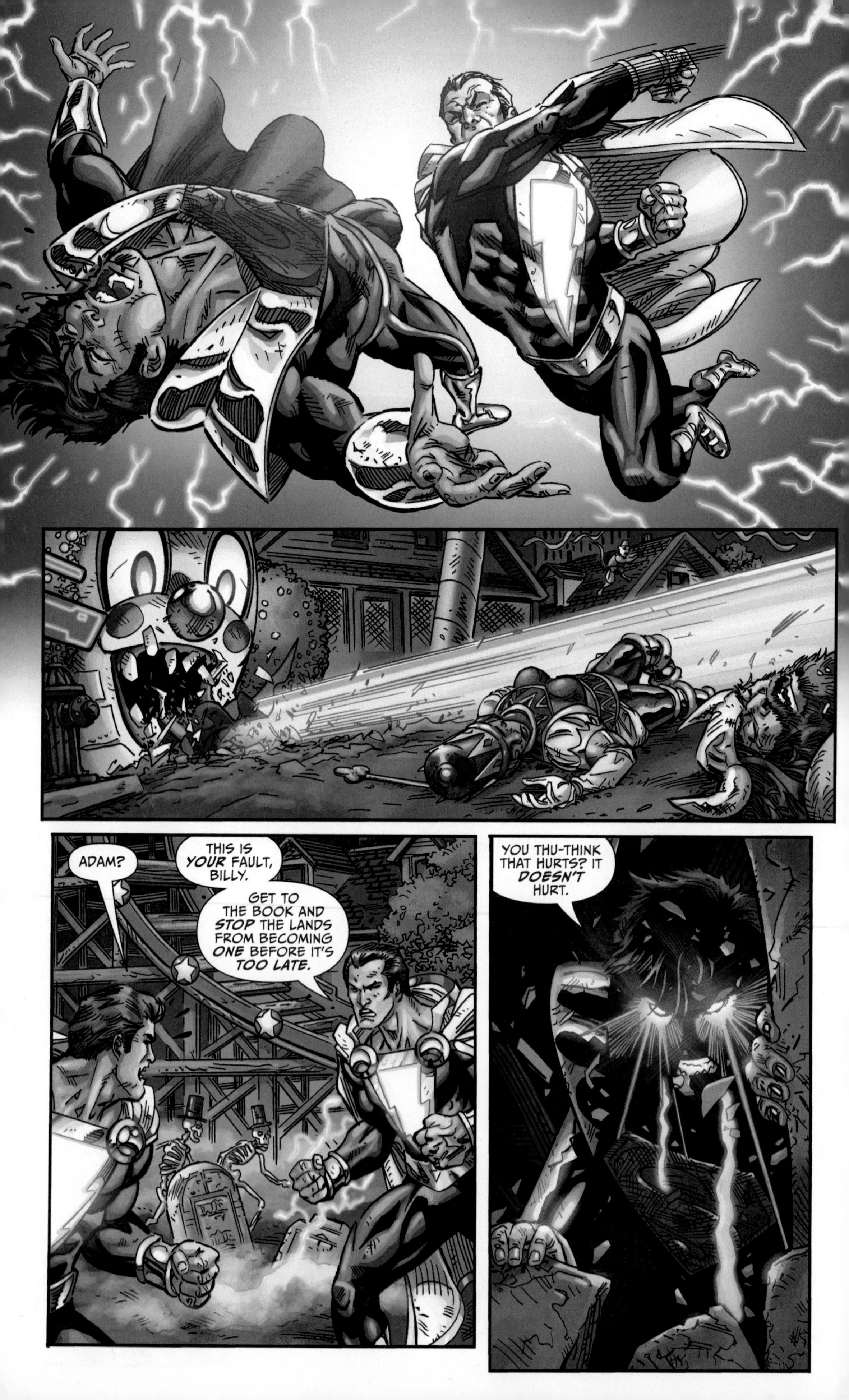
ADAM?
THIS IS YOUR FAULT, BILLY.
GET TO THE BOOK AND STOP THE LANDS FROM BECOMING ONE BEFORE IT'S TOO LATE.
YOU THU-THINK THAT HURTS? IT DOESN'T HURT.

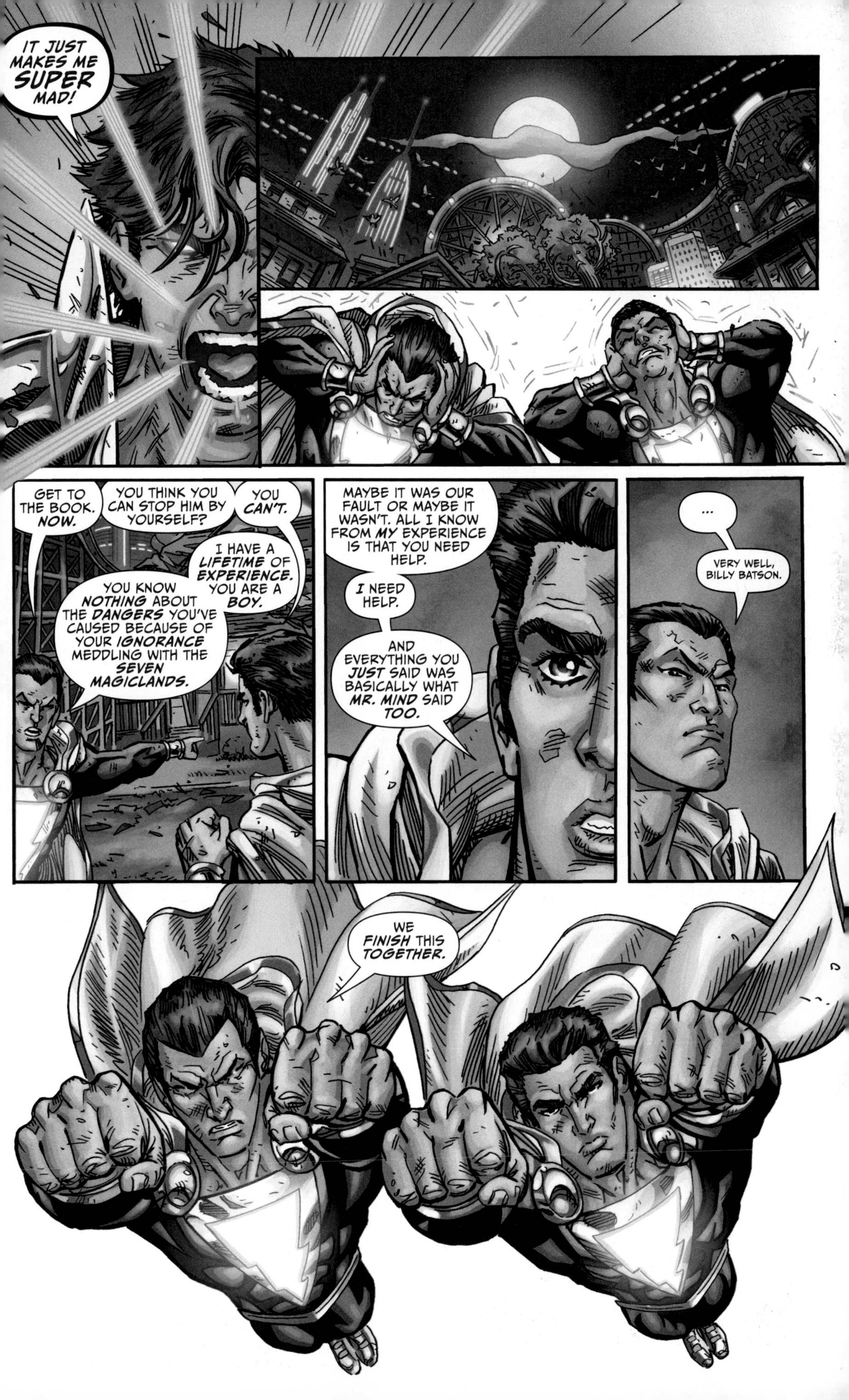
IT JUST MAKES ME SUPER MAD!
GET TO THE BOOK. NOW.
YOU THINK YOU CAN STOP HIM BY YOURSELF?
YOU CAN'T.
I HAVE A LIFETIME OF EXPERIENCE. YOU ARE A BOY.
YOU KNOW NOTHING ABOUT THE DANGERS YOU'VE CAUSED BECAUSE OF YOUR IGNORANCE MEDDLING WITH THE SEVEN MAGICLANDS.
MAYBE IT WAS OUR FAULT OR MAYBE IT WASN'T. ALL I KNOW FROM MY EXPERIENCE IS THAT YOU NEED HELP.
I NEED HELP.
AND EVERYTHING YOU JUST SAID WAS BASICALLY WHAT MR. MIND SAID TOO.
...
VERY WELL, BILLY BATSON.
WE FINISH THIS TOGETHER.

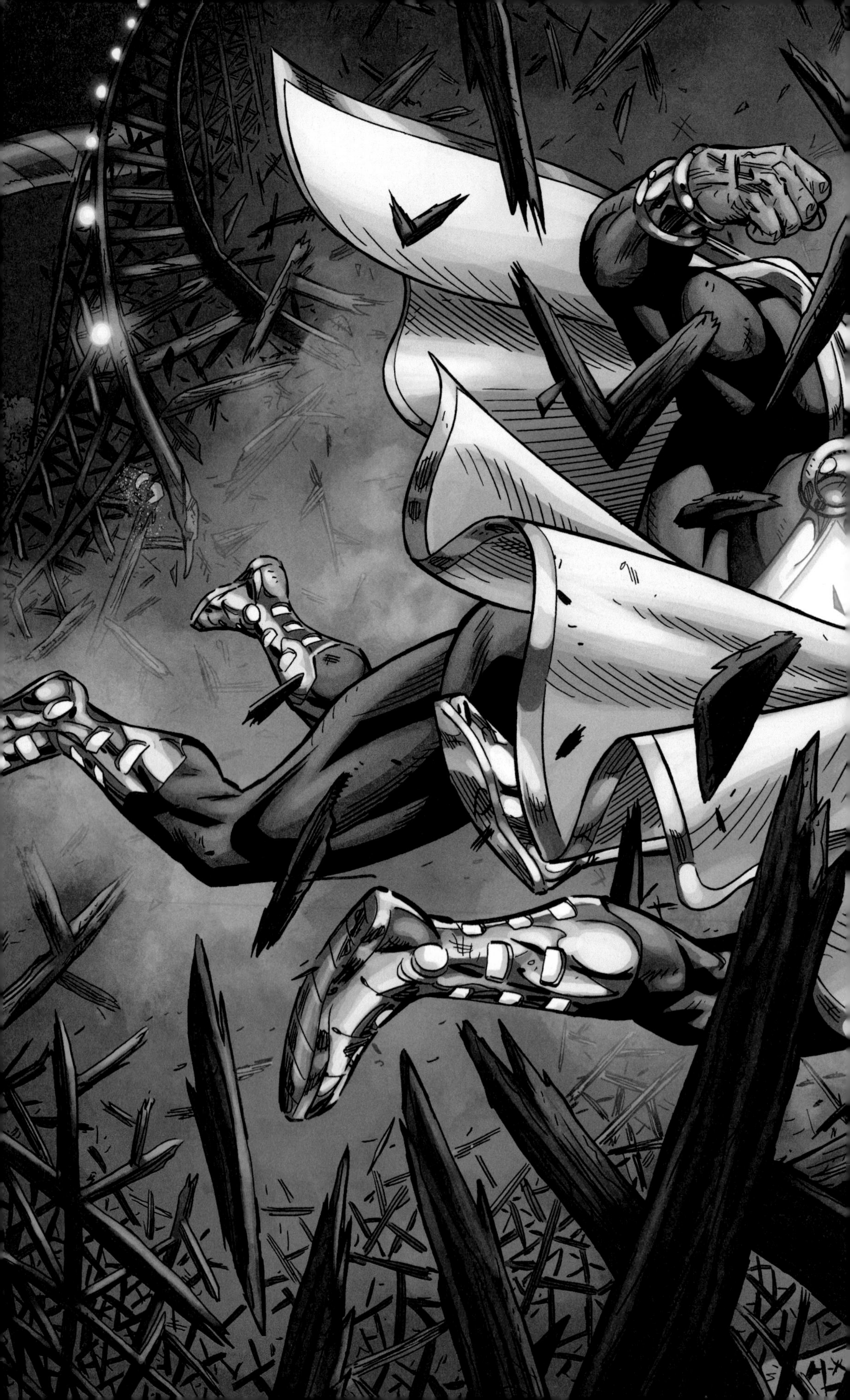

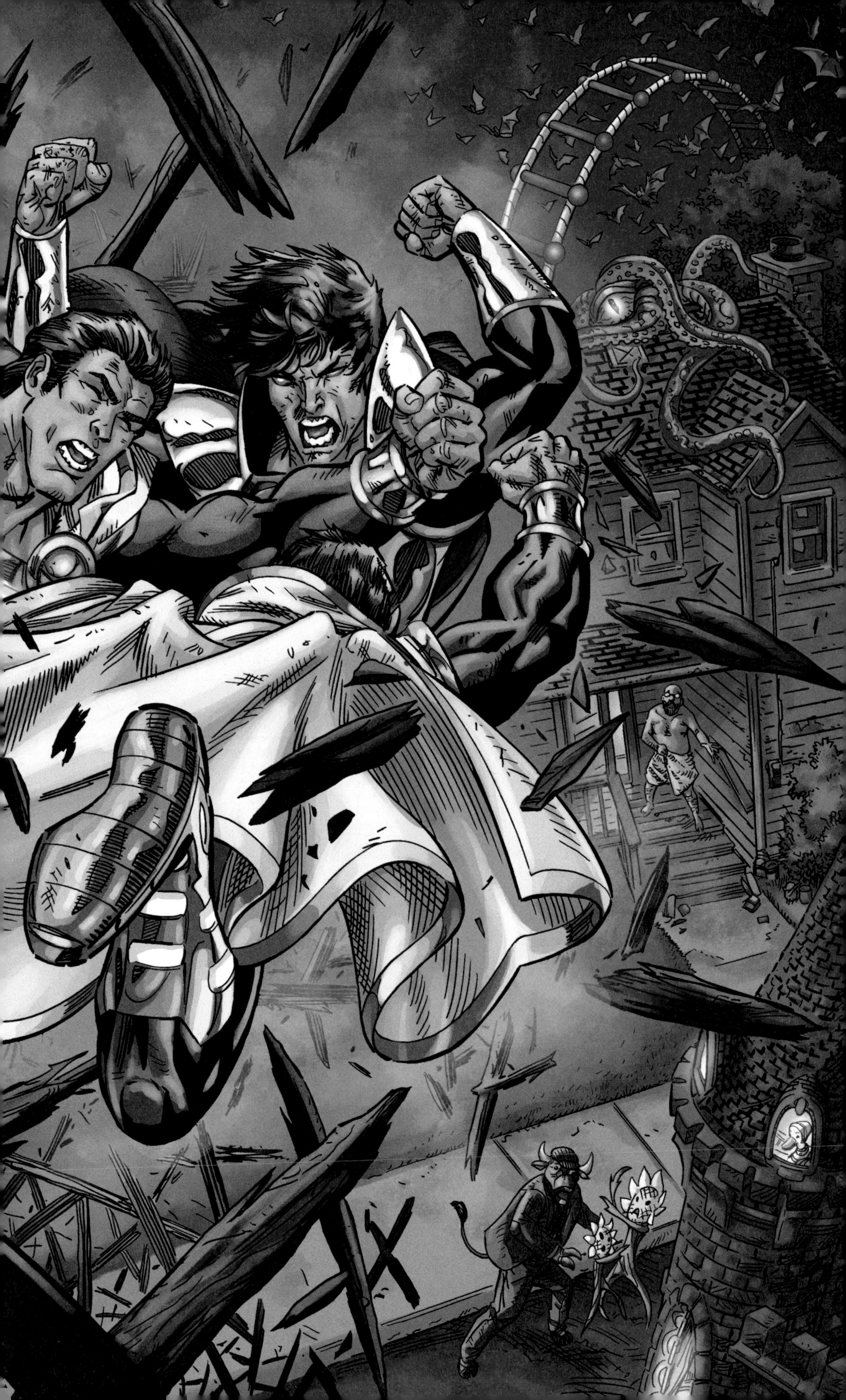

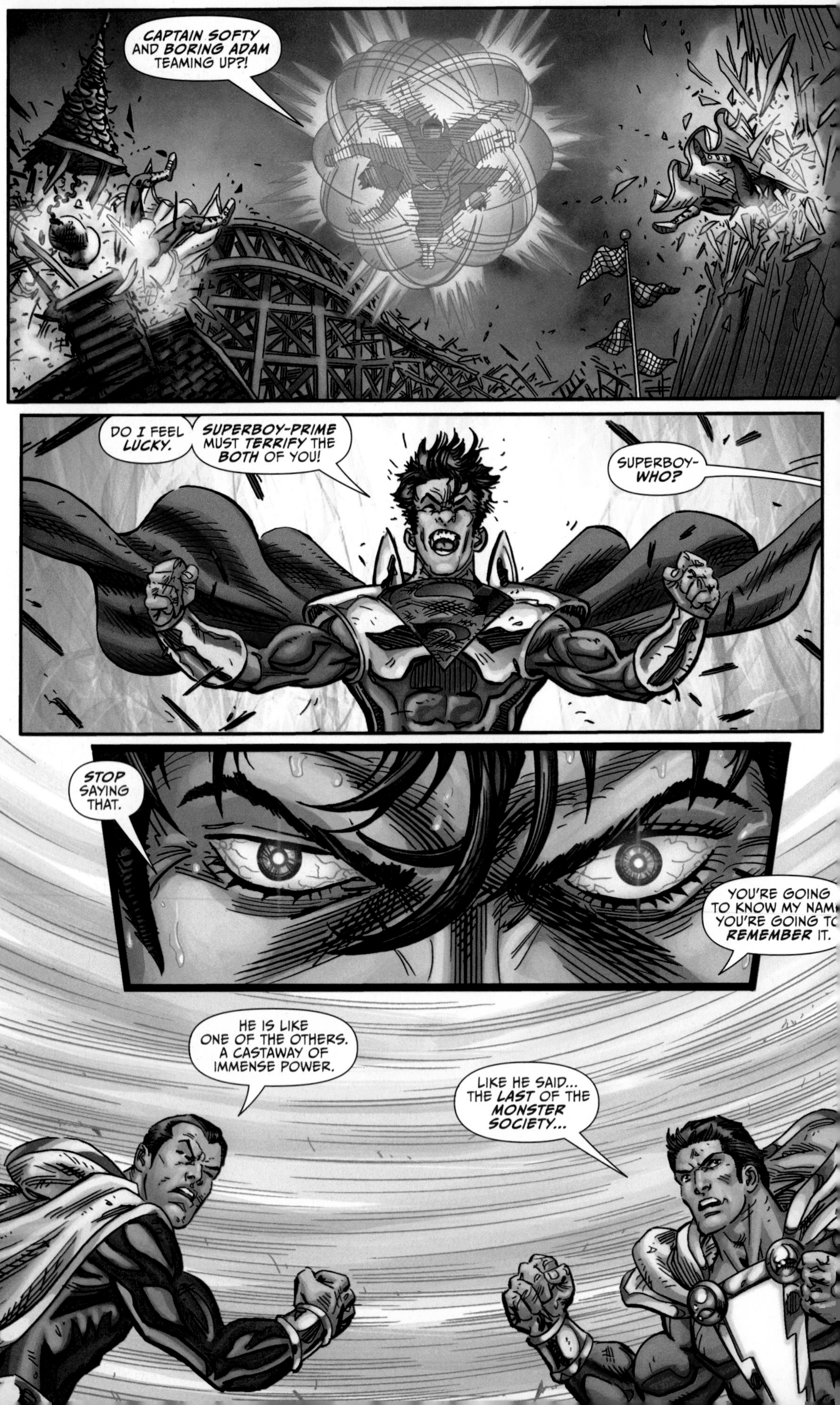

CAPTAIN SOFTY AND BORING ADAM TEAMING UP?!
DO I FEEL LUCKY.
SUPERBOY-PRIME MUST TERRIFY THE BOTH OF YOU!
SUPERBOY-WHO?
STOP SAYING THAT.
YOU'RE GOING TO KNOW MY NAM YOU'RE GOING TO REMEMBER IT.
HE IS LIKE ONE OF THE OTHERS. A CASTAWAY OF IMMENSE POWER.
LIKE HE SAID... THE LAST OF THE MONSTER SOCIETY...

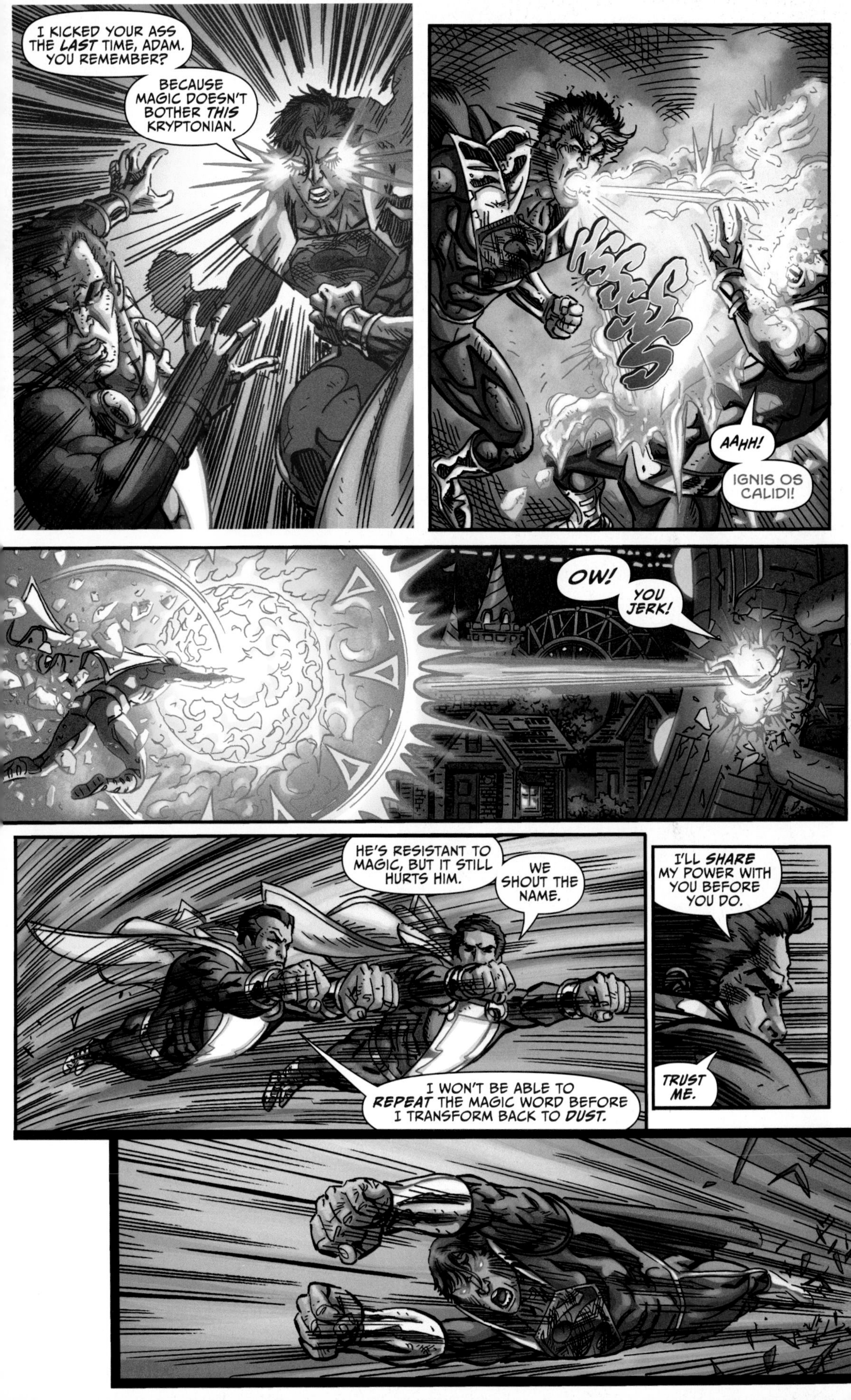
I KICKED YOUR ASS THE LAST TIME, ADAM. YOU REMEMBER?
BECAUSE MAGIC DOESN'T BOTHER THIS KRYPTONIAN.
HSSSSS
AAHH!
IGNIS OS CALIDI!
OW!
YOU JERK!
HE'S RESISTANT TO MAGIC, BUT IT STILL HURTS HIM.
WE SHOUT THE NAME.
I WON'T BE ABLE TO REPEAT THE MAGIC WORD BEFORE I TRANSFORM BACK TO DUST.
I'LL SHARE MY POWER WITH YOU BEFORE YOU DO.
TRUST ME.

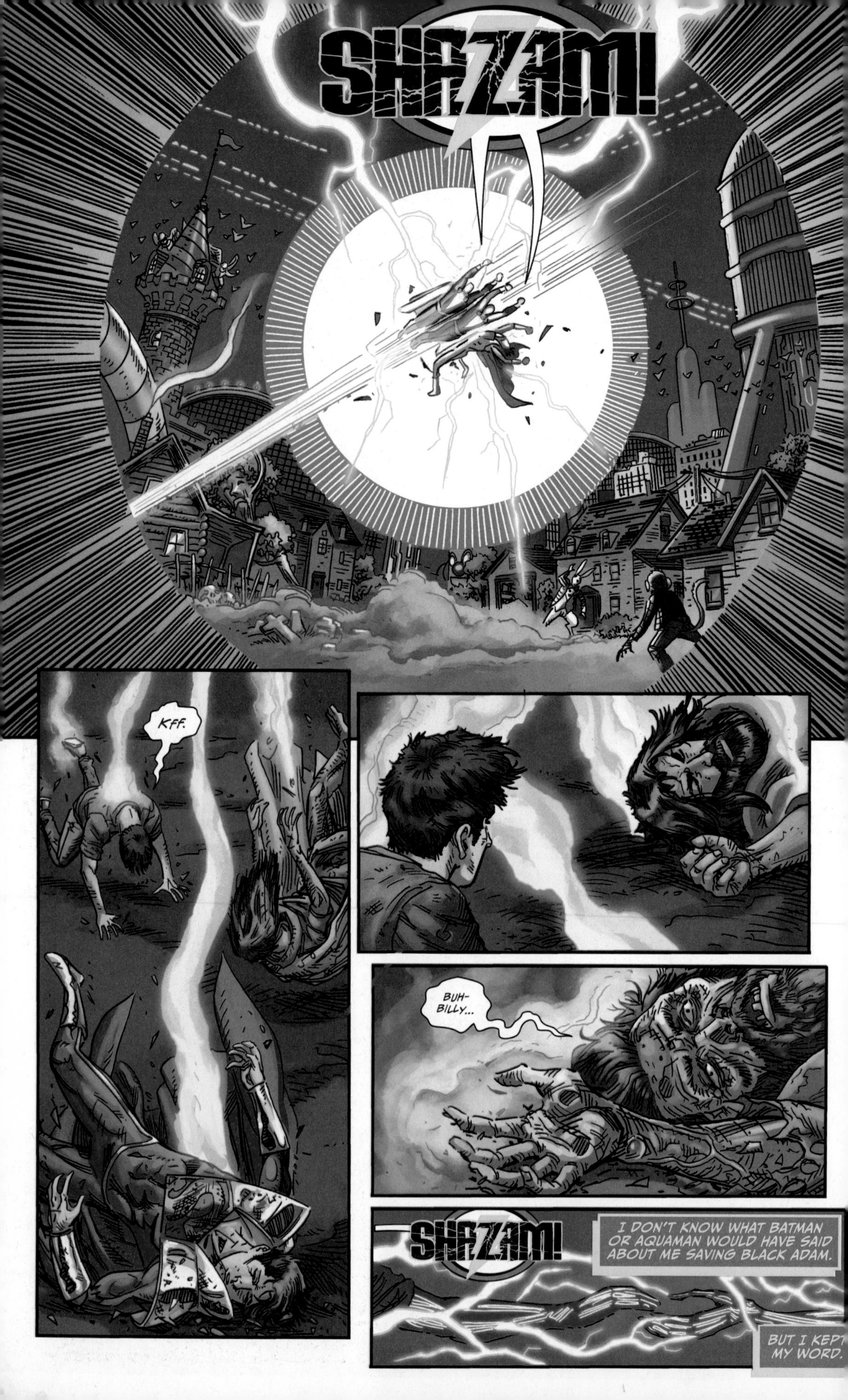
SHAZAM!
KFF.
BUH-BILLY...
SHAZAM!
I DON'T KNOW WHAT BATMAN OR AQUAMAN WOULD HAVE SAID ABOUT ME SAVING BLACK ADAM.
BUT I KEPT MY WORD.

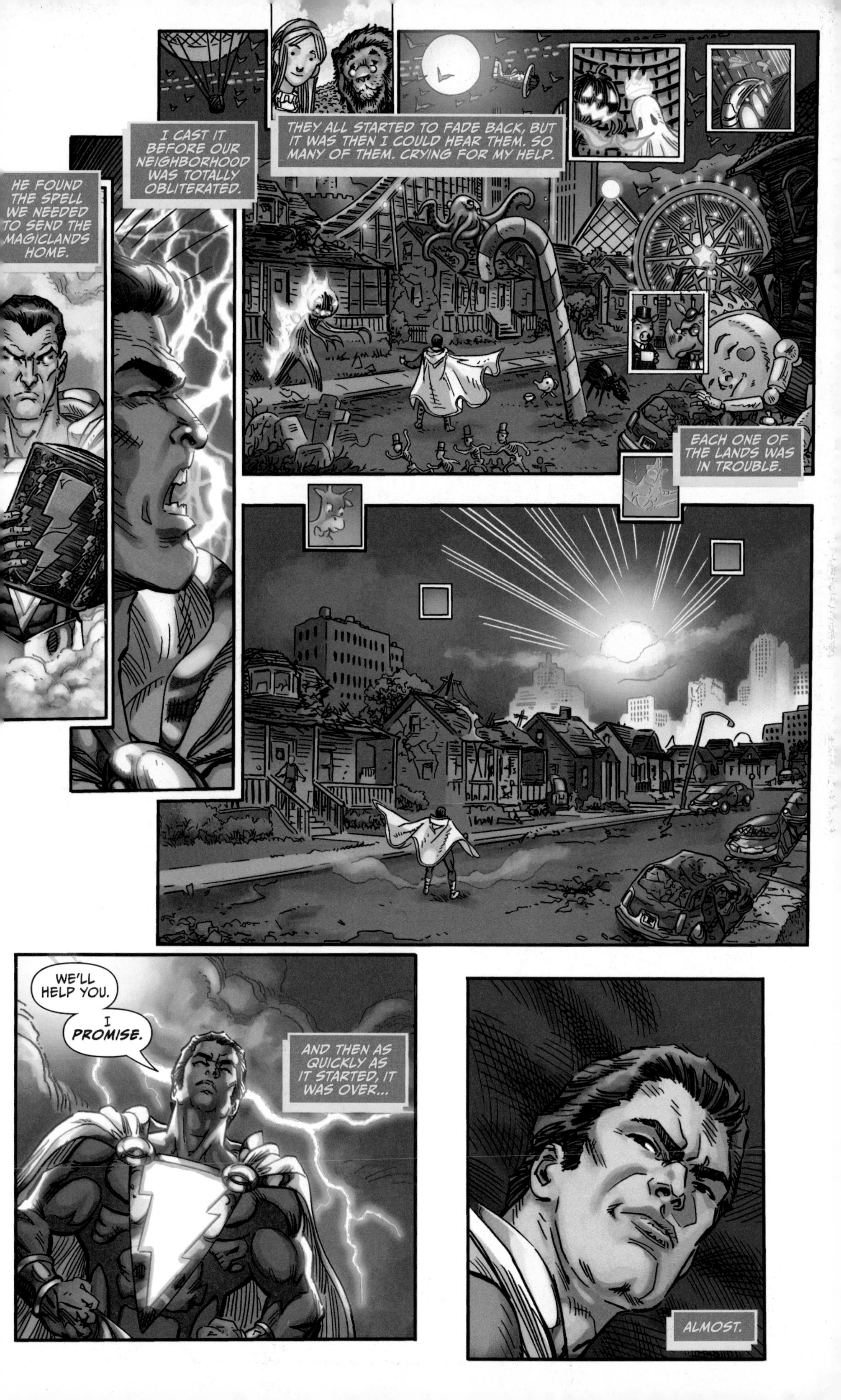
HE FOUND THE SPELL WE NEEDED TO SEND THE MAGICLANDS HOME.
I CAST IT BEFORE OUR NEIGHBORHOOD WAS TOTALLY OBLITERATED.
THEY ALL STARTED TO FADE BACK, BUT IT WAS THEN I COULD HEAR THEM. SO MANY OF THEM. CRYING FOR MY HELP.
EACH ONE OF THE LANDS WAS IN TROUBLE.
WE'LL HELP YOU.
I PROMISE.
AND THEN AS QUICKLY AS IT STARTED, IT WAS OVER...
ALMOST.

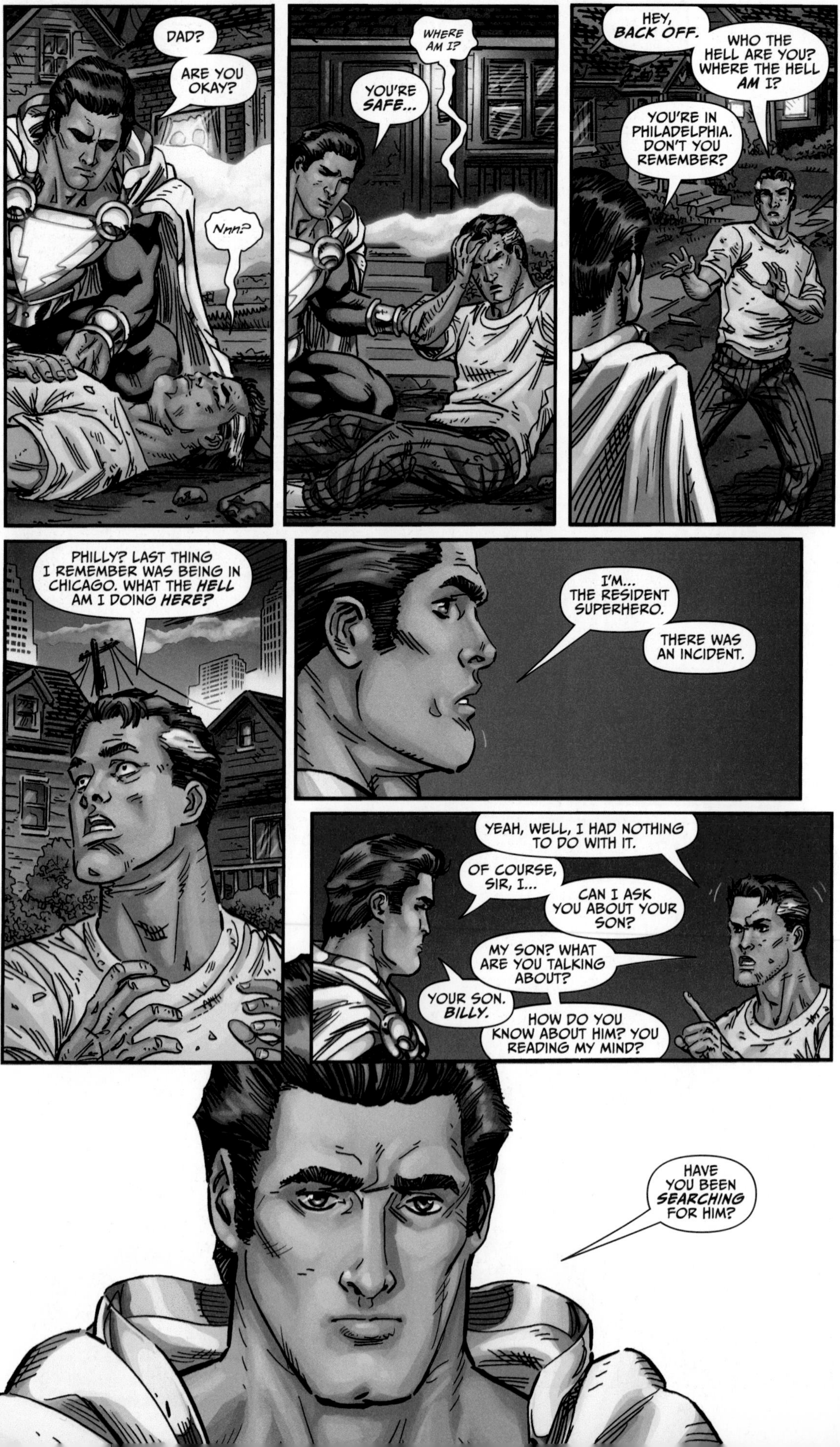

DAD?
ARE YOU OKAY?
Nnn?
WHERE AM I?
YOU'RE SAFE...
HEY, BACK OFF.
WHO THE HELL ARE YOU? WHERE THE HELL AM I?
YOU'RE IN PHILADELPHIA. DON'T YOU REMEMBER?
PHILLY? LAST THING I REMEMBER WAS BEING IN CHICAGO. WHAT THE HELL AM I DOING HERE?
I'M... THE RESIDENT SUPERHERO.
THERE WAS AN INCIDENT.
YEAH, WELL, I HAD NOTHING TO DO WITH IT.
OF COURSE, SIR, I...
CAN I ASK YOU ABOUT YOUR SON?
MY SON? WHAT ARE YOU TALKING ABOUT?
YOUR SON. BILLY.
HOW DO YOU KNOW ABOUT HIM? YOU READING MY MIND?
HAVE YOU BEEN SEARCHING FOR HIM?

SEARCHING FOR HIM? LISTEN...MY EX AND I GAVE THAT KID UP A LONG TIME AGO. WEREN'T REALLY THE PARENT TYPES AND WE WEREN'T GETTING ALONG. I MEAN, SHE'S A *MESS*.

HEY, IF YOU'RE *JUDGING* ME FOR THAT, ASKING IF I FEEL *BAD*... SURE, I GUESS.

BUT I'M BETTER OFF WITHOUT HIM.

I MEAN, THE KID'S BETTER OFF WITHOUT ME.

LOOK, SUPERHERO. CAN I *GO* NOW?

I GOT A *LIFE* TO GET BACK TO, YOU KNOW?

YEAH. SURE.

YOU'RE FREE TO GO.

HE STOOD THERE FOR AWHILE, NOT SURE WHAT TO DO...I WASN'T EITHER... AND THEN HE LEFT.

I WANTED TO SAY SO MANY THINGS, GOOD AND BAD, BUT I FELT FROZEN.

BILLY?

WE STOPPED MR. MIND AND THE MONSTER SOCIETY, BUT IT WASN'T THE HAPPIEST DAY OF MY LIFE.

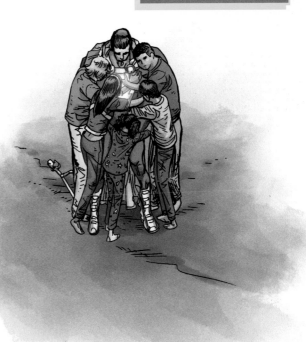

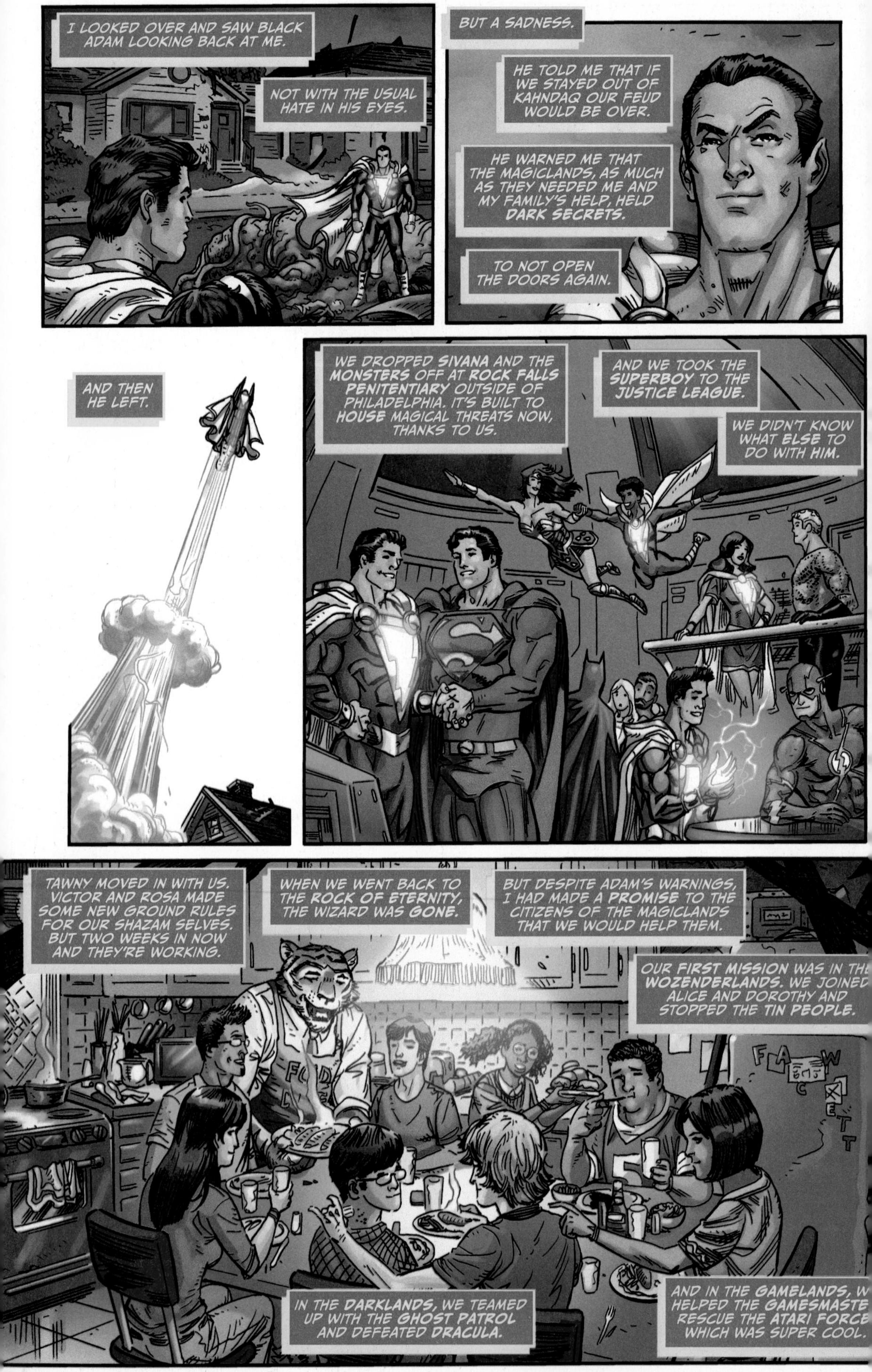
I LOOKED OVER AND SAW BLACK ADAM LOOKING BACK AT ME.
NOT WITH THE USUAL HATE IN HIS EYES.
BUT A SADNESS.
HE TOLD ME THAT IF WE STAYED OUT OF KAHNDAQ OUR FEUD WOULD BE OVER.
HE WARNED ME THAT THE MAGICLANDS, AS MUCH AS THEY NEEDED ME AND MY FAMILY'S HELP, HELD DARK SECRETS.
TO NOT OPEN THE DOORS AGAIN.
AND THEN HE LEFT.
WE DROPPED SIVANA AND THE MONSTERS OFF AT ROCK FALLS PENITENTIARY OUTSIDE OF PHILADELPHIA. IT'S BUILT TO HOUSE MAGICAL THREATS NOW, THANKS TO US.
AND WE TOOK THE SUPERBOY TO THE JUSTICE LEAGUE.
WE DIDN'T KNOW WHAT ELSE TO DO WITH HIM.
TAWNY MOVED IN WITH US. VICTOR AND ROSA MADE SOME NEW GROUND RULES FOR OUR SHAZAM SELVES. BUT TWO WEEKS IN NOW AND THEY'RE WORKING.
WHEN WE WENT BACK TO THE ROCK OF ETERNITY, THE WIZARD WAS GONE.
BUT DESPITE ADAM'S WARNINGS, I HAD MADE A PROMISE TO THE CITIZENS OF THE MAGICLANDS THAT WE WOULD HELP THEM.
OUR FIRST MISSION WAS IN THE WOZENDERLANDS. WE JOINED ALICE AND DOROTHY AND STOPPED THE TIN PEOPLE.
IN THE DARKLANDS, WE TEAMED UP WITH THE GHOST PATROL AND DEFEATED DRACULA.
AND IN THE GAMELANDS, W HELPED THE GAMESMASTE RESCUE THE ATARI FORCE WHICH WAS SUPER COOL.

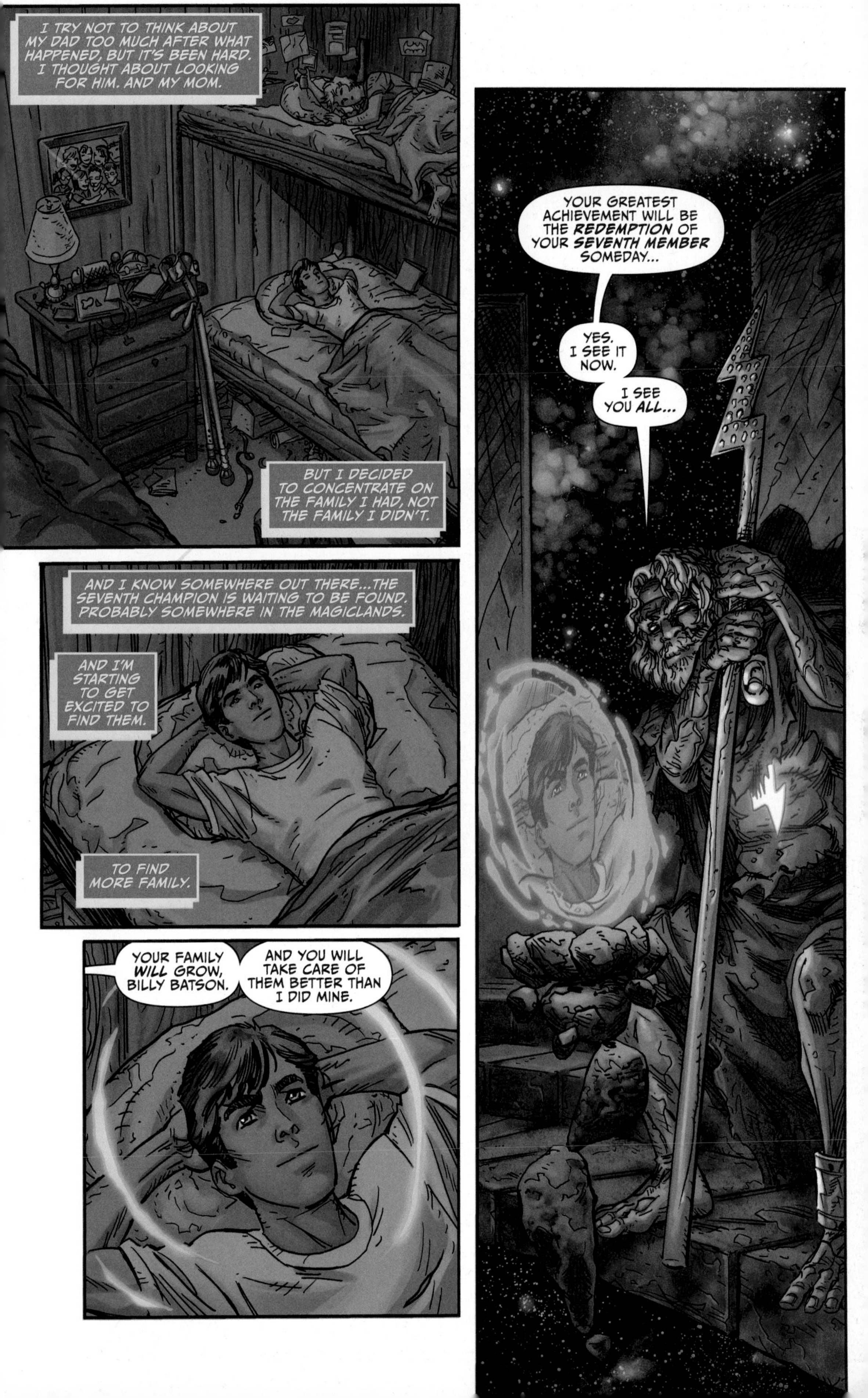
I TRY NOT TO THINK ABOUT MY DAD TOO MUCH AFTER WHAT HAPPENED, BUT IT'S BEEN HARD. I THOUGHT ABOUT LOOKING FOR HIM. AND MY MOM.
BUT I DECIDED TO CONCENTRATE ON THE FAMILY I HAD, NOT THE FAMILY I DIDN'T.
AND I KNOW SOMEWHERE OUT THERE...THE SEVENTH CHAMPION IS WAITING TO BE FOUND. PROBABLY SOMEWHERE IN THE MAGICLANDS.
AND I'M STARTING TO GET EXCITED TO FIND THEM.
TO FIND MORE FAMILY.
YOUR FAMILY WILL GROW, BILLY BATSON.
AND YOU WILL TAKE CARE OF THEM BETTER THAN I DID MINE.
YOUR GREATEST ACHIEVEMENT WILL BE THE REDEMPTION OF YOUR SEVENTH MEMBER SOMEDAY...
YES. I SEE IT NOW.
I SEE YOU ALL...

"THE SEVEN CHAMPIONS. THE COUNCIL OF ETERNITY. THE SHAZAM FAMILY.
"LONG MAY YOU REIGN."
WHO WANTS PIZZA?
OH, I DO, ADAM! BUT NO PINEAPPLE THIS TIME!
BUT I *LOVE* PINEAPPLE! I NEVER GET MY WAY!
PIZZA!!!
END

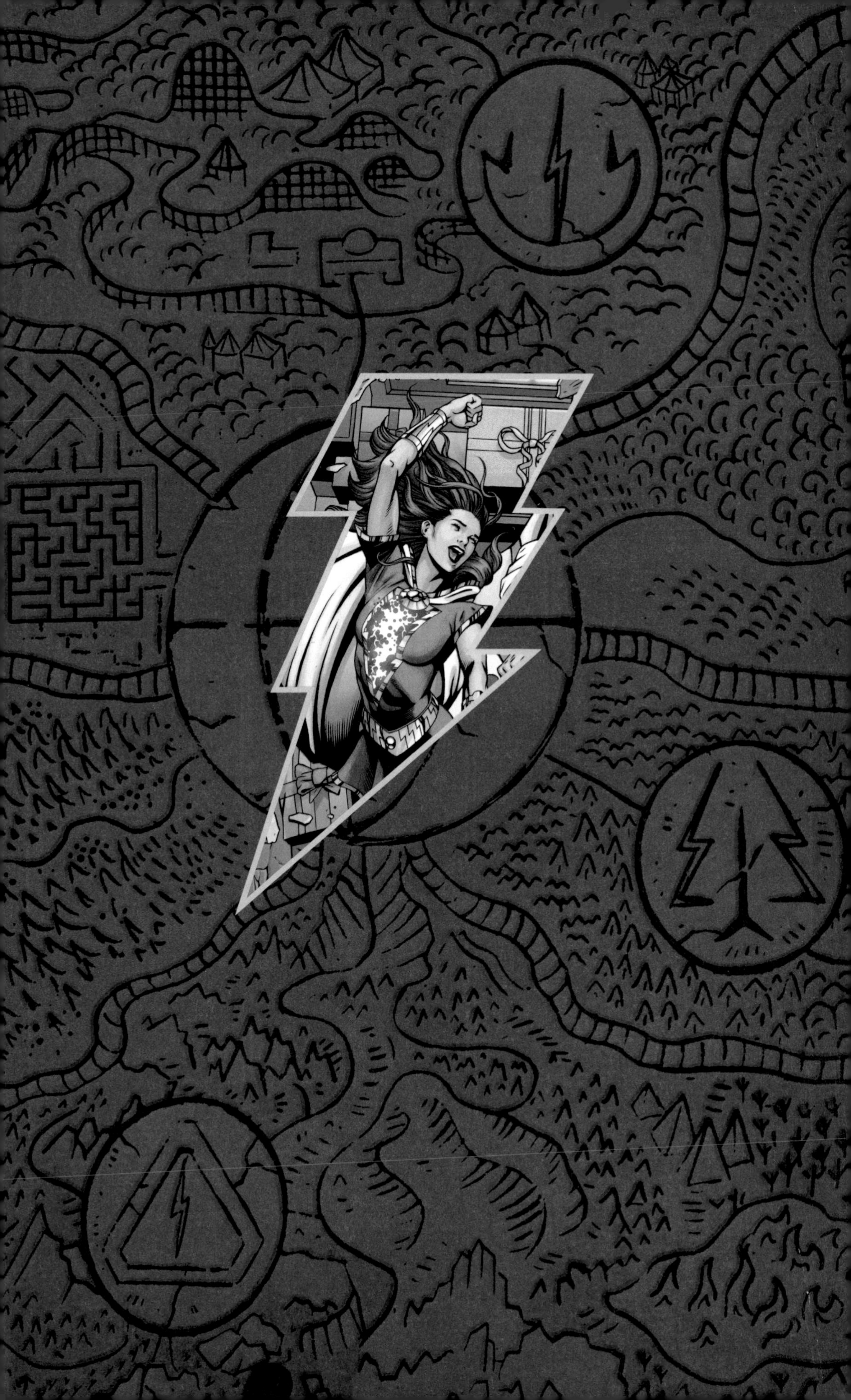

# MARY

GEOFF JOHNS
Writer

MAYO "SEN" NAITO
Artist

ROB LEIGH
Letterer

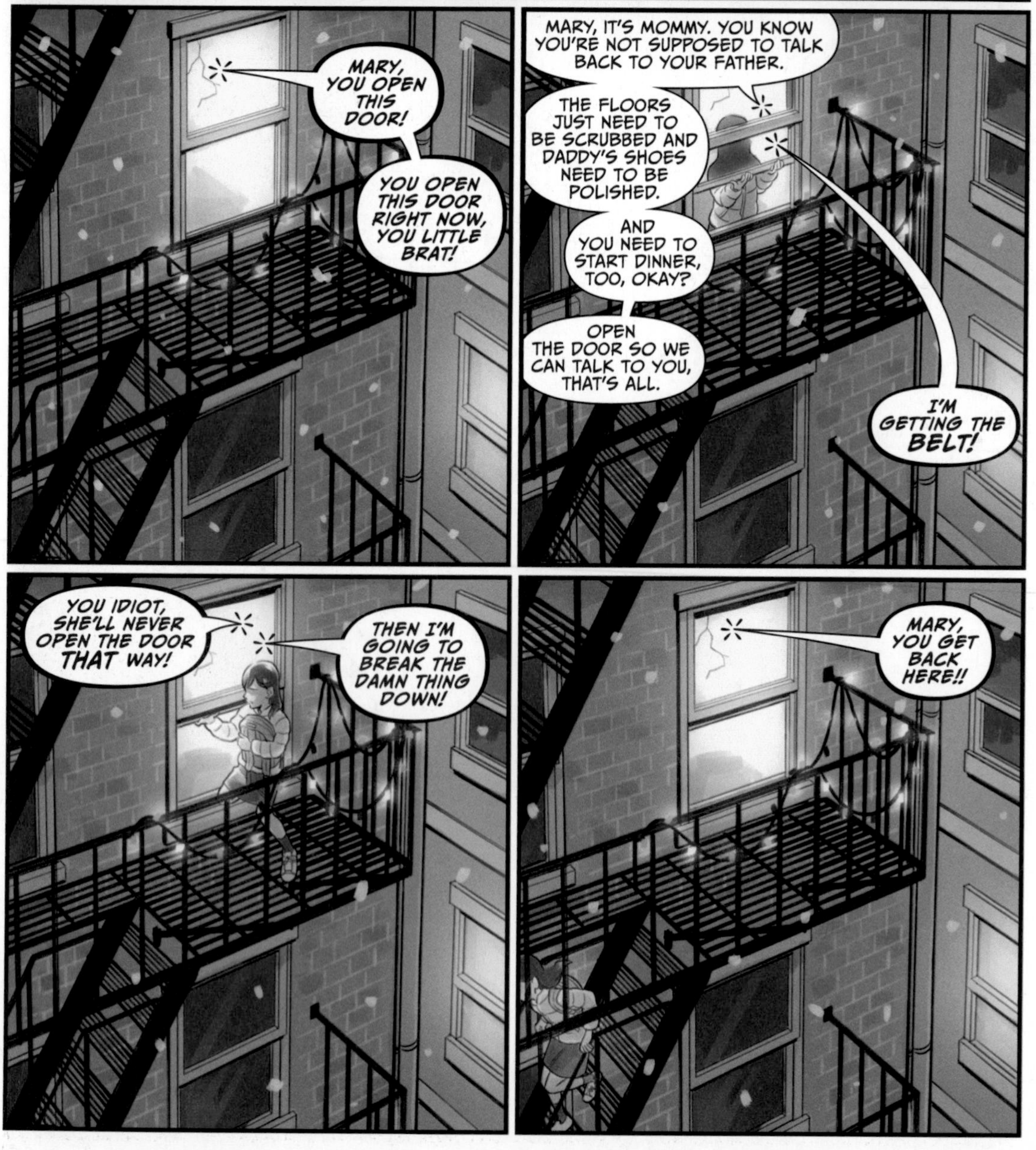
MARY, YOU OPEN THIS DOOR!
YOU OPEN THIS DOOR RIGHT NOW, YOU LITTLE BRAT!
MARY, IT'S MOMMY. YOU KNOW YOU'RE NOT SUPPOSED TO TALK BACK TO YOUR FATHER.
THE FLOORS JUST NEED TO BE SCRUBBED AND DADDY'S SHOES NEED TO BE POLISHED.
AND YOU NEED TO START DINNER, TOO, OKAY?
OPEN THE DOOR SO WE CAN TALK TO YOU, THAT'S ALL.
I'M GETTING THE BELT!
YOU IDIOT, SHE'LL NEVER OPEN THE DOOR THAT WAY!
THEN I'M GOING TO BREAK THE DAMN THING DOWN!
MARY, YOU GET BACK HERE!!

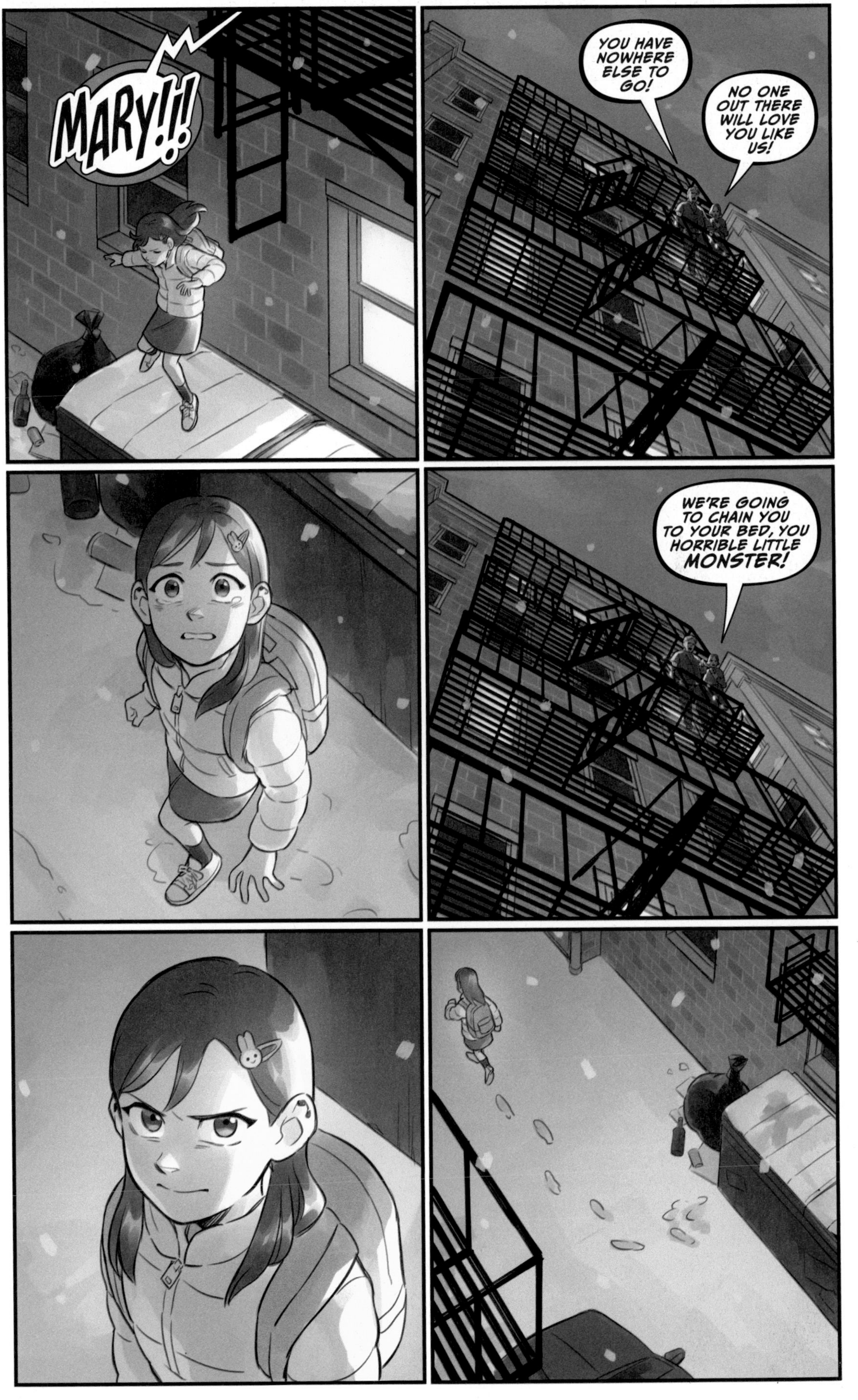
MARY!!!
YOU HAVE NOWHERE ELSE TO GO!
NO ONE OUT THERE WILL LOVE YOU LIKE US!
WE'RE GOING TO CHAIN YOU TO YOUR BED, YOU HORRIBLE LITTLE MONSTER!

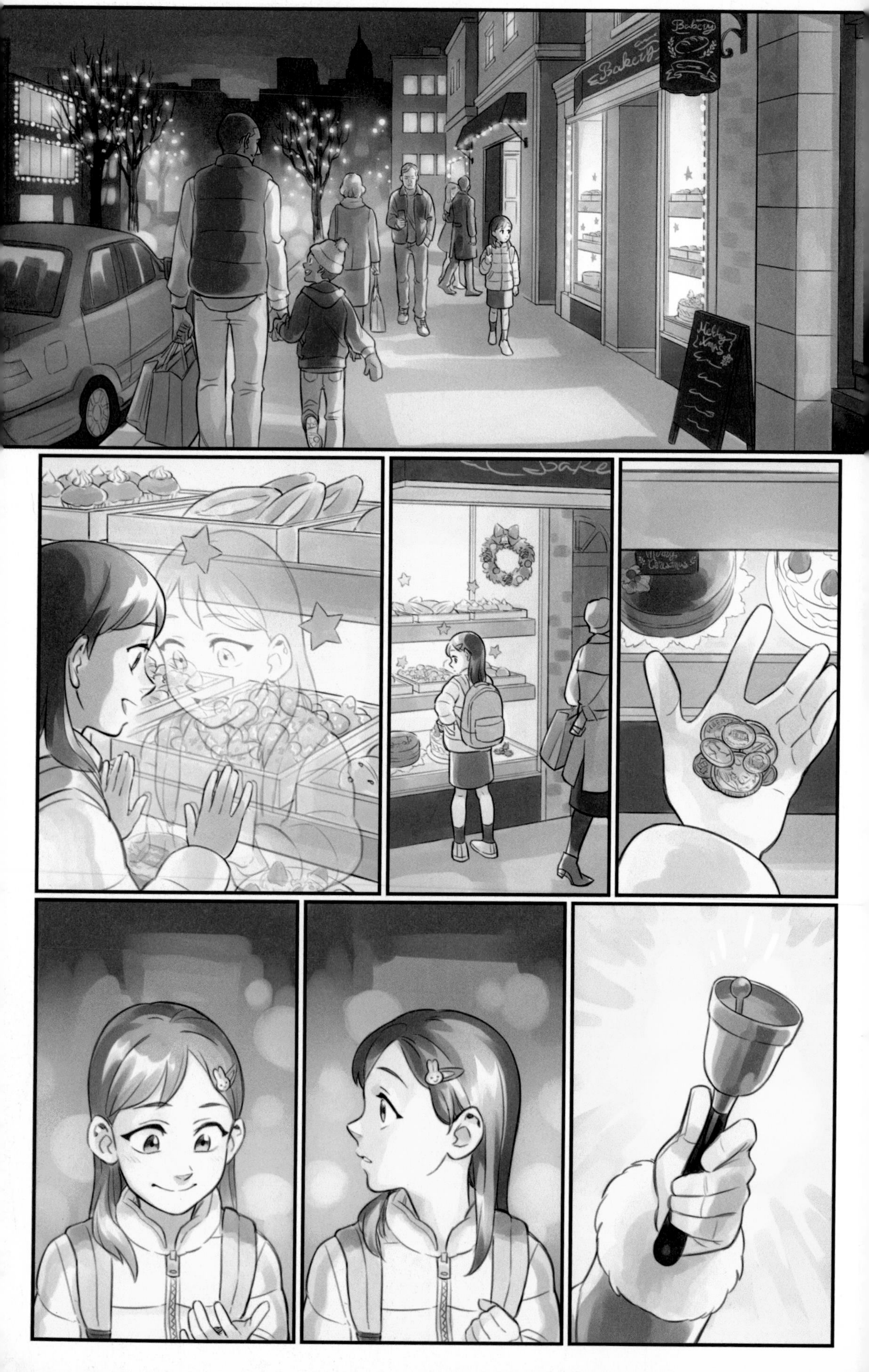
Bakery
Bakery
Merry Xmas
Merry Christmas

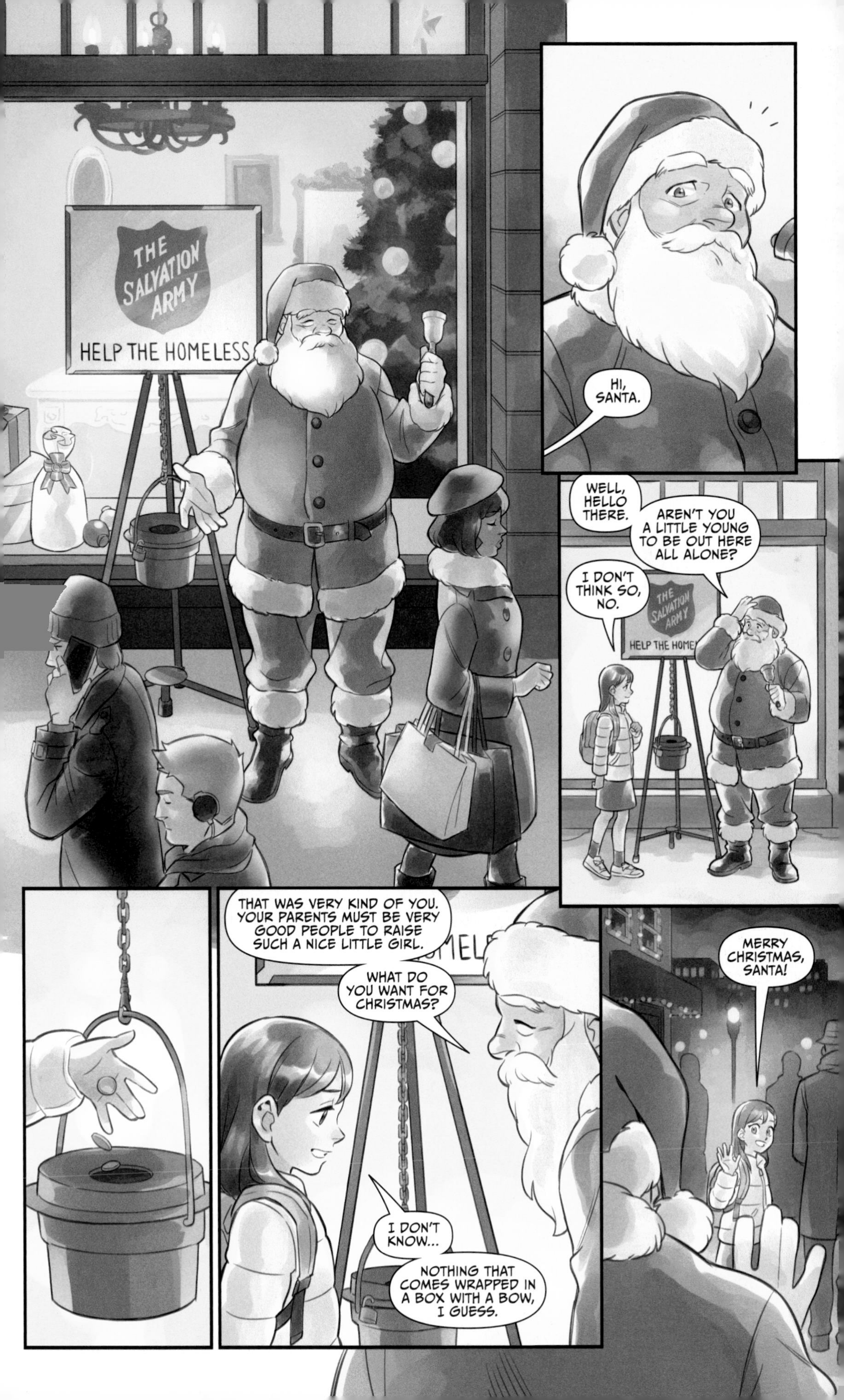
THE SALVATION ARMY
HELP THE HOMELESS
HI, SANTA.
WELL, HELLO THERE.
AREN'T YOU A LITTLE YOUNG TO BE OUT HERE ALL ALONE?
I DON'T THINK SO, NO.
THE SALVATION ARMY
HELP THE HOME
THAT WAS VERY KIND OF YOU. YOUR PARENTS MUST BE VERY GOOD PEOPLE TO RAISE SUCH A NICE LITTLE GIRL.
WHAT DO YOU WANT FOR CHRISTMAS?
I DON'T KNOW...
NOTHING THAT COMES WRAPPED IN A BOX WITH A BOW, I GUESS.
MERRY CHRISTMAS, SANTA!

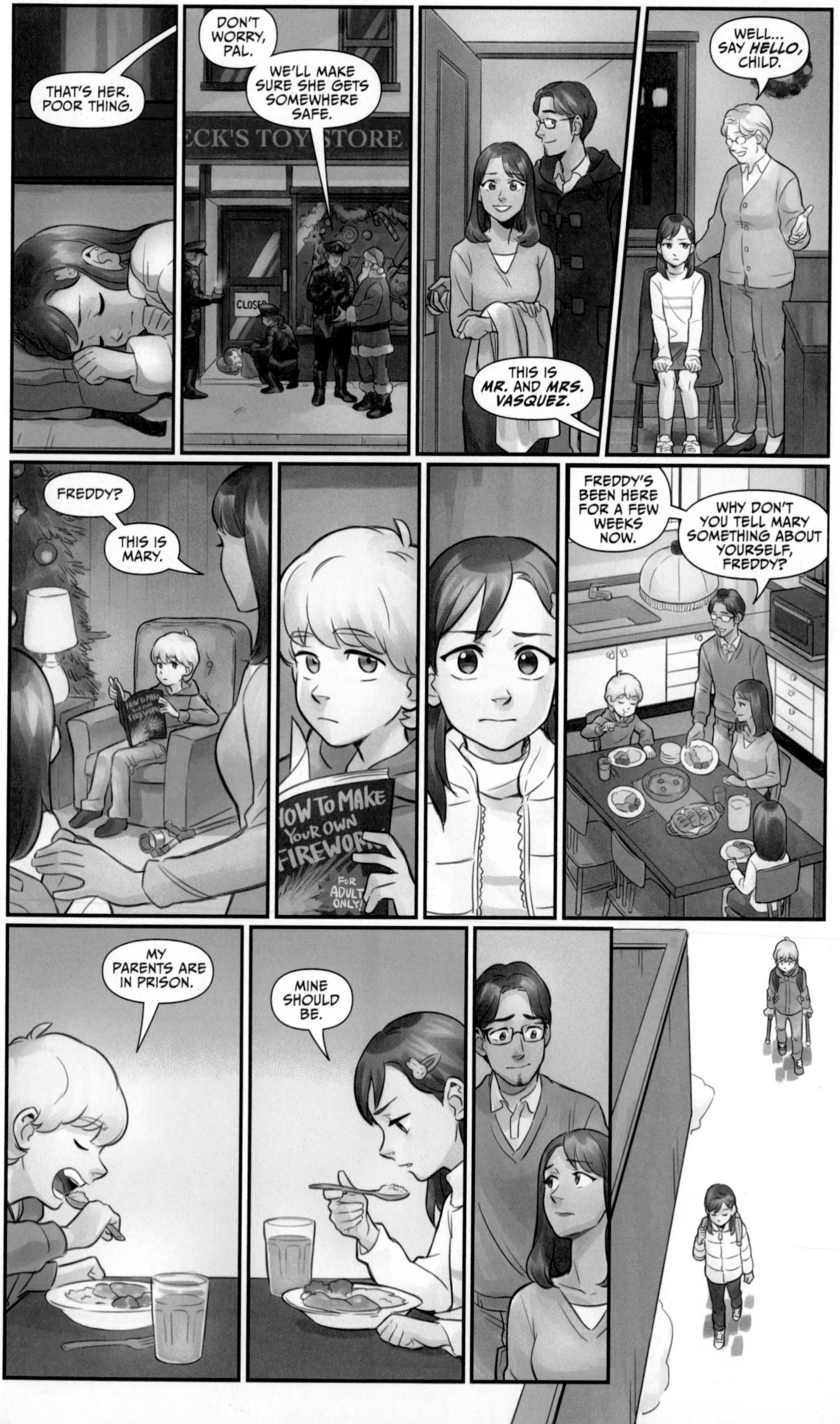
THAT'S HER. POOR THING.
DON'T WORRY, PAL.
WE'LL MAKE SURE SHE GETS SOMEWHERE SAFE.
ECK'S TOY STORE
CLOSED
THIS IS MR. AND MRS. VASQUEZ.
WELL... SAY HELLO, CHILD.
FREDDY?
THIS IS MARY.
HOW TO MAKE YOUR OWN FIREWORKS
FOR ADULTS ONLY!
FREDDY'S BEEN HERE FOR A FEW WEEKS NOW.
WHY DON'T YOU TELL MARY SOMETHING ABOUT YOURSELF, FREDDY?
MY PARENTS ARE IN PRISON.
MINE SHOULD BE.

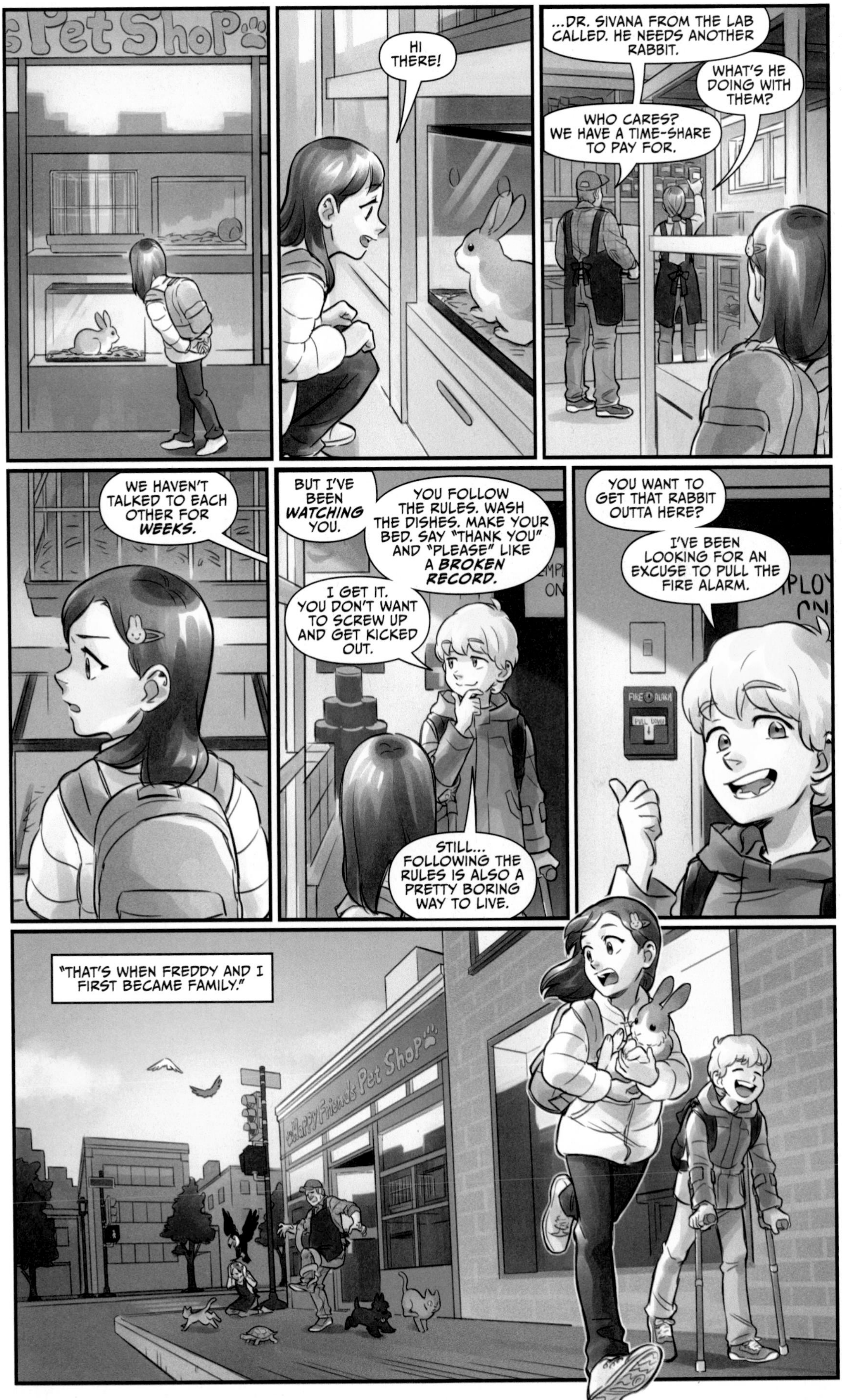
Pet Shop
HI THERE!
...DR. SIVANA FROM THE LAB CALLED. HE NEEDS ANOTHER RABBIT.
WHAT'S HE DOING WITH THEM?
WHO CARES? WE HAVE A TIME-SHARE TO PAY FOR.
WE HAVEN'T TALKED TO EACH OTHER FOR WEEKS.
BUT I'VE BEEN WATCHING YOU.
YOU FOLLOW THE RULES. WASH THE DISHES. MAKE YOUR BED. SAY "THANK YOU" AND "PLEASE" LIKE A BROKEN RECORD.
I GET IT. YOU DON'T WANT TO SCREW UP AND GET KICKED OUT.
STILL... FOLLOWING THE RULES IS ALSO A PRETTY BORING WAY TO LIVE.
YOU WANT TO GET THAT RABBIT OUTTA HERE?
I'VE BEEN LOOKING FOR AN EXCUSE TO PULL THE FIRE ALARM.
FIRE ALARM
PULL DOWN
"THAT'S WHEN FREDDY AND I FIRST BECAME FAMILY."
Happy Friends Pet Shop

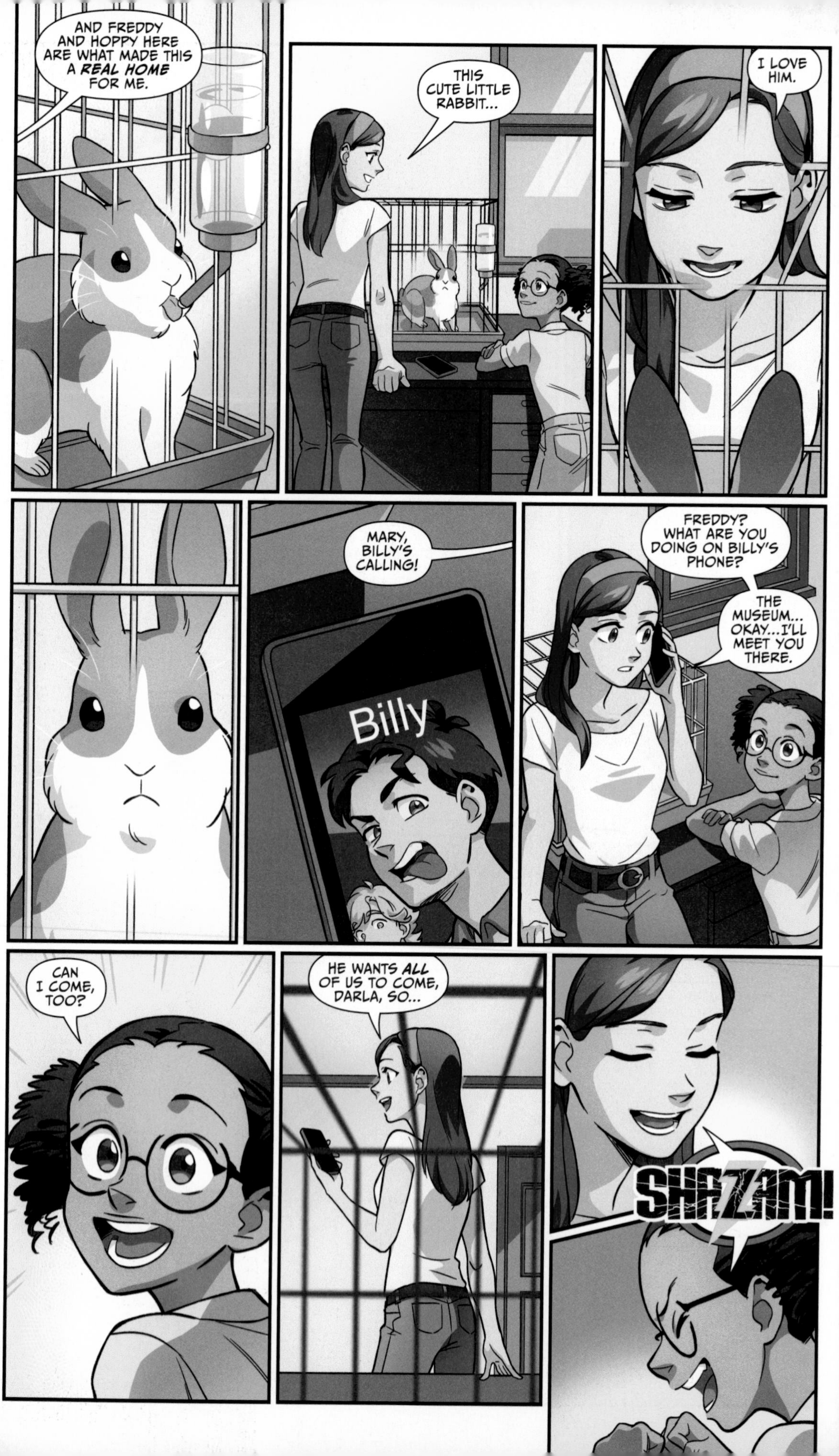
AND FREDDY AND HOPPY HERE ARE WHAT MADE THIS A ***REAL HOME*** FOR ME.
THIS CUTE LITTLE RABBIT...
I LOVE HIM.
MARY, BILLY'S CALLING!
Billy
FREDDY? WHAT ARE YOU DOING ON BILLY'S PHONE?
THE MUSEUM... OKAY...I'LL MEET YOU THERE.
CAN I COME, TOO?
HE WANTS ***ALL*** OF US TO COME, DARLA, SO...
SHAZAM!

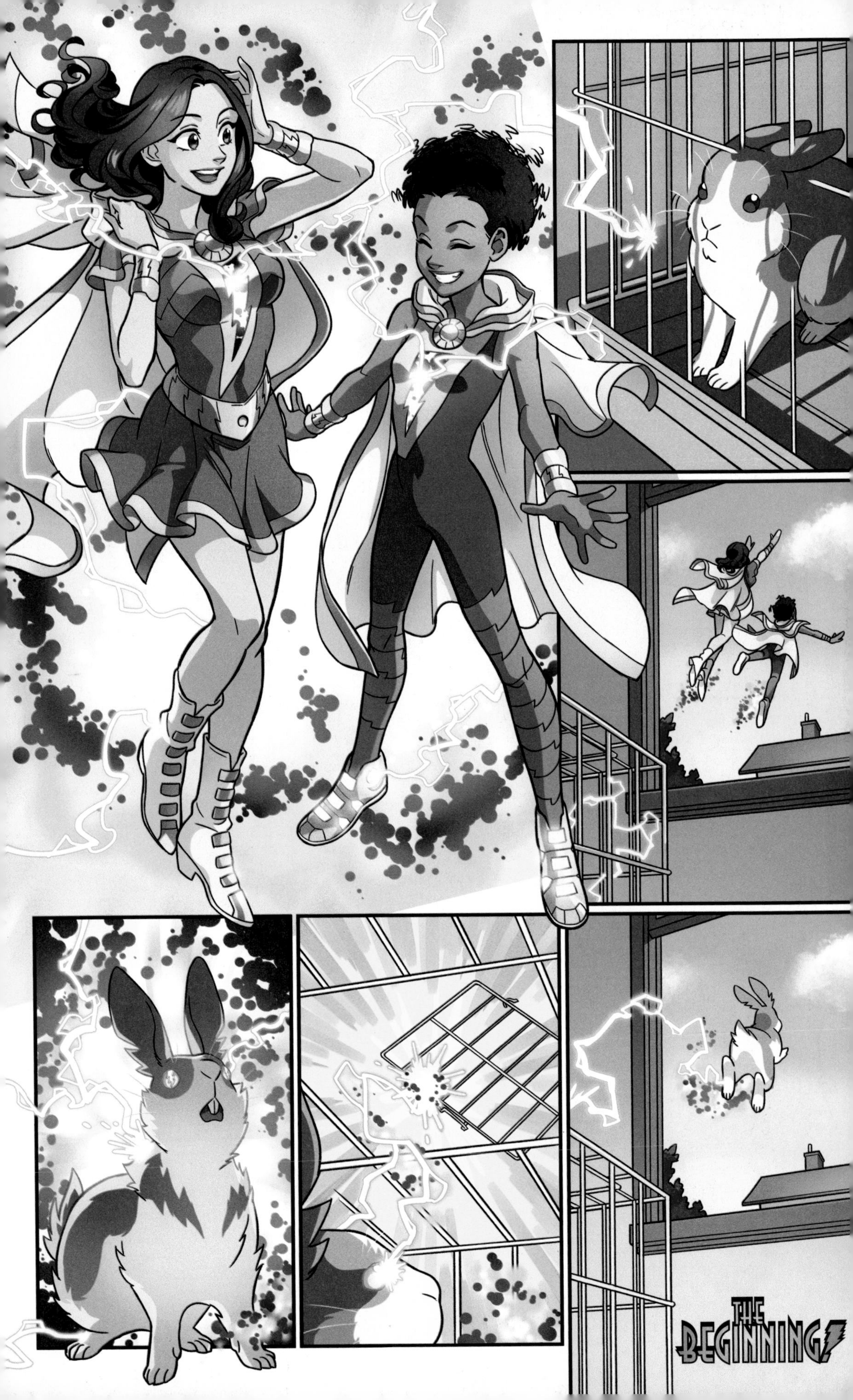
THE BEGINNING

VARIANT COVER
GALLERY

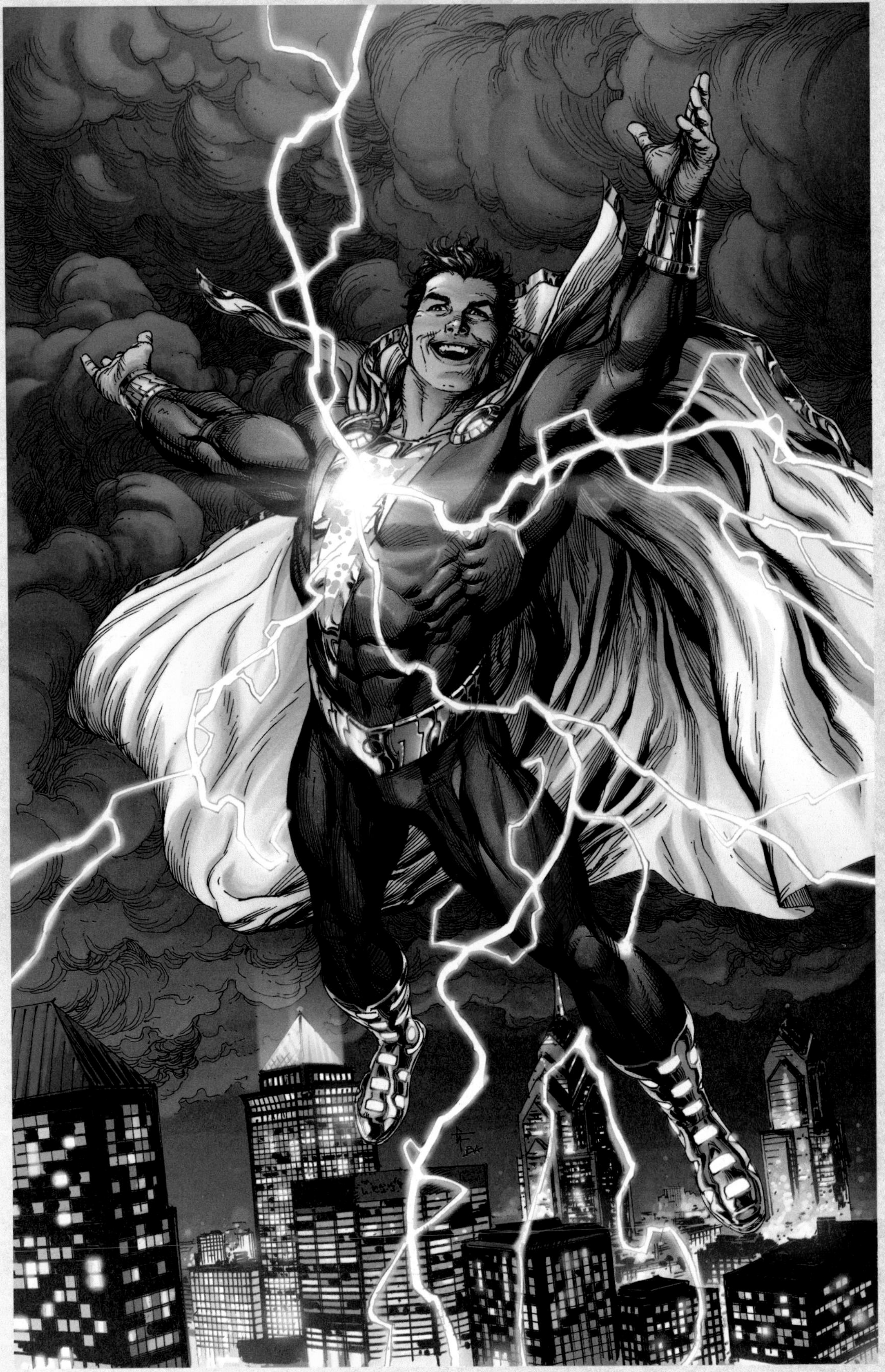

*Shazam!* #1 variant cover by Gary Frank and Brad Anderson

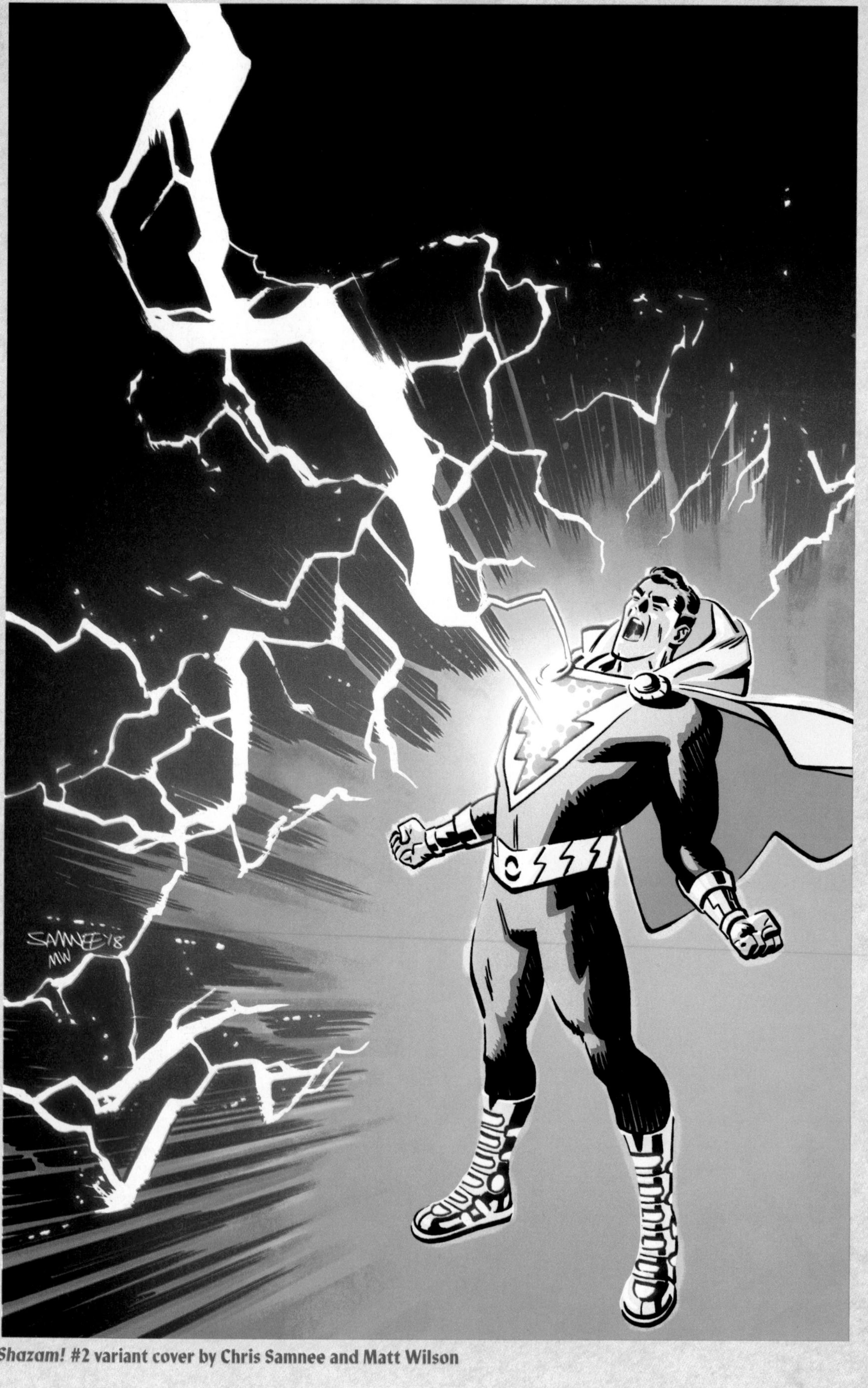
SAMNEE'18
MW

*Shazam!* #2 variant cover by Chris Samnee and Matt Wilson

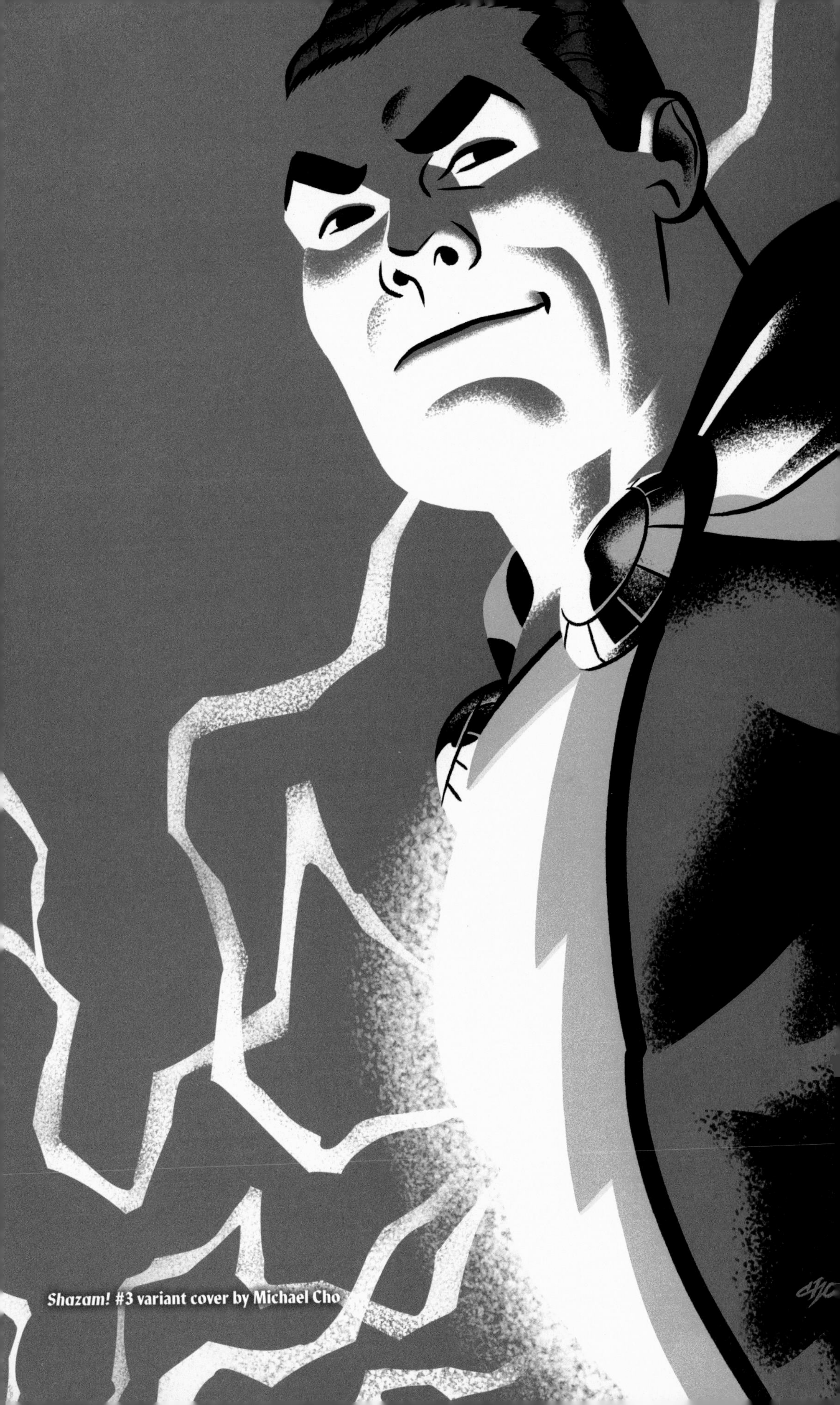

*Shazam!* #3 variant cover by Michael Cho

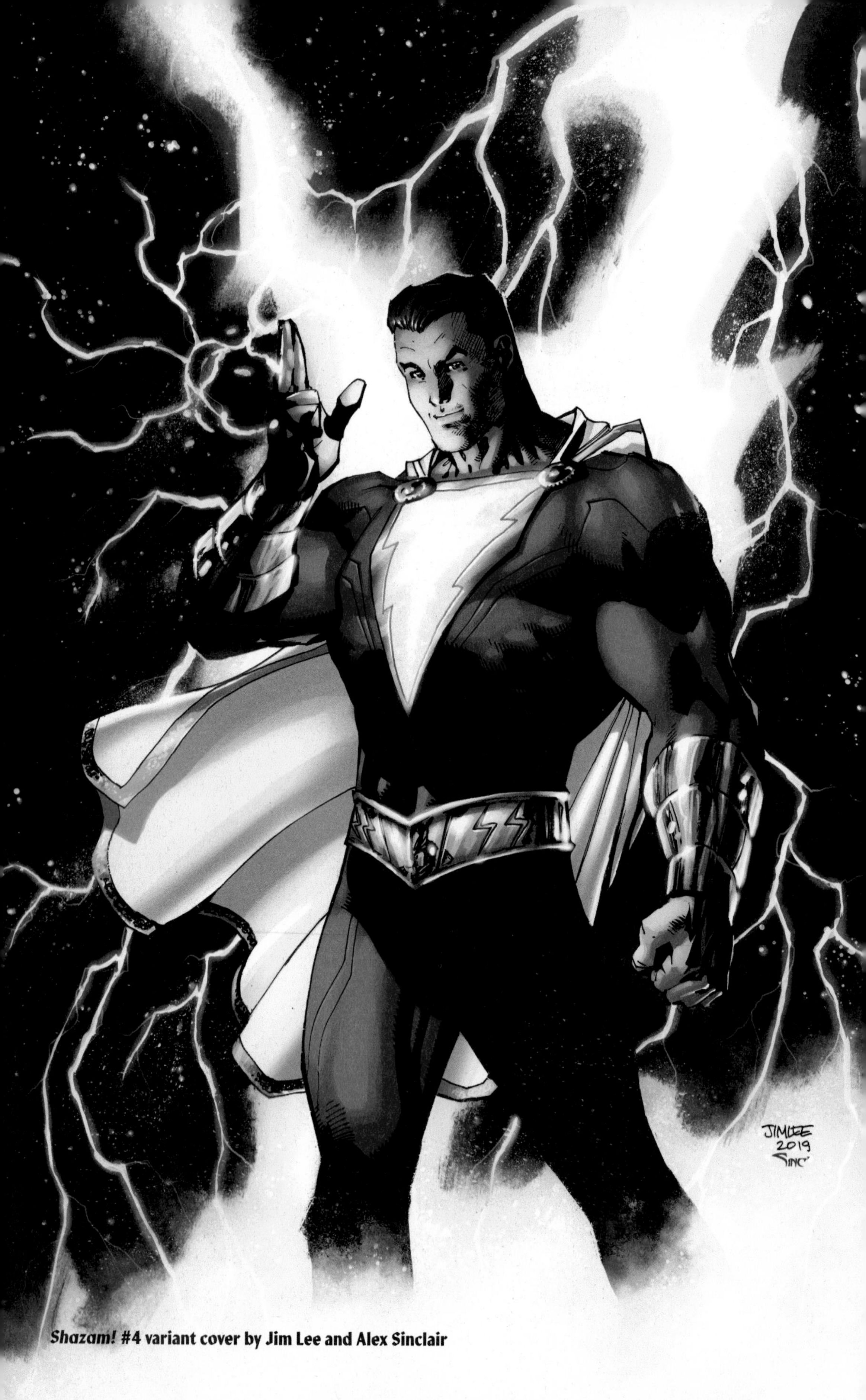
JIMLEE
2019
SINC

*Shazam!* **#4 variant cover by Jim Lee and Alex Sinclair**

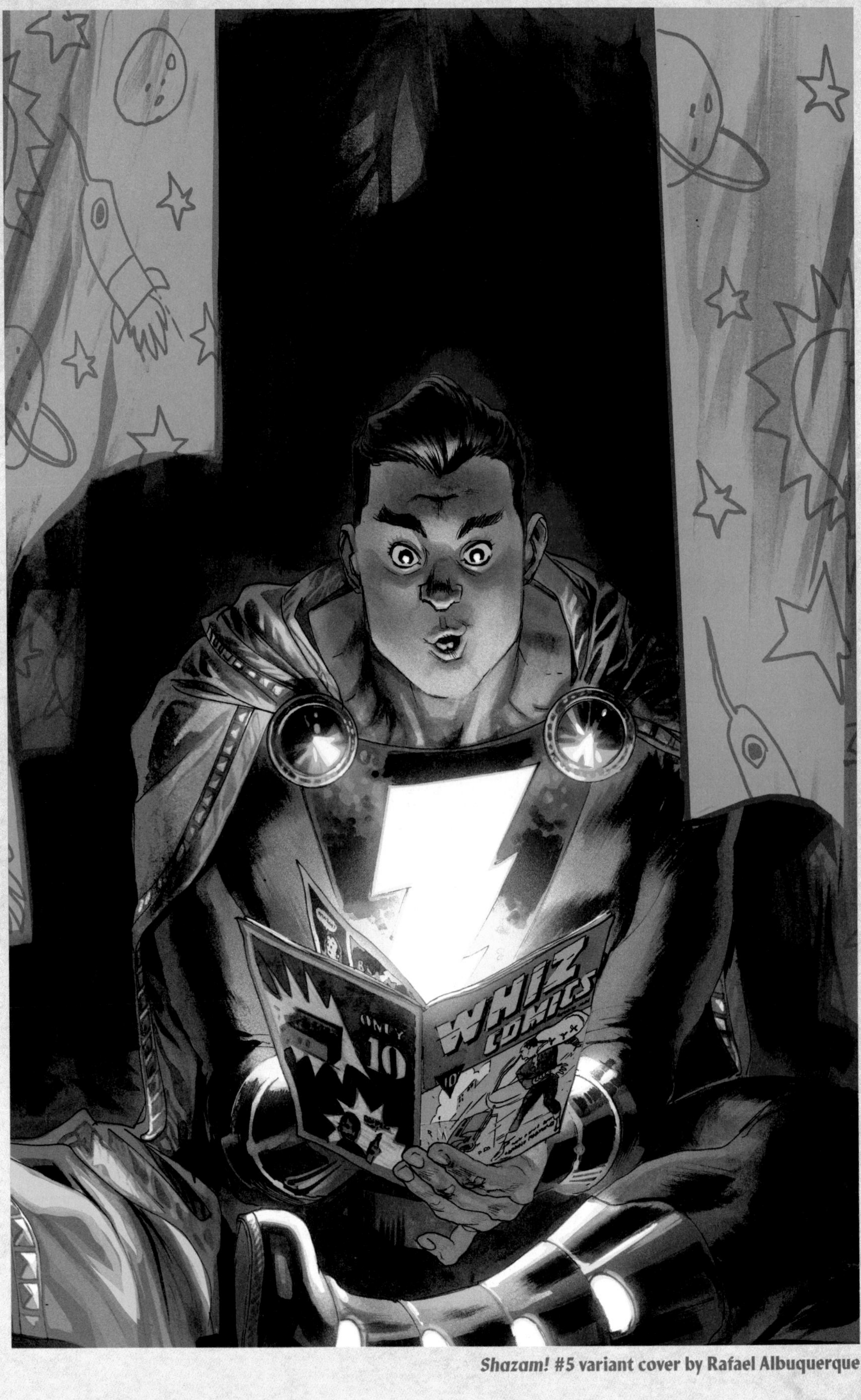
WHIZ COMICS

***Shazam! #5* variant cover by Rafael Albuquerque**

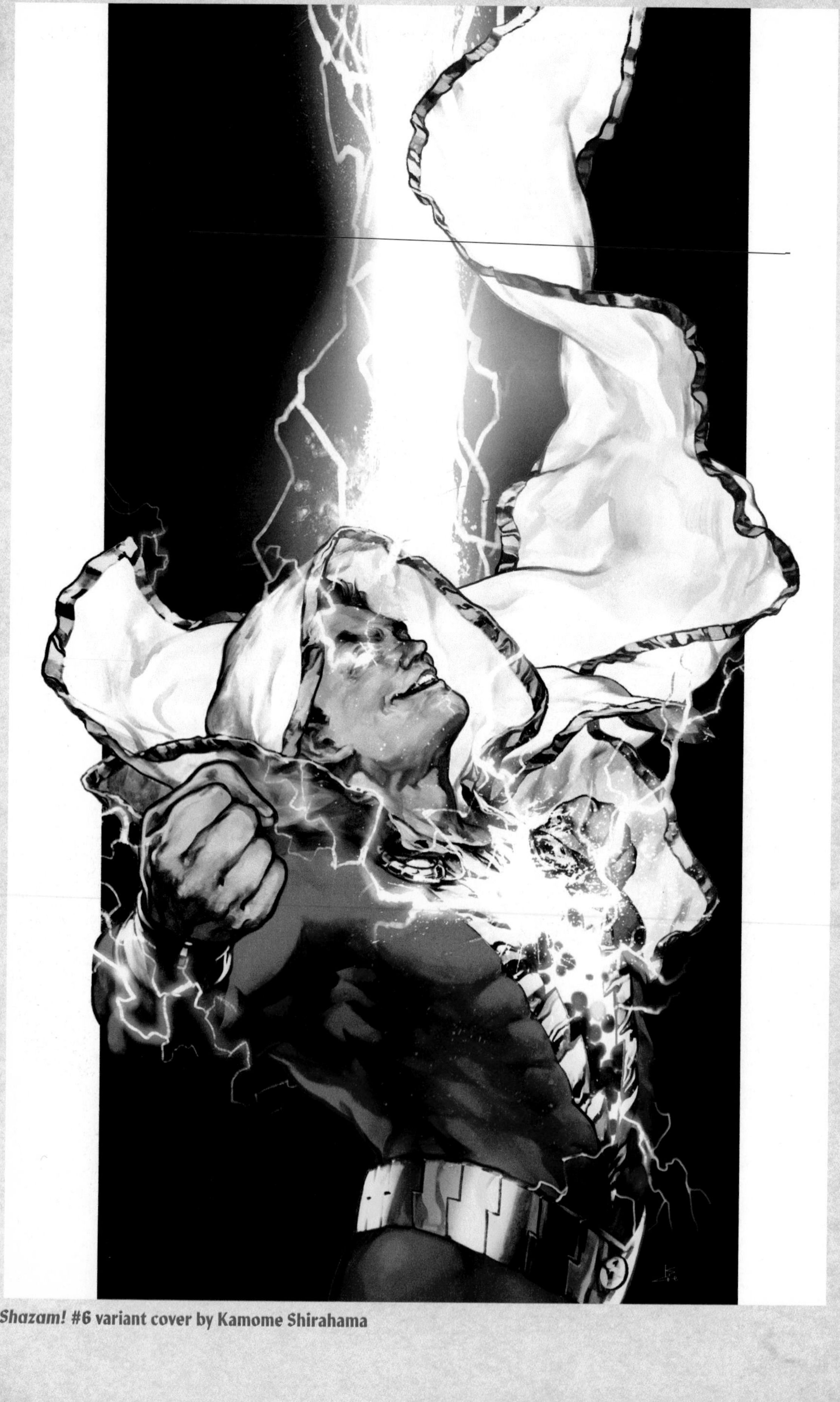

***Shazam! #6*** **variant cover by Kamome Shirahama**

*Shazam!* #7 variant cover by Ivan Reis, Oclair Albert, and Marcelo Maiolo

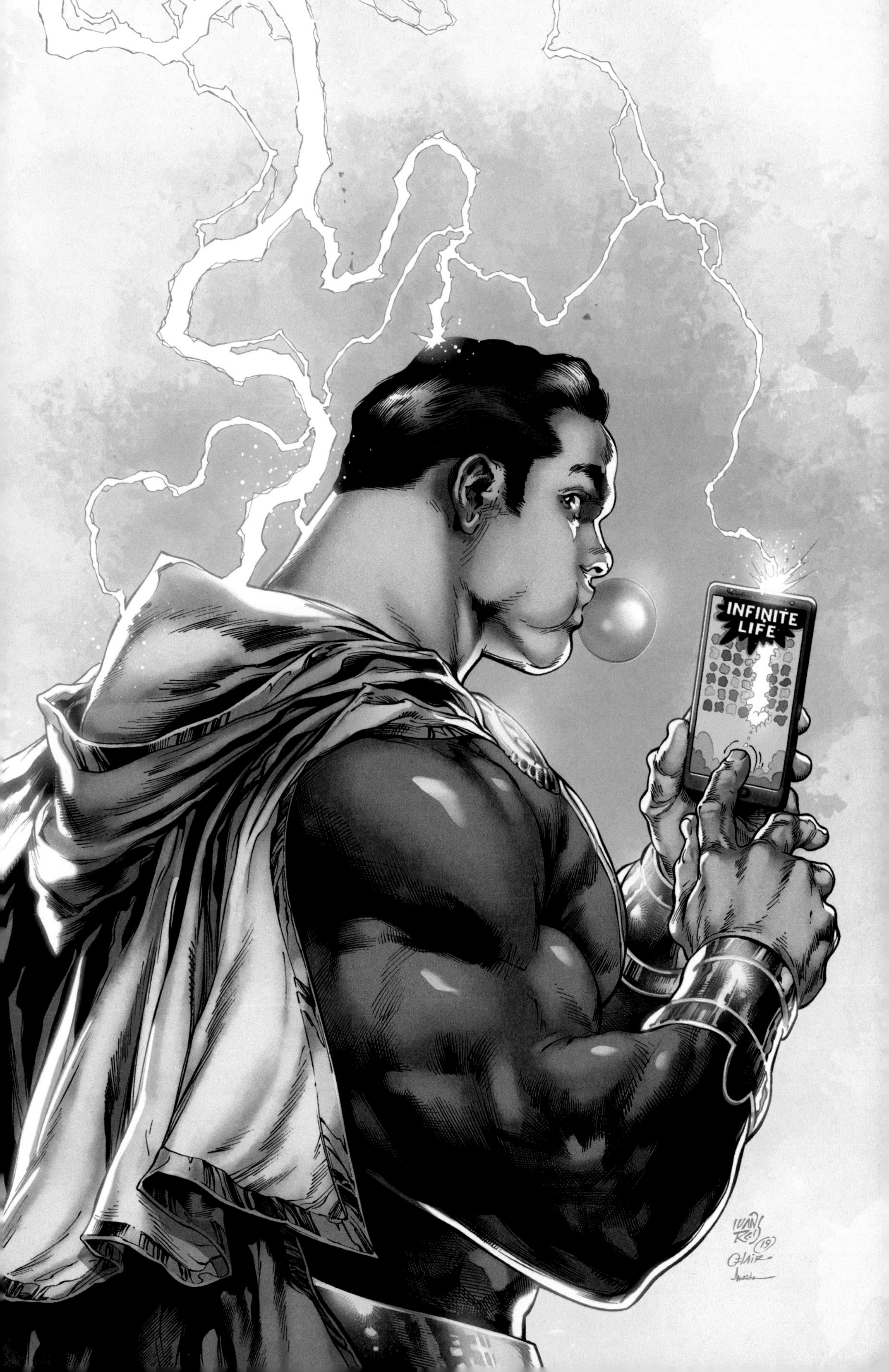
INFINITE
LIFE

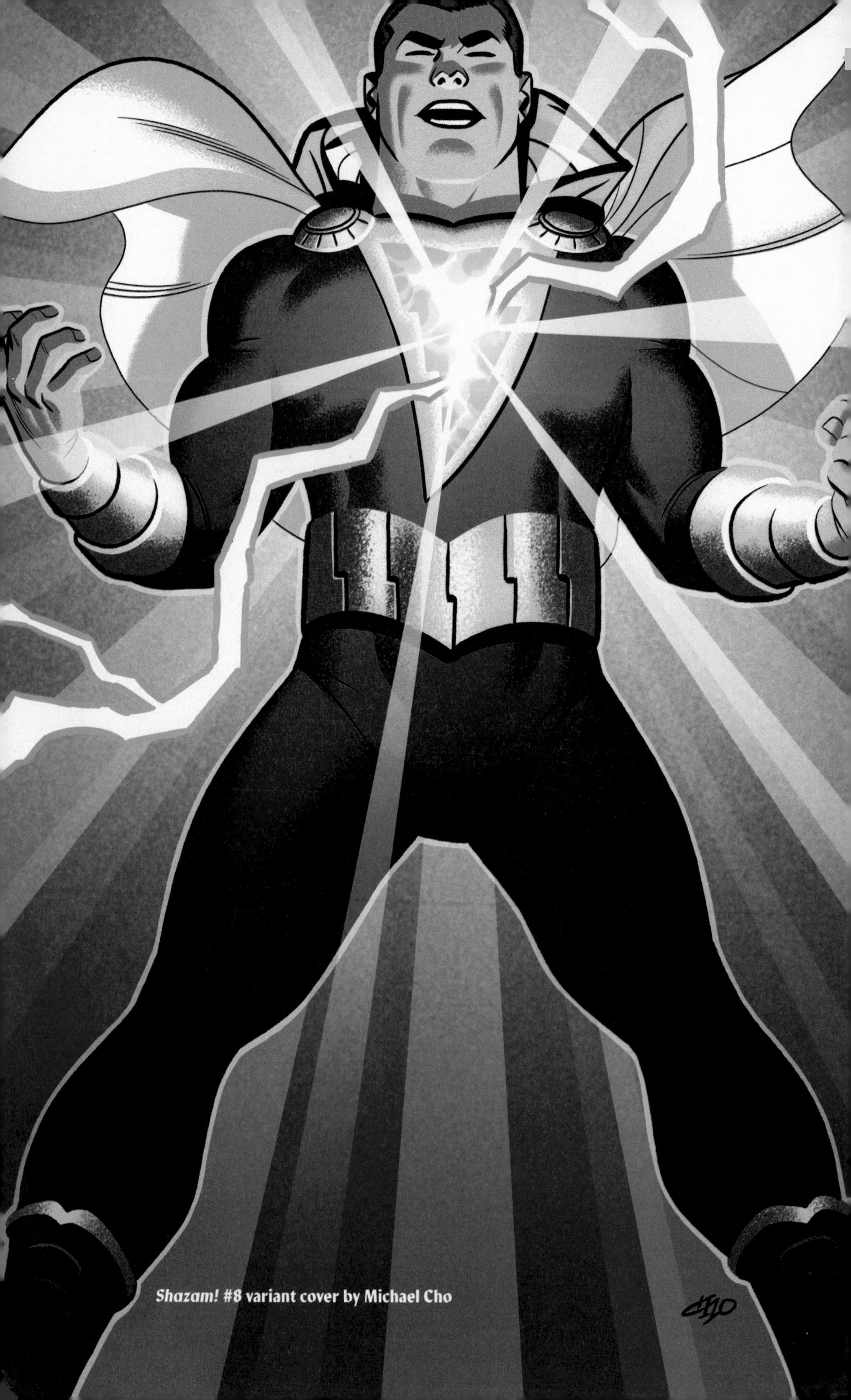

*Shazam! #8 variant cover by Michael Cho*

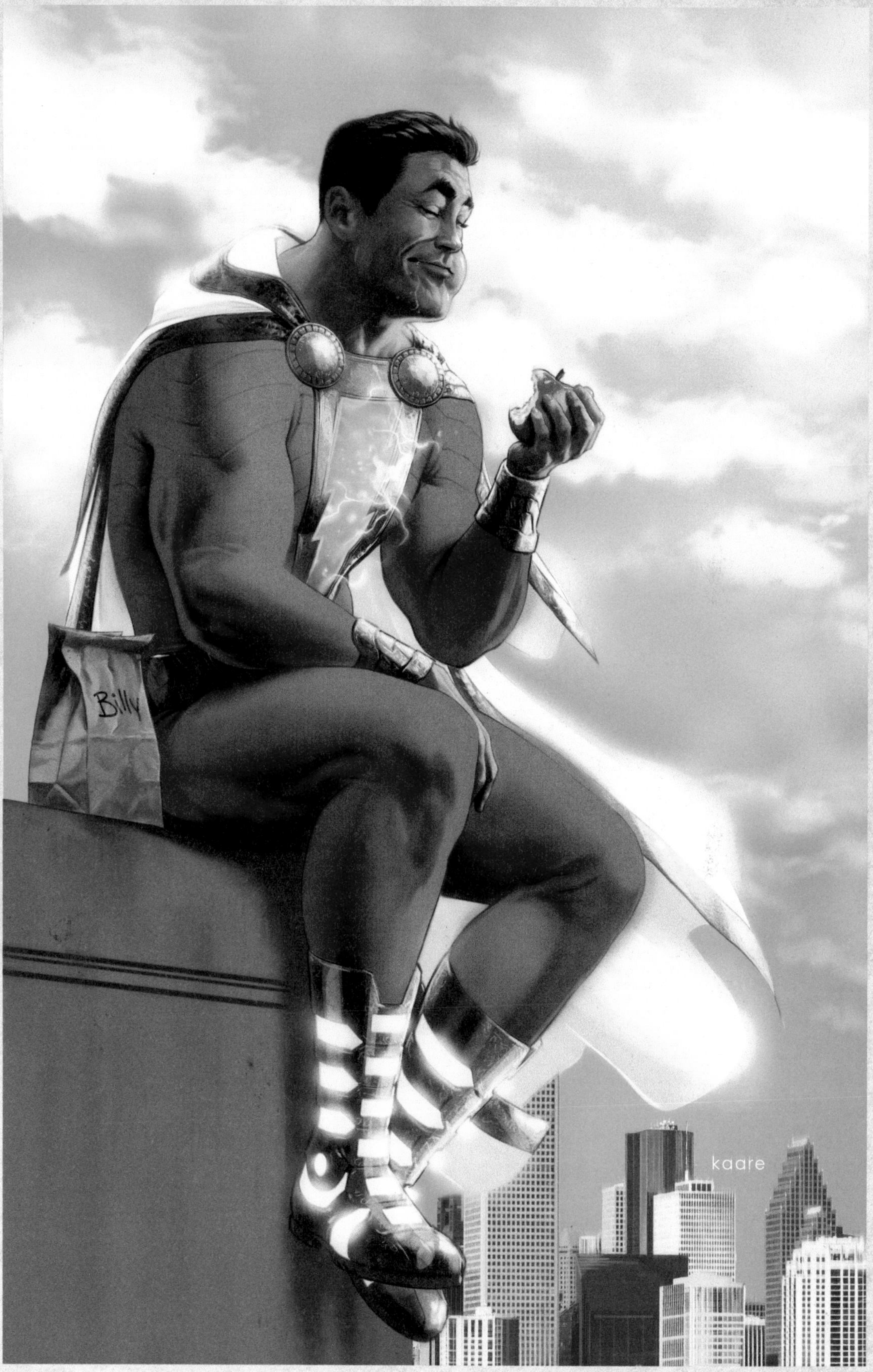
Billy
kaare

***Shazam!* #9 variant cover by Kaare Andrews**

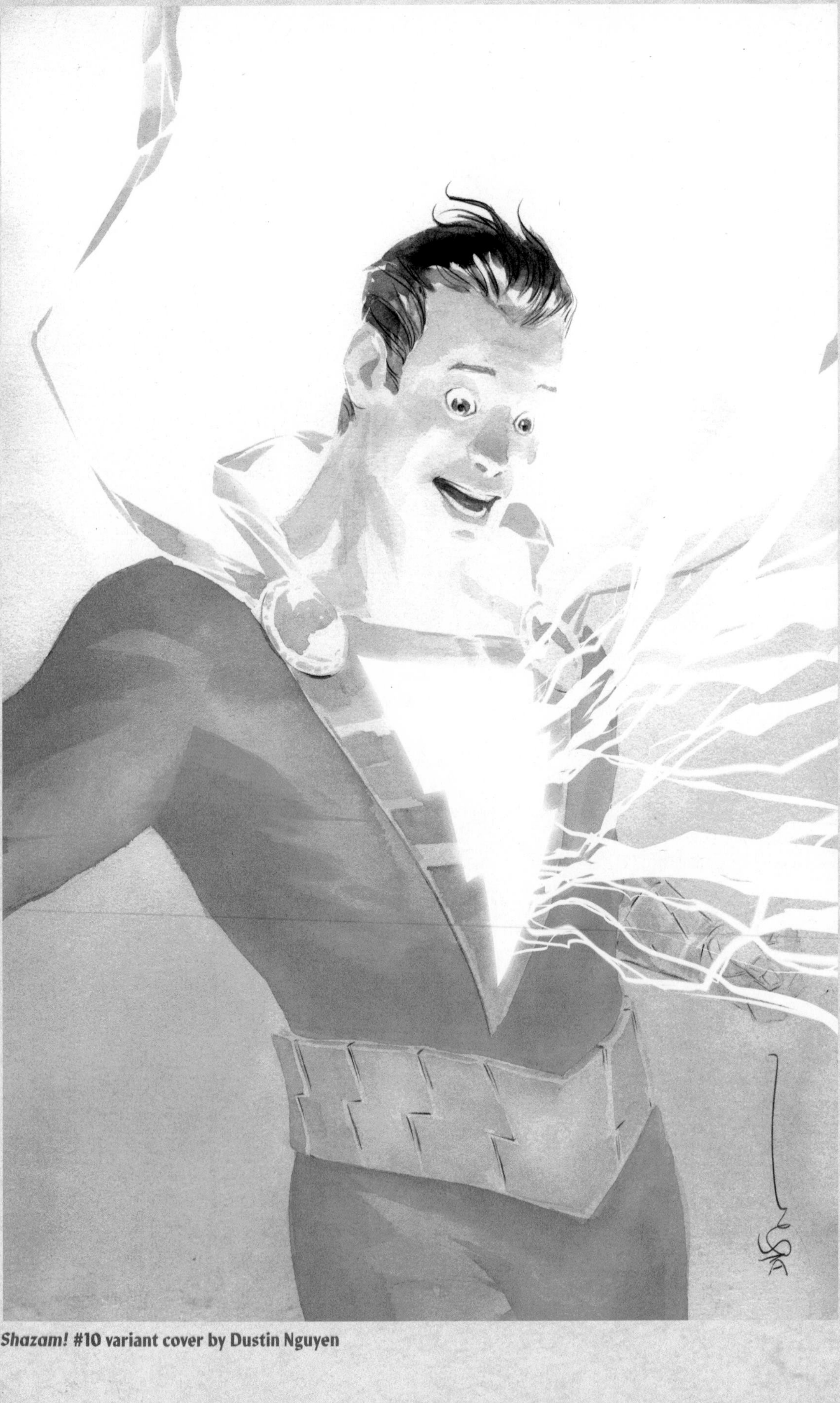

*Shazam!* #10 variant cover by Dustin Nguyen

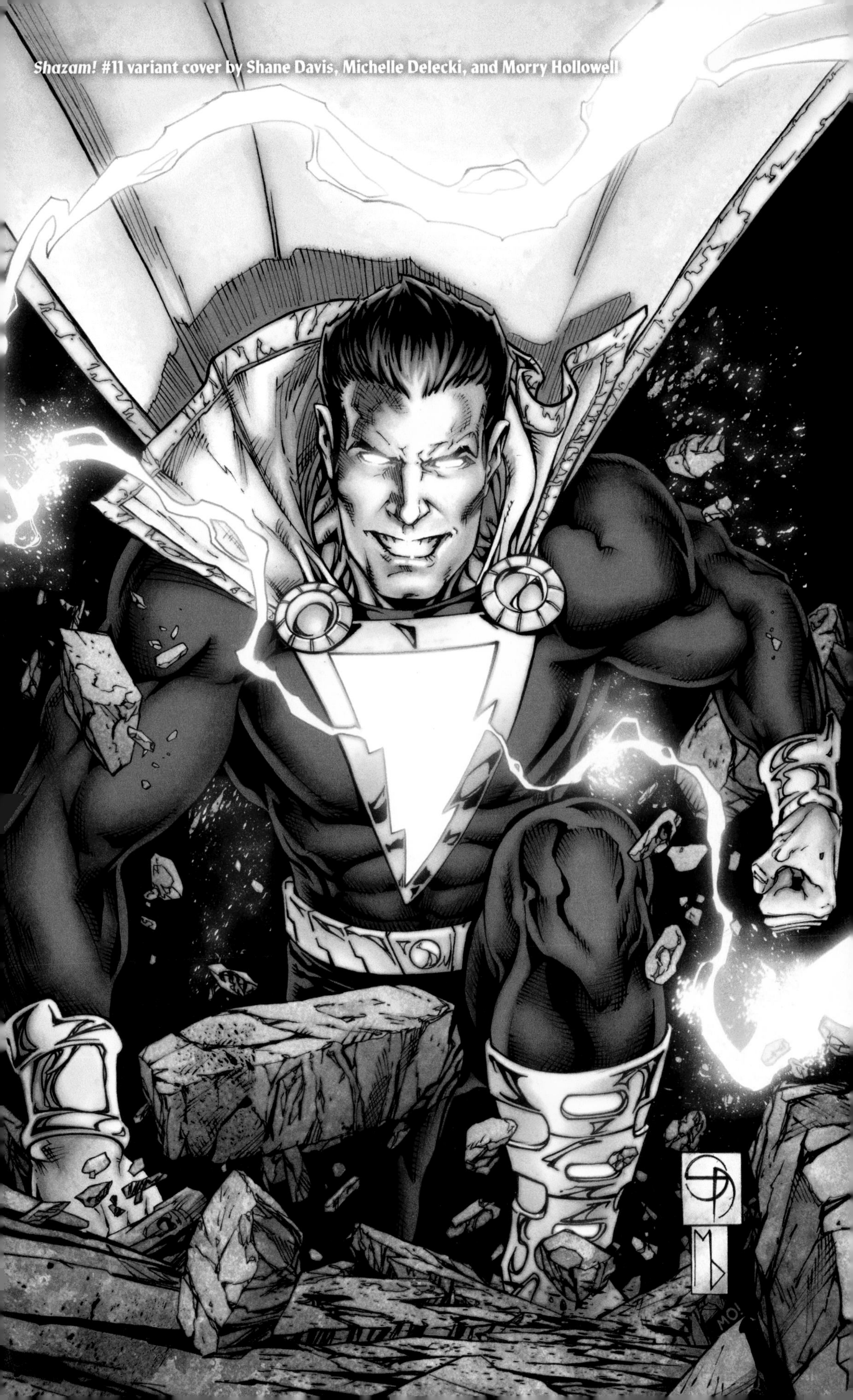

*Shazam!* #11 variant cover by Shane Davis, Michelle Delecki, and Morry Hollowell

*Shazam!* #13 variant cover by Julian Totino Tedesco

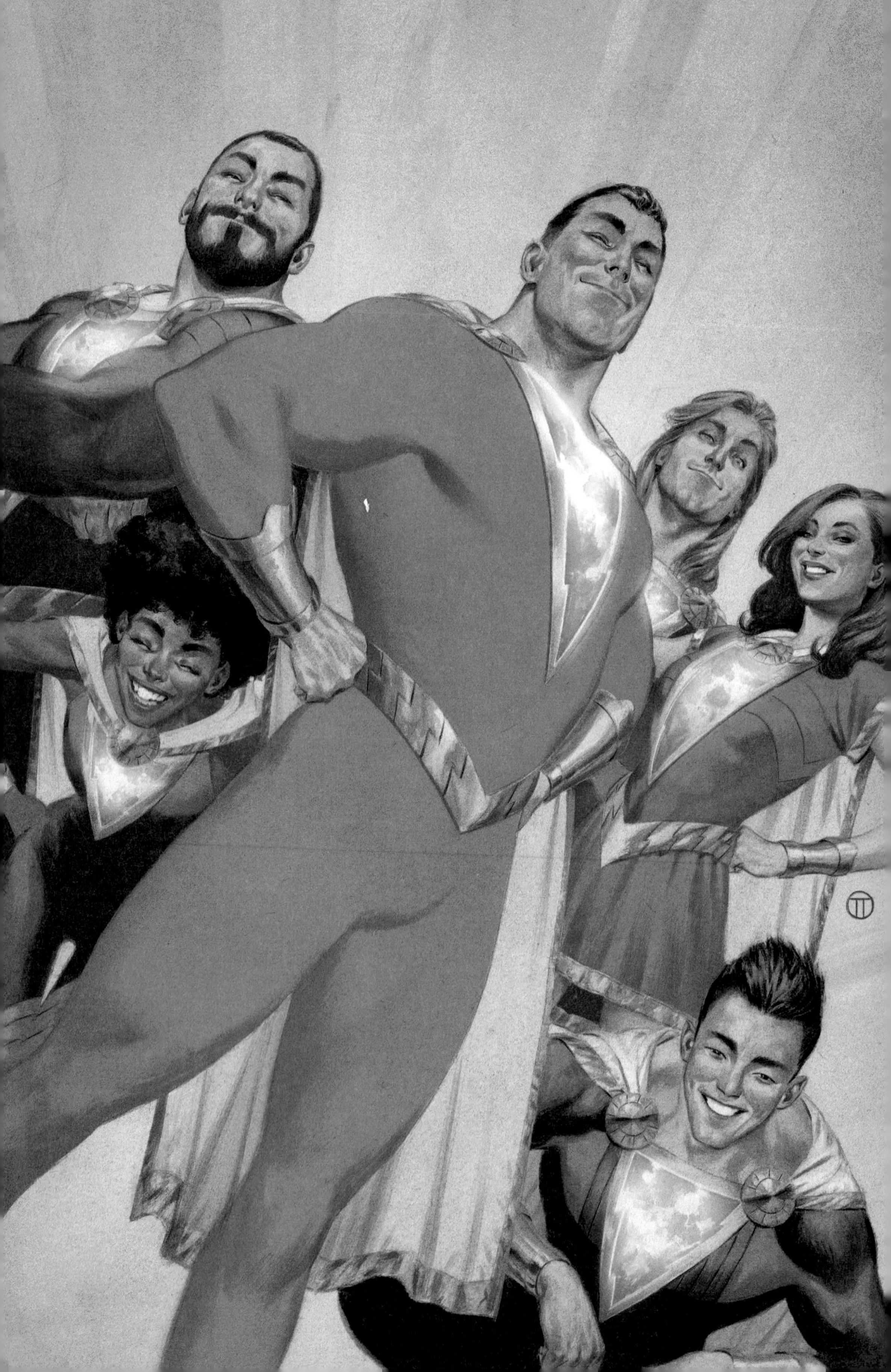

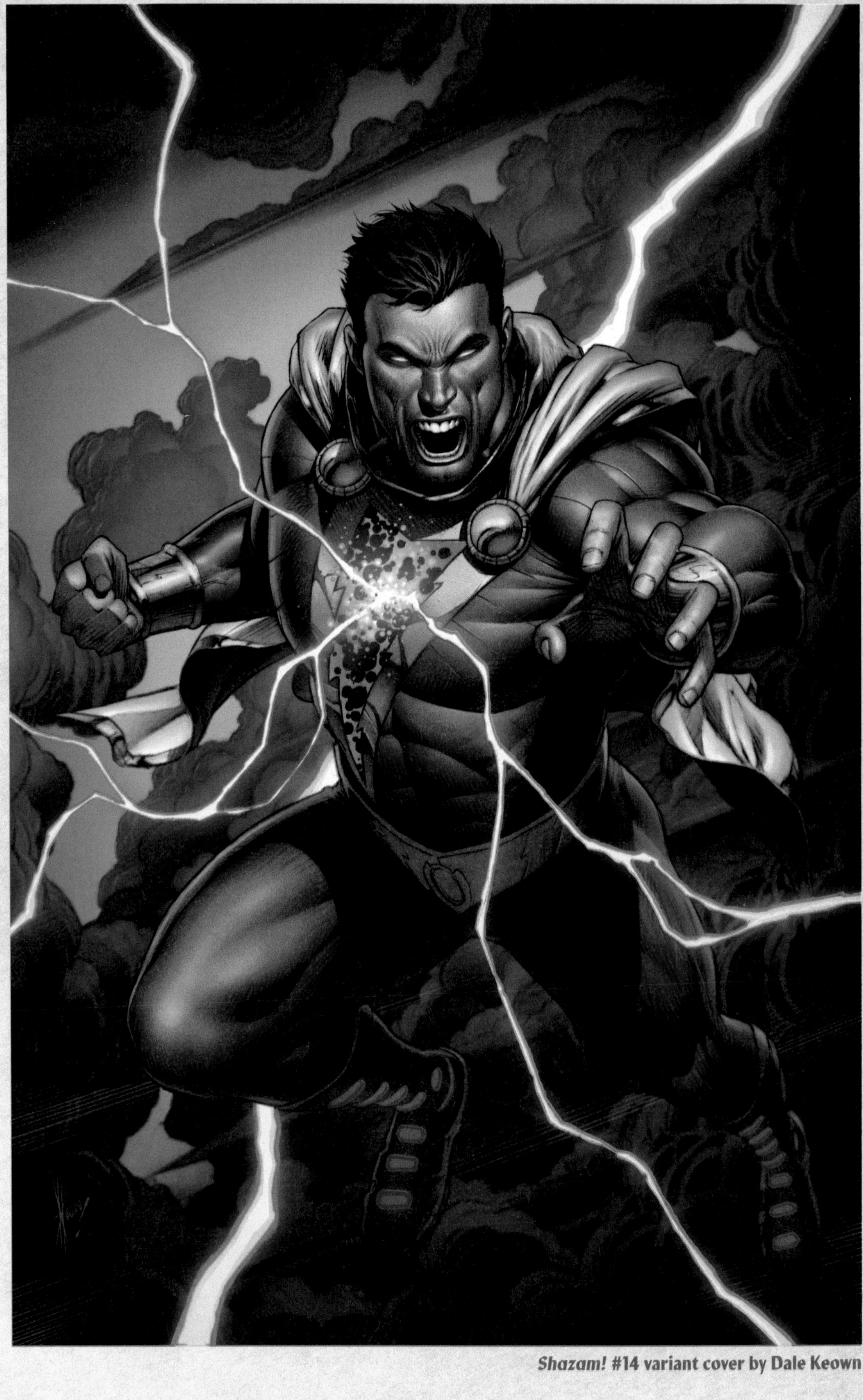

*Shazam!* #14 variant cover by Dale Keown

GEOFF JOHNS is an award-winning screenwriter and producer and one of the most successful comic book writers of his time. He has written dozens of *New York Times* bestselling graphic novels, including some of the most recognized and highly acclaimed stories featuring Superman and the Justice League. He has also reinvented lesser-known characters with great commercial and critical success. Under his Mad Ghost Productions banner, Johns is currently in various stages of production on an extensive list of projects in television and film. Among his recent projects, he is writing and producing *Stargirl* and writing the anticipated *Green Lantern Corps* feature; he has also produced the second installment of the *Wonder Woman* film franchise, *Wonder Woman 1984*, which he co-wrote with director Patty Jenkins. On the comic book side, he developed the commercial and critical hit *Doomsday Clock*.

DALE EAGLESHAM has worked for various comics companies including Marvel, Dark Horse, and CrossGen, among others, though he is best known for his work at DC Comics, where his credits include *Justice Society of America*, *Green Lantern*, *Secret Six*, *The Terrifics*, *Scooby Apocalypse*, *Sinestro*, and *Villains United*.

SCOTT KOLINS, the award-winning comic book creator known for his art on *The Flash*, *The Avengers*, *Justice League*, *Final Crisis: Rogues' Revenge*, and many more, hails from Central Wisconsin. He studied at the Joe Kubert School and was a Romita Raider. Scott has written and drawn his own book, *Adam.3*, as well as *Solomon Grundy*, *Citizen Cold*, *Superman/Batman*, *JSA*, and *Batman: Legends of the Dark Knight*. Scott has also worked for Lucasfilm and for the *Flash* TV show. In case you haven't guessed, Scott loves comics. He lives in Arizona but travels the world at various conventions, dreaming up new comics and sketching his days away. You can contact Scott on Facebook, Twitter, and Instagram.